Narrating and Constructing the Beach

spectrum
Literaturwissenschaft/
spectrum Literature

Komparatistische Studien/Comparative Studies

Herausgegeben von/Edited by
Moritz Baßler, Werner Frick,
Monika Schmitz-Emans

Wissenschaftlicher Beirat / Editorial Board
Sam-Huan Ahn, Peter-André Alt, Aleida Assmann, Francis Claudon,
Marcus Deufert, Wolfgang Matzat, Fritz Paul, Terence James Reed,
Herta Schmid, Simone Winko, Bernhard Zimmermann,
Theodore Ziolkowski

Band 68

Narrating and Constructing the Beach

An Interdisciplinary Approach

Edited by
Carina Breidenbach, Tamara Fröhler, Dominik Pensel,
Katharina Simon, Florian Telsnig and Martin Wittmann

DE GRUYTER

ISBN 978-3-11-112547-3
e-ISBN (PDF) 978-3-11-067224-4
e-ISBN (EPUB) 978-3-11-067229-9
ISSN 1860-210X

Library of Congress Control Number: 2020936588

Bibliographic information published by the Deutsche Nationalbibliothek
The Deutsche Nationalbibliothek lists this publication in the Deutsche Nationalbibliografie;
detailed bibliographic data are available on the Internet at http://dnb.dnb.de.

© 2022 Walter de Gruyter GmbH, Berlin/Boston
This volume is text- and page-identical with the hardback published in 2020.
Typesetting: bsix information exchange GmbH, Braunschweig
Printing and binding: CPI books GmbH, Leck

www.degruyter.com

Inhalt

Acknowledgements —— IX

Carina Breidenbach, Tamara Fröhler, Dominik Pensel, Katharina Simon, Florian Telsnig, Martin Wittmann
Measuring the Beach: Processes, Practices and Discourses —— 1

Yoko Tawada
Gedanken über unsichtbare Inselgruppen —— 53

(Precluded) Arrivals/Departures

Virginia Richter
Stranded. The Beach as Ultimate Destination in Joseph Conrad's *Amy Foster* and Thomas Mann's *Death in Venice* —— 57

Jeannot Moukouri Ekobe
Dystopie, Utopie, Heterotopie: Die Imagination des Strands in der Literatur von Afropäerinnen —— 82

Thérèse De Raedt
Figuring Senegalese Beaches in Moussa Sène Absa's Films —— 100

Drawing and Crossing Lines

Carmen Ulrich
Strandbekanntschaften in Georg Forsters *Reise um die Welt* und das europäische Projekt ‚Zivilisation' —— 123

Désirée Mangard and Miriam Strieder
Wechselnde Gezeiten: Der Strand als Schauplatz für Wendepunkte in Heldendichtung und höfischer Literatur des Mittelalters —— 146

Elsa Devienne
'There's Law on the Beach!': Law and Order on Los Angeles's Beaches,
1910s–1970s —— 171

Carol Bunch Davis
Always on Duty: Galveston's African American Beaches and
Lifeguards —— 194

Building Structures & Assembling Elements

Dietrich Erben
Sand, Spuren, Architektur – Zur gebauten Ökologie des Strandes —— 213

Wiebke Kolbe
Strandburgen: Eine deutsche Lust? Zum Strandurlaub seit dem späten neunzehnten Jahrhundert —— 236

Robert Bauernfeind
Der Strand als Schauplatz weltweiter Fauna. Exotische *naturalia* auf Stranddarstellungen Jan van Kessels d.Ä. —— 255

Nadja Grasselli
SHORELINES & SPACES —— 276

Bodies in Time: Littoral Rhythms of Death and Desire

Roxanne Phillips
Time and Tide Again. Traces, Permeable Spaces and Sensory Perceptions of the Beach in Theodor Storm's *Aquis submersus* and HBO's *Big Little Lies* —— 285

Alberto Napoli
"Stile balneare." Singing the Italian Summer by the Seaside (1960s–1980s) —— 311

Acknowledgements

This collection of essays is based on the interdisciplinary conference *Narrating and Constructing the Beach* which took place on 14–16 June 2018 at the Amerikahaus München. We are very grateful to everyone who helped to make this event a success.

First, we would like to take this opportunity to thank our colleagues and friends Stefan Brückl, Ines Ghalleb, Jeannot Moukouri Ekobe and Roxanne Phillips for co-organizing the conference with us. Over the many months – and through more than one sleepless night – that we spent conceptualizing and planning this event together, we complemented and inspired each other, learned from one another, and, along the way, became a great team – a veritable 'beach-taskforce.'

We are greatly indebted to the Graduate School Language and Literature (GS L&L) at LMU Munich, whose generous support made the conference and this publication possible in the first place. We especially want to thank our coordinators Markus Wiefarn and Katharina Wagner, as well as the GS L&L's advisory board members Stephan Kammer, Annette Keck and Susanne Lüdemann for their encouragement and support. We gratefully acknowledge the funding for the event provided by the Graduate Center at LMU Munich, Duke Gin, and Brillen Schneider.

The board of the Bayerische Amerika-Akademie (BAA) and its director Heike Paul deserve our gratitude for the co-organization of the conference, as well as the co-sponsorship of Michael Taussig's keynote lecture. We would like to extend our particular thanks to the BAA's Margaretha Schweiger-Wilhelm and Markus Faltermeier, who not only opened up the doors of the Amerikahaus München to us and thereby provided us with a splendid location for our conference, but who also generously offered us their invaluable advice regarding the organization of the event in the months leading up to it.

We thank all the conference participants for their intriguing and thought-provoking presentations. A special thank you goes to our keynote speakers Virginia Richter and Michael Taussig.

The assistance provided by Helen Baur, Christiane Bayer, Anna-Marie Merkle, Janna Meyer-Schwickerath, Antonia Pensel, Sara Russo and Johanna Vejvoda during the conference was greatly appreciated. We would also like to offer a special heartfelt thanks to Heidi Kühn at the Amerikahaus for her kindness and dedication.

We warmly thank our editors at De Gruyter, Marcus Böhm and Anja Michalski for their expertise, guidance and counsel throughout the editorial process of this volume and their insightful answers to our manifold and incessant questions. We would also like to offer our thanks to the rest of the editorial team at De Gruyter for their help in turning our manuscript into an actual book. We are grateful to the editors of De Gruyter's *Spectrum Literature* for accepting our collection into the series.

We would like to express our gratitude to Myrto Aspioti, Daniel Brookman and Lucas-Jan Dörre for their valuable comments on the introduction.

Last but not least, we want to thank all of our authors for making this volume what it is with their inspiring contributions.

Munich, February 2020,

Carina Breidenbach, Tamara Fröhler, Dominik Pensel, Katharina Simon, Florian Telsnig and Martin Wittmann

Carina Breidenbach, Tamara Fröhler, Dominik Pensel,
Katharina Simon, Florian Telsnig, Martin Wittmann
Measuring the Beach: Processes, Practices and Discourses

1 Introduction: *Sun & Sea (Marina)*

A crowded beach was the main theme, material scenery and central poetic image of the performance art piece that won the Golden Lion at the 2019 Venice Biennale. For *Sun & Sea (Marina)*, Lithuanian artists Rugilė Barzdžiukaitė, Vaiva Grainytė and Lina Lapelytė constructed an elaborate artificial beach in the basement of an old warehouse on the periphery of the Venice Arsenale. The beach is inhabited by 22 individuals, labelled as 'North African refugees' in the stage directions, lying on the sand and hunched up in sleeping bags. The audience's first impression of the piece is purely auditory: when entering the foyer of the building, visitors cannot see the beach because it is located in the main warehouse space; instead, they encounter a constantly surging and swelling soundscape, created by the shivering, muttering and crying of the actors behind the closed doors of the foyer. These sounds acoustically guide the audience via a metal staircase to a mezzanine balcony from which they can observe the beach scenery below. There, the listeners turn into spectators of the refugees' distress. Aided by its choreographed lighting – the beach scenery is illuminated while the balcony is left in the dark – the setting of the warehouse produces and uncovers a hierarchy of visibility that both activates voyeuristic practices inherent to Western notions of the beach as a 'vacationscape' (Gunn 1972) and marks a shift away from such notions.

As an area of unregulated movement and an institutionalized border, the beach has been receiving growing media interest in the period of increased migration to Europe since 2015, which has in turn changed its public perception significantly. By showing the beach not as a scene of leisure but as the stage for a fight for survival, the performance addresses this shift and thereby marks the beach as a site where power relations become visible. By vertically separating performers and audience, and reenacting the misery of the stranded, their objectification by passive bystanders and the failed communication between these two groups, *Sun & Sea (Marina)* deals with questions of displacement and the failure of civic courage in 'Fortress Europe.' – However, the catch with the preceding description is that it is based on a conceptual idea by the artists ("Lithuanian Pavilion Receives" 2019) that was never actually staged.

In fact, the art installation *Sun & Sea (Marina)* as it *was* staged at the 2019 Venice Biennale does not focus on displaced individuals but rather on a different, though not unrelated, concern central to contemporary discourse: climate change and ecological issues. Instead of refugees, the inhabitants of the beach are swimwear-clad tourists sprawled across colorful beach towels and deckchairs. They are surrounded by numerous paraphernalia of leisure typical of a casual day on the beach in the twenty-first century: straw hats, plastic water bottles, food in Tupperware boxes, books and magazines, sunglasses, inflatable balls, children's toys, and, of course, smartphones and tablets.

Fig. 1: *Sun & Sea (Marina)* in the Lithuanian pavilion at the 2019 Venice Biennale.

As the invisible audience watches from an elevated, decidedly voyeuristic position on the warehouse mezzanine, the performers engage in manifold mundane beach practices like building sandcastles, reading, eating, or applying suntan lotion, while singing what the artists described as "broken pop songs,"[1] "everyday songs, songs of worry and boredom, songs of almost nothing."[2] Catchy, often almost sickly-sweet melodies accompany a libretto comprised of 24 songs that unfold a panorama of dramas big and small: from the most mundane concerns of everyday life like sunburns and missing one's flight to existential anxieties about mortality and contemporary tragedies on a planetary scale like climate change and the extinction of animal species.

The 2019 Lithuanian pavilion, which has been called an "ecological work at its very core"[3] by its makers, shows us a beach "populated by people to be observed as if they were in a museum's diorama of the Anthropocene" (Barone 2019) and performs "a pop song on the very last day of the earth" (Halperin 2019) by staging Western vacation practices permeated by the imminent danger of an ecological catastrophe. Amongst the vacationers there are characters such as the "Workaholic," lamenting his exhaustion and thereby unveiling the deceptiveness of the promise that "after vacation / your hair shines, / your eyes glitter, / everything is fine," or the "3D Sisters," twin sisters whose braided pigtails pay homage to teenage climate activist Greta Thunberg and who sing about how they "cried so much" when they "learned that corals will be gone" and that "bees are massively falling from the sky" since these manifestations of the current ecological crisis made them aware of their own mortality (Grainytė "no 6," "no 16," "no 8," "no 20," "no 1," "no 23"). The characters of the opera performance create the impression of an ordinary vacation scene and simultaneously uncover "the slow creaking of an exhausted earth" (*Sun & Sea* 2019) below them, their "tired bodies" are "offering a metonym for a tired planet" (Evans 2019). With the opera incessantly starting-over, trapped in a loop of constant repetition and replicating the perpetual rhythm of a rising and falling tide along the shore, this threat scenario becomes even more exhaustive. In *Sun & Sea (Marina)* there is no larger narrative arc, no climax, no turning point at which the superficial peace of the beach scene is irreversibly destroyed, and accordingly, there is no catharsis. Instead of staging a fiery apocalypse, the Lithuanian artist trio paints the picture of a world "ending in quiet complacency" (Barone 2019). As French philosopher Bruno Latour remarked in a conversation with the piece's

---

1 Rugilė Barzdžiukaitė und Lina Lapelytė in a public conversation with Lucia Pietroiusti and Bruno Latour at the event *Speaking from the Beach* at the Lithuanian Pavilion at the 58th Biennale on 10 July 2019.
2 Leaflet handed out on site to visitors of the pavilion on 10 July 2019.
3 Leaflet handed out on site to visitors of the pavilion on 10 July 2019.

creators and its curator, the installation captures the simultaneous "tragedy and lightness of the current situation in the Anthropocene."[4]

It was not always clear that the Lithuanian Pavilion would look like this. When the artists arrived in Venice, they saw their entire concept challenged by the environmental conditions of the Biennale's host city. Due to insufficient heating, performing in bathing suits and creating the atmosphere of a sunny day of leisure did not seem feasible to the artists and curators. Instead, they considered – as Rugilė Barzdžiukaitė stated in an interview with the theater-blog *Menų faktūra* – installing a "beach full of refugees huddled in sleeping bags" ("Lithuanian Pavilion Receives" 2019), in a set-up inspiring the hypothetical one discussed in the beginning. Equipped with electric heaters to warm up the warehouse, the Lithuanian team was eventually able to realize the installation with a focus on ecological issues as planned, but paradoxically at the cost of negatively influencing its ecological balance.[5] This additionally shows how the mechanisms of a global art market come to bear on artistic production.

What strikes us as most interesting here is the imaginative overlap, only partially motivated by causal links, of different political and social debates that are taking place on and around the beach. In both the actual and the hypothetical realization of the installation, the beach functions as a site of sociocultural debate and an indicator of trends in sociocultural criticism. While in the past few years there has been a focus on the critical appraisal of Western refugee politics, current societal perceptions seem to be shaped by the era of the Green New Deal or Fridays for Future. This shift in public and artistic interest, which is reflected in the considerations to alter the conceptual framework of the project *Sun & Sea (Marina)*, can be observed on the beach and in discourses on the beach and points to the imaginative potential as well as the multiple semantic layers of littoral space. It testifies to the importance of the beach as a scene that confronts us with crucial issues of our time. Migration and climate change are among numerous conflicts, discourses and practices that manifest themselves on the beach and find their focal point there. Others are postcolonial power structures and mass tourism, environmental pollution as well as gender and burkini swimwear controversies. Taking these multiple dimensions of the beach in contemporary discourse as its point of departure, this volume concentrates

---

[4] Bruno Latour at the event *Speaking from the Beach* at the Lithuanian Pavilion on 10 July 2019.

[5] For the paradoxal tension between ecocritical art pieces and their own – often poor – ecobalance, see Hanno Rauterberg's article "Die Kunst der Scheinheiligkeit" [The Art of Hypocrisy] (2019), for which a photograph of *Sun & Sea (Marina)* serves as illustration.

on the beach as a focal point in various contexts by analyzing its historically and geographically specific varieties.

Just as *Sun & Sea (Marina)* tries to approach the semantic and aesthetic complexity of the beach by means of a diverse range of artistic forms, from theater to poetry to music, this volume takes an interdisciplinary look at the changing image of 'the beach' to explore how its topographies, its cultural significations, and the experiences associated with it are constructed through art, society and culture and how 'the beach' shapes poetics and aesthetic strategies in literature, film, photography, painting, music and performance. It sets out to analyze the beach as a cultural phenomenon that is constantly changing, transforming and diversifying in its semantic texture.

2 Shifting Signifiers

The omnipresence and polysemy of the beach in current political and cultural discourses create a desire to understand what 'the beach' is in the first place, in order to then trace the specific cultural ideas and evaluations that are attached to this basic concept in different contexts. It might appear like a promising endeavor to highlight some facets of 'the beach' and attempt to open up a spectrum of its meanings by studying the variety of signifiers that are associated with 'the beach' – both through conventions of translation as well as through explorations of etymological contexts – and by then considering the semantic dimensions of these signifiers in different languages and different cultures.

The *Oxford English Dictionary* lists three meanings for the word 'beach' (2019): One referring to a specific matter that can be found at the sea-shore: "[t]he loose water-worn pebbles of the sea-shore; shingle"; another obsolete meaning pointing to "a ridge or bank of stones or shingle"; and thirdly, what presents itself as the most common use of the word: "the shore of the sea, on which the waves break, the strand; *spec.* the part of the shore lying between high- and low-water-mark. Also applied to the shore of a lake or a large river. In *Geology* an ancient sea-margin."[6] While all these definitions situate the prototypical beach at the sea-shore, the *Oxford Dictionary of English Etymology* (1992, 82) notes that, although "it is difficult to determine the date of the emergence of the present sense," the word 'beach' goes back to the sixteenth century and probably derives from the Old English *bæċe, beċe*, denoting 'brook' or 'stream.'

---

[6] There is also an additional meaning 3b in the *OED* that specifies the use in nautical language: "The shore, any part of the coastline off which a ship is at anchor."

In its etymological origins the word 'beach' is thus linked to bodies of flowing water and not the sea.

In the Romance and most of the Slavic languages, the terms that have a semantic content similar to the third *OED*-meaning of 'beach,'[7] such as French *plage*, Spanish *playa*, Portuguese *praia*, Italian *spiaggia*, Polish *plaza*, Czech *pláž*, Hungarian *plaža* or Russian пляж *(plyazh)*, all find their origin in the Latin word *plaga* ('open expanse of land, sea or sky') and are therefore not etymologically associated with a concept of situatedness next to bodies of water but rather with a concept of spatial extension. In contrast to this, the Hawaiian term *'ae kai*, commonly defined as "[p]lace where sea and land meet" (Pukui and Ebert, 4), or the Vietnamese word *bãi biển*, denoting a 'flat expanse' *(bãi)* at the 'sea' *(biển)*, point to a space at the ocean specifically.

The aspect of spatial expansion stressed in these terms can be juxtaposed to other approximate translations for 'beach' (*OED*-3) that circle around the notion of a spatial 'border'-'line' towards the water, as is suggested by the Latin word *litus*, which refers to a border between land and water without distinguishing between the shores of the sea, rivers or lakes, as well as the German *Strand*, which is etymologically connected to New High German words for 'edge' and 'rim' (Grimm and Grimm 1957), or the Hebrew חוֹף (*ḥof*, corresponding to Arabic حوف [*ḥauf*], 'border,' 'rim'; see Klein 1987, 211).

In other languages, signifiers used for referring to the 'beach' (*OED*-3) are directly connected to information about its material texture: The ancient Greek word ἀκτή (*aktḗ*) as well as θίς (*this*), which Homer mostly uses, or the Chinese 沙滩 (*shā tān*), for example, specifically address the rocky or sandy qualities of the littoral spaces they denote (Beekes 2010, 58; Frisk 1973, 61). A trace of salt (λός) can be detected in the most common ancient Greek term αἰγιαλός (*aigialós*), which can be described as conceptualizing the 'beach' (*OED*-3) as a place where the waves of the sea break (Beekes 2010, 31–32; Frisk 1960, 31, 78–79). Material beach processes are also evoked by the Hawaiian words *kahakai* or *kahaone*, which envision a place formed by the scratching (*kaha*, 'scratch,' 'place') of 'sea' (*kai*) and 'sand' (*one*) through the movement of waves (Pukui and Ebert, 110).

Finally, the German *Strand* as well as the English *strand* can be traced back to the Norse word *strǫnd*. Etymologically linked to terms for 'border' or 'edge,' *strǫnd* is associated with an image of the 'beach' (*OED*-3) as threshold, but it also denotes the 'edge of a shield,' thus invoking the image of military combat and inviting the notion of the beach as a contested zone of contact or conflict. (Grimm and Grimm 1957)

---

[7] From now on referred to as *OED*-3.

A form of situatedness next to the water in general or the sea specifically, a spatial extension, a separating border, an accumulation of a specific material substance: A short trip through the streams of linguistic association already reveals a disorienting variety of semantic approaches. It remains impossible to determine, however, whether this result can really be attributed to a multifaceted or ambiguous character of the beach, or whether it should be understood as an effect of the method of description. An investigation into meaning and etymology seems unable to establish a definition of 'the beach' that can serve as a reference point; rather, the diversity of cultural and local perspectives revealed in this examination results in an erosion of the referent. The idea that all these different terms are in fact referring to the same 'beach' emerges as problematic. This calls for a methodology that, instead of distinguishing between a core concept of 'the beach' and additional layers of cultural meanings, concentrates on operations of narration and construction to illuminate the interplay between different modes of constructing the beach.

3 Narrating and Constructing the Beach

The destabilization of the referential relation pointed to above poses a significant challenge to the project of the present volume, which is to explore the beach as a focal point for various processes, practices and discourses of far-reaching impact. Since there is no objective 'beach' separate from what is happening or what is said and done on and around it, its relation to these processes, practices and discourses must be conceptualized as one of reciprocal construction. As the language-related analysis in the last section has already revealed, reflections on spatial aspects are an almost ubiquitous element of attempts to think the beach, but they are also highly contingent on cultural, discursive and geographic contexts. In addition to this, descriptions of 'the beach' as a specific space are haunted by a paradoxical tension between the necessity for and the impossibility of demarcation (literally and figuratively speaking): on the one hand, they have to outline in how far the beach can be understood as a space with its own characteristics and distinctive processes that set it apart from land and sea, as well as from other coastal formations or spaces like the harbor. In view of the beach as a prevalent figure of in-betweenness, as a border zone, as a space of transition, on the other hand, it appears as evident and has to be taken into account that the beach can only be conceptualized in relation to other spaces.

Spatial aspects, however, are not the only factor that must be considered as constitutive of the beach. Examining the beach always means examining ontologically heterogeneous ensembles and what may appear as such: spatial *and* temporal, natural *and* cultural components, material objects and data of perception not only encounter each other on the beach – in a sense, their encounter *is* the beach.

Building on these considerations, the collection's title *Narrating and Constructing the Beach* gives expression to the awareness that there is no (space of the) beach as an objective point of reference that would orient a foundational analysis and allow one to compare geographically and historically specific shapes in culture and art with it. Instead, this volume examines different ways in which 'the beach' is constructed: On a first level, the beach is constructed in perception by organizing sensory data into a coherent whole: strands of images, sounds, smells, tactile and gustatory sensations are interwoven to form the complex and unique texture of experience that becomes identified with the beach. But 'construction' can also take on a very literal meaning, as the experience of the beach is also framed by material structures built on the beach. The construction of the beach as a site of experience operates through the construction of more or less permanent architectural interventions. In a similar manner, the beach experience is 'built' through other forms of art and cultural production, may it be sculpture, visual media, music, dance, performance art, lecture performance or writing.

'Construction' here is not conceived as implying "a culture or an agency of the social which acts upon a nature, which is itself presupposed as a passive surface, outside the social and yet its necessary counterpart" (Butler 1993, xiv). There is neither a single nor a collective subject that would be free to choose to construct the beach in whatever way it felt inclined to at a given moment. The constructed character of the beach also does not impinge on its reality, since every single 'thing' (including the beach) only becomes materialized through a specific construction. And the implications of any particular construction of the beach are just as real: Ecological problems caused or accelerated by mass tourism at the beach make the unintended dimensions and uncontrollable effects that each construction entails particularly visible and tangible. Moreover, on a more abstract level, there are always specific erasures and foreclosures produced through every particular (mode of) construction; they produce an excess that, even though – or rather because – it figures as unreadable in and through the system of binary oppositions that founds a given construction, continues to haunt it (ibid., xvii). This predicament is of special relevance in the case of the beach since its construction is closely connected to the production of differences organizing orders of race, class and gender (among others).

As the title already indicates, the present volume puts specific emphasis on narrative as "a form not only of representing but of constituting reality" (Bruner 1991) – i.e. as a specific mode of construction that involves "cultural artefacts that tell a story" (Bal 2017, 3). This is relevant beyond the contributions in which narratives – in a narrow sense of the word, as literary narratives – are discussed. Narratives, in a broader sense of the word, are essential constituents of every cultural and social construction of reality. A critical evaluation of the role these 'cultural narratives' play in the construction of such a highly contested and symbolically charged space as the beach requires one to break away from the formalistic approach of structuralist narratology, which treats questions of voice, perspective and temporal organization as politically neutral structural traits or techniques, and to explore instead their function as "explicit or implicit carriers of cultural meaning and ideology" (Nünning 2009, 168). This allows for the study of the beach as trope or topos in its changing imaginations, one of them being the 'invention of the beach' itself in the eighteenth century. Constituted by narration, the beach always figures as a setting for the interplay of socially and culturally differentiated voices and perspectives (following Bakhtin's analysis of novelistic discourse in Bakhtin 1981). The diversity of these voices, the antagonisms between these perspectives prevent a stable cultural image or final essentialist definition of the beach. The beach therefore remains always open to reevaluation and reconceptualization.

Following this line of thought, this volume not only interrogates the ways in which the beach is constructed through processes of cultural and artistic creation but also asks how the work of art itself takes a specific shape in this act of construction. This inescapable interdependence constitutes what could be called a 'poetics of the beach.' To account for the multifaceted character of the beach and the plurality of practices taking part in its construction, an interdisciplinary approach proves to be not only productive but necessary. In this volume, perspectives from history, cultural studies, literary studies and musicology as well as art studies, visual culture and architecture are brought into dialogue. In order to make cross-disciplinary affinities and common thematic interests palpable, the arrangement in different sections deliberately avoids reproducing disciplinary boundaries.

The volume *The Beach in Anglophone Literatures and Cultures*, edited by Ursula Kluwick and Virginia Richter (2015), provides a constitutive comprehensive systematization of thematic dimensions of the beach. Our collection combines the reflection on its spatial dimensions with a more pronounced exploration of material and temporal aspects. It also makes a sustained effort to interrogate the consequences that the geographical and historical diversity of beaches, together with and in relation to culturally and socially diverse positions, has for a definition of the beach.

4 Uncertain Borders: Liminality and the Politics of (De-)Regulation

In thinking about the beach, one is confronted right away with the difficulty to understand the relation of the beach to mechanisms of regulation and control on the one hand, and to emancipatory potential, liberty and freedom on the other. How to negotiate these two relations, is itself contested, especially since this emancipatory potential in its transformative quality is often linked to concepts of liminality, which in turn can be read as either empowering or overwhelming (even though it can be argued that these concepts often constitute a hypostatization of early conceptions of liminality, insofar as they extrapolate an ambiguity that is the effect of a relational system into a state of being). While in one context the beach is viewed as a paradigmatic example of an in-between space, in another, it is viewed as a paradigmatic example of ordered space. At times, these two tendencies in perceiving the beach can become contradictory. (See Samuelson 2015; Burdsey 2016) They are tied up with geographical and geological imaginaries, differences in cultural perspective and access to power, the individual and intersecting histories of disciplines and peoples and the discourses that derive from them, as well as the functions that those discourses serve in specific settings. While they cannot always be neatly aligned with the perspectives of the Global North and the Global South, it is apparent that those theoretical positions implicate sociopolitical consequences.

The notion of the beach as an in-between space is tied to a specific sensory experience, which is supported by a specific geological discourse. Situated where land and water meet and merge and constituted by the dynamic interplay of these complementary elements, the littoral space is viewed as a 'borderland' *par excellence*. The boundary formed by the beach is not static and clearly defined, it is a blurred or fluid borderline that is constantly erased and then redrawn with the rhythm of the ebb and tide, rendering the beach a processual phenomenon rather than a fixed territory with stable coordinates. The beach as a hybrid in-between space denies not only geographical but also semantic fixation: As John Fiske put it in the chapter "Reading the Beach" of his study *Reading the Popular* (1989, 43), the beach "simply has too much meaning, an excess of meaning potential."[8]

The concept of 'liminality' (from the Latin *limen* for 'threshold') has featured prominently in many of the existing studies of littoral spaces from different disciplinary angles,[9] and there is a plurality of artistic representations that conceptualize the beach as a 'liminal space' in which 'liminal' or 'liminoid' experience is possible. As a theoretical concept, 'liminality' was first introduced by ethnographer Arnold van Gennep (1960 [1909]) in the context of his research on religious rituals. Drawing on van Gennep's work, Victor Turner (1969) conceptualized 'liminality' as the transitory and transformational middle stage of a 'rite of passage.' The 'liminal persona' is temporarily situated beyond the symbolic order and the rules and regulations that govern day-to-day social life; thus, 'liminality' is a sphere of full potentiality and possibility, a "time of enchantment when anything might, even should happen" (Turner 1979, 465).

The liminal experience is by definition a transient one, and the beach, as a zone that is incessantly constituted anew by the changing tides as well as natural processes of sedimentation and erosion, has an affinity to transitoriness rather than permanence. It is a place of coming and going, of entries and exits; those who arrive at the beach from the land or from the sea – settlers, explorers, refugees – seldom come to stay and are often on the brink of beginning a new life and leaving an old one behind.[10] At the ever-changing threshold of land and water, the vital processes of becoming, being and decaying are eminently manifest. Built on various mythic sediments, artistic and scientific discourses alike often portray the beach as a space closely associated with life and (pro-)creation, birth and rebirth as well as death, violence and destruction: One can think of the iconic scene of birth depicted in Botticelli's *Birth of Venus*, which captures the moment of the goddess's arrival at the beach of Cyprus, following her emergence from the foam the waves created after Cronus cut off his father Uranos's genitals and threw them into the sea – a brutal act of violence, which Botticelli's idyllic representation only hints to in its title. Taking up and rewriting these mythopoetic traditions, an influential current of thought in nineteenth

---

8 In a footnote from *Mythologies*, Barthes (1972 [1957], 221) constructs a contrast between beach and sea based on their signifying potential (focusing on the classic arsenal of semiology): "Here I am, before the sea; it is true that it bears no message. But on the beach, what material for semiology! Flags, slogans, signals, sign-boards, clothes, suntan even, which are so many messages to me."
9 For studies of the beach as a liminal space, see for example Shields (1990 and 1991); Andrews and Roberts (2012); for an application of the concept of liminality to the beach in conjunction with questions about race, see Burdsey (2016).
10 In contrast, see Richter in this volume for the beach as a place of impossible departures.

century natural and historical sciences conceptualizes the "mucus of sea water" at the beach as "the result of the numberless deaths which furnish forth materials for new lives" and invents the beach as the origin of all life: "at once an Alpha and an Omega, a beginning and an end" (Michelet 1861, 117).[11]

Drawing from this imaginary discussed above, essentializing and idealizing notions of an in-betweenness of the beach are frequent and persistent, performing a metonymical shift away from a relational understanding of it to its hypostatization into a quality attached to the space of the beach. These notions often find expression in portrayals of the beach as a zone beyond the habits of quotidian life. Greg Dening, reinterpreting Turner's theory of liminality, 'reads' the beach as an "in-between space in an in-between space" that can become a "space of crossing," of cultural transfer and "transformation," "an unresolved space where things can happen, where things can be made to happen" (Dening 2002, 8–9). The symbolic construction of the beach as a quasi-utopian space, in which a suspension of the rules and regulations that govern the mundane sphere opens up possibilities for transgressive encounters with the 'other,' is well attested in a long tradition of works of art and literature: Theodor Fontane's *Effi Briest* or Joaquín Sorolla's paintings, for example, portray beach-crossings as holding a potential to weaken existing power hierarchies as well as social and cultural demarcation lines in order to allow encounters and transitions beyond social categories such as race, class, gender, nation or religion.

From a different discursive perspective, it can be argued, however, that the origin of the concept of liminality in ethnology already points to a cultural coding of the liminal conception of the beach and the fantasies associated with it. Imaginations revolving around the transgression of borders are themselves already inserted into a structure of difference. Borders that determine the existence of some subjects can become invisible to others who are not restricted by them. Entering the space of shipwreck of the European project of 'civilization,' the impossibility of a neutral position *vis-à-vis* the question of a liberating potential of the beach becomes all the more jarring.[12] Fantasies and realizations of freedom and control are bound together in depictions of beach and harbor, which contrast and complement each other.

In Georg Forster's *Ansichten vom Niederrhein* [Views of the Lower Rhine] (1791–1794), for instance, the harbor is depicted as an ideal "image" of manmade

---

[11] See in this volume: Begemann's discussion of theories of primeval mud and the beach as a place where life and death overlap in the work of Theodor Storm.
[12] In the South African setting, it is exactly the relation between the beach as a site of segregation and as the site of transforming encounter that has to be negotiated (Samuelson 2015, 121–123, 130 and passim).

"meticulous and wonderful order" (as cited in Ette 2017, 39)[13] where, as Corbin notes, "nature has retreated before the labour of man, who had cut stones and reshaped the boundaries" of land and water (Corbin 1994, 187). In this sense, "eight thousand pillars" demarcate a clear and strict borderline between the sea and the harbor's geometrical grid of zones and squares, streets and canals. Tableau-like, everything has its proper place: the buildings, the larger and smaller ships, or "vessels coming and leaving the port," the "lanterns, compasses, flags," "anchor cables and smaller ropes, pulleys and sails," the sailors and workers with their repetitive actions, "in a word, every single part of the smallest piece" is ordered and regulated. What might seem small and insignificant is in fact perfectly integrated into the "astonishing structure" of this "ungeheuren Maschine" [monstrous machine]. (Citations in Ette 2017, 39–40) The harbor is a hybrid network of objects, people, signs and practices, whose individual actors are only small springs of a machine ("nur kleine Triebfedern einer Maschine"; Forster 1958, 300). Forster, however, is very aware that he himself contributes to this perfectly functioning order through his perspective in reflecting and describing: "nicht dem Auge allein, sondern auch dem Verstand erscheint Amsterdam von der Wasserseite im höchsten Glanze" [not only to the eye, but also to the mind Amsterdam appears from the water's side in the highest splendor] (ibid., 299). Thus, the regulated and ordered harbor space correlates with the observer's regulating and ordering gaze. Only in the mind, in fantasy, by imaginatively transforming the "Aussicht" [view] into a distanced total over-view from the center of the port, it can be united into a whole ("zu Einem Ganzen vereinigt"; ibid., 300). As such a view, following Claude Lorrain's and Joseph Vernet's well-known paintings, the harbor assembles both the human microcosm and the macrocosm of the whole world, finding its structure in the colonial economico-political network of "Handel und Schiffahrt" [trade and seafaring] spanning the entire globe (ibid.; see also Blumenberg 1997, 8).

Whereas this 'safe harbor' serves as model of regulation, control and predictability, the description and production of an order of the beach, in contrast, are a lot more difficult. Here, zones and squares, different spaces and spheres overlap, interfere, come into conflict and provoke the need for demarcation lines, for description (and rewriting) and thus for processes of construction and narration. In his *Journey Round the World* (1777), Georg Forster reflects on these processes by describing what could be interpreted as the primal scene of (b)order

---

[13] Since there is no English translation of Forster's text (Forster 1958) available, all paraphrases or translations are either ours or quoted from Ette (2017).

demarcation on the beach:[14] Having finally reached the beach of the island Tanna after many unsuccessful attempts (and just as many attempts on Forster's part to describe it), the Europeans, led by James Cook, intend to "prevent any unhappy differences with the natives, by apprizing them of [their] power" (Forster 1968, 486). Consequently, they are drawing "a line [...] on the sand" which the locals "should not transgress" (ibid., 488). In other words, they establish "authority" (ibid., 486) – or authorship – by literally writing (on) the beach. Referring to a distinct act of making "signs" (ibid.), of signification in order to demarcate and regulate the allegedly unregulated space, the passage obviously depicts a "writing scene" (Campe 1991). Accordingly, the described scene reflects on the one hand Forster's own act of 'writing the beach' and reveals it, once more, as an act of signification and symbolization, i. e. as an act of narrative construction rather than mimetic description. With this line on the strand, he also deliberately inscribes himself into the strand of the long tradition of Western imaginaries of the beach beginning with Vitruvius's report of the shipwrecked Aristippus, who "recognized that there were humans nearby when he saw geometrical figures traced on the sand" (Blumenberg 1997, 12). If Forster therefore aesthetically overwrites the beach of Tanna with the Western history of the beach, this reminds us that this borderline, on the other hand and in a very real sense, aims at ordering, (sub-)dividing and controlling the alleged "wild" space by a sort of European *divide et impera* (Forster 1968, 488). As "a violence without ground," this clearly semanticized act of demarcation therefore also represents a colonialist law-writing scene, a violent inaugural act of institution of law that functions through writing and over-writing on the beach, which becomes ground of the law (Derrida 1990). If the harbor can be described as "a *limes* whose safety must be protected" (Corbin 1994, 187), the Europeans obviously use hierarchical binary structures in order to enforce within this sandy zone a colonial 'safe harbor'-like legal order that is supposed to transform the beach into a territory of power and of regulated encounters and trade.

Looking at Forster's texts, it becomes more than apparent how the interaction between processes of regulation and deregulation can offer a relevant framework for understanding the space of the beach. Especially in contrast with the harbor, one can appreciate how the density of structures on the one hand and the "territoire du vide" (Corbin 1994) on the other can trigger different imaginations of control and freedom. While the harbor can be conceived as a model of structure or as a Moloch that exceeds control and precludes visibility, the beach can be viewed as a space outside of reified structures of society or as

---

14 For a detailed analysis of Forster's Tanna episode, see Ulrich's article in this volume.

a space whose very emptiness and accessibility to scrutiny make it an ideal place of inscription for even more rigid demarcations.[15]

In this context, the beach can be considered to be part of the network of dominant structures of capitalism or society and, simultaneously, as a space beyond them. Its imagination as a space apart from society has a long cultural history: The beach is configured and marketed as an untouched, primordial paradise, in which nakedness and idleness point to the condition before the Fall.[16] An image that movies like Danny Boyle's *The Beach* or Terrence Malick's *The Thin Red Line* then turn on its head or use as a foil for contrast. However, even this space beyond established orders can then again become part of competing (shadow) networks of goods and trade that are not regulated by government institutions – though one may argue that this fantasy of the beach as an unmarked space of subversion already masks its constructedness and underlying hierarchizing structures.

That the emptiness of the beach is in itself the result of a certain way of looking can be developed with recourse to a passage from Italo Calvino's *The Invisible Cities* that tells the parable of a city dweller and a goatherd. While the city dweller does not perceive the modulations of the territory, the markers that order space in the countryside, the man from the countryside is incapable of orienting himself in the urban space, which appears distinctionless to his eyes, whereas orientation in the countryside poses no problem to him (Calvino 1974, 129). As a territory of fluctuating borders, the beach, of course, presents an interesting limit case.

Building on this, the aforementioned line in the sand is an example of microstructures that visualize and translate orders of gender, race, class and (dis-)ability in a society on/into the closed-off space of the beach (a process that also holds the potential to work against them).[17] While this organization of space can occur through built structures – from piers and pavilions to whole vacation villages – it can also occur through, often object-related, practices. The building of sandcastles[18] can be considered to occupy a compelling in-between position: While sandcastles can be understood as an echo of the bunker structures

---

[15] See Bunch Davis's article in this volume about the phenomenon of segregated beaches in the US; on the segregation of South African beaches in its relation to literature, see Samuelson (2015); also see Foucault's description of Bentham's panopticon (Foucault 1977, 200).
[16] See on the semiotics of the naked body, Vinken in this volume; on the uneasy relationship of political transformation and its representation to nakedness, see Haselbeck in this volume.
[17] See Devienne in this volume on the factors governing the increased policing of beaches in the twentieth century.
[18] See Kolbe in this volume.

defending the outer lines of territory, as is visible in Normandy to this day, the practice of building them also opens our eyes to the more ephemeral beach practices that establish hierarchies, borders and relations: from the placing of towels, the collecting of sea shells or flotsam and jetsam, to the formation of a specific cultural repertoire of looks exchanged, furtive glances and instances of dominating gaze (Löw 2005; Kaufmann 1995). Further, the different levels of competency for those practices create distinctions among groups and a division of tasks, at the same time reshaping, restricting or expanding the space of the beach: It is foremost swimming that comes to mind, a practice that regulates the access to parts of the territory and determines the extent of space that can be appropriated – and thus moves the line dividing the accessible and inaccessible portions of the beach. The gendered and racialized profiles of specific competencies, or rather the stereotypes now attached to the topic, constitute the backdrop for the biographies of African American lifeguards that Carol Bunch Davis's article in this volume focuses on, while *Insecure*, Issa Rae's TV series, takes up these stereotypes to present the beach as a space of limited access for young African Americans. However, a variation in spatial extent can also occur when an area placed far away from the coast is transformed into a beachscape through practices that mirror typical beach practices.[19] In analogy to the argument made by Burkhardt Wolf (2013, 295), and in an ironic inversion of it (since Wolf precisely argues that it is the water that becomes limitless in extent), one can say that the beach is made to stretch beyond its own borders.

Already in Forster's description, the regulatory practices discussed above are intrinsically connected to the function of the beach as a site of (post-)colonial encounter, often commercial in nature, as it is configured in cultural imaginations. The beach is the site of the first encounter between local inhabitants and colonial explorers, which, especially in postcolonial literature, may then become the point of origin of a hybridized (and brutalized) 'self' and the point of contact with an enigmatic predecessor who becomes visible here for the first/last time in the operation of separation and the establishment of a new order.

The relation of postcolonial literature and theory to these voices and figures beyond the written accounts of explorers, scientists and colonial administrators is highly contested and dependent on the specific historico-geographical context. A reading based on the Caribbean or African context may conclude, in keeping with Frantz Fanon (2008, 70), that the perspective of this 'other' on the beach has to remain uncommunicable forever, all imaginings of his/her standpoint prosthetic and after-the-fact, belatedness their constitutive mode (Döring 2015, 109–111). For the South Pacific context, scholars often prefer to sharply

---

[19] See Butz's account of skateboarding as an urban correlate of surfing in this volume.

distance themselves from theories of 'fatal impact' and their claims of inaccessibility and further emphasize that viewing those historical events as disruptions in local history is not the only option, since they can also be understood to participate in its continuities (Calder, Lamb and Orr 1999, 10, 17; see also Balme 2007, 19, 35). Tracey Moffatt's video installation *The White Ghosts Sailed In* at the Australian Pavilion at the Venice Biennale of 2017 ironically comments on this contested question by showing a view of the coast and water presented as an indigenous documentary of the arrival of Captain James Cook in 1788 (see Moffatt 2017 and also Wright 2017). However, all of those differing positions share in the common matrix of a dual perspective that finds its imagined origin in the encounter on the beach.

A late echo of these scenes seems to inform a self-reflexive scene in Fanon, who describes the community waiting at the docks for the returnee from the capital to assess if he – in this scene, the returnee is always a man – has been transformed in his ways (Fanon 2008, 24). In a larger sense, though, for Fanon, writing on the French Antilles, there is no alternative to a hybridized culture that has been transformed by the contact with the colonial other (ibid., 70, passim). In this sense, the beach is the setting for the primal scene of postcolonial literature.

While this primal scene already includes negotiation and trade, the beach moreover serves as a space of exchange, a *marketplace* in the broadest sense, where goods, knowledge, cultural assets, practices and even identities are negotiated. From Forster's men – exchanging languages, (hi-)stories and even their names with the locals (Forster 1968, 498) – to contemporary forms of (eco-)tourism; the beach as such a marketplace might serve as a space for cultural exchange and transformations, while at the same time this marketplace is ruled by postcolonial regulations. In this sense, Fanon's "The Pitfalls of National Consciousness" highlights the problem that the "national bourgeoisie" in newly decolonized states "organizes centers of rest and relaxation and pleasure resorts to meet the wishes of the Western bourgeoisie," coming "to it as tourists avid for the exotic" (Fanon 2001 [1961], 153). With this he refers to the aforementioned old (Western) fantasy of an exotic, untouched paradisiacal space, which has been reinvented since the 1950s through tourist marketing strategies as "vacationscape" (Gunn 1972; Taussig 2000, 252).[20] Under "the name of tourism," Fanon continues, tourist destinations like the "beaches of Rio" are increasingly being transformed into "brothel[s] of Europe" (Fanon 2001 [1961], 153–154). In other words, Forster's line on the beach as a "sign" of (post)colonial "power" (Forster 1968, 486) is still running through the sand and tourist encounters

---

[20] See also on the tourist imagination and its erasures of visibility Urbain (2003).

constantly reenact the primal scene of postcolonial literature. "Organized around the pursuit of sun, sea, sand, 'exotic' culture, and sex" (Carrigan 2010, XII–XIII), postcolonial tourism also perpetuates existing power hierarchies since it is built on the economic and cultural hegemony of the former colonial power marginalizing and exploiting the (formerly) colonized people and states.

The beach serves, in this respect, as "brothel of Europe" in a very literal sense. In fact, as can already be seen in Bougainville's *Voyage Round the World* (1771) or Diderot's "Supplement to Bougainville's *Voyage*" (1796), the tourist imagination of a paradisiacal virgin beach has from the outset been closely linked to the idea of "erotic spectacle" (Balme 2007, 29) and "easily accessible sexual fulfilment" (Richter and Kluwick 2015, 7). Accordingly, in contemporary novels, like *Turtle Nest* (2003) by the Sri Lankan author Chandani Lokugé, the beach is a tainted paradise:[21] Set in a fishing village on Sri Lanka's south-west coastline, the novel depicts the beach as the 'place to be,' where locals as well as tourists gather and converse as they would do on a marketplace in a town center. This beach is, however, also and especially a marketplace in an economic sense: "outside the fence" of the hotels (Lokugé 2017, 12) and dominated by a gang of "beach boys," shady deals are made, drugs are traded and, above all, bodies are bought and sold between tourists and locals, who try "to keep all the family from starving" (ibid., 95). Lokugé's beach is "not safe" (ibid., 46), it is literally the dark flip side of the 'safe harbor': a place of crime, of "drugs, prostitution, pimping," terror and rape (ibid., 87, 83, 112, 225). While the locals meet "the white men on the beach" (ibid., 72) and use and "live[] off the tourists" (ibid., 83), these, in turn, "abuse [them], one after another, and then drive [them] onto the streets" (ibid., 87). The beach as *such a* marketplace sheds light on the mostly invisible hegemonic and violent dynamics of (post-)colonialism, capitalism and tourism.

5 Tourist Beachification: Material and Imaginary Constructions of Littoral Space

The language and ideas through which the beach is perceived are, at least in Western Europe, highly influenced by tourist modes of constructing the beach, as has already come into view above. Their emergence in the eighteenth century – initially coupling a shift in cultural attitudes around the element of water with the erection of material structures along the coastline – can be retraced by

---

21 For a more detailed analysis, see Carrigan (1999, 151–191).

focusing on small coastal villages and the ways they were refashioned in the course of these processes. Today, tourist modes of beach construction impact social, cultural and natural environments of and around beaches on a global scale. While connected to an imaginary that endows the beach with an appeal derived from notions of emancipation and alternative ways of living, these modes also result in relations of economic dependence and processes of destruction.

5.1 Designing the Urban Beach

> Such a place as Sanditon, sir, I may say was wanted, was called for. Nature had marked it out, had spoken in most intelligible characters. The finest, purest sea breeze on the coast – acknowledged to be so – excellent bathing – fine hard sand – deep water ten yards from the shore – no mud – no weeds – no slimy rocks. Never was there a place more palpably designed by nature for the resort of the invalid – the very spot which thousands seemed in need of! The most desirable distance from London! (Austen 2008 [1817], 143)

With these words, Mr. Parker – one of the main characters in Jane Austen's last and unfinished novel *Sanditon* – describes and advertises his coastal hometown: Sanditon, a place "designed by Nature" (ibid., 143), undergoes a process of change and transformation. The former "quiet village of no pretensions" has become "a profitable speculation" for Mr. Parker and other landowners (ibid., 146), who try to turn the fisherman's village into a modern and commercial seaside town by constructing "new buildings" (ibid., 159): bathing houses, seaside resorts and other sites of leisure. In its representation of Sanditon, the novel ironically depicts the institutionalizing of bathing in eighteenth-century Britain and the cultural practices associated with it. The developments in Britain can be regarded as paradigmatic in the context of the social and material transformations of the coast which amount to what could be termed 'beachification' of the beach. This process follows a shift in the notion of the sea, which is no longer thought of only as a site of overpowering danger, profound alienation and potentially fatal seduction by sirens and other mythological water creatures (Schmitz-Emans 2003) but also as a site of recreation and revitalization, a shift which, as Alain Corbin has shown in his study *The Lure of the Sea* [*Le Territoire du vide*], occurs from the mid-eighteenth century onwards. The eighteenth century's great interest in hydrotherapy and seaside recuperation, however, not only affects the cultural imagination of the sea, but – even more so – that of the coastal area itself: With the construction of resorts and bathing houses, the beach receives increasing interest, turning from a mere part of the maritime landscape to the iconic center of seaside travelling, which produces its own set of regulations and cultural practices. This perceptional shift is captured in Jane Austen's *Sanditon* – a novel that inscribes the materiality of the beach into both its title as well as its setting, and, thus, shows how this materiality enters into economic speculation and becomes the scenery of architectural development.

The processes described above appear as a first manifestation of the commodification of seaside travelling that also lies at the heart of the contemporary global tourist industry. While seaside travelling had been reserved for the English upper class up to the 1850s, rising standards of living, the emergence of voluntary holiday associations and the establishment of (paid) vacation days accomplished by labor movements in the second half of the nineteenth century eventually led to a rapidly increasing number of working-class visitors at British beach resorts (Walton 1981; Walvin 1987): "working-class demand became the most important generator of resort growth in northern England in late Victorian times" (Walton 1983, 30). Together with this 'democratization'[22] (Pearson 1991, 61) of seaside travelling, the cultural practice of summer holidays prepared the ground for further processes of commodification and the large-scale development of infrastructure. With the invention and expansion of the railway in the course of the nineteenth century, beaches became increasingly integrated into the "Machine Ensemble" of railways as well as trams, subways and buses (Schivelbusch 1986, 39). As a result, even the beaches of the periphery, such as Normandy or Brittany, were incorporated into the infrastructural network of the center and thus into the city, so that "the station" literally "became the entrance to those regions," which subsequently became more and more urbanized (ibid.).

Nineteenth-century French painting reflects (on) this urbanization and commercialization of the seaside in a condensed form: In the 1860s and early 1870s, Eugène Boudin, Claude Monet and Édouard Manet paint on the Normandy Coast and develop a distinctive variant of the "beach scene" which depicts "the fashionable holidaymaker at the beach" (House 2007, 13).[23] Dippel (1996) especially stresses the close link of these depictions to the parallel development of notions of urban modernity in the capital. These beach scenes refashion the beach as an urbanized environment.

---

[22] Even though increasing mobility and workers' rights bring high numbers of working-class visitors to the beach, social diversification of seaside travelling scarcely indicates 'democratization' but produces strict segregation along the shores: Resorts, towns and even seaside regions launched class-specific advertisement, spatially separating the upper class from the middle and working class (Barton 2005, 136–138).

[23] For an overview on impressionist beach painting, see also Handyside (2015, 18–22); see for the British context Payne (2015).

In the Mediterranean area, which in many aspects can be regarded as a paradigmatic tourist region, tourism evolved along different lines. First and foremost, tourism in the Mediterranean area has been from the very beginning an international affair, while versions of domestic tourism predominantly constitute the backdrop for the developments traced above, and was characterized by a fascination for historically and geographically distant cultural artefacts and habits. Already in the Middle Ages, contemporaneous discourses on pilgrimages reflect on (and express their theological concerns about) the psychological intertwinement of religious piety with a certain *curiositas*, an enjoyment of travelling itself and an excitement for foreign environments (Stagl 1995, 47). From the seventeenth century onwards, young men of the European aristocracy visit the Mediterranean region as part of their so-called 'Grand Tour,' in order to taste the sublime pleasure of being close to the remnants of ancient Greek and Roman culture. In the nineteenth century, new stimuli for this interest in classical antiquity are created with the rediscovery of Pompeii, the idealization of classical beauty in the works of Winckelmann, popular at the time, and Byron's participation in the Greek War of Independence. (Gordon 2003, 207; Löfgren 1999, 157; Stagl 1995, 47–94) The gradual remodeling of this initial form of tourism as an educational experience for social elites into the mass tourism economy at the Mediterranean coast that was consolidated in the middle of the twentieth century and still exists today was driven by a variety of concurrent processes, among others: the colonization of North African countries at the south coast and the subordination of their economies to European interests, the enormous technological advancements in the field of transportation, the introduction of labor reforms that included paid vacation time and the establishment of a huge hotel and gastronomy industry (Gordon 2003, 207–220). In the 1970s, a growing awareness for the negative effects of tourism in general and Mediterranean tourism in particular enters public discourse. It becomes obvious that tourism only integrates underdeveloped regions into global markets at the cost of reinforcing relations of economic dependency between core and periphery. (Holden 2006, 120) One important aspect of this dynamic is the ecological damage caused by tourism, which not only impacts coastal ecospheres but also the local communities, who lose access to natural resources due to over-extraction or pollution (ibid., 171–175).

Today, the Mediterranean is still the most popular tourist destination in the world. The World Tourism Organization (UNWTO) reported 342 million international tourist arrivals in 2014, which amounts to a share of 30 per cent of arrivals worldwide (*UNWTO Tourism Trends* 2015). But to assess the charm still emanating from the Mediterranean, it is not enough to merely take into account the visitors of the region. Rather, market economy has long since discovered the potential of the concept 'Mediterranean' as a label applicable to all kinds of consumer products. The notion of a Mediterranean cuisine in particular is connected to a powerful cultural idea centered around a phantasmatic reconciliation of health and hedonism, authenticity and cultural refinement. In this fashion, the beaches of the Riviera or the Adria lose their ties to a specific geographical space and become a feature of everyday experience even for people living far away from a coast.[24]

The construction of artificial beaches represents the development analogous to this process: Often built in cities (such as Paris Plages) or as part of hotel complexes, artificial beaches blur the formerly constitutive opposition of coastal and urban existences and transport the promise of the recreational *retreat from* everyday life *into* everyday life. This occasional 'beachification' of the city mirrors the increasing urbanization of beaches. While the opposition between beaches and cities becomes blurred, the distinction between the beach and the coast is sharpened: functional architecture associated with the coast – including lighthouses, harbors or piers – bears almost no similarity to tourist-related structures, like beach pavilions or vacation resorts. Tourism drives the 'reformatting' of the seaside into a beach.[25]

5.2 Utopian Nightmares: The Janus-Faced Beach

Paradoxically, the increasing interdependence and intertwining of urban and littoral space is linked to a gradually developing imaginary of the beach as a realized utopia outside quotidian life. The beach has been perceived, as in Orvar Löfgren's *On Holiday* (1999, 7), as a "cultural laboratory where people have been able to experiment with new aspects of their identities, their social relations, or their interaction with nature." Beyond being associated with transgressive cross-cultural exchange, the beach is often imagined as a space for transformative encounters with the self, as a sphere where sensual experience is heightened, self-perception is intensified and affects and desires that are deemed unacceptable and are repressed or sublimated in day-to-day social contexts are allowed to come to the surface.

---

24 Filmic representations from Federico Fellini's *La dolce vita* (1960) and Jean-Luc Godard's *Le Mépris [Contempt]* (1963) to Fatih Akin's *Auf der anderen Seite [The Edge of Heaven]* (2007) have played an important role in underscoring, reflecting and updating the myth of the Mediterranean and the life associated with it.

25 See Erben in this volume: "Architektur macht mit solchen Pavillons unübersehbar, dass die Küste zum Strand umformatiert wurde." [With such pavilions, architecture makes it obvious that the coast has been reformatted into a beach.] (p. 225)

The tourist imaginary can draw upon influential models from a tradition of experimentations with alternative forms of social organization, in which the beach was also thought of as a space of unlimited possibilities, a (utopian) free space of liberation *beyond* or *beneath* social orders and regulations. From monasteries, built on islands at the sea like Le Mont-Saint-Michel, to hippie communes at the beaches of Goa, the gay community on the beaches of Fire Island/New York[26] or artist colonies like Ahrenshoop in the North of Germany, beaches have repeatedly served as imaginary spaces and as real places of an alternative community trying to overcome social differences. Perhaps the most famous example that comes to mind is the slogan "Sous les pavés, la plage!" [Beneath the paving stones, [is] the beach!], which was painted across Parisian walls during the May–June 1968 protests in France, when revolutionary students tore up paving stones from the strictly ordered Parisian streets and literally uncovered the sand underneath.

The tourist imagination takes up this notion of the beach as a space in which the norms of society are suspended or set aside. Case studies examining the cultural significance and social function of different geographic beachscapes have suggested that the beach, especially in Western tourist and consumerist contexts, has come to be constructed as a 'liminal zone' (Shields 1991, 5–6),[27] which opens up opportunities for "illicit or disdained social activities" (ibid., 3) such as excessive drinking and transgressive sexual activity.[28] After its development into a resort and amusement park starting in the nineteenth century, the Coney Island Beach in Brooklyn acquired its notorious nickname as the 'playground of the world.' In his research on the British seaside town Brighton, sociologist Rob Shields demonstrated how, through the superimposition of an "imaginary geography filled with both myths and realities" (Shields 1990, 39) onto its material geography, Brighton Beach "has come to have a particularly powerful and enduring association with the liminal and with the

---

26 See Parlett in this volume.
27 See the more detailed discussion of liminality in the section "Uncertain Borders" above.
28 Tourism in the Soviet Union, on the contrary, remained connected to a paradigm of physical training and patriotic education. From the late Stalin era onwards, an increasing number of Soviet citizens travelled to the beaches of the Black Sea or Estonia to strengthen their body through swimming and to enjoy a somehow exotic, yet safely Sovietized cultural environment. (Gorsuch 2011) *Turizm*, as a purposeful, self-improving activity, was usually sharply distinguished from *otdykh*, a form of rest and relaxation mostly reserved to people with health issues – or those who had the connections to be declared as such (Gorsuch 2011, 8). This gradually changed when, in the Brezhnev years, so-called 'wild tourists' (*dikie turisty*) began to outnumber the tourists travelling with government vouchers (Noack 2019).

carnivalesque" (ibid., 39–40), and with the promise of "freedom from the constraints of social position (both high and low)" (ibid., 39), and thereby

> became the locus of an assemblage of social practices and of customary social norms, which, attached to the notion of 'Beach' transformed its nature into a socially defined zone appropriate for specific behaviours and patterns of interaction outside of the norms of everyday behaviour, dress and activity. (Ibid., 40–41)

In a similar vein, Anette Pritchard and Nigel Morgan (2010, 138) examine how the 'resort beach' functions as the site for a "contemporary form of carnival." They analyze televised "representations of the (un)dressed beach body" (ibid., 128) in the US-American TV formats *Wild On* and *Naked Wild On 2*, which were filmed mainly at beaches in Florida and the Caribbean, and cite Mikhail Bakhtin's theory of the 'carnivalesque' to uncover how the beach is "marked by unrestrained excess and embodied celebrations" and becomes a space of "exaggerated exoticism, eroticism" and "escapism" (ibid., 138). As Shields notes, the image of the beach as the quintessential site for leisure, fun and excess has been so pervasive in Western cultures that "'Beach' became a metaphor for a wider circle of discourses on pleasure and pleasurable activities – discourses and activities without which our entire conception of a beach would be without meaning" (Shields 1990, 41). At the same time, this societal construct relies on the deliberate obliteration of all traces pointing to the work processes required to keep up the outward appearance of an undisturbed paradise.[29]

However, the very phantasmatic imagination of a paradisiacal space of liberation and freedom always provokes the inversion into its reverse image since the same mechanisms that constitute these utopias necessarily imply their dystopian counterpart. Alex Garland's 1996 novel *The Beach* and Danny Boyle's 2000 film adaptation starring Leonardo DiCaprio develop the dystopian corruption of this fantasy of an Eden-like escapist refuge in a systematical fashion. In *The Beach*, a remote island in the Gulf of Thailand with its hidden lagoon and pristine beach becomes the site for the development of a self-sufficient community of backpackers who, far removed from the constraints of their former lives in the Western world, live the dream of an alternative, utopian society devoted to pleasure, leisure, a love of nature and ultimate freedom. Garland's protagonist Richard, who is accepted into the exclusive group of people living the "beach life" (Garland 2016 [1996], 116), initially experiences that "escape through travel works" (ibid., 115). Soon, his "life in England" becomes "meaningless," and he fully immerses himself into the seemingly ideal new mode of existence and does not "really question anything about the beach" (ibid.). The

---

[29] See Richter in this volume.

expulsion from the escapist littoral paradise on earth is, however, inevitable, as fun and peace on the beach give way to violence, insanity and death: Power struggles and increasing tensions between the beach-dwellers lead to a splitting up of the community into smaller groups which eye each other with suspicion; several community members who were tasked with fishing fall victim to fatal shark attacks; and a violent run-in with the local Thai cannabis farmers ends in the murder of a newly arrived group of backpackers looking to join the community. In the end, Richard, who is suspected of having given away the secret of the island's location to fellow tourists and thereby putting the community's survival in jeopardy, barely makes it out alive when he escapes from the precarious cosmos of 'beach life' at the last minute, after a group of intoxicated community members has attempted to kill him, and flees back to the mainland on a raft. The utopian dream of a space freed from all hierarchy and convention is perverted, gives rise to new and more brutal authoritarian relations and ultimately turns into a nightmare – the vacationscape becomes a 'thanatoscape' (see Kluwick 2015).

The beach as thanatoscape may disrupt the phantasmatic invisibilization of labor: In the 2015 terror attacks in Sousse Beach, Tunisia, 38 people, a majority of them British tourists, were tragically killed. More deaths were only prevented by the employees of a nearby hotel forming a line with their unarmed bodies to protect the tourists on the other side of the beach. Ironically, at the very moment when the idyllic and peaceful holiday scenario collapsed, the only thing that provided a barrier of safety for the tourists was the physical presence of the local workers, which, as a reminder of the labor that is required to keep the beautiful appearance of the beach intact, must be invisibilized under regular circumstances. At the same time, in these attacks, which were specifically directed against the democratization of the country and its integration into international diplomatic relations,[30] the escalation of a production of difference inherent in the system of globalized tourism is rendered palpable. By turning beaches into globalized spaces through its imaginary and material constructions, international tourism has also put them at risk of becoming the scenes of violent counter-reaction to globalization.

---

[30] We are grateful to Ines Ghalleb for pointing our attention to this issue in her introduction to Virginia Richter's keynote at the conference *Narrating and Constructing the Beach* on 15 June 2018 in Munich.

6 Vanishing Sands: Precarious Habitats and the Economy of Dematerialization

In recent theoretical thinking, more and more attention has been paid to the ways in which the mediated materiality of the beach in its relation to a system of (limited) natural resources is exploited by a global capitalist economy of which tourism forms a vital part. In this context, the question of how concepts of habitability and human intervention into a natural sphere are configured across different media – e. g. photography, film and writing – acquires particular relevance. Geological and geographical discourse provides an important backdrop for a discussion of those questions. Definitions originating from the discipline of physical geography condition debates on the material disappearance of the beach (or rather its sands), while the discourse on the Anthropocene refers to stratigraphic dimensions of the geological discipline. The problematization of humanity's relation to its material environments opens into the discussion of the beach as a zone of inhabitability.

If one attempts to describe it from a geological and geographical perspective, the beach appears as a body with various zones and borders that consists of superimposed sediments and is constantly shifting.[31] In its definitional approximations, geology addresses from a phenomenological and theoretical perspective a referent that exceeds the dry strip of sand next to the water often associated with the word 'beach.'

Geologically, oceanic beaches are part of the coastal area, which in addition to the backshore also includes the foreshore and shoreface. Apart from dry strips of land, this area also comprises zones which are temporarily or permanently submerged by the ocean. The beach, as a transition between two ecosystems, includes both the eulittoral zone as well as the supralittoral zone (splash zone), while the sublittoral zone reaches down to the edge of the continental shelf. The eulittoral zone is located between high-water line and low-water line. This is the area that is rhythmically washed over by the ebb and flow of the tides. The shoreline marks the transition between land and sea, but it does so as a dynamic boundary, even though it is mapped as a precise line. In fact, beaches are constantly moving and the border between sea and dry land is more of an area than a line. The morphological properties of beaches (and coasts in general) cause their littoral drift. Due to their dynamic and spatial

---

[31] On geological and geographical definitions and models related to the beach, see Gierloff-Emden (1990); Davis and Duncan (2004).

character, it is, strictly speaking, impossible to define beaches from a geodetic perspective.

The extension and expansion of common notions of the beach presented by this geological discussion can be further accentuated through relational thinking: In relation to the maritime world on the one hand and to the human world on the other, the beach has its own quality, although the beach cannot be viewed separately from them: the beach as a coincidence of both is connection and disconnection between land and sea, *neither* land nor sea and *both* land and sea, all at the same time. Land and sea are different from each other, but the beach in its in-betweenness is something that differs. Although the beach stands out from both land and sea, it cannot be distinguished as separate from them, because neither can its spatial character be reduced to a link between those two relata (in the sense of a mediation or a self-existing space in-between) nor can it be defined as something that exceeds them.

Further, every beach is different and differs over time. The beach alters its appearance and character dramatically with the changing of the tides and of the water level in the intertidal zone. The beach slope affects the wave run-up and *vice versa*. The ecosystem of the beach is not only dependent on the tides but also strongly influenced by the degree of salinity, which increases rapidly as water evaporates on the way from the open sea to the coast. Every beach as an ecosystem is a singular configuration which is the result of specific local circumstances, ranging from climatic to hydro-geographic or geological conditions as well as flora and fauna to human interventions.

Those interventions especially concern the stuff the beach is made of: sand. In contrast to other coastal or shore formations, such as cliffs consisting of rock formations or artificial solution bottoms as part of harbor structures, the beach is composed of moving rock that is pressed against the shore by the waves and constantly shifting. The appearance of the beach is determined by the erosion of this unconsolidated rock by wind and waves and its deposition on the beach either in the form of grains of sand or as gravel or pebbles.[32] The actual habitat of the beach is less on its sandy surface than in the cavities between the grains of sand. Kōbō Abe, in a passage in *The Woman in the Dunes*, captures the reality of movement constitutive of the beach, which is conditioned by its materiality: "Sand not only flows, but this very flow is the sand" (as cited in Urbain 2003, 323).

---

[32] 'Sand' as a term is used when the grain size is between 0.063 mm and 2 mm. Grains that are smaller are referred to as 'silt' or 'clay,' depending on the degree of fineness, while larger grains are referred to as 'gravel.'

Sand is a clastic sediment (Greek: *klastein*, 'fracture') which is formed by weathering processes. Each grain of sand is in a certain sense a toy of waves and tides and has undergone a journey of up to a thousand years and various stages of the cycle of erosion. From a geological perspective, sand on the beach comes from the rivers carrying granite or sandstone, which is slowly weathered by rain, snow and ice, into the sea. Much of the sand is formed when glaciers melt. The granular material of the beach consists of a mineral mixture that varies from beach to beach: There are beaches of quartz sand, volcanic sand, limestone sand (e.g. originating from the shells of marine organisms) and relatively rare gypsum sand (Duran 2000).

The uncountable countability of the grains of sand represents a popular metaphor for picturing the universal or the infinite. There is as much of something, as the saying goes, "as there is sand by the sea" (Gen. 22,17; Gen. 41,49; Rom. 9,27). The number of grains of sand, on the basis of which Archimedes, in the third century B.C., revolutionized the numeral system with his text *The Sand Reckoner* (1897), was no less a synonym for infinity in ancient times. In the book *Sirach*, written about 175 B.C., it says: "If we live a hundred years, we have lived an unusually long time, but compared with all eternity, those years are like a drop of water in the ocean, like a single grain of sand" (Ecclus. 18,10).

Like water, sand not only functions as a popular image for the embodiment of infinity, but above all, it represents one of the most important raw materials for humankind. Sand is indispensable, for example, in the glass industry, the electronics industry, in hydraulic fracturing for the extraction of shale gas and shale oil, in cosmetics and health products and especially in the construction of buildings and civil engineering. (Welland 2009) Meanwhile however, the grains of sand on the beach are numbered: Scientific studies predict that a large number of the world's beaches, sometimes whole islands, are about to disappear (Vousdoukas et al. 2020).

This loss, even though it has many reasons, is entirely caused by the human species: The natural retreat of the coast is blocked by the construction of cities or hotel complexes on the beach, while the anthropogenic climate emergency leads to global warming and a rise in sea levels that will eventually result in the flooding of coastal regions and the disappearance of habitat, which will first affect the people in the Global South. Further, the supply of sand from rivers is severely impaired by hydroelectric power plants. The main cause, however, is the global construction boom, which will continue to have immense geopolitical, economic and ecological consequences. Sand beaches are usually preceded by highly dynamic and mobile sandbanks, which serve as a natural buffer against the forces of wind and waves released by storms and tsunamis. These sand dunes, which are located in front of the beaches, are the main objects of desire for the construction industry. Their degradation has fatal consequences not only for the ecosystem formed by the beach. Because fine drifting sand of the desert is not (yet) suitable as a raw material for construction, concrete consists mainly of gravel and the coarse-grained sand from rivers and beaches, where it is (often illegally) mined by the so-called 'sand mafia.' This problem has gained broader attention through the instructive documentary *Sand Wars* (2013) by Denis Delestrac.

The affected countries are also aware of this: the protection of coasts and preservation of beaches through so-called 'beach nourishment' has become a worldwide phenomenon. Despite the enormous financial means spent on these practices, however, the success achieved is exclusively cosmetic and very short-lived.[33] It is not uncommon that after two years all the artificially deposited sand (as beach renourishment or sand replenishment) has disappeared.

> A fundamental problem is not simply that this is treating the symptoms rather than effecting a cure, but that the wrong kind of medicine is often used. Beach sand is, after all, the specific local product of local processes, and replacing it with sediment dredged from offshore is replacing it with something else entirely – finer-grained sand, differently sorted sand, or mud. A typical 'nourished' beach erodes much faster than a natural one. (Welland 2009, 118)

Beach nourishment not only contributes to the scarcity of sand, in the end, it also exclusively serves the profit interests of the sand industry.

The beach itself has offered a possible solution to the problems associated with the exploitation of sand. It is well known that glass is made of sand and has the same properties when it comes into contact with water. This is shown by the existence of beaches which consist of fine glass grains, as the Glass Beach in MacKerricher State Park, California, and the Steklyannaya Bukhta [Glass Bay] close to Vladivostok in the east of Russia. Created by pollution, these beaches are now popular for their kaleidoscopic reflections. The recycling of glass, however, cannot become a viable and competitive alternative to the industrial exploitation of beaches and rivers as long as the extraction of sand stays unregulated and almost free of charge. The same applies to the recycling

---

[33] According to Michael Welland, a mile of beach costs about 10 million dollars. "On the US east coast barrier island chain, from the southern end to Long Island to southern Florida, the equivalent of 23 million dump trucks of sand has been spread over 195 beaches on more than seven hundred separate occasions. Virginia Beach has been 'renourished' more than fifty times." (Welland 2009, 118)

of building debris, which is much more expensive than the (largely) illegal mining of sand.[34]

This dematerialization of the beach due to sand mining can be regarded as paradigmatic for an impact on nature which runs so deep that it is no longer possible to conceptualize humanity and its environment as two separate entities. Within the debates trying to theoretically capture and negotiate this development, the concept of the 'Anthropocene' is prominent. It posits that humankind has become the most formative geological factor on a planetary scale, which has led to a new geological age. This notion is supplemented by the argument that it is far from unlikely that humanity not only as an 'idea,' as Foucault's famous 'bet' at the end of *Les mots et les choses* in 1966 suggests, but also as an entire species could disappear in the near future "like a face drawn in sand at the edge of the sea" (Foucault 2002, 422).

With regard to the Anthropocene, the geologist Peter K. Haff recently added the "technosphere" to the "classic Earth spheres – atmosphere, hydrosphere, litosphere and biosphere" (Haff 2019, 139; 2014), meaning the sphere as a system – and not as a collection of artifacts and technological objects made by humans – with all that is living in it. Unlike the biosphere, it is difficult to recycle. The physical technosphere on the one hand is vital for the survival of humanity because of the size of the world's population and on the other hand threatens the biosphere and thus the survival of humans, animals and plants due to its toxic elements. In the form of plastiglomerates of future fossils, as is already visible in 'beach rocks' on the beach, it may inscribe itself into the earth's layers of rock strata (Zalasiewicz 2008). Non-degradable materials such as plastic constitute one of the greatest environmental burdens facing humankind, as is evidenced by the fact that the plastic waste in the oceans is already forming gigantic garbage vortices directly beneath the ocean surface (as the Great Pacific Garbage Patch), which have been designated as the 'eighth continent.'

Just as the microplastics in the ocean, which have become a 'fixed' part of our food chain and are now detectable in almost all fish, are invisible, so, too, are the microplastics on the beaches, even though every tenth grain of sand on various beaches already consists of them. Whether in the sea or on the beach, the plastic microparticles are not the object of immediate observation but are only visible in the sense of a "hyperobject" (Morton 2013) – as a 'weird' entity that is not really recognizable in one specific place but at the same time spreads

---

[34] On the importance of sand for human culture and civilization, its widespread use in tech and other industries, its illegal exploitation and the environmental crises caused by the latter, see the essential works by Welland (2009) and Beiser (2018) as well as the documentary by Delestrac (2013).

out immensely spatio-temporally, and therefore only becomes intelligible through the consequences it evokes. (Kramm and Völker 2017; Leinfelder and Assunção Ivar do Sul 2019) In this context, art represents a form of intervention that can reflect on the changed ecological conditions and make them visible or tangible.[35] In recent years, images of the beach as a place of death and decay have garnered attention in connection with contemporary political, social and environmental crises: photographs of dead whales washed ashore with their bodies full of plastic and birds hobbling about the sand helplessly with their feathers covered in black oil have been engrained into the collective imagination as illustrations for the disastrous effects of environmental pollution.

Implicit in the popular discourse on the Anthropocene is above all the moral consideration that all human beings are equally responsible for environmental pollution, global warming and climate change after the dawn of the age of humanity. This notion is accompanied by the imperative that all people must be aware of their responsibility. Andreas Malm and Alf Hornborg (2014), Jason Moore (2016b) and Donna Haraway (2016), on the other hand, have argued that it is not so much an undefined 'humanity' as such who is responsible for these developments but rather the organization and objectification of nature through the system of capitalism in general and through industrialization in particular, in which agency is distributed asymmetrically.[36] For these scholars, the ecological crisis cannot be separated from questions of production, social reproduction, commodification, capital accumulation and the oppression of humans by humans (e. g. the objectification of humans as cheap labor). By rehistoricizing the debate, they reveal the political dimensions of the biosphere catastrophe, which they capture with a term coined by Malm (Moore 2016a, xi), "Capitalocene" – 'the age of capital.'

Not only on the scale of species but also on the scale of individual lives, has the relationship between humans and the beach environment been a precarious one: The coast has always been an important habitat for humans. Two thirds of the world's population live no more than 300 kilometers away from the ocean (Bruns, Petretto and Petrovic 2013, 9). Paul Virilio sees the main reason why people have always been settling close to the coast in the fact that water allows for a combination of mobility and mass(es) (Virilio 2010, 20). Although a

---

35 See Auerochs in this volume; on art as an epistemic factor in relation to the maritime habitat, see Bauernfeind in this volume.
36 "'[T]he Anthropocene' might be a useful concept and narrative for polar bears and amphibians and birds who want to know what species is wreaking such havoc on their habitats [...]. Within the human kingdom, on the other hand, species-thinking on climate change is conducive to mystification and political paralysis. It cannot serve as a basis for challenging the vested interests of business-as-usual." (Malm and Hornburg 2014, 67)

remarkable amount of people lives close to the water, the beach in itself, and especially the intertidal zone of the ocean, is not a place in which humans usually find their homes. Even though new ways of constructing beach houses have changed this somewhat, the almost cyclical destruction of these structures, accelerated by climate change (Gillis and Barringer 2012), is a testimony to the fact that the beach is in most cases too exposed and too shifting in its topography, too inhospitable to make it a 'natural' home for humans (a condition the architectural designs of Dionisio González react to). It is thus no accident that beach architecture and the 'built ecology' of the beach are situated between the stable and the ephemeral.[37] If humans do live there, something has been thrown out of joint (one may think of the beginning of Shakespeare's *Macbeth* with its battle "lost and won" (1.1.4, Shakespeare [1623] 1984), which the Polánski adaptation from 1971, preparing the ground for key scenes in Kurzel's version from 2015, locates at the beach). In the works of Marguerite Duras, it is the memoryless protagonists' continued presence on the beach, as in *L'Amour* (2013 [1972]) and *La Femme du Gange* (1973), that serves to underscore their status beyond life and death but also outside human society. The interplay of light and weather that captures the figures in a kind of objectless epiphany plays an important part in this transience. In Léonora Miano's and Marie Ndiaye's novels, the beaches on both sides of the Mediterranean are portrayed as 'heterotopias of violence.' From the arrested movement of captured Africans who are deemed 'superfluous' within the inhuman workings of international slave trade on the beaches of Africa to that of migrants and refugees at the coasts of Europe some hundred years later, living in those spaces becomes impossible, in a sense that takes the form of a political appeal.[38] One of the most haunting beach images distributed by mass media in recent years is a photograph of three-year-old Syrian refugee Alan Kurdi lying face-down on the beach after drowning in the Mediterranean Sea in September 2015.

The term 'Fortress Europe' (*Festung Europa*) is used again in this context today, not only by right-wing politicians but also among conservatives (Schmitz-Berning 2007; Mayrhofer 2010). It mobilizes a rhetoric originating from National Socialist parlance, which was in use until 1943 and then replaced with the term *Atlantikwall*, due to its less defensive character. The Atlantic Wall was a line of defense with which the Nazis intended to protect the western coastline with bunkers against the invasion of the Allied Forces. As opposed to

---

[37] See Erben's contribution "Sand, Spuren, Architektur – Zur gebauten Ökologie des Strandes" [Sand, Traces, Architecture – On the Built Ecology of the Beach] in this volume.
[38] On the dehumanization of African characters and the regulation of their movements in Miano and Ndiaye, see Ekobe in this volume.

more temporary buildings such as bathing cabins, kiosks or small huts, and alongside the piers protruding into the sea, bunkers are one of the few architectural types that have a permanent claim to the beach.[39]

Declaring the age of borders to be over, Virilio (1994, 12; see also 2010, 19) dedicated an 'archeology' to these relics of bygone warfare, shown as an exhibition at the Centre Pompidou in 1975, and published as a book the same year. The erection of walls and borders can be viewed as a desperate attempt to protect oneself from the actions of virtual powers and their consequences on a global scale. According to 'media geography,' however, financial and ecological crises have led to a "remedialization of geography," a renewed awareness of the fact that our understanding of spaces, such as the beach, is always constituted through specific media (Döring and Thielmann 2009, 10; Graham 2004). Fortress Europe, which Virilio saw as being dismantled militarily by the weathering of the bunkers, is rebuilding itself and its borders today – against the backdrop of the 'migration crisis,' which in Virilio's sense confirms that having power means being able to control movement.

Virilio's *Bunker Archeology* (1994) contains a chapter entitled "An Aesthetics of Disappearance," which shows images of sanded bunkers. This Aesthetics of Disappearance designates a process that returns the bunkers to that from which they were originally formed. As they slowly sink into the beach, they erode into the granular medium they once were: sand.

7 The 'Oscillating Pendulum': Resonances of 'Beach-Time'

In the Western European (and US-American) imaginary, the Normandy bunkers have acquired a symbolic function of peripeteia within the course of European and World history: They iconically mark the turning point of World War II and the beginning of the end of the deadly Nazi domination of Europe, and as such are depicted time and again and tied into a standardized plot in the Blockbuster war movies of Europe and Hollywood – among them the multinational European production *The Longest Day* (1962), Sam Fuller's grim autobiographically inspired satire *The Big Red One* (1980) and Steven Spielberg's redefinition of the combat movie genre *Saving Private Ryan* (1998) (see Basinger 2003; Bronfen

---

[39] Bunkers and bunkeresque fortresses that should have protected against an invasion of Napoleon's troops that ultimately never took place can be found on the southern coast of England, they can also be found on the Adriatic coast, dating back to the time of Tito.

2012; Kappelhoff 2006). In this narrative, the D-Day landing at Omaha Beach begins with a massacre: The Allied soldiers arriving from their boats are caught in the crosshairs of the German-held bunkers and die in masses, the beach becomes a space of liminality and death in the most radical sense. When the breach of the German defense lines finally succeeds and the territory of the beach can be left behind, the tide of the war has been turned with the tide of the battle.

Far beyond this example, beach scenes prominently feature as essential turning points or moments of peripeteia in narratives:[40] In Ian McEwan's novel *On Chesil Beach*, the dysfunctional relationship of a newly married couple culminates and ends in a final confrontation on the beach; in Jordan Peele's acclaimed horror movie *Us* (2019), the traumatic encounter with the protagonist Adelaide's doppelganger occurs in a funhouse located on Santa Cruz Beach; in Moussa Sène Absa's films the beach figures as a space of new beginnings;[41] and in David Lynch's TV-drama *Twin Peaks* (1990–1991), the central mystery of the show begins when Laura Palmer's dead body is found washed ashore on the beach.

For these works of fiction, the beach seems to play an important role not only because of its spatial characteristics but also as a temporal agent that is able to initiate, accelerate or turn around series of events. No discussion of the beach would be complete, therefore, without addressing it as the figure of a unique temporality. The beach can be considered as much as a temporal phenomenon as in its spatiality. Its temporal character must not be reduced to the situatedness of individual beaches in time, to their being affected by historical changes taking place in the surrounding world. Rather, it can be argued that the beach is related to a specific mode of temporality, a 'beach-time,' whose basic components can be described as follows:

'Beach-time' is mainly structured by two back-and-forth movements, two distinguishable but related repetitions, each generating their own form of time: The macro-time of the tides, the periodic but alternating (Gierloff-Emden 1990) ebb and flow connects 'beach-time' to processes taking place on a cosmic scale, to the gravitational forces between astronomical bodies and their orbital movements through space. Organizing a regular material exchange between land and sea, the tides, besides being an important factor in the lives of many maritime animals and of people living and working at the coast, are associated with both the threat of being drawn into the ocean and drowned as well as the

---

[40] For a study of the beach as a turning point in medieval literature, see the article by Mangard and Strieder in this volume.
[41] See De Raedt in this volume.

opposing threat of being stranded and thrown onto the shore like a piece of debris. These are not only literal dangers that beachgoers or ship travelers have to deal with but also powerful metaphors for existential conditions of immersion into or exposure to radically alien circumstances. 'Beach-time' provides conceptual metaphors through which changes taking place in the biographies of human individuals can be viewed and represented.

The micro-time of the surf, the back-and-forth movement of waves hitting the shore and subsequently withdrawing into the ocean, creates the characteristic – sometimes soothing, sometimes threatening – sensory impression of the beach that constitutes a key element of its aesthetic appeal. The acoustic experience of the surf in particular renders beach-time perceptible to human ears. The beach as a temporal phenomenon is above all a rhythmic phenomenon. Structuring time through the regularity of rhythmic repetition, the sound of the surf invites a comparison with the kind of segmentation accomplished by the tick-tock of a clock. However, in contrast to the monotonous music of the clock, the surf also allows for sonic variations, for alterations in tempo, volume or timbre caused either by changes in the weather or by the resonations of a multitude of objects contained within the waves, forming the most heterogeneous orchestra imaginable, as Jules Michelet points out:

> The pendulum of the clock oscillates less regularly than that alternating moan and roar of the Ocean in its grand unrest. And this latter, let me repeat it, has *not* the monotony of the pendulum, for in 'what those wild waves are saying,' we feel, or fancy that we feel the thrilling intonations of life. And in fact, at high flood, when wave rears its crest upon wave, immense, electric, there mingles with the tumultuous roaring of the fiercely rushing waters, the sound of the shells and pebbles, and the thousand things animate as well as inanimate that they carry with them in their shoreward rush. (Michelet 1861, 17–18)

Sometimes roaring or rumbling, sometimes murmuring or mumbling, the surf can be associated with the full spectrum of rhythmic organization. There is no objective and constant sound of the surf but continuous variation as a function of exterior circumstances as well as of subjective perception. As a result of this variation, any sensual suggestion of a transcendental and uniform time 'at' the beach is disrupted by an undercurrent of a dynamics of rhythmical oscillation, extension and contraction that makes the experience of 'beach-time' resist any effort to apply an abstract and exterior measure to it.

Henri Bergson's philosophy of temporality is centered around the opposition between a mechanistic notion of 'time' that is made quantifiable by reducing it to a succession of uniform movements between stable positions in a homogenous space (e.g. the movement of the hands of a clock) and his concept of 'duration' that consists of a fluid and immeasurable process of qualitative change (Bergson 1950, 75–139). 'Beach-time,' however, seems to be situated on both sides of the opposition. It is characterized by both regularity and variation, is both comparable to a clock and fundamentally different from it. It renders time perceptible by relating it to repetitive spatial movements – the back-and-forth of the tides and the waves – but these movements cannot be described as mere changes of location, as crossings of a border between two areas, because it is the borderline itself that is constantly moving. The spatial configuration of the beach does not precede these movements but is constituted by them, shaped by them and potentially submitted to the impact of their variations. 'Beach-time' transfers aspects of 'duration' into a spatialized form of time.

One significant advantage of Bergson's concept of 'duration,' according to Gilles Deleuze (1991, 32), is that it allows us to think encounters between different 'durations' as interactions between singular modes of temporal existence: "[M]y own duration, such as I live it in the impatience of waiting, for example, serves to reveal other durations that beat to other rhythms, that differ in kind from mine." In this manner, the beach inscribes its own temporality into the lives of individuals who are passing through its sphere of influence, letting the rhythms of 'beach-time' resonate in their bodies and minds.

There is an abundant and complex cultural imagery linking the structure of traumatic memory to the movement of waves at the beach. The oscillating waterline of the beach is imagined as constantly renegotiating various interconnected oppositions that are crucial for the conceptualization of psychic processes of remembering: back-and-forth, proximity and distance, depth and surface, latency and manifestation.[42] These are not superficial analogies between the beach and the human psyche providing us with metaphorical terms for the understanding of unconscious mechanisms. When relics of a distant and repressed past are suddenly washed onto the shore (Klooss 2014, 197), the beach literally participates in traumatic memory by violently inserting its own rhythms of disappearance and reappearance into the psychic economies of human subjects.

This example shows that 'beach-time' is inseparable from its relatedness to humanly produced modes of temporality. It enters into psychic or social contexts not without shaping their inherent rhythmical organization. In artistic representations of the beach in literature, film or music, this contagious effect of

---

[42] See Phillips's analysis of visual and auditory strategies in the HBO-series *Big Little Lies* in this volume. Phillips maps out the correlations between the rhythmic quality of the beachscape and the role of repetition in trauma.

'beach-time' becomes particularly transparent when the whole texture of the artwork is seized by its rhythmical vibrations.[43]

The beach is never simply 'in' time, if time is understood as a transcendental framework where phenomena appear and disappear. Rather, it generates its own unique time, which it then injects into the world, affecting the temporal constitution of all surrounding beings, including humans. In contrast to the imaginary 'time machines' we know from science fiction literature, which are usually mere vehicles moving through time, the beach can be regarded as a veritable time machine.

This capacity to temporally affect its surroundings and to make 'exterior,' 'natural' rhythms on the one hand and 'interior,' psychic rhythms on the other hand interact with each other is a particularly striking example for the reconfiguration of difference that occurs at or in relation to the beach. As this introduction has shown, differential relations are at the core of every discussion that revolves around the beach. These can involve the geological difference between sea and land, social and cultural differences between people, which are connected to and can be interpreted from different social and cultural perspectives, differences between imaginary and material constructions, between urban and littoral space. These differences are reconfigured on, around and by the beach in multiple ways: by being reflected or represented, accentuated or obscured, established or erased, by being associated with transgression or separation, by entering into relationships with other differences and forming social or narrative structures and processes. Since the beach is a focal point for various processes, discourses and practices, and since all these bring into play their own differences, studying the beach always means dealing with complexity on many levels. This constitutes both the challenge and the fascination of the beach as an object of study.

Contributions

The majority of the contributions are based on the papers that were presented at the conference *Narrating and Constructing the Beach* held in Munich in June 2018. The articles in the first section, "(Precluded) Arrivals/Departures," approach the beach as a transitional zone of coming and going and discuss the

---

[43] See Napoli's article in this volume for a discussion of the temporal trope of *villeggiatura* in Italian popular music.

multiplicity of conditions, opportunities and perils associated with the acts of entering and exiting the littoral borderland. Traditionally, the beach is thought to offer salvation in the form of a *terra firma* to those who are shipwrecked, but especially in recent years, European beaches have become sites at which refugees experience humiliation and unregulated violence. While socio-economic as well as psychological factors can preclude the departure from the beach and thereby turn the seasonal and temporary stay into permanent 'imprisonment,' the act of a successful departure from the beach figures as an imaginative generator for socio-political progress.

In her article "Stranded. The Beach as Ultimate Destination in Joseph Conrad's *Amy Foster* and Thomas Mann's *Death in Venice*," Virginia Richter compares two works of modernist narrative fiction and argues that in both narratives the beach is a place of stasis and degradation that exerts a "negative transformational power" on the respective protagonists and is inextricably linked to notions of death and decay. In *Amy Foster* the beach, which is construed not as a commodified vacationscape but as a sphere associated with hard work, poverty and the lethal dangers of the sea, comes to symbolize its protagonist Yanko's abject status in England as a Carpathian emigrant, who is, by all means, both literally and 'socially shipwrecked.' Mann's protagonist Gustav Aschenbach, on the other hand, gets 'stranded' on Venice's Lido only in a figurative sense, as he is captivated by the beauty of young Tadzio, gradually descends into decadence and moral decline and ultimately dies on the beach, turning his journey to Italy into a 'voyage of no return.'

The association of the beach with experiences of degradation is also revealed as central to the two novels analyzed by Jeannot Moukouri Ekobe in "Dystopie, Utopie, Heterotopie: Die Imagination des Strands in der Literatur von Afropäerinnen" [Dystopia, Utopia, Heterotopia: Imaginations of the Beach in the Literature of Female Afro-European Authors]. In Léonora Miano's *La Saison de l'ombre*, the African beach appears as the site of the first colonial encounter between the Mulongo people and European slave traders and as the place where European colonizers symbolically assert power over the 'other.' While Miano's historical novel depicts its protagonists as being forced into 'mobility' as they are deported from their homes, Marie Ndiaye's *Trois femmes puissantes*, which is set in the present time, tells the tale of African emigrant Khady Demba, who is forced into 'immobility' when, after a long and strenuous journey, she is shot and killed by soldiers on a beach at the European border, which acquires the status of an 'invisible fence.' As Ekobe's epoch-spanning analysis demonstrates, both novels paint a dystopian picture of the beach as a 'heterotopia of violence,' where agency and the power of decision over one's own movements are taken away from their African protagonists.

In "Figuring Senegalese Beaches in Moussa Sène Absa's Films," THÉRÈSE DE RAEDT, in a diachronic study of four of Absa's films, shows that the Senegalese filmmaker's cinematographic representations of beaches are not limited to the portrayal of the littoral zone as a 'thanatoscape.' Rather, these representations are as multifaceted as the liminally configured space of the beach itself and play an essential role for Absa's filmic poetics. De Raedt reveals how the history of Senegal and the socio-political situation of the country at large become visible and tangible in the filmic representation of the development of Senegalese beaches in the twentieth and twenty-first century. In Absa's films, the liminal and ever-fluctuating space of the beach reflects the tensions and paradoxes that characterize post-colonial Senegal, and symbolizes both life and death, nature and pollution, hope and despair, leisure and work.

The section "Drawing and Crossing Lines" interrogates the beach in relation to the production of difference and enforcement of hierarchies. It looks at the operations through which the beach becomes an ordered space and/or is functionalized to contribute to the ordering of societies, global systems and narrative representations.

CARMEN ULRICH's contribution "Strandbekanntschaften in Georg Forsters *Reise um die Welt* und das europäische Projekt 'Zivilisation'" [Beach Encounters in Georg Forster's *Reise um die Welt* and the European Project of 'Civilization'] is placed at the beginning of the chapter since it deals with the basic operation and archetypical scene of ordering processes: the drawing of a line in the sand, which is here described in Forster's *Voyage around the World* (in its later, German version), thus already inscribing it into the context of cultural encounter and the colonial expansion of European countries. This gesture simultaneously establishes the distinction between nature and culture, law and lawlessness. Ulrich stresses the fictionalizing element in Forster's depiction of this scene and investigates it as an attempt at ordering space that contrasts with the destabilizing qualities of the island's volcano, which always looms in the background. The transgression beyond this line proves irreversible in its deadly consequences but is cast in an ambiguous light by Forster.

DÉSIRÉE MANGARD's and MIRIAM STRIEDER's study of the beach motif in medieval literature, "Wechselnde Gezeiten: Der Strand als Schauplatz für Wendepunkte in Heldendichtung und höfischer Literatur des Mittelalters" [Changing Tides: The Beach as a Setting for Watershed in Medieval Heroic Poetry and Courtly Romance], interrogates its role for the ordering of narrative representation. Building on previous studies on the topic, they analyze the presence of the beach motif in a broad geographical and temporal range of texts. Mangard and Strieder draw on Lotman's framework, which describes the function of borders and their transgression for the plot. They expand the definition of the beach motif by establishing the beach as a space of peripeteia, a turning point in the action, or foreshadowing of the same and develop how the appearance of the beach in the texts may often coincide with decisive scenes of battle but may also serve to establish the heroic identity of the hero.

The two contributions by Elsa Devienne and Carol Bunch Davis treat beaches in the United States of the twentieth century and in relation to distinctions of sex, sexual orientation and age but especially race and class. In "'There's Law on the Beach!': Law and Order on Los Angeles's Beaches, 1910s–1970s," ELSA DEVIENNE looks at the history of regulations of beach behavior and their enforcement in the L. A. area and distances herself from linear narratives of a growing policing of behavior throughout the twentieth century. She especially stresses economic factors in determining the shape of those laws (which differentially affect white beachgoers and black and Latino beachgoers). Among those factors, the distribution of jurisdiction, practical police capacities and the development of the local housing market figure prominently. In tracing these developments, Devienne also tracks the construction of a history of the beach with regard to regulation and freedom.

In "Always on Duty: Galveston's African American Beaches and Lifeguards," CAROL BUNCH DAVIS examines the history of the segregated beaches of Galveston, a former center of the slave trade at the Mexican Gulf, and the memorial politics with which the city now commemorates its black history. She considers the biographies of Galveston's first two black lifeguards at the city's black beaches through the notion of 'sitting up,' which has its point of origin in the idea of tending to an illness and constitutes a model of "black care" that addresses the continued devaluation of black lives. In also targeting the continued disavowal of Galveston's history with regard to the commemoration of Juneteenth, she extends her examination up into the present of a segregated cityscape and sheds light on the place of beaches and their history in Galveston's commemorative landscape. Bunch Davis's contribution thus also finds itself at the limits of the category of "Drawing Lines," at the intersection where the devastating institutionalization of difference translates itself into the literal 'building structures' of the city.

The section "Building Structures & Assembling Elements" focuses on the material structures and conglomerations of objects or matter that are built or brought together on the beach. These arrangements between ephemerality and permanence, between order and seeming arbitrariness are bound up with larger networks of appropriation (of the beach and its beyond) and are heavily saturated with theoretical, historical and allegorical meaning. Within these processes and relations, the contributions show the interplay between the construction of the beach in cultural imagination and a variety of material constructions. Spanning littoral architecture as well as accumulations of objects on the beach, they make visible that the material that makes up the 'beach' not only extends beyond sand and water as its 'natural basis' to the stones and concrete of beach buildings like hotels and holiday homes and to the debris or exotic and curious items brought onto it by chance or deliberation, but that the practices articulated through them and situated on the beach form an integral part of it as well. The topics explored by the articles range from the development of the ecological system 'beach' through repetitive cultural patterns and practices to the creation of a holiday experience through sand structures as material products of a practice of building that are at the same time contested sites of interpretation, to the beach as pictorial setting for a Wunderkammer of (allegorical) animals on the verge of the inanimate that is itself folded back into the practice of collection (of objects and by extension of knowledge) underpinning and underwriting a colonial world and its power structures.

Taking as its point of departure the architectural constructions in Daniel Defoe's novel *Robinson Crusoe*, DIETRICH ERBEN discusses the beach as a 'built ecology' that transforms the coastal area into a beach zone. Along the categories of sand, trace and building, the article "Sand, Spuren, Architektur – Zur gebauten Ökologie des Strandes" [Sand, Traces, Architecture – On the Built Ecology of the Beach] follows the spatial organization of the beach through social routines, from setting up deckchairs and sunshades to visiting beach restaurants and bathing houses. Thereby, Erben shows that not only can the beach be seen as a liminal zone between water and land, but also can its built ecology be considered an interspace between solid construction and a 'situational occupancy of space.'

A particular form of building on the beach is examined by WIEBKE KOLBE. In her article "Strandburgen: Eine deutsche Lust? Zum Strandurlaub seit dem späten neunzehnten Jahrhundert" [Sand Castles: A German Pleasure? On Beach Vacation from the Late Nineteenth-Century Onwards], she addresses the academic narrative of sandcastle-building as a 'German' practice between the 1880s and 1970s. Kolbe counters this perspective by reading the building of sandcastles not as a nationally specific beach practice but as a paradigmatic metaphor that reveals the ambivalence of beach tourism between familiarity and strangeness, proximity and distance, work and leisure, center and margins, while also exploring the symbolic function of sandcastles in the German Empire, the Weimar Republic and National Socialism.

In ROBERT BAUERNFEIND's article "Der Strand als Schauplatz weltweiter Fauna. Exotische *naturalia* auf Stranddarstellungen Jan van Kessels d.Ä." [The Beach as Setting for World-Spanning Fauna. Exotic *naturalia* in Beach Representations of Jan van Kessel the Elder] objects suspended between the animate and inanimate are assembled at the beach: In the analyzed representations of the Flemish Baroque painter, the beach space becomes a heavily coded setting for an array of different shore and water animals, linking it to practices of collection and classification fueling and solidifying a European project of global colonial expansion. Bauernfeind shows how the beachscape becomes something akin to a painted cabinet of natural curiosities, which is underscored by the self-reflexive reference made within the central images of the allegories to the study of depictions of animal species and the *mise en abyme* of the Kunst- or Wunderkammer, into whose collections the paintings could then become reinserted. He argues that the representations frame the beach as the prerequisite for trade in the Americas while simultaneously promoting the claim to universality made by European science and the role of painting as an epistemological tool in this process of scientific and geographical 'discovery.' His article reveals the allegorical potential of this likewise newly discovered space, which is articulated through the arrangements of natural specimens within this setting.

The section "Bodies in Time: Littoral Rhythms of Death and Desire" is dedicated to tracing the specific temporal modes associated with the beach as well as their aesthetic manifestations in literature, film and music. In the works analyzed, the back-and-forth of the waves seems to resonate through the bodies of fictional characters, intermingling its own rhythmic line with their corporeal rhythms of death and desire.

In "Time and Tide again. Traces, Permeable Spaces and Sensory Perceptions of the Beach in Theodor Storm's *Aquis submersus* and HBO's *Big Little Lies*," ROXANNE PHILLIPS, through a comparative analysis of a novella by Storm published in 1876 and a recent TV series, retraces an intricate structure of correspondences between representations of the beach in its rhythmic appearance and patterns of repetition in traumatic memory. The incessant blurring of the line between land and sea performed by the waves coincides with the crossing of the boundaries between past and present, latency and manifestation in the psyches of characters haunted by transgenerational stories of violence and death.

Rhythmic repetition also figures prominently, albeit in a seemingly much more cheerful way, in ALBERTO NAPOLI's "'Stile balneare.' Singing the Italian Summer by the Seaside (1960s–1980s)." The escapist fantasies and erotic desires associated with the beach are modulated by the social convention of *villeggiatura*, the habit of annually returning to the same coastal location for summer vacations, which inscribes itself even into the very musical structure of the songs.

As Napoli further shows, the fantasies and desires expressed in Italian summer hits are always refracted by categories of race and gender and not as sunny and innocent as they might appear upon first impression.

The "constitutive bind [between] death and desire" is a central motif in Jack Parlett's "The Boys on the Beach: Andrew Holleran's Fire Island," a reading of Holleran's 1978 novel *Dancer from the Dance*. In this novel, the beach of Fire Island, a vacation spot close to New York City, functions as the point of contact of multiple temporal dynamics, shaping the existence of individuals within a local gay community. Tropes of seasonal repetition and variation, like the alternation of fashion and beauty standards from summer to summer, are inextricably linked to tropes of transience, the recurrence of death through suicide or drug abuse. Thereby, the line between the seemingly trivial aspects of a hedonistic gay lifestyle and existential threats to gay lives is blurred in a way that foreshadows the HIV/AIDS epidemic of the 1980s.

In "Stimmen über der Tiefe, gärender Schlamm, Wasserleichen – Theodor Storms Strände" [Voices over the Depths, Fermenting Mud, Drowned Bodies – Theodor Storm's Beaches], Christian Begemann provides an extensive analysis of the beach in the oeuvre of the nineteenth-century German writer. As Begemann shows, the various topographical types of Northern German beaches are reflected in a variety of textual models for narrating the overlap between life and death. This overlap not only invites comparisons between Storm's writing and contemporaneous scientific theories of primeval mud, it can also be shown to constitute the beach as a 'Raum eines Unheimlichen' [space of an uncanny], a space that allows for the spectral return of the metaphysical within a post-metaphysical world.

The section "Social and Material Transformations" focuses both on processes of change that take place at the beach and, in contrast or at the same time, processes that are initiated through the specific materiality of the beach. These manifestations of transformations, on the one hand, can be understood as modifications of the material condition of the beach triggered by ecological contamination. Material transformations are in many cases not as much contingent events as they are results of human interactions with their environment. The massive rise in mobility during the last century is one of the keys to the understanding of these developments. On the other hand, artistic or political practices, among others, are as capable of transforming something else into a beach as they are of transforming the beach into something else. At the same time, the beach plays the role of a catalyst of trans- and deformatory processes in the context of drastic actions and events in which historical figures or fictitious characters are involved as actors or affected. This section reveals that the agency of the beach affects social transformations, while in turn social transformation affects the material development of the beach.

In his petrocritical reading, FLORIAN AUEROCHS unearths the dismal and dark side of beaches, showing them as marine habitats marked by fossil energy culture. By analyzing the differences between Allan Sekula's oil spill photography and Alejandro Durán's visually highly expansive plastic-spill photography, in his article "Sisyphos am Strand: Beachcleaning und die litoralen Figurationen fossiler Energiekultur in der zeitgenössischen Umweltfotografie" [Sisyphus on the Beach: Beachcleaning and the Littoral Figurations of Fossile Energy Culture in Contemporary Environmental Photography], Auerochs regards the beach as a space of overlapping and reciprocal interpenetration of various spill events where the "environmental development and cultural transformation" in the age of the Anthropocene are made visible.

In his article "The Ephemeral Beachscape: Skateboarding and the Appropriation of Suburban Concrete," KONSTANTIN BUTZ reads the skateboard as an emancipatory device that is capable of creating a beach wherever someone is surfing the sidewalk in the suburban sphere. For the duration of his/her interaction with the neighborhood, the skateboarder as a sidewalk surfer does not as much construct the beach in an imaginary way through social practices as he/she gives form in a concrete and physical sense to "an ephemeral beachscape."

In his contribution "Beached. The Awkward Beginnings of Weimar Democracy," SEBASTIAN HASELBECK exposes the complex and multi-layered tensions that prevailed between the old monarchic and the new democratic order in early twentieth-century Germany, analyzing a 1919 photograph of President Friedrich Ebert and Gustav Noske, Minister of Defense, clad in swimsuits on the beach. As an aesthetic reflection of the recent political transformation, the controversies around this image reveal the political imaginary of Weimar Germany. The beach, as a public and democratic space where social equality is possible at least to a certain extent, functions around the time of the new government's inaugural ceremony in Weimar as a symbol of a new form of political representation to which contemporaries reacted with discomfort.

In her essay "Der Strand: What to wear on the beach / Was am Strand anziehen?," BARBARA VINKEN takes the Burkini debate as a point of departure to reflect in a more general sense on the repoliticization of beachwear as an example for the transformations of the cultural semiotics of the clothed/naked body. Rereading Bernardin de Saint-Pierre's *Paul et Virginie* and Theodor Fontane's *Effi Briest*, she views the so-called 'beach body' as a secularized promise of paradisiac innocence and redemption: The 'beach body' functions as a second skin both in the sense of a sublimated body whose nudity and naturalness is carefully constructed and of a cipher for the transformation into the new man.

Finally, three artistic approaches frame, complement and expand the interdisciplinary academic contributions by exploring beaches and beach experiences through an alternative, aesthetic mode. This volume opens with the poem "Gedanken über unsichtbare Inselgruppen" [Thoughts about Invisible Archipelagos] by the German-Japanese writer YOKO TAWADA. As is, not least, reflected in her poetics lecture *Fremde Wasser* [Foreign Waters] (Tawada 2012), the beach and coastal or harbor spaces function as significant places and models with both cultural and poetic relevance in Tawada's work. In its literary form, which is rich in references and allusions, the poem allows for an initial encounter with many of the aesthetic, cultural, social and political questions that constitute the material for academic discussion in the following articles.

NADJA GRASSELLI's "SHORELINES & SPACES" is based on a performance presented together with Federico Robol at the *Narrating and Constructing the Beach* conference. The text is deliberately placed in the middle of the volume, between the academic contributions, since it is characterized by the idea that a particularly adequate approach to the fluid and transitory beach space might be the employment of an equally permeable, ephemeral form at the interface between art and science.

The book concludes with MARK OLIVAL-BARTLEY's sonnet "Revisited," revisiting many previously discussed aspects, opening up spaces and leaving traces for multiple associations and reconsiderations. The Hawaiian poet transforms his personal perspectives on an often-revisited place into a polychrome recollection of the beach landscape of Kailua – and in doing so, narrates and performatively constructs it as a "storied" space.

Bibliography

Andrews, Hazel, and Les Roberts (Eds.). *Liminal Landscapes. Travel, Experience and Spaces In-Between*. London and New York: Routledge, 2012.

Archimedes. *The Sand-Reckoner*. Translated by Thomas L. Heath. Cambridge: Cambridge University Press, 1897.

Auf der anderen Seite [*The Edge of Heaven*]. Directed by Fatih Akin. Pandora Filmproduktion, 2007.

Austen, Jane. "Sanditon" [1817]. *The Cambridge Edition of the Works of Jane Austen. Later Manuscripts*. Ed. Janet Todd. Cambridge: Cambridge University Press, 2008. 137–209.

Bakhtin, Mikhail. "Discourse in the Novel." *The Dialogic Imagination*. Edited by Michael Holquist. Austin: University of Texas Press, 1981. 259–422.

Bal, Mieke. *Narratology. Introduction to the Theory of Narrative*. Toronto, Buffalo and London: University of Toronto Press, 2017.

Balme, Christopher. *Pacific Performances. Theatricality and Cross-Cultural Encounter in the South Seas*. Hampshire: Palgrave Macmillan, 2006.

Barone, Joshua. "In Venice, an Opera Masks Climate Crisis in a Gentle Tune." *The New York Times Online* (14 July 2019): https://www.nytimes.com/2019/07/14/arts/music/sun-and-sea-lithuania-venice-biennale-review.html (31 July 2019).

Barthes, Roland. *Mythologies* [1957]. Translated by Richard Howard and Annette Lavers. New York: Hill and Wang, 2012.

Barton, Susan. *Working-Class Organisations and Popular Tourism, 1840–1970*. Manchester: Manchester University Press, 2005.

Basinger, Jeanine. *The World War II Combat Film. Anatomy of a Genre*. Middletown, CT: Wesleyan University Press, 2003.

"beach, n." *OED Online*. www.oed.com/view/Entry/16443. Oxford: Oxford University Press, 2019 (17 February 2020).

Beekes, Robert (ed.). *Etymological Dictionary of Greek, Vol. 1*. Leiden and Boston: Brill, 2010.

Beiser, Vince. *The World in a Grain: The Story of Sand and How It Transformed Civilization*. New York: Riverhead Books, 2018.

Bergson, Henri. *Time and Free Will. An Essay on the Immediate Data of Consciousness* [*Essai sur les données immédiates de la conscience*, 1889]. Translated by F. L. Pogson. London: George Allen & Unwin LTD, 1950.

The Big Red One. Directed by Samuel Fuller. United Artists, 1980.

Blumenberg, Hans. *Shipwreck with Spectator. Paradigm of a Metaphor for Existence* [*Schiffbruch mit Zuschauer. Paradigma einer Daseinsmetapher*, 1979]. Translated by Steven Rendall. Cambridge/MA and London: MIT Press, 1997.

Bougainville, Louis-Antoine de. *Voyage round the World* [*Voyage autour du monde par la frégate du roi La Boudeuse et la flûte L'Étoile*, 1771]. Translated by J. R. Forster. Amsterdam: Da Capo, 1967.

Bronfen, Elisabeth. *Specters of War. Hollywood's Engagement with Military Conflict*. New Brunswick: Rutgers University Press, 2012.

Bruner, Jerome. "The Narrative Construction of Reality." *Critical Inquiry* 18 (1991): 1–21.

Bruns, Sebastian, Kerstin Petretto and David Petrovic. "Zum Geleit." *Maritime Sicherheit*. Eds. Sebastian Bruns, Kerstin Petretto and David Petrovic. Wiesbaden: Springer, 2013. 9–15.

Burdsey, Daniel. *Race, Place and the Seaside: Postcards from the Edge*. London: Palgrave Macmillan, 2016.

Butler, Judith. *Bodies That Matter: On the Discursive Limits of 'Sex.'* London and New York: Routledge, 2011.

Calder, Alex, Jonathan Lamb and Bridget Orr. "Introduction. Postcoloniality and the Pacific." *Voyages and Beaches. Pacific Encounters, 1769–1840*. Eds. Alexander Calder, Jonathan Lamb and Bridget Orr. Honolulu: University of Hawaii Press, 1999. 1–23.

Calvino, Italo. *Invisible Cities*. Translated by William Weaver. Orlando et al.: Harvest, 1974.

Campe, Rüdiger. "Die Schreibszene. Schreiben." *Paradoxien, Dissonanzen, Zusammenbrüche. Situationen offener Epistemologie*. Eds. Hans Ulrich Gumbrecht and Karl Ludwig Pfeiffer. Frankfurt/Main: Suhrkamp, 1991. 759–772.

Carrigan, Anthony. *Postcolonial Tourism. Literature, Culture, and Environment*. New York and London: Routledge, 2011.

Corbin, Alain. *The Lure of the Sea. The Discovery of the Seaside in the Western World 1750–1840* [*Le Territoire du vide. L'Occident et le désir de rivage*, 1988]. Translated by Jocelyn Phelps. Berkeley and Los Angeles: University of California Press, 1994.

Davis Jr., Richard A., and Duncan M. Fitzgerald. *Beaches and Coasts*. Malden and Oxford: Blackwell Publishing, 2004.
Deleuze, Gilles. *Bergsonism* [*Le Bergsonisme*, 1966]. Translated by Hugh Tomlinson. New York: Zone Books, 1991.
Dening, Greg. "Performing on the Beaches of the Mind. An Essay." *History and Theory* 41 (2002): 1–24.
Derrida, Jacques. "Force of Law: The 'Mystical Foundation of Authority.'" *Cardozo Law Review* 11.5–6 (1990): 920–1045.
Diderot, Denis. "Supplement to Bougainville's *Voyage*" [*Supplément au voyage de Bougainville*, 1796]. *Rameau's Nephew. And Other Works*. In new translations by Jacques Barzun and Ralph H. Bowen. With an introduction by Ralph H. Bowen. Indianapolis and Cambridge: Hackett, 1956. 179–228.
Dippel, Andrea. *Von Paris an den Ärmelkanal. Der Städter am Strand bei Manet, Monet, Morisot, Degas und Renoir*. Cologne, 1996 [PhD dissertation, Universität zu Köln].
La dolce vita. Directed by Federico Fellini. Cineriz, 1960.
Döring, Jörg, and Tristan Thielmann. "Mediengeographie: Für eine Geomedienwissenschaft." *Mediengeographie. Theorie – Analyse – Diskussion*. Eds. Jörg Döring and Tristan Thielmann. Bielefeld: transcript, 2009. 11–66.
Döring, Tobias. "Caribbean Beachcombers." *The Beach in Anglophone Literatures and Cultures. Reading Littoral Space*. Eds. Ursula Kluwick and Virginia Richter. Farnham and Burlington: Ashgate, 2015. 107–119.
Duran, Jacques. *Sands, Powders, and Grains. An Introduction to the Physics of Granular Materials*. Translated by Axel Reisinger. New York: Springer, 2000.
Duras, Marguerite. *L'Amour* [*L'Amour*, 1972]. Translated by Kazim Ali and Libby Murphy. Rochester: Open Letter, 2013.
Duras, Marguerite. *Nathalie Granger. Suivi par La Femme du Gange*. Paris: Gallimard, 1973.
Ette, Ottmar. "Travel/Landscapes. Wor(l)ds on Their Way to Transareal Travel Literature." *Travel, Agency, and the Circulation of Knowledge*. Eds. Gesa Mackenthun, Andrea Nicola and Stephanie Wodianka. Münster and New York: Waxmann, 2017. 39–74.
Evans, Miles. *Sun & Sea (Marina)*. Press Release. https://drive.google.com/drive/folders/1gj5_oeUan6syc06FQIMwcbW-wHhFXZzR (22 August 2019).
Fanon, Frantz. *Black Skin, White Masks* [*Peau noire, masques blancs*, 1952]. Translated by Charles Lam Markmann. London: Pluto, 2008.
Fanon, Frantz. *The Wretched of the Earth* [*Les Damnés de la Terre*, 1961]. Translated by Constance Farrington. London: Penguin, 2001.
Fiske, John. "Reading the Beach." *Reading the Popular*. Boston: Unwin Hyman, 1989. 34–62.
Fontane, Theodor. *Effi Briest* [1894–1895]. Translated by Hugh Rorrison. London: Penguin, 2000.
Forster, Georg. "A Voyage Round the World." *Werke. Sämtliche Schriften, Tagebücher, Briefe*, Vol. 1. Ed. Robert L. Kahn. Berlin: Akademie-Verlag, 1968.
Forster, Georg. "Ansichten vom Niederrhein, von Brabant, Flandern, Holland, England und Frankreich im April, Mai und Junius 1790." *Werke. Sämtliche Schriften, Tagebücher, Briefe*, Vol. 9. Ed. Gerhard Steiner. Berlin: Akademie-Verlag, 1958.
Foucault, Michel. *The Order of Things. An Archaeology of the Human Sciences* [*Les mots et les choses. Une archéologie des sciences humaines*, 1966]. London and New York: Routledge, 2002.

Foucault, Michel. *Discipline and Punish. The Birth of the Prison* [*Surveiller et punir. Naissance de la prison*, 1975]. Translated by Alan Sheridan. New York: Vintage, 1977.
Frisk, Hjalmar. *Griechisches etymologisches Wörterbuch, Vol. 1*. Heidelberg: Winter, 1973.
Garland, Alex. *The Beach* [1996]. Reissued with a new introduction. London: Penguin, 2016.
Gennep, Arnold van. *The Rites of Passage* [*Les Rites de Passage*, 1909]. Chicago: Chicago University Press, 1960.
Gierloff-Emden, Hans-Günter. *Geographie des Meeres – Ozeane und Küsten. Lehrbuch der Allgemeinen Geographie, Vol. 5.2*. Berlin: de Gruyter, 1990.
Gillis, Justin, and Felicity Barringer. "As Coasts Rebuild and U. S. Pays, Repeatedly, the Critics Ask Why." *New York Times* online (18 November 2012): https://www.nytimes.com/2012/11/19/science/earth/as-coasts-rebuild-and-us-pays-again-critics-stop-to-ask-why.html (05 September 2019).
Gordon, Bertram M. "The Mediterranean as a Tourist Destination from Classical Antiquity to Club Med." *Mediterranean Studies* 12 (2003): 203–226.
Gorsuch, Anne. *All This is Your World: Soviet Tourism at Home and Abroad after Stalin*. New York: Oxford University Press, 2011.
Graham, Stephan. "Beyond the 'Dazzling Light': From Dreams of Transcendence to the 'Remediation' of Urban Life: A Research Manifesto." *New Media Society* 6.1 (2004): 16–25.
Grainytė, Vaiva. "Song no. 1, Sunscreen Bossa Nova I." *Sun & Sea (Marina). Libretto*. Translated by Rimas Užgiris. https://www.sunandsea.lt/Sun-and-Sea_libretto.pdf (22 August 2019).
Grainytė, Vaiva. "Song no. 6, Wealthy Mommy Song I." *Sun & Sea (Marina). Libretto*. Translated by Rimas Užgiris. https://www.sunandsea.lt/Sun-and-Sea_libretto.pdf (22 August 2019).
Grainytė, Vaiva. "Song no. 8, Song of Exhaustion. Workaholic's Song I." *Sun & Sea (Marina). Libretto*. Translated by Rimas Užgiris. https://www.sunandsea.lt/Sun-and-Sea_libretto.pdf (22 August 2019).
Grainytė, Vaiva. "Song no. 10, Dream." *Sun & Sea (Marina). Libretto*. Translated by Rimas Užgiris. https://www.sunandsea.lt/Sun-and-Sea_libretto.pdf (22 August 2019).
Grainytė, Vaiva. "Song no. 15, The Couple's Distance Song." *Sun & Sea (Marina). Libretto*. Translated by Rimas Užgiris. https://www.sunandsea.lt/Sun-and-Sea_libretto.pdf (22 August 2019).
Grainytė, Vaiva. "Song no. 16, Wealthy Mommy Song II." *Sun & Sea (Marina). Libretto*. Translated by Rimas Užgiris. https://www.sunandsea.lt/Sun-and-Sea_libretto.pdf (22 August 2019).
Grainytė, Vaiva. "Song no. 20, Song of Exhaustion. Workaholic's Song II." *Sun & Sea (Marina). Libretto*. Translated by Rimas Užgiris. https://www.sunandsea.lt/Sun-and-Sea_libretto.pdf (22 August 2019).
Grainytė, Vaiva. "Song no. 22, 3D Sister's Song." *Sun & Sea (Marina). Libretto*. Translated by Rimas Užgiris. https://www.sunandsea.lt/Sun-and-Sea_libretto.pdf (22 August 2019).
Grainytė, Vaiva. "Song no. 23, Sunscreen Bossa Nova II." *Sun & Sea (Marina). Libretto*. Translated by Rimas Užgiris. https://www.sunandsea.lt/Sun-and-Sea_libretto.pdf (22 August 2019).
Grainytė, Vaiva. "Song no. 24, Vacationer's chorus III." *Sun & Sea (Marina). Libretto*. Translated by Rimas Užgiris. https://www.sunandsea.lt/Sun-and-Sea_libretto.pdf (22 August 2019).

Grimm, Jacob, and Wilhelm Grimm. "Strand." *Deutsches Wörterbuch, Vol. 19.* http://www.woerterbuchnetz.de/DWB?lemma=strand. Leipzig: S. Hirzel, 1957 (01 September 2019).

Gunn, Clare A. *Vacationscape. Developing Tourist Areas.* Washington/D. C.: Taylor & Francis, 1997.

Haff, Peter. "Technology as a Geological Phenomenon: Implications for Human Well-Being." *A Stratigraphical Basis for the Anthropocene. Geological Society London, Special Publication* 395 (2014): 301–309.

Haff, Peter. "The Technosphere and Its Relation to the Anthropocene." *The Anthropocene as a Geological Time Unit: A Guide to the Scientific Evidence and Current Debate.* Eds. Jan Zalasiewicz, Colin N. Waters, Mark Williams and Colin P. Summerhayes. Cambridge: Cambridge University Press, 2019. 138–143.

Halperin, Julia. "It's Hard to Make Good Art About Climate Change. The Lithuanian Pavilion at the Venice Biennale is a Powerful Exception." https://news.artnet.com/exhibitions/lithuanian-pavilion-1543168 (22 August 2019).

Handyside, Fiona. *Cinema at the Shore. The Beach in French Film.* Oxford et. al.: Peter Lang, 2014.

Haraway, Donna. "Staying with the Trouble: Anthropocene, Capitalocene, Chthulucene." *Anthropocene or Capitalocene? Nature, History, and the Crisis of Capitalism.* Ed. Jason Moore. Oakland: PM Press, 2016. 34–76.

Holden, Andrew. *Tourism Studies and the Social Sciences.* London and New York: Routledge, 2006.

House, John. "Preface." *Impressionists by the Sea.* Ed. John House. Catalog of the exhibition. London: Royal Academy of Arts, 2007. 13.

Insecure. Season 1, episode 3: "Racist as Fuck." Created by Issa Rae and Larry Wilmore. HBO, 2016.

Kappelhoff, Hermann. "Shell shocked face. Einige Überlegungen zur rituellen Funktion des US-amerikanischen Kriegsfilms." *Verklärte Körper.* Eds. Nicola Suthor and Erika Fischer-Lichte. München: Fink, 2006. 69–89.

Kaufmann, Jean-Claude. *Corps des femmes regards d'hommes: sociologie des seins nus.* Paris: Nathan, 1995.

Klein, Ernest. *A Comprehensive Etymological Dictionary of the Hebrew Language for Readers of English.* Jerusalem: Carta, 1987.

Klooss, Wolfgang. "Coast and Beach: Contested Spaces in Cultural and Literary Discourse." *Navigating Cultural Spaces. Maritime Places.* Eds. Anna-Margaretha Horatschek, Yvonne Rosenberg and Daniel Schäbler. Amsterdam and New York: Rodopi, 2014.

Kluwick, Ursula. "Food for Sharks. Abjection on the Beach." *The Beach in Anglophone Literatures and Cultures: Reading Littoral Space.* Eds. Ursula Kluwick and Virginia Richter. Farnham and Burlington: Ashgate, 2015. 139–154.

Kramm, Johanna, and Carolin Völker. "Plastikmüll im Meer: Zur Entdeckung eines Umweltproblems." *APUZ – Aus Politik und Zeitgeschichte* 67.51–52 (2017): 17–22.

Leinfelder, Reinhold, and Juliana Assunção Ivar do Sul. "The Stratigraphy of Plastics and Their Preservation in Geological Records." *The Anthropocene as a Geological Time Unit: A Guide to the Scientific Evidence and Current Debate.* Eds. Jan Zalasiewicz, Colin N. Waters, Mark Williams and Colin P. Summerhayes. Cambridge: Cambridge University Press, 2019. 147–155.

"Lithuanian Pavilion Receives Golden Lion Award at Venice Biennale" (15 May 2019). http://www.menufaktura.lt/en/?m=23613&s=62581 (01 September 2019).

Löfgren, Orvar. *On Holiday. A History of Vacationing*. Berkeley, Los Angeles and London: University of California Press, 1999.
Lokugé, Chandani. *Turtle Nest*. Melbourne: Arcardia, 2017.
The Longest Day. Directed by Ken Annakin et. al. Twentieth Century Fox, 1962.
Löw, Martina. "Die Rache des Körpers über den Raum? Über Henri Lefèbvres Utopie und Geschlechterverhältnisse am Strand." *Soziologie des Körpers*. Ed. Markus Schroer. Frankfurt/Main: Suhrkamp, 2005. 241–270.
Macbeth. Directed by Justin Kurzel. StudioCanal, 2015.
Macbeth. Directed by Roman Polański. Columbia Pictures, 1971.
Mack, John. *The Sea. A Cultural History*. London: Reaktion, 2011.
Malm, Andreas, and Alf Hornborg. "The Geology of Mankind? A Critique of the Anthropocene Narrative." *The Anthropocene Review* 1.1 (2014): 61–69.
Mayrhofer, Petra. "'Festung Europa?' Grenzikonographien im europäischen Raum." *Europabilder. Innen- und Außenansichten von der Antike bis zur Gegenwart*. Eds. Benjamin Drechsel, Friedrich Jaeger, Helmut König, Anne-Katrin Lang and Claus Leggewie. Bielefeld: transcript, 2010. 307–321.
McEwan, Ian. *On Chesil Beach*. London: Vintage, 2007.
Le Mépris [Contempt]. Directed by Jean-Luc Godard. Cocinor, 1963.
Michelet, Jules. *The Sea [La Mer, 1861]*. New York: Rudd & Carleton, 1861.
Moffatt, Tracey. "Tracey Moffat Talks with Simone Brett about The White Ghosts Sailed In." *Tracey Moffatt: My Horizon*. Ed. Natalie King. London: Thames & Hudson, 2017. 113 and 140–141.
Moore, Jason (ed.). *Anthropocene or Capitalocene? Nature, History, and the Crisis of Capitalism*. Oakland: PM Press, 2016a.
Moore, Jason. "The Rise of Cheap Nature." *Anthropocene or Capitalocene? Nature, History, and the Crisis of Capitalism*. Ed. Jason Moore. Oakland: PM Press, 2016b. 78–115.
Morton, Timothy. *Hyperobjects. Philosophy and Ecology after the End of the World*. Minneapolis: University of Minnesota Press, 2013.
Noack, Christian. "Coping with the Tourist: Planned and 'Wild' Mass Tourism on the Soviet Black Sea Coast." *Turizm: The Russian and East European Tourist under Capitalism and Socialism*. Eds. Anne E. Gorsuch and Diane P. Koenker. Ithaca/NY: Cornell University Press, 2019. 281–304.
Nünning, Ansgar. "Narrativist Approaches and Narratological Concepts for the Study of Culture." *Narratology in the Age of Cross-Disciplinary Narrative Research*. Eds. Sandra Heinen and Roy Sommer. Berlin: de Gruyter, 2009. 145–182.
The Oxford Dictionary of English Etymology. Ed. Charles T. Onions. Oxford: Clarendon Press, 1992.
Payne, Christiana. "Visions of the Beach in Victorian Britain." *The Beach in Anglophone Literatures and Cultures. Reading Littoral Space*. Eds. Ursula Kluwick and Virginia Richter. Farnham and Burlington: Ashgate, 2015. 21–35.
Preston-Whyte, Robert. "The Beach as a Liminal Space." *The Blackwell's Tourism Companion*. Eds. Alan Lew, Michael Hall and Allan Williams. Oxford: Blackwell, 2004. 249–259.
Pritchard, Anette, and Nigel Morgan. "'Wild On' the Beach: Discourses of Desire, Sexuality and Liminality." *Culture, Heritage and Representation. Perspectives on Visuality and the Past*. Eds. Emma Waterton and Steve Watson. Farnham and Burlington: Ashgate, 2010. 127–144.

Pukui, Mary Kawena, and Samuel H. Ebert (eds.). *Hawaiian Dictionary. Hawaiian–English, English–Hawaiian*. Honolulu: University of Hawaii Press, 1986.
Richter, Virginia, and Ursula Kluwick. "Introduction: 'Twixt Land and Sea: Approaches to Littoral Studies." *The Beach in Anglophone Literatures and Cultures. Reading Littoral Space*. Eds. Ursula Kluwick and Virginia Richter. Farnham and Burlington: Ashgate, 2015. 1–20.
Samuelson, Meg. "Literary Inscriptions on the South African Beach. Ambiguous Settings, Ambivalent Textualities." *The Beach in Anglophone Literatures and Cultures. Reading Littoral Space*. Eds. Ursula Kluwick and Virginia Richter. Farnham and Burlington: Ashgate, 2015. 121–138.
Sand Wars. Directed by Denis Delestrac. PBS International and Green Planet Films, 2013.
Saving Private Ryan. Directed by Steven Spielberg. DreamWorks Distribution, 1998.
Schivelbusch, Wolfgang. *The Railway Journey. The Industrialization and Perception of Time and Space*. Berkeley and Los Angeles: University of California Press, 1986.
Schmitz-Berning, Cornelia. "Festung Europa." *Vokabular des Nationalsozialismus*. Berlin: de Gruyter, 2007. 232–233.
Schmitz-Emans, Monika. *Seetiefen und Seelentiefen: Literarische Spiegelungen innerer und äußerer Fremde*. Würzburg: Königshausen & Neumann, 2003.
Shields, Rob. *Places on the Margin. Alternative Geographies of Modernity*. London: Routledge, 1991.
Shields, Rob. "'The System of pleasure.' Liminality and the Carnivalesque at Brighton." *Theory, Culture & Society* 7 (1990): 39–72.
Sun & Sea (Marina). https://sunandsea.lt/en. Official Website (22 August 2019).
Stagl, Justin. *A History of Curiosity: The Theory of Travel 1550–1800*. London: Routledge, 1995.
Taussig, Michael. "The Beach (A Fantasy)." *Critical Inquiry* 26.2 (2000): 248–278.
Tawada, Yoko. *Fremde Wasser. Literarische Essays*. Ed. Ortrud Gutjahr. Tübingen: Konkursbuchverlag, 2012.
The Thin Red Line. Directed by Terrence Malick. Twentieth Century Fox, 1998.
Turner, Victor. *The Ritual Process. Structure and Anti-Structure*. Chicago: Aldine, 1969.
Turner, Victor. *Liminal to Liminoid, in Play, Flow, and Ritual. An Essay in Comparative Symbology*. Houston: Rice University Studies, 1974.
Turner, Victor. "Frame, Flow and Reflection: Ritual and Drama as Public Liminality." *Japanese Journal of Religious Studies* 6.4 (1979): 465–499.
Twin Peaks. Created by David Lynch and Mark Frost. CBS Television, 1990–1991.
UNWTO Tourism Trends Snapshot: Tourism in the Mediterranean, 2015 edition. https://www.e-unwto.org/doi/pdf/10.18111/9789284416929. Madrid: World Tourism Organization, 2015 (17 June 2020).
Urbain, Jean-Didier. *At the Beach* [*Sur la plage*, 1994]. Translated by Catherine Porter. Minneapolis: University of Minnesota Press, 2003.
Us. Directed by Jordan Peele. Universal Pictures, 2019.
Virilio, Paul. *Bunker Archeology* [*Bunker archéologie*, 1975]. Translated by George Collins. New York: Princeton Architectural Press, 1994.
Virilio, Paul. "Le littoral, la dernière frontière. Entretien avec Jean-Louis Violeau." *Esprit* 370 (2010): 17–24.
Vousdoukas, Michalis I. et al. "Sandy coastlines under threat of erosion." *Natural Climate Change* 10 (2020): 260–263.

Walton, John K. "The Demand for Working-Class Seaside Holidays in Victorian England." *The Economic History Review* 34.2 (1981): 249–265.
Walton, John K. *English Seaside Resort. A Social History 1750–1914*. London: Palgrave Macmillan, 1983.
Walvin, James. *Beside the Seaside. A Social History of the Popular Seaside Holiday*. London: Allen Lane, 1987.
Welland, Michael. *Sand. A Journey Through Science and the Imagination*. Oxford: Oxford University Press, 2009.
Wolf, Burkhardt. *Fortuna di mare. Literatur und Seefahrt*. Zürich and Berlin: diaphanes, 2013.
Wright, Alexis. "Odyssey of the Horizon." *Tracey Moffatt: My Horizon*. Ed. Natalie King. London: Thames & Hudson, 2017. 114–121.
Zalasiewicz, Jan. *The Earth After Us: What Legacy Will Humans Leave in The Rocks?* New York: Oxford University Press, 2008.

List of Figures

Fig. 1: *13_Sun&Sea (Marina). Opera-performance by Rugilė Barzdžiukaitė, Vaiva Grainytė, Lina Lapelytė at Biennale Arte 2019, Venice*. Picture: Andrej Vasilenko.

Yoko Tawada
Gedanken über unsichtbare Inselgruppen

Jemand spielte Klarinette,
als ich im Wind schmeckte das Meeressalz.

Auf der ozeanischen Metallplatte
ein rasselnder Erbsentanz.

Im Sand strandete eine Zigarette,
zerquetscht im ozeanischen Schmutz.

Durchnässt die Papierröhrchen-Skelette.
Ein Kind verdorrt ohne Schutz.

Es bettelt vor jeder Gaststätte.
Der Traum auszuwandern: sein einziger Schatz.

Krallige Wellen schwingen alte Sklavenkette.
Das Schmuggelgut Mensch spuckt Umsatz.

Im Abendrot las ich eine Silhouette
und die Flaschenpost ein fremder Kratz.

Wenn ich angesprochen hätte
die Toten von diesseits und jenseits,

wäre ich angstfrei wie eine Marionette,
würde ich tanzen auf einem versteinerten Gesetz.

Ist der Globus ein Diamant oder nur eine Fassette?
Eine andere Melodie auf jedem Stehplatz.

Der Atlas ist die Bühne deiner Operette.
Wer reisend schreibt, bekommt im Traum einen Korallenkranz.

—
(Precluded) Arrivals/Departures

Virginia Richter
Stranded. The Beach as Ultimate Destination in Joseph Conrad's *Amy Foster* and Thomas Mann's *Death in Venice*

Whereas the modern beach is predominantly conceived as a vacation site, and hence as a transitional space, this essay looks at the narrative construction of the beach as a place from which departure is not possible, be it for socioeconomic or psychological reasons. Comparing two very different modernist short stories that are set on a Northern, isolated coast and a Southern seaside resort respectively, this essay seeks to expand the understanding of the beach as a heterogeneous space, and advocates an intersectional, multisensorial and interdisciplinary approach to the literary study of the beach.

Während der moderne Strand überwiegend als Urlaubsziel und damit als ein Raum vorübergehenden Aufenthalts aufgefasst wird, widmet sich dieser Beitrag dem erzählerischen Entwurf des Strands als einem Ort, von dem die Abreise nicht mehr möglich ist, sei es aus sozioökonomischen oder psychologischen Gründen. Durch den Vergleich zweier sehr unterschiedlicher Erzählungen der modernen Literatur, deren jeweilige Handlung an einem einsamen nördlichen Strand respektive einem südlichen Urlaubsort angesiedelt ist, versucht dieser Aufsatz den Begriff des Strands als einem heterogenen Ort zu erweitern und plädiert für eine intersektionelle, multisensorielle und interdisziplinäre Auseinandersetzung mit dem Strand in der Literaturwissenschaft.

1 Coming, going, staying

> One day I wrote her name upon the strand
> But came the waves and washed it away:
> Again I wrote it with a second hand,
> But came the tide, and made my pains his prey.
> (Spenser 2008 [1595], V. 1–4)

Edmund Spenser's "Sonnet LXXV" captures an essential quality of the beach, the way it is formed by elements in flux, the incessant movement of the waves, wind, sunshine and rain, silting and erosion.[1] Because of its "immutable mutability" resulting from the constant interaction of the elements (Lenček and Bosker 1998, 5), the beach is a space inviting and inspiring creation, and

---

[1] For a reading of "Sonnet LXXV" in terms of its setting on a sandy beach, which denotes constant change and impermanence as well as the enmeshment between inorganic and biotic particles, see Mentz (2013, 195–197).

https://doi.org/10.1515/9783110672244-003

simultaneously hostile to it – obliterating, destructive, the softly lapping waves erasing human inscription. Defined as the "shore of the sea, on which the waves break, the strand; *spec.* the part of the shore lying between high- and low-water-mark" (OED 2018), the beach forms that part of the coastal territory that lies precisely at the intersection between the sea (or a large lake or river) and the land, a constantly shifting line. Not all bodies of water, and not even all seas, are tidal, of course; the tidal action in the Baltic Sea, for example, is minimal. But even in such instances the waterline is fluctuating, shifted by currents, storms and rising sea levels. This instability is one of the topographical features most frequently stressed in conceptualisations of the beach; another is its liminality, as the threshold between land and sea. These constitutive characteristics give the beach its peculiarly generative and transformative quality, in topographical, evolutionary and cultural terms:

> The beach is an ambiguous place, an in-between place. It is a place where for much of the time nothing much seemingly happens: the tide comes and goes; people arrive to pass time in leisure activities; occasional ships anchor there. But at the same time, the beach is a place where everything transformational in the cultures of coastal peoples begins and ends. The tides create a shifting boundary between sea and land. Their effect is to emphasize the liminality of the beach as parts of it are successively revealed and then swamped by tidal action. The boundary between sea and land alters on a daily basis. It is a neutral space, neither properly terrestrial nor yet thoroughly maritime, awaiting a metamorphic role. (Mack 2011, 165)

John Mack's much-quoted definition ascribes various attributes to the beach: an alternative temporality, that is, a rhythm and temporal regime determined by the tides and hence, by the moon rather than the sun; a spatiality marked by stasis ("nothing much [...] happens") as well as by constant change and shifting boundaries; a geographical instability that connotes a transformative potential. In social terms, the beach is a place of coming and going, of arrival and departure, of random encounters. As a vacation site, the beach is also demarcated as a heterotopia of industrialised modernity, that is, a "real space" functioning as a counter-site in which "the other real sites that can be found within the culture are simultaneously represented, contested, and inverted" (Foucault 1986, 24). Specifically, the beach is a place of leisure, not work, both sustaining – by offering necessary recreation – and undermining – by offering a glimpse of paradise – capitalist work ethics (see Kluwick and Richter 2020). Predominantly, the beach denotes transformation, movement and mobility. As a holiday destination, it is visited for limited amounts of time. Arriving at the beach already evokes the moment of departure. However, it is also a place where one can get stuck.

In this paper, I want to look at the beach as a site of coming and going, and of staying, voluntarily or otherwise. The dynamic between mobility and "sedentarism" (Cresswell 2006, 55), I suggest, underpins most littoral writing in Western literature.[2] The two founding texts of this tradition, *The Odyssey* and *Robinson Crusoe*, are clearly examples of the interaction between seafaring and being stranded; but curiously, Odysseus is always thought of as "the Wanderer," the embodiment of the restless man, whereas Crusoe is the epitome of the castaway. But he is no more sedentary than Odysseus: his 28-year sojourn on the desert island is framed by, and the direct consequence of, several long-distance sea voyages in the pursuit of early modern entrepreneurship. Robinson travels from London to Guinea and back, from London to Morocco, from Morocco to Brazil; he is on his way from Brazil to Guinea, on a slave-trading expedition, when he is ship-wrecked and cast away on the island. Odysseus, on the other hand, spends seven out of his ten travelling years with the nymph Calypso on the island of Ogygia. Ogygia is transformed from a place of confinement to a site of departure only by the intervention of the gods. When Hermes, at the gods' behest, arrives at Ogygia to speed Odysseus' return, he finds the hero on the beach, bewailing his detention by the nymph:

> But Hermes did not find great-hearted Odysseus indoors,
> but he was sitting out on the beach, crying, as before now
> he had done, breaking his heart in tears, lamentation, and sorrow,
> as weeping tears he looked out over the barren water. (Homer 2007, V. 81–84)

In these two grand narratives on being stranded, the beach is constructed as a place of waiting, of enforced immobility, of despair. The "barren water" across which both Odysseus and Robinson gaze during their captivity constitutes a barrier hindering their getting away, rather than a space of connections. This sedentary and settled status, however, is unstable; very quickly, the beach can be transformed into a place of arrival, when successive waves of visitors begin to invade Robinson's island, or of departure, when Hermes bids Odysseus to build a raft and set out to sea.[3] Sometimes, the reasons for remaining stranded

---

[2] Tim Cresswell distinguishes between a "metaphysics of sedentarism" and a "metaphysics of nomadism" that privilege, respectively, rootedness, stability and belonging, and mobility, flux and change (2006, 55). Because of its attributes, the beach can be seen as a paradigmatic site on which sedentarism and mobility interact; in other words, the beach functions as a contact zone suited to the analysis of the "dialectic of cultural persistence and change" which Stephen Greenblatt (2009, 2) describes as vital for an understanding of contemporary culture – in fact, any culture.

[3] For an analysis of Odysseus and Robinson Crusoe as crafty mariners embodying practical reason in Western literature, see Cohen (2010).

can be psychological just as well as material. One wonders why Odysseus, if he was pining so much for Ithaca, did not build his raft much earlier. As will be discussed below, Joseph Conrad's protagonist Yanko Goorall is restrained in the area where he was shipwrecked by his poverty, but also by his lack of information and his traumatised state. Thomas Mann's Gustav von Aschenbach is stranded, of course, only in a figurative sense, bound to the Lido beach by the presence of his beloved Tadzio.

As the threshold between the sea and the land, the beach has always been suspended between these two options: it can be a place of withdrawal whose solitude is threatened, by unwelcome arrivals – from cannibals and pirates to loud, vulgar tourists – or by one's own necessity to leave; or it can be a transit space, intended for a temporary visit and a speedy departure, which then changes by force of circumstance into a permanent or long-term dwelling place. In the nineteenth and early twentieth centuries, the beach acquired a particular resonance as a site of leisure and vacation, which defined it as a place of temporary residence. As the quintessential holiday destination, the beach has become an indelible part of an economy of everyday life divided between work and leisure.[4] To sustain its promise of freedom and sensuous enjoyment, the beach needs to enter this polarised economy in a particular way; it needs to tie itself to leisure and therefore to erase its association with work. According to John Gillis (2012, 150), "[t]he appeal of the beach lies in the fact that it excludes all that is 'workful.' Its relation to nature and history must always be concealed, for it functions in modern culture as a primary place of getting away, of oblivion and forgetting." In fact, this can be considered the particularly modern aspect of the modern beach: its dissociation from work, and its realignment as a space of recreation, a vacationscape – "a place of regeneration and of withdrawal from everyday life" (Richter and Kluwick 2015, 2). In consequence, all allusions to work processes, including the workers who keep the beach in good order, have to be excised:

> Whether pictorial or novelistic, this worldly socialization of the beach, 'cleansed,' as it were, of its native population, is a sign that presupposes a fundamental historical inversion of psychological and cultural relations at the seaside. This space now serves not for use but for exchange, not for labor but for contemplation, not for work but for play, not for production but for consumption, finally, so that the child's sandcastle comes to replace the fisherman's boat, and the bather's umbrella replaces the seaweed harvester's rake. (Urbain 2003 [1994], 45)

---

[4] For the history of seaside tourism, see Anderson and Tabb (2002); Hassan (2003); Lenček and Bosker (1998); Payne (2002); Urbain (2003 [1994]); Walton (1983).

As Jean-Didier Urbain suggests, the modern beach is pitted against a capitalist economy of expediency and the rational employment of time, not only through an association with philosophical practices – contemplation – but even with childish play. What can be more wasteful of time, more useless, and yet more pleasurable than the building of sandcastles that will be washed away by the tides? Conversely, if a literary or visual depiction of the beach focuses on the toilers of the sea, it follows that the function of the seaside as a vacationscape recedes into the background, and its pre-modern associations – with hard work, nautical disasters and a dangerous topography – come to the fore.[5] These two diverging aspects of the beach are explored in the two narratives at the centre of this essay, Thomas Mann's *Death in Venice* (1912) and Joseph Conrad's *Amy Foster* (1901).

Vacations, by their very nature, come to an end. In the following, however, I want to consider some ways in which the beach – and the seaside more generally, with its adjacent settlements and hinterland – escapes the pattern of the limited vacation stay, either by transforming the vacation into a voyage of no return, as in Mann's *Death in Venice*, or by altogether resisting the codification of the beach as a modern vacationscape, as in Conrad's *Amy Foster*. Published only ten years before *Death in Venice* – at a time when the transformation of the British seaside into a tourist destination had already happened – *Amy Foster* depicts the beach as 'pre-modern,' in the sense of a land undeveloped for tourism and barely touched by industrialisation. None of the local inhabitants have an eye for the beach or spend any time there. Rather than belonging to a corpus of modernist texts exploring the beach as a site of sensuous pleasure, aesthetic enjoyment and freedom from obligations, *Amy Foster* can be aligned with the older shipwreck literature depicting the horrid shore. The castaway's interminable stay is enforced by external circumstances, by fatality and poverty, rather than by the psychological seduction of the seaside, as in Mann's novella. Conrad's construction of the beach thus points to the asynchronicity of modernist practices – such as the leisured mobility that is a prerequisite of seaside vacations, but which is not available to everyone – as well as to the non-coincidence of experience that is bound up with class and nationality.

The juxtaposition of these two tales can elucidate the narrative construction of the beach in several ways. First, by describing two very different littoral topographies – a Northern, barren, isolated strip of mud and shingle, and a Southern, sandy beach associated with sensuality, luxury and cosmopolitanism – the texts also show two modes of psychological and aesthetic engagement with the

---

[5] For a study of the seaside as a fearful territory before its "discovery" in the mid-eighteenth century, see Corbin (1994 [1988]).

beach. Interestingly, in both cases this has to do with degradation, but in significantly different ways. By crawling on shore, on all fours like an animal, Conrad's castaway is not only disappointed in his hope of finding a better life in America, but loses whatever human dignity he had in his home country. Mann's vacationing man of letters, by contrast, debases himself by his half-voluntary descent into decadent eroticism. In both cases, it is the beach that exerts a *negative* transformational power on the protagonists. Second, in both stories we see a temporality at work that differs from the temporal structure of modernity, conceived as a forward-moving trajectory.[6] Rather than being a spatiotemporally mobile site, the beach denotes both temporal stasis and spatial sedentarism. In *Amy Foster*, the seashore has been bypassed by modern developments; in *Death in Venice*, the stasis is psychological, consisting of Aschenbach's luxurious abandonment of work. And finally, in both tales we can observe a certain hierarchy of practices, tied to social distinctions and narrative power. Working-class people, if present at all, fulfil practical tasks on the beach: in Conrad's story, it is their job to salvage the drowned bodies after the shipwreck; in *Death in Venice*, they appear as subaltern hotel employees and beach attendants. Only the middle-class, educated characters who, in the case of *Amy Foster*, are also the narrators, are ever found gazing out at the sea. Trained in the post-romantic appreciation of nature, they are the only ones capable of transcending the limited locality of the beach and travelling mentally to the horizon, and beyond.

2 Mud: Littoral Topography and Narrative in Conrad's *Amy Foster*

Joseph Conrad's short tale *Amy Foster* was first published in 1901 in the *Illustrated London News*; in 1903 it was reprinted in Conrad's collection *Typhoon and Other Stories*. The narrative, set in "Colebrook, on the shores of Eastbay" and the near-by village of Brenzett (Conrad 1963 [1901], 228), is told by an anonymous first-person narrator, who in turn hears the story of Amy Foster and Yanko Goorall from his friend, the country doctor Kennedy. The narrative situation is, in other words, similar to that in Conrad's Marlow stories, and similarly to *Heart of Darkness*, the narrative unfolds at the boundary between land and sea. Dr Kennedy's narration is triggered by an encounter with Amy as the doctor

---

[6] According to Bruno Latour (1993, 69), the moderns sensed "time as an irreversible arrow, as capitalization, as progress." See also Assmann (2013, esp. 58–69).

is doing his rounds in his friend's company, but he unfolds the bulk of the story in the late evening in his house, while the extradiegetic narrator, now the intradiegetic narratee, sits "by the open window," observing, "after the windless, scorching day, the frigid splendour of a hazy sea lying motionless under the moon" (ibid., 234). The close-by sea provides from the start a framework for the narrative: it is the topographical edge of the story-world, furnishing a constant sense of its limited and enclosed character; it sets the mood, often one of haziness, indistinctness and obscurity; and it offers a vanishing point for the storytelling process itself, as the narrator and narratee, the doctor and his friend, gaze at the horizon. Their unique ability to look into the distance suggests that they are the only ones who are capable of comprehending and generalising, of seeing "that there is a particle of a general truth in every mystery" (ibid., 229).[7] The protagonists in the hypodiegetic narrative lack precisely this ability; to them, events simply happen. This lack of consciousness corresponds to their relation to the sea: to the farmers and shepherds of Brenzett, the sea and the beach remain nearly invisible. The beach is experienced only metonymically through the mud that denotes both the passage through the littoral borderland and the distinction between humanity and bare life, belonging and exclusion.

Despite the importance of the littoral setting, the positioning of the unfolding events is curiously landbound. The beach as a space where anything happens is described directly only once, albeit at a highly significant moment – after the shipwreck that brings Yanko to Eastbay. But the way the proximity to the sea determines the story's topography as well as the inhabitants' character is established in the text's opening paragraph:

> The high ground rising abruptly behind the red roofs of the little town crowds the quaint High Street against the wall which defends it from the sea. Beyond the seawall there curves for miles in a vast and regular sweep the barren beach of shingle, with the village of Brenzett standing out darkly across the water, a spire in a clump of trees; and still farther out the perpendicular column of a lighthouse, looking in the distance no bigger than a lead pencil, marks the vanishing-point of the land. The country at the back of Brenzett is low and flat; but the bay is fairly well sheltered from the seas, and occasionally a big ship, windbound or through stress of weather, makes use of the anchoring ground a mile and a half due north from you as you stand at the back door of the Ship Inn in Brenzett. A

---

7 On the epistemological limitations of the narrator Kennedy and the supportive function of the more 'objective' extradiegetic narrator, see Andreach (1965). A critical response picking apart Andreach's argument is offered by Griem (1992) who underlines Kennedy's soundness as a medical man and careful observer, and hence a reliable narrator. I would argue that Kennedy is largely reliable, but his insights are limited by the gaps in Amy's and Yanko's narratives. More significantly, Kennedy's desire to fully penetrate into their secrets is indicative of a certain epistemological violence, against which their partial silence functions as a screen.

dilapidated windmill near by, lifting its shattered arms from a mound no loftier than a rubbish-heap, and a Martello tower squatting at the water's edge half a mile to the south of the coastguard cottages, are familiar to the skippers of small craft. (Conrad 1963 [1901], 228)

This passage stresses the closed-in, almost claustrophobic character of Colebrook and environs. The town itself is squeezed between the rising ground inland and the seawall defending and separating it from the sea. The various buildings mentioned in the passage, in particular the lighthouse, the Martello tower and the coastguard cottages, partake of this defensive character, marking the boundary between the land and the sea, dedicated to warn and deter approaching ships. The latter seem likely to draw nearer to this part of the coast only if constrained by circumstances, if "windbound or through stress of water." The coast around Colebrook is only peripherally linked to navigation – the bay is "sheltered from the seas" – and hence to the wider world of commerce and migration. But the area is equally untouched by industrialisation; even the windmill, not exactly denoting the vanguard of industrial production, is dilapidated. The words chosen to describe its broken condition and its location, the comparison of the mound to a rubbish-heap, just like the "squatting" shape of the Martello tower, repudiate any associations with the sublime. This is a very unpoetic bit of seashore. The village inn itself, its name harking back to more glorious days of seafaring, allows a view of the sea only from its back door. Finally, there are no signs of seaside tourism; the "barren beach of shingle" appears as uninviting as the rest of the countryside. Despite its closeness to the shore, this is a cut-off, backward region, turning its back resolutely to the sea and anything that might come in from it.

Dr Kennedy has a past as an explorer and scientist; he relates the story of Amy and Yanko as a case-study, not only of human behaviour, but of the way it is determined by geographical conditions and conditioning. Amy Foster, a shepherd's daughter and servant to a farmer, is the personification of the dreary country that bred her: she is "a dull creature" with a "squat figure," reminiscent of the "squatting" Martello tower, and a "dull face" (Conrad 1963 [1901], 229); she is "very passive" (ibid., 230). By contrast, Yanko, her deceased husband, "came from there" (ibid., 233), the doctor says pointing to "the level sea far below us [...] ending in a belt of glassy water at the foot of the sky" (ibid.). Like a mythological creature, the young man came across the sea; in fact, he was a Polish emigrant shipwrecked on the English shore on his way to America. His name is disclosed only three quarters into the tale. Yanko's long-lasting namelessness is one of the narrative strategies to mark him as an outsider, a stranger, even, in the view of the locals, as scarcely human. Of equal importance is his language, that is, his initial lack of English on the one hand, his own native tongue on the other. This language, only late defined as Polish, is incomprehensible to the peasants who apprehend it only as "a sudden burst of rapid, senseless speech" (ibid., 240). But even to the better educated inhabitants who try their German, French, Spanish and Italian on the stranger, the sounds he emits appear as "pleasant, soft, musical," but mainly as "utterly unlike anything one had ever heard" (ibid., 245). These descriptions are strikingly different: Yanko's speech is perceived as cacophonous by the working-class people, as euphonious by the middle class. In other words, those who, like the doctor, received an aesthetic education and can appreciate Yanko's physical beauty as well as the beauty of the sea, can also note the melodious quality of his native language, but cannot progress to a further degree of understanding. In both cases, Yanko's speech is a token of his otherness.

Yanko's initial inability to communicate is one of the reasons why the dramatic event that triggers the plot, the shipwreck of the Hanseatic emigrant ship Herzogin Sophia-Dorothea, is pushed to the farthest edge of the narrative and seems at first completely unconnected to the sudden appearance of the stranger. But Yanko never becomes an Odysseus narrating his adventures at sea; even years later he cannot and will not speak about the disaster: "The man himself, even when he learned to speak intelligibly, could tell us very little" (Conrad 1963 [1901], 242). He only remembers the emotions he felt during his voyage, sea-sickness, loneliness, fear, and from the night of the shipwreck only "the darkness, the wind, and the rain" (ibid., 238).[8] Even these bits are not told in Yanko's own words; his story is "learned fragmentarily" (ibid., 237) by the doctor over the course of two or three years, and then pieced together, with other eye-witness reports, as Kennedy communicates it to the narratee. This has two effects: Yanko disappears behind several narrative layers and never becomes the subject of his own story, and the shipwreck, with the location where it takes place – the shallow waters and the beach – retains the uncertain quality of a rumour, an obscure incident the precise nature of which can never be ascertained:

> A completeness without a clue, and a stealthy silence as of a neatly executed crime, characterize this murderous disaster, which, as you may remember, had its gruesome celebrity. The wind would have prevented the loudest outcries from reaching the shore; there had been evidently no time for signals of distress. It was death without any sort of fuss. The Hamburg ship, filling all at once, capsized as she sank, and at daylight there was not even the end of a spar to be seen above water. She was missed, of course, and at

---

[8] The traumatic impact of this experience, and its link with "the trauma of cultural, geographical, and linguistic displacement" is analysed by Shaffer (2000, 167).

> first the Coastguardmen surmised that she had either dragged her anchor or parted her cable some time during the night, and had been blown out to sea. Then, after the tide turned, the wreck must have shifted a little and released some of the bodies, because a child – a little fair-haired child in a red frock – came ashore abreast of the Martello tower. By the afternoon you could see along three miles of beach dark figures with bare legs dashing in and out of the tumbling foam, and rough-looking men, women with hard faces, children, mostly fair-haired, were being carried, stiff and dripping, on stretchers, on wattles, on ladders, in a long procession past the door of the Ship Inn, to be laid out in a row under the north wall of the Brenzett Church. (Ibid., 241–242)

The shipwreck is surrounded by a triple silence: the cries of the victims are drowned by the storm, communication with the coastguard fails, and the completeness of the ship's disappearance, with the exception of the bodies washed ashore, prevents a proper investigation of the case despite its short-lived celebrity as a great nautical disaster. In Yanko's fragmentary narrative as reported by Kennedy, his passage across the sea and his landfall remain untold, subject to speculation.[9] Similarly, the beach where the landing of the living and the dead takes place remains a marginal, unseen, almost repressed part of the landscape. The passage quoted above is the only one where the beach is described as a location with which the shore-dwellers have any contact, but even here, it is perceived from a distance, and mediated by a beholder standing apart. Only at a second glance does it become clear what is happening: the "dark figures with bare legs" are rescuers who carry the drowned passengers on shore. Significantly, these corpses are not marked in any way as exotic or ethnically different; on the contrary, it is mentioned twice that the children are "fair-haired," thus including them in a circle of European and Northern blondness and innocence that marks their death, within a logic of racial hierarchy, as tragic. The hair and skin colour of their drowned parents is not specifically mentioned, but other traits connect them to the labouring population of Eastbay: the reader can assume that the "rough-looking men" and "women with hard faces" are not very distinct from the Englishmen who carry them on shore. This is in sharp contrast to the only survivor of the disaster, Yanko, who is so black-haired and dark-skinned that he is thought to be a Hindu or a Basque (ibid., 244).[10] Can he really have belonged to this group of fair, hard-faced emigrants?

---

9 Over the years, Yanko does tell the story of his recruitment as a migrant worker, and of his conveyance from Poland to Hamburg, and then across the North Sea to the South of England (Conrad 1963 [1901], 234–237). However, the actual journey is only described in fragmented sketches expressing his bewilderment and traumatisation.

10 The rescuers' description as bare-legged dark figures momentarily links them to Yanko who is also dark and, at first, barefooted (see below). Without entering into a Freudian discussion of

He seems to have been as solitary during his journey as he is during his sojourn at Brenzett.

The inhabitants of Eastbay are slow, unsmiling, downcast peasants, described by Kennedy as children of the earth who are "uncouth in body and as leaden of gait as if their very hearts were loaded with chains" (Conrad 1963 [1901], 232). In contrast, Yanko is "a being lithe, supple and long-limbed, straight like a pine, with something striving upwards in his appearance as though the heart within him had been buoyant" (ibid.). But although he crossed the sea, he is not a creature of the sea which he abhors as a frightening and deadly element. Yanko's light-footedness and upward striving derive from his origins in a mountainous region which defines him to the extent of giving him a new surname: "as he would also repeat very often that he was a mountaineer (some word sounding in the dialect of his country like Goorall) he got it for his surname" (ibid., 250). As a mountain dweller, he is as indifferent to the sea as the Brenzett peasantry. He does not share with Kennedy and the narrator the ability to gaze at the horizon and thus comprehend his place in the universe: "He looked upon the sea with indifferent, unseeing eyes" (ibid., 253).

The mystery Kennedy tries to elucidate by telling this story is how plodding Amy and light-footed Yanko got together in the first place, and why their relationship ended tragically. According to the doctor's psychological explication, Amy possesses, despite the constitutional "inertness of her mind" (Conrad 1963 [1901], 230), a capacity that distinguishes her from her fellow countrymen: imagination. It is imagination that allows her to perceive beauty in the other and thereby to surmount, alone among the inhabitants of Brenzett, her inherited preconceptions; for, as Kennedy comments, "you need imagination to form a notion of beauty at all, and still more to discover your ideal in an unfamiliar shape" (ibid., 231). In this quality, he even sees a link between Amy and himself, as they "alone in all the land, I fancy, could see his very real beauty" (ibid., 251). However, Amy's appreciation is a kind of spell rather than an aesthetically informed choice, and indeed sustained by a vague desire for the exotic, mirrored by a similar kind of "positive fascination" for the "peculiarities" of her employer's grey parrot (ibid, 231). Yanko's death by negligence is prefigured in the fate of this "outlandish bird" whom Amy fails to save from the cat, although the parrot "shrieked for help in human accents" (ibid.). Her love for Yanko may be a similar kind of fascination for his otherness that elicits rejection in everyone else. In both cases, it is the sound of a voice that is situated between the human and animal – the parrot's human accents, Yanko's

the uncanny, it may be this subliminal similarity between the villagers and Yanko that reinforces their strong rejection of the stranger.

incomprehensible Polish as he pleads for water during his terminal illness – that triggers the lapse of Amy's imagination, and with it her pity, replacing it by "the unaccountable terror of a brute" (ibid., 232), and prompts her to run out of the house, away from that voice. Amy's panicked reaction signals a failure of her humanity – in the sense of humaneness – that brings her, in turn, closer to a brute.

The negotiation of the human-animal boundary is essential for Amy's relationship with Yanko, and for the latter's treatment by the villagers. As he tries to find shelter after the shipwreck, the castaway is not only perceived as a stranger, but as a strange creature outside the pale of humanity. In a series of encounters, he is abused, beaten and driven away, until he reaches a stage of deprivation and exhaustion that makes him indeed behave and look like an animal. A cause of his abject status, apart from his already mentioned inability to make himself understood, is the mud with which he is covered after crawling on shore. The mud literally erases the human face that would successfully appeal to hospitality.[11] Rather than seeing in him somebody who needs help, the people he meets only perceive a "wet and muddy" tramp, potentially drunk and dangerous, "babbling" in a frightening voice and moving across country in an irrational manner (Conrad 1963 [1901], 239). Finally, the stranger arrives at New Barns Farm, the place where Amy works as a servant. Again, he is treated like a dangerous animal; Amy's employer, farmer Smith who ends up locking him in the barn, is scared by the encounter with a being who looks like "some nondescript and miry creature […] swinging itself to and fro like a bear in a cage," "one mass of mud and filth from head to foot" (ibid., 239). Smith, otherwise described as humane, does not feel compassion but "the dread of an inexplicable strangeness" (ibid., 240). The generally shared reaction to this strangeness is to treat the "creature" as a source of danger, precluding even the most basic gestures of humanity such as offering him food and drink. But even after the first stage he continues to be consigned to a not-quite-human realm. He is handed over to Smith's wealthy neighbour, Mr Swaffer, where Yanko is "kept" (ibid., 245) in the coach-house, sleeping on "a straw pallet," covered with "a couple of horse-blankets" (ibid., 244); as he regains his strength, he goes about barefoot, works for Mr Swaffer without wages and is given his food at the back door. To

---

[11] Douglas Kerr (2016, 337–338) offers a Derridean reading of hospitality in "Amy Foster": Yanko's lack of language excludes him from common hospitality, but is the prerequisite for Amy's unconditional hospitality in Derrida's sense, a risky hospitality offered without knowing the other's intentions. I follow this interpretation, but disagree with Kerr's further claim that the "most splendid hospitality in the tale is afforded to Yanko by the narration of Dr Kennedy" (ibid., 339). This overlooks the desire for appropriation inherent in Kennedy's treatment of Yanko as a case study.

Dr Kennedy, who now sees him for the first time, the stranger appears like "a wild bird caught in a snare" (ibid.); Mr Swaffer, though not unkind, speaks of him offhandedly "as if the other had been indeed a sort of wild animal" (ibid.).

Within this circle of people who treat Yanko like an animal, Amy stands out by her intuitive understanding of his situation. She alone shows no fear but an active compassion exercised by handing him "half a loaf of white bread," an action that makes her appear "to his eyes with the aureole of an angel of light" (Conrad 1963 [1901], 243). This not only saves the starving man's life, but has a deep psychological impact: "Through this act of impulsive pity he was brought back again within the pale of human relations with his new surroundings. He never forgot it – never" (ibid.). This gesture is the germ of a courtship essentially predicated on a mutual misunderstanding of each other's being; but despite their incongruity, Amy continues to be the link that ties Yanko precariously to the community of Brenzett, and to humanity in general. Their marriage is eventually enabled by Swaffer's gratitude, expressed through proper wages and the gift of a cottage, upon Yanko's saving Swaffer's granddaughter from drowning in the village pond. The danger is in fact not so much of drowning, as the "pond was not very deep," but of suffocating "in the foot or so of sticky mud at the bottom" (ibid., 248). The calamity Yanko prevents is thus a reminder of the fate he narrowly escaped, and a prolepsis foreshadowing his own death in a muddy puddle. It is no wonder that the mud marking his passage from sea to land is so scary: it is a reminder of the horrors of the sea which the shore-dwellers, with their protective walls and earthbound gaze, are trying to suppress.

The estrangement between Yanko and Amy begins after the birth of their son. Both try to claim the boy for their own language and extraction. In particular, Yanko tries to teach him the prayers and songs of his country – an appropriation by the father, and an assimilation to his lost homeland, which Amy not only resents but perceives as a threat to the child: "His wife snatched the child out of his arms one day as he sat on the doorstep crooning to it a song such as the mothers sing to babies in his mountains" (Conrad 1963 [1901], 253). Gradually, the fascination Amy felt precisely for Yanko's strangeness transmutes into its opposite, and she adopts the position originally occupied by her fellow countrymen: fear and repulsion. Yanko's home-sickness and growing isolation, as he finds himself abandoned even by the one being who once saved him, undermine his health until he comes down with "lung trouble" (ibid., 254), an illness aggravated, as Dr Kennedy suspects, by Amy's neglect. As the doctor subsequently reconstructs the events, Yanko's fever causes him to switch from English to Polish, and it is his strange talk which increases Amy's terror "of that man she could not understand" (ibid., 255). Their initial encounter is re-capitulated; but this time,

Amy withholds any compassion and help as Yanko keeps pleading, in his strange-sounding native language, for a drink of water. As with the parrot shrieking for his life, Yanko's "terrible voice" makes her run away from the house and abandon her husband to his fate (ibid.).

Yanko has now come full circle. Again, he is utterly alone, feared and shunned for his strangeness. In the end, he reverts to the abject state he was in during his wanderings after the shipwreck. His ultimate failure to settle and establish himself as a social being is again indicated by a covering of mud. The next morning, the doctor finds him outside his cottage "lying face down and his body in a puddle"; "[h]e was muddy" (Conrad 1963 [1901], 256). The puddle, insufficiently deep to drown in, seems nevertheless like a token from the sea, marking his escape from the mud of the beach as temporary. If Yanko does not die by drowning, he is the victim of a social shipwreck, doomed "to perish in the supreme disaster of loneliness and despair" (ibid., 257). In *Amy Foster*, the beach and its synecdoche, the mud that sticks to Yanko even on dry land, denote disaster, death and the expulsion from the human community. At first glance, therefore, the littoral setting appears as the complete antithesis of the sociable, hedonistic beach of the Venetian Lido in Mann's novella.

3 Sand: Mann's *Death in Venice*

Tod in Venedig, written in 1911 and first published in a private edition of 100 signed copies (Hyperionverlag Hans von Weber, 1912), was reprinted in the literary magazine *Die Neue Rundschau* (1912) and finally published as a monograph with S. Fischer Verlag in 1913. Thomas Mann's greatest success after his novel *Buddenbrooks* (1901), the novella has generated a vast secondary literature, exploring in depth the themes of homoeroticism (also in relation to Mann's private life), mythology, aestheticism and décadence, and the Nietzeschean influence on Mann's writing.[12] The Venetian setting has also received some attention, but the beach as a specific location less so.[13] An exception is Michael Taussig who

---

[12] This literature is too extensive to be referenced here, but for a comprehensive survey, see Shookman (2003).
[13] In her encompassing study of Venice in literature, Angelika Corbineau-Hoffmann (1993, 309) describes Aschenbach's story as an existential alienation – in the psychoanalytic sense – of the usual tourist experience ("eine [...] ins Existentielle hineinreichende Verfremdung dessen, was einem Touristen widerfahren kann"). While she analyses Venice as a place in which the town's classical heritage and decay coalesce to produce a spatial alterity which in turn facilitates Aschenbach's homoerotic fantasy (ibid., 401–404), Corbineau-Hoffmann virtually ignores the specific setting and function of the beach.

connects Venice, "the ur-scene of capital" also associated with sexual licence and the commodification of sexuality, with the beach as a collective fantasy of Northern people of "our paradise, our Eden, from which we have been banished and to which we eternally return" (2006, 116). This conjunction of capitalist, decadent Venice with the sensuous beach results in a setting "where the repression sustaining civilization takes a transgressive dive and where, moreover, it is to be seen doing so where children play building sandcastles and adults play at being children on their way to being sea-creatures" (ibid.). It is precisely the apparent return to a state before the fall (and hence, before the rise of a Protestant work ethics), expressed in the adults' reversion to childhood and to a state of partial nakedness, that enables Gustav von Aschenbach's transgression of the rigid rules that hitherto dominated his life. According to Clayton Koelb, it is the novella's watery setting that induces the liquefaction of Aschenbach's rigidity:

> Aschenbach's experience in Venice is a steady, ruinous process of letting go in which the protagonist, as he becomes more and more dissolute, comes closer and closer to dissolving into formlessness. Mann gives this fusion a local habitation and a name in the figure of the 'Pontos,' Aschenbach's beloved sea. The ocean is clearly identified in the story both as the scene of sensuous abandon (the 'nakedness' of the beach society) and as the elemental 'ground of all being' to which the soul returns in death. The setting in Venice, a city completely dominated by water, provides an opportunity for numerous variations on this theme. Canals, fountains, and the great lagoon separating the city from the barrier island of the Lido all provide locations for important events in the tale. The whole city is presented as a 'sunken queen' in the process of nearly dissolving in the waters that surround and sustain it. (Koelb 2004, 107–108)

The omnipresence of water dissolves the boundaries between the firm land and the sea, and leads to a metaphorical as well as bodily "dissolving into formlessness" of Aschenbach's very being. From this perspective, the distinction between Venice, the city built on water, and the beach of the Lido di Venezia does not seem to be vital. While I agree that the amphibian configuration of Venice – as well as its geopolitical position at the intersection between the West and the East, the North and the South (see Elsaghe 1997, 27) – plays a vital role for the unfolding of the narrative, I argue that the story's beach setting deserves more attention in its own right than it has received so far.

The Lido (from Latin *litus*, 'coast') is not just any of the city's many islands, it is the spit separating the Venetian lagoon from the open sea, and therefore its beach epitomizes the function of an ambiguous territory, separating land and sea but with a constantly shifting boundary, that is constitutive of the beach in general (see Mack's definition quoted at the beginning of this essay). As a geographically dynamic place that is simultaneously positioned outside the temporal and social regimes of modern society, the Lido beach attains a productive as well as destructive agency in the narrative. It is the main location of Aschenbach's fantasizing about the Polish boy Tadzio, it is the site of heightened aesthetic experience and consequently of Aschenbach's most exquisite literary production, but it is also the scene of his moral deterioration and, finally, his death.[14] In addition, it fulfils many criteria of the perfect, paradisiacal beach, especially the presence of sand rather than shingle; this is one of the features that distinguishes the Lido beach from the pebbly and muddy beach in *Amy Foster*. As John Gillis has pointed out, at the modern seaside, dedicated to consumption and pleasure, sand, "principally white sand, has become the universal standard for beaches even where it is wholly unnatural and has to be imported" (2012, 143). In Mann's novella, the criteria of the perfect beach are first defined *ex negativo* during Aschenbach's first stopover at a resort off the Istrian coast. What Aschenbach desires but does not get in Istria is a balmy climate, a cosmopolitan clientele and, above all, "that restful intimate contact with the sea which can only be had on a gentle, sandy coast" (Mann 1998 [1912], 209). He is also in search of an "other place," a heterotopia different from his working life, or in his words "a fantastic mutation of normal reality" (ibid.), epitomised by Venice.

After his transfer across the Adriatic Sea, Aschenbach does find in the well-maintained beach of the Hotel des Bains the desired place demarcated as separate from work, although the weather continues sultry and the sea is grey:

> The scene on the beach, the spectacle of civilization taking its carefree sensuous ease at the brink of the element, entertained and delighted him as much as ever. Already the grey, shallow sea was alive with children wading, with swimmers, with assorted figures lying on the sand-bars, their crossed arms under their heads. Others were rowing little keelless boats painted red and blue, and capsizing with shrieks of laughter. In front of the long row of *capanne*, with their platforms like little verandahs to sit on, there was animated play and leisurely sprawling repose, there was visiting and chattering, there was punctilious morning elegance as well as unabashed nakedness contentedly enjoying the liberal local conventions. Further out, on the moist firm sand, persons in white bathing-robes, in loose fitting colourful shirtwear, wandered to and fro. On the right, a complicated sandcastle built by children was bedecked by flags in all the national colours. (Mann 1998 [1912], 223)

In some ways, however, this description deviates from the perfect beach of travel brochures, combining white sand, blue sky and the absence of other

---

[14] Kasia Boddy stresses the importance of the beach as a site of erotic flaneurism and aesthetic education in the writings of modernist authors such as Marcel Proust, James Joyce and Thomas Mann. For Mann's Aschenbach, she claims, the beach is the locus of transformation from a literary toiler to a "symbolist poet" (2007, 26).

visitors. The Lido beach does have the required element of fine, in this case "wax-yellow" sand (ibid.), but it is not an isolated natural place, nor is it empty. On this beach, the transformation from an empty to an overcrowded space that Kasia Boddy sees as constitutive of the modern beach, and that turns it into one of the paradigmatic spaces of modernity, has already taken place (2007, 22–23). In fact, the working population associated with tourism, such as the gondoliers, the waiters at the hotel, and most importantly, the bathing attendant, "a barefooted old man with linen trousers, sailor's jacket and straw hat" who conducts Aschenbach "to his reserved beach cabin" and sets up his table and chair "on the sandy wooden platform in front of it" (Mann 1998 [1912], 223), are described with great care. The bathing attendant's sailor's jacket and, even more so, the "English sailor's suit" (ibid., 220) the boy Tadzio usually wears, are traces pointing to the loss of utility, and hence disappearance, of the old maritime professions in the service economy of seaside resorts (see Urbain 2003 [1994], 45). In *Death in Venice*, the machinery of tourism is not hidden, but rather foregrounds the luxury of the Hotel des Bains. In this sense, the marked presence of hotel employees does not denote everyday work, but underscores the guests' separation from the necessity of breadwinning. As Taussig has suggested, the beach, with its associations of paradisiacal innocence and childish play, is predicated on capital, being affordable only to the wealthy, while simultaneously operating as the scene of the modern person's desire to escape from the logic of capitalism (2006, 116). This double function is further underscored by the private nature of the beach, that is, the fact that it is owned by the hotel and exclusively reserved for its guests. The "spectacle of civilization" Aschenbach enjoys observing from his deck-chair is thus not an unrestricted mingling of nations and classes, but only of the privileged segment of European society. For the visitors, the beach is clearly a place of leisure, as shown by the various activities they engage in: swimming, sunbathing, incompetently rowing boats, sauntering along the beach and building sandcastles. These are the classic practices that construct and hallmark the beach as a leisure site. A general relaxation of sartorial rules, allowing the guests to appear in anything from "punctilious morning elegance" to "unabashed nakedness" (Mann 1998 [1912], 233), contributes to the construction of the beach as a heterotopia of leisure where different norms and rules apply.

As a writer, not restricted to a work-place and defined office-hours, Aschenbach's position in relation to the work-leisure divide is ambiguous. His journey to the South is described as "an urge to escape, to run away from his writing" (ibid., 200–201), but he also carries books and writing material with him. Despite his longing for "intimate contact with the sea" (ibid., 209), Aschenbach does not enter it once; he does not swim, nor does he engage in any other of the usual beach practices. Settled in his deck-chair, he takes out "his travelling writing-case" and begins to deal with his correspondence (ibid., 225); by working on the beach, he collapses the regimes of work and leisure. But he is seduced away from his work by, as it were, the beach itself, "this most enjoyable of all situations" (ibid.), and in particular by its scopic appeal, its nature as a spectacle that involves all senses, but sight in particular (see Koné 2014). There is one paradigmatic beach practice that Aschenbach does take up, in which, in fact, he indulges to excess, and that is sea-gazing. The intimate contact he desires is, as it seems, not immersion into the sea but the look directed at it. Sea-gazing, from his hotel window but mostly from his deck-chair on the beach, becomes his pre-eminent activity, but one that is closely linked to passivity, to letting something happen rather than doing: "he gazed out over the beach, uncovered at this time of the afternoon, and over the sunless sea which was at high tide, its long low waves beating with a quiet regular rhythm on the shore" (Mann 1998 [1912], 218); "he let his eyes wander in the sea's wide expanse, let his gaze glide away, dissolve and die in the monotonous haze of this desolate emptiness" (ibid., 224); and after his failed attempt to leave Venice, "Aschenbach gazed out, his hands folded in his lap, pleased to be here again" (ibid., 233). The more extended and, in the end, unlimited his stay becomes, the more does Aschenbach give himself up to the complete passivity induced by sea-gazing: "Thus he sat for about an hour, resting and idly daydreaming" (ibid.).

Soon, however, Aschenbach's gaze is deflected "from limitless immensity" to the sand beach immediately beneath his feet: "the horizontal line of the seashore was suddenly intersected by a human figure" (ibid., 224). His gaze is from now on riveted on the figure of the Polish boy he had observed earlier in the hotel. He watches as Tadzio engages in the various beach activities – "sauntering, wading, digging, snatching, lying about and swimming" (ibid., 236) – that Aschenbach himself refrains from. In this way, they represent two types of beach visitors, the active and the passive, the practitioner of beach pleasures and the voyeur for whom Tadzio soon begins to perform. The writer imagines, and nobilitates, his infatuation with Tadzio in terms of the Greek model of older master and ephebe.[15] This whole cultural apparatus surrounding the relationship, the philosophy and aesthetic theory Aschenbach evokes to justify himself,

---

[15] As various commentators have observed, Tadzio takes on a number of classical and mythological roles, as "Eros, Phaedrus, Hyacinthus, Narcissus" (Boddy 2007, 26), and finally Hermes (Koelb 2004). What has been overlooked, to my knowledge, is Tadzio's similarity with Nausikaa who appears on the beach, like the Polish youth, surrounded by a group of deferential companions. This would place Aschenbach in the position of the stranded Odysseus whose subsequent rejuvenation is wrought, however, not by Athena's magic but by the art of the coiffeur.

this level of constant if perhaps disingenuous self-reflection, constitutes one of the crucial differences between Aschenbach's obsession and Amy's unreflected fascination with Yanko. There is no reason to suppose that Mann was familiar with *Amy Foster*,[16] so that the fact that in both stories the object of obsession is a beautiful young Pole is coincidental. As the only son of an aristocratic family, Tadzio is of course at the opposite social pole from Conrad's poor emigrant.[17] Nevertheless, it is instructive to note the different role of the Polish language:

> Aschenbach understood not a word of what he said, and commonplace though it might be, it was liquid melody in his ears. Thus the foreign sound of the boy's speech exalted it to music, the sun in its triumph shed lavish brightness all over him, and the sublime perspective of the sea was the constant contrasting background against which he appeared. (Ibid., 236)

As noted above, the middle-class characters in *Amy Foster* were appreciative of the melodious quality of Yanko's native language, but this did not save him from being an outcast, and finally, his relapse into Polish led to his fatal estrangement from Amy. In *Death in Venice*, the effect is different, but not quite dissimilar: the perception of Tadzio's speech as pure "melody" and "music" contributes to his transformation into an aesthetic entity, a figure of beauty contrasting with the sublime sea, but effectively also robs him of any discursive power. What Tadzio may have to say does not matter. If Yanko's strange language is a source of alienation and even of terror, in Tadzio's case it contributes further to Aschenbach's enchantment, or one could say, prevents his disenchantment, because it sustains the opacity of Tadzio's probably "commonplace" boyish mind, and thus allows him to continue to function as an object of fantasy. In Yanko's case, by contrast, the spell his exotic beauty casts on Amy is broken precisely by his functional muteness, his incomprehensible "terrible voice" (Conrad 1963 [1901], 255).

However young and beautiful Tadzio is, he is no more than a suitable, but coincidental object on which Aschenbach's desire for youth and beauty fastens. It is not a specific individual that lures the aging writer away from his dedication to work; rather, this is the effect of the place and the situation, the life at the beach: "The lulling rhythm of this existence had already cast a spell on him; he had been quickly enchanted by the indulgent softness and splendour of this way of life" (Mann 1998 [1912], 234–235). The careful calibration between

---

[16] Mann was familiar with some of Conrad's work and wrote the preface to the German translation of *The Secret Agent* (1926), but as he states there, this was a fairly late discovery (Lorenz 2015; Vidan 1993).
[17] The implications of Tadzio's Polishness in the context of Mann's shifting political allegiance are discussed in Foster (1998, esp. 199–201).

leisure and work, the ancillary function of leisure for work, breaks down as Aschenbach, under the influence of the sun, the sea and the sand, turns from the personification of Protestant, in his case specifically Prussian, work ethics into an old faun, a voyeur who cannot prevent himself from following his fantasized boy-lover around on the hotel grounds and through the streets of Venice:

> The sun was browning his face and hands, the stimulating salty breeze heightened his capacity for feeling, and whereas formerly, when sleep or food or contact with nature had given him any refreshment, he would always have expended it completely on his writing, he now, with high-hearted prodigality, allowed all the daily revitalization he was receiving from the sun and leisure and sea air to burn itself up in intoxicating emotion. (Ibid., 241)

The vacation no longer serves the reinvigoration necessary for Aschenbach's creative work. On the contrary, the capital he had accumulated by his writing is now squandered, equally to his vital powers, to subsidize his never-ending vacation: "He was no longer keeping tally of the leisure time he had allowed himself; the thought of returning home did not even occur to him. He had arranged for ample funds to be made available to him here" (ibid.). It is only consistent that Aschenbach eschews the possibility of an honourable retreat by informing Tadzio's mother of the spreading cholera, thus hastening the family's departure and allowing himself the return to his former self. But Aschenbach does not want to return to his life of hard work: "the thought of returning home, of levelheadedness and sobriety, of toil and mastery, filled him with such repugnance that his face twisted into an expression of physical nausea" (ibid., 259). Aschenbach wants to stay at the beach, forever. And so he stays and dies there, gazing out at the sea and "follow[ing] the movements of the walking figure in the distance" (ibid., 267). If Yanko dies a miserable, lonely death in a puddle, marked as abject by his covering of mud, Aschenbach, despite his possible infection with cholera, is allowed to die a dry death on the sand. Collapsing in his deckchair on the Lido's sandy beach, he wanders gently into infinity, as Tadzio undergoes his final transformation into the mythological soul-summoner – Hermes, who helped Odysseus escape from Ogygia, and now leads Aschenbach from the beach to the realm of the dead.

4 Conclusion: Literary Littoral Studies

The differences between *Amy Foster* and *Death in Venice* can be described in a series of dichotomies, pertaining to the setting, narration, characters and the function of the beach. Colebrook and environs is enclosed, provincial and untouched by industrialisation; consequently, the landscape and the lives of its inhabitants are dominated by agricultural production, hard work and poverty. This pre-industrial lifestyle is linked with psychological traits such as lack of imagination and distrust of strangers. Venice, by contrast, is open and cosmopolitan – easily reached by ship and train, and connected to the world by telegraph and newspapers. Especially the hotel world of the Lido is presented as a modern service economy, dedicated to providing leisure and luxury to its well-to-do clients. At the same time, the city has lost its ancient political significance and is in a state of decay, providing a suitable setting for Aschenbach's moral decline. Corresponding to these social and spatial parameters, the main protagonists of *Amy Foster* belong to the agricultural working class, but they are not given a voice of their own; their story is presented by a pair of middle-class narrators who both arrived from the outside, and whose reconstruction of the events is fragmentary and speculative. *Death in Venice* is narrated by a heterodiegetic narrator who is unmarked but certainly shares Aschenbach's level of education; there is also zero focalisation, so that the reader has total insight into Aschenbach's life story, emotions and even dreams. This has the effect that the aging writer becomes the object of a scrutiny that is far more radical than his own observation of Tadzio, which stops at externals. In fact, both Dr Kennedy and the narrator of *Death in Venice* share a clinical, dissecting attitude towards the objects of their case studies, but as a homodiegetic narrator Kennedy has only limited insight into their inner lives. Conversely, Amy and Yanko can be said to be more resistant to the process of narrative appropriation than Aschenbach; if they cannot tell their own stories, they nonetheless retain some of their opacity in face of the doctor's alleged ability to extract "a particle of a general truth in every mystery" (Conrad 1963 [1901], 229).

These features have certain consequences for the respective constructions of the beach. Whereas in *Amy Foster* the beach forms only a marginal part of the story's topography, and can be described as the repressed within its narrative economy, it is the main setting in *Death in Venice*. This differing status of littoral space is, I have argued, closely tied to the different socio-economic conditions in the story-worlds. If the literary (and visual) representation of the modern beach requires the effacement of work and working people, as claimed by Urbain and others, then it is only to be expected that a narrative focusing on characters from the working class can represent the beach only through metonymy and synecdoche, in the shape of the mud that seeps into Yanko's story. By contrast, the sandy beach of the Lido is a classic modern beach, functioning as a stage for the display and observation of beach practices. It is the perfect beach of seaside tourism, available for leisure and consumption, exclusive in the sense of being reserved for the hotels' clientele, and of representing work only if it is in the service of these clients. There is, however, one element connecting these two contrasting constructions of the beach: the presence of death. The beach in *Amy Foster* is the site where the drowned bodies from the *Herzogin Sophia-Dorothea* are washed ashore. While Yanko himself does not die on the beach, his death, associated with mud and water, is the eventual result of this disaster, and is described as a social shipwreck. In *Death in Venice* this situation is reversed: the one individual death, that of Aschenbach, takes place on the beach, but it is the growing number of the anonymous dead, the spread of the cholera in Venice, that endangers the city's flourishing tourist economy. The international traffic that is the precondition of tourism is the cause of the epidemic, and threatens to depopulate the perfect beach not only of those who work, but also of those who pay and enjoy. Finally, the metamorphic power scholars ascribe to the beach is in both cases negative or at least ambivalent: Yanko is transformed from an emigrant seeking a better life into a debased and ostracised creature, close to an animal. Aschenbach, while momentarily experiencing new sensual pleasure and heightened aesthetic powers, succumbs to a moral shipwreck that turns him into a ludicrous *faux jeune homme* without dignity and self-control.

The juxtaposition of two so different tales allows for some generalisations on narrating and constructing the beach, and the directions littoral studies in literature could take. First, the different treatments of the beach in stories belonging to literary modernism, and being chronologically close, show that its functions are diverse, despite the apparent dominance of the beach as a vacation site after the late nineteenth century. Conrad's tale echoes earlier disaster literature and the robinsonade, where the beach is constructed as a site of rescue as well as a horrid place, a site of deprivation and solitude. The fascination of this genre persists to the present day; a recent example is Isabelle Autissier's *Soudain, seuls* (2015) in which a pair of circumnavigators strand on an island off Patagonia and fight for survival on the hostile beach. Second, my analysis of the two stories has shown the importance of class, income, nationality and education for the privilege of accessing, enjoying and narrating the beach. To these categories should of course be added gender, race, ethnicity and sexual orientation. Beaches are often segregated along these categories – for example, the beaches in Apartheid South Africa – but they can also function as sites of women's and LGBTIQ people's regeneration and emancipation, in novels as diverse as Elizabeth Gaskell's *Sylvia's Lovers* (1863), Kate Chopin's *The Awakening* (1899), Christopher Isherwood's *Goodbye to Berlin* (1939) and Colm Tóibín's *Blackwater Lightship* (1999). In short, I plead for an intersectional and multifaceted approach to littoral studies. Third, in a space that functions like a stage, scopic regimes – the rules of seeing and being seen – play a crucial role, as can be seen in relation to *Death in Venice* in particular. However, scholarship on the beach has stressed the importance of the five senses and the coenesthetic experience, the feeling of inhabiting one's body resulting from the stimulation by physical contact with the sea (Urbain 2003 [1994], 70). Littoral studies should therefore pursue a multisensorial approach, rather than one exclusively dedicated to vision. Fourth, an interdisciplinary approach suggests itself for littoral studies. The beach as a literary setting can be fruitfully analysed with the help of tools deriving from spatial theory and cultural geography, recent studies in history that focus on routes, trade and traffic – and therefore, on oceans and coasts rather than territories – and the study of linguistic landscapes, to name but a few. And finally, a combination of formal analysis and cultural studies seems indicated. The precise study of form, for example of narratological aspects, rhetorical tropes and the rhythm and sound of language, is crucial to show in what ways literary texts construct the beach. But the beach is not only textual; it is also particularly saturated with the social world. The materiality of the seaside is crucial: analyses can include concrete topographies, architectural features, beach fashions, postcards and objects associated with the seaside. Evidently, not all of these directions can be pursued in a single study. But more studies will come: littoral studies is poised to become an emergent field that will have a particular resonance across different disciplines and perhaps beyond academia.

Bibliography

Anderson, Susan C., and Bruce H. Tabb. *Water, Leisure and Culture: European Historical Perspectives*. Oxford and New York: Berg, 2002.

Andreach, Robert J. "The Two Narrators of 'Amy Foster.'" *Studies in Short Fiction* 2 (1965): 262–269.

Assmann, Aleida. *Ist die Zeit aus den Fugen? Aufstieg und Fall des Zeitregimes der Moderne*. München: Hanser, 2013.

Autissier, Isabelle. *Soudains, Seuls*. Paris: Editions Stock, 2015.

"beach, n." *OED Online*. www.oed.com/view/Entry/16443. Oxford: Oxford University Press, 2019 (30 October 2018).

Boddy, Kasia. "The Modern Beach." *Critical Quarterly* 49.4 (2007): 21–39.
Chopin, Kate. *The Awakening* [1899]. Ed. Marco Culley. 2nd ed. New York and London: W. W. Norton, 1994.
Cohen, Margaret. *The Novel and the Sea*. Princeton and Oxford: Princeton University Press, 2010.
Conrad, Joseph. "Amy Foster [1901]." *The Nigger of the 'Narcissus,' Typhoon and Other Stories.* Harmondsworth: Penguin, 1963. 228–257.
Corbin, Alain. *The Lure of the Sea. The Discovery of the Seaside in the Western World, 1750–1840* [*Le Territoire du vide. L'Occident et le désir de rivage*, 1988]. Translated by Jocelyn Phelps. Berkeley and Los Angeles: University of California Press, 1994.
Corbineau-Hoffmann, Angelika. *Paradoxie der Fiktion: Literarische Venedig-Bilder 1797–1984.* Berlin and New York: De Gruyter, 1993.
Cresswell, Tim. *On the Move: Mobility in the Modern Western World*. New York and London: Routledge, 2006.
Defoe, Daniel. *The Life and Strange Surprizing Adventures of Robinson Crusoe* [1719]. Ed. J. Donald Crowley. Oxford: Oxford University Press, 1983.
Elsaghe, Yahya A. "Zur Sexualisierung des Fremden im 'Tod in Venedig.'" *Archiv für das Studium der Neueren Sprachen und Literaturen* 149.1 (1997): 19–32.
Foster, John Burt Jr. "Why is Tadzio Polish? *Kultur* and Cultural Multiplicity in 'Death in Venice.'" *Death in Venice: Complete, Authoritative Text with Biographical and Historical Contexts, Critical History, and Essays from Five Contemporary Critical Perspectives.* Ed. Naomi Ritter. Boston and New York: Bedford Books, 1998. 192–210.
Foucault, Michel. "Of Other Spaces" ["Des Espaces autres," 1984]. Translated by Jay Miskowiec. *Diacritics* 16.1 (1986): 22–27.
Gaskell, Elizabeth. *Sylvia's Lovers* [1863]. Edited and with an introduction by Shirley Foster. London: Penguin, 2004.
Gillis, John R. *The Human Shore: Seacoasts in History*. Chicago and London: University of Chicago Press, 2012.
Greenblatt, Stephen. "Cultural Mobility: An Introduction." *Cultural Mobility: A Manifesto.* Ed. Stephen Greenblatt. Cambridge: Cambridge University Press, 2009. 1–23.
Griem, Eberhard. "Physiological Possibility in Joseph Conrad's 'Amy Foster': The Problem of Narrative Technique." *Conradiana* 24.2 (1992): 126–134.
Hassan, John. *The Seaside, Health and the Environment in England and Wales since 1800.* Aldershot: Ashgate, 2003.
Homer. *The Odyssey of Homer.* Translated and with an introduction by Richmond Lattimore. New York: Harper Perennial, 2007.
Isherwood, Christopher. *Goodbye to Berlin* (1939). *The Berlin Novels*. London: Vintage, 1999.
Kerr, Douglas. "Conrad and the Immigrant: The Drama of Hospitality." *Review of English Studies* 67.279 (2016): 334–348.
Kluwick, Ursula, and Virginia Richter. "Of Tourists and Refugees: The Global Beach in the Twenty-First Century." *Heterotopia and Globalisation in the Twenty-First Century*. Eds. Simon Ferdinand, Irina Souch and Daan Wesselman. London: Routledge, 2020. 116-130.
Koelb, Clayton. "Death in Venice." *A Companion to the Works of Thomas Mann.* Eds. Herbert Lehnert and Eva Wessell. Rochester/NY: Camden House, 2004. 95–113.
Koné, Christophe. "Aschenbach's Homovisual Desire: Scopophilia in 'Der Tod in Venedig' by Thomas Mann." *Thomas Mann: Neue kulturwissenschaftliche Lektüren*. Eds. Stefan Börnchen, Georg Mein and Gary Schmidt. München: Fink, 2014. 95–106.

Latour, Bruno. *We Have Never Been Modern* [*Nous n'avons jamais été modernes*, 1991]. Translated by Catherine Porter. Cambridge/MA: Harvard University Press, 1993.
Lenček, Lena, and Gideon Bosker. *The Beach: The History of Paradise on Earth*. New York: Viking, 1998.
Lorenz, Matthias N. "Joseph Conrad und die Deutschen: Ein Bericht." *IASL* 40.1 (2015): 222–265.
Mack, John. *The Sea: A Cultural History*. London: Reaktion Books, 2011.
Mann, Thomas. *Buddenbrooks. Verfall einer Familie* [1901]. Ed. Eckhard Heftrich. Frankfurt/Main: Fischer, 2015.
Mann, Thomas. "Death in Venice" ["Tod in Venedig," 1912]. *Death in Venice and Other Stories*. Translated and with an Introduction by David Luke. London: Vintage Books, 1998. 197–267.
Mann, Thomas. "Vorwort zu Joseph Conrads Roman *Der Geheimagent* [1926]." *Rede und Antwort: Über eigene Werke. Huldigungen und Kränze: Über Freunde, Weggefährten und Zeitgenossen*. Ed. Peter de Mendelssohn. Frankfurt/Main: Fischer, 1984. 572–585.
Mentz, Steve. "Brown." *Prismatic Ecology. Ecotheory Beyond Green*. Ed. Jeffrey Jerome Cohen. Minneapolis and London: University of Minnesota Press, 2013. 193–212.
Payne, Christiana. "Seaside Visitors: Idlers, Thinkers and Patriots in Mid-nineteenth-century Britain." *Water, Leisure and Culture: European Historical Perspectives*. Eds. Susan C. Anderson and Bruce H. Tabb. Oxford and New York: Berg, 2002. 87–104.
Richter, Virginia, and Ursula Kluwick. "Introduction: 'Twixt Land and Sea: Approaches to Littoral Studies." *The Beach in Anglophone Literatures and Cultures: Reading Littoral Space*. Eds. Ursula Kluwick and Virginia Richter. Farnham and Burlington/VT: Ashgate, 2015. 1–20.
Shaffer, Brian W. "Swept from the Sea: Trauma and Otherness in Conrad's 'Amy Foster.'" *Conradiana* 32.3 (2000): 163–176.
Shookman, Ellis. *Thomas Mann's 'Death in Venice': A Novella and Its Critics*. Rochester/NY and Woodbridge: Camden House, 2003.
Spenser, Edmund. *Amoretti* [1595]. Ed. Teresa Page. Kent: Crescent Moon, 2008.
Taussig, Michael. "The Beach (a Fantasy)." *Walter Benjamin's Grave*. Chicago and London: University of Chicago Press, 2006. 97–119.
Tóibín, Colm. *Blackwater Lightship*. London: Picador, 1999.
Urbain, Jean-Didier. *At the Beach* [*Sur la plage*, 1994]. Translated by Catherine Porter. Minneapolis and London: University of Minnesota Press, 2003.
Vidan, Ivo. "Conrad and Thomas Mann." *Contexts for Conrad*. Eds. Keith Carabine, Owen Knowles and Wiesław Krajka. Boulder: East European Monographs, 1993. 265–285.
Walton, John K. *The English Seaside Resort: A Social History, 1750–1914*. Leicester and New York: Leicester University Press and St. Martin's Press, 1983.

Jeannot Moukouri Ekobe
Dystopie, Utopie, Heterotopie: Die Imagination des Strands in der Literatur von Afropäerinnen

The present work analyses the construction of the beach in two novels of contemporary Afro-European authors. While the aesthetic reconstruction of slavery's memory constitutes the framework for this construction in Léonora Miano's *La Saison de l'ombre*, the depiction of contemporary migration flows to Europe offers the background for the narration in Marie Ndiaye's *Trois femmes puissantes*. In this regard, the two novels imagine the beach in contexts where African characters encounter Europe. The article's main hypothesis is that the beach is conceived and lived by African characters as the place where human dignity is lost. It is a place of transformation of the human being into an illegal being, into a subhuman. Furthermore, the beach also appears as a break with normality because physical and moral violence as well as profound humiliation become a banality there. In the two novels, the beach seems to have dystopic features. It is a heterotopia of violence.

Das Ziel des vorliegenden Artikels besteht darin, zu untersuchen, wie der Strand in zwei Romanen von zwei Afropäerinnen konstruiert wird. Während sich diese Rekonstruktion in Léonora Miano's *La Saison de l'ombre* vor dem Hintergrund des Gedenkens an die Sklaverei vollzieht, liefert der zeitgenössische Migrationsstrom nach Europa den Rahmen der Narration in Marie Ndiayes *Trois femmes puissantes*. So gesehen, wird der Strand in den beiden Werken im Kontext der Begegnung der Völker geschildert. Die Arbeit basiert auf der zentralen Hypothese, dass der Strand von afrikanischen Figuren als der Ort wahrgenommen, vorgestellt und erlebt wird, an dem eine tiefe Erniedrigung und Entmenschlichung erfahren wird. Am Strand werden Herabwürdigung und Gewalt zur Normalität. Deswegen weist er dystopische Züge auf. Der Strand ist eine Heterotopie der Gewalt.

1 Einführung

Schon seine physische Struktur weist auf die Tatsache hin, dass der Strand keine unmittelbar eindeutige Bedeutung besitzt. Er liegt nämlich irgendwo zwischen Meer und Festland, zwischen Verschließung und Öffnung, zwischen Anfang und Ende. Deswegen ist seine soziale Wahrnehmung breit gefächert.

Was europäische Gesellschaften angeht, hat sich nach und nach eine Vorstellung des Strands etabliert, bei der der Strand als ein öffentlicher transitorischer Raum betrachtet wird, welcher der Entspannung gewidmet ist. Er befindet sich in einem Nirgendwo, außerhalb der normalen Zeitlichkeit, wo sich der

Mensch von einem der wichtigsten Zeichen der Zivilisation befreien kann, der Kleidung.

Doch wenn es um die Begegnung der Völker geht, zum Beispiel zwischen Europäer*innen und Afrikaner*innen, scheint der Strand nicht die gleiche Bedeutung zu besitzen. Sei es während der Zeit der Sklaverei, der Kolonialzeit oder in der Gegenwart mit der sogenannten ‚illegalen Migration', der Strand ist der unvermeidliche Ort der ersten Begegnung mit dem Anderen. Die Reiseliteratur ist voll von Berichten über solche Begegnungen. Diese werden aber vorwiegend aus der Perspektive der weißen Forschungsreisenden, der Sklavenhändler(*innen), der Missionar*innen, der Tourist*innen etc. dargestellt. Deswegen ist es bei diesen Begegnungen wichtig, sich für die Wahrnehmung des Strands aus der Perspektive der afrikanischen Figuren zu interessieren. Demgemäß verfolgt der vorliegende Artikel das Ziel, die Art und Weise zu analysieren, wie der Strand von afrikanischen Figuren in zwei Werken von zwei zeitgenössischen Afropäerinnen wahrgenommen, vorgestellt und erlebt wird.

In ihrem Werk *La Saison de l'ombre* inszeniert Léonora Miano die erste Begegnung des Volks der Mulongo mit den europäischen Sklavenhändler(*innen)[1] an einem Strand irgendwo in Afrika. Marie Ndiaye wiederum stellt in *Trois femmes puissantes* die Erfahrung einer jungen Afrikanerin dar, die sich über das Meer auf den Weg nach Europa macht.

Die hier vorliegende Arbeit basiert auf der zentralen Hypothese, dass der Strand von afrikanischen Figuren als ein Ort wahrgenommen, vorgestellt und erlebt wird, wo eine tiefe Erniedrigung und Entmenschlichung erfahren wird. Für sie hat der Strand dystopische Züge. Konzepte von ‚Heterotopie' (Foucault), ‚Raumproduktion' (Lefebvre) und ‚Einzäunen' (Mbembe) stellen den theoretischen Rahmen der Analyse dar.

2 Ambivalenz

Die von Daniel Defoe (2000 [1719],128) geschilderte Strandszene zwischen Robinson Crusoe und dem indigenen Mann, bei welcher der britische weiße Held seinem neuen Gesprächspartner einen Namen, Freitag, zuweist, ist symptomatisch für die asymmetrischen Beziehungen im Kontext der Begegnung der Völker jener Zeit. Nicht nur beschreibt sie den Besitzanspruch der europäischen Figur auf den Anderen als selbstverständlich, sondern sie stellt auch das Modell

---

[1] Für das nicht eindeutig zu entschlüsselnde generische Maskulinum des französischen Originals ist hier und an den folgenden Stellen die Schreibung mit Genderstern gewählt.

einer lange andauernden Erzähltradition von Herrschaftsbeziehungen aus der Perspektive des weißen Helden dar. Doch scheint Léonora Mianos *La Saison de l'ombre* (2013), ein von einer ‚Afropäerin' (Miano 2008) fast dreihundert Jahre später verfasster Roman bzw. Schilderung einer Begegnung der Völker, eines mit Defoes berühmtem Text gemeinsam zu haben: Beide beschreiben den Strand als einen Raum der Gewalt, wo eine herrschaftsfreie Begegnung zwischen Europäer*innen und den Anderen unmöglich scheint. Miano entfernt sich aber sowohl von der Tradition der Erzählung aus der Machtposition als auch von der der Erzählung des Sklavenhandels aus der Perspektive der Sklav*innen (Mokam 2015, 69). Vielmehr legt sie den Akzent auf die Familie, der Verwandte geraubt wurden.

Léonora Miano's *La Saison de l'ombre* erzählt die Geschichte des Volksstamms bzw. der Gemeinschaft der Mulongo, die damals irgendwo in Äquatorialafrika lebte. Nach einem großen Brand fehlen eines Nachts zwölf Männer unter den Mitgliedern des Volkes, zehn Jugendliche und zwei ältere Männer. Die Mütter der Jugendlichen wurden verhaftet und müssen in einem kleinen Haus bleiben, während die Männer versuchen, das Verbrechen aufzuklären. Niemand versteht, was passiert ist. Nach einigen Tagen entscheidet sich Eyabe, eine der inhaftierten Frauen, das Hafthaus zu verlassen, um sich auf die Suche nach den verschwundenen Männern zu machen. Sie begibt sich auf die Suche außerhalb des Dorfs, wohin nur wenige Mulongo zu gehen wagen. Die Suche nach einer Erklärung hilft ihr dabei, die Situation nach und nach zu verstehen: Es gibt einen epochalen Bruch. Die Gegend erlebt gerade den Anbruch einer neuen Epoche. Da sie noch keinen Begriff dafür hat, bezeichnet Eyabe diese Epoche als die Zeit der Verfolgungsjagd, ‚die Zeit der Menschenjagd durch den Menschen' (Miano 2013, 138–139). Mianos Roman entsteht in einem Kontext großer Debatten über die Gedächtnisforschung in Hinblick auf die Sklaverei und die Bildung der Nation in Frankreich. Ihr Verfahren ist aber transnational, da sie versucht, den Akzent auf die Herkunftsländer von einstigen Sklav*innen und Kolonisierten zu setzen. Dabei nehmen afrikanische Strände maßgebliche symbolische Bedeutungen an. In dem Roman werden sie mal als Quelle der Macht, mal als Ende der bekannten Welt und auch als Ort der Neugeburt geschildert.

Um die Bedeutung des Strands als Quelle der Macht zu verstehen, lohnt es sich, die Beschreibung der verschiedenen afrikanischen Völker des Romans zu berücksichtigen. Im Roman werden vier afrikanische Gruppen beschrieben, die sich in Hinblick auf die „géographie littéraire" [literarische Geographie] (Ferré 1954, 145) voneinander klar unterscheiden. In Hinblick auf den ‚wahrgenommenen Raum' (Simo 2010, 21) ist beispielsweise Bekombo, die Hauptstadt der Bwele, eine erfolgreiche Stadt mit prächtigen Häusern. Seinerseits ist Mulongo ein kleines, bescheidenes Dorf. Dagegen verfügt Isedu über neue militärtechnische

Mittel, die das Dorf von den Fremden bekommt. Bebayedi wiederum hat nur Pfahlbauten, die es gegen Angriffe schützen.

Dass die Erzählerin so einen großen Akzent auf Unterschiede zwischen den afrikanischen Gemeinschaften legt, ist von maßgeblicher Bedeutung. Die besondere Erzählsituation erscheint als eine Kritik an der Tendenz zur Verallgemeinerung, die in der Kolonialbibliothek afrikanische Menschen undifferenziert betrachtet (Mokam 2015, 69). Die so im Text akzentuierten Unterschiede zwischen den afrikanischen Gemeinschaften dienen weiterhin auch als Hilfsmittel für das Verständnis des regionalen Machtspiels, das sich mit der Ankunft der Europäer*innen zugespitzt hat. Dieses Machtverhältnis zwischen den verschiedenen Gruppen im Text ist stark von der Entfernung vom Strand bzw. von der Küste abhängig. Dies kommt beispielweise bei einem Gespräch zwischen Mutango, einem Prinz der Mulongo, mit Bwemba, einem General der Bwele, zum Vorschein:

> Ceux qui vivent sur les limites du monde connu sont[...] terriblement prétentieux. Depuis qu'ils ont rencontré les étrangers venus par les eaux, ils se croient les égaux du divin. Leurs nouveaux amis les fournissent en étoffes inconnues dans cette partie de misipo. Ils leur donnent aussi des armes, des bijoux et des choses qu'on ne saurait nommer. Enfin, les Côtiers[...] se prétendent aujourd'hui frères des hommes aux pieds de poule.[2] (Miano 2013, 79–80)

Der vorliegende Textauszug macht das strategische Spiel von Allianzen sichtbar, das sich vor dem Hintergrund der Nähe/Ferne vom Strand abspielt. Die Europäer*innen, die über neue militärische Mittel verfügen, schließen Verträge mit den König*innen der Küste. Dank diesen Handelsverträgen bekommen diese moderne Gewehre und andere europäische Produkte, die ihre Macht in der Region vergrößern. Wenn nun die Europäer*innen Sklav*innen brauchen, wenden sie sich diesen König*innen zu, die Raubangriffe im Hinterland organisieren, Menschen fremder Völkergruppen entführen und gegen europäische Produkte eintauschen:

> Jadis, d'après ce que j'ai compris, ils leur procuraient de l'huile rouge et des défenses d'éléphants. Désormais, ils donnent des gens, même des enfants, en échange de marchandises. Il paraît que les Côtiers possèdent maintenant un roseau qui crache la foudre, lance

---

[2] „The people who live on the brink of the world are terribly pretentious[...]. Ever since they met the foreigners who came across the waters, they see themselves as equals of the gods. Their new friends provide them with fabric unknown in this part of Misipo. They also give them weapons, jewellery and things for which we have no names. Finally, the coastal residents [...] now claim to be brothers of the men with hen feet." (Miano 2018, 73)

des projectiles mortels. Cette arme, fournie par les hommes aux pieds de poule, leur permet de soumettre aisément leurs captifs.³ (Ebd., 132 [im Original kursiv])

So äußert sich ein Überlebender der Entführung. Aus dem oben Ausgeführten geht hervor, dass afrikanische Völker der Küste, die als erste Europäer*innen begegnet sind, eine deutlich privilegierte Position haben und dadurch vermeiden können, selbst als Sklav*innen entführt zu werden. Die Nähe zur Küste bzw. zum Strand entpuppt sich somit als eine strategisch vorteilhafte Position. In diesem Zusammenhang sind Völker des Hinterlandes, wie beispielsweise die Mulongo, dazu verurteilt, Opfer des neuen Typs von Handel zu sein, weil sie keinen Zugang zum Strand bzw. keinen Kontakt mit Europäer*innen haben. Die Mitglieder ihrer Völker werden geraubt und versklavt. Somit versucht der Text einen Aspekt des Sklavenhandels zu enthüllen, der von afrikanischen Forscher*innen meist zu behandeln versäumt wird: die afrikanische Verantwortung am Sklavenhandel (Diakité, 2008). Doch die genaue Analyse der Machtverhältnisse in der Gegend, so wie sie im Text zum Vorschein kommen, legt vielmehr nahe, diese Verantwortung differenziert zu betrachten. Sie tritt eigentlich als eine Komplizenschaft unter Druck auf, bei der die Völker in Strandnähe keine andere Wahl haben, als Völker des Hinterlands zu verkaufen. Ansonsten laufen sie Gefahr, selbst versklavt zu werden. Europäer*innen, die meistens in ihren Schiffen oder am Strand bleiben, greifen nämlich immer an, wenn die Alliierten sich weigern, mit ihnen zusammenzuarbeiten. Dies scheint Wolfgang Klooss' (2014, 203) Überlegung über die Produktion des Strandes zu bestärken, wenn er behauptet: „The beach is turned into a battleground where ‚duels to the death [are] waged between races and cultures'". Was Klooss hier auf den Raum des Strands allein beschränkt, gilt bei Miano in *La Saison de l'ombre* für das ganze afrikanische Territorium des Romans. Die Machtspiele, die am Strand bzw. an der Küste stattfinden, also die „colonial encounters, conquest, defeat, appropriation, and destruction" (Kloos 2014, 195), bedeuten eine tiefgreifende Umwälzung für die ganze Region. Die neue Epoche, die sich von der Küste her abzeichnet, ist durch Plünderung, Raub, Razzien, Kriege, Massaker, allseitige Verschleppung und Terror gekennzeichnet.

Die Betrachtung des Strandes als einem Ort des Leidens, aber auch gleichzeitig als einem Ort der Machtausübung scheint Lefebvres (1974) These des Raums als soziales Produkt zu bekräftigen. Als soziales Produkt wird der Strand im Text unterschiedlich ‚vorgestellt' (Simo 2010, 21) und erlebt. Dies kann

---

3 „From what I have understood, they used to supply them with red oil and elephant tusks. Now they give them people, even children, in exchange for merchandise. It seems the Coastlanders now have a reed that spits fire, shoots deadly projectiles. The men with hen feet supplied these to them to help them subjugate their captives." (Miano 2018, 126)

anhand der geographisch binären Opposition zwischen den Dörfern Isedu und Mulongo veranschaulicht werden. Die Isedu, die am Strand bzw. an der Küste wohnen, leben harmonisch in diesem Umfeld. Sowohl ihre Mythologie als auch ihr Alltag sind stark von Strand und Meer beeinflusst, so dass sie sich als „fils de l'eau" [Söhne des Wassers] (Miano 2013, 79) betrachten, deren Götter in einer unterirdischen Wasserwelt leben sollen. Somit erscheint der Strand als ihr natürliches Umfeld, das sie schützt und ihnen das Gefühl der Geborgenheit gibt. Eine solche symbolische Besetzung des liminalen Orts Strand durch das Volk der Küste wird der Figur Eyabe sofort bewusst, als sie den Strand auf der Suche nach den entführten Mulongo-Männern endlich erreicht. In einer Episode, in der sie unerlaubt der offiziellen Trauerfeier eines Prinzen der Küste beiwohnt, kann sie die Verankerung der lokalen kulturellen und alltäglichen Erfahrung in dem Küstenumfeld erleben. Die Trauergemeinde hat sich nämlich am Strand versammelt, um das Begräbnisritual durchzuführen. Bei der Zeremonie sind nicht nur alle führenden Kräfte der Isedu, sondern auch König*innen von alliierten Dörfern und Europäer*innen anwesend. Auch das einfache Volk und die Knechte aus fremden Dörfern nehmen an der Zeremonie teil. Nach zahlreichen religiösen und traditionellen Ritualen werden sowohl der verstorbene Prinz als auch seine noch lebendigen Frauen und Knechte begraben. Die Wahl des Strands als Schauplatz solcher wichtiger Ereignisse ist insofern bedeutungsvoll, als sie unter anderem auf den sakralen Charakter des Strands bei den Isedu hinweist. Der Strand wird somit zum Bindeglied zwischen den Isedu und ihren Ahnen bzw. zwischen dem Diesseits und dem Jenseits.

Nicht nur das ganze Ritual und besonders das Begräbnis der noch lebendigen Menschen, sondern auch die so starke symbolische Bindung zum Strand sind Eyabe völlig fremd. Vor der Ankunft der Europäer lebten die lokalen Völker relativ getrennt voneinander. Kontakte zwischen ihnen gab es kaum und dann nur zu direkt benachbarten Gruppen. Die Figur Eyabe kannte daher nur ihr direktes Umfeld. Genauso wie viele Mulongo hatte sie damals keine Stranderfahrung und wusste nicht, dass die Region sehr groß und in sich unterschiedlich ist. Statt eines Gefühls der Geborgenheit empfindet sie eine tiefgreifende Erschütterung bei ihrer ersten Stranderfahrung. Der Strand und das Meer erwecken bei ihr Angst, Schrecken, Kränkung und Unruhe. Die Art und Weise, wie die bekannte Welt so plötzlich am Strand in einem ungeheuren Ausmaß an Wasser verloren geht, ist symbolisch für den epochalen Bruch, der sich durch die Ankunft der Europäer*innen in der Region und die Entführung der Brüder und Söhne jener Nacht annonciert. Wurde bis dahin der Strand als Grenze der (bekannten) Welt bezeichnet, so entwickelt er sich für die Entführten und ihre Familien nach und nach zum Ende der bekannten Welt, was an Foucaults Konzept von Heterotopie denken lässt.

Die Heterotopie ist eine Kategorie zur Beschreibung imaginierter Orte, von Utopien, die aber zur realen Welt gehören, auch wenn sie von ihr getrennt zu sein scheinen. Sie funktionieren nach eigener Logik, die manchmal im Widerspruch zu gewöhnlichen bzw. gesellschaftlich als ‚normal' betrachteten Praktiken steht. Sie dienen unter anderem mal der Regulierung von Krisen, mal der Begleitung einer Transformation und haben ein besonderes Verhältnis zu Zeit und Raum. Michel Foucault unterscheidet sechs Prinzipien der Heterotopie. Die Heterotopie der Krise bezeichnet Orte, die für Menschen reserviert sind, die sich in einer Krisenphase befinden: Jugendliche, Frauen in der Periode der Menstruation, alte Menschen etc. An diesen Orten wird die Transformation bzw. der Übergang von einer Lebensphase zu einer anderen vorbereitet und erlebt. Heutzutage wird eher von Heterotopie der Abweichung gesprochen. Sie bezeichnet Orte, die für Menschen reserviert sind, deren Verhalten den sozialen Normen folgend als abweichend betrachtet wird: Gefängnisse, Altersheime, psychiatrische Kliniken usw. Das zweite Prinzip der Heterotopie ist ihre Wandelbarkeit in der Zeit. Einem Ort werden je nach Epoche unterschiedliche Bedeutungen zugeschrieben. Das dritte Prinzip betrifft die Überlappung von widersprüchlichen Orten. Das vierte Prinzip bezieht sich auf ihr besonderes Verhältnis zur Zeit, das man als ‚Heterochronie' bezeichnet. Das fünfte Prinzip weist auf ihre Ambivalenz hin: zwischen Öffnung und Schließung, Anfang und Ende, Hoffnung und Hoffnungslosigkeit. Das letzte Prinzip betrifft ihre imaginative Funktion. Die Heterotopie hilft dabei, sowohl utopische gut organisierte, vollkommene Orte, als auch illusorische Orte außerhalb gesellschaftlicher Normen zu imaginieren. (Foucault 1984 [1967], 46–49)

Afrikanische Figuren der nicht alliierten Völker werden im Hinterland entführt und an den Strand verschleppt. Der Verwandlungsprozess von Mensch zu Untermensch, der mit einer solchen Entführung begann und sich unterwegs fortsetzt, verwirklicht sich schließlich am Strand. Die Mulongo, die bisher eine fast unbegrenzte Freiheit in ihrem Dorf genossen, erfahren jetzt am Strand eine menschenunwürdige Behandlung. Die Transformation zu Nicht-Menschen, um die es hier geht, ist in vielerlei Hinsicht manifest. Am Strand werden alle aus diversen angegriffenen Nachbardörfern Entführten zusammengepfercht. Sie werden als Vieh behandelt, gefesselt, geschlagen, vergewaltigt und in Schlepperhäusern inhaftiert. Die Entführten, die sich selbst noch nicht als Sklav*innen sehen und die ganze Aufeinanderfolge von merkwürdigen Ereignissen noch nicht verstehen, erleben die Wartezeit am Strand als Bruch mit der normalen Zeitlichkeit. Der Zerfall der bekannten Welt geht mit dem Zusammenbruch des gewohnten Verhältnisses zur Zeit einher. In dieser Hinsicht scheint der wiederkehrende Ausdruck: Zeit der „Mwititi"[4] (Miano 2013, 25), also Zeit der ‚Finsternis', in den das Erzählgefüge komplett eingebettet ist, darauf hinzuweisen, dass die Zeit in ihrem natürlichen Ablauf gestoppt worden ist. Die Gegenwart wird zu einer außerzeitlichen Realität. An die Vergangenheit und ihre Vertrautheit können sich die Entführten nun nur vergeblich erinnern, ohne zu wissen, ob sich die damals für sie gewöhnlichen und alltäglichen Praktiken und Gesten werden wiederholen können. Die Zukunft ist ihrerseits von Finsternis bedeckt und scheint in diesem großen Ausmaß an Wasser zu versinken, jenseits dessen keiner sich projizieren kann. Niemand weiß, was aus ihm werden soll: „cela n'avait pas de sens" (ebd., 187), das ergab keinen Sinn. Die Suche nach einem Sinn, um sich dieser Heterochronie zu entziehen, die sich als Zeitstillstand ausdrückt, mündet vielmehr in die eingangs erwähnte erste Form der Heterochronie/Heterotopie: die Verwandlung, die Transformation.

Dem Zerbrechen einer normalen Zeitlichkeit entsprechend werden die Entführten und bisher Inhaftierten und Zusammengepferchten den Europäer*innen in offenen Ställen am Strand verkauft. Doch scheint diese Form der Verdinglichung und Vertierung nicht die absurdeste Situation am Strand zu sein. Menschen, die aus verschiedenen Gründen nicht verkauft werden konnten, erleben nämlich eine rätselhafte Situation. Sie leben im Gefängnis, aber sie können sich am Strand frei bewegen. Ihr Leben erweist sich als überflüssig, da ihre neue Gesellschaft keine Rolle für sie gefunden hat. Trotzdem dürfen sie nicht zurück in ihre Dörfer. Die meisten würden wahrscheinlich den Heimweg nicht wiederfinden können. Wie aus der Aussage der Figur Mukudi hervorgeht, haben sie ihr Selbst verloren: „Ne m'appelle plus ainsi [...]. Ce nom était le mien dans un autre monde. Dans celui-ci, je ne suis ni un fils, ni un frère. La solitude est mon logis et mon seul horizon."[5] (Ebd., 201 [im Original kursiv]) Trotz der Illusion der Offenheit ist der Strand tatsächlich ein geschlossener Raum, weil auch Menschen wie Eyabe, die als freie Person an den Strand kamen, in der Hoffnung, die Ihrigen zu retten, den Ort nicht mehr verlassen dürfen. Die Stranderfahrung wird zur Dystopie, insofern als sie den Anfang einer langen dunklen Epoche voller Leiden für afrikanische Protagonist*innen ankündigt.

Da im Text besonders über Frauenfiguren gesprochen wird, ist es wichtig, sich kurz eigens auf sie zu konzentrieren: Die Schilderung der Figur Eyabe und einiger anderer weiblicher Figuren im Roman könnte sich in die Tradition des

---

4 Ein weiteres Zeichen der Wichtigkeit dieses Worts im Roman ist die Tatsache, dass es sich sogar schon im Titel befindet. Wenn man den französischen Titel, *La Saison de l'ombre*, in Duala, die Muttersprache der Autorin und die Sprache des Volks der Mulongo im Roman, übersetzt, ergibt sich Folgendes: *Ponda'a Mwititi* [meine Übersetzung].
5 „Do not call me that any more. That was my name in another world. In this one, I am neither a son nor a brother. Solitude is my abode and my only horizon." (Miano 2018, 197)

‚Writing back' (Ashcroft und Griffiths 1989) einordnen lassen. Im Gegensatz zu Vorurteilen über die putative natürliche Unmündigkeit und Unterdrückung von Frauen in der traditionellen afrikanischen Gesellschaft schildert die Autorin selbstbewusste Frauen. Die Situation der Frauen im Text ist nicht auf einen gemeinsamen Nenner zu bringen, insofern als sie breit gefächert ist. Doch auch wenn diese Situation je nach Dorf und seinem jeweiligen Verhältnis zur Genderrolle variiert, muss man feststellen, dass die Frauen eine zentrale Position in den verschiedenen Dörfern haben.

Njanjo, die Königin der Bwele, etwa lebt in einer klar matriarchalen Gesellschaft, die um und von Frauen organisiert ist. Hier verfügen die Frauen über die politische und militärische Macht. In derselben Hinsicht soll unterstrichen werden, dass die Königin Njanjo die einflussreichste Figur des Romans ist. Sie herrscht über das größte Königreich der Region. Die Tatsache, dass es ihr gelungen ist, strategische Allianzen mit den Königen der Küste abzuschließen, die ihr Volk vor der Verheerung der Sklaverei schützen, ist ein Zeugnis davon, dass sie eine schlaue Politikerin ist. Auch in anderen Völkergruppen sind die Frauen keine passiven Figuren. Das Volk/Dorf der Mulongo etwa wurde vor langer Zeit von einer Frau, Emene, gegründet, auf die Frauen sich immer bei Schwierigkeiten beziehen (Miano 2013, 46). Auch wenn es jetzt von Männern geführt wird, bleibt die Gesellschaft matrilinear (ebd., 13). Hier haben Frauen eine zentrale symbolische Stellung. Und gerade, weil sie geschätzt sind, gibt es zahlreiche Verbote, die darauf abzielen sollen, sie zu schützen[6] (ebd., 43). Einige Frauen aber brauchen keinen Schutz, da sie den Männern gleichrangig sind. Ebeise, die Matrone, ist aufgrund ihres Alters eine von ihnen. Die Figur Ebeise erscheint als die meistgeachtete Person im Dorf der Mulongo. Sie übt eine symbolische und praktische Autorität über das ganze Volk aus, die sich unter anderem durch ihren maßgeblichen Einfluss auf die Entscheidungen des Königs bzw. der Ältesten ausdrückt (ebd., 12). Sie ist diejenige, die Eyabe erlaubt und hilft, das Dorf auf der Suche nach ihrem Sohn zu verlassen, obwohl es den Frauen verboten ist.

Seinerseits bestärkt das Textschema diesen Prozess des ‚Writing back' (Ashcroft und Griffiths 1989). Eyabe verwirft das patriarchale System und trifft die Entscheidung, selber Untersuchungen außerhalb des Dorfes anzustellen, um ihren Sohn wiederfinden zu können. Sie ist die Figur unter den Mulongo, die als erste den Sinn der Epoche versteht; lange Zeit bevor sich die Männer entscheiden, verspätete Nachforschungen zu beginnen. Besonders die Tatsache, dass Eyabe der/die einzige Zugehörige der Mulongo ist, der/die den Strand als freie Person erreicht, ist von ausschlaggebender Bedeutung. Die weibliche Figur

---

6 Das kann man natürlich ambivalent betrachten.

Eyabe eignet sich den Diskurs über sich selbst an und vollzieht somit eine Brechung des Narrativs über die Passivität bzw. Unmündigkeit von Frauen in der traditionellen afrikanischen Gesellschaft.

Mitten in den Trümmern zerbrochener Leben, und während die bekannte Welt zusammenbricht, entsteht jedoch ein Hoffnungsschimmer, der sich paradoxerweise an einem anderen Strand langsam gestaltet. Bebayedi ist dieses kleine Dorf an einem anderen Strand, das nach und nach Züge der Negation des Absurden annimmt. Sowohl seine Zusammensetzung als auch die symbolische Aneignung des geographischen Umfelds durch die neue Bevölkerung zeugen von der Ambivalenz der Bedeutung, die der Strand/die Küste haben können. Von dieser Zusammenstellung erfährt Eyabe, als sie einen der ehemaligen Entführten zufällig in diesem neuen Dorf wiedertrifft:

> Il lui apprend que ce peuple accueillant n'en est pas un, au sens où la chose s'entend habituellement. Ici, les gens n'ont pas de mémoire commune. Leur clan n'a ni fondateur, ni ancêtres tutélaires. Chacun a apporté ses totems, ses croyances, ses connaissances en matière de guérison. Tout cela, mis en quelque sorte dans un pot commun, forme une spiritualité à laquelle tous se conforment. Hommes et femmes se sont réparti les tâches de façon claire et simple : ils chassent, pêchent, préservent l'intégrité physique du clan ; elles cultivent, se chargent de la vie intérieure. Tous joignent leurs forces pour construire les habitations. Il n'y a pas de lignée régnante. La communauté s'est choisi un chef qu'elle congédiera s'il ne se montre pas à la hauteur des attentes.[7] (Miano 2013, 131)

Die Aussage, dass das besprochene Volk kein Volk im üblichen Sinne sei, weist darauf hin, dass seine Mitglieder aus diversen Kontexten kommen. Bebayedi, das eigentlich ein Kompositum darstellt, besteht aus Menschen, die dem Chaos der neuen Epoche entflohen sind und hier Zuflucht gefunden haben. Menschen mit Sklaverei-Erfahrung, Menschen, die Razzien entkommen sind, ehemalige Gefangene in europäischen Schiffen usw. sind Personen, die dieses Dorf bzw. dieses neue Volk aus dem Nichts erfunden haben. An diesem ‚espace autre' [Gegenort] (Foucault 1984 [1967], 46) versuchen sie erneut, aber mit erfundenen Modi, Sinn zu finden. Die Verbindung von diversen Praktiken, Erfahrungen und Gesten dient der Erzeugung einer neuen Realität. Um weiterleben zu können

---

[7] „She learns that these welcoming people are not really a [one, amendation] people, in the usual sense of the term. They do not share a common memory. Their clan has neither founder nor ministering ancestors. They have all brought their own individual totems, beliefs, methods of healing. All this, put together in a common pot of sorts, forms a spirituality to which they all adhere. The men and women divide up the tasks in a clear, simple way: the men hunt, fish, safeguard the physical integrity of the community; the women grow crops, take charge of the interior life. They all work together to build the dwellings. There is no reigning lineage. The community choses for itself a chief that it can dismiss if the person does not live up to their expectations." (Miano 2018, 125)

bzw. sich wieder zurechtzufinden, drängt sich die Notwendigkeit der Wiedergeburt auf. Bebayedi ist in dieser Hinsicht „un peuple neuf" (Miano 2013, 138), ein neues Volk. Der Strand wird somit zur Quelle der Sinnfindung. Das Dorf, das eigentlich vom Sumpf umgeben ist, ist ein friedlicher Ort mitten in dieser seit der Ankunft der Europäer*innen chaotisch gewordenen Gegend, wo Raub, Mord, Razzien und weitere Grausamkeiten herrschen. Die neuen Bewohner*innen versuchen, sich der neuen Umgebung vorteilhaft anzupassen bzw. sich diese anzueignen:

> Le terrain est inconfortable, mais les habitants ont appris à y vivre, savent désormais bâtir leurs cases sur pilotis, pêcher dans la rivière, chasser dans la brousse avoisinante. Les enfants savent débusquer les crustacés, les faire sortir de leurs trous creusés dans la vase. Les adultes connaissent les plantes comestibles ou vénéneuses, certaines herbes médicinales. Leur langue mêle toutes celles qui se sont rencontrées sur ce sol boueux.[8] (Ebd., 133–134)

Die neuen Praktiken, die sich an diesem neuen Strand entwickeln, ermöglichen, dass das Volk fortbesteht. Während der umgebende Sumpf ein natürlicher Schutz gegen Feinde ist, bauen die Bewohner*innen Pfahlhäuser, die ihnen helfen sollen, eventuelle Angriffe aus dem Meer oder Fluss früher zu sehen und diese entweder zu vermeiden oder hinauszuzögern. Daneben ist die Anpassung ihrer kulinarischen, medizinischen usw. Gewohnheiten an das Angebot ihrer neuen Umwelt ein Beweis dafür, dass sie sich ihre neuen Realitätsbedingungen angeeignet haben. Die Erfindung eines neuen Kommunikationsmittels durch die Vermischung von unterschiedlichen Sprachen und die an diesem Ort ähnlich entstandene Spiritualität bestärken die Idee des Strands als Heterotopie der Verwandlung, der Transformation.

Die Beschreibung des Dorfs Bebayedi ähnelt einer Vorausdeutung. Sie erscheint als eine utopische Vision – hier die Spiegelfunktion der Heterotopie – des Werdens der Völker nach der Begegnung mit den Fremden. Sie könnte als Möglichkeit betrachtet werden, darauf vorauszuweisen, wie es einigen Gesellschaften gelungen ist, sich nach ihrer gewaltvollen Begegnung mit Europa neu zu erfinden. Die Erfahrung der Dislokation, das Erlebnis des Verfalls der bekannten Welt und der Verlust/das Verschwinden des Vertrauten stellen eine beängstigende Situation dar, die man trotzdem überleben kann. In der jüngsten Geschichte der Menschheit haben die oben erwähnten Phänomene der Dislokation

---

[8] „The terrain is uncomfortable but they have learnt to live here. They now know how to build huts on stilts, fish in the river, hunt in the surrounding bush. The children know how to find shellfish, tease them out of the holes in the bog. The adults know which plants are edible, which are poisonous, which can be used for medicinal purposes. The language is a mix of all the tongues that came together on this muddy ground." (Miano 2018, 128)

und des Zerfalls der vertrauten Welt durch die Begegnung mit den Fremden hauptsächlich nicht-europäische Völker auf ihrem eigenen Boden betroffen. Dabei haben diese Völker eine gewisse Resilienz an den Tag gelegt. Sie haben sich neu erfunden, um sich der neuen Sachlage produktiv anzupassen. Daher scheint sich die Vorausdeutung an Europa zu wenden, da es zum ersten Mal in dieser jüngsten Geschichte aufgrund der Migration aus der nicht-europäischen Welt durch die Angst des Verfalls, die Gefühle der Dislokation und der Desorientierung beklommen zu sein scheint. Wie es David Simo (2010, 17) anmerkt: Das Neue in der jetzigen Begegnung der Völker „ist die Tatsache, dass die Erfahrung der Dislokation im Zuge der Immigration von der Peripherie in das Zentrum der europäischen Metropole transportiert wird." Diese neue Erfahrung löst sowohl Angst als auch Panik aus. Die Begegnung mit dem Anderen auf eigenem Boden, also zu Hause, verbindet sich mit der Angst vor dem Aussterben des Eigenen. Diesem Narrativ der Hoffnungslosigkeit entgegen ist die Schilderung des Dorfs Bebayedi eine starke Botschaft: An dem Verschwinden der vertrauten Welt stirbt man nicht. Man kann sich neu erfinden, genauso wie es andere vor uns getan haben. Anhand dieser Ambivalenz, die heterotopischen Orten eigen ist, liefert der Text eine hoffnungsvolle Botschaft.

3 Die Logik des Zauns

In Marie Ndiayes *Trois femmes puissantes* (2009) werden afrikanische Figuren nicht mehr gegen ihren Willen aus Afrika entführt.[9] Ihre Bewegung wird vielmehr eingegrenzt und gestoppt. Der gemeinsame Nenner, der von Roman zu Roman bzw. von Epoche zu Epoche unverändert bleibt, ist, was man als ‚Prinzip der externen Entscheidung' bezeichnen könnte. In den beiden Geschichten werden nämlich die Entscheidungen zur Bewegung und Nicht-Bewegung[10] von Dritten getroffen, ohne den Willen bzw. den Wunsch der Figuren zu berücksichtigen. Dies führt zu der Schlussfolgerung, dass man von einem Mobilitäts- zu einem Immobilitätszwang übergegangen ist.

Im dritten Teil des Romans *Trois femmes puissantes* wird die Geschichte von Khady Demba erzählt, die allerdings schon im ersten Teil des Romans erwähnt wurde. Nach dem Tod ihres Mannes versucht sie, eigentlich am Anfang widerwillig, nach Europa zu kommen. Nach einer langwierigen Reise durch die

---

9 Dabei wäre aber die Ansicht richtig, dass sie gegen ihren Willen (unfaire internationale Wirtschaftsstrukturen, postkoloniale militärische Konflikte, Suche nach besseren Erziehungssystemen usw.) zur Migration getrieben werden.
10 Von einem Kontinent zu einem anderen.

Wüste und durch feindselige Gegenden erreicht sie einen Strand, wo sie mit vielen anderen Reisenden mehrmals erfolglos versucht, die andere Seite des Ufers zu erreichen. Irgendwann gelingt es ihr, vor einer Grenzmauer den ersten europäischen Boden zu erreichen. Sie wird aber von Soldat*innen erschossen, bevor sie die Mauer erklimmen kann. Der Strand, der in der westlichen Imagination vorwiegend als Urlaubs- und Entspannungsraum verstanden wird (Coëffé 2010, 53), nimmt in dieser Geschichte paradoxale Züge an.

Der Strand tritt in Ndiayes Roman als der Raum für das Einsperren des ‚überflüssigen Lebens' (Mbembe 2017 [2016], 73) auf. So wie das Konzept in den verschiedenen Texten, und zwar „Necropolitics" (2003), *Ausgang aus der langen Nacht* (2016 [2010]), *Kritik der schwarzen Vernunft* (2014 [2013]) und *Politik der Feindschaft* (2017 [2016]), behandelt wird, bezeichnet der Zaun bzw. das ‚Einzäunen' zuerst die „*Einfriedung [enclos, J.E.] durch die Rasse*" (Mbembe 2016 [2010], 87) und die entsprechende Behandlung. Eine Behandlung, die sich hauptsächlich in der Form der Verneinung der Menschlichkeit des Andren auf der Basis einer bio- bzw. nekropolitischen Logik äußert. Sie regelt die Aufteilung von Privilegien je nach der Zugehörigkeit zur Gruppe der Gleichartigen und Andersartigen und mündet sogar in die Erklärung der Wertlosigkeit des Lebens des Anderen, den man unbedingt von den Eigenen trennen will. Der Zaun bzw. das Lager, als Paradigma der Modernität (Giorgio Agamben 2002 [1995], 125), tritt in seinen vielfältigen Formen als radikales Mittel der Separation auf. (Mbembe 2016 [2010], 103) Die ungleiche Verteilung des Rechts auf Freizügigkeit scheint nach einer ethnischen Logik zu funktionieren. Der Ausbau bzw. die Verstärkung von politischen, juristischen sowie militärischen Mitteln, um bestimmte Personen zu zwingen, an einem Ort, möglichst weit weg von Europa, zu bleiben, folgt der Logik des Zauns bzw. des Lagers. In dieser Hinsicht vermehren sich die Lager überall und die Grenzen von Europa, die sich seit einiger Zeit in südliche Richtung bewegt haben, befinden sich nun auf dem afrikanischen Kontinent, um den Weg nach Europa vor Ort zu versperren. Der Kontinent wird somit zu einem großen Gefängnis (im Sinne des *enclos*).

Um diese Deutungsweise zu erhellen, will ich zuerst auf Foucaults (1984 [1967]) Kategorie der ‚Heterotopie der Abweichung' zurückgreifen. Für den französischen Philosophen verfügt jede Gesellschaft über spezialisierte Orte, wo Menschen, deren Verhalten von der gesellschaftlich geltenden Norm abweicht, eingesperrt sind. Beispiele dafür sind, wie schon erwähnt wurde, Altenheime, psychiatrische Kliniken und natürlich Gefängnisse. Heterotopien der Abweichung dienen also dazu, Menschen mit abweichendem Verhalten fern von der Gesellschaft zu halten, weil man fürchtet, dass ihre Anwesenheit inmitten der Gesellschaft, unter sogenannten ‚normalen' Menschen, die Kohäsion derselben stören würde. Das ‚überflüssige Leben' (Mbembe 2017 [2016], 73) soll in einem eingegrenzten, zwar realen, aber mit utopischen, hier vielleicht besser: dystopischen, Mustern gefüllten Raum zusammengepfercht werden. Es soll die Illusion erzeugt werden, dass diese Orte und ihre Bewohner*innen nicht existieren. Einen psychisch Kranken, eine Großmutter im Altenheim, einen Gefangenen besucht bzw. sieht man nicht jeden Tag. Somit können sogenannte ‚normale' Menschen dem normalen Lauf ihres Lebens folgen. Eigentlich sind diese Orte meistens Wartezimmer des Todes, weil die Gesellschaft ohne diese Menschen angeblich besser funktioniert.[11] Die Figuren des Romans, deren Leben überflüssig scheint, sind keine psychisch Kranken, keine Kriminellen oder Menschen mit Behinderung, wie man es im üblichen Sinne versteht. Doch müssen sie möglichst fern von der sogenannten ‚normalen' Gesellschaft gehalten werden.

Schon lange Zeit vor ihrem gescheiterten Reiseversuch nach Europa ist Khady Demba von ihrer Wertlosigkeit überzeugt. Dies gründet unter anderem auf der Tatsache, dass ihr niemand den Eindruck vermittelt, ihre Anwesenheit zu schätzen. Die Großeltern, bei denen sie aufwächst, nachdem ihre Eltern sie verlassen haben, verheiraten sie früh. Dieses Gefühl wird später nicht nur durch ihre extreme materielle Armut bestärkt, sondern auch durch ihre Unfähigkeit, schwanger zu werden. Der Wunsch, schwanger zu werden, wird zu einer Besessenheit, die aber mit dem Tod ihres Mannes unerfüllt bleibt:

> Khady évitait de se montrer dans la cour car elle redoutait encore les paroles sarcastiques sur la nullité, l'absurdité de son existence de veuve sans biens ni enfants, et quand elle était obligée de s'y tenir pour éplucher les légumes ou préparer le poisson elle se rencognait si bien, ne laissant dépasser de sa mince silhouette accroupie dans son pagne, resserrée sur elle-même, que ses doigts rapides et, de son visage baissé, les hauts méplats de ses joues, qu'on l'oubliait, comme si ce bloc de silence et de désaffection ne valait plus l'effort d'une apostrophe, d'un quolibet.[12] (Ndiaye 2009, 265)

Ihr magerer Körper, der Folge einer lebenslangen materiellen und psychischen Not ist, genügt nicht, sie unsichtbar zu machen, sodass die Familie ihres Mannes an die Nichtigkeit ihrer Existenz ständig erinnert wird. Davon ausgehend schreibt sich die Entscheidung, ständig zu schweigen, in das Projekt ein, sich

---

11 Der Artikel vertritt natürlich diese Position nicht.
12 „Khady vermied es, sich im Hof zu zeigen, denn sie hatte noch Angst vor den sarkastischen Sprüchen über die Nichtigkeit, die Sinnlosigkeit ihres Lebens als Witwe ohne Habe und ohne Kinder, und wenn sie gezwungen war, sich dort aufzuhalten, um Gemüse zu putzen oder Fisch auszunehmen, kauerte sie sich so sehr zusammen, dass aus der schmalen, in ihrem Wickeltuch auf den Fersen hockenden Gestalt nur die flinken Finger hervorschauten und von ihrem gesenkten Gesicht nur die hohen Wangenknochen sichtbar blieben, weshalb man sie bald nicht mehr beachtete, man vergaß sie, als wäre dieser Block Schweigen und Abkehr nicht einmal mehr einen Zuruf, eine Bemerkung wert." (Ndiaye 2010, 273)

selbst unhörbar, unbemerkbar zu machen. In dieser Hinsicht scheinen die langen, aufeinanderfolgenden Sätze der Erzählerin die Anhäufung von Erfahrungen auszudrücken, die Khady Demba passiv erleidet. Sie signalisieren die Gewöhnung an die Erniedrigung und an das Unglück. Dies scheint jedoch die Voraussetzung für die Reise über das Meer nach Europa zu sein. Denn die Figuren, die sich auf die Suche nach besseren Lebensbedingungen machen, scheinen die Auffassung passiv angenommen zu haben, dass sie Menschen zweiter Klasse sind. Deswegen erscheinen die Episoden ihrer Reise durch die Wüste, wo sie in großer Zahl in kleinen, alten, kaum funktionsfähigen Autos zusammengepfercht sind und somit immer zu sterben riskieren, keine außerordentlichen Ereignisse zu sein. Auch können sie reibungslos von Schlepper zu Schlepper übergeben werden, die dann über ihr Schicksal entscheiden.

Die Körper, die letztlich den Strand erreichen, sind gebrochene Körper. Körper, die Zeugen von schmerzhaften Existenzen sind. Körper, die jegliche Art des Leidens erleben müssen und die trotz aller Hindernisse ununterbrochen nach dem anderen Ufer des Meers, als Erlösung für ihre minderwertige Existenz, streben.

Im Sinne des Konzepts des ‚vorgestellten Raums' (Simo 2010, 21) können sich die Migrant*innen den Strand als Hoffnungsort vorstellen, von dem aus sich ihr Europa-Traum verwirklichen kann. Doch wird der Strand konkret als Zaun erlebt, wo überflüssige, minderwertige Leben eingesperrt werden, um sie an der Reise nach Europa zu hindern. In diesem Zusammenhang kann der Hof in Strandnähe (Ndiaye 2009, 305) als Symbol für das ganze Küstengebiet betrachtet werden, das Züge eines unsichtbaren Zauns aufweist. Auf diesem Hof sammeln sich jeden Tag zahlreiche Menschen, die aus unterschiedlichen afrikanischen Regionen kommen. Schwangere Frauen, Frauen mit kleinen Kindern, junge Männer und andere sind Teil der Gruppe von Menschen, deren Reise nach Europa hier monatelang bzw. jahrelang blockiert wird oder sogar endet. Genauso wie der Zaun dient dieser Hof dazu, die Scharen von ungewollten Menschen in Schach zu halten. Auf dem Hof am Strand und in Strandnähe entsteht bald eine neue Form der Vergesellschaftung, die scheinbar ausschließlich in diesem Raum Geltung besitzt. Neben nicht geahndeten Menschenrechtsverletzungen müssen Figuren ständig neue Tricks entwickeln, um überleben zu können. Diebstahl, Gewalt und Prostitution werden zur Normalität.

Hier bekommt die genderspezifische Gewalt eine ganz andere Dimension. Die Gefahren, denen weibliche Figuren während der Migrationserfahrung begegnen, sind zum Teil anders als die ihrer männlichen Leidensgenossen. Weibliche Figuren erleben als Frauen und als Migrantinnen eine Situation von doppelter Verwundbarkeit. Sie sind der Gewalt besonders ausgesetzt. Dies betrifft vor allem die sexuelle Gewalt, wie es das Beispiel von Khady Demba zeigt. In der Migrationssituation wird ihr Körper sehr schnell zum Objekt und zur Einkommensquelle. Er wird sowohl von ihrem neuen Freund Lamine, einem Mitreisenden, als auch von einer sogar selbst weiblichen Zuhälterin ausgenutzt. Sie versprechen Khady dafür Zuneigung bzw. geben ihr eine Unterkunft. (Ebd., 320) In diesem Ausnutzungsprozess erreicht die Gewalt gegen den weiblichen Körper ihren Höhepunkt. Sie kennt keine Grenze. Von dem so verdinglichten und entmenschlichten Körper wird nichts anderes als Geldproduktion erwartet: weder Schmerz noch Müdigkeit. Deswegen muss Khady Demba Sex mit Kunden haben, obwohl ihre Vagina durch eine schwere, stark stinkende und eitrige Verwundung verwüstet ist (ebd., 312). Kunden lassen sich von der Verwundung nicht entmutigen. Doch zeigen sie ihr eine tiefgreifende Verachtung vor, während und nach dem Geschlechtsverkehr. In diesem Zusammenhang erweist sich das regelmäßige Spucken aus Ekel in ihr Gesicht während des Geschlechtsverkehrs nur als zusätzlicher Beweis ihrer Unbedeutendheit (ebd., 319). Mit dem Raub ihrer Ersparnisse durch ihren Freund (ebd., 323) ist der Zirkel der totalen Verwundbarkeit vollendet: ökonomisch, physisch (sexuell) und psychologisch.

Am anderen Ufer des Meers werden die sogenannten ‚illegalen Migrant*innen' von Soldat*innen wie Tiere gejagt, als sie sich, nachdem sie die natürliche Barriere, das Meer, überquert haben, vorbereiten, die Grenzmauer zu erklimmen. Dabei werden sie von den Soldat*innen ermordet.

> Vie superflue donc, celle dont le prix est si faible que cette vie n'a aucune équivalence marchande, et encore moins humaine, propre ; cette espèce de vie dont la valeur est hors économie, et qui n'a pour équivalent que la sorte de mort qu'on peut lui infliger.[13] (Mbembe 2016, 55)

So könnte man mit Achille Mbembe die Situation von afrikanischen Migrant*innen am Strand zusammenfassen.

Im Gegensatz zu üblichen Annahmen, nach denen der Strand einen transitorischen Raum darstellt (Coëffé 2010, 52), wird er in diesem Roman zum Inbegriff der Übergangslosigkeit. Der Immobilitätszwang, der afrikanische Figuren betrifft, beeinflusst ihr Verhältnis zur Zeit, die zur Heterochronie wird. Khady Demba und ihre Freunde müssen nämlich am Strand bzw. in Strandnähe so lange auf den besten Moment für die Reise warten, dass sie den Eindruck haben, dass die Zeit angehalten wurde. Doch werden sie nicht von diesem langsamen Ablauf der Zeit entmutigt, auch wenn sie schnell dünner bzw. magerer werden.

---

13 „Ein überflüssiges Leben also, dessen Preis so niedrig ist, dass dieses Leben keinerlei Marktwert und erst recht keinen eigenen menschlichen Wert besitzt; jene Art von Leben, dessen Wert außerhalb der Ökonomie liegt und dessen Äquivalent allein in der Art von Tod liegt, den man ihm zufügen kann." (Mbembe 2017 [2016], 73)

Der Strand (besonders das Meer) erweckt zwar Angst und Schrecken, aber er wird bloß als eines der letzten Hindernisse auf dem Weg nach Europa betrachtet. Die Verletzung von Khady Demba am Bein während der ersten gescheiterten Überquerung des Meers tritt als Symbol für den hier besprochenen Immobilitätszwang auf. Die Tatsache, dass sie von da an nur unter Schmerzen gehen kann, ist symbolisch für den mühseligen Reiseversuch. Der Sand, der an ihrer Wunde klebt, markiert die Verbindung des Strands mit schmerzhaften Erfahrungen. Um den Immobilitätszwang definitiv durchzusetzen, wird sie vor dem Zaun erschossen. Die Raben, die sie im Laufe der Handlung ständig begleiten und so ihren Tod mystisch vorhersagen, fliegen im Himmel. Während sie sich über die Grenzmauer bewegen können, ist Khady Dembas Hoffnung auf Mobilität endgültig zunichtegemacht: Eine Leiche bewegt sich nicht. Die vorsätzliche Tötung, die ungestraft bleibt, erscheint hier als endgültiges Mittel, um das überflüssige Leben (Mbembe 2017 [2016], 73) von Europa fern zu halten.

4 Fazit

Aus der Untersuchung der beiden Werke geht die Rekurrenz des Motivs der Herrschaft und des Leidens hervor, das die Erfahrung des Strands für afrikanische Figuren kennzeichnet. In dieser Hinsicht stellt die besondere Betrachtung der Frage der Bewegung die Ähnlichkeit zwischen der Epoche der Sklaverei und der jetzigen Epoche heraus. In den beiden Werken sind afrikanische Figuren nicht Herr ihrer Körper. Ihre Bewegung wird stark kontrolliert. Einerseits erleben sie einen Bewegungszwang, andererseits einen Immobilitätszwang. Am Strand erfahren sie eine tiefe Erniedrigung und Herabwürdigung. Die besondere Leistung der beiden Romane besteht darin, den Lesenden zu ermöglichen, einen Einblick in die Gefühle ihrer afrikanischen Figuren zu gewinnen. Im Gegensatz zu den Texten der Kolonialbibliothek, in denen die Eingeborenen Afrikas als Nicht-Menschen bzw. Untermenschen dargestellt wurden, dient die ausführliche Beschreibung ihrer Gefühle in den Werken dazu, diejenigen, deren Leben bzw. Leben als Mensch für überflüssig gehalten wurde, in ihrer vollkommenen Menschlichkeit zu schildern. Der Gestus scheint aber widersprüchlich zu sein, insofern als der Strand als symbolischer Ort auftritt, wo sich einerseits die Verwandlung des Menschen zum Untermenschen durch den Verkauf als Sklav*in, also als Objekt, und die Herabsetzung zu illegalen (Migrant*innen) Menschen vollzieht. Der Strand ist aber gleichzeitig, aufgrund der genauen Beschreibung von Empfindungen, Gefühlen und Gedanken, der Raum, in dem sich das Menschliche in seiner tiefsten Schwäche zeigt.

Literaturverzeichnis

Agamben, Giorgio. *Homo Sacer. Die souveräne Macht und das nackte Leben* [1995]. Übersetzt von Hubert Thüring. Frankfurt/Main: Suhrkamp, 2002.

Ashcroft, Bill, und Gareth Griffiths. *The Empire Writes Back. Theory and Practice in Post-Colonial Literatures*. London: Routledge, 1989.

Coëffé, Vincent. „La plage, fabrique d'une touristi(cité) idéale". *L'information géographique* 74.3 (2010): 51–68.

Defoe, Daniel. *Robinson Crusoe* [1719]. Wien: Tosa, 2000.

Diakité, Tidiane. *La traite des Noirs et ses acteurs africains*. Paris: Berg International, 2008.

Ferré, André. „Le problème et les problèmes de la géographie littéraire". *Cahiers de l'Association internationale des études françaises* 6 (1954): 145–164.

Foucault, Michel. „Des espaces autres, Hétérotopies" [1967]. *Architecture, Mouvement, Continuité* 5 (1984): 46–49.

Klooss, Wolfgang. „Coast and Beach: Contested Spaces in Cultural and Literary Discourse". *Navigating Cultural Spaces: Maritime Places*. Hg. Anna-Margaretha Horatschek, Yvonne Rosenberg und Daniel Schäbler. Amsterdam und New York, NY: Rodopi, 2014. 195–220.

Lefebvre, Henri. „La production de l'espace". *L'Homme et la société* 31–32 (1974): 15–32.

Mbembe, Achille. *Politik der Feindschaft* [*Politiques de l'inimitié*, 2016]. Übersetzt von Michael Bischoff. Berlin: Suhrkamp, 2017.

Mbembe, Achille. *Politiques de l'inimitié*. Paris: La Découverte, 2016.

Mbembe, Achille. *Ausgang aus der langen Nacht. Versuch über ein entkolonisiertes Afrika* [*Sortir de la grande nuit. Essai sur l'Afrique décolonisée*, 2010]. Übersetzt von Christine Pries. Berlin: Suhrkamp, 2016.

Mbembe, Achille: *Kritik der schwarzen Vernunft* [*Critique de la raison nègre*, 2013]. Übersetzt von Michael Bischoff. Frankfurt/Main: Suhrkamp, 2014.

Mbembe, Achille: *Critique de la raison nègre*. Paris: La Découverte, 2013.

Mbembe, Achille. *Sortir de la grande nuit. Essai sur l'Afrique décolonisée*. Paris: La Découverte, 2010.

Mbembe, Achille. „Necropolitics". *Public Culture* 15.1 (2003): 11–40.

Miano, Léonora. *Season of the Shadow*. Übersetzt von Gila Walker. London, New York und Calcutta: Seagull Books, 2018.

Miano, Léonora. *La Saison de l'ombre*. Paris: Grasset et Fasquelle, 2013.

Miano, Léonora. *Afropean Soul et autres nouvelles*. Paris: Flammarion, 2008.

Mokam, Yvonne-Marie. „Polar historique et mémoire de la capture des esclaves". *Revue critique de fixxion française contemporaine* 10 (2015): 64–72.

Ndiaye, Marie. *Drei starke Frauen*. Übersetzt von Claudia Kalscheuer. Berlin: Suhrkamp, 2010.

Ndiaye, Marie. *Trois femmes puissantes*. Paris: Gallimard, 2009.

Simo, David. „Migration, Imagination und Literatur, die Literatur der Migration als Ort und Mittel des Aushandelns von neuen kulturellen Paradigmen". *Weltengarten: Migrationen heute und gestern. Deutsch-Afrikanisches Jahrbuch für interkulturelles Denken* (2009–2010): 7–58.

Thérèse De Raedt
Figuring Senegalese Beaches in Moussa Sène Absa's Films

My essay analyzes the representation of beaches in four feature-length films by the Senegalese director Moussa Sène Absa: *Ça twiste à Popenguine* [Rocking Popenguine] (1994), *Tableau ferraille* (1997), *Madame Brouette* (2002), and the docufiction *Yoolé* [Sacrifice] (2010). I argue that in these films the beach crystallizes the socio-political and economic changes that have occurred in postcolonial Senegal, starting in the early years after independence and moving into the contemporary epoch. I show how in the liminal space of the beach tensions between work and leisure, bad and good, pollution and nature, despair and hope, corruption and integrity, destruction and redemption, poverty and prosperity, imprisonment and freedom, and death and life come together and sometimes intersect.

Mein Artikel analysiert die Darstellung des Strandes in vier Filmen des senegalesischen Regisseurs Moussa Sène Absa: *Ça twiste à Popenguine* [Rocking Popenguine] (1994), *Tableau ferraille* (1997), *Madame Brouette* (2002), sowie die Doku-Fiktion *Yoolé* [Sacrifice] (2010). Ich möchte zeigen, dass in diesen Filmen der Strand als Kristallisationspunkt der sozio-politischen und ökonomischen Veränderungen im post-kolonialen Senegal, beginnend mit den ersten Jahren nach der Unabhängigkeit bis in die gegenwärtige Epoche, fungiert. Im liminalen Raum des Strandes begegnen und überkreuzen sich Spannungen zwischen Arbeit und Freizeit, Gut und Böse, Umweltverschmutzung und Natur, Verzweiflung und Hoffnung, Korruption und Integrität, Zerstörung und Erlösung, Armut und Wohlstand, Gefangenschaft und Freiheit, Tod und Leben.

1 Opening Remarks

Dakar, the administrative, political, and economic capital of Senegal, is located in the Cap-Vert peninsula, the westernmost point of the African continent. It is surrounded by beaches. Its first inhabitants were Lebou fishermen.[1] The coast which stretches from the Cap-Vert peninsula to the Saloum Delta near the Gambian border is called *Petite Côte* [Little Coast] and is occupied by traditional fishing villages of mainly Serer people.[2] For many local inhabitants of that region the beaches represent places of work, although the artisanal fishing industry is now declining. The tourist industry is developing, and these days the Cap-Vert peninsula and the *Petite Côte* are known by tourists for their holiday resorts.

---

[1] The Lebou people are related to the Wolof, the largest ethnic group in Senegal. The second largest ethnic group are the Fula people.
[2] The Serer people are the third largest ethnic group in Senegal.

Since 1999–2000 some of those beaches have also become places from which immigrants are trying to escape Senegal in hope of a better future in Europe. And in recent decades, several beaches have become polluted.

The Senegalese director Moussa Sène Absa, who was born in 1958 in the suburb of Dakar called Tableau Ferraille, describes himself as follows: "Je suis de Tableau Ferraille avec l'océan devant moi et une mémoire remplie de choses d'ici et d'ailleurs" [I am from Tableau Ferraille with the ocean in front of me and with memories from here and from anywhere else in the world] (De Raedt 2015, 180).[3] His identification with Tableau Ferraille and the ocean helps us understand the important role the beach plays in his cinema and more generally in his artistic oeuvre. It represents home and a place where one can realize oneself.

Absa's overarching filmic project is the creation of a collective memory for postcolonial Senegalese society. "[P]our [lui], l'artiste a une fonction sociale, un devoir de société" [For [him], an artist has a social role to play, has a duty towards his society] (ibid., 179). Being a socially engaged artist, he makes films for his people: "je pense à ce que je peux apporter à mon peuple pour lui dire combien je l'aime et pour l'aider à grandir" [I think about what I can bring to my people in order to tell them how much I love them and to help them grow] (Pfaff 2010, 200). His cinema is made for the people and inscribed within neo-realism. The beaches he portrays are therefore inhabited by Senegalese people (not by Western tourists, for example). Consequently, the Senegalese people can relate to the stories they see on screen. Through the film narratives that take place at the beach, Absa looks in a lucid way at his society, which is made up of contrasts and paradoxes, and tackles complicated and difficult social issues on which he wants his audience to reflect.

In a certain perspective, the beach with its natural phenomenon of ebb and flow contains – literally and symbolically – the threat of erasure and destruction as much as potentiality. In this in-between space of transformation and change, nothing is ever fixed but always in flux. I contend that Absa uses the liminal space of the beach, which is "'betwixt and between'" (Turner 1967, 97)[4],

---

3 Absa comments on the name Tableau Ferraille for the suburb of Dakar: "Il y a trois noms: Yarakh pour les autochtones, Hann pour le colon et Tableau Ferraille pour les gens de ma génération" [There are three names: Yarakh for the autochtonous people, Hann for the colonizers, and Tableau Ferraille for the people of my generation] (De Raedt 2015, 175). All translations from the French are mine.
4 I take the term 'liminality' from Victor Turner who implemented Arnold van Gennep's theory on the three phases of *"rites de passage"* [transition rites]. Van Gennep defined *"rites de passage"* as "rites which accompany every change of place, state, social position and age" and "are marked by three phases: separation, margin (or *limen*), and aggregation" (van Gennep

wedged between land and sea, to capture Senegalese society's contrasts and paradoxes made of tensions between bad and good, destruction and redemption, and death and life. I will show how those tensions come together at the beach and sometimes intersect. Thus, the beaches Absa presents in his films, though specific, also articulate universal meanings.

Although Absa is best known as a film director, he is also an accomplished painter, musician, writer, and actor. His wide-ranging interests in the visual, musical, literary, and performing arts come to the fore in his cinematographic productions. His films are dominated by a bright color palette reminiscent of his paintings. The music that he employs to accompany his films is also vibrant and cheerful.

I will consider four feature-length films as case studies to show how the beaches within them reflect the socio-political and economic changes that have occurred in postcolonial Senegal: the fiction films *Ça twiste à Popenguine* [Rocking Popenguine] (1994), *Tableau ferraille* (1997), and *Madame Brouette* (2002) and the docufiction *Yoolé* [Sacrifice] (2010). The first film takes place in 1964 in Popenguine, a village located at the Atlantic Ocean in the region of the *Petite Côte*, whereas the next two films take place in Dakar and its immediate suburbs of Tableau Ferraille and Niayes Thiokeert in the mid-1990s and early 2000s, respectively. Most scenes of the docufiction were shot in Dakar and its surroundings in 2009.

2 *Ça twiste à Popenguine* – Coming of Age, Identity Crisis, and Dreams

Ça twiste à Popenguine is set around Christmas 1964 in the fishing village of Popenguine. It recreates the joyful atmosphere of the years following the independence from France. Back then, Léopold Sédar Senghor was Senegal's first president.[5] Most scenes of the film take place at the white sandy beach of the village of Popenguine. In this coastal village, people live off the local fishing

---

1960 cited in Turner 1967, 94). Turner explains that transitional beings "are neither one thing nor another; or may be both; or neither here nor there; or may even be nowhere (in terms of any recognized topography), and are at the very least 'betwixt and between' all the recognized fixed points in space-time of structural classification" (Turner 1967, 97). For Turner, liminality is not only associated with changing life stages but also with certain places.

5 Léopold Sédar Senghor was Senegal's president from 1960 until 1980. He graduated with an *agrégation* in French grammar. He was a poet and one of the instigators of the *négritude* movement.

industry. Bacc, a smart ten-year-old orphan educated by the entire community, is the protagonist of the film. In many ways he resembles the director Moussa Sène Absa, who does the narrative voice-over of Bacc.[6] This upbeat film should be considered as a nostalgic depiction of the director's youth, but also as a representation of the collective experience of a generation.

As its title indicates, *Ça twiste à Popenguine* is imbued with the rock 'n' roll music of the mid-1960s. Those were the days of yé-yé music and bell-bottoms.[7] Within Popenguine, two gangs of adolescents compete: the "Inséparables" or "Ins," who identify with French music and take on the celebrity names of Sylvie Vartan, Sheila, Johnny Hallyday, Cloclo (for Claude François), and Eddy Mitchell; and the "Kings," who listen to African American music and call themselves James Brown, Otis Redding, Ray Charles, and Jimmy Hendrix. Both gangs gather in hide-outs at the beach. The Ins get together in a shed covered with pictures taken from the popular French magazine *Salut les Copains*.[8] The Kings meet in an abandoned gas station, whose walls are decorated with graffiti of American symbols and iconic monuments, like the Statue of Liberty. Bacc acts as a mediator between the two gangs. Unlike the Ins, the Kings have no female members, but they do own a coveted record player, the *teppaz*. Named after its creator, the French engineer Marcel Teppaz, the *teppaz* became the very symbol of rock 'n' roll music in the 1960s. The film's plot is set into motion when Bacc brings a letter to Eddy Mitchell from his girlfriend, Tina, who has left for France with her parents. At that moment, the Ins sit together at the beach. In the letter, Tina explains that she will not come back to Senegal for the holidays. Consequently, the Ins won't get the *teppaz* Tina had promised to bring back from France.

The story turns around the Ins trying to get money to purchase a *teppaz*. Bacc suggests that they organize a surprise party, an American concept that he knows through reading the magazine *Salut les Copains*. With the help of his negotiations, the Ins rent the *teppaz* and records from the Kings. The party in the

---

[6] In an interview Absa said that with a few exceptions "Bacc, c'est moi, totalement" [Bacc is me, exactly] (De Raedt 2015, 175). Though Absa now lives in Popenguine, he grew up in Dakar's suburb of Tableau Ferraille. He thus transferred his childhood memories a couple of kilometers south on the same shoreline.

[7] Yé-yé music was a popular musical genre in the 1960s which had its origins in the radio show *Salut les Copains*, transmitted every day on *Europe 1*. The best-known artists are Johnny Hallyday, Sylvie Vartan, Chantal Goya, Françoise Hardy, Sheila, France Gall, Michèle Torr, Claude François, and later Jacques Dutronc and Michel Polnareff.

[8] Created in 1962, the very successful magazine *Salut les Copains* was a written extension of the eponymous radio show. Every month the magazine contained a poster of the cover-page artist.

Ins' shed is just getting started when the religious shopkeeper El Hadj Gora discovers that they are using electricity from the mosque and abruptly puts an end to it. The Kings, who are very angry that they now cannot be paid for lending the *teppaz* and records, start a fight which continues in the ocean and set fire to the Ins' shed. The elders of the village punish both the members of the Ins and the Kings. Jabeel, El Hadj Gora's aid, exacts this punishment with a belt in the village's main square.

In a later sequence, the male members of the Ins take an old, broken pirogue, which subsequently sinks, out on the water to prove to the girls that they are strong. A memorable night scene shows the village anxiously waiting at the beach that elderly fishermen rescue them. The Ins are, again, reprimanded. Though the elder generation punish (and even beat) the younger generation, it is to help them become responsible adults, so the film seems to suggest.

Intertwined with these misadventures of the teenagers, the film depicts the identity crisis of the French teacher Monsieur Benoît, who does not know where he feels more at home, in Popenguine or in his native Breton town of Guilvinec. He often goes to the only existing canteen at the beach to get a beer. That canteen is owned by Madame Ginette, the other French person in the village. In the three scenes that take place in the canteen, the evolution of his confusion can be observed. In the first scene, Mr Benoît is happy and talks to friends from the village community; in the second scene, he is drunk and acts out his discontent with everybody, but especially with himself. In the last canteen scene, he has regained his serenity thanks to the help provided by the entire village community and writes placidly to his sister, who still lives in Guilvinec.

The film ends with Johnny, Cloclo, and Eddy from the Ins going to Johnny's father, who works at the modern holiday resort *Les Filaos,* a place seemingly owned by a French person, to get back the small amount of money they had given to him to purchase a *teppaz*. Walking along the pristine beach, they dance to the catchy song "Viens danser le twist" [Come and dance the twist] by Johnny Hallyday, who was extremely popular in West Africa.

The song is the French version of the African American song, "The Twist," by Chubby Checker. The three friends rhythmically twist their pelvises while their half-folded arms accompany the movement. Their legs are alternately stretched or flexed. (Fig. 1) The song and the dance inspired the original French title of the film and epitomize the film's depiction of the lively atmosphere of the mid-1960s music scene. It is being sung at the liminal, imaginary frontier between the two beaches: the beach of the village's permanent community of fishermen and the beach of the tourists' transient community. At the latter of *Les Filaos,* local inhabitants serve the tourists, who are sunbathing or sitting around the bar. Those tourists are presumably French. For them, the Senegalese beach represents leisure and hedonism.

Fig. 1: The Ins dancing at the beach in *Ça twiste à Popenguine*.

At the holiday resort, the Ins meet Frank Larry, a "grand musicien de Paris" [great Parisian musician], and Johnny persuades him to come to Popenguine to sing for the annual Christmas party. The film concludes with the village community dancing happily together: both gangs' members dance with each other, all generations mingle, and Mr Benoît, who is reconciled with himself, dances with a Senegalese woman Jabeel has introduced him to.

At the beach of the village of Popenguine women sell the fish the men have brought back in their dugout boats. It is the place where young people hang out in their free time and where they play out their dreams by imitating their musical idols. The elders relax at the beach in Madame Ginette's canteen, of which Mr Benoît is a regular. The beach also incarnates the place where the story's pivotal moments happen: the scene where the Ins receive Tina's letter, where they have their surprise party, where they fight with the Kings, but also where their shed burns, where the villagers anxiously wait for them to be rescued, and where Mr Benoît's identity crisis is revealed.

In this film, the beach crystallizes the bifurcated or liminal epoch when colonial rule has ended, but neo-colonial culture is still very much influenced by France. Mr Benoît's identity crisis is being foregrounded in Mme Ginette's canteen. The narrative focuses much more on the lives of the members of the Ins, who revere and mimic French musical icons, than on the lives of the Kings, who are obsessed with African American music. What appealed to the younger generation came mainly from France, like the *teppaz*, or via France: the 'surprise party' became known thanks to the magazine *Salut les Copains* and rock 'n' roll music mainly via French singers. Johnny's father works at the resort, owned most probably by a French person, and one of the French tourists, Frank Larry, brings the entire village together on Christmas Eve. The scene with Johnny, Eddy, and Cloclo twisting along the beach metaphorically represents this liminal period of post-independence. They go to Johnny's father, who works at the French tourist resort, to get their money back. This image is a metaphor for the country as a whole, which still relies on France economically.

3 *Tableau Ferraille* – Pollution, Death, and Redemption

Tableau Ferraille takes place in the mid-1990s. By that time, the popularity of Abdou Diouf, Senegal's second president, had eroded.[9] The country had lost some of the hopes and possibilities that the years after independence seemed to hold.

This film is structured around flashback sequences and narrates the political ascent and then downfall of Daam, an idealistic and well-intentioned politician, who comes back to his native Tableau Ferraille after having been trained in France. He falls into disgrace because the owner of the local fish cannery, nicknamed 'Président,' who used to be one of his close friends, betrays him with the complicity of his own second wife Kiné.[10] All flashback sequences return to the initial narrative moment of Daam's first wife, Gagnesiri, reflecting on her life with Daam in front of the grave of Anta Saar, her best friend. While she remembers her past, Daam and Anta's husband Biraan stay outside the cemetery.

The film opens with a shot of the beach of the Dakar neighborhood of Tableau Ferraille. Though Tableau Ferraille is the name of a location, it also has a symbolic value since *ferraille* in French means 'scrap heap.' Indeed, unlike the pristine white, sandy beach of *Ça twiste à Popenguine*, this beach is polluted: black smoke comes out of rusty barrels. Dwellings built without regulation impinge on the beach. Against this background, a young boy pulls a small hand-made truck in which he puts a crab. Symbolically, it is the last animal to

---

9 The International Monetary Fund had required structural-adjustment measures and the West African currency of the CFA franc had been devaluated, which caused economic hardships for the population because the wages did not rise accordingly. This led to increased poverty and corruption.
10 In Africa in general, and in Senegal in particular, it is very common to give nicknames to people.

survive ecological disaster. The way this beach is represented is emblematic of Senegal's neo-colonial society, where corruption and poverty are rampant in daily life at the local level. This will be made clear in a later scene. While Daam and his friend Biraan are waiting for Gagnesiri outside the cemetery, a man carrying barrels on a cart passes by. He tells them that at the seaport he can make money fast because Président pays him handsomely to dump barrels. Since these barrels are at the harbor and some are radioactive, they are likely to come from richer countries overseas.[11] The carter proudly says that he throws the content of those barrels into the sea and then sells them to dry cleaners or to women as water containers while gullibly emphasizing that some hold radioactive waste. Daam is visibly upset and condemns him for contaminating innocent people, but Biraan, eager to get easy money, leaves to get barrels at the harbor. The flashback that follows shows Anta's funeral march, followed by a ceremony at the cemetery. When one considers the opening sequence with the smoking rusty barrels, the carter's barrels sequence and the burial flashback sequence, one detects a direct causal link between the dumping of toxic waste that is overlooked and even permitted due to social and economic corruption and Anta's illness and death at age fifty.

In the first flashback sequence, Gagnesiri remembers that Daam asked her to marry him during his election campaign. She agreed to marry him if her father would give his blessing. Their wedding ceremony was traditional. In a later flashback sequence, she recalls how Daam decided to marry a second wife, Kiné, because Gagnesiri could not give him children. Kiné is not only more modern than Gagnesiri but also ambitious. For her, "il faut de l'argent pour être heureux" [one needs money to be happy]. Kiné, who is a close friend of Président, will give him confidential documents that her husband possesses in exchange for a huge amount of money. In a flashback sequence, Président proposes this transaction of stealing the documents to Kiné. This sequence takes place at an isolated beach with sand of immaculate white that looks very different from the polluted beach of the opening sequence.

The unspoiled white beach and their white clothes contrast with what they are brazenly plotting since Kiné decides to conspire with Président and consequently causes her husband's downfall. Kiné wears a modern, alabaster white dress and golden, ostentatious jewelry and Président an ivory white suit and a cowboy hat. (Fig. 2) These fashion choices indicate their complicity and allude to her expensive taste and his admiration of American capitalist culture. He di-

---

11 Président has likely signed secret agreements with foreign companies. In the late 1980s, several West African countries accepted toxic waste from Europe and the USA (see Brooke 1988).

rects his fish cannery shamelessly and makes profit to the detriment of the workers, who very often have to look for a second job to get by.¹² Those hard-working and innocent people don't have access to those unsullied beaches – unlike Président and Kiné, who are sullied.

Fig. 2: Kiné and Président conspiring at the beach in *Tableau Ferraille*.

This beach sequence contrasts with the final beach sequence, in which Gagne-siri leaves the cemetery while Daam is sleeping peacefully on a bench behind the cemetery's wall. The little boy with the handmade truck, who has followed them, asks Gagnesiri what he should tell Daam when he wakes up, to which the Baye Fall chorus sings her reply in Wolof: "Neko Demna" [Tell him I've gone].¹³ She is on her way to the beach, where there are several pirogues owned by fishermen waiting, which indicate that there are problems with the fishing business due to corruption and pollution. She is quickly joined by the Baye Fall chorus, who continue their song "Neko Demna." The childless Gagnesiri, who has just reevaluated her situation, realizes that she has to become an active agent of her life. Though she departs, she leaves Daam everything and retains her values and love, as evidenced by her keeping the same bright orange boubou, similar to the color of his polo shirt. The beautiful, majestic, and determined Gagnesiri heads with the chorus to a pirogue, wading into the water. (Fig. 3)

---

12 Anta Saar's daughter starts to be a prostitute on the fifteenth of the month because her salary at the fish cannery doesn't suffice, especially since she has to take care of her child.
13 The Baye Fall chorus appears at key moments, commenting on the dramatic action. The historical Baye Fall movement had as spiritual leader Cheikh Ibrahima Fall (1855–1930). He was one of the disciples of the Muslim Sufi leader Cheikh Amadou Bamba (1853–1927), founder of the Mouride Muslim brotherhood.

Fig. 3: Gagnesiri leaving the beach in *Tableau Ferraille*.

The lead Baye Fall, played by Moussa Sène Absa himself, helps Gagnesiri enter the pirogue. She leaves the beach and embarks on a journey, becoming a 'liminar.' According to Turner, the 'liminar' "passes through a symbolic domain that has few or none of the attributes of his past or coming state" (Turner 1974, 232). The boat takes a diagonal route, which symbolizes a long and endless journey. According to Baye Fall beliefs, it is not necessary to pass through death to reach paradise, an unspoiled locale which can be terrestrial and does not need to be celestial. Gagnesiri moves away from all toxic influences, the barrels, Président, and her co-wife, which the parked fishermen's pirogues on the beach incarnate.

By the end of the film, with the liminal state of Gagnesiri's blissful voyage, Absa's message becomes clear:

> Dans ce film, je veux dire: Afrique réveille-toi. On te demande d'aller trop vite. [...] L'Afrique s'est embarquée dans un train sans savoir où il mène. Je préférerais qu'on attende un autre train où l'on trouve notre place en sachant où le train va. [In this film, I want to say: Africa wake up. You are being asked to go too fast. [...] Africa has embarked on a train without knowing where it goes. I would prefer that we wait for another train in which we find our place while knowing where the train goes.] (Barlet 2002)

This metaphor of the train also appears in the Baye Fall song's lyrics, in which Gagnesiri asks to tell Daam that she left before the train departed. Her departure reveals an alternative personal and social path, and though the path is unknown, it indicates possible improvement and hope for a better future. Daam on the other hand has embarked on a train without knowing where it is going. His political and material ascent was precipitated. Dishonest people took advantage of his position, but he remains sincere and faithful to his ideals.

In *Tableau Ferraille*, the fish trade is no longer depicted through women selling fish at the beach but through Président's fish cannery. Culturally, Senegal has distanced itself from France, and economically it is now part of global capitalism, where profit at all costs seems to be the driving force. All the negative consequences of capitalism, materialism, and neo-colonialism come to the fore at beaches and are linked to the character of Président: waste and pollution (the smoking barrels at the beach and the dumping of the toxic barrels into the sea), corruption (making illegal contracts and transactions), treachery (betraying his best friend), etc. Daam's second wife, the ambitious and modern Kiné, conspires with Président walking along a pristine beach. The faithful and traditional Gagnesiri departs from a fishermen's beach in a pirogue. At both beaches, the real identity and dichotomy of both of Daam's wives come to the fore: the negative – even toxic – one of Kiné and the positive one of Gagnesiri.

4 *Madame Brouette* – Corruption, Imprisonment, and Freedom

The story of *Madame Brouette* occurs in the early years of the twenty-first century, when Abdoulaye Wade, who had promised *sopi* or 'change,' was Senegal's third president.[14] He defended a free-market economy, supported the private sector, and modernized Dakar by launching big construction projects.

'Madame Brouette' is the nickname for Mati, who supports herself and her daughter Ndèye by selling goods from her wheelbarrow (*brouette* in French) around the streets of Dakar. The film starts in the early morning light in Dakar's Niayes Thiokeert neighborhood, located at the beach. There Mati shot her lover Naago, a very charming but corrupt policeman, who had entered her room drunk, unkempt, and dressed as a woman, following the tradition of *tadiabone*.[15] The frame narrative consists of journalists interviewing people to

---

[14] Abdoulaye Wade (born in 1926), from the Senegalese Democratic Party (Parti Démocratique Sénégalais), became Senegal's third president on 1 April 2000. His election marked the end of 40 years of socialism. He had led the party since its creation in 1974, had been the opposition leader since 1978, and ran for president four times. He was re-elected in 2007 but then defeated in 2012.

[15] *Tadiabone* is a typical Senegalese tradition of cross-dressing. *Tadiabone* is celebrated during the night of Tamxarit, a Muslim holiday marked by abundance and prayer. It could be compared to Carnival.

understand Mati's act of killing Naago. These interviews, which lead to flashback scenes, take place at the beach, soon after the murder, close to where the murder happened, i. e. near Mati's room and her adjacent canteen.

The important flashback sequences also take place at the beach. Soon after having met Naago, Mati makes out with him at the beach on New Year's Eve and becomes pregnant. Mati wants to open a canteen to give her daughter, who had been complaining about their difficult life conditions, and the baby she is expecting, a better life. She is able to purchase a canteen by reselling merchandise, bought in Gambia on the black market, via one of Naago's shady friends, the hustler London Pipe. She has negotiated the sale of the contraband merchandise at the beach. Though she regrets that she has to engage in this illegal transaction, she claims that she had no other choice because the money she made honorably from selling the goods from her wheelbarrow was not sufficient. In order to obtain her operating permit, she also had to bribe different official authorities.

Mati's canteen resembles Ginette's canteen in *Ça twiste à Popenguine*, but Ginette's canteen was the only canteen at the beach in Popenguine, whereas there are several canteens in Niayes Thiokeert. It is notable that, while in 1964 the canteen was owned by a French woman, in the early 1990s, the owners are Senegalese women. Similar to the way the Ins' shed at the beach in *Ça twiste à Popenguine* was decorated with pictures taken from the French magazine *Salut les Copains*, Mati's room next to her canteen is decorated with luxury advertisements and images from Western magazines. Sheila Petty explains that this "discordant collage of consumerism seems incongruous when considered against the poverty of this Senegalese setting," and adds, "the spectator is simultaneously confronted with the implications of Mati's emotional state as well as the ideological context within which it has arisen" (Petty 2009, 103). In an era of increasing economic neoliberalism in Senegal, Mati appears to be a product of those political, economic, and social transformations. Wade's *sopi* and its ramifications for the country are explored through these new values, which Mati embraces.

When Mati has her canteen, she is very happy because she is independent and can be part of the Niayes Thiokeert community at the beach. She swims in the sea with her friend while her daughter Ndèye makes sandcastles (or better sand shacks) with Samba, her friend from the neighborhood (fig. 4).

Fig. 4: Children building sandcastles in *Madame Brouette*.

In this sequence, the beach is untarnished and beautiful. Absa seems to imply that the shacks made from sand allude to home, community, and stability but also to fragility. Just as – we imagine – they will be demolished by the rising tide later, so, too, Mati's canteen will be destroyed. From the moment London Pipe and his cronies start to use her canteen as a hangout for drug trafficking and prostitution, its business goes down steadily.

In one later sequence, walking along the beach with her friend, Mati discusses her concern that she is losing clients. Mati still pushes her wheelbarrow, which indicates that she continues to work in an honest way. All other people are doing construction work, which refers to Dakar's growing population and to shacks being built without urban planning, in an unregulated way, overrunning the beach. Mati then tells her friend the nightmare she had: it was dark and raining heavily, a herd of hyenas was chasing Naago and herself. Naago asked her to hide in the bushes and to wait for him. He never came back, and she felt 'strangely free' ("étrangement libre"). This dream foreshadows the events that occurred in the early morning after *tadiabone*.

Before the murder happened, London Pipe had asked Naago, who owed him a lot of money, to burn down Niayes Thiokeert in order to pay him back and wipe the slate clean. In the spirit of modernizing Dakar instigated by 'the president' – the reference is to president Wade who is not named – the mayor had decided to build a new housing-development complex in Niayes Thiokeert. However, the poor residents did not want to leave. Hence London's demand to Naago to force them out. Clearly, corruption has infiltrated all levels of society, as is evident from the fact that London and the local politicians have been conspiring. Naago eventually sets the houses in Niayes Thiokeert on fire during the night of *tadiabone*. Mati, who has just come home with her new-born baby, wakes up and sees her neighborhood in flames. Several dwellings at the beach are on fire. In *Ça twiste à Popenguine*, the Kings had put the Ins' shed at the beach on fire because the Ins could not give them back the money they owed them for renting their *teppaz* and records. In this scene, the fire has been ignited because Naago was indebted to London Pipe. Whereas the village elders of Popenguine had punished both gangs, it is not clear if anyone will face justice for prompting this fire. Though London Pipe is arrested, he is protected by and complicit with power-hungry politicians and greedy industrialists.

At the very end of the film, Mati confesses to the police inspector that she shot Naago because she had no other alternative. A flashback shows that her daughter Ndèye, who held her new-born baby brother on her lap, shot Naago in the arm first. (She shot him because she had been attacked by Naago's friends during the *tadiabone* celebration. Though she was very scared, Naago did not interfere to help her.) Naago tries to take the gun. In order to defend her daughter, Mati kills him. Before following the police inspector to his car without any resistance, Mati frees the pet partridge that is in a cage hanging next to her room, saying, "Je suis comme une perdrix, j'aime la liberté." [I am like a partridge. I love freedom.] Absa has compared a woman to a partridge:

> I compare her to a partridge. In the days of royal courts, the partridge was a sacred animal, used in mystical practices because it brought luck and happiness. This bird could not be eaten by just anyone. You had to deserve it. Like a woman. You must deserve her. (Moyes 2013)

Naago didn't deserve Mati. After having freed the partridge, Mati asks Samba to take care of Ndèye since he had defended Ndèye against Naago's friends during *tadiabone*. The film ends with a shot of the partridge flying at sunset above the ocean, following a spiraling and slightly diagonal route towards the horizon. As symbolized by the spirals, it is obviously on a long and difficult journey towards paradise.

Like the ebb and the flow of tides transform the liminal space of the beach, above which the partridge flies, the notions of freedom and imprisonment are linked and blurred, as Mati's liminal situation attests. Although Mati committed illegal acts by buying contraband goods, she did so to improve the life of her children, and she shot Naago to protect her daughter. The beach in *Madame Brouette* is thus characterized by Mati's emancipatory hopes for a better future for herself and her children but also for freedom from corrupting influences.

These are present not only at the local level but also at the national level, including the administration, the police, and the politicians. Like Gagnesiri in the previously discussed film, and though Mati will very likely be imprisoned for having killed Naago, she remained true to herself all along, and, if not physically, psychologically she is keeping her freedom.

The dwellings and Madame Brouette's canteen at the beach in Niayes Thiokeert materialize the political, economic, and social transformations that have taken place in Senegal in the 40 years since the sheds of the teenage gangs and Madame Ginette's canteen in *Ça twiste à Popenguine*. There are no French people on the beach of Niayes Thiokeert. The Senegalese population has increased, and the beach is occupied by haphazardly built dwellings in which people live. At the same time, the beach has become a much coveted, exploitable, and lucrative space.

5 *Yoolé* – Despair, Disillusion, and Hope

Moussa Sène Absa made the docufiction *Yoolé* after he learned about a tragic event. In April 2006, a boat containing eleven dead bodies was discovered adrift along the coast of Barbados. In the pocket of one of the bodies was a little note with names and phone numbers from Senegal. A Senegalese inhabitant of the island helped with the investigation and found out that these eleven people together with forty-three others had departed from Senegal four months earlier, in December 2005, in the hope of reaching Europe via the Canary Islands. Their dugout boat deviated from its trajectory and went westwards, eventually to reach Barbados. Absa was enticed to make the film to answer a simple question that the Senegalese inhabitant of Barbados asks in the film: "[W]hy do young people leave their home country, Senegal, where there is no civil war, no famine, no genocide?" At that time, Abdoulaye Wade, the defender of *sopi*, was finishing his first seven-year term as president.[16]

Absa shot his film between December 2008 and December 2010. The title of the film, *Yoolé* [Sacrifice], indicates that parts of the young generation are being sacrificed. Its subtitle "les ailes perdues des anges" [the lost wings of angels] corroborates this further. The film consists of several interviews, some of which were conducted in Barbados and Portugal, but the majority of them were done in Senegal. Those interviews are interspersed with black and white footage of

---

[16] Wade's first term as president lasted 7 years, from 2000 until 2007. He was re-elected in March 2007 for a 5-year term because the constitution had been changed.

Abdoulaye Wade's political discourses, with Serigne Mor Mbaye, a Senegalese psychologist, explaining the reasons why young people leave their home country, and with beautiful scenes of the glimmering ocean. During those ocean scenes, Absa reads in voice-over an imaginary letter that one of the men who died in the pirogue could have written to his mother. Absa thus tries to put himself in the shoes of one of those young unfortunate migrants. He said in an interview that making this film was extremely hard on him psychologically. "Ce film a fait basculer ma vie, m'a ouvert les yeux sur la fragilité de nos vies" [This film turned my life upside down. It made me realize how fragile our lives are] (De Raedt 2015, 179). In *Ça twiste à Popenguine*, he had given the narrative voice-over to Bacc, a fictional character inspired by his own life. In this film, he gives his compassionate voice to one of the real-life persons who have perished in the dugout boat. A fascinating shot shows the waves coming and drifting on the beach while the voice-over in the background reads the fictional letter. He describes his friends in the dugout boat. Interestingly, one of them, Ibrahima, had chosen 'Johnny' as his nickname. He had brought his tape recorder and his tapes with him since he loved music and dance. Absa thus creates a link with his first feature-length film and shows how life has changed: in *Ça twiste à Popenguine* the male members of the Ins had taken to the sea on an old, broken pirogue to impress the girls, whereas here it is not so much to show their bravery as to look for a better future in Europe. The fictional Johnny of this film plans on a one-way trip because he is convinced that he will stay in Europe.

In Bridgetown, Absa interviewed a journalist (Tim Slinger) at the beach, perhaps to underscore that the pirogue went from one side to the other side of the Atlantic Ocean. In Senegal, he interviewed young people at the beach close to dugout boats. They had voted for Abdoulaye Wade and now felt betrayed by his government.[17] Indeed, during his election campaign, Wade had promised that, once elected, he would give everyone a job, that Dakar would become a new Paris, that everyone would profit from the political change and from the economic recovery he had announced. But once he became President, he didn't keep any of his promises. After five years, those young people who had helped him win the elections didn't notice any change, on the contrary, they saw an old president surrounded by his French family ruling over the country and people from his entourage becoming rich overnight.[18]

---

[17] The voting age in Senegal is 18 years. There is currently discussion to put the age down from 18 to 16. Senegal is a very young country with half of its population being less than 20 years old.
[18] Abdoulaye Wade's wife, Viviane Vert, is French, and their two children were educated in France (and in the French schools in Senegal) and barely speak Wolof, the most widely spoken

Some of those young people who had left Senegal and arrived at the Canary Islands felt betrayed twice. After a few days in the Canary Islands, they were asked to enter a plane. They thought they would be sent to mainland Spain. Through the loudspeaker, they learned that they were going to Dakar because, as they were told, the president and the country needed them. President Wade's government had negotiated with the Spanish government to repatriate them. Once they arrived in Dakar, they were not taken care of and were left to their own fate. The film shows how traumatized they are: they lost everything and came back to their community as having failed to emigrate. This terrible stigma of failure continues to haunt them. Their faces are closed and express exhaustion, depression, and dejection.[19]

A memorable sequence in the film shows the construction of the big monument celebrating the "Renaissance africaine" [African Renaissance], located on one of Dakar's volcanic hills, overlooking the Atlantic Ocean and the neighborhood of Ouakam. Documentary footage shows Wade praising this monument that he had conceived. He explains that he wants it to have an iconic value comparable to the Statue of Liberty in New York.[20] Not only does he stress the monument's symbolism of African rebirth, he also accentuates that it should be considered as an investment since it will attract tourists, who will pay to visit it. He further insists that, though the monument belongs to the state of Senegal, the intellectual property rights are his and will always remain his.[21] This long sequence represents the paradox of the current socio-political situation. On the one hand, there is a greedy president with grandiose dreams who has lost touch with the daily reality of the Senegalese population. On the other hand, there are young fishermen from Ouakam who are leaving in pirogues for Europe in the hope of finding a better life there because fishing is no longer profitable.[22] Indeed, Wade's government gave fishing licenses to big foreign factory ships, with the consequence that the local fishermen had to go further and further offshore to find fish and by doing so came close to the Canary Islands.

---

national language. Wade gave his son several ministerial appointments and put his daughter in charge of several organizations.

19 The psychologist explains that the young people leave especially because they want to find work, because they are profoundly disappointed and frustrated by the new government, and because they no longer find their place in society.

20 The monument has received criticism from different people (see De Jong and Foucher 2010).

21 Abdoulaye Wade has claimed 35 per cent of the monument's profits under the pretext of 'intellectual property rights.'

22 Historically, Ouakam's neighborhood is predominantly populated by Lebou people, who are known to be excellent fishermen.

At the end of the film, a scene shows the sea at night while the fictional letter writer explains in voice-over that several of his fellow companions have died or are about to die. He wonders who would have thought that, at age 25, he would pray in the middle of the ocean for death. A scene follows in which young people are wrestling at the beach.[23] As the outcome of a wrestling match is never predictable, neither is the outcome of the journey to Europe. Metaphorically, the wrestling suggests fighting against natural elements, against sickness and death. In the subsequent scene, two young people draw a big heart, with "I love you" written within it, on the sand at the beach. A Catholic song in the background accompanies that scene.

In the last ocean scene, the fictional letter writer says in voice-over that he becomes weaker and that his hands can barely hold his pen. He declares that he is about to embrace a long night and that he is at the doorway of death but that he is no longer afraid to die. He finishes by saying: "Je défierai la mort comme j'ai défié la mer, en homme digne" [I will defy death as I challenged the sea, as a worthy man]. Clearly, Moussa Sène Absa has given him a tremendous capacity for resilience. At that moment, a shot shows the image of a mother superimposed over the waves at the beach, where a shoe is washed ashore (fig. 5). This shot refers to the all too well-known images of immigrants washed ashore by the sea. Symbolically, it represents the death of the eleven immigrants who have died in a dugout boat along the coast of Barbados and the forty-three others who had accompanied them. It could perhaps also refer to Absa no longer being able to put himself in the shoes of the person he had incarnated. The waves bringing back the shoe contain the threat of erasure, rejection, and destruction but perhaps also of a symbolic return to home and redemption.

The drawing of the big heart on the beach in the previous scene could then be read as a testimony to the fact that people continue to love those who have left and that they will never be forgotten. The accompanying Catholic choir music corroborates this idea of redemption further. Arguably, the film ends on a hopeful note.

In this docufiction, the consequences of post-modernity and global inequality come together at the beach. Absa, who is a socially engaged director, denounces the effects of a political system which neglects its youth. He portrays the grandiose dreams of its president, symbolized by the monument of African Renaissance overlooking the ocean. The liminal space of the beach incarnates the hope of long-term (and often permanent) migration from Senegal to Europe but also the despair of its failure.

---

23 Senegalese wrestling, or *làmb*, is Senegal's most popular sport and is often practiced at the beach.

Fig. 5: Image of a mother superimposed over the waves, where a shoe is washed ashore, in *Yoolé*.

6 Figurations of the Beach in Absa's Films

In this tetralogy, we have seen how the Senegalese beachscape of the Cap-Vert peninsula and the *Petite Côte* has changed in almost half a century. In the years following independence, it is still strongly dominated by France's influence, as *Ça twiste à Popenguine* attests. At the turn of the century, as evidenced in *Tableau Ferraille* and *Madame Brouette*, it is marked by poor dwellings and pollution. In more recent years, as shown in *Yoolé*, Dakar's beachscape is transformed by the imposing and controversial monument of the African Renaissance.

For Moussa Sène Absa, who grew up with the ocean in front of him, the beach is a sign of home, as *Ça twiste à Popenguine* clearly illustrates, but also of the self and of self-realization. The beach signals the place of home for Daam and of self-realization for the protagonist Gagnesiri in *Tableau Ferraille*. It represents home and self-realization for Mati in *Madame Brouette*. One could contend that the beach also incarnates home and hope for self-realization in *Yoolé*.

Through his depictions of beaches, Absa denounces what is happening in Senegalese society and compels his audience to ponder the situation. At the same time, he sends a message of hope, even if the hope has often not yet taken a concrete shape and remains undetermined. Though the film narratives happen in concrete locations on the beach and illustrate specific concerns, the significance of these stories transcends the local and is universal: childhood memories, a mother wanting the best for her children, people moving somewhere else for a better future, etc. The liminality of the beach is represented by movement and stability, and escape and voyage. At the beach, work and leisure, pollution and nature, despair and hope, corruption and integrity, destruction and redemption, poverty and prosperity, imprisonment and freedom, death and life come together and sometimes intersect.[24]

Bibliography

Absa, Moussa Sène. "Leçon de cinéma: Niit Nitki 'Éclairer l'humain.'" Talk given at the University Gaston Berger. 5 December 2018 [Unpublished manuscript].

Barlet, Olivier. "À propos de *Madame Brouette*. Entretien d'Olivier Barlet avec Moussa Sène Absa." *Africulture* (7 March 2003): http://africultures.com/a-propos-de-madame-brouette-2810/ (25 January 2019).

Barlet, Olivier. "À propos de *Tableau Ferraille*. Entretien d'Olivier Barlet avec Moussa Sène Absa." *Africulture* (2 September 2002): http://africultures.com/a-propos-de-tableau-ferraille-2498/ (25 January 2019).

Bob, Bigué. "Le procès Barça-Barsax. Projection *Yoolé* de Moussa Sène Absa." *Enquête+* (2 March 2013): http://www.enqueteplus.com/content/projection-yool%C3%A9-de-moussa-s%C3%A8ne-absa-le-proc%C3%A8s-bar%C3%A7a-barsax (25 January 2019).

Brooke, James. "Waste Dumpers Turning to West Africa." *The New York Times* (17 July 1988): https://www.nytimes.com/1988/07/17/world/waste-dumpers-turning-to-west-africa.html (26 August 2019).

Ça twiste à Popenguine. Directed by Moussa Sène Absa. California Newsreel, 1994.

Chirol, Marie-Magdeleine. "Tableau Ferraille ou le mirage de la modernité." *Cinémas africains, une oasis dans le désert?* Ed. Samuel Lelièvre. Condé-sur-Noireau: Charles Corlet, 2003. 101–105.

De Jong, Ferdinand, and Vincent Foucher. "La tragédie du roi Abdoulaye? Néomodernisme et Renaissance africaine dans le Sénégal contemporain." *Politique africaine* 118 (2010): 187–204.

De Raedt, Thérèse. "Entretien avec Moussa Sène Absa." *The French Review* 89.1 (2015): 172–184.

Gennep, Arnold van. *The Rites of Passage*. Translated by Monika B. Vizedom and Gabrielle L. Caffee, with an introduction by Solon T. Kimball. Chicago: University of Chicago Press, 1960.

Madame Brouette. Directed by Moussa Sène Absa. TLA Releasing, 2002.

Moyes, Bea. "Feature Film *Madame Brouette*." *Litro* (11 January 2013): https://www.litro.co.uk/2013/01/feature-film-madame-brouette/ (10 February 2019).

---

[24] I would like to thank Katharina Gerstenberger for letting me know about the conference "Narrating and Constructing the Beach" and for her careful reading of an earlier draft. I also would like to express my gratitude to Jerry Root for his critical advice, and to Katharina Simon and Martin Wittmann for their excellent editing.

Petty, Sheila. "The Rise of the African Musical: Postcolonial Disjunction in *Karmen Geï* and *Madame Brouette*." *Journal of African Cinemas* 1.1 (2009): 95–112.

Pfaff, Françoise. *À l'écoute du cinéma sénégalais*. Paris: L'Harmattan, 2010.

Tableau Ferraille. Directed by Moussa Sène Absa. California Newsreel, 1998.

Turner, Victor. *Dramas, Fields, and Metaphors. Symbolic Action in Human Society*. Ithaca and London: Cornell University Press, 1974.

Turner, Victor. *The Forest of Symbols: Aspects of Ndembu Ritual*. New York: Cornell University Press, 1967.

Yoolé. Directed by Moussa Sène Absa. Absa Films, 2010.

List of Figures

Fig. 1: Still from *Ça twiste à Popenguine*. Directed by Moussa Sène Absa. California Newsreel, 1994.

Fig. 2: Still from *Tableau Ferraille*. Directed by Moussa Sène Absa. California Newsreel, 1998.

Fig. 3: Still from *Tableau Ferraille*. Directed by Moussa Sène Absa. California Newsreel, 1998.

Fig. 4: Still from *Madame Brouette*. Directed by Moussa Sène Absa. TLA Releasing, 2002.

Fig. 5: Still from *Yoolé*. Directed by Moussa Sène Absa. Absa Films, 2010.

Drawing and Crossing Lines

Carmen Ulrich
Strandbekanntschaften in Georg Forsters *Reise um die Welt* und das europäische Projekt ‚Zivilisation'

In Georg Forster's *A Voyage Round the World* (1777) the South Pacific beach sceneries function as an intercultural meeting space and a provisional space for different actions. For the Europeans the beach seems to be a lawless territory where they negotiate their own rules. Gestures of hospitality alternate with gestures of power. We have to deal with a multi-coded field of experimentation where the project 'civilization' develops in three directions: 1) through introduction of social norms, 2) through exchange and trade, 3) through processes of education in the name of the Enlightenment. The project becomes questionable, especially in the moment of a manslaughter. On the basis of current perspectives, this article sheds light on cultural paradigms, concepts and discourses in Forster's journey description, in particular on the liminal and multiple phenomenon of the beach.

In Georg Forsters *Reise um die Welt* (1787, 1789) fungieren Inselstrände im Südpazifik als eine interkulturelle Begegnungsfläche und als provisorischer Handlungsraum. Für die Europäer ist der Strand ein rechtloser Raum, in dem sie ihre eigenen Regeln aufstellen. Gesten der Gastfreundschaft alternieren mit Machtdemonstrationen. In diesem mehrfach kodierten Experimentierfeld entfaltet sich das Projekt ‚Zivilisation' in drei Richtungen: 1) zur Etablierung von gesellschaftlichen Normen und Strukturen, 2) durch Handel und Warenaustausch, 3) durch Prozesse der Bildung im Zeichen der europäischen Aufklärung. Das Projekt wirft, spätestens mit der Tötung eines Insulaners, Fragen auf. Der Beitrag beleuchtet die kulturellen Paradigmen, Konzepte und Diskurse in Forsters Reisebeschreibung und perspektiviert insbesondere das liminale und multiple Phänomen des Strandes.

1 Natur und Kultur

Inselstrände im Südpazifik boten im achtzehnten Jahrhundert nicht nur ein Projektionsfeld für die Utopien empfindsamer Intellektueller, sondern auch ein Experimentierfeld für realpolitische Ziele, wie das Projekt ‚Zivilisation'. Der vorliegende Beitrag beleuchtet in Georg Forsters *Reise um die Welt*[1] einige Episoden und Begegnungen am Strand, einer spannungsreichen Grenzlandschaft, in der sich das Projekt ‚Zivilisation' – in intendierter Abgrenzung von

---

[1] Originaltitel: *Dr. Johann Reinhold Forster's und seines Sohnes Georg Forster's Reise um die Welt, auf Kosten der Grosbrittannischen Regierung, zu Erweiterung der Naturkenntniß unternommen und während den Jahren 1772 bis 1775 in dem vom Capitain J. Cook commandirten Schiffe the Resolution, ausgeführt.*

kolonialpolitischen Eroberungszügen und religiösen Missionsbewegungen – in drei Richtungen hin entfaltet: 1) durch Handel und Warenaustausch, 2) zur Etablierung von gesellschaftlichen Normen und Strukturen, die als zivilisiert und wünschenswert für alle Völker galten, 3) durch Prozesse der Bildung (*libido sciendi*) im Zeichen der europäischen Aufklärung.

Innerhalb des deutschen Wissenschaftsdiskurses begründet sich der Begriff ‚Zivilisation' seit dem neunzehnten Jahrhundert bekanntlich aus der Entwicklung der Ökonomie und Technik und wird scharf abgegrenzt vom Begriff der ‚Kultur', die den geistigen, künstlerischen, religiösen und moralischen Bereich umfasst.[2] In der englischen und französischen Tradition hat sich diese Unterscheidung nicht durchgesetzt, so dass auch Wissenschaft, Weltanschauung und menschliches Verhalten unter den Begriff der ‚Zivilisation' fallen (Lethen 1994, 31). *Die Reise um die Welt* – verfasst vor jener Begriffsdifferenzierung, entstanden in einem internationalen Kontext von verschiedenen, sich überlappenden Wissenschaftsgeschichten – folgt einem weitgefassten Begriff von ‚Zivilisation', der mit dem der ‚Kultur' und des ‚Fortschritts' durchaus verschränkt ist.[3] Indem Forster die natürlichen Voraussetzungen von Zivilisationen mittels der beobachteten Geographie rekonstruiert, verknüpft er die Naturgeschichte mit der Kulturgeschichte (Garber 2000, 202).

Mit siebzehn Jahren überquerte Georg Forster an Bord von James Cooks Resolution den Äquator als Hilfskraft seines Vaters Johann Reinhold, dessen Aufgabe es war, „eine *philosophische Geschichte der Reise*" zu verfassen,

> von Vorurtheil und gemeinen Trugschlüssen frey, worinn er seine Entdeckungen in der Geschichte des Menschen, und in der Naturkunde überhaupt, ohne Rücksicht auf willkührliche Systeme, blos nach allgemeinen menschenfreundlichen Grundsätzen darstellen

---

2 Nach Jörn Garber vereinigen sich ab 1750 im Begriff ‚Kultur' zwei Konzeptionen der „verhältnismäßigen" Bestimmung des Menschen: „In der Synchronie aller räumlichen Elemente einer Kultur deutet die Geographie den ‚zusammengesetzten' Zustand von Gesellschaften an. In einer zeitlich angeordneten ‚Stufentheorie' der menschlichen Entwicklung erfaßt die Menschheitsgeschichte alle bisher ausgebildeten Formen der materiellen und ideellen Kultur." (Garber 2000, 193; vgl. Starobinski 1990, 9–64)

3 Der Begriff der ‚Zivilisation' ließe sich auch rezeptionsästhetisch erörtern mittels eines Vergleiches englischer und deutscher Kritiken auf die *Reise um die Welt*. Nach seinem Tod, 1794, wurden Forsters Werke zunächst nicht weiter publiziert, ein Grund dafür war auch sein Engagement für die Französische Revolution. Seine – namentlich nicht genannte – Tochter gab zusammen mit Georg Gottfried Gervinus die erste Gesamtausgabe seiner Werke heraus (Forster 1843). Jacob Moleschott stellt Forster in den 1860er-Jahren in eine Reihe mit Goethe, Lessing und Schiller (Moleschott 1862, III). Während des aufkeimenden Nationalismus im nachnapoleonischen Deutschland und der nationalsozialistischen Herrschaft verschwand Forster aus der Öffentlichkeit.

sollte; das heißt, eine Reisebeschreibung, dergleichen der gelehrten Welt bisher noch keine vorgelegt worden. (Forster 1989a, II, 8)

Der junge Georg hatte die Aufgabe, unter Anleitung seines Vaters, die noch unbekannte Botanik, die Tier- und Pflanzenwelt der Südsee zu zeichnen. Die Reise begann im Juli 1772 und führte zunächst in den Südatlantik, über den Indischen Ozean und die antarktischen Gewässer in den Südpazifik, zu den Inseln Polynesiens und schließlich um Kap Horn wieder zurück nach England, wo die Expedition im Juli 1775 eintraf.

Als weder die erste Berichterstattung Johann Reinhold Forsters noch die zweite an den Vorgaben des Admirals-Präsidenten Graf Earl of Sandwich orientierte Textfassung auf Wohlwollen stößt und der Vater schließlich von einer Publikation gänzlich ausgeschlossen wird, hält es der junge Georg für seine „Schuldigkeit, wenigstens einen Versuch zu wagen, an seiner Stelle eine philosophische Reisebeschreibung, auch unter Einbezug der Aufzeichnungen des Vaters, zu verfertigen" (Forster 1989a, 9; vgl. Graczyk 2001, 103). Innerhalb von acht Monaten füllt Forster zwei Quartbände auf Englisch. Im März 1777 erscheint *A Voyage Round the World*. Zum Klassiker wird jedoch erst die deutsche Fassung, die keine Übersetzung ist, sondern ein eigenes Original (darin z. B. Erörterungen nautischer Spezialprobleme weggelassen sind), erschienen in zwei Bänden 1778 und 1780. Sie macht Forster mit einem Schlag einem größeren Publikum bekannt.

Im Fokus steht die Natur. Seinen Naturbegriff verdankt Forster, der kaum eine Schule besucht hat, seinen eigenen Anschauungen und Erfahrungen. Alles, was er sieht, hat für ihn nicht nur eine materielle Bedeutung, sondern steht vielmehr in einem engen Zusammenhang mit menschlichen Handlungen, Kräften und Trieben. Seine Wahrnehmungen und Eindrücke von Bewohnern anderer Erdteile und deren Landschaften verdichten sich stellenweise zu einer Metaphorik, die zu mehrdeutigen Lesarten einlädt. Die Naturgewalt, die Forster am eigenen Leib erlebt, wird ihm zum Schlüssel seines Geschichtsverständnisses: die Gewalt als dauernde und antreibende Kraft der Geschichte. (Goldstein 2016, 166) Die der Natur innewohnende Gesetzlichkeit, ihre Ursachen- und Wirkungszusammenhänge, erkennt Forster auch im Sozialen: die Gesellschaft als ein natürliches System, dessen kausale Entwicklung als Teil der Naturgeschichte gelesen werden kann. Forster ist der Auffassung, dass „gewaltsame Bewegungen von einem Extrem zum andern eine gefährliche Stockung in dem großen Gange der Menschheit verhüten" (Forster 1989b, 86). Ähnliche Vorstellungen finden sich bei Johann Gottfried Herder (Herder 1989) oder in Goethes Naturbetrachtungen, in denen auch gesellschaftsrelevante oder sogar politische Ansichten vermittelt werden.

Die Annahme einer selbsttätigen Entwicklung der Menschheit, die als Organismus ihre gegensätzlichen Eigenschaftsmengen sukzessive entfaltet und die sinnliche Natur zur sittlichen Kultur verwandelt, gewinnt weniger Einfluss auf die universitären Fachdisziplinen als auf die universale Kulturgeschichte und Anthropologie der Spätaufklärung (Garber 2006, 55). Forsters literarisch versierte Reisebeschreibung weckt allerdings auch Zweifel an einer zu starren Analogiesetzung von körperlichen und geistigen Kräften, die womöglich Teil eines essayistischen Spiels mit den Metaphern des biologisch gebildeten Lesers des achtzehnten Jahrhunderts ist, der die Geschichte der Menschheit – ohne theologische oder metaphysische Voraussetzungen – zu einem selbstreferentiellen Organisationsprozess erklärt (ebd., 64).

Zu Forsters einschlägigsten Naturerlebnissen während seiner Weltumseglung zwischen 1772 und 1775 gehört der Blick auf den aktiven Vulkan Mount Yasur auf der Insel Tanna, die zur Inselgruppe der Neuen Hebriden gerechnet wird.[4] Das Panorama des ausbrechenden Vulkans prägt seine Bildsprache, mit der er später den revolutionären Umbruch in Frankreich[5] begrüßt – gleich einer naturhaften, notwendigen Veränderung (ähnlich dem Topos des Erdbebens, der nach der Zerstörung Lissabons auf politische Umwälzungen übertragen wurde). Im Kapitel über die Insel Tanna nimmt Forster sieben Anläufe, um den Vulkan zu beschreiben. Aus der Ferne, vom Schiff aus, ist zunächst nur der Gipfel zu sehen:

> Er war zur Zeit unsers Hierseyns gerade in vollem Ausbruch, und lag 5 bis 6 Meilen weit im Lande, so daß man, verschiedener dazwischen befindlicher Hügel wegen, vom Schiffe aus, nichts als den rauchenden Gipfel desselben sehen konnte. Dieser war an mehreren Stellen geborsten und am äußeren Rande gleichsam ausgezackt. (Forster 1989a, II, 208)

Vom Schiff aus betrachtend, gleichwohl dem Strande immer näher kommend, wird der flammende Vulkan auch hörbar, „mit donnergleichem Krachen", ein „unterirrdisches Getöse" verursachend (ebd., 208–209). Die „Gewalt des unterirrdischen Feuers" schleudert „aus dem Innersten des Berges" Felsenklumpen empor, „zum Theil so groß als unser größtes Boot [...], als ob es gleichsam nur Kiesel wären" (ebd., 232). Spürbar wird zudem die „mit Rauch und schwarzer Schörl-Asche" angefüllte Luft, die im Auge „einen beissenden Schmerz" auslöst

---

4 Vgl. Forsters naturkundliche Überlegungen zu Vulkanen im Allgemeinen (Forster 2003, 951–953).

5 In *James Cook, der Entdecker* (1787) schreibt Forster bspw.: „Der Gang so vieler Revolutionen, die sich immer ähnlich sind, so manches auch die Verhältnisse des Orts und der Zeit darin ändern, zertrümmert also offenbar jene idealischen Systeme, die auf eine grundlose Hypothese erbauet sind." (2008, 12)

und „das ganze Schiff" bedeckt, „und auch der Strand lag überall voll kleiner Bimssteine und ausgebrannter Kohlen" (ebd., 208–209, vgl. 231, 238, 256).

Führen wir uns die Szenerie einen Moment vor Augen, vom Blickpunkt des Betrachters Georg Forster aus, der zuvor mit der Schiffsmannschaft wochenlang im Pazifik unterwegs war. Hinter ihm liegt der unberechenbare Ozean, „prächtig und fürchterlich zugleich", und die Erfahrung, „ein vollkommenes Spiel der Wellen" zu sein, von ihrer entsetzlichen Gewalt „bald hier, bald dorthin" verschlagen zu werden, in die „unzählbar tiefe[n] Furchen" des Meeres, gepeitscht von starken Winden und heftigen Stürmen (ebd., 358–359), die mit eigenen Worten kaum beschreibbar sind. Ausdruck dafür findet Forster in der Literatur Shakespeares, aus der er zitiert: „*which took the ruffian billows by the top / Curling their monstrous heads and hanging them / With deafning clamours in the slippery clouds.*" (Ebd., 423) Das Meer nun im Rücken, mehreren drohenden Schiffsunglücken mit letzter Kraft entkommen, betrachtet Forster vom Strand aus das Innere einer fremden Insel, im Zentrum der aktive Vulkan, der ebenso verlockend wie gefährlich erscheint. Sein Standpunkt erscheint nicht weniger prekär: ein Sandstrand – nichts Festes, nichts Bewohnbares, ausgesetzt der Sonne und den Blicken der Inselbewohner, die sich ihrerseits immerhin verbergen können.

2 Ort und Raum

Der Strand – ein „Territorium der Leere", wie Alain Corbin behauptet, „wo es kein Eigentum gibt, wo die Dinge wie im Urzustand frei zur Verfügung stehen" (Corbin 1990, 287)? Ungeachtet der Tatsachen, dass es lange vor Cooks Reisen ausgeklügelte Berechnungen darüber gab, wie weit der Besitz einer Insel ins Meer hineinragt und die Insel Tanna durchaus schon bewohnt war und der Begriff ‚Territorium' auf Besitzverhältnisse hindeutet (verwendet für Hoheits- oder Staatsgebiete), welche die Engländer – allein durch Betreten des Landes – zweifellos für sich beanspruchten, haben wir es nur bedingt mit einem Territorium der Leere zu tun, eher mit dem Anspruch auf Leere im Sinne einer vorübergehenden Unbestimmtheit, die Möglichkeiten bietet, das Unbestimmte in eine Bestimmung zu überführen. Denn so leer und weiß wie jener Teil der Landkarten zu dieser Zeit vermeintlich war – tatsächlich vermutete das englische Königshaus einen großen südlichen Kontinent, den James Cook im geheimen Auftrag entdecken sollte –, so bedingt leer wie uneindeutig waren auch die Ansprüche auf das Territorium des Strandes, Ansprüche, die sich aus ungesicherten Annahmen, Mythen oder sogar Fiktionen speisten.

Reisebeschreibungen von ersten Entdeckerfahrten, hier die Entdeckung einer Insel, die von keinem Europäer bislang betreten wurde, haben keine literarische Vorlage und in dem Sinne keine vorgeschriebenen Handlungen und Praktiken, die den Raum gliedern. Vielmehr stehen sie selbst vor der Aufgabe, ein Memorandum zu schaffen in Form von geographischen Karten mit Deskriptoren von Wegstrecken und einer künftigen Erinnerungsliteratur, die sich fortschreiben lässt. Jedoch stellt sich schon hier, in den Anfängen der Entdeckerliteratur, die Frage, ob der Strand überhaupt jemals ‚geschichtslos' war. Geht es um die Darstellung eines bislang ungeschriebenen Raumes oder nicht vielmehr um die Fiktion oder sogar um die Darstellung der Fiktion eines bislang nicht beschriebenen, für alle Denkbarkeiten offenen Raumes? Die Idee des Fortschritts, nicht nur zeitlich gedacht, sondern auch als Raum mit intensiven Kommunikationsbeziehungen, setzt, so Garber, die Vorstellung eines zuvor leeren, d. h. unterkomplexen Raumes voraus (Garber 2000, 224). Dies zu erörtern und zu hinterfragen, würde uns in postkoloniale Diskurse und in die Problematik des Beobachterstandpunkts führen. Weltreisebeschreibungen des späten achtzehnten Jahrhunderts, so lässt sich festhalten, stellen die Geschichte der Menschheit als eine Raumgeschichte dar, die immer auch den Gegenwartsstatus der Menschheitsgeschichte – als ein „thesaurus temporum" – widerspiegelt (ebd., 205).

Für unser Thema relevant ist der zuerst betretbare Raum zwischen Meer und Festland, der Strand als Übergang, als „Linie, an der die konstitutiven Elemente der Welt miteinander in Berührung kommen" (Corbin 1990, 23). Dabei haben wir es in doppelter Weise mit einer Erzählung von Raum, einer Raum-Erzählung zu tun, die vor allem auch jenen Gründungsakt des Raumes beschreibt oder vielmehr die Metamorphose von einem vorgefundenen, fremden Ort hin zu einem Raum, den man gestalten kann nach eigenen Vorstellungen. Rückgreifend auf Michel de Certeaus *Kunst des Handelns* können wir unterscheiden zwischen Räumen und Orten. Während der Ort als „eine momentane Konstellation von festen Punkten" die Ordnung der Beziehungs- und Koexistenzverhältnisse der Elemente bezeichnet, besteht der Raum aus einem Geflecht von beweglichen Elementen und Aktivitäten, die von zeitlich beschränkter Dauer sind (Certeau 1980, 345, 351–352). Räume sind folglich geschichtlich, im Sinne von ‚geworden'. Im Gegensatz zum Ort, definiert durch seine Objekte, ist der Raum weder stabil noch eindeutig, da er auf Handlungen von vergänglichen Subjekten beruht.

Der Strand, der die Schwelle zwischen Meer und Land anzeigt und daher in besonderem Maße als liminal bezeichnet werden kann, lässt sich in dem Sinne als Raum begreifen. Allerdings gilt der Strand auch als peripher, da die Natur *per se* jeglichen Eingriff in diesen Raum zu einem vorläufigen macht, das heißt, der Strand kann nur bedingt ein politischer oder soziokultureller Handlungsraum sein. Und insofern mag die stete naturbedinge Veränderung (infolge der Gezeiten, Winde und Regenfälle) womöglich etwas Statisches, im Sinne von ‚Undurchdringlichem' gewinnen, was eher Orte kennzeichnet. Doch können Orte durch Erzählungen zu Räumen und umgekehrt Räume zu Orten werden. Die Grenze ist fließend und die Wahrnehmung vom Standpunkt des Betrachters abhängig: Entweder man erkennt eine statische Anordnung von Objekten, die als Bild beschreibbar ist, oder man nimmt Dinge in Bewegung und in Bezügen zueinander wahr. Beide Arten der Erzählung – eine Erzählung des Raumes wie auch eine Erzählung des Ortes – können sich überlappen. Und dies ist in Forsters naturanthropologischer Beschreibung der Insel Tanna und in seiner „völlig neuartigen Vorstellung des ‚Strandes'", auf die Takashi Mori, allerdings ohne nähere Erläuterung, verweist (Mori 2011, 68), durchaus der Fall.

Der Standort zwischen bewegtem Meer und aktivem Vulkan erscheint aus der Perspektive Forsters als ausgesprochen vielseitig:[6] So dient der Strand der Vulkaninsel des südwestpazifischen Inselstaates Vanuatu Cooks Seefahrern in erster Linie der Beschaffung neuer Wasser- und Nahrungsvorräte. Zugleich ist er aber auch eine interkulturelle Begegnungsfläche und ein provisorischer Handlungsraum, der mit eigenen Regeln versehen und genutzt wird für das Aushandeln von materiellen und immateriellen Werten. Wie Bödeker (2006, 149) schreibt, nimmt der Handel eine zentrale Bedeutung in der Begegnung zwischen Europäern und Einheimischen ein – ob Forster aber dadurch den Fortgang der Zivilisation wirklich so sehr befördert sieht, bleibt fragwürdig.

Einerseits fungiert der Strand als Peripherie, Grenzgebiet, Niemandsland und andererseits als semiotisch übersetzter Raum (vgl. Lotman 1990), in dem militärische Demonstrationen und Friedensverhandlungen, der Austausch von Waren und kulturellem Wissen, wissenschaftliche Erkundungen und amouröse Abenteuer, Grenzziehungen und Grenzauflösungen stattfinden. Inmitten dieser südpazifischen Grenzlandschaft verbreiten die Europäer nicht nur ihre Geschlechtskrankheiten, sondern werben auch für das Projekt ‚Zivilisation', das sich zunächst einmal von kolonialistischen Eroberungsfeldzügen deutlich abzugrenzen sucht. Schließlich unterstand Kapitän Cook klaren „Verhaltensbefehle[n]": träfe man Einwohner an, so sollten deren Charakter, Temperament, Genie und Anzahl bemerkt und „wo möglich freundschaftliche[r] Umgang mit ihnen" gesucht werden (Forster 1989a, I, 36–37). Als Hauptzweck der Expedition gilt die wissenschaftliche Erkundung. So zumindest lautet der Auftrag an

---

[6] Forsters positive, nahezu verlockende Beschreibungen der Küstenregionen kontrastieren das von Edmund Burke (1990 [1757], 65–76) verbreitete Bild des Strandes als ‚privation', ‚vastness', ‚infinity' und ‚sublime'.

Cook und dementsprechend – als Beispiel *par excellence* für die friedlichen Absichten dieses Entdeckungszeitalters – wurden seine Reisen und Berichte auch rezipiert (vgl. Peitsch 2005, 78; Ritter 2003, 20).

Der junge Forster hat trotz – oder womöglich wegen – seiner geringen Schulbildung eigene Ansichten zur Zivilisation. Zwar stellt er an keiner Stelle seine Zugehörigkeit oder Funktion unter der britischen Krone in Frage (wie sollte er auch?), doch ist sein Reisebericht – die distanzierte, sacht ironische Beschreibung der Europäer, wie sie am Strand der Tanneser, deren Kultur sie nicht kennen, ihre eigenen Regeln aufstellen – mit Skepsis grundiert.

> Von Westen kam ein Haufe von etwa 150 Wilden her, die allesammt, in der einen Hand Waffen, in der andern aber grüne Palmzweige trugen. Diese überreichten sie uns als Friedenszeichen, und wir beschenkten sie dagegen mit Medaillen, Tahitischem Zeug und Eisenwerk, tauschten auch für dergleichen Waaren etliche Cocosnüsse ein […]. Hierauf verlangten wir, daß sie sich alle niedersetzen mögen, welches auch zum Theil geschahe, und alsdann ward ihnen angedeutet, daß sie eine in den Sand gezogene Linie nicht überschreiten sollten […]. (Forster 1989a, II, 206–207)

Gilt seit dem *spatial turn* schon der Raum an sich nicht mehr als ein Objekt oder Behälter, in dem sich Menschengruppen und Kulturen befinden, sondern vielmehr als das Ergebnis sozialer Beziehungen, die ein Interesse und Handeln einzelner Menschen oder Gruppen voraussetzen, so trifft dies insbesondere für den Raum des Strandes bei Forster zu: Der reale Naturraum zwischen Meer und Festland ist nicht dauerhaft bewohnbar und kann allenfalls eine Stellvertreterfunktion einnehmen. Umso entschiedener formieren sich die Ansprüche auf Durchsetzung der eigenen sozialen und kulturellen Werte. Die in den Sand gezogene Linie übernimmt die Funktion der Normen und Institutionen, durch welche eine Gesellschaft ihre Werte zu legitimieren und umzusetzen sucht. Da es sich aber um einen liminalen Naturraum handelt, ohne allseits anerkannte Besitzrechte, muss der Anspruch an die anderen, eine bestimmte Normsetzung (die Sandlinie) und das damit verbundene Wertesystem anzuerkennen, erst ausgehandelt werden. Infolge der topologischen Wende, des sogenannten *topographical turn* (Weigel 2002), wird der Raum nicht mehr nur als Objekt betrachtet. Es wird konsequenterweise auch nicht *der* Raum gedacht, vielmehr gilt es, *räumlich zu denken* und in dem Sinne den Raum Strand als eine eigene Analysekategorie zu fassen (Bachmann-Medick 2013, 697). Und genau dies scheint Forster zu tun: Der Strand ist nach seiner Beschreibung nicht einfach gegeben, er wird vielmehr permanent produziert, d. h. kulturell konstituiert, und ist infolgedessen in seiner Bedeutung veränderbar.

3 Grenzziehung und Grenzüberschreitung

Ausgehend von der Erfahrung, die Forster zuvor monatelang auf dem Meer gemacht hat und die auch im Hinblick auf den feuerspeienden Vulkan greifbar nahe liegt – eine sich permanent in Bewegung befindende Natur, auf die der Mensch angemessen zu reagieren hat –, erscheint auch der Strand als Bewegungsbild. Er vermittelt die Erfahrung einer flüchtigen Gleichzeitigkeit von divergenten Ordnungen, Selbst- und Fremdbildern. Und mitten hinein ziehen Cooks Seesoldaten eine Linie in den Sand und verbieten den Insulanern, diese zu überschreiten.

Bildlich gesprochen, haben wir es mit der Errichtung eines Stilllebens zu tun, mitten in einem bewegten, sich stets verändernden Naturraum. Allerdings entsteht mit der Grenzziehung kein friedliches Stillleben, vielmehr eine militärisch durchgesetzte Ordnung, die vom Wasser aus geschützt wird mit quergestellten Schiffen, „damit die Kanonen das Land bestreichen", während die „See-Soldaten" mit „einer wohlbewafneten Parthey Matrosen" an Land gehen (Forster 1989a, II, 210).

> Während dieser Zeit hatten die Soldaten sich in Ordnung gestellt, und die Indianer bezeigten so viel Furcht vor ihnen, daß sie, bey der geringsten Bewegung derselben, allemal eine Ecke fortliefen; nur etliche alte Männer waren so herzhaft sich dadurch nicht erschrecken zu lassen. Wir verlangten, daß sie ihre Waffen von sich legen sollten, welcher Forderung, so unbillig sie an sich auch seyn mochte, dennoch von mehresten Genüge geleistet wurde. (Ebd., 207)

Diese ,unbillige' Forderung und das mit starkem Geschütz aufgebotene Bemühen um Selbstvergewisserung registriert Forster durchaus kritisch. Mit Genugtuung beschreibt er, angesichts der militärischen Aufstellung, die Reaktion und Verwegenheit eines Insulaners, „uns den Hintern zu zeigen und mit der Hand darauf zu klatschen, welches, unter allen Völkern im Süd-Meer, das gewöhnliche Zeichen zur Herausforderung ist" (ebd., 210). Dass zumindest einige Insulaner den Befehl der gerüsteten Engländer, die Waffen niederzulegen, ignorieren, verwundert Forster keineswegs: „vielleicht kam es ihnen gar unbillig und lächerlich vor, daß eine Handvoll Fremde sich's beygehen ließ, ihnen, in ihrem eigenen Lande, Gesetze vorzuschreiben." (Ebd., 211) Indessen gelingt es den Europäern auf dem beinahe leeren Sandstrand „See-Soldaten in zwei Linien" aufzustellen, um „Pfähle in die Erde" zu schlagen und einen „Strick dazwischen" zu ziehen,

> so daß die Wasserschöpfer einen Platz von wenigstens 150 Fus breit inne hatten, wo sie ihre Arbeit ohngestört vornehmen konnten. Nach und nach kamen die Einwohner, aus

dem Gebüsch, auf den Strand; wir winkten ihnen aber jenseits unsrer Linien zu bleiben […]. Der Capitain wiederholte nun seine vorige Zumuthung, daß sie ihre Waffen niederlegen mögen. (Ebd., 212)

Der Text lässt Fragen offen, z. B. nach der Legitimation dieser Grenzziehung, die einen politischen Diskurs eröffnen kann. Der Anspruch auf den fremden Raum inkludiert die Durchsetzung mitgebrachter Ordnungsmuster, die als Platzhalter für Europa fungieren, das mit Zivilisation und zivilisatorischer Überlegenheit gleichgesetzt wird. Noch bemerkenswerter aber ist die *Beschreibung* dieser Grenzziehung. Die gewaltsam geforderte Einhaltung der in den Sand gezogenen Grenze verschleiert nur unzulänglich die Willkür der Grenzziehung. Sie erscheint umso kontroverser und widersprüchlicher, je mehr Durchsetzungskraft die Europäer für ihre Verteidigung aufbringen. Um den gegenseitigen Handel (z. B. Nägel gegen Lebensmittel oder die auf der Insel befindlichen Schweine) durchzusetzen, erinnert Cook die Insulaner zunächst „durch Zeichen" an ihr gegebenes Wort, und wo dies nicht die erwünschte Wirkung hervorruft, greift er zur „Flintenkugel", was man wiederum „auf dem Schiffe für ein Signal hielt", das „grobe Geschütz" aufzufahren und mit einem Male „5 vierpfündige[] Kanonen, zwey halbpfündige[] Dreh-Bassen", und „vier Musketons" abzufeuern (ebd., 211). „Die Kugeln pfiffen über die Indianer weg, und kappten etliche Palmbäume; dadurch erreichten wir unseren Zweck, daß nemlich in wenig Augenblicken nicht ein Mann mehr auf dem Strande zu sehen war." (Ebd., 211)

Allerdings signalisiert die Grenze nicht nur Macht und Feindseligkeit, sie markiert zugleich den Anspruch auf ein eigenes Territorium als Schutzraum und zur lebensnotwendigen Nahrungsbeschaffung. Und gegenüber den Tannesern, die, stets mit Keulen bewaffnet, den Seeleuten die Wege ins Innere der Insel verwehren, wird mit der Grenzziehung auch eine Verhandlungsbasis geschaffen, die eine gewisse Gleichheit zwischen den verschiedenen Völkern, durch Ausgleich der Besitzverhältnisse, etabliert. Darüber hinaus ließe sich im Rückgriff auf den zeitgenössischen philosophischen Diskurs behaupten, dass die Wahrnehmung der Welt erst infolge von Grenzen und Grenzziehungen möglich wird.

Vier Jahre bevor Forster mit Cooks Mannschaft in See sticht, erscheint Immanuel Kants Abhandlung „Von dem ersten Grunde des Unterschiedes der Gegenden im Raum" (1768). Darin verknüpft Kant die Möglichkeit, die Welt zu erkennen an eine vorausgehende Funktionalität des Raumes und der Zeit (Kant 1912, 375). Der Raum gilt bereits im achtzehnten Jahrhundert als operatives Element des Verstandes, mit dem die Wirklichkeit konstruiert wird. Unser Logos, oder besser gesagt, die Logozentrizität, von der Kant ausgeht, ist räumlich vorstrukturiert und umgekehrt der Begriff Raum als eine reine Anschauung und daher in eine Vernunftidee zu fassen. Zwar ist der Raum, nach Kant, sowohl von empirischer Realität als auch von transzendentaler Idealität und somit offen für ganz unterschiedliche Inhalte, doch folgt die Vernunft zugleich dem Gesetz des Widerspruchs, demzufolge Entgegengesetztes zu gleicher Zeit nicht möglich ist. Die in den Sand gezogene Linie markiert eine Unterscheidung zwischen dem Einen und dem Anderen, dem Eigenen und dem Fremden. Sie fungiert als Grenze und Abgrenzung und zugleich als eine Kategorie zur Herstellung von Ordnung, die einen Standort, eine Perspektive ermöglicht.

Anders als Kant, geht Forster allerdings nicht von binären Differenzstrukturen aus, sondern – darin ähnlich unserer postkolonialen Moderne – von einem offenen „Kontingenzfeld, wo politische und kulturelle Differenzen nicht auf bleibende Weise aufhebbar, sondern höchstens vorübergehend verhandelbar erscheinen" (Mehigan und Corkhill 2013, 15). Die von den Europäern gezogene Linie in den Sand ist nicht nur lesbar als der Anspruch auf einen eigenen mit Bedeutung erfüllbaren Raum in Abgrenzung zum Raum der Anderen, sondern auch als ein Versuch, dem Strand insgesamt eine Ordnung zu verleihen. In ihrer offensichtlichen Unbeständigkeit und Vergänglichkeit stellt die Sandlinie allerdings die nicht an sich erkennbare, sondern gewaltsam erhobene Ordnung bereits in Frage. Der Strand bleibt das Kontingenzfeld – offen für unterschiedliche (soziale) Ordnungen, die von der unberechenbaren Natur jederzeit aufgehoben werden können. Aufgrund der Liminalität der Grenze innerhalb dieses liminalen Raumes ließen sich Grenzziehungen als solche womöglich überhaupt in Frage stellen – wäre es nicht zu einer Grenzüberschreitung gekommen, mit nicht wieder gut zu machenden Folgen. „Keine Grenze ohne Grenzübertritt", behauptet Dieter Lamping in seiner Schrift zur literarischen Topographie (Lamping 2001, 12–13). Ohne ihre eigene Überwindung, ihre eigene Aufhebung ist die Grenze folglich nicht zu denken. Die Grenzüberschreitung am Strand zu Tanna hat – anders als die Grenzziehung – unumkehrbare Folgen und kann daher nicht als vorläufig betrachtet werden.

Hinzu kommt die einseitige Ahndung der Grenzüberschreitung, welche die Frage aufwirft nach der Legitimität der Grenze, ihrer Überschreitung und der Bestrafung infolge der Überschreitung.

> Man hatte, wie gewöhnlich, eine Schildwacht ausgestellt, die den Platz, den unsere Leute zu ihren Geschäften brauchten, von Indianern rein halten mußte, dahingegen die Matrosen diese Scheidelinie ohne Bedenken überschreiten, und sich nach Belieben unter die Wilden mischen durften. (Forster 1989a, II, 271)

Das Bizarre an dieser Szene wird mit dem einleitenden Hinweis auf das gewöhnliche, alltägliche Vorgehen zusätzlich gesteigert: Für die eigenen Geschäfte muss der Platz „von Indianern rein" gehalten werden. Die Idee der Reinheit entstammt dem Sakralen, in dessen Kontext eine heilige Stätte nur dann betretbar ist, wenn die Person sich zuvor rituell gereinigt hat. Hier aber gehört die ‚heilige Stätte' den profanen Geschäften der fremden Ankömmlinge, die sich ihrerseits „unter die Wilden mischen", sich also völlig zwanglos und schamfrei hybridisieren.

Als folgenschweres Defizit europäischer Verständigung in dieser ohnehin äußerst misslichen Situation beschreibt Forster das Verhalten seiner Landsleute gegenüber einem „Indianer[], der vielleicht seit unserm Hierseyn noch nie am Strande gewesen seyn mochte" und „den freyen Platz" zu betreten sucht.

> Weil aber unsere Leute diesen für sich allein zu haben meynten; so nahm die Schildwache den Indianer beym Arm, und stieß ihn zurück. Dieser hingegen glaubte mit Recht, daß ihm, auf seiner eigenen Insel, ein Fremder nichts vorzuschreiben habe, und versuchte es daher von neuem, über den Platz wegzugehen, vielleicht blos um zu zeigen, daß er gehen könne, wo es ihm beliebe. Allein, die Schildwache sties ihn zum zweytenmal, und zwar mit solchem Ungestüm zurück, daß wohl ein minder jähzorniger Mann, als ein Wilder, dadurch hätte aufgebracht werden müssen. Kein Wunder also, daß er, um seine gekränkte Freyheit zu vertheidigen, einen Pfeil auf den Bogen legte, und damit nach dem, der ihm angegriffen, zielte. Dies ward der Soldat nicht sobald gewahr, als er sein Gewehr anschlug, und den Indianer auf der Stelle todt schoß. (Ebd., 272)

Angesichts dieser empörenden, jeder Humanität entbehrenden Grenzüberschreibung der Europäer vermag Forster die eigenen Werturteile nicht zurückzuhalten: Die „gekränkte Freyheit" habe den Indianer veranlasst, seine Rechte zu verteidigen, während die „grausamen" Gäste „auf fremdem Boden sich solche Ungerechtigkeiten erlaubten" (ebd.).

Dabei war Forster während des Geschehens gar nicht zugegen. Er selbst war nämlich im Inneren der Insel unterwegs, und zwar allein, ohne sich vor den Eingeborenen – die sich mehrfach „durch die deutlichsten Zeichen [...] für Menschenfresser ausgaben" (ebd., 245, vgl. 208, 234) – zu fürchten. Und während er so in den Wäldern und entlang der Äcker spaziert, „mit dem herzerhebenden Gedanken an Freundschaft und Volksglückseligkeit", wird ihm die Insel Tanna „im Säuseln des kühlen Seewindes" zu einem leibhaftigen „Gemählde", einem „Sinnbild des Friedens und Überflusses" (ebd., 269–270). Er verliert sich in eine „Reihe von Betrachtungen über den Nutzen, den unser hiesiger Aufenthalt unter den Insulanern gestiftet haben könnte" und findet unermessliches „Vergnügen" in dem „beruhigende[n], damals noch ganz ahndungsfreye[n] Gedanke[n], daß wir uns hier, zur Ehre der Menschheit in einem sehr vortheilshaften Lichte gezeigt hätten!" (Ebd., 270)

> Wir hatten nun vierzehn Tage unter einem Volke zugebracht, das sich anfänglich äußerst mißtrauisch und ganz entschlossen bewieß, auch die geringste Feindseligkeit nicht ungeahndet zu lassen. [...] Sobald wir es einmal *dahin* gebracht hatten, jenen heftigen, aufbrausenden Naturtrieb, der allein die Wilden so argwöhnisch, scheu und feindselig macht (Selbsterhaltung) zu besänftigen, sobald sahe man auch schon in ihren rohen Seelen jenen zweyten, nicht minder starken Naturtrieb – Geselligkeit – aufkeimen und sich entwickeln. [...] Nach wenig Tagen begannen sie sogar, an unsrer Gesellschaft Vergnügen zu finden, und *nun* öffnete sich ihr Herz einem neuen uneigennützigen Gefühl von überirdischer Art, der Freundschaft! Welch ein schätzbares Bewußtseyn, rief ich aus, auf solche Art das Glück eines Volkes befördert und vermehrt zu haben! welch ein Vortheil, einer gesitteten Gesellschaft anzugehören, die solche Vorzüge genießt und anderen mittheilt! (Ebd., 270–271)

Die kurz vor der Erschießung des Insulaners mit so viel Pathos vorgetragene Lobeshymne auf die interkulturelle Kompetenz der Europäer wirkt aus Forsters Mund doppelbödig, wenn nicht gar verräterisch. Die Betrachtungen über den Nutzen ihres Aufenthaltes unter den indigenen Völkern erscheinen schon an dieser Stelle kaum glaubwürdig. Nach dem Mord, den Forster als „die offenbahreste Grausamkeit" beschreibt (ebd., 273), verkehren sich schließlich die Zuschreibungen von Sittlichkeit ins Gegenteil, und es folgt der zum geflügelten Wort avancierte Ausruf der Verzweiflung: „Was mußten die Wilden von uns denken?" (Ebd.) Damit kennzeichnet Forster die Entdeckungsreise nicht nur als eine Bewährungsprobe für Aufklärung und Zivilisation, er konfrontiert den Leser zugleich auch mit der Perspektive der ‚Entdeckten' (May 2005, 4), die womöglich gar nicht „den Wunsch hatten, erforscht, noch das Bedürfnis, entdeckt, noch das Verlangen danach, ausgebeutet zu werden, ausgetrickst und ausmanövriert" (Gomsu 2006, 323). So bleibt es auf prekäre Weise unbestimmt, welches Bewusstsein welches Glück von welchem Volk zu fördern vermag.

Das eben noch mit Stolz verkündete Selbstbewusstsein, als Glücksbringer fremder Völker unterwegs zu sein, wird augenblicklich abgelöst von der Scham, sich in eine Gemeinschaft voll unschuldiger Menschen „unter dem Schein der Freundschaft eingeschlichen [zu haben], um sie hernach als Meuchelmörder zu tödten" (Forster 1989a, II, 273). Schon die Pluralsetzung verrät, dass es sich hierbei – nämlich „das vornehmste Gebot der Gastfreyheit so schändlich aus den Augen" verloren zu haben (ebd., 272) – um keinen Einzelfall handelt: „Dergleichen Übereilungen waren uns fast aller Orten begegnet, und der Schade nirgends gut zu machen gewesen." (Ebd., 273) Und auch wenn es dieses Mal ‚nur' einen einzigen Einwohner traf, sei es „darum doch nicht weniger zu bedauern, daß Europäer sich so oft ein Strafrecht über Leute anmaßen, die mit ihren

Gesetzen so ganz unbekannt sind." (Ebd., 457) Ist das Projekt ‚Zivilisation' am Strand von Tanna also gescheitert – aufgrund jener Gewalttat, die aller Vernunft und Sittlichkeit widerspricht?

4 Im Vorhof des Vulkans

Für den jungen Reisenden, gerühmt als einfühlsamer Ethnologe (vgl. Fischer 2006, 177), wird jener unbestimmte und zugleich von divergierenden Vorstellungen, Dynamiken, Praktiken und Ästhetiken überladende Strandraum zum Prüfstein der Frage nach den Bedingungen und Folgen des europäischen Zivilisationsprojekts, das, nach Forsters Beschreibung, von Anfang an in einem Dilemma zu stecken scheint – mit tragikomischen Zügen.[7] Auffallend ist dazu das gewaltige Bühnenbild, der Vulkan, der mehrfach und immer so beschrieben wird, als sähe Forster ihn zum ersten Mal: „Um den Faden dieser Erzählung nicht zu unterbrechen, habe ich von einem merkwürdigen Phänomen, dem auf dieser Insel vorhandenen Volcan, bisher noch nichts erwähnen können" (Forster 1989a, II, 208), obwohl er dies wenige Seiten zuvor getan hat. Forster beschreibt den Vulkan hier weder zum ersten Mal noch setzt er eine „Erzählung" fort. Oder doch?

Dem Satz unmittelbar voraus geht die Beschreibung der ersten Kontaktaufnahme:

> Sobald die Fässer gefüllt waren, kehrten wir ans Schiff zurück, ganz erfreut, daß der erste Schritt zur Bekanntschaft mit den Eingebohrnen glücklich geschehen und so ruhig abgelaufen sey. Am folgenden Morgen zeigte sich aber, daß die Insulaner nur in Ermangelung einer größern Anzahl so friedlich gegen uns verfahren, im Grunde aber keineswegs gesonnen waren, uns freyen Zugang in ihre Insel zu gestatten. Sie befürchteten, daß wir auf ihr Land und anderes Eigenthum Absichten hätten, und machten daher Anstalt, beydes zu vertheidigen. Um den Faden dieser Erzählung [...]. (Ebd.)

Handelt es sich hierbei tatsächlich um eine Erzählung, und wenn ja, in welchem Sinne – womöglich im Sinne der Narration, einer literarischen Gattung, die neben dem Inhalt auch einen Subtext transportiert, der sich nicht erschöpft in der historischen Berichterstattung, sondern auch Elemente der Poetik, der Fiktion enthält?

Ins Auge fallen die zahlreichen Zitate aus der Literatur der antiken Dichter Plinius, Horaz und Vergil, aus Shakespeares *Henry IV* und Miltons *Paradise*

---

[7] Jan Philipp Reemtsma (1998, 30–31) beschreibt den Aufenthalt zu Tanna als ein Drama in fünf Akten.

Lost, dazu intertextuelle Verweise auf Louis Antoine de Bougainvilles *Reise um die Welt* (1766–1769), die Forster vor der eigenen Reise ins Englische übersetzt hatte. Auch seine Naturbeschreibungen wirken ungewöhnlich poetisch und für die zeitgenössischen Rezensenten irritierend[8] – exemplarisch die Ankunft auf Tahiti, dem „locos laetos & amoena vireta", mit der bekannten Einleitung: „Ein Morgen war's, schöner hat ihn schwerlich je ein Dichter beschrieben." (Forster 1989a, I, 155; vgl. Fischer 2006, 185; Görbert 2015)

Was hier, im Kapitel zu Tanna, die ‚Erzählung' unterbricht und gleichzeitig fortsetzt, ist die immer wiederkehrende Rede über den Vulkan, dessen ungeheure Macht als „ein angenehmes und zugleich prächtiges Schauspiel" rezipiert wird (Forster 1989a, II, 219). Dem ästhetischen Genuss geht ein an den wissenschaftlichen Erkenntnissen dieser Zeit orientiertes Naturverständnis voraus. Jenes Naturereignis, das bis ins 18. Jahrhundert hinein verbunden wird mit dem Konzept eines religiösen Gefühls des Erhabenen, wird einerseits demystifiziert (vgl. Begemann 1987, 111); andererseits widersetzt sich die Natur, in Forsters Beschreibung, einer von kolonialen Interessen ausgehenden Wahrnehmung und Verfügbarmachung. Zwar löst der Vulkan weder Schrecken noch Schmerz aus (vgl. Burke 1990), doch verlockt er zu einer Denkfigur, in der verschiedene Ordnungen und Wahrnehmungskategorien aufeinander stoßen und sich teilweise gegenseitig überschreiten. So vermag der Vulkan im Reisenden, Ende des 18. Jahrhunderts, nicht unbedingt eine religiöse Ergriffenheit auszulösen, aber doch ein Erstaunen, das zu einer Erweiterung der Kategorien der Beurteilung führt: Die ungestüme, lebensbedrohliche Naturgewalt (und nicht mehr nur die übermäßige Naturgröße) wird zum ästhetischen Genuss (vgl. Weber 2015, 220), der sich im Falle Forsters allerdings nicht aus der Annahme der Moderne begründet, die Natur sei von nun an beherrschbar. Vielmehr erweckt die unbeherrschbare Natur auch deshalb sein Gefallen, weil Forster, ab 1789 Anhänger der Französischen Revolution, sie als Gleichnis für die Unbeherrschbarkeit und Freiheit des Menschen versteht. Die aufklärerische Vernunft befähigt das empfindsame Subjekt, Korrelationen zwischen dem Einzelnen und dem Ganzen zu erstellen, als Teil dieser begrifflich unerschließbaren Totalität fühlt sich das Subjekt in seiner Existenz berauscht (ebd., 233). Der aktive Vulkan wird hier zu einer ästhetischen Orientierungsgröße, die eine ständige Bezugnahme erlaubt und so auch die Erzählung mit strukturiert. „Je dunkler dieses [d. i. die Regennacht die Finsterniß machte, desto mahlerischer war es anzusehen, wie das

---

8 So wirft der Rezensent Johann Friedrich Gmelin in der *Allgemeinen deutschen Bibliothek* (1777) Forster vor: Er „spielt zu sehr, und oft ganz am unrechten Orte den empfindsamen Jüngling [...], streuet hin und wieder solche Raisonnements, die nicht zur Sache gehören, und hat die Gabe, mit vielen Worten wenig zu sagen" (zit. nach: Fischer 2006, 171).

Feuer des Volcans den aus dem Gipfel emporsteigenden dicken Rauch vergoldete." (Forster 1989a, II, 230)

Das malerische Bild von der vergoldeten Rauchsäule setzt also eine besonders ‚dunkle Finsternis' voraus – so dunkel, dass man die eigene Hand vor Augen nicht sieht, in der die unmittelbare Umgebung und der Beobachter selbst unkenntlich werden, dafür aber die Ferne, das Fremde in deutlicher Klarheit erstrahlen, gleich einem Gemälde, wie es heißt, das immer auch ein Kunstwerk und von Menschen erschaffen ist. Der ausbrechende Vulkan als Gemälde, welches die besagte ‚Erzählung' unterbricht, womit zugleich zwei Künste sich einander überlagern und der ‚Erzählung' einen doppelt fiktionalen Rahmen verleihen. Die Realität, das mit allen Sinnesorganen Wahrgenommene, empirisch Überprüfbare gewinnt an dieser Stelle eine neue Dimension, wird zu einer Surplusrealität, welche die Möglichkeiten der Imagination und vor allem unterschiedliche Verfahrensweisen mit der Realität miteinschließt. Der Bericht einer Reise um die Welt wird erweitert oder vielmehr eingebettet in eine Erzählung, die sich literarischer Verfahrensweisen bedient, und zwar um der Wahrheit willen. Und wovon handelt die ‚Erzählung'? – Von der Scheinfriedlichkeit der Insulaner, die tatsächlich „aber keineswegs gesonnen waren, uns freyen Zugang in ihre Insel zu gestatten" und ihr Land und Eigentum „zu vertheidigen" suchten; erzählt wird also die *story* von der Unzivilisiertheit der Wilden.

Diese *story* entspricht der Vorlage der Engländer und dem angefertigten Bericht Johann Reinhold Forsters, den der Sohn nur geringfügig auszuschmücken hatte. Georg Forster übernimmt also die Denkweisen und Ansichten der Entdecker, und indem er sie mittels poetischer Versatzstücke einbettet und nicht ohne Raffinesse zugleich als Erzählung ausweist, hat er alles – ohne plumpen Widerspruch – gesagt. Die Schilderung der barbarischen Südseebewohner, denen die Europäer dank ihrer Menschenliebe die Zivilisation bringen, wird mittels zarter Verweise auf literarästhetische Strategien als eine der Realität nicht entsprechende und auch nicht wünschenswerte Utopie erkennbar. Es handelt sich um die Darstellung einer Fiktion, die sich selbst als solche entlarvt durch Widerspiegelung und Umkehrung ins Gegenteil.

Und so entwirft Forster keinesfalls, wie in der Forschungsliteratur behauptet, seine Idealvorstellung von einer Lernbeziehung zwischen ‚zivilisierten Europäern' und ‚wilden Bewohnern' der Südsee, auch seine Mitleidsbekundungen sind viel zu widersprüchlich und ambivalent, als dass sie moralische Urteile bilden könnten (vgl. dagegen Ritter 2003, 29, 36–37). Vielmehr greift er auf die vorhandenen und mitgebrachten Bilder, Stereotypen, Klischees zurück, entwirft Gegenbilder und steigert die Antagonismen, Widersprüche durch ironische Übertreibung bis ins Absurde hinein, so dass auch das Gegenstück zu den ‚menschenfressenden Tannesern', nämlich das Bild von den beiden Männern im

Gras, die das Opfer des besagten ‚Meuchelmordes' in ihren Armen halten, kaum glaubhaft wird: „Zween Männer saßen im Grase und hielten einen Dritten, todt, in ihren Armen. Sie zeigten uns eine Wunde, die er von einer Flintenkugel in die Seite bekommen hatte und sagten dabey mit dem rührendsten Blick: ‚er ist umgebracht'." (Forster 1989a, II, 271)

Diese rührende Szene erinnert in der Tat, wie Ritter bemerkt, an die christliche Pietà. Allerdings erscheint es fragwürdig, ob sich dadurch das Opfer, der Fremde, der Eingeborene zu einem Jesus Christus eurozentrischer Wahrnehmung formiert (vgl. Ritter 2003, 38). Greift Forster nicht genau diese einseitigen Wahrnehmungsmuster – die Idealisierung des Opfers einerseits, die Idealisierung der interkulturellen Kompetenzen und Zivilisiertheit der Europäer andererseits – auf, um sie durch Übertreibung ins Lächerliche zu ziehen?

Immerhin beschreibt er an anderer Stelle das Verhalten der sogenannten „Wilden" – die ihm und seinem Begleiter während ihrer einsamen Inselspaziergänge „nicht das geringste Leid" zufügen, gleichwohl „sie doch den Mord ihres Landmannes an uns beyden aufs nachdrücklichste hätten rächen können" – als eine „seltne Mäßigung" (Forster 1989a, II, 272). Nun ließe sich dies als glücklicher Ausnahmezustand, als idyllisches Gegenbild zu den ‚wilden Barbaren' oder als Relativierung alles zuvor Behaupteten lesen (vgl. Fischer 2006, 173). Doch nicht nur die Beschreibung der Insel Tanna, vielmehr der gesamte Reisebericht changiert zwischen Kritik an der europäischen Zivilisation und pathetischen Lobeshymnen auf die Vorteile von Zivilisation und Fortschritt (vgl. Prinz 2008, 78), lesbar als eine Textstrategie, die auf folgende Erkenntnis abzielt: Forster erörtert ganz unterschiedliche Beobachtungen und Möglichkeiten, Denkbarkeiten von Verhaltensweisen, für die es jeweils Gründe und Geschichten gibt, nicht aber durch Ethnie oder Nation begründete Eigenschaftsmerkmale.

Und damit wären wir wieder beim Vulkan, dessen Ausbruch auch die Erzählungen vom ‚edlen Wilden' wie auch vom ‚menschenfressenden Insulaner', vom ‚zivilisierten Europäer' wie auch vom ‚kriegerischen Eroberer' stets unterbricht. Der Vulkan, zugleich Faszination wie auch Verstörung auslösend, lässt sich nicht zu einem Stillbild formieren. Er bleibt aktiv, in Bewegung, widersetzt sich in dem Sinne der Verortung, der Kategorisierung. Er ist vielmehr selbst die Kategorie, nach der die Wirklichkeit wahrgenommen wird: als immer wieder einbrechendes Ereignis, das in seiner Maßlosigkeit alle Ordnungsmuster übersteigt und in dem Sinne die Handlung fortsetzt.

Vor dieser Kulisse erscheint die in den Sand gezogene willkürliche und vorläufige Grenze, mit der die Europäer unbedingten Gehorsam einfordern, wie ein künstliches Requisit, das ganz offenbar nicht hierher passt. Gegenüber dem Aufgebot der Insulaner, die Ankömmlinge mit Bitten, Erklärungen und Drohungen vom Inneren der Insel fernzuhalten, sie notfalls totzuschlagen und aufzufressen, wirkt die durch den Sand gezogene Grenze, die sich aus nichts anderem begründet als der Herrschergeste der Engländer, schlichtweg künstlich. Und diese künstliche Grenze, die sowohl eine Trennung zwischen Zivilisierten und Wilden, Eigenem und Fremdem postuliert als auch Unterschiede proklamiert, steht im Gegensatz zur Natur, die weder gut noch schlecht ist, sondern schlichtweg gewaltig und durch ihre selbstverständliche Kraft ihre Relevanz zu behaupten vermag.

Indem sich Forster literarischer Stilmittel und narratologischer Spannungsmuster bedient, indem seine Beschreibungen der Europäer und Insulaner sich als situationsabhängig entpuppen und keinesfalls den Anspruch auf zuverlässige Charakterstudien erheben, sich vielmehr widersprechen, und indem sich Forster als Augenzeuge eines Mordes vorstellt, obwohl er ganz offensichtlich nicht dabei gewesen ist, inszeniert und entlarvt er sich als ‚unzuverlässiger Erzähler', und zwar ganz gezielt: so unzuverlässig wie unbeständig, unstet und wechselhaft, Zeiten und Gezeiten ausgeliefert wie die Sandkörner des Küstenstreifens, der „überall von verschiedener Gestalt und Beschaffenheit" ist (Forster 1989a, II, 209).

Der Strand wird in seiner naturbedingten Fragilität und Vorläufigkeit nicht nur beschrieben, sondern gleichsam in Sprache gesetzt. Ein Zwischenraum, in dem Dinge aufgebaut und wieder verworfen werden, in dem Bedeutungen geschaffen werden, die sich als fragil erweisen, in dem Zuschreibungen gemacht und als widersprüchlich erkannt werden. In dem alles stattfindet, was auch in gewachsenen Gesellschaften stattfindet – aber eben im Bewusstsein der Vorläufigkeit, im Bewusstsein, dass alles vergeht, wie die Spuren im Sand verwehen oder alles auch ganz anders sein kann. Und jeder Versuch der Selbstvergewisserung umso größere Selbstzweifel nach sich zieht. Und wo die aufgeklärte Vernunft an ihre Grenzen kommt – angesichts des permanent vorläufigen, fluiden und unberechenbaren Standortes zwischen Meer und Festland, der dem Menschen immer auch die eigene Sterblichkeit vor Augen führt. Und wo sich die Frage nach einer anthropologischen Konstante stellt, die aber weder sozial noch politisch oder ästhetisch eindeutig zu beantworten ist. Mitten in dieser Offenheit und Unabschließbarkeit, im Approximativen und Versuchhaften von Inhalt und Form (Ewert 1993, 8–9), fungiert der Strand so auch als Möglichkeitsraum, in dem Handlungsoptionen durchgespielt werden (Mein 2007, 53) und immer auch die Möglichkeit besteht, diesem ganzen Dilemma zu entschwinden, die Fahne zu hissen und – wie Cooks Seemannschaft – wieder abzusegeln.

5 Fazit

Zum Schluss noch einmal auf unsere Eingangsfrage nach dem europäischen Projekt ‚Zivilisation' zurückzukommen, stellt sich die Frage: Was bleibt von diesen frühen Entdeckungen, Begegnungen, Auseinandersetzungen an diesem Küstenstreifen im fernen Südpazifik und was ließe sich heute damit anfangen? Georg Forsters Konzeption des Strandes ist heute aktueller denn je. Sie ist lesbar als Sinnbild unserer Zeit, die Foucault als eine Epoche des Raumes, des Simultanen, „des Nahen und Fernen, des Nebeneinander, des Auseinander" beschreibt (Foucault 1990, 34). Die errichteten und wieder verworfenen Ordnungen am Strand, die dem Raum die Signatur materieller und symbolischer Praktiken verleihen, können als prototypisch gelten; sie stehen für die wirklichen wie auch wirksamen Orte einer Zivilisation, die sich unter dem Begriff der „Heterotopie" bündeln lassen: realisierte Utopien, in denen Plätze repräsentiert, bestritten, entgegengesetzt oder zu Orten außerhalb aller Orte werden, gleichwohl sie geortet werden können. (Foucault 2001, 39)

Wenn es Heterotopien, also Räume mit unterschiedlichen gesellschaftlichen Bedeutungen und Zuschreibungen gibt, so mag es auch nicht nur einen, sondern unterschiedliche Wege zur Zivilisation und Moderne geben.[9] Forster schreibt sich einerseits in den zeitgenössischen hegemonialen westlichen Diskurs über die Entdeckung und Nutzbarmachung der Welt ein, entwickelt zugleich aber dialektische Diskursstränge, die sich der britischen Spielart des Imperialismus widersetzen.[10]

Die sichtbar gewordenen kulturellen Besonderheiten bleiben vage, fluide, ohne ins Manifeste überzugehen – beschreibbar als ein Dialog der Differenzen, in dem es Annäherungen, Überlagerungen wie auch Vertauschungen gibt. Der Vergleich zwischen Europäern und den Bewohnern der südpazifischen Inseln wird stets neu ausgehandelt und unterschiedlich konturiert. Keineswegs gesteht Forster den Europäern, bei all ihrer Fortschrittlichkeit, einen

---

[9] Joseph Gomsu (2006, 324), der sich auf Stuart Halls Annahme von verschiedenen möglichen Wegen zur Modernität beruft, stellt die Frage, ob es im Westen selbst andere Diskursstränge gab, die auf eine Modernität mit weniger Hegemonie, weniger Zerstörung und stattdessen mehr Anerkennung und Respekt für außereuropäische Gesellschaften zielten.

[10] In seinen philosophischen und zeitgeschichtlichen Schriften entwickelt Forster die Begriffe vom Globalen und Lokalen, um den Prozess der Angleichung und des Widerstands gegen die Angleichung zu entfalten. Während die Denkfigur des Globalen sich auf den Prozess der Homogenisierung richtet, versteht sich das Lokale als Widerstand gegen jegliche Globalisierungstendenzen zur Bewahrung heterogener Elemente von Ethnizität. Aus dieser Wechselwirkung zwischen Globalem und Lokalem lassen sich Prozesse der Hybridisierung rekonstruieren (Forster 1974; vgl. Gomsu 2006, 329).

unangefochtenen Führungsanspruch zu (dagegen May 2006, 352–353). Dagegen sprechen Textstruktur wie auch literarische Strategien und vor allem das Zusammenspiel von Erkenntnisfunktion und ästhetischer Relevanz. Alexander Gottlieb Baumgarten, Begründer einer eigenständigen Ästhetik als Fach, schrieb Mitte des achtzehnten Jahrhunderts der vergleichenden Praxis zwei Ordnungsfunktionen von Welt zu: eine abbildende (im Sinne der Nachahmung von Natur) und eine erprobende (im Sinne der Konstruktion von Zusammenhängen). (Müller 2017, 76) Gelesen mit Baumgarten, erschöpfen sich Forsters Augenzeugenberichte keineswegs in der faktischen Beschreibung oder dogmatischen Rede, vielmehr gewinnen sie auch eine visionäre und utopische Dimension, gerade wenn es um zwischenmenschliche Begegnungen geht, die mitunter so berührend sind, dass sie die mitgebrachten Wahrnehmungskategorien in Frage stellen. Für besonders bemerkenswert hält Forster das Ritual der freundschaftlichen Begegnung:

> [E]iner, dem die andern mit gewisser Achtung zu begegnen schienen, nahm meines Vaters Namen an, indem er ihm dafür den seinigen beylegte. Er hieß Umbjegan. Dieser Gebrauch, durch gegenseitige Vertauschung der Namen, Freundschaft mit einem andern zu errichten, ist auf allen Inseln des Süd-Meeres, so viel wir deren bisher besucht hatten, eingeführt, und hat würklich etwas verbindliches und zärtliches an sich. (Forster 1989a, II, 222)

Die mit der Vertauschung der Namen erwirkte Identifizierung mit dem Anderen lässt die abendländische Philosophie des Solipsismus merkwürdig karg erscheinen. Der freundschaftlich-verlockende Perspektivenwechsel unterläuft auf subtile Weise die Selbstgewissheit des aufgeklärten Europäers. Denn es geht nicht um die gewaltsame Entmachtung des Subjekts, sondern – was als durchaus schwerwiegender erlebt werden kann – um die zärtliche Verbindung des Einen mit dem Anderen, mit der jede Grenzziehung obsolet wird. Aus der Berührung resultiert der Wunsch nach Verbindlichkeit. So erweist sich die zarte Geste der Humanität als nicht minder wirksam als die Macht der Natur, dessen Inbegriff der Vulkan mit seinem rauchenden Gipfel und faszinierenden Farbenspiel ist, das immer wieder zu jener Bewegung zwischen Annäherung und Entfernung verlockt... und auch noch in der späteren Niederschrift der *Reise um die Welt* eine emphatische Erinnerung auszulösen vermag, die dem Leser seinerseits als stets aktualisierbare Imagination verfügbar bleibt.

Literaturverzeichnis

Bachmann-Medick, Doris. „Spatial turn". *Metzler Lexikon Literatur- und Kulturtheorie. Ansätze – Personen – Grundbegriffe*. Hg. Ansgar Nünning. 5. Aufl., Stuttgart und Weimar: J. B. Metzler, 2013. 697–698.

Begemann, Christian. *Furcht und Angst im Prozeß der Aufklärung: zu Literatur und Bewußtseinsgeschichte des 18. Jahrhunderts*. Frankfurt/Main: Athenäum, 1987.

Bödeker, Hans Erich. „Die ‚Natur des Menschen so viel möglich in mehreres Licht [...] setzen'. Ethnologische Praxis bei Johann Reinhold und Georg Forster". *Natur – Mensch – Kultur. Georg Forster im Wissenschaftsfeld seiner Zeit*. Hg. Jörn Garber und Tanja van Hoorn. Hannover-Laatzen: Wehrhahn, 2006. 143–170.

Burke, Edmund. *A Philosophical Enquiry into the Origin of Our Ideas of the Sublime and Beautiful* [1757]. Oxford und New York: Oxford University Press, 1990.

Certeau, Michel de. *Kunst des Handelns*. Aus dem Französischen von Ronald Voullié. Berlin: Merve, 1988.

Corbin, Alain. *Meereslust. Das Abendland und die Entdeckung der Küste 1750–1840*. Berlin: Fischer, 1990.

Ewert, Michael. *„Vernunft, Gefühl und Phantasie, im schönsten Tanze vereint". Die Essayistik Georg Forsters*. Würzburg: Königshausen & Neumann, 1993.

Fischer, Tilmann. „Denklust und Sehvergnügen. Zum Rollenwechsel in den Reisebeschreibungen Georg Forsters". *Natur – Mensch – Kultur. Georg Forster im Wissenschaftsfeld seiner Zeit*. Hg. Jörn Garber und Tanja van Hoorn. Hannover-Laatzen: Wehrhahn, 2006. 171–196.

Forster, Georg. *Sämmtliche Schriften*. Hg. von dessen Tochter, begleitet mit einer Charakteristik Forster's von Georg Gottfried Gervinus. Leipzig: Brockhaus, 1843.

Forster, Georg. *Kleine Schriften zu Philosophie und Zeitgeschichte. Werke. Sämtliche Schriften, Tagebücher, Briefe*. Bd. 8. Bearbeitet von Siegfried Scheibe. Berlin: Akademie-Verlag, 1974.

Forster, Georg. *„Reise um die Welt". Werke. Sämtliche Schriften, Tagebücher, Briefe*. Bd. 2–3. Bearbeitet von Gerhard Steiner. Berlin: Akademie-Verlag, 1989a.

Forster, Georg. *Ansichten vom Niederrhein, von Brabant, Flandern, Holland, England und Frankreich, im April, Mai und Junius 1790*. Hg. Ulrich Schlemmer. Stuttgart: Erdmann, 1989b.

Forster, Georg. *Schriften zur Naturkunde. Zweiter Teil. Werke. Sämtliche Schriften, Tagebücher, Briefe*. Bd. 6,2. Herausgegeben und bearbeitet von Klaus-Georg Popp. Berlin: Akademie-Verlag, 2003, 901–953.

Forster, Georg. *James Cook, der Entdecker und Fragmente über Capitain Cooks letzte Reise und sein Ende*. Herausgegeben und mit Nachwort Frank Vorpahl. Frankfurt/Main: Eichborn, 2008.

Foucault, Michel. „Andere Räume". *Aisthesis. Wahrnehmung heute oder Perspektiven einer anderen Ästhetik*. Hg. Karlheinz Barck, Peter Gente, Heidi Paris und Stefan Richter. Leipzig: Reclam, 1990. 34–46.

Garber, Jörn. „‚So sind also die Hauptbestimmungen des Menschen [...]'. Anmerkungen zum Verhältnis von Geographie und Menschheitsgeschichte bei Georg Forster". *Wahrnehmung – Konstruktion – Text. Bilder des Wirklichen im Werk Georg Forsters*. Hg. Jörn Garber. Tübingen: Niemeyer, 2000. 193–230.

Garber, Jörn. „Von der naturalistischen Menschheitsgeschichte (Georg Forster) zum gesellschaftswissenschaftlichen Positivismus (Friedrich Buchholz)". *Natur – Mensch – Kultur. Georg Forster im Wissenschaftsfeld seiner Zeit.* Hg. Jörn Garber und Tanja van Hoorn. Hannover-Laatzen: Wehrhahn, 2006. 53–78.

Görbert, Johannes. „,Ein Morgen war's, schöner hat ihn schwerlich je ein Dichter beschrieben.' Zur Textgenese von Georg Forsters literarischer Tahiti-Inszenierung". *Georg-Forster-Studien XX.* Hg. Stefan Greif und Michael Ewert. Kassel: Kassel University Press, 2015. 1–6.

Goethe, Johann Wolfgang. *Die Schriften zur Naturwissenschaft.* Hg. Dorothea Kuhn, Wolf von Engelhardt und Irmgard Müller. Begründet von Lothar K. Wolf und Wilhelm Troll. Weimar: Böhlau, 1947–2011.

Goldstein, Jürgen. *Georg Forster. Zwischen Freiheit und Naturgewalt.* Berlin: Matthes & Seitz, 2016.

Gomsu, Joseph. „,Über lokale und allgemeine Bildung': Georg Forsters Projekt einer anderen Moderne". *Georg-Forster-Studien XI/2.* Hg. Horst Dippel und Helmut Scheuer. Kassel: Kassel University Press, 2006. 323–334.

Graczyk, Annette. „Forschungsreise und Naturbild bei Georg Forster und Alexander von Humboldt". *Georg-Forster-Studien VI.* Hg. Horst Dippel und Helmut Scheuer. Kassel: Kassel University Press, 2001. 89–116.

Herder, Johann Gottfried. *Ideen zur Philosophie der Geschichte der Menschheit* (1784–1791). *Werke. 10 in 11 Bände, Bd. 6.* Hg. Martin Bollacher. Frankfurt/Main: Suhrkamp, 1989.

Hoorn, Tanja van. *Dem Leibe abgelesen. Georg Forster im Kontext der physischen Anthropologie des 18. Jahrhunderts.* Tübingen: Niemeyer, 2004.

Kant, Immanuel. „Von dem ersten Grunde des Unterschiedes der Gegenden im Raum". *Vorkritische Schriften II: 1857–1777. Kant's Gesammelte Schriften, Bd. I/2.* Hg. Königlich Preußische Akademie der Wissenschaften. Berlin: Reimer, 1912. 379–383.

Lamping, Dieter. *Über Grenzen – Eine literarische Topographie.* Göttingen: Vandenhoeck & Ruprecht, 2001.

Lethen, Helmut. *Verhaltenslehren der Kälte. Lebensversuche zwischen den Kriegen.* Frankfurt/Main: Suhrkamp, 1994.

Lotman, Juri M. „Über die Semiosphäre". *Zeitschrift für Semiotik* 12.4 (1990): 287–305.

May, Yomb. „,Was mußten die Wilden von uns denken?' – Georg Forster, der Entdecker als Kritiker". *Georg-Forster-Studien X.* Hg. Horst Dippel und Helmut Scheuer. Kassel: Kassel University Press, 2005. 1–20.

May, Yomb. „Pluralität und Ethos in Georg Forsters Anthropologie". *Georg-Forster-Studien XI/2.* Hg. Horst Dippel und Helmut Scheuer. Kassel: Kassel University Press, 2006. 335–357.

Mehigan, Tim, und Alan Corkhill. „Vorwort". *Raumlektüren. Der Spatial Turn und die Literatur der Moderne.* Hg. Tim Mehigan und Alan Corkhill. Bielefeld: transcript, 2013. 7–21.

Mein, Georg. „Raum als Analysekategorie in den Humanwissenschaften. Überlegungen im Spannungsfeld von Regionalität und Globalität". *Forum für Politik, Gesellschaft und Kultur* 272 (2007): 52–54. https://www.forum.lu/wp-content/uploads/2015/11/6311_272_Mein.pdf (12. Oktober 2018).

Moleschott, Jacob. „Vorrede". *Georg Forster, der Naturforscher des Volks.* Hamm: G. Grote'sche Buchhandlung, 1862. I–XIII.

Mori, Takashi. *Klassifizierung der Welt. Georg Forsters Reise um die Welt.* Freiburg/Breisgau et al.: Rombach, 2011.

Müller, Dorit. „Vergleichen als epistemische und ästhetische Praxis bei Georg Forster und Adelbert von Chamisso". *Forster – Humboldt – Chamisso. Weltreisende im Spannungsfeld der Kulturen.* Hg. Julian Drews, Ottmar Ette, Tobias Kraft, Barbara Schneider-Kempf und Jutta Weber. Göttingen: Vandenhoeck & Ruprecht, 2017. 75–90.

Peitsch, Helmut. „Zum Verhältnis von Text und Instruktionen in Georg Forsters *Reise um die Welt*". *Georg-Forster-Studien X.* Hg. Horst Dippel und Helmut Scheuer. Kassel: Kassel University Press, 2005. 77–123.

Pickerodt, Gerhart. „Forster als Mittler zwischen Antike und Moderne". *Georg-Forster-Studien IX.* Hg. Horst Dippel und Helmut Scheuer. Kassel: Kassel University Press, 2004. 1–15.

Reemtsma, Jan Philipp. *Mord am Strand. Allianzen von Zivilisation und Barbarei. Aufsätze und Reden.* Hamburg: Hamburger Edition, 1998.

Ritter, Christian. „Darstellungen der Gewalt in Georg Forsters *Reise um die Welt*". *Georg-Forster-Studien VIII.* Hg. Horst Dippel und Helmut Scheuer. Kassel: Kassel University Press, 2003. 19–51.

Starobinski, Jean. „Das Wort Zivilisation". *Das Rettende in der Gefahr. Kunstgriffe der Aufklärung.* Frankfurt/Main: Fischer, 1990. 9–64.

Weber, Christoph. *Vom Gottesgericht zur verhängnisvollen Natur. Darstellung und Bewältigung von Naturkatastrophen im 18. Jahrhundert.* Hg. Deutsche Gesellschaft für die Erforschung des achtzehnten Jahrhunderts. Hamburg: Felix Meiner, 2015. 219–262.

Weigel, Sigrid. „Zum ‚topographical turn'. Kartographie, Topographie und Raumkonzepte in den Kulturwissenschaften". *KulturPoetik* 2.2 (2002): 151–165.

Désirée Mangard und Miriam Strieder
Wechselnde Gezeiten: Der Strand als Schauplatz für Wendepunkte in Heldendichtung und höfischer Literatur des Mittelalters

The beach is a setting of permanent change. In medieval literature, the beach often serves as a setting of arrival and departure or as a liminal space so that it tends to be the location of a turning-point in the plot: As the coastline changes with the force of nature the plot changes with the impact of the newly arrived or departed. The following thoughts are concerned with the beach as a setting in heroic poetry (*Beowulf, Battle of Maldon, Kudrun*) as well as in courtly literature (Gottfried's *Tristan*, Konrad's *Schwanritter, Alliterative Morte Arthur*). The beach as a setting is not only a formulaic pattern stemming from oral tradition with a mnemonic function but also serves as a setting of change in medieval literature and contributes to the structure of the plot.

Der Strand ist Schauplatz ständiger Veränderung und dient in der mittelalterlichen Literatur häufig als Kulisse für Ankunft und Aufbruch oder als liminaler Raum. Er wird als Ort des Übergangs und Wendepunkt der Handlung aufgeladen: So wie die Küstenlinie unter der Gewalt der Elemente ihre Gestalt verändert, ändert sich auch die Handlung unter dem Einfluss der Neuankömmlinge oder Aufgebrochenen. Die folgenden Überlegungen beschäftigen sich mit dem Strand als *setting* in der Heldenepik (*Beowulf, Battle of Maldon, Kudrun*) sowie in der höfischen Literatur (Gottfrieds *Tristan*, Konrads *Schwanritter, Alliterative Morte Arthur*). Der Strand als Handlungsschauplatz beinhaltet nicht nur ein formulaisches Muster (*formulaic pattern*) aus der mündlichen Tradition, das eine mnemotische Funktion übernimmt, sondern markiert auch Veränderung in der mittelalterlichen Literatur und trägt zur Struktur der Handlung bei.

1 Einleitung

1.1 Kulturwissenschaftliche Vorbemerkungen zum Strand im Mittelalter

Strand und Hafen sind besonders im Frühmittelalter und im *heroic age*, in dem heldenepische Erzählungen situiert sind, nicht so streng unterschieden, wie man dies vielleicht argwöhnen könnte. Aus einem Strand, der über günstige naturräumliche Bedingungen verfügt, kann sich im Laufe der Jahrhunderte ein florierender Hafen entwickeln.¹ Gleichzeitig können aber auch bereits bestehende Häfen versanden und so wieder der Natur überlassen werden. Die Küstenlinien der Anrainergebiete rund um die Nordsee sind heute noch von Erosion betroffen, waren es jedoch in wesentlich größerem Ausmaß im Mittelalter. Aber auch besonders große Sturmfluten formten die Küstenverläufe dramatisch und oftmals irreversibel, sodass Gebäude oder sogar ganze Siedlungsgebiete dem Meer preisgegeben werden mussten.² Das Grenzgebiet zwischen Festland und Meer, das auch den Strand umfasst, wurde so als unfester und latent bedrohter Ort wahrgenommen, der für das mittelalterliche Weltbild besonders deutlich das Liminale zum Ausdruck brachte.

Sowohl der Strand als auch der Hafen bilden das Einfallstor für Neues in Wirtschaft und Kultur, aber auch für gesellschaftliche Umwälzungen. Der Schiffsbau der Zeit reagiert auf diese Voraussetzungen, indem Schiffstypen entworfen werden, die entweder aktiv stranden oder sich durch Ebbe trocken fallen lassen konnten – dazu gehören Koggen und Holke (Meier 2016, 28). Frühere Schiffstypen verfügen bis etwa ins siebte Jahrhundert nicht über einen Kiel (Simek 2014, 74–75), sodass das Stranden problemloser möglich ist und damit praktisch jeder Ort, der über einen Strand verfügt, erreichbar ist. Je beständiger die Küstenlinie durch Eindeichung³ und Entwicklung von festen Häfen wird, über desto mehr Tiefgang verfügen die Schiffe: Sind es um 1300 gerade einmal 70 cm, so weisen Schiffe um 1500 im Durchschnitt bereits 3,50 m an Tiefgang auf (Wagenführ 2015, 21). Der Strand verändert im Laufe der technischen, gesellschaftlichen und kulturellen Entwicklung im Mittelalter seine Bedeutung, denn auch wenn Sturmfluten bis in unsere Zeit ein gravierendes Problem für die Küstenbewohner*innen bleiben, so ist doch der Strand nicht mehr länger der gefährliche und unfeste Ort, der das Element des Ungewissen so dezidiert beinhaltet. Während des gesamten Mittelalters ist dieser Abschnitt zwischen Land und Meer der Ort, an dem wertvolles Strandgut oder Händler aus fernen Ländern mit lukrativen Waren anzutreffen sind. Aber hier landen auch fremde Krieger an, die die küstennahen Siedlungen überfallen, oder monströse Wesen

---

1 Vgl. Jeutes (2015, 241) Zusammenschau der Grabungsfunde der Hafenorte im Gebiet des heutigen Bremens sowie den Artikel für das altnordische „*hafnleysi*: hafenlose Küste, Strand, an dem man nicht anlegen kann" in Baetke (2006, 223). Auch das nhd. ‚Haff' verweist darauf.
2 Bekannteste Beispiele dürften hier der untergegangene und im 17. Jahrhundert wiederentdeckte Nehalennia-Tempel im heutigen niederländischen Domburg und das in Detlev von Liliencrons Ballade „Trutz, blanke Hans" (1882/1883) verewigte Rungholt sein, das sich durch vom Watt freigegebene archäologische Funde mehr und mehr vom sagenhaften moralischen Lehrstück zu einem realen Ort entwickelt.
3 Rieken (2005, u. a. 64) gibt an, dass der Deichbau etwa im elften Jahrhundert beginnt und so sind die geologischen und technologischen Folgeentwicklungen zeitlich durchaus realistisch.

der Tiefe, die als Seeungeheuer klassifiziert werden und unter Umständen als böses Vorzeichen für drohendes Unheil interpretiert werden (Corbin 1994, 14; Sandmo 2018, 15). Zudem ist der Strand das Einfallstor für das Meer, das Fluch und Segen zugleich ist, indem es mit mächtigen Fluten fruchtbares Land für Jahre zerstört oder aber als ‚Wellenstraße'[4] Verkehrsweg und damit Lebensader für den mittelalterlichen Menschen sein kann (vgl. u. a. Kellenbenz 1991, 286–287). Der Strand ist somit von einem kulturwissenschaftlichen Standpunkt aus ein höchst ambivalenter Ort,[5] der innerhalb des Erfahrungshorizontes der Rezipierenden mittelalterlicher Texte mit den oben skizzierten Assoziationen verbunden ist und in der früh- und hochmittelalterlichen Literatur entsprechend reflektiert und nach poetologischen Merkmalen umgeformt und neubesetzt wird. Im Gegensatz zum postmodernen Strand, der wie der mittelalterliche ambivalent besetzt ist (für die Postmoderne als Urlaubsresort und Schauplatz von Katastrophen wie Klimawandel oder Sterbeort von Flüchtlingen), und dem modernen Strand, der als gesundheitsbeförderndes Freizeitvergnügen für Privilegierte firmiert, weist der Strand im Mittelalter nur einen sehr eingeschränkten ‚Freizeit- oder Erlebniswert' auf, da diese Konzepte für die mittelalterliche Kultur nur sehr bedingt zur Verfügung stehen. Wie in der Moderne kann der Strand aber ständisch besetzt werden, wenn der adlige Protagonist von dort auf seine Reise aufbricht oder das wilde Gestade als unangemessener Aufenthaltsort für Figuren charakterisiert wird.

1.2 Der Strand unter poetologischen Gesichtspunkten

Dass der Strand gerade in der Heldenepik, aber auch in der um 1200 neu entstehenden Gattung des höfischen Romans eine durchaus prominente Rolle als *setting* übernimmt, ist innerhalb der Forschungsdiskussion bereits häufiger herausgearbeitet worden, besonders für altenglische Texte. Crowne hat mit seinem Ansatz von 1960 die Diskussion für Jahrzehnte befeuert und seine Kriterien für das *theme*, „[a] mnemonic unit [...], [...] not restricted by metrical considerations, [...] part of a recurrent piece of narrative" (Crowne 1960, 363) sollen auch hier Beachtung finden; zum *theme* ‚Strand' gehören „(1) a beach, (2) the

---

4 Diese Kenning erscheint in *Beowulf* (V. 228), vgl. S. 152.
5 Diese Ambivalenz zeigt sich eindrücklich in der altnordischen Mythologie, wenn die ersten Menschen Askr und Embla zwar an einem Strand erschaffen werden und dieser somit zum Ort des Lebens wird, zugleich aber auch Nástrandir der Leichenstrand von Helheim ist und als Ort der Bestrafung für Mörder, Ehebrecher und Eidbrüchige dient. Vgl. *Völuspá* sowie *Snorris Prosaedda*.

comitatus-relationship, (3) a bright light, and (4) a voyage" (ebd., 371).⁶ Diese Elemente können variiert, aber auch abgeschwächt werden, sodass Crowne (1960, 371) allein für den *Beowulf* sechs Beispiele ausmachen kann. Renoir (1964, 72) überträgt dann Crownes Überlegungen auf das *Nibelungenlied* und bringt das Element der Türschwelle als Zeichen für das Liminale ins Spiel: „the juncture between two worlds – that of the finite inside and that of the infinite outside" (ebd., 73). Fry (1966) ergänzt eine Stelle im ae. *Finnsburh-Fragment* als Missing Link und Higley (1986) transferiert eher wenig überzeugend das *theme* von der menschlichen in die außermenschliche Sphäre, indem sie den Bericht über den Hirschen, der Grendels Pfuhl meidet, untersucht. Schließlich greift Renoir das *theme* noch einmal auf und etabliert eine Parallelstelle im 8. Buch der *Ilias* (vgl. Renoir 1989, bes. 113), um so nachzuweisen, dass es sich um ein indoeuropäisches Versatzstück handeln könnte. Anscheinend ohne Notiz zu nehmen von der Debatte um das *beach/threshold-theme* arbeitet Shippey (1985) eine Unterscheidung der ae. Helden heraus, indem er sie in die Kategorien „boar" und „badger" einteilt. Dabei referiert er ebenfalls auf das *setting* im Türrahmen (Shippey 1985, 221, explizit für *Cynewulf und Cyneheard*), übergeht aber den Punkt des Liminalen, der für seine Argumentation nur wenig beizutragen gehabt hätte.

Allgemeiner formuliert kann man mit Lotman (1993, 316) feststellen, dass „das räumliche Modell der Welt in diesen Texten zum organisierenden Element wird, um das herum sich auch die nichträumlichen Charakteristiken ordnen". Dazu gehört zum einen, dass sich der Held/Protagonist mittelalterlicher erzählender Texte seinen Raum erschließt (Störmer-Caysa 2007, 34–75, bes. 65), zum anderen zählt dazu aber auch die Strukturierung des Textes anhand der Mnemotechniken, die für Vortragende und Rezipierende Signale sind und an die bestimmte Erwartungen an die Handlung geknüpft werden. Innerhalb des Lotmanschen Raumkonzepts spielt die Grenze eine entscheidende Rolle. Von einer Grenze spricht Lotman dann, wenn sie drei Aspekte erfüllt: Erstens hat sie „den Raum in zwei disjunkte Teilräume" zu teilen, zweitens hat sie „unüberwindlich" zu sein und drittens soll durch die Teilung „die innere Struktur der beiden Teile verschieden" sein (Lotman 1993, 327). Um im Bild des Strandes zu bleiben, trennt das Liminale in diesem *theme* (*hero on the beach*) das Meer der Erzählmöglichkeiten von einer konkret auserzählten Variante; dass dabei Meer und

---

6 Der *comitatus* bezeichnet die Gefolgschaft eines Kriegsherrn, seine Gefährten, die mit ihm in den Kampf ziehen und ihm zur Seite stehen. Innerhalb des *comitatus* gibt es eine enge Bindung der Krieger untereinander und an ihren Herrn, der sich ihrer Loyalität u. a. durch das Verteilen von Beute versichert. Im germanischen Kulturkreis ist der *comitatus* eine der engsten Gemeinschaften und Ansprüche, die sich daraus ableiten, übersteigen auch die der Familie. Vgl. dazu *Cynewulf and Cyneheard*.

festes Land im zeitgenössischen Rezipierenden unterschiedliche Assoziationen wie ‚Reise' und ‚Gefahr' sowie ‚Ortsfestigkeit' und ‚konkrete Handlung' hervorrufen, machen sich die Erzählungen zu Nutze. Diese Grenze, die die mittelalterlichen Erzählungen in Räume teilt,[7] ist nur für den Helden durchlässig, worauf auch Lotman aufmerksam macht (ebd., 346).[8]

Vom Raum in literarischen Texten ausgehend entwickelt Lotman seine Überlegungen zum Sujet und erklärt:

> [H]inter der Darstellung von Sachen und Objekten, in deren Umgebung die Figuren des Textes agieren, zeichnet sich ein System räumlicher Relationen ab, die Struktur des Topos. Diese Struktur des Topos einerseits ist das Prinzip der Organisation und der Verteilung der Figuren im künstlerischen Kontinuum und fungiert andererseits als Sprache für den Ausdruck anderer, nichträumlicher Relationen des Textes. Darin liegt die besondere modellbildende Rolle künstlerischen Raums im Text. (Ebd., 330)

Diese Definition des Topos lässt sich mühelos auf den Strand in der mittelalterlichen Literatur beziehen, der die Erzählung in ein Vorher-Nachher, Hier-Dort strukturiert und auf diese Weise Figuren und Dinge zuordnet und dem Helden die Möglichkeit gibt, sich einen Raum zu gestalten und zu seinem zu machen. Diese Eigenart mittelalterlicher Texte widersetzt sich Lotmans Unterteilung in sujetlose und sujethafte Texte (ebd., 337–338), da die oben erwähnte Grenze, die der Strand oftmals bildet, für den Helden zwar überschreitbar ist und auch eine Rückkehr für ihn möglich ist, aber andere Figuren, insbesondere Frauen, ortsgebunden sind und Grenzen, nicht nur den Strand, nicht oder nur durch große Opfer wie Preisgabe des eigenen Status (vgl. *Kudrun*) überschreiten können. Die hier betrachteten mittelalterlichen, heldenepischen und höfischen Texte changieren dabei zwischen diesen beiden Polen und verweisen auf Besonderheiten der vormodernen Erzählungen.

Eine Zusammenschau über Sprach- und Gattungsgrenzen sowie Jahrhunderte hinweg, wie sie hier angestrebt wird, hat die ergiebige Forschungsdiskussion allerdings nie unternommen. Obwohl die mittelalterliche europäische Literatur, gerade in den Gattungen Heldenepik und höfischer Roman, inhärente Parallelen, Beeinflussungen, Übertragungen etc. aufweist, ist eine wie auch immer geartete Zusammenschau immer mit Problemen behaftet, die zum einen aus den unterschiedlichen Sprachen resultieren, zum anderen aber auch Quellenfragen, Stoff- und Motivgenese, Probleme der *oral poetry* usf. tangieren. Vergleichende Arbeiten sind deshalb zwar erstrebenswert, weil sie die engen

---

[7] Dies ist nicht nur der Strand, sondern auch Hof und Wald werden dezidiert voneinander getrennt, so u. a. in der eingängigen Doppelformel „ze hove und ze holze".
[8] So auch der psychoanalytische Ansatz Campbells (1953).

Verwandtschaften innerhalb der mittelalterlichen Literatur Europas aufzeigen, zugleich bergen sie aber auch immer das Risiko der Zuschreibung, da ein Weg *ad fontes*, zur ersten, originalen Version eines Textes, Motivs u. Ä. in den meisten Fällen verstellt ist. Trotz dieser Einwände soll dieser Beitrag zum einen versuchen zu zeigen, dass das *setting* Strand eine bekannte, immer wieder verwendete Komponente der mittelalterlichen Literatur ist und zum anderen soll, ergänzend zu der bereits etablierten Hypothese vom *theme*, deutlich gemacht werden, dass der Strand inhaltlich als Wendepunkt aufgeladen werden kann. Dieser folgt klaren poetologischen Grundlagen und konnte so für die Rezipierenden mittelalterlicher Literatur, die größtenteils mündlich vorgetragen wurde, als Signal für eine Änderung des Handlungsverlaufs dienen. Das Liminale des Strandes wird dabei nicht nur durch die mnemotechnische Ausgestaltung des *theme* unterstützt, sondern durch den besonderen Charakter des *setting* wird der Wendepunkt in der Erzählung auch wirkungsvoll in Szene gesetzt.

2 Der Strand in der Heldenepik

2.1 Sandiger Start in Beowulfs Heldenbiografie

Wie bereits erwähnt, hat Crowne im *Beowulf* bereits sechs Szenen ausgemacht, auf die seine Merkmalsliste des Strand-*setting* passt. Dazu zählen die Ankunft des Helden in Heorot, die Breca-Episode sowohl aus der Sicht von Unferth als auch aus der Sicht von Beowulf, Beowulfs Abreise von Heorot und seine darauffolgende, zweimal erzählte Ankunft bei seinem Gefolgsherrn Hygelac (Crowne 1960, 371). Crowne geht es darum, die Strand-Episoden als *theme* zu etablieren und erst mit der Ergänzung um das Liminale kommen die Überlegungen in die Nähe eines Wendepunkts, der für Crowne noch keine Rolle spielt. Dementsprechend wird in diesem Beitrag eine Stelle betrachtet, die für die frühe Forschung zum *theme*, die sich auf A. Lords Überlegungen zu Memorierungstechniken stützt,[9] noch nicht von Bedeutung ist: Beowulfs Abreise von Hygelac und seine (noch unbeobachtete) Ankunft im Land der Dänen. Diese wird so geschildert:

Fyrst forð gewāt;	flota wæs on ȳðum,
bāt under beorge.	Beornas gearwe
on stefn stigon;	strēamas wundon
sund wið sande;	secgas bæron
on bearm nacan	beorhte frætwe

---

9 Zur Unterscheidung zwischen *theme* und *formula* vgl. Lord (2001, 30–98).

gūð-searo geatolīc; guman ūt scufon
weras on wil-sīð wudu bundenne.
gewāt þā ofer wǣg-holm winde gefȳsed
flota fāmī-heals, fugle gelīcost,
oðþæt ymb ān-tīd, ōþres dōgores,
wunden-stefna gewaden hæfde,
Þæt ðā līðende land gesāwon,
brim-clifu blīcan, beorgas stēape,
sīde sǣ-næssas; þā wæs sund liden,
ēoletes æt end. Þanon up hraðe
Wedera lēode on wang stigon,
sǣ-wudu sǣldon, sycran hrysedon,
gūð-gewǣdo, Gode þancedon
Þæs þe him ȳð-lāde ēaðe wurdon.[10] (*Beowulf*, V. 210–228)

Um Crownes Ansprüchen an ein *theme* Genüge zu tun, sei hier kurz erwähnt, dass sowohl der *comitatus* („beornas gearwe") als auch der Strand („sande") als Ausgangspunkt einer Reise („wil-sīð") und das Leuchten („beorhte frætwe") in dieser Abfahrtszene vorkommen. Auch bei der Ankunft im Land der Dänen finden wir das Leuchten („blīcan"), eine strandähnliche Topographie, ohne die das Verlassen des Schiffs in Rüstung nur sehr schwer möglich wäre („sund"), das Ende der Reise („sund liden, ēoletes æt end") und der *comitatus* („Wedera lēode").

Eine Betrachtung der Stelle zeigt zum ersten, dass der Stabreim die Inhaltswörter bzw. bedeutungstragenden Wörter eng zusammenbindet und sie in einem Vortrag den Zuhörenden umso präsenter erscheinen lassen wird.[11] Hier sind dies besonders landschaftliche Merkmale wie „flota" (stabend mit „fyrst" und „forð" bzw. „fāmi" und „fugle"), „sund" und „sande" (stabend mit „secgas") usf. Zum zweiten tritt dazu die Charakterisierung von Strand und

---

10 „Zeit verging. Die Flut war in den Wellen, / das Schiff unterhalb der Klippen. Gerüstete Männer / stiegen in den Steven; Strömungen wanden / das Meer gegen den Strand; die Männer trugen / in den Bauch des Schiffes leuchtende Schätze, / kostbare Waffen. Die Männer stießen das Boot vom Ufer ab, / Leute auf glücklicher Reise im gut gearbeiteten Schiff. / Da wurde abgelegt über die kabbelige See mit eiligen Winden, / das Meer von Gischt umströmt, wie ein Vogel / zur rechten Zeit am zweiten Tage / das Schiff mit dem hohen Steven war es gegangen, / sodass die Reisenden Land sahen, / die Seeklippen leuchteten, die steilen Berge, / die großen Kaps; da war die Meerfahrt / über das Wasser zu Ende. Da stiegen / die wedischen Leute sofort an Land, / das Seeholz vertäuten sie sicher, ihre Rüstungen klapperten, / die Kampfesausrüstung, Gott dankten sie, / dass die Wellenstraße leicht für sie [zu überqueren] gewesen war." [eigene Übersetzung]
11 Dass der Stabreim natürlich für den Vortragenden eine Memorierhilfe darstellt und er anhand der so einprägsam gewordenen landschaftlichen Merkmale die Reise besser im Gedächtnis behalten kann, versteht sich.

Meer als Gegensatz: Ist das Meer etwas potentiell Gefahrvolles, dessen sichere Bewältigung keineswegs normal ist („Gode þancedon þæs þe him ȳð-lāde ēaðe wurdon"), sind Strand und Klippen als Elemente der festen Erde Landmarke für Anfang und Ende der Reise und werden daher auch mit positiven Zuschreibungen wie „brim-clifu blīcan" belegt. Drittens ist die Verquickung von Zeit und Raum durch „[f]yrst forð gewāt; flota wæs on ȳðum" bemerkenswert: Die Zeit wird durch den Raum bestimmt und bildet damit einen Bachtinschen Chronotopos. Ebbe und Flut machen die Reise des Helden möglich oder unmöglich und dieses Phänomen ist eng gebunden an (Mond-)Zeit und Landschaft. Hier ist die Geographie Beowulf wohlgesonnen und befördert sein Fortkommen in der erzählten Welt wie auch im Handlungsverlauf so leicht wie das eines „fugle". Im Gegensatz dazu steht zum Beispiel Grendels Pfuhl, dessen abschreckende Geographie den Helden bei der Vollendung seiner Aufgabe behindern wird (*Beowulf*, u. a. V. 1357–1366).

Der Wendepunkt in der Erzählung stellt eben genau jene Reise dar, die Beowulf mit seinen Heergesellen unternimmt und mit der er nun zum ersten Mal eine Heldentat vor Zeugen vollbringen wird,[12] womit er seine Heldenbiografie sozusagen im Licht der Öffentlichkeit beginnt. Dabei wird Beowulf sofort vom Küstenwächter als der im Wortsinne herausragendste der Neuankömmlinge erkannt (*Beowulf*, V. 247–251); deswegen und wegen seines heroischen Verhaltens wird ihm sein Heldentum zugetraut. Damit hat nicht nur die Erzählung ihren Helden und Protagonisten gefunden, sondern auch Beowulf seine Rolle als heldenhafter Krieger. Zuvor nämlich war von den Dänen die Rede gewesen (besonders Scyld, Beow und Hrothgar; *Beowulf*, V. 4–85) und erst in Vers 194 und damit 15 Verse vor der bereits geschilderten Abfahrtsszene findet die Erzählung ihren noch namenlosen Protagonisten, der aufbricht, um über das Meer zu segeln und es mit Grendel aufzunehmen. Das Heldenhafte, das zuvor Scyld, Beow und auch Hrothgar anhaftete, wird nun auf diesen neuen Protagonisten übertragen, der das menschliche Umfeld immer wieder verlassen wird, um Heldentaten zu vollbringen, und dem die Erzählung fast 3000 Verse lang folgen wird.

---

[12] Die Breca-Episode kann eben deshalb von Unferth rhetorisch disqualifiziert werden, weil es keine Augenzeugen der Geschehnisse auf dem Meer gibt.

2.2 Der Strand als schlachtentscheidendes Merkmal im *Battle of Maldon*

Dass der historisch belegte Battle of Maldon im Jahre 991 ausgerechnet an den Ufern der Mündung des heutigen Blackwaters, eines von den Gezeiten beeinflussten Flusses, stattfand, dürfte dem Verfasser des *Battle of Maldon* (*BoM*) nur stimmig vorgekommen sein, wenn ihm memorierbare Versatzstücke, die die Forschung ausgemacht hat, aus heldenepischen Texten vertraut waren. Zugleich wird ihm auch die Signalwirkung des *setting* am Ufer des Wassers nicht entgangen sein, sodass er eben genau dort das topische *flyting* stattfinden lässt,[13] das sich unter diesen geographischen Bedingungen vermutlich gar nicht umsetzen ließ.

Die topographischen Gegebenheiten, mit denen uns der Text konfrontiert, ermöglichen erst das heroische Handeln des Anführers der Angelsachsen, Byrhtnoth, und eröffnen zudem eine Bewertung des Protagonisten, mit der sich die Forschung bis dato schwergetan hat.[14] Es scheint aber unumstritten, dass der Wendepunkt des Textes dort liegt, wo Byrhtnoth das unbehellige Übersetzen der Wikinger von der Gezeiteninsel auf den Flussstrand zulässt und die folgende Schlacht sowie sein Leben verliert. Der Strand wird damit zum schlachtentscheidenden *setting*.

Zugleich muss auch konstatiert werden, dass im Sinne eines *theme* hier nicht alle Elemente ausgestaltet wurden: Sowohl das *setting* am Flussstrand mit der Furt (*BoM*, u. a. V. 25, 28, 74) als auch die Anwesenheit des Helden mit seinen Gefährten (besonders auffällig in V. 24) sind klar herausgearbeitet, aber das helle Licht sowie der Beginn oder das Ende einer Reise fehlen, auch wenn diese leicht zu erschließen sind. Die Ausrüstungsgegenstände der Angelsachsen, besonders Byrthnoths kostbares Schwert (*BoM*, V. 161), werden sicherlich das Licht reflektieren, und dass das zusammengerufene Heer, die sogenannte *fyrd*, aus verschiedenen Landesteilen angereist und somit am Strand des Blackwaters am Ende seiner Reise angekommen ist, erscheint auch deutlich.[15] Dass das literarische *theme* nicht vollständig umgesetzt wurde, kann unter Umständen damit begründet werden, dass der *Battle of Maldon* auf einer historischen Begebenheit basiert und so kein rein literarischer Text vorliegt, sondern nur

---

13 Vgl. zum *flyting* im *BoM* u. a. Clark (1968, 66) sowie Parks (1990, 69).
14 Zur *ofermod*-Diskussion vgl. u. a. Shippey (1985, 220) sowie Gneuss (1976, 117–137).
15 Dies lässt sich besonders gut an Æschferth, der Geisel aus Northumbria, festmachen. Die Reise von Byrhtnoth und seinen Gefährten kann hier durchaus auch metaphorisch gelesen werden, da die Herdgesellen des Protagonisten (ae. ‚heorðwerod') zum Großteil ihr Leben in der Schlacht lassen und so ihre Lebensreise am Strand des Blackwaters zu Ende geht.

eine literarische Überformung historischer Vorkommnisse. Deshalb muss das *theme* nicht vollständig ausgeformt werden, da es nicht nur dem mündlichen Gedächtnis von Vortragenden anvertraut wird, sondern auch Chroniken und sonstigen schriftlichen Quellen. Unter anderem Anklänge an das *hero-on-the-beach*-Motiv deuten aber ganz klar auf die Nähe zur Heldenepik.

2.3 Der Strand in der *Kudrun* als heldenepischer Reflex

Über die genaue Lokalisierung der Handlungsschauplätze der *Kudrun* ist in der einschlägigen Forschung viel diskutiert worden.[16] Ob es realhistorisch verortbare *settings* gibt, ist hier aber nicht im Fokus des Interesses, sondern vielmehr soll an dieser Stelle der Handlungsschauplatz Strand auf seine Funktion als Wendepunkt befragt werden und damit wiederum Beweise dafür liefern, dass der Strand in der Heldenepik eine eindeutige Zuordnung im Rahmen einer poetologischen Konzeption aufweist.

Obwohl mehrere Strände in der *Kudrun* geschildert werden, sollen an dieser Stelle zwei Szenen an zwei verschiedenen Stränden in den Blick genommen werden, die beide im letzten Handlungskursus (der eigentlichen Kudrun-Erzählung) eine Rolle spielen – zum einen die Schlacht auf der Sandinsel Wülpensand und zum anderen das Zusammentreffen von Kudrun mit ihrem Verlobten auf dem Strand an der Küste der Normandie.[17] Für alle Strände in der *Kudrun* schlägt Bleumer (2014, 116) vor, sie im Kontext der Brautwerbungserzählung als Verlängerung des Schiffs zu lesen und so als eine „Verbildlichung einer sozialen Ordnung [mit] den Herausforderungen von schicksalshaften oder zufälligen Ereignissen" zu verstehen. Zugleich plädiert er auch dafür, den Strand als Ort des „Konflikt[s] mit einer Gegenpartei und ihrer Gesellschaftsordnung" (ebd.) zu interpretieren, wobei dieser Konflikt zumeist in heldenepischer Manier als Kampf ausgetragen wird und so einen Wendepunkt innerhalb der Erzählung darstellt: Wer als Sieger und wer als Verlierer vom Sand geht, ist für die Handlung von entscheidender Bedeutung.

Für Wülpensand lassen sich leicht die Merkmale des *theme* ausfindig machen; einer der Helden (in diesem Falle der antagonistische) und seine Heergesellen werden in 847,1–3 bezeichnet:

---

[16] Eine konzise Zusammenfassung bietet Bleumer (2014, 100, Anm. 19).
[17] Für den Kampf am Strand von Waleis in der Hetel-Hilde-Werbung vgl. *Kudrun* (465,1–524,4) sowie Bleumer (2014, 118).

> Nu was künic Ludewîc und ouch her Hartmuot
> Mit ir landes volk bî des meres fluot
> Beliben durch ir ruowe ûf den wilden griezen.[18]
> (*Kudrun*, 847,1–3)

Und auch die Protagonistin, Kudrun selbst, findet sich auf dem Strand als Ort der Entscheidung wieder:

> Die vil edele gîsel von Hegelinge lant
> Die hête man gewîset ûf den wilden sant.[19]
> (*Kudrun*, 849,1–2)

Das Leuchten kommt von den Feuern, die entzündet worden sind, um das Lager auf der verlassenen Insel angenehmer zu machen: „Die fiur man allenthalben bî dem sande sach" (*Kudrun*, 850,1) und die Reise der Widersacher wird auf Wülpensand unterbrochen, um von dort aus dann auch wieder fortgeführt zu werden. Zweimal wird der Strand als „wild" charakterisiert und damit als nicht für menschlichen (und besonders adligen) Aufenthalt geeignet. Dies gilt ganz besonders für Kudrun selbst, deren Anwesenheit auf dem Strand besonders betont wird, womit verdeutlicht wird, dass für adlige Damen der höfischen Gesellschaft das Ufer des Meers weder als Aufenthaltsort noch als Lagerplatz angemessen ist. Die „fiur", die entzündet werden, bringen nicht nur eine menschliche Kulturtechnik in diese Wildnis, sondern heben die Wildnis gleichzeitig auch hervor. Diese unzivilisierte Gegend scheint auf die Figuren überzugreifen: Sie kampieren im Freien, kämpfen und sterben auf einer sandigen Insel und perpetuieren das Unrecht, das mit Kudruns doppelter Entführung begonnen hat. Auf den ersten Blick führt das *setting* damit die Handlung nur fort.

Einen Wendepunkt erhält die Erzählung aber dadurch, dass in der Schlacht von Wülpensand der Brautvater Hetel erschlagen wird, die Hegelinge und der Verlobte Herwig die Verfolgung von Kudrun und Hartmut abbrechen und sie darauf warten müssen, bis neue Krieger nachgewachsen sind.[20] Für Kudrun bedeutet das viele Jahre des Leids in der Normandie, zugleich aber auch eine Ausdehnung der erzählten Zeit um mehrere Jahre. Auch hier fließen Ort und Zeit zusammen, allerdings nicht wie im *Beowulf* als für den Protagonisten vorteilhaft.

---

[18] „Nun waren der König Ludwig und auch der Herr Hartmut mit ihrem Kriegsvolk nahe bei dem Meer geblieben auf dem wilden Strand um der Ruhe willen." [eigene Übersetzung]
[19] Die königliche Geisel aus dem Land der Hegelinge hatte man auf den wilden Strand geschickt.
[20] Dass die Szenen auf Wülpensand, die zudem verdoppelt werden, offensichtlich ein Reflex auf die rekonstruierte Hildesage sind, zeigt Bleumer (2014, 117, 119) sehr eindrücklich.

Ebenfalls Beachtung finden soll der Beginn der schlussendlichen Befreiung Kudruns in der Normandie, die sich am Strand als Ort der Begegnung abspielt. Weil Kudrun und ihrer Gefährtin Hildburg die demütigende Arbeit von Waschfrauen übertragen wurde, befinden sich die beiden am Strand: „Kûdrûn und Hildburc die wuoschen alle zît ûf einem sande." (*Kudrun*, 1165,4) Der Strand in der Normandie wird wie auch bei der Schlacht auf Wülpensand als ein Ort des Leids charakterisiert, der auf diesen rückverweist.[21] Zugleich wird hier aber auch wieder explizit auf die Zeit verwiesen, die aus der Sicht der Protagonistin nicht zu vergehen scheint, sondern in einem Zirkel („alle zît") angelegt ist, der erst durch die Ankunft ihrer Befreier durchbrochen werden kann, wodurch sowohl die lineare Zeit als auch eine anders konnotierte Geographie wieder eingeführt werden.

Am Strand begegnet ihnen ein Engel Gottes, der die Gestalt eines Vogels angenommen hat und ihnen nun von den Verwandten berichtet (*Kudrun*, 1167,1–1186,1). Obwohl keine genauere Beschreibung des Vogels gegeben wird, können wir doch annehmen, dass es sich sicherlich um ein Tier mit weißem Gefieder handelt und ihn ein göttlicher Glanz umgibt,[22] denn Kudrun erkennt den himmlischen Boten und reagiert auf ihn, indem sie sich in Kreuzform vor ihm auf den Sand wirft (*Kudrun*, 1170,1–2). Die frohe Kunde, dass sich eine Wende in Kudruns Schicksal einstellen wird, erfährt sie also am Strand, wo dann auch Herwigs Reise enden wird, denn er sieht Kudrun und Hildburg dort beim Waschen und initiiert das Erkennen der Verlobten über die Schönheit der beiden Frauen:

> [Der Verlobte Herwig spricht]: Wes disiu rîchen kleider ûf dem sande sîn
> Oder wem ir waschet. Ir beide sît sô schœne.[23]
> (*Kudrun*, 1221, 2–3)

Anders als auf Wülpensand werden hier nicht alle Elemente des *theme* verbalisiert, können aber in den beiden Szenen erschlossen werden: Das Ende der Reise des göttlichen Boten, der in himmlischem Glanz auftritt, Kudrun und ihre Gefährtin als Heldin mit Gesellin, die oft mit Glanzmetaphorik bedachte weibliche Schönheit der beiden Frauen sowie das Ende der Reise von Herwig und dessen

---

[21] Interessant ist, dass die beiden Frauen an einem Meeresstrand waschen, obwohl das Salzwasser für die Reinigung der Kleider ungeeignet ist. Der Strand ist hier also als *setting* bewusst gewählt worden.
[22] Vgl. dazu die Gralstaube in 470,7 in Wolframs *Parzival*, die „durchliuhtec blanc" (strahlend weiß) ist.
[23] „Wem gehören diese prächtigen Kleider am Strand oder für wen wascht ihr? Ihr beide seid so schön." [eigene Übersetzung]

Heer bilden genügend Indizien, um das altvertraute *theme* zu identifizieren. Dass diese beiden letzten Strandszenen eindeutig einen Wendepunkt markieren, wird deutlich, wenn man bedenkt, dass danach Kudrun aus ihrer Gefangenschaft befreit, dem Verlobten zurückgegeben und in ihr Heimatland gebracht wird.

3 Die Funktion des *hero-on-the-beach*-Motivs abseits der Heldenepik

Bislang wurden in der Forschung in Hinblick auf das *hero-on-the-beach*-Motiv fast ausschließlich altenglische Texte untersucht und bearbeitet – eine sprachliche Ausnahme bildet hier die Arbeit von Alain Renoir (1964) über das *Nibelungenlied*. Zudem standen bei den bisher publizierten Überlegungen zum *theme* Strand fast immer heldenepische Texte im Vordergrund (u. a. Crowne 1960; Renoir 1964; Fry 1966), allerdings lässt sich dieses auch in höfischen Texten finden. Gerade die Aufladung des Strandes als Wendepunkt ist bei höfischen Romanen besonders gut nachvollziehbar. Verglichen mit der Heldenepik steht das *hero-on-the-beach*-Motiv bezogen auf die höfische Literatur wohl weniger als Memorierungs- und Erinnerungshilfe im Vordergrund, sondern erfüllt verstärkt die (Wieder-)Erkennungsfunktion als Einordnungshilfe für die Rezipierenden.

Im Rahmen der vorliegenden Zusammenschau soll die Bedeutung des *setting* Strand für die höfische Literatur exemplarisch anhand dreier Werke und vierer Szenen dargestellt werden. Bei zweien handelt es sich um mittelhochdeutsche Werke, Gottfrieds von Straßburg *Tristan* und Konrads von Würzburg *Der Schwanritter*, der dritte Text, der *Alliterative Morte Arthure*, ist wiederum in (mittel)englischer Sprache verfasst.[24]

---

[24] An dieser Stelle würde es zu weit führen, eine Diskussion zur Definition eines Helden zu eröffnen und fundiert darzulegen, ob und inwieweit die Protagonisten der höfischen Epik mit den Helden der Heldenepik unter dem Begriff des ‚Helden' vereint werden dürfen. Wenn in der hier vorgestellten Umlegung des *theme* des *hero-on-the-beach* auf die höfische Epik im Folgenden die Rede von ‚Helden' ist, ist dies lediglich der begrifflichen Vereinfachung und der Tatsache geschuldet, dass es sich in beiden Fällen um die männlichen Hauptfiguren der jeweiligen Erzählung handelt.

3.1 Unfreiwilliger Aufbruch zu neuen Ufern und zur wahren Identität Tristans

Dadurch, dass der entführte Waisenjunge Tristan von seinen Entführern aus Angst vor der Strafe Gottes, als die sie ein Gewitter interpretieren, an einem menschenleeren, fremden Stand abgesetzt wird, wird die daran anschließende Handlung in eine Richtung gelenkt, von der zu diesem Zeitpunkt noch niemand etwas weiß. Die aufmerksame, das Strand-*theme* erkennende Hörer- und Leserschaft kann diesen Wendepunkt aber bereits sehr wohl erahnen, als die Entführer nach einem aufkommenden Sturm die Küste Cornwalls erreichen und in der Beschreibung die Komponenten des *hero-on-the-beach*-Motivs aufgerufen werden:

> dô wart ir kumberlîchiu vart
> gesenftet an der stunde:
> wint unde wâc begunde
> sich sâ zerlœsen und zerlân,
> daz mer begunde nider gân,
> diu sunne schînen lieht als ê.
> hie mite enbitens ouch dô nimê,
> wan der wint hete sî geslagen
> innerhalp den ahte tagen
> in daz lant ze Kurnewâle
> und wâren zuo dem mâle
> bî dem stade sô nâhen,
> daz sîn bereite sâhen
> und stiezen ûz ze lande aldâ.
> Tristanden nâmen si sâ
> und sazten den ûz an daz lant
> und gâben ime brôt an die handt
> und ander ir spîse ein teil.[25]
> (*Tristan*, V. 2458–2475)

Der Junge wird bei erstbester Gelegenheit an Land abgesetzt und es handelt sich hier eindeutig um einen Strand, nicht etwa um einen Hafen, denn er befin-

---

[25] „Da kam ihre beschwerliche Fahrt / mit einem Mal zu sanfter Ruhe. / Wind und Wogen begannen / sich aufzulösen und zu legen, / das Meer begann sich zu beruhigen, / die Sonne schien wieder so hell wie zuvor. / Nun mussten sie auch nicht mehr länger warten, / denn der Wind hatte sie in den acht Tagen / in das Land Kurnewal verschlagen. / Sie waren bereits / dem Strand so nahe, / dass sie ihn schon sehen konnten / und so begaben sie sich dort an Land. / Sie nahmen Tristan und setzten ihn am Ufer aus / und versorgten ihn mit Brot / und ein wenig von ihren anderen Nahrungsmitteln." [eigene Übersetzung]

det sich abseits jeglicher Zivilisation.[26] Das *flashing-light*-Motiv kann einerseits bereits im Vorfeld verbunden mit dem Gewitter gesehen werden, das zur An-Land-Setzung Tristans führt, andererseits auch in der beschriebenen hell leuchtenden Sonne gefunden werden (V. 2463).

Somit sind nach Crownes Definition des Strand-*theme* alle Merkmale erfüllt: Tristan kommt mit dem Schiff mit seinen Begleitern am Strand („stade"; *Tristan*, V. 2469) an und beendet damit eine unfreiwillig angetretene Reise. Gleichzeitig beginnt er anschließend eine solche, indem er sich auf die Suche nach menschlicher Zivilisation begibt, was sein weiteres Schicksal maßgeblich beeinflussen wird. Wir haben es hier daher mit einem wichtigen Wendepunkt zu tun, denn durch seine Ankunft in Cornwall wird die folgende Handlung erst möglich und seine wahre Identität kommt (auch für ihn selbst) kurz darauf ans Licht. Bereits bevor dies geschieht und die tatsächliche Auswirkung dieser Anlandung offenbart wird, können aufmerksame Rezipierende diesen drastischen Handlungseinschnitt bereits als solchen wahrnehmen. Der liminale Charakter des Strandes, der als Übergangsort zwischen der Wildheit des Meeres und der Zivilisiertheit des Königshofes fungiert, spiegelt gewissermaßen auch die persönliche Situation Tristans, der seine bisherige Identität aufgeben muss und seine neue, eigentlich wahre Identität als Mitglied der Königsfamilie noch nicht gefunden hat. Insofern stellt der Strand hier einen markanten Kontrast zum Hof dar, der für Tristan als Adeligen das eigentlich zugedachte Umfeld wäre, und weist Parallelen zum Strand in der Kudrun auf, in der die Königstochter niedere Dienste am Strand verrichtet und damit bewusst aus der Hofgesellschaft ausgeschlossen wird.

3.2 Neuordnung alter Hierarchien im *Tristan* durch einen Kampf am Strand

Als Tristan am Hof seines Onkels bereits gut integriert ist und seine Herkunft offengelegt wurde, kommt es zu einer weiteren einschneidenden und zukunftsweisenden Episode, in der erneut auf das Strand-*theme* zurückgegriffen wird. Môrolt, der Bruder der irischen Königin, kommt nach Cornwall, um den Zins für Irland einzutreiben, was Tristan nicht akzeptieren will. Er meldet sich freiwillig, um gegen Môrolt zu kämpfen und damit Cornwall von dieser Last zu befreien.

---

26 Vgl. hierzu auch die Ausführungen Ingrid Hahns, die für den *Tristan* Gottfrieds von Straßburg feststellt: „*stat* hat immer die ganz präzise Bedeutung von Ufer und Küste [...] Für den Anlegeplatz der Schiffe steht ausschließlich *habe*" (Hahn 1963, 25).

Daher kommt es zum Kampf der beiden und bereits bei der Beschreibung von Tristans Ausrüstung sowie der Aufmachung seines Pferdes wird mehrfach das Motiv des Leuchtens aufgerufen (z. B. „wîziu decke"; *Tristan*, V. 6681 und „liehte unde lûter alse der tac"; *Tristan*, V. 6682).

Besonders ist in dieser Sequenz der Schauplatz des Kampfes, der auf einer kleinen, dem Strand vorgelagerten Insel stattfindet und folgendermaßen beschrieben wird:

> Sus was den kempfen beiden
> ein kampfstat bescheiden,
> ein kleiniu insel in dem mer,
> dem stade sô nâhe und dem her,
> daz man dâ wol bereite sach,
> swaz in der insele geschach.
> und was ouch daz beredet dar an,
> daz âne diese zwêne man
> nieman dar în kæme,
> biz der kampf ende næme.[27]
> (*Tristan*, V. 6725–6734)

Es handelt sich in dieser Szene nicht nur um eine ganz bewusste Platzierung auf einem Strand, sondern um dessen Verdoppelung: Der Kampf findet auf einer kleinen Insel statt und somit auf einem Strand – zusätzlich ist dieser Kampfschauplatz vom Strand des Festlandes zu sehen, weswegen sich dort die Gefolgschaft beider Männer versammelt.

Das *flashing-light*-Motiv ist bereits vor dem Kampf durch die Beschreibung der schimmernden Ausrüstung von Pferd und Reiter erkennbar, es finden sich jedoch auch bei der Beschreibung der Kampfeshandlung weitere Indizien. Durch die reiche Gestaltung der Rüstungen und die Lichtbrechungen auf den schimmernden Waffen sind Glanzreflexe vorprogrammiert. Es wird sogar ein Vergleich zu einem Gewitter („dunre"; *Tristan*, V. 6909) gezogen, mit dem meist auch Blitze einhergehen.[28]

Der Kampf Tristans mit Môrolt ist von vornherein als entscheidender Wendepunkt markiert und durch die Verdoppelung des Strandes besonders

---

[27] „Nun wurden den beiden Kämpfern ein Kampfplatz zugewiesen: Eine kleine Insel im Meer, dem Strand und dem Heer so nahe, dass man da sehr gut sehen konnte, was auf der Insel geschah. Und es wurde auch vereinbart, dass niemand außer diesen zwei Männern dorthin kommen würde, bis der Kampf beendet wäre." [eigene Übersetzung]

[28] In der mittelalterlichen Gedankenwelt gehen Donner und Blitz Hand in Hand, weswegen man bei der Nennung von Donner oder einem Gewitter auch die damit einhergehenden Blitze mitdenken muss, selbst wenn diese nicht explizit Erwähnung finden. So liegt es nicht fern, bei der Nennung von ‚dunre' auch an ‚dunresblic', ‚Blitz', zu denken.

ausgezeichnet: Einer der beiden Kämpfer – gleichzeitig auch adeliger Vertreter eines Landes – wird sterben, und es entscheidet sich, wie die Tributforderungen Irlands in Zukunft gehandhabt werden. Somit sind der Ausgang dieses Kampfes bzw. die damit verbundenen Konsequenzen ein drastischer Einschnitt sowohl für die jeweilige Herrscherfamilie wie auch für deren Herrschaftsbereich. Selbst der letztlich eindeutigen Äußerung Tristans, dass der Tod von einem der beiden Kämpfer unvermeidlich sei (*Tristan*, V. 6802–8610), wird durch das *setting* des Kampfes eine Bühne geboten, indem sie die Erklärung für das Treibenlassen des Bootes ist, was wiederum durch den Schauplatz am Strand ermöglicht und motiviert wird.

Wie sich herausstellt, ist das Ende des Kampfes auf dem Strand auch gleichzeitig der Beginn einer Reise Tristans nach Irland, weil dies die einzige Möglichkeit darstellt, seine von Môrolt mit einer vergifteten Waffe verursachte Wunde versorgen zu lassen. Gleichzeitig schafft dieser Wendepunkt am Strand auch erst die Grundlage für den längerfristigen Handlungsverlauf, indem erst durch diese Reise Tristans die Figur der weiblichen Protagonistin Isolde ins Spiel gebracht wird. Auch Monika Schulz (2017, 59) schreibt dem Kampf am Strand zweierlei entscheidende Funktionen zu: „1. Er installiert Tristan als Befreiungshelden im Reich König Markes und weist damit diesen und nicht König Marke als den superioren Aktanten aus. [...] 2. Der Moroldkampf ist die unverzichtbare Vorgeschichte für die spätere Brautwerbung." Durch das *hero-on-the-beach-theme* wird die Bedeutung des Kampfes für die weitere Erzählung dabei bereits hervorgehoben und implizit wird auch Tristans Vorrangstellung deutlich gemacht.

3.3 Der Schwanritter als Retter in der Not

Nicht nur in den umfangreicheren epischen Werken des Mittelalters, wie bspw. dem *Tristan*, kommt dem Strand-*theme* eine narrative Funktion zu, sondern auch in wesentlich kürzeren Erzählungen wie etwa dem *Schwanritter* Konrads von Würzburg. Witwe und Tochter eines auf einem Kreuzzug verstorbenen Ritters wurden von dessen Bruder um ihr Erbe gebracht. Während die beiden Frauen dieses Unrecht dem König vorbringen, geschieht ein seltsames ‚Wunder': Über das Wasser kommt ein weißer Schwan angeflogen, der an einer silbernen Kette ein kleines Boot mit einem Ritter darin Richtung Ufer zieht:

> Der künec blicte nebensich
> aldurch ein venster wünniclich:
> dô spürte er daz ein wîzer swan
> flouc ûf dem wazzer dort herdan
> und nâch im zôch ein schiffelîn
> an einer keten silberîn,
> diu lûter unde schône gleiz.
> der vogel sich des harte fleiz
> daz er die cleinen arken
> gezüge ab dem vil starken
> wilden wâge unmâzen tief.
> ein ritter in dem schiffe slief:
> der hæte sich darîn geleit,
> darüber ein spalier was gespreit
> daz liehten schîn den ougen bar,
> von palmâtsîden rôsenvar,
> in dem diu sunne spilte.[29]
> (*Schwanritter*, V. 245–261)

Sowohl die Glanzmetaphorik („die lûter unde schône gleiz", V. 251; „liehten schîn", V. 259 bzw. „sunne spilte", V. 261) als auch die mit dem (Schwan-)Gefährten beendete Reise runden das *theme* rund um die Ankunft am Strand ab. Um einen solchen handelt es sich eindeutig, im Gegensatz zur Anlandungsszene im *Tristan* ist diese Uferstelle jedoch in unmittelbarer Zivilisationsnähe zu lokalisieren, wie die Inszenierung der Einführung des Protagonisten in die Erzählung zeigt: Der sogenannte Schwanritter wird vom König höchstpersönlich entdeckt und ehrenvoll am Strand empfangen (*Schwanritter*, V. 352–359). Er wird von der höfischen Gesellschaft bereits intuitiv als besonderer Ritter erkannt und von vornherein sehr positiv aufgenommen – er bekommt somit verfrühtes Lob, bevor er seinen Heldenmut überhaupt unter Beweis stellen kann. Motiviert wird das Erkennen der Besonderheit des Ritters nicht im Speziellen, dies wird vom gesamten Figurenpersonal jedoch auch nicht in Frage gestellt. Durch das Strand-*setting* wird bereits eine Vorausdeutung auf die handlungstragende Funktion des Ritters impliziert, die zumindest für die Rezipierenden nicht ausschließlich intuitiv fassbar ist, sondern aufgrund der hinweisenden Funktion des *hero-on-the-beach*-Motivs als solche markiert ist. Diese Ankunftsszene

---

29 „Der König schaute beiseite / durch ein schön verziertes Fenster: / Da bemerkte er einen weißen Schwan, / der über dem Wasser heranflog / und ein kleines Schiff hinter sich her zog / an einer silbernen Kette, / die hell und strahlend glänzte. / Der Vogel gab sich große Mühe, / den kleinen Kahn / durch die wilden weiten Wellen zu ziehen, / die sehr tief waren. / Ein Ritter schlief in dem Schiff: / der hatte sich hineingelegt, / bekleidet mit einem Untergewand / aus rosenfarbener Seide, / auf dem die Sonne widerschien / und den Augen einen hellen Schimmer bot." (Konrad von Würzburg 2016, V. 245–261)

wird sehr ausführlich beschrieben und die Besonderheit der Passage und des Protagonisten mehrfach erwähnt. Welcher Art diese Ausnahmestellung ist, stellt sich erst kurz darauf heraus, denn lediglich der Schwanritter erklärt sich bereit, für die beiden Frauen in einem Zweikampf um deren Erbe anzutreten, gewinnt diesen und wendet damit das Schicksal. Das Auftauchen des Ritters lässt für das Figurenpersonal und auch die Rezipierenden einen radikalen Wendepunkt erahnen und wird durch das *hero-on-the-beach-theme* in seiner Bedeutung hervorgehoben, die tatsächliche Tragweite ist aber erst danach erkennbar.

3.4 Gawains Tod am Strand im *Alliterative Morte Arthur*

Obwohl das *theme* des *hero on the beach* in der altenglischen Literatur häufig vorkommt, ist es in der mittelenglischen Literatur fast gar nicht greifbar. Johnson schreibt: „[I]t might be expected that a theme so abundant in Old English poetry would also have been popular in the later English alliterative poetry. But such does not appear to be the case." (Johnson 1975, 272) Eine Ausnahme gibt es im Mittelenglischen aber doch, auf die auch schon Johnson hinweist. Laut ihm taucht das Motiv nur in einem einzigen mittelenglischen Werk auf, dem *Alliterative Morte Arthure*, und ist dort sogar in sehr deutlicher Ausprägung zu finden (ebd., 272). Dies betrifft aber nicht ausschließlich dieses *theme*, sondern allgemein weist der *Alliterative Morte Arthure* Ähnlichkeiten mit der altenglischen Literatur auf, wie beispielsweise Benson (1966, 76) konstatiert. Allerdings dürfen diese Parallelen nicht über die dennoch vorhandene Eigenständigkeit des *Alliterative Morte Arthure* hinwegtäuschen, da sich das Werk durchaus auch als Produkt seiner eigenen Zeit zeigt und in seiner Ausgestaltung an einem zeitgenössischen Publikum orientiert ist, wie etwa Keiser (1974, 133–144) am Beispiel der Eröffnungsszene darlegt.

Den anderweitig mit Eroberungszügen beschäftigten König Arthur erreichen alarmierende Nachrichten: Der Thron wurde usurpiert, der königliche Schatz geplündert und Guinevere als Frau/Geliebte beansprucht. Arthur kehrt mit seiner Armee nach England zurück und es kommt zu einer Seeschlacht, in der Arthur und seine Männer siegen. Gawain und seine kleine Truppe sind die ersten an Land und Gawain stürmt Richtung Strand, um den Verräter Mordred anzugreifen.

Then Sir Gawain the good	a galley he takes
And glides up at a gole	with good men of armes;
When he grounded, for gref	he girdes in the water
That to the girdle he goes	in all his gilt weedes,
Shootes up upon the sand	in sight of the lordes,
Singly with his soppe,	my sorrow is the more!
With banners of his badges,	best of his armes,
He braides up on the bank	in his bright weedes[30]

(*Alliterative Morte Arthure*, V. 3724–31)

Gawain und seine Männer stehen dem Usurpator Mordred und seine Söldnerarmee ohne die Unterstützung von Arthurs Truppen gegenüber. Das Ergebnis dieses Kampfes ist für eine Erzählung dieser Art und die Ausnahmestellung Gawains jedoch ausgesprochen ungewöhnlich: Gawain wird umzingelt und es folgt die Niederlage durch Mordred – dieser Kampf endet also mit dem Tod Gawains. Jeder, sogar Mordred, beklagt Gawains Tod, denn er soll der beste aller Ritter gewesen sein. Arthur betrauert ebenfalls diesen Verlust und schwört, Gawains Tod zu rächen.

Gawains heroische Gestalt scheint im *Alliterative Morte Arthure* oft sogar die von König Arthur zu übertreffen, wenn der Dichter ihn im Laufe der Erzählung beispielsweise in einem ausgedehnten Zweikampf mit Sir Priamus sowie zahlreichen anderen Begegnungen zeigt, in denen Gawain die dominierende Rolle spielt.[31] Selbst nachdem Gawain getötet wird, genügt ein kurzer ‚Lebenslauf' seines edlen Lebens, um Mordred dazu zu bringen, seine verräterischen Taten zu bereuen. Wer daher von einem wundersamen Sieg des scheinbar überragenden Helden gegen eine Übermacht ausgeht, wird enttäuscht, hätte diese Wendung des Schicksals aber durch die Ausgestaltung des Strand-*theme* erahnen können, das bereits auf das Unerwartete oder in diesem Fall zumindest nicht Erhoffte vorausdeutet.[32]

---

30 „Dann nimmt Sir Gawain, der Gute, eine Galeere / und segelt einen schmalen Meeresarm hinauf mit guten Kämpfern. / Als er strandete, stürzt er aus Bedrängnis (oder auch: ‚Wut') ins Wasser, / sodass er darin bis zum Gürtel ist in seiner goldverzierten Kleidung (Rüstung), / stürmt auf den Strand in Sichtweite der Lords (Adeligen), / alleine mit seiner Truppe, zu meinem großen Leidwesen! / Mit seinem Wappenbanner, seinen besten Waffen / springt er ans Ufer in seiner glänzenden Rüstung." [eigene Übersetzung]
31 Vgl. hierzu auch die Ausführungen von Johnson (1975, 272).
32 Konkretisiert wird diese Vorausdeutung kurz darauf, als der Erzähler einen seiner wenigen Kommentare in der ersten Person einarbeitet: „*For had Sir Gawayne the grāce tō hǫld the green hill, / Hē had worship, īwis, wonnen forever!*" [„Wenn Sir Gawein das Glück gehabt hätte, den grünen Hügel zu halten, / Hätte er Ruhm, ich weiß es, für immer gewonnen!"] (V. 3768–3769; eigene Übersetzung). Bezogen auf diese Passage meint Ziolkowski: „Whether the word grace in

Als er sich und seine Männer von einer Übermacht von sechzigtausend Männern Mordreds umzingelt sieht, wird auch Gawain selbst sich dessen bewusst, dass sein Schicksal sich gewendet hat. Zu diesem Zeitpunkt wird Gawain klar, dass er sich und seine Männer durch seinen überstürzten Angriff, ohne auf Arthur und seine Truppen zu warten, zum Scheitern und damit zum Tod verurteilt hat (Finlayson 1968, 270). Der Wendepunkt, der durch das Strand-*theme* somit bereits zu erahnen war, wird nun auch dem Helden selbst klar.

Wie erwähnt, sinnt Arthur auf Rache und setzt seine Ankündigung auch in die Tat um, was wiederum auf einen bedeutenden Kampf hinausläuft. Auch dieser endet durchaus ungewöhnlich (vgl. Johnson 1975, 274) mit dem Tod beider Anführer, wovon einer Arthur ist. Fichte (1981, 114) deutet hier einen direkten Zusammenhang zwischen Gawains Tod und jenem von Arthur an: „Once he [Gawain] is killed, his death precipitates Arthur's own downfall, since the king, bent on revenge, is now deaf to any sensible advice."

In Hinblick auf das *hero-on-the-beach-theme* und die vier von Crowne festgelegten Kriterien stellt Johnson (1975, 272) bezogen auf die Verse 3724–3731 des mittelenglischen *Alliterative Morte Arthure* fest: „This passage satisfies almost perfectly the four criteria [...] for the theme of ‚the hero on the beach'". Gawain kommt mit seinen Begleitern (V. 3725 und 3728–3729; vgl. Johnson 1975, 273) am Strand an und beendet damit eine lange Heeresfahrt in der Gefolgschaft Arthurs sowie eine Seereise. Das *flashing-light*-Motiv ist eher in einer Andeutung versteckt – in der Beschreibung des Glanzes seiner Ausrüstung: „gilt weedes" (V. 3727) und „bright weedes" (V. 3731).[33] Das Adjektiv *bright* taucht vier Verse darauf (als „bryghte wapyne" nach der Zitation Johnsons bzw. „brigth wēpen" nach der Ausgabe Bensons) erneut auf. Zwar kommt dieses Adjektiv gerade in diesen Kombinationen nicht selten in der alliterierenden Funktion vor, dennoch ist eine solche Häufung innerhalb so weniger Zeilen auffällig. Somit scheint der Hinweis auf den Glanz diverser Objekte besonders nachdrücklich.

Für viele Passagen des *Alliterative Morte Arthure* können die benutzten Vorlagen recht gut benannt werden,[34] dies gilt jedoch nicht für die hier angeführte

---

this line means ‚good fortune' or ‚the favor of God', the poet gives a plain indication that Gawain's string of victories is near its end." (Ziolkowski 1988, 240)

33 Vgl. Johnson (1975, 273), der jedoch eine andere Ausgabe verwendet und entsprechend „gylte wedys" und „bryghte wedys" nennt.

34 Für die Eingangsszene legt dies beispielsweise Keiser (1974) dar und geht dabei von einer Abhängigkeit von Waces *Brut* aus. Keiser verweist dabei auch auf die 1963 an der University of Cambridge eingereichte, allerdings unpublizierte Dissertation von John Finlayson, der darin seiner Meinung nach überzeugende Beweise dafür liefert, dass Wace als die Hauptquelle des *Alliterative Morte Arthure* anzusehen sei.

Passage. Auch Johnson (1975, 271) konstatiert: „no wholly satisfactory written source for this passage has been identified". Fichte (1981, 108) stellt in seiner Beschäftigung mit der Figur Gawains ebenfalls fest: „In none of the three sources [Laȝamon, Geoffrey of Monmouth, Wace] do we find an account of Gawain's desperate fight against Mordred – a fight provoked by Gawain's monomaniacal desire for revenge." Durch die Einführung der sogenannten ‚oral formulaic theory' und deren Anwendung für die Interpretation von alt- und mittelenglischen Werken wurde das Phänomen des Aufgreifens bekannter Muster in mittelalterlicher Dichtung in einem neuen Licht gesehen (Göller 1981, 10). Bezogen darauf ist es denkbar, dass sich die besprochene Passage des *Alliterative Morte Arthure* rein aus der mündlichen Tradition speist und gar nicht auf einer schriftlichen Quelle basiert.[35] Dass sich dieses Motiv über Jahrhunderte halten konnte, könnte wiederum also ein Indiz für den Erfolg als Memorierungshilfe sein (vgl. Johnson 1975, 275–280), was uns zum Beginn der Forschungsgeschichte des *hero-on-the-beach-theme* zurückbringt.

4 Fazit

Insgesamt kann sowohl für die Heldenepik als auch für die höfische Literatur festgestellt werden, dass das *hero-on-the-beach*-Motiv zutrifft, nämlich insofern, dass das *setting* ‚Strand' formelhaft als Memorierungs-, Erinnerungs- und (Wieder-)Erkennungshilfe dient. Somit werden mit dem Strand üblicherweise ganz bestimmte Dinge verknüpft, die in dieser Erzählsituation aufgerufen werden können. Dies erleichtert einerseits die Strukturierung und Befüllung mit Inhalt für den Vortragenden, andererseits aber auch die Einordnung und gedankliche Gliederung für die Rezipierenden.

In vielen Fällen gehen vier Merkmale Hand in Hand: Zum einen der eine Reise antretende oder beendende Protagonist, meist mit seinen Begleitern, zum anderen der Übergangsraum Wasser-Land, der sich im Strand manifestiert, und schließlich das *flashing-light*-Motiv, das sich in sehr unterschiedlichen Ausformungen zeigen kann. Nicht alle Elemente müssen zwingend vorhanden bzw.

---

[35] In diesem Kontext ist zu bedenken, dass sich der Arthur-Stoff grundsätzlich stark aus mündlichen keltischen Erzählungen speist (Birkhan 2004, 40–41). Daher wäre es unter Umständen lohnend, Renoirs (1989) Ansatz, das *hero-on-the-beach-theme* als indoeuropäisches Versatzstück zu sehen, auf den *Alliterative Morte Arhure* anzuwenden, wobei sich gerade für Passagen ohne Vorlage möglicherweise eine Interpolation aus dem Keltischen und Germanischen herausstellen könnte.

explizit benannt sein, können aber unter Umständen interpretiert bzw. durch die übrige Beschreibung der Szenerie und Handlung assoziiert werden.

Zusätzlich kann festgestellt werden, dass der Strand das *setting* für inhaltlich äußerst wichtige und einschneidende Wendepunkte darstellt, die die weitere Handlung teils massiv beeinflussen bzw. erst ermöglichen. Somit fungiert der Strand nicht nur als reine Memorierungs- und Strukturierungshilfe, sondern ihm kommt auch die Funktion der Vorausdeutung auf einen essentiellen Handlungseinschnitt und eine drastische Wendung der Erzählung zu.

Die Verbindung zwischen wichtigem inhaltlichen Wendepunkt und diesem *setting* ist jedoch keine rein literarische Erfindung. Das Strand-*setting* wird nicht nur literarisch mit der Funktion aufgeladen, eine bedeutende Veränderung einzuläuten, sondern ist auch realhistorisch damit verknüpft, wodurch aufgrund von Alltagserlebnissen – wie der Anlandung eines Handelsschiffes, die Ankunft fremder Krieger, die generelle Nutzung als Verkehrsweg etc. – wiederum in der Literatur zusätzliche Assoziationen rund um einen Wendepunkt aufgerufen werden können.

Literaturverzeichnis

„Battle of Maldon". *The Cambridge Old English Reader*. Hg. Richard Marsden. Cambridge: Cambridge University Press, 2006. 254–269.

Beowulf. Bilingual Edition. Herausgegeben und übersetzt von Howell D. Chickering, Jr. New York: Anchor Books, 1989.

Kudrun. Zweisprachige Ausgabe. Herausgegeben und übersetzt von Uta Störmer-Caysa. Stuttgart: Reclam, 2010.

„Alliterative Morte Arthure". *King Arthur's Death. The Middle English Stanzaic Morte Arthur and Alliterative Morte Arthure*. Hg. Larry D. Benson und Edward E. Foster. Kalamazoo: Medieval Institute Publications, 1994. 113–238.

Gottfried von Straßburg. *Tristan*. Hg. Karl Marold. Berlin und New York: De Gruyter, 2004.

Konrad von Würzburg. *„Schwanritter". Das Herzmære und andere Verserzählungen. Mittelhochdeutsch/Neuhochdeutsch*. Nach der Textausgabe von Eduard Schröder. Hg. Lydia Miklautsch. Stuttgart: Reclam, 2016.

Baetke, Walter. *Wörterbuch zur altnordischen Prosaliteratur. Vollständiges Faksimile der 1. Auflage (Berlin 1965–1968) zusammen mit Titelei und beiden Vorwörtern der zweiten, durchgesehenen Auflage (Darmstadt 1976) samt Korrekturen, erweitert um einen alphabetischen Stichwortindex aller im Wörterbuch verzeichneten altnordischen Wörter mit Flexions- und Wortklassenangaben*. Bearbeitet von Hans Fix in Verbindung mit Norbert Endres und Andrej Schabalin, unter Mitwirkung von Andreas Braml, Sebastian Holtzhauer, Jana Ilgner, Ann-Kathrin Müller und Fabian Schwabe. Greifswald: o. V., 2006 [digitalisierte Ausgabe].

Benson, Larry D. „The Alliterative ‚Morte Arthure' and ‚Medieval Tragedy'". *Tennessee Studies in Literature* 11 (1966): 75–87.

Birkhan, Helmut. *Keltische Erzählungen vom Kaiser Arthur*. Teil 1. Wien: LIT Verlag, 2004.

Bleumer, Hartmut. „Diagramm und Dimension. Zum Raumproblem heldenepischer Narrationen am Beispiel der Kudrun". *Zeitschrift für Literaturwissenschaft und Linguistik* 44.4 (2014): 93–126.

Campbell, Joseph. *Der Heros in tausend Gestalten*. Frankfurt/Main: Fischer, 1953.

Clark, George. „The Battle of Maldon: A Heroic Poem". *Speculum* 43.1 (1968): 52–71.

Corbin, Alain. *The Lure of the Sea. The Discovery of the Seaside in the Western World, 1750–1840*. Berkeley: University of California Press, 1994.

Crowne, David K. „An Example of Composition by Theme in Anglo-Saxon Poetry". *Neuphilologische Mitteilungen* 61.4 (1960): 362–372.

Fichte, Jörg. O. „The Figure of Sir Gawain". *The Alliterative Morte Arture. A Reassessment of the Poem*. Hg. Karl Heinz Göller. Cambridge: D. S. Brewer, 1981. 106–116.

Finlayson, John. „The Concept of the Hero in ‚Morte Arthure'". *Chaucer und seine Zeit. Symposion für Walter F. Schirmer*. Hg. Arno Esch. Tübingen: Niemeyer, 1968. 249–274.

Fry, Donald K. „The Hero on the Beach in ‚Finnsburh'". *Neuphilologische Mitteilungen* 67.1 (1966): 27–31.

Gneuss, Helmut. „*The Battle of Maldon* 89: Byrhtnōð's ‚Ofermod' Once Again". *Studies in Philology* 73.2 (1976): 117–137.

Göller, Karl Heinz. „A Summary of Research". *The Alliterative Morte Arture. A Reassessment of the Poem*. Hg. Karl Heinz Göller. Cambridge: D. S. Brewer, 1981. 7–14.

Hahn, Ingrid. *Raum und Landschaft in Gottfrieds Tristan. Ein Beitrag zur Werkdeutung*. München: Eidos, 1963.

Higley, Sarah Lynn. „‚Aldor on Ofre'. Or the Reluctant Hart: A Study of Liminality in ‚Beowulf'". *Neuphilologische Mitteilungen* 87.3 (1986): 342–353.

Jeute, Gerson H. „Zwischen Piratennest und Bischofssitz. Die Hafenorte im Bremer Becken". *Häfen im 1. Millenium AD. Bauliche Konzepte, herrschaftliche und religiöse Einflüsse. RGZM-Tagungen Bd. 22*. Hg. Thomas Schmidts und Martin M. Vučetić. Mainz: RGZ, 2015. 231–246.

Johnson, James D. „‚The Hero on the Beach' in the Alliterative ‚Morte Arthure'". *Neuphilologische Mitteilungen* 76.2 (1975): 271–281.

Keiser, George R. „Narrative Structure in the Alliterative ‚Morte Arthure', 26–720". *The Chaucer Review* 9.2 (1974): 130–144.

Kellenbenz, Hermann. *Die Wiege der Moderne. Wirtschaft und Gesellschaft Europas 1350–1650*. Stuttgart: Klett-Cotta, 1991.

Lord, Albert B. *The Singer of Tales*. Hg. Stephen Mitchell und Gregory Nagy. 2. Aufl. Cambridge/MA: Harvard University Press, 2001.

Lotman, Jurij M. *Die Struktur literarischer Texte*. Übersetzt von Rolf-Dietrich Keil. 4. Aufl. München: Fink, 1993.

Meier, Dirk. „Mensch und Umwelt im Rungholt-Gebiet des hohen und späten Mittelalters". *Rungholt. Rätselhaft und Widersprüchlich*. Hg. Jürgen Newig und Uwe Haupenthal. Husum: Husum Druck- und Verlagsgesellschaft, 2016. 19–31.

Parks, Wards. *Verbal Dueling in Heroic Narrative. The Homeric and the Old English Traditions*. Princeton/NY: Princeton University Press, 1990.

Renoir, Alain. „Oral-Formulaic Theme Survival: A Possible Instance in the ‚Nibelungenlied'". *Neuphilologische Mitteilungen* 65.1 (1964): 70–75.

Renoir, Alain. „The Hero on the Beach: Germanic Theme and Indo-European Origin". *Neuphilologische Mitteilungen* 90.1 (1989): 111–116.

Rieken, Bernd. *Nordsee ist Mordsee. Sturmfluten und ihre Bedeutung für die Mentalitätsgeschichte der Friesen*. Münster: Waxmann, 2005.

Sandmo, Erling. *Ungeheuerlich. Seemonster in Karten und Literatur 1491–1895*. Übersetzt von Sylvia Kall. München: Nagel & Kimche, 2018.

Schulz, Monika. *Gottfried von Straßburg. ‚Tristan'*. Stuttgart: Metzler, 2017.

Shippey, Tom. „Boar and Badger. An Old English Heroic Antithesis". *Leeds Studies in English* 16 (1985): 220–239.

Simek, Rudolf. *Die Schiffe der Wikinger*. Stuttgart: Reclam, 2014.

Störmer-Caysa, Uta. *Grundstrukturen mittelalterlicher Erzählungen. Raum und Zeit im höfischen Roman*. Berlin und New York: De Gruyter, 2007.

Wagenführ, Philip. *Schiffsrouten und Navigation im spätmittelalterlichen Nordeuropa. Instrumente und Methoden*. Hamburg: Diplomica, 2015.

Ziolkowski, Jan. „A Narrative Structure in the Alliterative ‚Morte Arthure' 1–1221 and 3150–4346". *The Chaucer Review* 22.3 (1988): 234–245.

Elsa Devienne
'There's Law on the Beach!': Law and Order on Los Angeles's Beaches 1910s–1970s

How is it possible to combine the hedonism of the beach setting and the necessity to maintain urban order? This is the question that Los Angeles beach authorities had to contend with throughout the twentieth century. At the intersection of the history of policing and the history of seaside leisure, this article analyzes the ways in which authorities, users, and coastal residents negotiated the seaside order from the beginning of the twentieth century – when the littoral was considered a sort of free-for-all space far from the authorities' gaze – until the 1970s, when the beaches, under the pressure of urban expansion, became part and parcel of the city. Based on a varied range of sources (press, municipal archives, etc.), the article shows that despite the emergence of a regime of 'seaside tolerance,' the increasing urbanization of the beaches made the coastline less accessible and less attractive to working-class beachgoers and ethnic and racial minority groups.

Wie lässt sich der Hedonismus einer Strandumgebung mit der Notwendigkeit vereinbaren, die städtische Ordnung aufrechtzuerhalten? Mit dieser Fragestellung mussten sich die für den Strand von Los Angeles zuständigen Autoritäten das gesamte zwanzigste Jahrhundert hindurch auseinandersetzen. Am Schnittpunkt der Geschichte von Überwachung und Kontrolle und der Geschichte von am Strand verbrachter Freizeit situiert, analysiert dieser Artikel die Arten und Weisen, auf die Autoritäten, Besucher*innen und Küstenbewohner*innen die Ordnung am Strand verhandelten. Der Zeitrahmen erstreckt sich dabei vom Beginn des zwanzigsten Jahrhunderts, als man die Küste noch als einen dem Blick der Autoritäten entzogenen Freiraum für alle betrachtete, bis zu den 1970er Jahren, als die Strände, unter dem Druck urbaner Expansion, zum Bestandteil der Stadt wurden. Unter Rückgriff auf eine große Bandbreite von Quellen (Presse, Stadtarchive etc.) zeigt der Artikel, dass trotz der Herausbildung eines Regimes der ‚seaside tolerance' die zunehmende Urbanisierung der Strände die Küstenregion weniger zugänglich und weniger attraktiv für Strandbesucher*innen der Arbeiterklasse sowie ethnische Minoritäten machte.

1 Introduction

"Have a good time at the beach this year! Go as often as you please! Stay as long as you please. Swim as much as you like. Eat what you want; and soak up the sunshine." (Hamilton 1936, 15) On July 5, 1936, *The Los Angeles Times* encouraged its readers to find refuge from the heat on the beaches of the metropolis. While the article celebrated the freedom the seaside offered, it also included stern words of warning: "But remember just this," cautioned the journalist, "there is law on the beach and you are expected to observe it to the letter!"

(Ibid.) Indeed, the rest of the article consisted of a list of the laws that applied to beachgoers.

Such an article throws into sharp relief the tensions surrounding the policing of beaches in a large metropolis: How is it possible, indeed, to combine the hedonism of the beach setting and the necessity to maintain urban order? In Los Angeles, the seaside attracted little attention from law enforcement as the city first developed inland, about fifteen miles from the ocean. Starting in the mid-1920s, Los Angeles experienced an economic boom that propelled urban growth towards the Pacific. The first laws specifically regulating beachgoing behavior appeared in that context, when the city's public beaches truly became *urban* spaces.

Today, many activities are banned on the beaches of Los Angeles, including drinking alcohol, walking dogs, begging, sleeping, building a fire, and setting up a tent. Moreover, the surveillance and repression of visitors' behavior have intensified, especially for some groups of beachgoers – namely, youths and racial minorities – who have historically been the object of intense scrutiny by the police. Indeed, in his famous 1990s opus on the City of Angels, Mike Davis claimed that its beaches were "virtually inaccessible" to young African Americans and Latinos (Davis 1992, 258).

At first glance, the history of beach policing in Los Angeles seems to correspond to a familiar narrative developed by social scientists: Public spaces in urban America, particularly starting in the 1970s, have become heavily policed and, as a result, less diverse and less accessible, especially for certain categories of people (Low and Smith 2005; Zukin 1991; Beckett and Herbert 2010). However, a closer look reveals that the process through which the L. A. coastline morphed from a sort of free-for-all space into a site of intense surveillance is more complex than it appears. Police control over urban space did not gradually expand from downtown to the city's margins in a mechanical fashion. Rather, the history of urban order – and seaside order is no exception – is one of constant negotiation and trial and error. Over the past ten years, historians of policing have highlighted both the ways in which police officers adapt laws to what happens on the ground and how citizens can occasionally question the legitimacy of city ordinances (e. g. Deluermoz 2012; Deluermoz et al. 2015). Moreover, discounting the coastline as just another space that the police eventually started to patrol does not account for the complex factors that accompanied the transformation of the city's beaches into urban spaces, fully integrated into the metropolitan matrix.

In this article, I analyze the evolution of beach laws and beach policing in twentieth-century Los Angeles. In doing so, I aim to avoid a teleological vision that overemphasizes the linearity of the process through which urban spaces in the US have become intensely policed. I also refuse the common narrative found in histories of the seaside that describes the beach as a space separate from everyday life, where relationships of domination and social and racial hierarchies are suspended. This project thus sits at the intersection of two historiographies that are rarely discussed at the same time: the history of policing and the history of the seaside.¹ Building on recent research on urban law enforcement (Milliot 2007; Dewerpe 2006; Blanchard 2011), I uncover the rationale behind the progressive (and imperfect) 'ordering' of the seaside.² In doing so, I contribute to the study of public order at the margins of cities (e. g. Fassin 2014). In addition, this article also sketches out the contours of a history of urban beaches – which has yet to be written. While there is a rich social and cultural history of seaside leisure (e. g. Corbin 2010; Désert 1983; Vincent 2007), historians have tended to consider beaches as spaces detached from everyday life and urban issues. By contrast, this study shows that the coastline of a large metropolis such as Los Angeles formed an integral part of the city, with typical urban problems such as security and crowd control.

I used different types of archives to carry out this study: Municipal archives include accounts of the debates that precede the adoption of new laws and give us an insight into residents' demands; local newspapers often relay the authorities' point of view, but they can also give a glimpse into everyday interactions between police officers and bathers; finally, while it is impossible for a historian to go back in time and follow a police patrol in its everyday activities, I was able to find accounts by sociologists and journalists who did so in the past.³

The study covers most of the twentieth century, from the 1910s – in other words, from the moment L. A.'s beaches started attracting large numbers of visitors – up until the 1970s – after the major shift of the 1960s, when crime rates in US cities soared. During this period, the management of public order on the beach did not change in reaction to increases or decreases in crime but because of economic factors – in particular, the rising value of coastal real estate – and socio-demographic changes – the increasing visibility of youths and ethnic, racial, and sexual minorities playing a major role in the postwar period. In

---

1 One exception is a sociological study of police surveillance on a public beach in Marseille, France, by Andréo (1990).
2 It is worth mentioning that, in France at least, historians of policing took their inspiration from sociologists, who produced the first studies on the police (e. g. Monjardet 1996). In the US, historians have recently explored the urban consequences of mass incarceration (e. g. Thompson and Murch 2015).
3 Police archives are usually not accessible to scholars in the US and historians often have to resort to newspapers, city archives, sociological studies, and interviews with police officers (e. g. Philippe 2007).

contrast to a linear vision of an ever more repressive system of surveillance, this history of L. A. beaches shows how the littoral 'entered' the city and how, in doing so, it altered law enforcement practices at the metropolitan scale.

2 A Lawless Space?

According to historians of the seaside, the beach of the nineteenth and early twentieth centuries amounted to a lawless space, where "the certainties of authority [were] diluted, and the usual constraints on behavior [were] suspended" (Walton 2000, 3). There is no doubt that the seaside in the Western world represented, at least until the Second World War, a space outside the ordinary, where both clothing and conduct followed looser rules. However, beaches located near or within large cities were carefully regulated, and they could become the site of violent confrontations that called for police intervention. The 1919 Chicago race riot, for instance, started on a Lake Michigan beach: The intrusion of black beachgoers into an area usually reserved to whites led to an altercation. Historians have shown that throughout the twentieth century leisure spaces in general (not just beaches) crystallized racial tensions because they encouraged playful flirting and could potentially become the site of interracial sexual encounters (e. g. Diamond 2009; Wiltse 2007; Wolcott 2012).

In early twentieth-century Los Angeles, however, beach policing did not represent a major issue for local authorities. For one, racial relations were not as tense as in Chicago, where the large numbers of African-American migrants arriving from the South during the First World War caused intense rivalries for access to housing and other urban attractions such as leisure spaces. By comparison, the black population in Los Angeles remained much smaller up until the Second World War.[4] In California, where there were no segregation laws, African Americans could, in theory, have access to the entire coastline. Yet in practice, they used two beaches – the 'Inkwell,' in Santa Monica, and 'Bruce's Beach,' in Manhattan Beach – where the risk of being chased off by white beachgoers was lower (Jefferson 2009). Racial violence did occur occasionally – some incidents were even started by the police[5] – but it paled in comparison to the daily, and often bloody, interracial encounters on Chicago beaches.

---

4 There were 7 600 African Americans in Los Angeles in 1910 and 15 500 in 1920 (Flamming 2006, 25).

5 In 1920, an African-American man was hit by three police officers for refusing to leave a beach traditionally closed off to black beachgoers (Flamming 2006, 183–184).

The police also considered beaches a low priority because of the relatively small number of year-round residents living in coastal communities (Davidson 2004). At the beginning of the twentieth century, beach resorts such as Santa Monica and Venice relied almost exclusively on the tourism and leisure industry.[6] Considering the stiff competition to attract visitors, municipalities did not wish to scare off beachgoers by enforcing strict laws on the seaside. On the contrary, tourist brochures touted "the exhilarating freedom which only the ocean [could] provide" (Long Beach Municipal Convention and Publicity Bureau 1932, 5). Moreover, considering the small size of their police forces, coastal communities chose to concentrate their officers where they were most needed – on the streets. Indeed, according to the Venice Chief of Police in 1917, "there were not enough police in the city to watch all the bathers" ("Will Permit" 1917, 1). The problem also existed in neighboring Santa Monica: In 1911, the resort town's mayor recommended that a police officer be stationed near the municipal bathhouse, only to be told by the city council that such a measure could not be financed ("Wear Skirts" 1911, II 1). As for the communities that were part of the city of Los Angeles, they were also underserved. A sprawling metropolis unlike any other at the time, Los Angeles had the lowest number of officers *per capita* in the country.[7] Finally, it was only in the 1920s and 1930s that the first professional lifeguard teams were organized (Verge 2005, 24; Verge 2007). In other words, at the beginning of the century, there weren't any authority figures on the coastline, and beachgoers could engage in all kinds of activities – walking their dog, drinking alcohol, or starting a fire – for which no regulation existed. This flexible legal regime, which characterized the coastline, explains why beaches were often the site of festive gatherings organized by schools, charitable organizations, and local residents. Overnight, the beaches could morph into vast encampments with large bonfires and parked cars on the sand.[8] Such events would never have been possible in urban parks, where behavior was much more tightly regulated. This was the case for instance in New York's Central Park, where, around the same period, guards were on the lookout for visitors who drank alcohol or dared set foot on the park's lawns (Rosenzweig and Blackmar 1998, 313).

---

[6] The commercial and industrial port of Los Angeles was located in San Pedro Bay.
[7] One officer for 1 300 inhabitants in 1900 (compared to 1 for 430 in New York for instance) (Reiss 1992, 56–57).
[8] See the L. A. newspaper *Santa Monica Evening Outlook* for the 1900–1920 period.

3 Negotiating Nudity

The only regulations that did exist on the city's beaches at the time concerned bathing suits. Historians of the seaside phenomenon have written much about the bathing-suit laws, but they have tended to focus exclusively on women's attire (e. g. Sohn 2006, 94; Granger 2009; for the US, see Latham 1995). Moreover, they have usually exaggerated the rigidity of such rules, probably because the most striking images of these 'beach battles' – police vans filled with flappers in revealing bathing suits, swimmer Annette Kellerman's arrest in 1907, etc. – greatly pleased the more 'modern' generations, for whom such prudishness was obvious proof of their superiority. A more nuanced analysis of these laws in Los Angeles shows that female (and male) bathers were able to negotiate the exact terms of such rules. For one, many municipalities, such as Santa Monica, did not enact any laws regarding bathing suits on the premise that the innate modesty of beachgoers rendered such ordinances unnecessary ("Girl Dares" 1916, 1). Such attitudes were widespread in the US: The Board of Recreation superintendent in Bridgeport, Connecticut, considered that "the public [was] fairly sane on [the] matter of [bathing suits] and prescribing the inches above the knee, etc. [was] all tommy-rot" ("Bathing Suit" 1923, 569). In other words, the existence of profoundly internalized social norms removed the need for a written rule (Elias 1978). Moreover, in metropolitan Los Angeles, enforcing bathing-suit laws was complicated by the fact (unknown to most beachgoers) that the beaches belonged to different municipalities and thus enforced different laws. In 1930, a 'Public Beach Coordinating Committee' attempted to formulate uniform bathing suit regulations for the entire coastline but ended up abandoning the idea "in view of new styles being turned out by manufacturers every year" ("Bathing Suit Modesty" 1930, A2). And even when police officers did take action, as in August 1929, when the city of Santa Monica cracked down on male beachgoers who stripped to their waists, the transgressors could escape punishment by hurriedly adjusting their shoulder straps, diving into the water, or disappearing into the crowd ("Eight Face" 1929, A1). The police, if only by its appearance on the beach, did force beachgoers to "discipline"[9] themselves, but in doing so they also expressed their opposition to what they believed were old-fashioned norms. While the encounters between officers and Angelenos did result in compliance, bathing-suit regulations remained fragile and contested.

Moreover, coastline municipalities were especially concerned with preserving their reputation with the public, for fear of losing visitors to other resorts. At the beginning of the twentieth century, the American society experienced a

---

9 Term used in accordance with Foucault (2014).

"revolution in manners and morals" (Allen 1997, 76) that challenged the dominant Victorian values of modesty and restraint, in particular with regards to the body and behavior of women (Fass 1977). In this context, residents in beach communities were divided: The younger generation – men and women who enjoyed the pleasures of the seaside on a regular basis (swimming, playing ballgames on the sand, etc.) – supported a flexible policy; on the opposing side, the members of the city council, who were usually male and much older, wished to uphold moral values and found support from local religious authorities and upper-class women's clubs. Bathers' daily acts of transgression and occasional public protests did, in some instances, force the latter to renounce their plans. In 1912, for instance, the Venice city council abandoned its plan to adopt an ordinance regulating the length of bathing suits when a petition opposing it gained traction ("Bathing Suits Up" 1912, 1). But the most effective weapon bathers possessed was the local press and its power to make or destroy a resort's reputation. In the 1910s, controversies arose over the ordinances that prohibited bathers from walking through the city uncovered. While the police arrested many bathers (both male and female) in the streets and shops of the metropolis up until 1919, they eventually stopped when beach resorts realized that reports of the arrests in local newspapers were earning the region a bad reputation among tourists. In 1919, following the arrest of a "very pretty and young matron" in Santa Monica, the local paper expressed fears the news would turn the beach city into "the laughing stock of liberal minded persons" ("Arrest" 1919, 1). Given such negative media coverage of the arrest, police felt compelled to drop the case and stop enforcing the ordinance.[10] On the beach, not only was strict policing impractical (police officers were too few and bathers too often misinformed), but it placed the tourism and leisure economy at risk.

4 The First Beach Laws

While the beaches of the early twentieth century benefited from a relatively flexible legal regime, the situation changed in the 1920s and 1930s when three phenomena altered the economic and socio-demographic standing of beach communities. First, the region experienced rapid demographic growth: From 930 000 residents living in the county in 1920, the population grew to 2.2 million ten years later (Fogelson 1967, 77). Second, right around that time, Los Angeles elites made the conscious decision to abandon the traditional concentric

---
[10] For more details on this controversy, see Devienne (2018).

configuration of the city in favor of a low-density, horizontal urban landscape (Axelrod 2009). By refusing to reproduce the planning decisions made in older industrial cities on the East Coast, which were plagued by congestion and pollution, they accelerated the demographic movement towards the Westside. By the end of the 1920s, the influx of new residents had turned the small beach resorts of the Westside into full-fledged residential communities. At the same time, the region's economy grew increasingly diverse, with the development of the movie business, oil, agriculture, and aircraft manufacturing. Attracting more visitors to the coast thus ceased to be the primary concern of beach cities, and bringing order to the seaside became increasingly important to local elites. Coastal homeowners began to see how their own interests, in particular the value of coastal real estate, were linked to the ways in which the beach was policed. As for local city leaders, they wished to project an image of respectability in order to attract wealthy residents and tourists.

Within a few years, a legal arsenal emerged that regulated behaviors on the beach and indirectly excluded the working class and any bathers who did not conform to the ideal image of a tourist. For instance, the presence of squatters on the beach – which up until then had never been mentioned in the sources – led to the adoption of several laws. By banning fires and *closed* tents, beach cities hoped to chase them off from the sands without inconveniencing tourists (who did use tents to protect themselves from the sun). In 1926, the superintendent of the Los Angeles Board of Playground and Recreation proposed such an ordinance, arguing that closed tents "resulted in committing nuisances, which have called forth numerous complaints" (Minutes of the BPRC, 17 June 1926). While the declaration remained allusive, it targeted both those who used the beach as a camping ground and those who used it for 'depraved' behavior. Similarly, in 1927, the Los Angeles City Council voted a new law banning beach fires. While many bathers did complain about the charcoal left buried in the sands, the law also discouraged squatters and working-class bathers, who enjoyed "wienie bakes" on the beach ("Beach Fires" 1927, 2). The law did not affect upper-class bathers, who had access to private beach clubs, where beach fires remained legal. In Redondo Beach, beach fires were banned in the 1930s after coastal residents complained of the odors wafting from the beach (Hamilton 1936, 15). For local homeowners, the beach was not merely a public space but their backyard, which they believed they had the right to supervise.

Beach laws multiplied in the next few years, often in response to the demands of local residents.[11] Some regulations pertained to bathers' safety, as was

---

[11] See for instance the petition by Venice residents sent on 19 September 1951 to the L. A. City Council.

the case with the beach fire ban and other laws banning dogs, alcohol, and hard balls from the sands. But others had little to do with safety: Peddling, organizing a meeting, begging, and boisterous behavior were all forbidden (Ordinance n° 90738 from 23 April 1946; "Beach Regulations" 1930, A1). All these laws had consequences beyond their apparent goals (reducing odors, keeping bathers safe, etc.): They framed the beach as a space exclusively reserved for the enjoyment of middle- and upper-class bathers. Up until then, the beach had always been a site of sociability for the working class and a temporary camping ground for homeless people as well as a recreational space for wealthier people. Starting in the 1930s, such mixture of different activities proved impossible. The integration of coastal municipalities into the metropolis thus represented a turning point in the history of seaside order: From that moment on, beaches became much more strictly policed. This change did not impact bathers equally. Only working-class visitors, who did not have access to private beaches and who could not afford a house by the sea, had to comply systematically with these new rules. In the following years, forms of resistance to these rules emerged. As a result, a certain tolerance towards minor transgressions persisted throughout the 1930s.

5 A Troubled Seaside Order

With new rules also came new enforcement measures: In Santa Monica, for instance, lifeguards gained the power to arrest bathers in 1932, and an officer was assigned on the pleasure pier starting in 1940 (Letter from 20 February 1963; *Santa Monica Evening Outlook*, 1 July 1940, 1). But in some other coastal cities beach supervision was not as well-funded, and, in the summer, none of the seasonal lifeguards were also police officers. Only on special holidays, such as New Year's Eve and Independence Day, were police officers specifically assigned to the beach ("Noise" 1940, A1). On more than one occasion, police representatives of the Westside had to explain to lawmakers that their new beach ordinances would not be enforced. On 18 August 1927, for instance, a representative of the L. A. Police Department warned the City Council that the beach fire ban would not be enforced considering the shortage of manpower (Minutes of the BPRC, 18 August 1927). One year later, the captain of the Sawtelle division used the same argument when facing the Recreation Commission (Minutes of the BPRC, 2 August 1928). The shortage of police in a rapidly expanding city was an acute problem at the time: In 1937, the L. A. police chief claimed that despite the city's rapid demographic growth, the number of officers had barely changed since 1926 (Los Angeles Police Department 1936–1937, 4).

Moreover, the enforcement of beach laws proved particularly difficult in the region because the coast was divided among several administrative entities, each with its own set of rules. It was precisely to avoid confusion that in 1936 the *Los Angeles Times* published its special report, mentioned above, on beachfront regulations. In this article, the journalist listed the different rules enforced along the coast, compiling a sort of guide for the wandering bather. The fact that a journalist saw the need for such a guide indicates that many bathers probably broke the law – consciously or not – on a regular basis.

Some rules, it was commonly acknowledged, were never truly enforced. In Venice and Ocean Park, for instance, bathers played all kinds of ballgames on the beach despite the existing ban on such activities: "Why do guards sit idly and watch these games in progress with no effort to interfere?," asked an angry mother in a letter to the Parks and Recreation Commission (Letter by Mrs. H. Frederickson, 7 July 1930). Similarly, a 1940 article published in a local newspaper demanded tougher measures against bathers who rode their bicycles on the pier or jumped from it ("What Goes" 1940, 4). Even when the city's safety was at stake, laws were disregarded: During the Second World War, many bathers failed to respect the region-wide ban on beach fires, which could have allowed the enemy to identify the coast and its habitations (Resolution adopted on 31 March 1942).

Sociologist Dominique Monjardet has shown that the gap between written law and its enforcement on the ground is not a failure but rather an integral part of police work. Rather than commenting on these divergences, scholars should analyze the mechanisms behind this 'selection process.' (Monjardet 1996, 38) The interviews given by Westside police chiefs to local newspapers, while essentially serving to legitimize police work, also give a glimpse into why the police focused on certain tasks rather than others. According to the Redondo police chief, who spoke in 1936 to the *Los Angeles Times*, only those ordinances that guaranteed bathers' safety needed to be systematically enforced (Hamilton 1936, 15). Similarly, in Manhattan Beach, the local police chief claimed he closed his eyes on minor violations but that he "[would] make arrests of anyone whom [he found] breaking bottles at the beach" since broken glass posed an obvious risk to barefoot visitors (ibid.). According to the *Los Angeles Times* journalist, this flexible approach to beach policing was linked to the necessity of maintaining the resorts' popularity: "The hot dog merchant, the games proprietor and the fishing barge owner depend upon the good will of the public toward their community. They must do a whole year's business in four months." (Ibid.) While the region's economy had grown more diverse over the years, coastal communities still relied largely on tourists' dollars.

Even without taking tourist spending into account, all police chiefs interviewed for this 1936 article agreed that on the beach police officers ought to be more patient and understanding: "Most people get into trouble because they play too hard. Beach judges and beach police proceed on that theory." What mattered in the end, explained the Santa Monica chief of police, was the bather's "attitude": If he was "sarcastic or surly when the officers made the arrest it may go hard with him." (Ibid.) Such comments, printed in a very public forum, had two consequences: First, they explicitly condoned the discretionary power of police officers in the field and authorized them to treat bathers differently based not only on their actions but also on their class, race, sex, and age; second, they retroactively justified the flexible approach adopted on the beach and, at the same time, responded to citizens' demands for tougher enforcement. Police leaders thus managed to defuse accusations of inaction from the citizenry, even though they themselves acknowledged their inability to enforce beach laws in their discussion with city lawmakers. While they may have wanted to believe (and make others believe) that their tolerant approach was chosen after careful consideration, police leaders revealed in those (confidential) exchanges that they were, for the most part, forced to adopt this pragmatic policy because of a lack of staff available to patrol such a vast public space. The adoption of new laws in the 1920s to 1930s thus did not put an end to the unique status of the coastline within the metropolis. Yet it did lead to the emergence of new justifying narratives, equating police flexibility on the seaside with pragmatism.

6 'Cleaning' the Beach of 'Undesirables'

The Second World War had a transformative effect on the city of Los Angeles: Massive federal defense spending led to the rapid influx of internal migrants (Verge 1993). Over the next few years, just as the baby boom was unfolding, many families settled in the region, attracted both by high-paying jobs in defense industries and the Southern California climate and lifestyle. In the postwar period, the seaside tolerance regime eroded and new beach laws emerged such as alcohol bans, nighttime closing, and curfews, revealing the new obsession of the police for 'youth' – a loosely defined entity which symbolized, in the media discourse, both the shiny future of the country *and* an uncontrollable group which needed to be tamed (May 2002). In the meantime, the emerging gay social scene in bathhouses and beach bars became the target of relentless police harassment.

By the 1950s, L. A. beaches had become, in the eyes of the authorities, a place of debauchery in need of a thorough 'cleanup.' Two factors explain this transformation. First, Cold War tensions focused the attention of the authorities on the 'enemy within': all non-normative behaviors – whether social or sexual – were perceived as threats to the nuclear family and the American society at large (May 1988). Second, at the local level, the popularity of suburban living, rapid population growth, and the state's massive spending on beach modernization and development led to rapid increases in the value of coastal real estate (Devienne 2016). As a result, the population in many coastal communities started changing. In just a few years, cities like Santa Monica, Redondo Beach, and Newport Beach, where a large working-class population used to live, took on the airs of upper-class suburbs. Beach policing consequently took on increasing importance. How could coastal cities attract investors and wealthy residents when beaches were called, as was the case in Santa Monica, "the Mecca of sex deviates" (*Santa Monica Evening Outlook*, 11 December 1958, 1)?

The police's obsession with youths and gay bathers in the postwar period was not a new phenomenon. In the 1930s, sociologists already noted the concern with which local authorities and parents looked at young people's habits of partying, drinking alcohol, and having sexual relations on the beach (Bogardus 1926, 71–72, 80, 88). Several factors explain why such behaviors became increasingly visible in the postwar period. The baby boom, the rapid influx of young families with children in the region, combined with the emergence of a subculture centered on beach parties and surfing, brought the attention of the police on the youth. Similarly, the beach was already a place of sociability for gay men in the early twentieth century. In the 1950s, the media obsession with the "sexual psychopath" (Freedman 1987) – a term which applied both to men who had consensual sexual relationships with other men and to sexual criminals – increased police scrutiny of public spaces such as beaches, public toilets, and parks.[12] The concurrent rise of a gay political movement gave increased confidence to gay men in public spaces and thus made them more visible to the mainstream society (Hurewitz 2007).

The postwar beach 'cleanup' unfolded differently depending on the local context. At Zuma Beach, for instance, the county adopted a string of strict regulations targeting surfers in 1960. The beach fire ban was intended to put an end to their wild parties, which left the beach in such a state that "the crews

---

[12] For a classic work on public restrooms as sites of sexual encounters for gay men, see Humphreys (1975).

couldn't get it cleaned up in time for the Sunday crowds" ("Beach Combings" 1954, 17). That same year, the county decided to ban access to the beach between midnight and 6:00 a.m. ("County Ok's" 1960, 8). Yet the ordinance, which initially made it illegal for people to "come into and remain" on the beach, could potentially affect the activities of early-risers and fishermen, "individuals who engaged in legitimate recreational pursuits" ("Dorn Seeks" 1960). County lawmakers quickly fixed this initial wording and made it illegal to "loiter" on the shore ("Ordinance Wording" 1960). In doing so, they defined the beach as the exclusive territory of the nuclear family and banned what they perceived to be illegitimate forms of recreation.

In Orange County's Newport Beach, a popular spring break destination, homeowners were the ones who initiated aggressive measures against young beachgoers. Throughout the 1940s, when year-round residents were few and absentee homeowners collected high rents from students, residents had tolerated the spring break phenomenon. By the 1950s, however, the situation gradually changed as the number of year-round residents increased and working-class youths joined the students in the festivities (*Newport News*, 15 April 1941, 1). In 1958, the Newport Beach Homeowners Association was formed with the explicit goal of limiting the number of young people who came to party on the beach during Easter break. The 'laissez-faire policy' of the past was not acceptable anymore. ("Newport" 1958, OC2) Under the pressure of local homeowners, the police started systematically enforcing curfew laws, fire bans, and nighttime closing (Ordinance n° 1079 from 27 January 1964).

In the case of Crystal Beach – the unofficial gay beach of Los Angeles – the 'cleanup' was the product of Cold War tensions and local politics. 'Crystal Beach' was the nickname given to a section of Santa Monica beach where a string of dilapidated bars and bathhouses served a mostly gay clientele. While the beach remained largely obscure throughout the 1940s and early 1950s, it suddenly became the object of public attention during the municipal elections of April 1955 when two candidates running for city council – Fred Judson, a reverend, and Rex Minter, a young lawyer – condemned the sitting council for allowing these establishments to prosper ("City Ordinance Aimed" 1955, 1). Their strategy worked: One year later, the freshly-elected city council nominated a new chief of police who organized a series of raids in Crystal Beach bars and bathhouses, leading to the arrest of over 200 gay men ("City-State Move" 1956, 1). In the following months, several of these establishments were closed down and, in some cases, bulldozed (ibid.).

Police harassment of gay beachgoers did not just serve moral ends. It was also part of a larger effort by the local elites to attract wealthy residents and investors. According to Rex Minter, a fervent supporter of the 'cleanup' campaign, Crystal Beach was "the logical place for development." There, he envisioned the building of "beautiful hotels and apartments with the aid of the state." ("Candidates" 1955, 1) In the postwar period, rapid economic growth, new techniques in coastal engineering, and the development of tourism and upscale housing transformed American coastlines into the new frontier of real estate development. The pro-business city council of Santa Monica hoped to capitalize on that trend. Beach policing and the exclusion of 'undesirable' visitors were largely determined by the ambitions of local business elites. In the following years, local authorities maintained their watch over youths and gay beachgoers, but not quite as intensely. Instead, they turned their attention towards non-white bathers, whose presence became increasingly conspicuous.

7 "Just another version of city life"

In the postwar period, the number of beach visitors soared thanks to the region's rapid demographic growth and a successful campaign of artificial beach enlargement. In 1948, 2.8 million people visited Santa Monica beach annually (Madigan & Hyland Consulting Engineers 1949, 26). Between 1960 and 1965, that figure increased to 15 million. On a summer day, over 300 000 visitors could be found enjoying the ocean in Santa Monica. (*Los Angeles County Beach Study* 1965, 14–15) Many new bathers were African American or Latino. Indeed, the number of black Angelenos increased rapidly during and after the Second World War, when many African Americans from the South migrated to the region, lured by high salaries in the war industries. In the immediate postwar years, black bathers remained few and far between. Due to decades of residential segregation, most black neighborhoods were located on the Eastside and Southside, far from the coast. Even when black Angelenos did come to the beach, they usually stuck to the 'Inkwell,' a stretch of beach in Santa Monica frequented primarily by black bathers until at least the 1950s. (Stapleton 1952, 67) Similarly, most Mexican Americans lived on the Eastside and thus only occasionally came to the beach. Young Chicano men could also become the target of racial slurs and violence perpetrated by white bathers.[13] In the 1960s, coastal development challenged the status quo. For one, the Inkwell, the historic black beach of Los Angeles, gradually lost its identity when a huge parking lot, which attracted white beachgoers from the suburbs, was built right next to it.

---

[13] See the letter of a young Mexican American man sent to a court judge in 1943, quoted in Sanchez (1993, 207).

Secondly, with the inauguration of the Santa Monica Freeway in 1966, which connected the ocean to Downtown, it became much easier for residents of the Eastside and Southside to come to the beach. (Nichols 1973, 73) Finally, the 1965 immigration reform led to an influx of immigrants from Latin America and Asia settling in the Los Angeles region (Grant 1999, 51–52). By the early 1970s, the beachgoing public was more diverse than it had ever been.

These changes occurred at a time when soaring crime rates in US cities became a "national dilemma" ("'We Must'" 1965, B4). The situation in Southern California was particularly gloomy, with some of the highest rates in the country (ibid.). On the beach as well, local authorities claimed, delinquency and crime were on the rise. It is no coincidence then that this is the moment UCLA anthropologist Robert Edgerton chose to study public order on Santa Monica Beach. Compared to the daily reports of violence in the rest of the city, the beach was a remarkably quiet and serene public space. Edgerton wanted to find out why, and, in 1975, he sent some of his students to interview local lifeguards and beachgoers. While the book that he eventually wrote based on his investigation must be analyzed critically – he tends to show more empathy towards the (mostly) white lifeguards than towards black and Latino bathers – it is an exceptional primary source, which gives a voice to all the participants in the seaside order (see Edgerton 1979). The book opens on the observation, largely shared by all lifeguards, that the beach is "less and less pleasant." All spoke of the "increasing intrusion of the 'city atmosphere'" since the inauguration of the freeway. The beach, they felt, was "becoming just another version of city life." (Ibid., 51) While rising crime rates could partially explain this impression, it was also inextricably linked to the increasing visibility of ethnic and racial minorities. Lifeguards systematically made a distinction between those bathers they called "the beach people" and "people from the inner cities." Such expressions, at a time when urban areas were becoming increasingly divided between "chocolate cities and vanilla suburbs," had evident racial connotations (Avila 2004, 1). While the "beach people," to whom the lifeguards felt closest, were obviously white, the "people from the inner cities" were either Latino or black. Using this coded language, lifeguards made distinctions between the behaviors of these different groups. "Beach people" "truly love[d] and respect[ed]" the beach, but there were fewer of them each year (Edgerton 1979, 51). Conversely, lifeguards felt that the number of black and Latino beachgoers was increasing: The beach, they felt, was turning into "a melting-pot at the end of a freeway, a playground for people from the inner city." (Ibid.)

While this binary opposition was based on perceptions, it did have a real impact on how lifeguards policed the beach. According to Edgerton, "lifeguards who work[ed] in areas where there [were] large numbers of Chicano or black beachgoers admit[ted] that they [were] often tense and uncomfortable." (Ibid., 44) Some of the immigrants who had recently settled in the region were not familiar with local rules and drank beer in front of lifeguards, who then interpreted such cavalier attitudes as a provocation. Moreover, lifeguards scrutinized non-white bathers more intensely and thus policed their behaviors more systematically. One of them explained: "We've been taught that you got to watch blacks and Mexican Americans because of their poor swimming ability. So automatically when a group comes to the beach you just go 'oh' and a mental image goes into your brain to keep an eye on those people." (Ibid., 45) This lifeguard thus candidly acknowledged the existence of differential treatments based on race and ethnicity on the beach. While paying more attention to non-white bathers did not matter so much when it came to lifesaving issues, it could have serious consequences for behaviors outside of the water. Historian Heather Ann Thompson has shown that the dramatic rise of incarceration rates for black and Latino men since the 1970s is directly linked to what she calls the "criminalization of urban space" – the multiplication of restricting laws (curfew laws, anti-drug laws) regulating bodies and behaviors in minority neighborhoods (Thompson 2010, 703–734). By paying closer attention to non-white beachgoers, lifeguards also took part in this process.

8 A 'Security Contract' Between Authorities and Beachgoers

Starting in the mid-1960s, the increasing visibility of ethnic and racial minorities on the beach, rising crime rates, and fear of gang violence led to more intense beach policing, with a notable increase in the number of lifeguards and officers on the beat. Coastal cities also tried new policing techniques such as 'camouflaged' units ("'Camouflaged' Police" 1960, OC1), mounted police ("Reaction" 1966, WS1) and adapting uniforms to the beach beat, with officers adopting sneakers, a shirt, and shorts, in the early 1970s (Edgerton 1979, 55). These measures served a double purpose: They were meant to make bathers feel safe and yet not frighten them – the presence of a police officer in a blue uniform or on a motorcycle being associated with city problems. In contrast, a policeman in shorts or on a horse gave off an air of tranquility. In the same spirit, in 1970, the county granted lifeguards – who benefited from a positive public image – the power to issue misdemeanor citations along the coast ("County Lifeguards" 1970, SF A9). Most lifeguards, however, acknowledged that they lacked proper police training. In 1974, the city of Santa Monica responded to this common complaint by introducing motorized mixed units, including lifeguards *and* police officers, on the beach. (Edgerton 1979, 50–55)

These innovative measures also responded to the contradictory demands of the beachgoing public. Most bathers interviewed by Robert Edgerton and his students claimed they felt safe on the beach, even women who came unaccompanied. Many of them were not aware of beach regulations, and, even when they were, they routinely violated them: In 1980, for instance, county lifeguards claimed that half of the beachgoers brought alcohol with them ("Drinking" 1980, F1). Moreover, while bathers did see lifeguards in a positive light, they were often unaware of their citation powers. Interestingly, some of the visitors interviewed in Edgerton's study went so far as to pronounce themselves against police presence on the beach because, the author claimed, "the sight of a police officer would make them think that there was something to fear, and would change the beach from a relaxing place to a tense one." (Edgerton 1979, 124) Yet at the same time, many residents and beach homeowners fought for more police protection and presence on the beach. They wrote to their local city councils and newspapers asking for the strict enforcement of beach ordinances regarding dog leashes, brawls, rough sleepers, etc. (Letter from 11 January 1963; Motion taken on 23 June 1965; "Ban Sought" 1969, CS1). Local authorities thus faced the impossible task of responding to such demands while making their activities and presence as discreet as possible.

The flexible approach adopted by local authorities also reflected the 'selection process' mentioned earlier in this paper. In Edgerton's study, many police officers claimed that they did not systematically enforce beach regulations. According to a female officer, enforcing laws against alcohol and marijuana use "would create more problems than it would solve." (Edgerton 1979, 59) Others talked of the right of visitors to enjoy themselves at the beach. Even the director of the Los Angeles County Department of Beaches freely admitted to a *Los Angeles Times* journalist that "[he himself] had drunk beer on the beach in the past." ("Drinking" 1980, F1) As for the lifeguards Edgerton interviewed, they all agreed that they would not be able to do their job – insuring bathers' safety – if they had to enforce all municipal ordinances. The county officially condoned this attitude by encouraging lifeguards to "cope with problems in a 'low-key' manner [so as not to] alienate themselves from the citizens." (Edgerton 1979, 48)

By the 1970s, beach policing was intense but not necessarily as aggressive as it had been two decades before, when the police chased gay men and surfers off the coast. Rather, the 1960s–1980s appear to be a period of compromises, with the emergence of a 'security contract' between bathers and the police, according to which minor violations were tolerated as long as security and good morals were preserved. While this flexible approach to law enforcement echoed the attitude adopted by the police in the 1930s, it actually responded to different 'selection processes.' For one, it was not a choice by default due to a shortage of staff. In the 1970s, Santa Monica, for instance, had 87 lifeguards equipped with 20 lifeguard towers and four vehicles, including a dune buggy (ibid., 34). Secondly, in the postwar period coastal homeowners were wealthier and thus had more influence over the police's actions than they did in the 1930s. Finally, coastal municipalities did not depend on tourists' dollars anymore. On the contrary, many residents now dreaded the arrival of summer crowds and the security problems they brought with them. Policing the beach had become a balancing act, which consisted in preventing serious offenses – in particular, thefts and sexual crimes – while tolerating minor violations. By turning a blind eye to visitors drinking alcohol on the beach, police officers and lifeguards sought to avoid needless confrontations and preserve the peace and quiet so many beachgoers loved. At the very least, that is how the authorities justified their flexible approach to law enforcement on the seashore, choosing to present it as an example of their ability to adapt to the field. Tolerance towards violators, however, did not apply to all bathers: Latino and black beachgoers, groups of young males in particular, rarely benefited from such lenience.

9 Conclusion

In the twentieth century, the dominant factor influencing rule-making and policing on the beaches of Los Angeles was their proximity to residential areas. At the beginning of the century, the beaches were spaces at the margins of urban life – both physically and metaphorically – and, as such, they allowed visitors a certain degree of freedom. Starting in the 1920s and 1930s, however, urban expansion towards the Pacific transformed small beach resorts into coastal municipalities where a local elite pushed for new beach laws. Yet the police struggled to enforce new ordinances: Local authorities lacked sufficient staff and knew better than to fine visitors, whose dollars were essential to the tourist economy. These difficulties persisted in the postwar period, when the police tried to rid the beach of 'undesirable' beachgoers. From the perspective of homeowners and residents, the beach had to be policed just like any other public space in the city. Ironically, when a new freeway opened up the beach to the city's ethnic and racial minorities in the 1970s, the coastline was suddenly perceived as too 'urban.' By then, lifeguards yearned for the good old days, when beachgoers (and police officers) were fewer and, more importantly, white.

Throughout the twentieth century, a uniquely flexible police regime existed along the Los Angeles coastline. Far from being a homogeneous 'fortress,' the modern American city proved a much more complex policing terrain for authorities. Rather than being a 'natural' characteristic of the beach, police tolerance on the seaside was constructed over a long period of time, first in response to economic imperatives and staff shortage and later, ironically, because of rising crime rates and a heightened police presence, which led to the emergence of a 'security contract' between authorities and *some* beachgoers. The narratives used by the police to justify the exceptional status of the beach contributed to establishing this status even more firmly.

Yet not all bathers benefited from police tolerance at the beach. In the 1920s–1930s, the first beach laws targeted activities associated with working-class visitors (barbecuing, loud noises, etc.) and vagrants (peddling and beach fire bans). In the postwar period, new laws were aimed at the youth (curfew laws, alcohol ban) and gay men. All social classes were concerned in this case, although those who had money could avoid police repression by going to private beach clubs and beach houses or driving to remote beaches. Starting in the 1960s, police took a tolerant approach to most white visitors, but they failed to apply it to minority bathers. Historically, then, stricter beach laws and tougher beach policing have made the coastline less accessible and less attractive to working-class and minority beachgoers. In other words, the urbanization of the coastline and the concomitant rise in value of coastal real estate has made the beach less accessible and inclusive.[14]

Bibliography

Allen, Lewis. *Only Yesterday: An Informal History of the 1920s*. New York: John Wiley & Sons, 1997.
Andréo, Christophe. "Surveillance et contrôle des jeunes des quartiers populaires sur une plage marseillaise à la fin des années 1990." *Genèses* 67.2 (2007): 89–108.
"Arrest of Woman is Black Eye to City." *Santa Monica Evening Outlook* (18 July 1919): 1.
Avila, Eric. *Popular Culture in the Age of White Flight: Fear and Fantasy in Suburban Los Angeles*. Berkeley: University of California Press, 2004.
Axelrod, Jeremiah B. C. *Inventing Autopia: Dreams and Visions of the Modern Metropolis in Jazz Age Los Angeles*. Berkeley: University of California Press, 2009.
"Ban Sought on Fraternity and Sorority Houses." *Los Angeles Times* (5 January 1969): CS1.

---

[14] This article was originally published in French as Devienne, Elsa. "'Il y a des lois sur la plage !': Régulation et surveillance des comportements sur les plages de Los Angeles, années 1910–1970." *Actes de la recherche en sciences sociales* 218.3 (2017): 10–25.

"Bathing Suit and Bathing Beach Regulations." *American City* (28 June 1923): 569.
"Bathing Suit Modesty Issue Left to Resorts." *Los Angeles Times* (11 March 1930): A2.
"Bathing Suits Up. That Is, They Are Down Too Far." *Santa Monica Evening Outlook* (27 June 1912): 1.
"Beach Combings." *Santa Monica Evening Outlook* (16 June 1954): 17.
"Beach Fires to Be Kept in Fireplaces." *Palisades Del Rey Press* (11 November 1927): 2.
"Beach Regulations Urged." *Los Angeles Times* (15 September 1930): A1.
Beckett, Katherine, and Steve Herbert. *Banished: The New Social Control in Urban America*. Oxford: Oxford University Press, 2010.
Blanchard, Emmanuel. *La police parisienne et les Algériens (1944–1962)*. Paris: Nouveau monde, 2011.
Bogardus, Emory. *The City Boy and His Problems: A Survey of Boy Life in Los Angeles*. Los Angeles: House of Ralston, 1926.
"Candidates Pledge Efforts to turn Ocean Park into 'Garden Spot.'" *Santa Monica Evening Outlook* (2 April 1955): 1.
"'Camouflaged' Police Enforce Law at Beach." *Los Angeles Times* (24 July 1960): OC1.
"City Ordinance Aimed at Sex Deviates Illegal under Ruling of Supreme Court." *Santa Monica Evening Outlook* (6 April 1955): 1.
"City-State Move Dooms Deviate Hangouts." *Santa Monica Evening Outlook* (4 December 1956): 1.
Corbin, Alain. *Le territoire du vide: L'Occident et le désir du rivage (1750–1840)*. Paris: Flammarion, 2010.
"County Lifeguards to Get Power to Issue Misdemeanor Citations." *Los Angeles Times* (24 May 1970): SF A9.
"County Ok's New Beach Safety Rules." *Los Angeles Examiner* (9 June 1960): 8.
Davidson, Ronald A. "Before 'Surfurbia': The Development of the South Bay Beach Cities through the 1930s." *APCG Yearbook* 66 (2004): 81–94.
Davis, Mike. *City of Quartz: Excavating the Future in Los Angeles*. New York: Vintage Books, 1992.
Deluermoz, Quentin. *Policiers dans la ville: La construction d'un ordre public à Paris*. Paris: Publications de la Sorbonne, 2012.
Deluermoz, Quentin, Arnaud-Dominique Houte, and Aurélien Lignereux. "Introduction". *Revue d'histoire du XIXe siècle* [special issue *Societies and forces of security in the 19th century*] 50 (2015): 7–21.
Désert, Gabriel. *La vie quotidienne sur les plages normandes du Second Empire aux Années folles*. Paris: Hachette, 1983.
Devienne, Elsa. "City Limits: Bather Arrests in Early 20th-century Los Angeles." *Modes pratiques. Journal of Clothes and Fashion History* (special issue, 2018): 174–193.
Devienne, Elsa. "Agrandir la plage: Une histoire de la construction des plages de Los Angeles (1930–1960)." *Aménagement et environnement*. Eds. Geneviève Massard-Guilbaud and Patrick Fournier. Rennes: Presses Universitaires de Rennes, 2016. 231–246.
Dewerpe, Alain. *Charonne 8 février 1962: Anthropologie historique d'un massacre d'État*. Paris: Gallimard, 2006.
Diamond, Andrew J. *Mean Streets: Chicago Youths and the Everyday Struggle for Empowerment in the Multiracial City, 1908–1969*. Berkeley: University of California Press, 2009.
"Dorn Seeks to Ease Beach Ban." *Los Angeles Examiner* (17 June 1960).
"Drinking at Beach is Hazardous to Your Life." *Los Angeles Times* (13 October 1980): F1.

Edgerton, Robert B. *Alone Together: Social Order on an Urban Beach*. Berkeley: University of California Press, 1979.
"Eight Face Legal Tanning." *Los Angeles Times* (12 August 1929): A1.
Elias, Norbert. *The Civilizing Process: The History of Manners*. Translated by Edmund Jephcott. New York: Urizen Books, 1978.
Fass, Paula S. *The Damned and the Beautiful: American Youth in the 1920s*. Oxford: Oxford University Press, 1977.
Fassin, Didier. "Pouvoir discrétionnaire et politiques sécuritaires." *Actes de la recherche en sciences sociales* 201–202.1 (2014): 72–86.
Flamming, Douglas. *Bound for Freedom: Black Los Angeles in Jim Crow America*. Berkeley: University of California Press, 2006.
Fogelson, Robert. *The Fragmented Metropolis: Los Angeles, 1850–1930*. Cambridge/MA: Harvard University Press, 1967.
Foucault, Michel. *Surveiller et punir: Naissance de la prison*. Paris: Gallimard, 2014.
Freedman, Estelle. "'Uncontrolled Desires': The Response to the Sexual Psychopath, 1920–1960." *The Journal of American History* 74.1 (1987): 83–106.
"Girl Dares Judge to Pinch Her." *Santa Monica Evening Outlook* (19 August 1916): 1.
Granger, Christophe. *Les corps d'été: Naissance d'une variation saisonnière, XXe siècle*. Paris: Autrement, 2009.
Granger, Christophe. "Batailles de plage: Nudité et pudeur dans l'entre-deux-guerres." *Rives méditerranéennes* 30 (2008): 117–133.
Grant, David. "A Demographic Portrait of Los Angeles County, 1970 to 1990." *Prismatic Metropolis: Inequality in Los Angeles*. Eds. Lawrence D. Bobo, Melvin L. Oliver, James H. Johnson, Jr., and Abel Valenzuela, Jr. New York: Russell Sage Foundation, 1999. 51–80.
Hamilton, Andy. "There's Law at the Beach." *Los Angeles Times* (5 July 1936): 15.
Humphreys, Laud. *Tearoom Trade: Impersonal Sex in Public Places*. Chicago: Aldine, 1975.
Hurewitz, Daniel. *Bohemian Los Angeles and the Making of Modern Politics*. Berkeley: University of California Press, 2007.
Jefferson, Alison Rose. "African-American Leisure Space in Santa Monica." *Southern California Quarterly* 91.2 (2009): 155–189.
Latham, Angela J. "Packaging Women: The Concurrent Rise of Beauty Pageants, Public Bathing and Other Performances of Female Nudity." *Journal of Popular Culture* 29.3 (1995): 149–167.
Letter by Mrs. H. Frederickson from 7 July 1930. Minutes of the Board of Playground and Recreation Commission (BPRC), 1930, volume 11. Box C0368, City of L. A. Archives.
Letter from 11 January 1963. Box A1513, file 89691, city council communications, City of L. A. Archives.
Letter from 20 February 1963. Box A1513, file 89691, city council communications, City of L. A. Archives.
Long Beach Municipal Convention and Publicity Bureau. "Souvenir of Long Beach California." Reprinted in 1984 by the Long Beach Heritage Museum. Box 40, Location 2G, Long Beach Historical Society, 1932.
Los Angeles County Beach Study. California: Division of Beaches and Parks, 1965.
Los Angeles Police Department. *Los Angeles Police Department Annual Report 1936–1937*. Available at the Los Angeles Public Library.
Low, Setha, and Neil Smith. *The Politics of Public Space*. London: Routledge, 2005.

Madigan & Hyland Consulting Engineers. *Recreational Development of the Los Angeles Area Shoreline.* New York: Madigan-Hyland, 1949.

May, Elaine Tyler. *Homeward Bound: American Families in the Cold War Era.* New York: Basic Books, 1988.

May, Kirse Granat. *Golden State, Golden Youth: The California Image in Popular Culture, 1955–1966.* Chapel Hill: University of North Carolina Press, 2002.

Milliot, Vincent. "Histoire des polices: L'ouverture d'un moment historiographique." *Revue d'histoire moderne et contemporaine* 54.2 (2007): 162–177.

Minutes of the Board of Playground and Recreation Commission (BPRC) from 17 June 1926. Box C0368, CLAA.

Minutes of the BPRC from 18 August 1927. Box C0368, CLAA.

Minutes of the BPRC from 2 August 1928. Box C0368, CLAA.

Monjardet, Dominique. *Ce que fait la police: Sociologie de la force publique.* Paris: La Découverte, 1996.

Motion taken on 23 June 1965. Box A1914, file 124633, city council communications, City of L. A. Archives.

Newport News (15 April 1941): 1.

"Newport Will Stiffen Beach Rule Enforcement." *Los Angeles Times* (11 May 1958): OC2.

Nichols, Woodrow. *A Spatio-Perspective Analysis of the Effect of the Santa Monica and Simi Valley Freeways on Two Selected Black Residential Areas in Los Angeles County.* Unpublished dissertation. UCLA, 1973.

"Noise but no Drunkenness, Police Edict for New Years." *Los Angeles Times* (30 December 1940): A1.

Ordinance n° 90 738, 23 April 1946. Box A893, file 23172, city council communications, City of L. A. Archives.

Ordinance n° 1079, 27 January 1964. Newport Beach city council online archives.

"Ordinance Wording Changed. Pre-6 am Fishing Legal on Beaches," *Los Angeles Examiner* (26 July 1960).

Petition by Venice residents sent on 19 September 1951 to the L. A. City Council. Box A1106, file 50103, city council communications, City of L. A. Archives.

Philippe, Yann. "L'enquête comme évocation du monde: Langages de l'enquête et légitimation du New York Police Department (1900–1940)." *Revue française d'études américaines* 113.3 (2007): 77–91.

"Reaction Mixed to Posse Beach Patrol." *Los Angeles Times* (13 November 1966): WS1.

Reiss, Albert J., Jr. "Police Organization in the Twentieth Century." *Crime and Justice, An Annual Review of Research* (1992): 51–97.

Resolution adopted on 31 March 1942. Box A803, file 11077, city council communications, City of L. A. Archives.

Rosenzweig, Roy, and Elizabeth Blackmar. *The Park and the People: A History of Central Park.* Ithaca: Cornell University Press, 1998.

Sanchez, George J. *Becoming Mexican-American: Ethnicity, Culture, and Identity in Chicano Los Angeles, 1900–1945.* New York: Oxford University Press, 1993.

Santa Monica Evening Outlook (1 July 1940): 1.

Santa Monica Evening Outlook (11 December 1958): 1.

Sohn, Anne-Marie. "Le corps sexué." *Histoire du corps. Vol. 3: Les mutations du regard. Le XXe siècle.* Eds. Jean-Jacques Courtine, Alain Corbin and Georges Vigarello. Paris: Seuil, 2006. 93–127.

Stapleton, Charles. *Recreation and Its Problems on the Santa Monica-Venice Shoreline*. Unpublished Master's Thesis. UCLA, 1952.
Thompson, Heather Ann. "Why Mass Incarceration Matters: Rethinking Crisis, Decline, and Transformation in Postwar American History." *Journal of American History* 97.3 (2010): 703–734.
Thompson, Heather Ann, and Donna Murch. "Rethinking Urban America through the Lens of the Carceral State." *Journal of Urban History* 41.5 (2015): 751–755.
Verge, Arthur C. *Santa Monica Lifeguards*. Chicago: Arcadia, 2007.
Verge, Arthur C. *Los Angeles County Lifeguards*. Chicago: Arcadia, 2005.
Verge, Arthur C. *Paradise Transformed: Los Angeles During the Second World War*. Dubuque: Kendall/Hunt, 1993.
Vincent, Johan. *L'intrusion balnéaire: Les populations littorales bretonnes et vendéennes face au tourisme (1800–1945)*. Rennes: Presses universitaires de Rennes, 2007.
Walton, John K. *The British Seaside: Holidays and Resorts in the Twentieth Century*. Manchester: Manchester University Press, 2000.
"'We Must Work to Find Solutions.'" *Los Angeles Times* (13 November 1965): B4.
"Wear Skirts, Panties, too." *Los Angeles Times* (1 August 1911): II 1.
"What Goes in an Ordinance?" *Manhattan Beach Pilot* (19 September 1940): 4.
"Will Permit Bathing Suit Parade." *Santa Monica Evening Outlook* (27 June 1917): 1.
Wiltse, Jeff. *Contested Waters: A Social History of Swimming Pools in America*. Chapel Hill: University of North Carolina Press, 2007.
Wolcott, Victoria W. *Race, Riots, and Roller Coasters: The Struggle over Segregated Recreation in America*. Philadelphia: University of Pennsylvania Press, 2012.
Zukin, Sharon. *Landscapes of Power: From Detroit to Disneyworld*. Berkeley: University of California Press, 1991.

Carol Bunch Davis
Always on Duty: Galveston's African American Beaches and Lifeguards

Reading African American beaches in the U.S. Gulf South city of Galveston, Texas, as contested sites where struggles over the racial and spatial politics of commemoration, normative whiteness, and anti-blackness collide, this article interprets print media accounts of Wavery Guidry and James Helton, who attended to beach patrons at the city's two African American beaches. Framing their physical and cultural work as 'sitting up' with anti-blackness' myriad personal, cultural, social, legal and structural attacks, this paper contends that Guidry's and Helton's experiences provide a critical opportunity to reconsider how racial discourses in the U.S. Gulf South impact the beach's transformative possibilities.

Dieser Aufsatz liest die Strände des an der texanischen Golfküste gelegenen Ortes Galveston als Schauplätze, an denen sich Konflikte um rassistische Diskriminierung und segregatorische Gewalt gegen Afroamerikaner*innen in besonderem Maße räumlich manifestieren. Dazu werden Berichte aus zeitgenössischen Printmedien über Wavery Guidry und James Helton, die als schwarze Rettungsschwimmer zwischen 1934 und 1957 die Badegäste an den beiden afro-amerikanischen Stränden der Stadt beaufsichtigten, herangezogen und kritisch interpretiert. Die Autorin deutet Guidrys und Heltons körperliche und kulturelle Arbeit als ‚sitting up', also als eine besondere Form des schwarzen Widerstandes im Angesicht der zahlreichen persönlichen, kulturellen, sozialen, gesetzlichen und strukturellen Angriffe auf Afroamerikaner*innen durch weiße Bürger*innen. Die Untersuchung der Fallbeispiele Guidry und Waverton bietet die Gelegenheit zur kritischen Neubetrachtung des transformatorischen Potentials des Strandes als eines besonderen Raumes im Kontext von Rassismus und Widerstand.

1 Introduction: 'Sitting Up' with Anti-Blackness

> It has been long since too well settled even for debate or discussion that you cannot mix white and colored people socially and that their segregation in all of their social matters and matters of pleasure such as enjoyed on the beach front at Galveston, is absolutely imperative and necessary for the protection of both races.[1]

Brantley Harris and A. G. Fish referenced the "well settled" notion that black bathers and white bathers on Galveston's Seawall beaches must be segregated as the rationale for the petition they delivered on behalf of the Lions Club of Galveston to the Mayor Charles A. Keenan, City Attorney Frank S. Anderson and the Galveston Board of Commissioners. Signed by the entire club and an additional 1870 white Galvestonians, it called on commissioners to racially

---

[1] Brantley Harris and A. G. Fish on behalf of the Lions Club of Galveston ("Officials" 1922, 1).

segregate what was then just under five miles of Seawall beachfront ("Seek" 1922, 1). Linking their argument for limiting blacks' beach access with the U.S. Supreme Court's 1896 Plessy v. Ferguson decision that provided for "separate but equal" public accommodations for the nation's black citizens, Harris and Fish argued that the court "decided that segregation is valid for transportation, public education and social relations; it applies equally as well to purposes of bathing" ("Officials" 1922, 1; "Plessy v. Ferguson"). Though their argument that segregation was vital to the protection of both black and white people was a familiar one made in support of racial segregation during the Jim Crow era in the U.S., when the mayor, city attorney and commissioners received the petition, the beach front was *already* racially segregated by social practice rather than through municipal ordinance. Less than half a mile of Seawall beachfront between 27th and 29th Streets was utilized by "negro bathers" ("Petition" 1922), west of the white tourist destinations including Joyland Park, which featured a merry-go-round, a theatre and concessions situated at 21st Street. As Anthony J. Stanonis' discussion of Galveston's early tourism development points out, black locals and tourists "enjoyed beaches at their peril and with a great deal of white hand-wringing" (Stanonis 2014, 125).

Still, the petitioners implored commissioners to "take such action as will speedily remove the negro concession and the throngs of negro people from the Boulevard or beachfront" ("Officials" 1922, 1). They suggested relocating the black beach to the far west end of the island and "out of proximity to any point frequented by white people" (ibid.). In short, the proposal sought municipal policy to enact African Americans' complete eradication from Galveston's Seawall beachfront which stood at the center of the city's nascent tourism industry – beginning at the island's East End beaches and continuing west to the beachfront at 21st Street.

On Police and Fire Commissioner A. P. Norman's recommendation, Galveston's city commissioners rejected the petition in July of 1922. Yet they didn't refuse because they fundamentally disagreed with racial segregation. Instead, Norman's recommendation argued that an ordinance was unnecessary because "more than five blocks separated white and negro bathers while bathing" and "the negroes had made no attempt to mingle with white bathers" ("Petition" 1922, 1). Norman's reasoning suggests that African Americans accepted racial segregation's social practices and its white supremacist underpinnings. Ironically, the West End beach would become the second beach in the city utilized by black beachgoers, but only because they began using it after a failed second attempt at a city ordinance in 1941 to designate it for black bathers. By the early 1950s, West Beach became known as a black beach and black patrons continued to use it well into the 1970s after the end of racial segregation in the city's public accommodations. In short, even as city and civic leaders wrangled over where African Americans should access the Galveston beachfront, African American beach patrons created places for themselves in the face of anti-black racism, or anti-blackness.

This brief history of Galveston's black beaches demonstrates how anti-blackness – or the systematic devaluing and marginalization of black people through personal, cultural, social, legal and structural attacks – instigated the push for segregation through municipal ordinance. I want to draw attention to how African Americans' terrestrial engagement with anti-blackness extended to the beachfront. Galveston's two historically African American beaches – at 28th Street, sometimes called Brown Beach, and at West Beach, also known as Sunset Camps – enabled a black 'sense of place' resonant with Katherine McKittrick's definition of it as "physical and ontological manifestations of space" that African American Galvestonians configured as a respite from anti-blackness (McKittrick 2011, 947–963). Drawing from John Mack's notion of the beach's transformative potential as "a neutral space, neither properly terrestrial nor yet thoroughly maritime, [and] awaiting a metamorphic role" (Mack 2011, 165), I read Galveston's two African American beaches as contested spaces where black beach users cultivated fugitive moments of reprieve and crafted the beach as a space to celebrate black life, even as they remained perpetually vulnerable to anti-blackness. African American lifeguards facilitated and mitigated these efforts as they assiduously worked to prevent drownings, to rescue those in danger, and in some instances, to recover the drowned. Yet terrestrial anti-black discourses extended to the beach and impinged upon their work. In short, black lifeguards were no less impacted by anti-blackness than the black beach patrons they were charged with protecting.

Taking cues from Daniel Burdsey's work on English seaside environments which interrupts "the normative assumptions of these settings as racially neutral, where race is absent and social structures and relations are not racialized" (Burdsey 2015, 22) this article renders blackness visible on Galveston's beaches by exploring print media accounts of African American lifeguards Wavery Guidry and James Helton, who worked on Galveston's two black beaches between 1934 and 1957. Both men contended with anti-blackness' systematic marginalization and devaluing of black people even as they aided in shaping ontological and physical space for black beach patrons to cope with anti-blackness' multiple and intersecting impacts.

Finally, the silencing and erasure of black voices and bodies on the beach has implications for interpreting Galveston's existing commemorative spaces on two fronts. While Galveston is well known for its significant role in Texas history and its commemorative space reflects that, there is a dearth of commemoratives that address how black people occupied, mobilized and otherwise impacted and engaged a multitude of spaces across the city. Turning our attention to the ways that African American lifeguards interrupt the framing of Galveston and its beachfront as what Elijah Anderson identifies as a "white space" where "black people are typically absent, not expected, or marginalized when present," I read blackness' visibility and invisibility in the city's commemorative spaces to show how a less overt but no less pernicious iteration of racial segregation undergirded by anti-blackness informs how such commemoratives are imagined, narrated and constructed (Anderson 2015, 10–21). Similarly, Simone Browne's notion of "racializing surveillance" that "reif[ies] boundaries, borders, and bodies along racial lines, and where the outcome is often discriminatory treatment of those who are negatively racialized by such surveillance" (Browne 2015, 16) aptly reflects the experiences of African American lifeguards on Galveston's segregated beaches as they navigated boundaries that were contingent upon how white people framed white spaces – particularly the beach as a white space – and black lifeguards continually encountered this framing. While I recognize that white supremacy and racism impact a broad range of intersectional identities, my use of anti-blackness signals the very specific and interlocking implications of normative whiteness mobilized by white supremacy for black people that acknowledges black bodies' myriad encounters with personal, cultural, social, legal and structural attacks. I read African American beaches and their lifeguards documented in the white mainstream and African American print media to interrupt African Americans' marginalization within Galveston's commemorative history, to include Galveston's black beaches in that history and to document the African American lifeguards' corporeal and cultural work.

Such recognition of Galveston's African American beaches and their lifeguards moves beyond what Andrew Kahrl has called a "segregation-as-congregation paradigm" within studies of the Jim Crow South that sometimes romanticize black segregated spaces as wholly restorative (Kahrl 2012, 18). Instead, I contend that African American lifeguards 'sat up with' anti-black violence at, through, and beyond the beach. Calvin Warren's notion of "black care" informs my formulation 'sitting up' with anti-blackness as Warren recognizes and takes seriously anti-blackness' metaphysical wounds and offers an ethic of black care to endure them (Warren 2016). Similarly, I use the idiom 'to sit up with' to describe a specific iteration of black care that parallels attending to an illness rooted in one iteration of black southern cultural practice. 'Sitting up' with anti-blackness differs from witnessing suffering and vigilantly attends and ministers to as well as monitors and cajoles those suffering under the weight of anti-blackness. 'Sitting up' with someone during an illness does not fundamentally change the illness, nor does it prevent its recurrence. Instead, it enables the ailing to withstand the illness and provides the ailing and the caregiver with a template to assist others and themselves.

Similarly, Wavery Guidry and James Helton, the two lifeguards who worked alternately at Brown Beach and West Beach, 'sat up' with anti-blackness in a number of ways. They were two among at least five African American lifeguards who between 1934 and 1965 framed the beach's liminal space as a staging area for the preservation of black lives and the recovery of black bodies in multiple registers. Attending to black lives and bodies in their capacity as African American lifeguards they 'sat up' with anti-blackness' spatial logic which necessitates black hypervisibility and invisibility for its legibility. Galveston's African American lifeguards neither cured nor fundamentally changed the nature and daily enactment of anti-blackness, but their corporeal and cultural work enabled endurance and offered something akin to respite from its mundane daily terror.

I offer three contexts in which to consider the guards' multimodal labor in order to clarify its multiple historical, commemorative and geographical trajectories. First, I will geographically and socio-historically situate Galveston as a 'chocolate city' within the Gulf South. I will then turn to the racial meanings within two commemorative spaces to explore their implications for remembering African American lifeguards and segregated beaches. Finally, I will read the lifeguards' efforts to 'sit up' with anti-blackness in all its manifestations on Galveston's beachfront.

2 Queen of the Gulf: Galveston as a Gulf South 'Chocolate City'

The Port of Galveston was founded in 1825 and by the time the city was established in 1836, Galveston had become the largest slave market west of New Orleans. Entering its so-called Golden Era in the late nineteenth century, the city became one of the biggest cotton ports in the U.S. which is to say that the labor of enslaved Africans and African Americans drove the island's economy and enabled it to become 'the Queen of the Gulf' as it was then known.

Situated at the northern end of the Texas Coastal Bend, I read Galveston as a Southern city, but I lean on its identity as a Gulf South city as well as its proximity to the Gulf of Mexico because that waterway enabled slavery's deep influence on politics, economics, and social life in the region. Richard Campanella describes the maritime driven interactions and their impact on the Gulf South as a region thusly:

> Communities along the Gulf Coast interact with each other via gulf waters, interconnecting with the Caribbean and Atlantic systems, more so than their interior-South counterparts. New Orleans was "closer" to Havana than to Shreveport. Mobile interacted more with Galveston than it did with Huntsville, and everyday life in Galveston resembled Pensacola's a whole lot more than it did San Antonio's (Campanella 2014, 17–32).

Yet it is precisely the slave trade that drives these maritime interactions and what links the cities Campanella cites. Galveston was one of 48 known ports of entry in the U.S. for enslaved Africans. Further, the French pirates and privateers Jean Lafitte and Louis-Michel Aury smuggled enslaved people to multiple Gulf South cities including New Orleans through Galveston. While it is geographically situated in the state of Texas, and the Gulf of Mexico enables its connections to other Gulf South cities, it is Galveston's connection to the slave trade that significantly contributed to the city's economic prowess during the eighteenth and nineteenth centuries. The hypervisibility and invisibility of black bodies in Galveston mobilizes its framing as a white space where black bodies are marginalized even as they drive economic opportunity.

This is illustrated in the life possibilities for enslaved black people and the formerly enslaved after Emancipation which hinged on the continually shifting political and social climate in Galveston. For example, the city's recovery from the Great 1900 Hurricane, the worst natural disaster in U.S. history, turned on fabricated reports of African American criminality derived from white fears of African Americans that justified not only white vigilante violence, but also informed the city's Galveston Plan that provided for a local government structure with at-large districts that effectively eliminated African American representation (Coulter 1900, 58). Another outcome of the 1900 Storm was the construction of the Galveston Seawall between 1902 and 1904 which protected the city from future devastating storms and also changed the city's tourism landscape.

Despite the Houston Ship Channel's opening in 1914 that would ultimately hasten the end of the 'Queen of the Gulf'-era in Galveston, the Galveston Ship Channel still offered economic opportunities for African Americans, which drew many African American men, particularly from southwestern Louisiana and other Gulf South states, during the mid-twentieth century for job opportunities as longshoreman and stevedores. This lateral migration from the interior south to the Gulf Coast south in the midst of the Great Migration of African Americans from the south to northern industrial cities deeply informs Galveston's 'chocolate city,' following Zandria F. Robinson and Marcus Anthony Hunter's claims about black enclaves and neighborhoods that are now being dissolved by gentrification in cities across the U.S. Further, Robinson and Hunter contend that chocolate cities are predicated on both the joy and pain of black life – constant surveillance in public spaces and simultaneous moments of creative celebration of black life. (Robinson and Hunter 2018, 12–15) Similarly, Galveston's African American lifeguards served an important, though largely undocumented, role in crafting Galveston's chocolate city – or in engaging and experiencing the joy and pain of black life. However, there is a historical precedent for their unacknowledged labor in the city's commemorative spaces.

While enslaved black people built the structures that compose Galveston's commemorative landscape, black bodies remained vulnerable to metaphysical and corporeal violence and in the current moment, go largely unacknowledged within the white commemorative landscape. Two examples illustrate the challenges of commemorating black life in Galveston in ways that complicate its prevailing racialized narratives.

3 Normative Whiteness and Commemorative Space in Galveston

The fallout from the collision of the commemorative landscape and the chocolate city functions in two ways: first, the black historical figure is confined to black commemorative spaces alone, rather than reflecting the full scope of spaces where black people impacted and influenced Galveston's spatial and cultural landscape. The city's commemoration of the U.S.'s first African American heavyweight champion and Galveston native Jack Johnson reflects that tendency. After more than 15 years of discussion, in 2014 the Texas Historical Commission granted a historical marker commemorating his life. It was placed next to sculptor Adrienne Isom's bronze statue of Johnson in the newly dedicated and opened Jack Johnson Park. The park is located behind Old Central Cultural Center, a community and cultural center located in the Carver Park/Old Central historically black neighborhood. Old Central itself is housed in one of the three locations of the former Central High School, the first African American high school in the state of Texas. Johnson was born in Galveston on 31 March 1878 and he grew up in a home located at 806–808 Broadway which was then a multi-ethnic and multi-racial neighborhood and is now a predominantly white East End neighborhood. While there was some debate about where the statue would be erected, both of the proposed locations were located in historically black neighborhoods. The site where he was born and grew up was never considered.

Second, white commemorative spaces engage in equivocation and hand-wringing resonant with the city commissioner's stance on the segregated beachfront. Galveston is the site where 250 000 enslaved men and women learned of the Emancipation Proclamation and their freedom on 19 June 1865 – two and a half years after it took effect in the U.S. Initially celebrated as Emancipation Day in Texas, it is now known to most people as Juneteenth and commemorates the announcement by Major General Gordon Granger as written in "General Order Number Three" that "all slaves are free" ("General Order Number Three"). The order was read in three locations in the city. One was the now demolished Osterman Building where the Confederate headquarters once stood. It was also read at Reedy Chapel, the first African American church in Texas established in 1848. The final location was Ashton Villa, one of the first brick homes to be built in the state. It is a Texas Historic Landmark, now owned and managed by the Galveston Historical Foundation (GHF) which purchased the home in 1970. It was built in 1859 as the private home of wealthy white merchant, Col. James Moreau Brown. Though it is not open for public tours, the GHF offers the first floor for rental and does provide a tour of the first floor of the home as part of that service. Both Reedy Chapel and Ashton Villa were built by enslaved people, but only one, Reedy Chapel, acknowledges that fact on its historical marker bestowed by the Texas Historical Commission. As with other sites within the city's commemorative landscape, Ashton Villa's historical marker emphasizes its construction and aesthetics, but omits the enslaved black men and women who built and labored in the home. The marker simply reads "Mediterranean style architecture. European materials. Confederate and Federal headquarters in Civil War. Recorded Texas Historic Landmark-1967" ("Ashton Villa, 1859").

Preserving the romance of the antebellum era turns on a white normative southern identity shaped by the black body's hypervisibility and simultaneous invisibility, or as Patricia G. Davis observes about the Civil War in cultural memory, "contemporary cultural productions of the era have been marked generally not by hostile or paternalistic and stereotypical depictions of Civil-War-Era-blackness – though these do indeed exist – but by symbolic annihilation or the lack of representation of African American experiences" (Davis 2016, 7). I include Ashton Villa as a cultural production and a commemorative space that equivocates on enslavement in its Juneteenth marker in addition to evading black enslaved peoples' role in the home's construction. Ashton Villa's Texas Historical Commission Juneteenth marker paraphrases "General Order Number Three," which reads:

> The people are informed that in accordance with a Proclamation from the Executive of the United States, all slaves are free. This involves an absolute equality of personal rights and rights of property, between former masters and slaves, and the connection heretofore existing between them, become that between employer and hired labor. The freed are advised to remain at their present homes, and work for wages. They are informed that they will not be allowed to collect at military posts; and that they will not be supported in idleness either there or elsewhere ("General Order Number Three").

The Juneteenth Marker at Ashton Villa omits the qualifications of freedom listed in the order – that the formerly enslaved may not collect at military posts and will not be supported in "idleness." It notes that despite the Emancipation Proclamation, it "would take the Civil War and passage of the 13th Amendment to the constitution to end the brutal institution of African American slavery." ("Juneteenth") It continues, addressing the celebration of Juneteenth thusly:

> Freed African American observed 'Emancipation Day,' as it was first known, as early as 1866 in Galveston. As community gatherings grew across Texas, celebrations included parades, prayer, singing, and readings of the proclamation. In the mid-20th century, community celebrations gave way to more private commemorations. A re-emergence of public observance helped Juneteenth become a state holiday in 1979. Initially observed in Texas, this landmark event's legacy is evident today by worldwide commemorations that celebrate freedom and the triumph of the human spirit. (Ibid.)

The marker's recognition of enslavement as a "brutal institution" is the only acknowledgment of enslavement on the site and it ultimately notes that the Juneteenth holiday celebrates "the triumph of the human spirit" (ibid.). Yet I want to trouble this narrative of transcendence by turning our attention to the irony underwriting it which rests on a disavowal of the black bodies whose labor built and sustained the home that literally stands behind the Juneteenth marker. The enslaved men and women who built and worked inside Ashton Villa, both in their exchange value and their labor, go unacknowledged. It is a doubly debilitating omission in that even the commemoration turns on the absent presence of black bodies. In short, even as Ashton Villa's Juneteenth historical marker signals Juneteenth as beginning the United States' collective move beyond enslavement, that journey only commences with a wholesale denial of the enslaved's labor and their contributions to Ashton Villa's existence. Enslavement's commemoration turns on black disavowal and, as such, narrates Ashton Villa as a 'white space' where black presence is structured as absence. It is a site where African Americans do not belong even as they literally and figuratively structure the building. It begs the question of what we must forget in order to remember. Collectively, Jack Johnson's commemorative and Ashton Villa make anti-black commemorative practices visible. These examples illustrate how such practices often turn on blackness' omission and evasion. Consequently, the implications of such commemorative practices for Galveston's African American beaches and the lifeguards who protected beachgoers utilizing them are multiple.

Galveston's African American lifeguards nor its historically African American beaches have not been commemorated even as both structure the city's commemorative space. Yet Wavery Guidry and James Helton offer possibilities for challenging the commemorative landscape's prevailing racialized narratives as well as reconsidering what constitutes a commemorative space. I argue for these lifeguards' encounters on the segregated beaches where they worked as a means of understanding African Americans' fraught relationship with terrestrial white spaces. Though the beach offers transformative possibilities for the racially unmarked, for black bodies, the beach remained contingent and fraught with a range of racial meanings. I now turn to the ways that Guidry and Helton 'sat up' with those meanings.

4 Always on Duty: Wavery Guidry (1912–1986)

When Wavery Guidry died in 1986 at the age of 74, the *Galveston Daily News'* obituary did not mention his 14 seasons as lifeguard at 28th Street Beach – or Brown Beach as it was sometimes called. It instead identified Guidry as "a self-employed vegetable man [and] a former merchant seaman" ("Obituaries" 1986, 4A). But Guidry was the second African American lifeguard to work at the 28th Street beach, stationed there from 1942 until 1957 and employed by the Galveston Police Department which had taken responsibility from the American Red Cross for the city's beach lifeguards. During his time as a seasonal guard from May through September, he made nearly 30 rescues and recoveries documented in local news media. In one example, on Memorial Day weekend 1943, he recovered two African American men's bodies from the Gulf of Mexico. One man, 27-year-old Earl Matthews McAlpine, died on his job at the Pleasure Pier, the city's top tourist attraction, when the scaffold he was standing on accidentally shifted and ejected him into the Gulf. The other was 73-year-old fisherman Benny Harris, a non-swimmer, whose friends were unable to rescue him when his boat capsized at the other, and at the time, unguarded African American beach at the West end of the Island called the Sunset Camps ("Two Negro" 1943, 3).

While obviously their deaths were tragic, their work and recreation on Galveston's beachfront offers evidence of African Americans' presence there and offers a counternarrative to the beach as a race neutral space. Further, Guidry's recovery of McAlpine at the Pleasure Pier also makes beach segregation's contingencies clear. Though he died while working in the heart of Galveston's white tourist district where at least two white lifeguards were on duty, Guidry was called away from Brown Beach to retrieve McAlpine's body from the Gulf. Despite searching for four hours with a grappling hook to recover McAlpine's remains, Guidry did not find his body until the next morning ("Body" 1943, 2). As both an iteration of "racializing surveillance" that inscribes racial boundaries and an example of 'sitting up' with anti-blackness, Guidry's labor to recover McAlpine's body exposes the black body as an absent presence in the white spatial imagination. In other words, Guidry's visibility as a black lifeguard turns on his ability to retrieve McAlpine's body from the white beach at 21st Street. Yet that labor effectively reifies racial segregation's logic as he was forced to leave his post protecting black bathers as two white lifeguards stood on duty at the 21st Street beach and declined to find McAlpine's remains. Guidry 'sat up' with anti-blackness as he located McAlpine's body when white lifeguards refused to and when he 'protected' the white beach from blackness. It also exposes the irony that Guidry as a black lifeguard was not only tasked with enforcing the beachfront's color line, but in so doing, necessarily traversed it.

While Guidry's work to recover black bodies and to save black lives on the Galveston beachfront garnered print media coverage, his testimony in the racial spectacle of Kilgore, Texas, native John Brown's 1944 10th District Court trials for the murders of Galvestonians Rose Anna Coleman and Robert Walker garnered more media attention than all of his rescues and recoveries combined. It illustrates how Guidry as an African American lifeguard mediates racial meanings between terrestrial and beach spaces.

Inscribing black criminality on the beachfront at 28th Street, the *Galveston Daily News* reported that the case involved "the killing of a negro man and a negro woman in a brawl in a negro beer tavern at 28th and Boulevard" ("Fate" 1944, 1). Brown argued self-defense when he stabbed Coleman, whom he claimed had attacked him with a knife at the Gulf View Tavern, a popular African American nightclub. Guidry testified on Brown's behalf saying that he arrested Brown and took him to the hospital to treat the injuries he sustained as a result of his altercation with Coleman. He also testified about an encounter with Coleman a week prior to the deaths at the 28th Street beach when he confiscated a knife from her in a confrontation with two women. However, cross examination revealed that he declined to arrest Coleman when that incident occurred. Before their deliberations, the all-white jury heard testimony that Brown's reputation was good, and he eventually received a five-year suspended sentence ("Kilgore" 1944, 1).

Guidry's status as a 'negro lifeguard' – as he is identified in every print media reference –complicates the trial's tangle of racial meanings in two significant ways. First, as a racial spectacle that circulates black suffering for white enjoyment, Guidry's testimony in the Brown case substantiates and authenticates evidence of black criminality that underwrites the anti-black and white supremacist ideologies that structure segregation. Second, his testimony jeopardizes his own status as a beach law enforcement officer in that he implicates himself in his refusal to arrest Coleman. In short, Guidry himself became a defendant in the court of white public opinion about African Americans and the burden of proof required to meet demands for full citizenship. In the logic of the terrestrial white space, African Americans must demonstrate their fitness for full citizenship and this trial provides those seeking it with evidence to refute such an argument. Even as Guidry worked to defuse a conflict on the 28th Street Beach, that action is ultimately pressed into the service of a broader anti-black narrative of black criminality that undermines his legitimacy as a lifeguard on Brown Beach and interrupts its restorative possibilities as a place that facilitates experiencing and engaging in the joy and pain of black life. As such, his testimony offers an instance of 'sitting up' with anti-blackness illustrating the confoundedness of the black experience on Galveston's Brown and West beaches. Ultimately, though 28th Street Beach offered provisional pleasures and freedoms, it was no match for the terrestrial white space of Texas' 10th District Court.

Guidry's testimony also speaks to the burden of black representation or "the homely notion that you represent your race, thus that your actions can betray your race or honor it" and I want to close with a discussion of how the burden of representation plays out on the 28th Street Beach for the city's first African American lifeguard James Helton (Gates 1997, xvii).

5 Always on Duty: James Helton (1914–1965)

Galveston's African American community first petitioned for a lifeguard at 28th Street in 1921 just two years after the Galveston Red Cross lifesaving corps was established. James Helton, a BOI – born on the island – worked unofficially as a volunteer lifeguard after graduating from Central High School in 1934 ("Central" 1934, 9). However, increasing numbers of African American beach visitors and calls for a black lifeguard by Galveston's black community leaders led to his hire as the first African American guard in 1935 for the six-week season. Helton, like Guidry, had a long history of work at the Port of Galveston where he worked as a stevedore. He ended his seasonal lifeguard work in 1943 and remained employed by SP Dock until his death in 1965 ("Obituaries" 1965, 7B).

Helton was also lauded for multiple rescues and recoveries. He held a Red Cross senior lifesaving certificate and had been trained by the Red Cross Corps prior to starting work at Brown Beach in early May 1935 ("Reports" 1935, 2). Shortly after he was trained and hired, he participated in a demonstration of lifesaving techniques put on by six lifeguards at the Hotel Galvez for the Board of City commissioners who had just taken over funding what was then known as the Galveston Police Beach Patrol. At the event, Beach Patrol Captain Stuart L. Reed emphasized the guards' training in taking preventative actions to avoid drownings on the Galveston beachfront and Helton employed those measures at the 28th Street Beach ("Life-saving" 1935, 4). His first rescues there occurred shortly after his hire during the Memorial Day weekend in 1935 where Reed estimated that between 350 to 400 African American beachgoers enjoyed the beach each day of the weekend ("Reports" 1935, 12). Helton rescued three 28th Street bathers, an unnamed black woman, an elderly man identified as Pop Simmons and an unidentified 11-year-old boy, all visiting Galveston from Houston (ibid.). According to Reed, all three "would have drowned" had Helton not been on duty (ibid.). Each one returned home to their loved ones and Helton received accolades from Captain Reed and others witnessing the rescue. These beach patrons would have further opportunities to experience the joy and pain of black life at the beach.

Yet parallel to Guidry's experiences with 'sitting up' with anti-blackness, Helton's work on the beach produced his own encounter with it. Almost a year before Helton was officially hired by the Galveston Police Beach Patrol, he worked at 28th Street Beach. He was on duty when Galveston County deputy sheriff O. G. Flake who was driving on Seawall Boulevard spotted a white woman accessing the 28th Street Beach stairway and "thought she was acting rather funny" so he decided to turn his car around ("Young" 1934, 1). The fully dressed white woman walked across the beach, into the water, and Helton saved her from "a watery grave in the Gulf" (ibid.). However, as reported in the *Galveston Tribune*, the rescue is attributed to "the intuition of a special deputy sheriff with the assistance of a negro lifeguard" who goes unnamed (ibid.). No other local papers reported the event. The rescue's reporting anticipates both the politics of black representation as well as how the logic of the terrestrial white space impinges upon the beachfront. In this iteration, the white terrestrial space's logic centers the protection of white femininity from an anti-black perception of black male predatory sexuality. In effect, Helton cannot be publicly credited for the rescue because such an admission upends the prevailing anti-black narratives around white femininity and black male sexuality. Given that white visitors like Dallas resident C. E. Ganson who angrily observed in his letter to the editor of the *Galveston Daily News* that Galveston is "the only city in the South where social equality and negro supremacy is so nearly a fact" and was equally frustrated by the "intermingling of whites and negroes" on the city's beaches because it necessitated "walking through a crowd of yelling, screeching, nude negroes of both sexes," omitting Helton's name in documenting the rescue recognized the racially charged optics it would likely pose to both white visitors and residents ("Complains" 1929, 6). The white woman Helton rescued, who also went unnamed, told Galveston Police Chief Toy Messina after the incident that she had planned to "end it all" and nodded in the negative when asked if she was glad to have been saved (ibid.). Her family was notified, she was released to their care, and they returned with her to Houston. Though another person is reunited with their loved ones due to Helton's labor, in the end, his work, much like the omission of the enslaved's labor at Ashton Villa, goes unacknowledged in order to adhere to normative whiteness' terrestrial social demands that were extended to the beachfront. Like Guidry, Helton 'sat up' with an iteration of anti-blackness that required a white intermediary in order to legitimize his work.

Wavery Guidry and James Helton collectively stood guard at Brown Beach and West Beach for 21 years – Guidry worked for 12 years and Helton for 9. Long before there was a national organization like the United States Lifesaving Association, they enacted its charge to "[m]aintain an unwavering dedication to the safety of those they are assigned to protect" and they did so despite the white normative spatial logic that shaped the Galveston beachfront where the people they were charged with protecting had picnics, built sandcastles, played cards, crabbed, fished, swam and sometimes died ("The USLA Code"). Guidry and Helton had peers and predecessors. They could be found in cities and beaches along the Atlantic seaboard such as Pea Island, North Carolina and on the Virginia coast. As Kevin Dawson notes, enslaved people in the U. S. labored as lifeguards and lifesavers to "reduce white drowning death rates" and were employed by European slave traders who hired "African lifeguards to protect their investments" when boats transporting them capsized and the enslaved people attempted to swim away (Dawson 2018, 62). Yet no matter the geographic location, they all encountered and 'sat up' with anti-blackness. Guidry and Helton's work has been buried under years of racialized sedimentation – not only was it ignored, occluded, or evaded in the previous historical moment, but it has been neglected in the current historical moment in the service maintaining a linear and easily consumed narrative about race in Galveston's commemorative landscape. Their experiences trouble that narrative and present an opportunity to uncover a rich, textured and dynamic history that exposes the ways that black lives mattered in early to mid-twentieth century Galveston and demonstrate their multiple implications in the current historical moment. Their ongoing omission from the commemorative landscape, so many years after their deaths, marks a final instance of Guidry and Helton 'sitting up' with anti-blackness. Ultimately, Wavery Guidry and James Helton were always on duty – attending to both beach patrons and to anti-blackness' multiple contingencies in their work on the beach. These lifeguards who protected *all* beachgoers at Galveston's Brown Beach, West Beach, bore witness to the joy and pain of black life, and 'sat up' with anti-blackness at these beaches each day of their six-week season. Their experiences echo the critical race studies tenet that experiential knowledge is "critical to understanding, analyzing and teaching about racial subordination" and provide a critical opportunity to reconsider how racial discourses in the U.S. Gulf South impact the beach's transformative possibilities (Yoss 2005, 69).

Bibliography

Anderson, Elijah. "The White Space." *Sociology of Race and Ethnicity* 1.1 (2015): 10–21.
"Ashton Villa, 1859." *Texas Historical Marker*: https://www.txhistoricalmarker.com/marker/8217 (24 July 2019).
"Body of Negro Drowned in Gulf Recovered." *Galveston Daily News* (27 May 1943): 2.
Browne, Simone. *Dark Matters. On the Surveillance of Blackness*. Durham: Duke University Press, 2015.
Burdsey, Daniel. *Race, Place and the Seaside. Postcards From the Edge*. London: Palgrave, 2015.
Campanella, Richard. "Gulf Souths, Gulf Streams and their Dispersions: A Geographer's Take." *The Southern Literary Journal* 46.2 (2014): 17–32.
"Central High Will Graduate Students." *Galveston Tribune* (2 June 1934): 9.
"Complains of Negro Bathers." Letter to the Editor. *Galveston Daily News* (1 August 1929): 6.
Coulter, John. *The Complete Story of the Galveston Horror*. New York: United Publishers of America, 1900.
Davis, Patricia G. *Laying Claim: African American Cultural Memory and Southern Identity*. Tuscaloosa: University of Alabama Press, 2016.
Dawson, Kevin. *Undercurrents of Power: Aquatic Culture in the African Diaspora*. Pittsburgh: University of Pennsylvania Press, 2018.
Gates, Henry Louis Jr. *Thirteen Ways of Looking at a Black Man*. New York: Vintage, 1997.
"General Order Number Three." Issued by General Gordon Granger. *National Juneteenth Observance Foundation*: http://nationaljuneteenth.com/General_Order.html (24 July 2019).
"Juneteenth." *Texas Historical Marker*: https://www.txhistoricalmarker.com/marker/12030 (24 July 2019).

Kahrl, Andrew. *The Land Was Ours: How Black Beaches Became White Wealth in the Coastal South*. Chapel Hill: University of North Carolina Press, 2012.
"Kilgore Negro Gets Suspended Sentence." *Galveston Daily News* (22 January 1944): 1.
"Life-Saving Methods Are Demonstrated." *Galveston Daily News* (5 September 1935): 4.
Mack, John. *The Sea. A Cultural History*. London: Reaktion Books, 2011.
McKittrick, Katherine. "On Plantations, Prisons and a Black Sense of Place." *Social & Cultural Geography* 12.8 (2011): 947–963.
"Obituaries." *Galveston Daily News* (24 December 1986): 4A.
"Officials Again Postpone Beach Segregation Action, Following Heated Argument." *Galveston Daily News* (18 July 1922): 1.
"Plessy v. Ferguson." *Oyez*: https://www.oyez.org/cases/1850-1900/163us537 (25 July 2019).
"Reports Show Red Cross Active Here" *Galveston Daily News* (16 October 1935): 12.
Robinson, Zandria F., and Marcus Anthony Hunter. *Chocolate Cities. The Black Map of American Life*. Berkeley: University of California Press, 2018.
"Seek Removal of Negro From Beach." *Galveston Daily News* (16 June 1922): 1.
Stanonis, Anthony J. *Faith in Bikinis. Politics and Leisure in the Coastal South Since the Civil War*. Athens: University of Georgia Press, 2014.
"Two Negro Men Are Drowning Victims." *Galveston Tribune* (26 May 1943): 1.
"The USLA Code of Ethics." https://www.usla.org/page/Ethics (25 July 2019).
Warren, Calvin. "Black Care." *Liquid Blackness* 3.6 (2016): 35–47.
Yoss, Tara J. "Whose Culture Has Capital? A Critical Race Theory Discussion of Community Cultural Wealth." *Race Ethnicity and Education* 8.1 (2005): 69–91.
"Young Houston Woman is Saved From Drowning." *Galveston Tribune* (6 August 1934): 1.

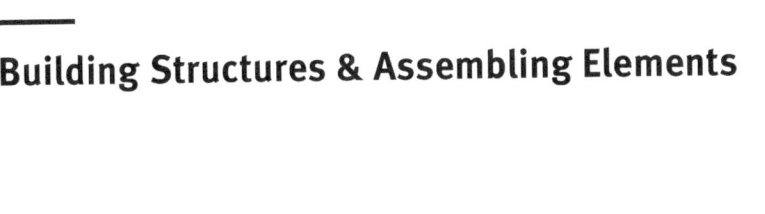

Building Structures & Assembling Elements

Dietrich Erben
Sand, Spuren, Architektur – Zur gebauten Ökologie des Strandes

This contribution will attempt to analyse the beach as an ecology viewed against the backdrop of the categories of sand, trace and building. The description of the beach in Daniel Defoe's *Robinson Crusoe* (1719) may be viewed as paradigmatic for the following consideration: do the architectures constructed by Robinson lead to a transformation of the coast into a beach; and do Friday's traces turn the island into a sociotope? Up until today, the spatial organisation of the beach has been coined by social routines of staying on the beach, which involve traces and architectures ranging from beach towels, sunbeds, parasols and bodily exercises to beach architectures of restaurants, bath houses and piers. If the beach could be considered a 'liminal' zone between water and land, the built ecology of beaches ought to be understood as interspace between stable buildings and situational occupancy of space.

In dem Beitrag wird der Versuch gemacht, den Strand als Ökologie anhand der Kategorien des Sandes, der Spur und des Gebäudes zu beschreiben. Als paradigmatisch für diese Überlegung kann die Schilderung des Strandes in Daniel Defoes *Robinson Crusoe* (1719) gelten, wo durch die von Robinson gebauten Behausungen die Küste zum Strand und durch die Spuren Fridays die Insel zum Soziotop wird. Bis heute ist die Raumorganisation des Strandes im Rahmen der sozialen Routinen des Strandaufenthalts durch Spuren und Architekturen geprägt – von Badetüchern, Liegestühlen über Sonnenschirme und Körperpraktiken bis zu Strandarchitekturen der Restaurants, Badehäuschen und Piers. Handelt es sich bereits beim Strand um eine ‚liminale' Zone zwischen Wasser und Land, so sollte auch die gebaute Ökologie von Stränden als Zwischenraum zwischen stabilen Gebäuden und situativer Raumbesetzung verstanden werden.

1 Erzählen und Handeln

Will man vom Strand ‚erzählen', so landet man offenbar unverzüglich in einer Paradoxie. Die einen sagen, ein Strand ist für eine Erzählung zu redundant, die anderen sagen, er ist durch sein Übermaß an Bedeutungen nicht mehr als Erzählung verständlich, wobei es sein könnte, dass beide Seiten vielleicht am Ende auf etwas Ähnliches hinauswollen. So gibt der Essayist Adrian A. Gill, der vor allem durch seine Reisereportagen bekannt geworden ist, zu bedenken, dass der Strand ein letztlich eindimensionaler Erlebnisraum sei. Sowieso gehöre es zum guten Ton, dass man über den Strand überheblich die Nase rümpfe; Strände provozierten ein kindliches Verhalten größter Direktheit; ein Strand gleiche ohnedies dem anderen und schließlich hätten Strände nichts Kohärentes zu erzählen:

> A beach is a sandpit for grown-ups. It's an infantilising experience where the crowds regress through childish, supine idiocy. [...] And all beaches are extension of the same beach; they have a repetitive primary simplicity. [...] Beaches dictate a certain sort of personality, a particular world view. It is, for instance, impossible to be sophisticated on a beach. [...] The reason I like beaches, and the reason travel writers don't, is that they have no narrative. They don't tell stories. (Gill 2012, 78, 80)

Die Stichworte von Serialität und Narration lassen sich, bei aller scheinbaren Beiläufigkeit in Gills Essay, durchaus auf die neueren Befunde der Narrationsforschung beziehen, wonach Wiederholungen zur Erzählung in Widerspruch geraten. Wenn es stimmt, dass es nur wenige Szenerien gibt, die keine Entwicklungslogik entfalten, so dürften dazu, wie der Rauch des Feuers und die dahinziehenden Wolken am Himmel, auch die Wellen des Meeres am Strand gehören. Solche Phänomene ohne Anfang, Mitte und Ende können, folgt man Aristoteles' Poetik, keine Erzählung ausprägen: Erst das „Ganze [d. i. einer Erzählung] ist, was Anfang, Mitte und Ende hat." (Aristoteles 1982, 7, 1450b) Der entsprechende erzähltheoretische Zusammenhang der Sequenzbildung wurde von Albrecht Koschorke erläutert (Koschorke 2012, 61–74). Laut Gill wird, wie die Naturgegebenheiten selbst, auch das Stranderlebnis im Wesentlichen von einer Wiederholungsstruktur bestimmt, nämlich von einer infantilen Regression weit unterhalb der Schwelle raffinierterer menschlicher Artikulation. Dabei liegt Gill jedwede Beurteilung aus höherer Warte fern – was er am Strand ausmacht, macht den Strand schätzenswert.

Auch der Kulturanthropologe John Fiske geht vom Gewöhnlichen des Strandes aus, doch für ihn ist er eine Sphäre implodierender, in ihrer Überfülle entropisch zusammenbrechender Bedeutungen. In seinem erstmals 1983 unter dem Titel „Surfalism and Sandiotics: The Beach in Australian Popular Culture" erschienenen Pionieraufsatz beschreibt und analysiert er den „suburban beach" (Fiske 2011 [1989], 44).[1] Beim Attribut ‚suburban' kann man daran denken, dass die topographische Bezeichnung im Sinne des Vorstädtischen (‚suburbia') auch mit einer Klassifizierung im Sinne des ‚Gewöhnlichen' verbunden ist. Beim ‚suburban beach' handelt es sich um ein künstliches Sozio- und Biotop, das sich durch erhebliche artifizielle Interventionen und durch ein teils damit verbundenes, teils daraus hervorgehendes soziales Verbotsregime auszeichnet. Sowohl Intervention als auch Verbotsregime stehen in scheinbar markantem Kontrast zur performativen ‚Natürlichkeit' des Strandes, sind jedoch letztlich deren Bedingungen. Bei Fiske ist die Rede von der Differenz zwischen der ‚Natur' („the nature") und dem ‚Natürlichen' („the natural") (ebd., 35). In der Sphäre des ‚Natürlichen' erzeugen die artifiziellen Dingwelten der Strandtücher,

---

[1] Siehe zu Fiske und zum Surfen auch den Beitrag von Konstantin Butz in diesem Band.

Liegestühle und Sonnenschirme, der Strandbuden und der Wegsysteme eine strikte kulturelle und räumlich zonierte Ordnung (Abb. 1). In sie fügen sich die Menschen durch Handlungsroutinen ein. Gemäß ihren Gewohnheiten entlassen sich Menschen am Strand durch ihre weitgehende Nacktheit und durch das Baden in Sonne und Meer einer gespielten Natürlichkeit. Es besteht kein Zweifel, dass sich kulturell kodierte ‚Natürlichkeit', Naturempfinden und Körperwahrnehmung einerseits und Disziplinierung andererseits wechselseitig bestärken: Die Ausgesetztheit der nackten Körper ist nur durch soziale Kontrolle überhaupt auszuhalten.[2] Soziale Observanz bildet die notwendige Voraussetzung für die Empfindung oder auch für die Illusion von Freiheit und Wohlbefinden in der ‚liminalen' Zone des Meeres. Laut Fiske resultiert aus diesen Bedingungsverhältnissen für den Strand ein „too much of meaning", ein „excess of meaning potential", ein „overflow of meaning" (ebd., 34).

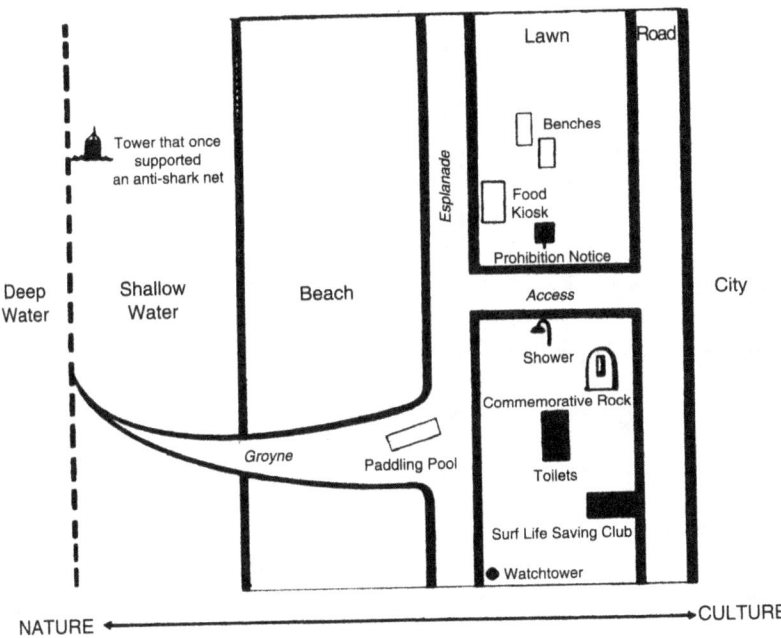

Figure 3

Abb. 1: John Fiskes Zonierungsdiagramm eines Strandabschnitts.

---

2 Siehe hierzu auch den Beitrag von Barbara Vinken im vorliegenden Band.

Die folgenden Überlegungen tragen der Skepsis gegenüber dem Narrativen Rechnung, indem sie den Endlosschleifen des Sozialen, nämlich den Handlungsroutinen als soziale Gegebenheit des Lebens am Strand, weiter auf der Spur sind. Dabei wird die Frage nach der Semantik des ‚suburban beach' keineswegs fallen gelassen. In den Blick genommen wird jedoch dazu der Wirklichkeitsstoff, aus dem der Strand gebildet ist, also dessen Komponenten der landschaftlichen Wasser- und Landflächen, der Bauten und anderer Flächenmarkierungen und nicht zuletzt der Menschen, die sich dort aufhalten. Es wird versucht, anhand dieser materiellen Wirklichkeiten den Strand als eine Szenerie zu beschreiben, der gleichsam durch das Zwischenmedium der Spur semantisch markiert wird. Diese Gesamtheit von realen Stoffen und von Imagination lässt sich meines Erachtens am besten – angeregt von dem Architekturhistoriker Reyner Banham, auf den noch zurückzukommen ist – als ökologisches System zur Synthese bringen.

Damit ist im Grunde schon gesagt, dass es im Folgenden um den Strand und ausdrücklich nicht um die Küste geht. Zur Sprache kommen weder der historische Wandel der Wahrnehmung der Küstenlandschaft, wie er in der klassischen Studie von Alain Corbin nachgezeichnet wurde (Corbin 1994 [1988]), noch die massiven Probleme, die in der Gegenwart für Lebensverhältnisse und damit auch der Architektur von ausgesprochener Relevanz sind. Hier sei nur an die im Zuge des Klimawandels immer drängenderen Planungen von Küstenschutzprojekten, für die beispielhaft der Wiederaufbau von New Orleans nach den Überschwemmungen durch den Tornado Katrina im August 2005 genannt werden kann (Hartman und Squires 2006; Falser 2008; Freireiss 2009), und an die weltweiten, neoliberal inspirierten Projekterschließungen von Küsten mit den damit oft einhergehenden Hafenkonversionen in Dienstleistungsareale erinnert. In der Unzahl der Beispiele stellen der Battery Park in New York, die Docklands in London, die Hamburger Hafen City und die Hafenkonversionen in Barcelona, Genua und Marseille die vielleicht bekanntesten Beispiele dar.[3] Zu diesen Problemfeldern zählt auch die Bewegung der Finanzökonomien in der Gegenrichtung, nämlich weg von den Küsten und hinaus auf das offene Meer. Das ist bei der Verlagerung von Finanzsektoren ‚offshore' der Fall, die ohne stabile Niederlassungen mit winzigen Atollen oder mit umso größeren Yachten auskommen (Kemp 2016, bes. 139–153). Und schließlich hat sich herumgesprochen, dass der Welt allmählich der Sand ausgeht. Es fehlt, genauer gesagt, an zum Bauen geeigneten, scharfkörnigen Sanden. Die Golfstaaten etwa haben zwar herrliche Wüsten und Sandstrände, müssen aber für ihre gigantomanischen

---

3 Vgl. als verhältnismäßig frühe Publikation Jaacks (2003) und als neuere Titel Hein (2011); Bullivant (2012).

Landaufschüttungen und Bauprojekte den für Beton tauglichen Gruben-, Fluss- und Küstensand aus Afrika oder Australien herankarren, wo der Abbau immense ökologische Schäden verursacht und wo, wie überall auf der Welt, der Bausand allmählich knapp wird. Von alledem ist, wie gesagt, im Folgenden nicht die Rede.

2 Spuren im Sand – Existenz in der ‚liminalen' Zone

Sand ist, nicht nur beim Bauen, ein Medium. Als solches wurde er im strand- aber keineswegs sandfernen Bielefeld von Niklas Luhmann beschrieben. Sand dient Luhmann, neben der Luft, zur Erläuterung eines seiner wichtigsten ästhetischen und wahrnehmungstheoretischen Probleme, nämlich der wechselseitigen Bedingtheit von Medium und Form.[4] Demnach ist die Form an das Medium gekoppelt, die kontingente Form bedarf des stabileren Mediums als Substrat. So ist es auch beim Sand und bei der Spur. Das Medium ist an sich formlos, die Form macht es spezifisch – der Abdruck des Fußes im Sand bewirkt eine rigidere Verbindung der Sandkörner, die sich zu einer Form, die wir Spur nennen, verfestigen und die wir als solche wahrnehmen können. Medien und Formen gibt es, darauf will Luhmann hinaus, nur in einer Koppelung. Die Luft ist nicht laut, sondern wir hören die von ihr getragenen Schallwellen. Die Wörter hören wir nicht, sondern nur die geformten, gesprochenen Laute. Den Sand können wir natürlich sehen, er ist aber ein vergleichsweise instabiles Medium, das erst durch Formen und deren besondere Ausprägungen, unter anderem als Spuren, prägnant wird.

Es hat offenbar viel mit diesem sinnfälligen und exemplarischen Gehalt von Sand und Spur zu tun, dass beide – also das Naturmedium des Sandes und die insbesondere vom Menschen erzeugte Form der Spur – nicht nur immer wieder Anlass zu medien- und zeichentheoretischen Überlegungen gegeben haben, sondern dass sie auch eine so reiche Entfaltung in der Symbolbildung im kollektiven und kulturellen Gedächtnis gefunden haben.

---

4 Erwähnungen des Sandes als Medium finden sich mehrfach in Werken von Luhmann im Zusammenhang mit seinen Erläuterungen zur Differenz von ‚Medium und Form'; ich nehme Bezug auf Luhmann (2011, hier bes. 200–202); vgl. auch den Eintrag „Form/Medium" in: Baraldi et al. (1997, 58–60).

Abb. 2: Robert Capa, Françoise Gilot, Pablo Picasso und Javier Vilato am Strand von Port-Juan (Foto 1948).

Sie möchte ich zunächst jenseits der touristischen Handlungsroutinen an ein paar ausdrücklich inszenierten Bildepisoden schildern, in denen es um den Maler Pablo Picasso und den Architekten Le Corbusier geht. Sie erinnern einmal mehr daran, dass Küstenorte nicht nur bevorzugte Aufenthaltsorte von Künstlerinnen und Künstlern der Moderne waren, sondern dass sie bis heute auch ein Topos der Moderne sind. Küstenorte sind Niederlassungsorte von KünstlerInnenkolonien wie auch in einem metaphorischen Sinn Gründungsorte der Moderne (Krüger 2014 sowie dessen in Arbeit befindliche Studie zum Lokalkolorit). Man denke nur an das Étretat der impressionistischen Künstlerinnen und Künstler in der Normandie oder an Pont-Avon in der Bretagne. Dort erträumte sich Paul Gauguin schon einmal die Ursprünglichkeit und Freiheit des Lebens, bevor er sich dann in den Kopf setzte, sie auf seinen Südsee-Reisen aufzusuchen. Bei der Ortswahl von Küstenorten spielten zunächst ökonomische Ausweichmanöver, das heißt konkret die Verfügbarkeit von billigem Wohn- und Atelierraum, eine Rolle. Hinzu kommt der Blick auf die Attraktivität des scheinbar unverbrauchten Lokalkolorits und der Landschaftsmotive. Darüber hinaus geht es um die Suche nach Ursprüngen im geographischen Abseits. So sind die Badenden am Strand ein spezielles Sujet der Moderne, an dem sich nicht nur dem homoerotischen Freikörperkult huldigen ließ, sondern auch dem künstlerischen Anliegen, die Malerei allmählich von den Gegenständen zu lösen und in die abstrahierten Gefilde der Formen vorzustoßen (Gallwitz und Ortuf 2003; Wallner 2018). Schließlich hielten die Künstlerinnen und Künstler gezielt nach einem Milieu Ausschau, das im Provinziellen und Peripheren zugleich die gesuchte gesellschaftliche Exzentrik und die ästhetische Modernisierung gerade jenseits der akademischen Kunstzentren, also besonders Paris und Berlin, zum Ausdruck bringen sollte.

All diese Motivationen waren auch nach dem Siegeszug der Moderne nach dem Zweiten Weltkrieg noch nicht obsolet geworden, es hat aber den Anschein, dass die Verarbeitungsmechanismen ironisch distanzierter geworden sind. Die unmittelbaren Erregungszustände haben der Inszenierung Platz gemacht. So ist die Photographie aufzufassen, die von Pablo Picasso mit seiner damaligen Lebensgefährtin Françoise Gilot und mit seinem Neffen, dem Maler Javier Vilato, am Strand von Port-Juan in der Provence entstand (Abb. 2). Das Foto stammt von dem berühmten Fotoreporter Robert Capa, der das Paar im Sommer 1948 in ihrem südfranzösischen Feriendomizil besuchte.[5] Es stellt die Szenerie einer ausgelassenen *joie de vivre* vor Augen, wobei es zu einem spielerischen Geschlechterkampf und zu einer teilweisen Inversion der Geschlechterhierarchien kommt. Der Malerfürst schreitet nicht nur im Respektsabstand hinter der Partnerin, sondern spendet ihr auch mit dem Sonnenschirm Schatten. Mit einem durchaus offenkundigen, gönnerhaften inszenatorischen Bewusstsein von seiner Aktion, bringt der Maler, der sich in seinem Œuvre lange genug mit Weltkunst und mit Barockmalerei auseinandergesetzt hat, hier ein höfisches Zeremoniell der Huldigung vor dem Fürsten zur Aufführung. Der Neffe mit der Harpune in Händen tritt als satyrnhafte Jägergestalt im Hintergrund hinzu. Konterkariert und durchkreuzt wird allerdings jedwede formale Feierlichkeit nicht nur durch die Kleidung und die Accessoires – also Strandkleidung und Sonnenschirm statt Baldachin –, sondern auch durch die Ausgelassenheit der Beteiligten und nicht zuletzt durch die gänzlich informelle Szenerie des Strandes. Aber solche Inversionen hin oder her – der Strand verführt dazu, das alte Thema von Maler und Muse noch einmal durchzuspielen. Ausnahmsweise stolziert die Muse dem Meister voran.

---

[5] Zu den Lebensumständen als Quelle Gilot und Lake (1980 [1964], bes. 78–79, 113–116, 302).

Abb. 3: Le Corbusier am Strand auf Long Island (Foto 1946).

Archaischer Ernst waltet hingegen über dem Foto von Le Corbusier am Strand von Long Island, das vermutlich im Rahmen von Le Corbusiers USA-Reise Anfang 1946 entstand (Abb. 3). Das Foto zeigt den seinerzeit knapp 60-jährigen Architekten in Badehose und mit seiner großen Brille auf der Nase in einer eigentümlich beschwörenden Haltung mit erhobenen Händen. Die Abdrücke im Sand vor ihm komplettieren die Pose zur Szene. Wir erkennen in der Sandgraphik zwei riesige pfotenartige Hände, unterhalb davon zwei Mulden und zwischen ihnen eine gewellte Linie. Die Füße des Architekten sind unmittelbar vor ihm in zwei Vertiefungen im Sand wiederholt. Die Anordnung von Person und Sandgraphik suggeriert, dass sich der Architekt am Strand niedergeworfen hat, nun wieder aufgestanden ist und das Verehrungsritual der Proskynese, also der Geste des Sich-Zu-Boden-Werfens als Zeichen der Ehrerbietung und Unterwerfung, mit dem Gebet in der Haltung des Oranten fortsetzt. Die Szene oszilliert zwischen einer unverkennbar theatralischen Inszenierung und einer beschwörenden Performanz, im Zuge derer tatsächlich authentische Erfahrungen evoziert werden sollen.[6]

---

[6] Zu diesem Verständnis von Performanz nicht allein als fiktionalisierte Inszenierung, sondern als gestisch oder sprachlich aktualisierter Wirklichkeit vgl. Pfister (2013).

Diese performativen Bezüge lassen sich detailliert eruieren (Maak 2010, bes. 23–29). Das Foto ist einerseits Teil einer persönlichen Imagekampagne von Le Corbusier, welche die vielen Bilder des Architekten in seinem technoiden Auftreten nun im Modus des Archaischen konterkariert und programmatisch komplementär zu einem Ganzen ergänzt. Damit deutet sich an, dass die Strandfotoserie andererseits eine tiefgründige architekturtheoretische Programmatik besitzt. Sie verdankt gerade in diesen Jahren der Nachkriegszeit einiges den Schriften von Paul Valéry, insbesondere dessen Architekturdialog *Eupalinos* und dem Essay „L'homme et la coquille" (beide 1923). In beiden Fällen handelt es sich um philosophische Reflexionen, die ihre Poetik und ihre Inhalte aus der antikisierenden Kultur der *méditerranée* und aus deren Ästhetisierung beziehen (Cachin 2000; Genge 2009, 167–186). Für Le Corbusier wurden sie, um es mit wenigen Schlagworten zu sagen, nicht nur deshalb, sondern auch in einem ganz konkreten Sinn bedeutsam: Er fand hier am Strand Begründungen für das kreative Prinzip des nicht-linearen Entwerfens, für die Inkorporation des Zufälligen, nämlich den Zufallsfunden von Naturobjekten wie Steinen oder Muscheln. Letztlich ging es um die Versöhnung von Natur und Kultur. Das Symbol dieser Synthese ist das Muschelgehäuse, die Ökologie dieser Synthese ist der Strand, das Medium dieser Synthese ist der Sand. Der Sand hat Le Corbusier, besonders in jenen Jahren, als das Foto entstand, nicht nur als Grundstoff des *beton brut* interessiert, sondern, wie seine zahllosen Fotos von Sandverwehungen zeigen (Benton 2012, 46–51), als zugleich naturwüchsige Hervorbringung und als extrem kontingentes Phänomen.

Im größeren Maßstab einer Sandverwehung erscheint die Düne in eindrucksvoller Prägnanz bei dem englischen Kunsthistoriker Michael Baxandall als Existenzmetapher – genauer gesagt als Metapher für die Möglichkeit und die Unmöglichkeit der Selbsterkenntnis und damit der Möglichkeit des Schreibens einer Autobiographie (Baxandall 2010, 15–21; Erben 2018). Das Buch zeichnet sich durch ein außergewöhnliches Maß an Selbstreferenzialität aus. Der Autor denkt in seiner Autobiographie unablässig über das Zustandekommen des autobiographischen Textes selbst nach. Zu dieser Reflexion gehört gleich zu Beginn des Buches die Umschreibung des eigenen Selbst (,self') mit der Metapher der Sanddüne. Er habe, so Baxandall, lange Zeit eine Postkarte von einer Sanddüne in der Wüste L'Erg Tihodaine in Algerien vor seinem Schreibtisch an die Wand gepinnt gehabt. An der Düne fasziniert den Kunsthistoriker nicht nur die sich stets wandelnde und daher letztlich unbeobachtbare Form. Die Düne ist darüber hinaus das ,Emblem' einer im stetigen Wandel begriffenen Identität, eines inkohärenten Selbst, bei dem es schwer sei, dieses „as something distinct, articulated and whole" zu sehen. (Ebd., 15) Die Emblematik der aus Sand gebildeten, gegenüber der Umgebung kaum zu definierenden und vom Wind unablässig verwandelten Düne verweist als Sinnbild des ‚Selbst' darauf, ‚die aktive Präsenz der Vergangenheit' anzuerkennen: „The virtue of the sand dune as emblem is that it acknowledges the active presence of the past." (Ebd., 15) Die Erinnerungen einer Person stammen nicht direkt vom ‚Selbst', sondern sind nur dessen ‚Fußabdrücke': „My experience is that memories are not often directly of oneself, but of what the self perceived or felt: footprints of the self. The identity is distributed through memory, not simply represented." (Ebd., 21)

Wenn uns das hier zunächst aufgenommene Phänomen der Spur überhaupt auffällt, und wenn wir überhaupt nicht nur über das Medium des Sandes, sondern auch über die Form der Spur reden, so sind wir – wie so oft – voreingenommen: In diesem Fall sind wir methodisch voreingenommen durch das Paradigma der Spur in der kulturalistischen Wende seit etwa 1970. Bei Jacques Derrida ist die Spur mit dem Konzept der „trace instituée" ein Kernbegriff von dessen Dekonstruktion (Derrida 1967, bes. 65–75; zur kulturtheoretischen Relevanz der Spur allgemein: Krämer et al. 2007). In Carlo Ginzburgs Überlegungen zur „Spurensicherung" ist die Spur ein Vehikel der Mikrohistorie und der „dichten Beschreibung" (Ginzburg 1986; zur Methodik Warnke 1981; Woolf 2011). Sie bietet eine gedankliche und theoretische Alternative zu den Gedächtniskonzepten von Quelle, Fragment, Figuration und Abstraktion. Eine Spur ist auf der einen Seite ein Präsenzphänomen, das auf der anderen Seite auf etwas Abwesendes oder Geschehenes schließen lässt. Sie fungiert als Index für etwas Vergangenes. Die Spur vermittelt damit zwischen der strikten Opposition von Absenz/Vergangenheit und Präsenz/Gegenwart; sie ist ein Überrest der Vergangenheit in der Gegenwart. Als Relikt verweist sie damit auch immer auf Urheberschaft oder Täterschaft. Spuren sind forensische Relikte, wobei aber – das ist am Ende vielleicht der springende Punkt – der Täter und der Detektiv Komplizen sind. Der situative Sachverhalt, in dem sich der Täter befand, ist niemals objektiv, sondern ist stets ein Produkt der Imagination des Spurensuchers. Im Paradigma der Spur rücken daher, das macht einen Gutteil von dessen kulturtheoretischer Faszination aus, Faktizität und Fiktion zusammen. Spuren sind Bruchstücke einer nicht mehr gänzlich erreichbaren Wirklichkeit, Fragmente eines Mosaiks oder Elemente eines Systems, das wir nicht mehr kennen, das wir aber als Ganzes dennoch voraussetzen müssen, denn nur so können wir die Spur als solche überhaupt lesen. Und dieses System nenne ich im Folgenden ‚Ökologie'. Ökologie soll dabei in einem recht weiten Sinn als eine Lehre von der Umwelt verstanden werden, in der Umwelt als Datensatz, von Ressourcen, Lebewesen, materiellen Beschaffenheiten, Klimagegebenheiten usw. innerhalb eines Beziehungsgefüges aufgefasst wird.

3 Architektur in der gebauten Ökologie

Der literarische Urahn einer ökologischen Konstellation des Strandes ist natürlich der 1719 erschienene *Robinson Crusoe*-Roman von Daniel Defoe. Hier findet sich paradigmatisch der Zusammenhang von Sandspur, Bauwerk und Umwelt ausgearbeitet. Defoe erfindet in seinem Roman eine eindringliche Architekturmetaphorik, durch die sich die einsame Insel zum Habitat verwandelt, während die Spuren von Friday dann dieses Habitat zum Soziotop machen. Der Protagonist durchlebt während der langen Jahrzehnte auf der einsamen Insel die Läuterung vom raubeinigen Draufgänger zu einer in Glaubensdingen und in seiner Verantwortung für die Gesellschaft gefestigten Persönlichkeit. Es ist dann der ‚Indian' Friday, dem das vermeintliche Glück dieser Persönlichkeits- und Glaubensfestigung missionarisch zu teil werden kann. So ist das Buch nur vordergründig eine Abenteuergeschichte, es lässt sich ebenso gut als Entwicklungsroman und als puritanisches Seelendrama lesen. Bei alledem wird im Einzelschicksal des Protagonisten zugleich der Prozess einer durchaus schon weltumspannend gedachten Aufklärung der Menschheit nachvollzogen. Hier kommt auch die Architektur sinnbildhaft zum Tragen, indem im Verlauf des Romans die vier Behausungen Robinsons ausführlicher beschrieben werden. Zunächst hatte der Schiffbrüchige Unterschlupf in einer Höhle gefunden (Defoe 1979 [1719], 49); dann richtet er sich, zwei Wochen nach seiner Ankunft, mit dem vom Schiffswrack geborgenen Segeltuch ein Zelt auf (ebd., 50–51). Nun beginnt er mit dem Bau einer festen Unterkunft, der ein volles Jahr in Anspruch nimmt. Geschildert werden die bedachte Wahl des Standortes, der Gebrauch der ebenfalls aus dem Wrack geretteten Werkzeuge, die Ausstattung des Hauses mit Möbeln und einer Feuerstelle sowie die Errichtung eines Vorwerks aus Palisaden, das der Verteidigung dient, in dessen Schutz Robinson aber auch den Hausgarten anlegt (ebd., 62–68). Die neue Unterkunft wird rückblickend im Buch als „home", „castle" und „residence" bezeichnet (ebd., 253). In späteren Jahren errichtet Robinson schließlich in einem anderen Teil der Insel einen „country seat", um von hier aus seine Plantagen mit den Feldfrüchten zu bestellen (ebd.).

Die Unterkünfte Robinsons sind eingängige und anspielungsreiche Symbole. In ihnen spiegeln sich ganz unmittelbar die schrittweise Naturbeherrschung und die Kultivierung der Insel wider, wie es dem zweckrationalen ökonomischen Denken der Zeit entsprach (Erben 2017, 47–48). Die Behausungen sind darüber hinaus Metaphern für die Charakterentwicklung ihres Bewohners. Sie stellen räumliche und zeitliche Ordnungen her und leiten Robinson damit zur Selbstreflexion an. Folgerichtig beginnt er, als er sein erstes wirkliches Haus (also seine dritte Unterkunft) vollendet hat, mit dem Schreiben jenes Tagebuchs, als das sich der Roman selbst ausgibt. Und schließlich rekapituliert die sukzessive Entstehung der Unterkünfte von der primitiven Zuflucht in der Höhle über das Zelt und die ‚Urhütte' bis zum Haus äußerst einprägsam eine Entwicklungsgeschichte, die sich nun ausdrücklich als Fortschrittgeschichte darstellt. Robinson hat auf seiner Insel die Zivilisation aus eigener Kraft noch einmal erschaffen und darin erweist er sich als der Paradefall eines Menschen, den sich die Aufklärung als *homo progressor et emancipator* erträumt. Der Strand ist die Topographie all dieser Progressionen und Selbstentwürfe.

Macht man von diesen Präliminarien aus einen weiten Sprung in die neueren Zeiten, so bleiben Sand und Spur aus meiner Sicht weiterhin die wesentlichen Elemente einer gebauten Ökologie des Strandes. Selbstverständlich hat es bebaute Küstenorte immer gegeben, aber es wird sich sagen lassen, dass sich die entsprechenden Architekturen über Jahrhunderte hinweg nicht von der jeweils zeitgenössischen Landarchitektur unterschieden. Es entwickelten sich spezielle Bauaufgaben wie Leuchttürme oder Hafenquais und Piers, die in der zweiten Hälfte des 19. Jahrhunderts aus dem Ingenieursbau hervorgingen (Grant 2018; Sattler 1976). Auch Ausreißer einer spleenigen Entertainment-Architektur wurden immer wieder an Badeorten gesehen. Beispielsweise wurde Portmeirion als bunte Architekturcollage in einem Bergnest über der walisischen Küste mit veritabler Kathedrale und Pantheon noch so klein in den tatsächlichen Dimensionen, aber dagegen groß im Maßstab der Ansprüche ans Entertainment errichtet (Pehnt 1983). Der Architekt des Städtchens hat sich ganz den „pleasures of architecture" verschrieben, so lautet der Titel seines Buches, das er in der Planungsphase geschrieben hat (Williams-Ellis 1924).

Eine moderne Fortsetzung findet diese Form der Unterhaltungsarchitektur, wie schon der modische Name Blue Moon signalisiert, in dem von Giancarlo de Carlo entworfenen Strandpavillon mit vorgelagertem Pier am venezianischen Lido.[7] Die gesamte, zwischen 1995 und 2005 geplante und errichtete, in Teilen schon wieder baufällige Anlage umfasst einen runden Pavillon mit Restaurantbetrieb und einer Dachterrasse sowie sich über dem Strand verzweigenden Piers (Abb. 4). Sie wurden auf Stelzen gestellt, um auf der einen Seite den Sandstrand nicht zu überbauen, und bieten auf der anderen Seite den Rundblick auf den Strand und den Meeressaum von erhöhter Warte aus. Unverkennbar wird auf die berühmte Rotonda a Mare in dem an der Adria gelegenen Senigallia Bezug genommen, die schon auf ein Projekt des späten 19. Jahrhunderts zurückgeht und in der heutigen Form 1935 im Stil des *razionalismo* umgebaut wurde. Solche

---

[7] Kurze Projektbeschreibung von Codello (2014, 108–111); zu Giancarlo De Carlo zuletzt die historischen Einordnungen bei Biraghi (2016, 346) und bei Mosco (2017, 41–44).

ausschließlich dem Strandaufenthalt dienende und schon lange nicht mehr als Teil einer Hafenanlage gedachten Piers bezeugen die allmähliche touristische Erschließung der Küstenregionen für auswärtige Reisende, nicht weniger aber auch für die Angehörigen der einheimischen Mittelschichten.[8] Architektur macht mit solchen Pavillons unübersehbar, dass die Küste zum Strand umformatiert wurde.

Abb. 4: Giancarlo De Carlos Strandpavillon Blue Moon auf dem Lido von Venedig (fertiggestellt 2005).

Richtig ernst wurde die Sache mit einer Strandarchitektur im flächendeckenden Maßstab erst im Zuge des Massentourismus seit den 1960er Jahren. Ich möchte für diesen zeitlichen und inhaltlichen Zusammenhang drei Theoriepositionen ins Feld führen. Mit den beiden Architekten Georges Candilis und Aldo Rossi und dem Architekturhistoriker Reyner Banham könnten die Autoren in Bezug auf ihre Zielsetzungen und auf ihr intellektuelles Temperament nicht unterschiedlicher sein. Doch alle drei entwickeln fast gleichzeitig eine gebaute Ökologie des Strandes.

Georges Candilis, ein zeitweiliger Mitarbeiter bei den Unités d'Habitation von Le Corbusier, war offenbar der erste, der die Bauaufgabe des Ferienresorts für den Massentourismus an den Mittelmeerstränden auf die theoretische Agenda setzte (zu Candilis zuletzt Weber 2017). Hintergrund war die Tourismuspolitik

---

8 Vgl. zum Tourismusprogramm nach 1945 mit Literatur Manning (2011). Siehe auch den Beitrag von Alberto Napoli im vorliegenden Band.

während der Präsidentschaften von De Gaulle und Pompidou, unter denen man den Südfrankreich-Tourismus besonders für die Bevölkerung im Großraum Paris ankurbelte und zugleich im Süden des Landes (Camargue, Languedoc, Pyrénées) gigantische Küstenentwicklungsprogramme startete (Savorra 2017). Candilis berichtet darüber im Kapitel „Les loisirs du plus grand nombre" seiner Autobiographie (Candilis 2012 [1997], 271–280). Bedingung war natürlich die nun voll entwickelte Freizeitgesellschaft mit Individualmotorisierung, gesetzlich geregelten Urlaubstagen und entsprechender Tarifpolitik. All diesen vielfältigen Gegebenheiten trägt Candilis in seinem Planungshandbuch, das 1972 als Foto- und Planband mit dreisprachigen, englischen, französischen und deutschen Texterläuterungen erschien, Rechnung und entwickelt daraus umsetzbare Planungsideen (Candilis 1972). Drei Leitgedanken sind dabei entscheidend: 1. Die Ressorts werden tatsächlich in den Maßstäben von Städten, und nicht von Dörfern, als durchgeplante Flächenanlagen mit autarker Infrastruktur konzipiert. Das Ganze wird abgewickelt in niedrigen strukturalistischen Teppichsiedlungen und hohen, scheibenartigen Wohnanlagen. 2. Es ist nicht mehr die Rede von Anverwandlungen regional-historisierender Erscheinungsbilder, sondern die Entwürfe sind gewonnen aus dem Formvokabular der Moderne und sie berücksichtigen die klimatischen Verhältnisse vor Ort, insbesondere mit den Verschattungssystemen bei den Balkonen, den Außentreppen und den Patios. Hier konnte Candilis auf Erfahrungen bei Wohnanlagen, die er in Algerien errichtet hatte, zurückgreifen. Und schließlich 3.: Die Architektur ist ganz auf die Hauptsache ausgerichtet, nämlich den Badestrand und die Lagunen. Candilis' Buch erscheint als theoretischer Flankenschutz für seine eigenen Bauprojekte, die er im Departement Pyrénées-Orientales errichtet hat. Hier werden die im Buch erläuterten Planungsprinzipien weitgehend umgesetzt (Abb. 5).

Die strukturalistischen Bodendecker von Candilis hat man freilich nicht überall nachgebaut. Es entstanden auch Superzeichen-Bauten wie in La Grande Motte, wo die Terrassenhäuser die Silhouetten von Segelschiffen mimen (Loyer 2006, 362–363). Verbindlich bleiben aber immer die stadtplanerischen Grundsätze hinsichtlich der Gegebenheiten vor Ort, wozu auch die Strandausrichtung gehört.

Sand, Spuren, Architektur – Zur gebauten Ökologie des Strandes —— 227

Abb. 5: Georges Candilis' Ferienresort von Le Barcarès-Port Leucate (errichtet 1964–72).

Eine Ökologie ganz anderer Art meint Reyner Banham in seiner Architekturmonographie über Los Angeles, die ebenfalls zu Beginn der 1970er Jahre erschien (Banham 2009 [1971]). Der Architekturhistoriker Banham[9] hatte – ganz im Gegensatz zu Candilis – alles andere als ein Planungshandbuch im Sinn. Ihm ging es um die Revision des Architekturbegriffs der Klassischen Moderne, und das lief bei ihm geradewegs auf die Dekonstruktion von autoritären architektonischen Normsetzungen hinaus. Banham war ein Unterstützer der Pop-Art, die er in der Londoner Independent Group mit aus der Taufe gehoben hatte. Sein 1971 erschienenes Buch *Los Angeles. The Architecture of Four Ecologies* ist ein Survey der kalifornischen Metropole, der sich – darauf will der Untertitel hinaus – entlang der Topographien der Stadt entwickelt und der sich um konventionelle Bautypologien nicht mehr schert. Banham identifiziert vier ‚Ökologien' ausgehend von den Niederungen des Strandes (a) über die Infrastrukturen (b) und die Bebauung in der Ebene (c) bis hin zur *villeggiatura* in den Hügeln (d). Er beschreibt ein Los Angeles, das heute natürlich schon längst untergegangen ist. Das gilt insbesondere für die damalige ‚Ökologie' des Strandes, der horrende Grundstückpreise den Garaus gemacht haben. ‚Ecologies' im Plural versteht der Autor gerade nicht als Singular der ‚Ökologie', wie er damals aufkam, also im Sinne von Umweltbewusstsein, Nachhaltigkeit oder Grüner Politik, sondern viel

---

9 Aus der umfangreichen Sekundärliteratur: zuletzt Whiteley (2002).

basaler, als Vielfalt von Habitaten und Topographien. Er beschreibt die Prozesse zwischen Topographie und Architektur und weiterhin die Überlagerung von Systemen – Landschaft, Architektur, Verkehr, Infrastruktur, Kommunikation, Versorgung, Freizeit und so fort. Das führt ihn dazu, den konventionellen Architekturbegriff aufzugeben. Banham geht es um, wie er es nennt, „polymorphous architectures" (Banham 2009 [1971], 5). Sie umfassen Wohnhäuser und Supermärkte, Hotdog-Buden und Tankstellen, Werbetafeln und Zäune. Banham schaut auf die Totalität von gebauten Artefakten und auf den andauernden Austausch dieses Gebauten. Die „ecologies" sprechen die „language of movement": „Mobility outweights monumentality." (Ebd., 5)

Abb. 6: Palisade aus Surfbrettern am Strand von Los Angeles.

Dies ist auch die Sprache des Strandes. Banham beschreibt hier die recht einfache Holzarchitektur der Häuser zwischen Strand und Highway sowie die Piers. Diejenige Architektur, welche die ‚Sprache der Bewegung' aber exemplarisch ausspricht, sind die aus Surfbrettern gebildeten Palisaden (Abb. 6): „The surfboard is the prime symbolic and functional artefact of those beaches where California surfing began." (Ebd., 31) Seit der Ankunft der Wikinger habe die Küstengeschichte nie etwas Farbigeres gesehen: „but few episodes of seaside history since the Viking invasions can have been so colourful." (Ebd.) Und weiter: „Leaning on the sea-wall or stuck in the sand like plastic magaliths, they [d. i. die Surfbretter] concentrate practically the whole capacity of Los Angeles to create stylish decorative imagery, and to fix those images with the panoply of modern visual and material techniques." (Ebd.) Wenn es Banham gelingt, die gebaute Ökologie des Strandes als ‚Surfurbia' überhaupt in den Blick zu nehmen, so verdankt sich das nicht nur den popkulturellen Vorzeichen einer Anerkennung der Massenkultur, sondern auch der Tatsache, dass ihn statt der *high brow*-Architektur nun die gebaute Ökologie des Strandes interessiert.

Abb. 7: Aldo Rossis *Cabine dell'Elba / Un'altra estate*.

Gleichzeitig mit den Bauten für die Massengesellschaft des Wohlfahrtsstaates bei Candilis und mit der Entdeckung der „polymorphous architectures" durch Banham erhob auch der italienische Architekt Aldo Rossi seine Stimme für die Strandarchitektur. Er schaut ausschließlich auf die Strandhäuschen. Die Strandkabinen sind unter anderem Reminiszenzen an die Strandurlaube als Jugendlicher, wie sie in dem, schon angesprochenen, Trend der Zeit des Massentourismus lagen. Rossi fertigte von den Strandhäuschen seit den frühen 1970er Jahren zahlreiche Zeichnungen an, die er in seiner zuerst englisch 1981 erschienenen Autobiographie beschreibt (Rossi 2009, 42, 47–48). Sie gelten ihm zunächst als Urformen, wenn er in ihnen die ‚Urhütte' Vitruvs wiedererkennt. Rossi geht es mit dieser Typologie im Wortsinne um den *oikos*, nämlich um das Haus bzw. den Herd, und er ist sich natürlich bewusst, dass im Begriff ‚Ökologie' dieses Wort nicht nur etymologisch, sondern auch historisch steckt – die Architektur begann mit dem Haus. In den Zeichnungen kommt es Rossi darauf an, die Einzelhäuschen in den wenigen Elementen der vier Wände und des Daches mit dem betonten Tympanon darzustellen (Abb. 7). Darüber hinaus werden die typologischen Einzelexemplare zu Gruppen versammelt und geradezu wie in Gesprächen zusammengeführt. Rossi nennt die Strandhütten „piccole case innocenti" (Rossi 2009, 48). Dabei sind ihm mehrere ‚liminale' Aspekte dieser Bauten wichtig. Einmal sind sie, dadurch dass sie aus dem gleichen Holz wie die Schiffe sind, gleichsam ein gebauter Vorposten der Artefakte des Meeres in der Randzone. ‚Liminal' ist aber auch das Verhältnis von Bau und menschlichem Körper. Die Strandkabine ist nicht nur ein Erinnerungszeichen der ‚Liebschaften des Sommers' („legata agli amori delle stagioni marine" [Rossi 2009, 47]). Sie ist auch Zeuge eines archaischen Rituals. Die Kabinen werden, wie Rossi schreibt, zu Beobachtern „bei der Unschuld des Sich-Entkleidens, bei dem sich stets die alten Bewegungen wiederholen, sie sehen die nassen Kleider, die Zärtlichkeiten und die Salzluft auf der Haut."[10] Alles in allem sind die Strandkabinen nicht nur Metaphern und Idealbilder einer archaischen Architektur, sondern eben auch deren gebaute, sinnliche Wirklichkeiten.

4 Schluss: Der Strand als Gegenpol und Todeszone

Blicken wir von all den hier referierten Theorieansätzen zurück auf den Normalfall einer „suburban beach", wie es John Fiske genannt hat (Fiske 2011 [1989], 44), so scheinen mir zu deren Verständnis die medialen Elemente von Sand, Spur und ‚polymorpher Architektur' weiterhin hilfreich, um sich der Ökologie des Strandes zu nähern (Abb. 8): Bis heute ist die Raumorganisation des Strandes im Rahmen der sozialen Routinen des Strandaufenthalts durch Spuren und Architekturen geprägt – wir hinterlassen Markierungen durch Badetücher, Liegestühle, Sonnenschirme und nicht zuletzt durch unsere Körper und wir nutzen die Strandarchitekturen der Restaurants, Badehäuschen und Piers. Handelt es sich bereits beim Strand um eine ‚liminale' Zone zwischen Wasser und Land, so sollte auch die gebaute Ökologie von Stränden als Zwischenraum zwischen stabilen Gebäuden und situativer Raumbesetzung verstanden werden.

Gibt es, so wäre am Ende zu fragen, in der Ära des Gebrauchs von Stränden als Territorien ökonomischer Wertschöpfung durch Tourismus, Freizeit-, Mode- und Körperindustrie dann überhaupt noch die Spur am Strand als Existenzmetapher? Zu befürchten ist, dass es sie öfter gibt, als wir uns das eigentlich wünschen. Und außer Zweifel steht, dass der Strand wie von jeher ein ‚liminaler' Bereich geblieben ist, über den immer wieder als Zone größter politisch-gesellschaftlicher Widersprüche und menschlicher Gefährdungen nachzudenken ist. So sind Strände in der Gegenwart zu räumlichen Gegenpolen von ‚Fliehkräften' nicht im naturwissenschaftlichen, sondern im sozialen Wortsinne geworden, denn wo wir als Touristen die fernen Strände in Afrika aufsuchen, kommen uns

---

[10] Übersetzung D. E.; die Passage im Original lautet: „Questo tornava nel disegno delle cabine come piccolo case innocenti: l'innocenza dello spogliarsi ripetendo antichi movimenti, gli indumenti bagnati, qualche gioco, un tepore acido del sale marino." (Rossi 2009, 48)

von dort an den südeuropäischen Stränden die Flüchtlinge entgegen (Holert und Terkessidis 2006). Am Ende mag der Blick auf zwei Zeitungsfotos genügen, um den Strand darüber hinaus als Todeszone einer global zerstörerischen Ökonomie und einer zerstörten Ökologie zu beschreiben.

Abb. 8: Massimo Vitalis *Papeete Beach Regatta* (Foto 2004).

Vor einigen Jahren tauchten Hunderte von fabrikneuen Fernsehapparaten an einem Küstenabschnitt in Japan auf (Abb. 9).[11] Angesichts der hübschen Reihung der Objekte mögen Freunde der Serialität, die noch dazu dem Appeal der Medienkunst verfallen sind, beim Betrachten des Fotos auf den Gedanken kommen, es handle sich um eine Kunstinstallation. Man ist aber ganz im Sinne von Carlo Ginzburg nur einem vorgängigen Tatgeschehen auf der Spur. Denn es handelt sich schlicht um eine Ladung von in China hergestellten, geschmuggelten Fernsehapparaten, die von der Schiffsmannschaft kurzerhand über Bord geworfen wurde, als die Küstenwache zur Inspektion auf den Frachter zusteuerte. Als Strandgut erscheinen uns die Fernseher wie Menetekel der massenweise produzierten Konsumgüter. Sie sind konfuse Relikte einer Ökonomie, die als globalisiertes Wirtschaften immense kriminelle Überschussenergien nicht nur des Gewinns, sondern auch der ökologischen Lasten erzeugt.

---

[11] Das Bild mit Bildunterschrift wurde publiziert in der *Süddeutschen Zeitung* vom 16./17. November 2002.

Abb. 9: Geschmuggelte Fernsehgeräte an einem Strand in Japan (Foto November 2002).

Und immer aufs Neue der Strand als Todeszone: Auf dem Foto (Abb. 10) sind Sandplastiken zu sehen. Ein paar Monate nach dem großen Tsunami im Indischen Ozean 2004, bei dem etwa 230 000 Menschen umkamen, wurden sie an einem Strand in Südindien von den Angehörigen der Ertrunkenen in den Sand geformt. Es sind Totenbildnisse der Wiederholung. Das Meer nahm nicht nur die Menschen mit sich fort, sondern wird es auch mit deren Bildern tun.

Abb. 10: Sandfiguren an einem Strand des Indischen Ozeans zum Gedenken an die Opfer der Tsunami-Flut 2004 (Foto 2006).

Literaturverzeichnis

Aristoteles. *Poetik*. Griechisch/Deutsch. Herausgegeben und übersetzt von Manfred Fuhrmann. Stuttgart: Reclam, 1982.
Banham, Reyner. *Los Angeles. The Architecture of Four Ecologies* [1971]. Berkeley, Los Angeles und London: University of California Press, 2009.
Baraldi, Claudio, Giancarlo Corsi und Elena Esposito. *GLU. Glossar zu Niklas Luhmanns Theorie sozialer Systeme*. Frankfurt/Main: Suhrkamp, 1997.
Baxandall, Michael. *Episodes. A Memorybook*. London: Frances Lincoln Publishers, 2010.
Benton, Tim. „Le Corbusier, der geheime Fotograf". *Le Corbusier und die Macht der Fotografie*. Katalog zur Ausstellung des Musée des Beaux-Arts von La Caux-de-Fonds. Hg. Nathalie Herschdorfer und Lada Umstätter. Berlin: Deutscher Kunstverlag, 2012. 31–53.
Biraghi, Marco. *Storia dell'architettura italiana 1985–2015*. Mailand: Einaudi, 2016.
Bullivant, Lucy (Hg.). *Masterplanning Futures*. London und New York: Routledge, 2012.

Cachin, Françoise (Hg.). *Méditerranée. De Courbet à Matisse*. Katalog zur Ausstellung der Galeries nationales du Grand Palais. Paris: Editions de la Réunion des musées nationaux, 2000.

Candilis, Georges. *Planen und Bauen für die Freizeit / Recherches sur l'architecture des loisirs / Planning and Design for Leisure*. Dokumente der Modernen Architektur 9. Stuttgart: Karl Krämer, 1972.

Candilis, Georges. *Bâtir la vie. Un architecte témoin de son temps* [1997]. Paris: infolio, 2012.

Codello, Renata. *Architetture contemporanee a Venezia*. Venedig: Marsilio, 2014.

Corbin, Alain. *Meereslust. Das Abendland und die Entdeckung der Küste* [Le territoire du vide, 1988]. Frankfurt/Main: Fischer, 1994.

Defoe, Daniel. *Robinson Crusoe* [1719]. London: Penguin, 1979.

Derrida, Jacques. *De la grammatologie*. Paris: Minuit, 1967.

Erben, Dietrich. *Architekturtheorie. Eine Geschichte von der Antike bis zur Gegenwart*. München: C. H. Beck, 2017.

Erben, Dietrich. „Erfahrung als Argument in Berufsautobiographien. Der Kunsthistoriker Michael Baxandall und der Architekt Louis Sullivan". *Das eigene Leben als ästhetische Fiktion. Berufsautobiographien und Professionsgeschichte*. Hg. Dietrich Erben und Tobias Zervosen. Bielefeld: transcript, 2018. 23–38.

Falser, Michael S. „Der Wiederaufbau von New Orleans nach Hurricane Katrina. Gedanken zum Status der Zivilgesellschaft im Kontext von Natur- und Kulturkatastrophen". *Kulturerbe und Naturkatastrophen / Cultural Heritage and Natural Disasters. Risk Preparedness and the Limits of Prevention*. Hg. Hans-Rudolf Meier. Dresden: TUDpress, 2008. 109–122.

Fiske, John. „Reading the Beach". *Reading the Popular* [1989]. London und New York: Routledge, 2011. 34–62.

Freireiss, Kristin (Hg.). *Architecture in Times of Need. Make it Right – Rebuilding New Orleans' Lower Ninth Ward*. Berlin: Prestel, 2009.

Gallwitz, Kaus, und Ortruf Westheider (Hg.). *Max Beckmann, Menschen am Meer*. Katalog zur Ausstellung des Bucerius Kunst Forums Hamburg. Ostfildern: Hatje Kantz, 2003.

Ginzburg, Carlo. „Spie. Radici di un paradigma indiziario". *Miti, emblemi, spie. Morfologia e storia*. Turin: Einaudi, 1986. 158–193.

Genge, Gabriele. *Artefakt, Fetisch, Skulptur. Aristide Maillol und die Beschreibung des Fremden in der Moderne*. Berlin und München: Deutscher Kunstverlag, 2009.

Gill, Adrian A. „Shore Thing". *Here and There. Collected Travel Writing*. London: Weidenfeld and Nicolson, 2012. 78–81.

Gilot, Françoise, und Carlton Lake. *Leben mit Picasso* [Life with Picasso, 1964]. Zürich: Diogenes, 1980.

Grant, Reg G. *Lighthouse. An Illuminating History of the World's Costal Sentinels*. London: Black Dog & Leventhal, 2018.

Hartman, Chester, und Gregory D. Squires (Hg.). *There Is No Such Thing as a Natural Disaster. Race, Class, and Hurricane Katrina*. London und New York: Routledge, 2006.

Hein, Carola (Hg.). *Port Cities. Dynamic Landscapes and Global Networks*. London und New York: Routledge, 2011.

Holert, Tom, und Mark Terkessidis. *Fliehkraft. Gesellschaft in Bewegung. Von Migranten und Touristen*. Köln: Kiepenheuer und Witsch, 2006.

Jaacks, Gisela (Hg.). *Der Traum von der Stadt am Meer. Hafenstädte aus aller Welt*. Katalog zur Ausstellung des Museums für Hamburgische Geschichte. Hamburg: Stiftung Museum für Hamburgische Geschichte, 2003.

Kemp, Wolfgang. *Der Oligarch.* Springe: Zu Klampen, 2016.
Koschorke, Albrecht. *Wahrheit und Erfindung. Grundzüge einer allgemeinen Erzähltheorie.* Frankfurt/Main: Fischer, 2012.
Krämer, Sybille, Werner Kogge und Gernot Grube (Hg.). *Spur. Spurenlesen als Orientierungstechnik und Wissenskunst.* Frankfurt/Main: Suhrkamp, 2007.
Krüger, Matthias. „Künstlerkolonien. Gründungsorte im Abseits der Moderne". *Gründungsorte der Moderne. Von St. Petersburg bis Occupy Wall Street.* Hg. Maha El Hissy und Sascha Pöhlmann. München: Fink, 2014. 161–176.
Loyer, François. *Histoire de l'architecture française. De la Révolution à nos jours.* Paris: Éditions Mengès, 2006.
Luhmann, Niklas. „Das Medium der Kunst". *Aufsätze und Reden.* Hg. Oliver Jahraus. Stuttgart: Reclam, 2011. 198–217.
Maak, Niklas. *Der Architekt am Strand. Le Corbusier und das Geheimnis der Seeschnecke.* München: Hanser, 2010.
Manning, Till. *Die Italiengeneration – Stilbildung durch Massentourismus in den 1950er und 1960er Jahren. Göttinger Studien zur Generationsforschung, Bd. 5.* Göttingen: Wallstein, 2011.
Mosco, Valerio Paolo. *Architettura italiana. Dal postmoderno ad oggi.* Mailand: Einaudi, 2017.
Pehnt, Wolfgang. „Das Schelmenstück von Portmeirion. Williams-Ellis, ein Postmoderner vor der Moderne". *Der Anfang der Bescheidenheit. Kritische Aufsätze zur Architektur des 20. Jahrhunderts.* München: Prestel, 1983. 203–211.
Pfister, Manfred. „*Performance*/Performanz". *Metzler Lexikon Literatur- und Kulturtheorie. Ansätze – Personen – Grundbegriffe.* Hg. Ansgar Nünning. Stuttgart und Weimar: Metzler, 2013. 590–592.
Rossi, Aldo. *Autobiografia scientifica.* Mailand: Il Saggiatore, 2009.
Sattler, Katharina. *Palace Pier Brighton, England.* Köln: DuMont, 1976.
Savorra, Massimiliano. „Il Mediterraneo per tutti. Georges Candilis e il turismo per il Grande Numero". *Immaginare il Mediterraneo. Architettura, arti, fotografia.* Hg. Andrea Maglio, Fabio Mangone und Antonio Pizza. Neapel: artstudiopaparo, 2017. 235–245.
Wallner, Julia (Hg.). *Zarte Männer in der Skulptur der Moderne. Katalog zur Ausstellung des Georg Kolbe Museums.* Berlin: Museumsverlag, 2018.
Warnke, Martin. „Vorwort". Carlo Ginzburg. *Erkundungen über Piero. Piero della Francesca, ein Maler der frühen Renaissance.* Berlin: Wagenbach, 1981. 7–14.
Weber, Korinna Zinovia. „Georges Candilis – Architect, Urban Planner and Author with Socialist Ideas in a Capitalist World". *French Artistic Culture and Central-East European Modern Art.* Hg. Ljiljana Kolešnik und Tamara Bjažić-Klarin. Zagreb: Institute of Art History, 2017. 302–318.
Whiteley, Nigel. *Reyner Banham. Historian of the Immediate Future.* Cambridge, MA.: Cambridge University Press, 2002.
Williams-Ellis, Clough, und Amabel Williams-Ellis. *The Pleasures of Architecture.* London: Jonathan Cape, 1924.
Woolf, Stuart. „Italian Historical Writing". *Oxford History of Historical Writing. Bd. 5: Historical Writing Since 1945.* Hg. Axel Schneider und Daniel R. Woolfe. Oxford: Oxford University Press, 2011. 333–351.

Abbildungsverzeichnis

Abb. 1: Zonierungsdiagramm eines Strandabschnitts. In: Fiske 2011 [1989], Fig. 3.
Abb. 2: Robert Capa, Françoise Gilot, Pablo Picasso, und Javier Vilato am Strand von Port-Juan. Foto 1948. In: Gilot und Lake 1980 [1964], 64.
Abb. 3: Le Corbusier am Strand auf Long Island. Foto 1946. Foto in: Maak 2010, 25.
Abb. 4: Giancarlo De Carlo. Strandpavillon Blue Moon auf dem Lido von Venedig, fertiggestellt 2005. Foto des Autors.
Abb. 5: Georges Candilis. Ferienresort von Le Barcarès-Port Leucate, errichtet 1964–72. Illustration in: Candilis 1972, 56.
Abb. 6: Palisade aus Surfbrettern am Strand von Los Angeles. Illustration in: Banham 2009 [1971], Fig. 14.
Abb. 7: Aldo Rossi. *Cabine dell'Elba / Un'altra estate*. Aquarellierte Zeichnung 1979. Illustration in: Rossi 2009, Taf. 12.
Abb. 8: Massimo Vitali. *Papeete Beach Regatta*. Foto 2004. Copyright Massimo Vitali.
Abb. 9: Geschmuggelte Fernsehgeräte an einem Strand in Japan. Foto November 2002. Foto Archiv des Autors.
Abb. 10: Sandfiguren an einem Strand des Indischen Ozeans zum Gedenken an die Opfer der Tsunami-Flut 2004. Foto 2006. Foto Archiv des Autors.

Wiebke Kolbe
Strandburgen: Eine deutsche Lust? Zum Strandurlaub seit dem späten neunzehnten Jahrhundert

From the 1880s until the ban of this practice in the 1970s, German vacationers built sandcastles, some of which were artfully decorated and awarded prizes in competitions by the spa administrations. Research regards this as a manifestation of a 'typical German' national character. The article counters this approach with an interpretation that understands sandcastles as metaphors for typical characteristics and principles of tourism, whose main feature is ambivalence. On the basis of the contrastive pairs familiarity – strangeness, proximity – distance, work – leisure, and centre – marginality, this ambivalence is carved out, and it is shown how it is applicable to the building of sandcastles since the late nineteenth century. At the same time, it is shown which meanings and functions sandcastles possessed in the respective historical contexts of the German Empire, the Weimar Republic and National Socialism.

Von den 1880er bis zum Verbot in den 1970er Jahren bauten deutsche Urlauber*innen Strandburgen, die teils kunstvoll verziert und von den Kurverwaltungen in Wettbewerben prämiert wurden. Dies wird in der Forschung als Manifestation eines ‚typisch deutschen' Nationalcharakters betrachtet. Dieser Deutung setzt der Artikel ein anderes Interpretationsangebot entgegen, das Strandburgen als Metaphern für typische Charakteristika und Funktionsweisen des Tourismus auffasst, deren Hauptmerkmal ihre Ambivalenz ist. Anhand der Gegensatzpaare Vertrautheit – Fremdheit, Nähe – Distanz, Arbeit – Freizeit und Zentrum – Marginalität wird diese Ambivalenz herausgearbeitet und gezeigt, wie sie auf den Strandburgenbau seit dem späten neunzehnten Jahrhundert zutraf. Dabei wird zugleich gezeigt, welche Bedeutungen und Funktionen Strandburgen im jeweiligen historischen Kontext des Kaiserreichs, der Weimarer Republik und des Nationalsozialismus besaßen.

Strandburgen – welch seltsames Thema für einen wissenschaftlichen Aufsatz, mag manche*r denken. Sind Strandburgen nicht viel zu banal, um wissenschaftlich behandelt zu werden: ein harmloses Vergnügen für Kinder, die sich mit Schäufelchen und Eimer an den Strand begeben, um dort eifrig die fragilen Gebäude aus Sand zu errichten? Zwar lässt sich die Zahl der wissenschaftlichen Publikationen über Strandburgen tatsächlich an einer Hand abzählen, doch bedeutet das nicht, dass das Thema keine sozial- und kulturwissenschaftliche Relevanz besäße. Diejenigen, die sich ausführlicher mit dem Phänomen Strandburg beschäftigen, versuchen sogar, mentalitätsgeschichtliche Theorien eines ‚typisch deutschen' Nationalcharakters daraus abzuleiten. In der Tat scheinen nur die Deutschen Strandburgen zu bauen – und zwar Kinder wie Erwachsene, mit ausgewachsenen Spaten, ungetrübtem Elan über einen Zeitraum von mehr als hundert Jahren und zum großen Verdruss der Angehörigen anderer Nationen, an deren Stränden sie dies tun. So betrachtet, sind Strandburgen nicht so unschuldig, wie es auf den ersten Blick scheint, im Gegenteil: Sie sind geradezu ein Politikum, ein umstrittenes Kulturgut, umkämpft nicht nur zwischen Strandurlauber*innen deutscher und anderer Nationalitäten, sondern auch unter deutschen Urlauber*innen sowie zwischen diesen und den Kurverwaltungen.

Im Folgenden werde ich einige kulturgeschichtliche Aspekte der Strandburg behandeln. Dabei geht es zunächst um eine genauere Definition des Gegenstands und um qualitative und historische Differenzierungen: Wer hat wann und wo welche Strandburgen gebaut? Anschließend werden die vorhandenen Interpretationen von Strandburgen als Manifestation deutscher ‚Identität' vorgestellt und schließlich ein alternativer Interpretationsansatz entwickelt, der die Strandburg nicht als typisch für die ‚deutsche Mentalität', sondern als Symbol für die Charakteristika von Urlaubsreisen betrachtet. Zugleich werde ich das Phänomen Strandburg historisieren und nach seinen Funktionen und Spezifika im Kaiserreich, in der Weimarer Republik und im Nationalsozialismus fragen.

1 Strandburgen: Wer, wo, wann, was? Systematik und Geschichte des Strandburgenbaus

Um Strandburgen zu bauen, musste der Strand zunächst als sozialer Raum entdeckt werden. Das geschah in Europa nicht vor dem letzten Drittel des neunzehnten Jahrhunderts im Zusammenhang mit veränderten Praktiken des Meerbadens. Das Baden im Meer war Mitte des achtzehnten Jahrhunderts in England als Heilmittel entdeckt worden und hatte sich von dort aus auf alle europäischen Strände ausgebreitet. Anfangs badeten Adel und gehobenes Bürgertum von Badekarren aus und überquerten den Strand rasch in Straßenkleidung, um zu den Karren zu gelangen, sich dort umzuziehen und dann damit ins Wasser gezogen zu werden. Ein längerer Aufenthalt am Strand war nicht vorgesehen. Als im letzten Drittel des neunzehnten Jahrhunderts die Zahl der Badegäste stetig wuchs, wurden feste Badeanstalten gebaut, um alle Badenden aufnehmen zu können. Allmählich wandelte sich das Baden nun von einem Heilmittel zu einem bürgerlichen Urlaubsvergnügen. Damit einher ging eine neue Nutzung des Strandes: Die Badegäste begannen, sich stundenlang am Strand aufzuhalten, allerdings noch immer in vollständiger Straßenkleidung. Dadurch entstanden neue kulturelle Praktiken und Bedeutungen des Strandes (Kolbe 2009,

24–26). An deutschen Stränden war eine von ihnen der Bau von Strandburgen. Wann es die ersten Strandburgen Erwachsener gab, lässt sich schwer feststellen. Vor den 1890er Jahren gibt es zumindest keine schriftlichen oder bildlichen Belege (Diers 1986, 139). Ab etwa 1895 tauchten Strandburgen dann als beliebtes Postkartenmotiv der deutschen Seebäder auf – zu dem Zeitpunkt, als Postkarten begannen, fotografische Motive zu zeigen, und damit einen raschen Aufstieg als neues kommerzielles Massenmedium nahmen (Walter 2001, 46, 48, 52–53). Schriftliche Quellen sind für die Zeit vor 1890 für die meisten deutschen Seebäder rar; viele Bäderzeitungen etwa wurden erst später gegründet oder sind nicht erhalten. Dennoch ist zu vermuten, dass der Strandburgenbau sich als Urlaubspraxis in größerem Umfang tatsächlich erst seit etwa den 1880er Jahren etabliert hat, denn der Burgenbau hängt unmittelbar mit dem genannten Wandel der Urlaubsaktivitäten in den Seebädern zusammen, der sich zu dieser Zeit vollzog.

Als Strandburgen bezeichnet man zunächst kleinere burgähnliche Sandgebilde, gegebenenfalls mit Türmchen und Wassergraben, die von Kindern mit Hilfe von Eimer und Schaufel am Strand errichtet wurden (vgl. z. B. die Abb. bei Diers 1986, 144). Diese Art von Strandburgen bau(t)en nicht nur deutsche, sondern auch Kinder anderer Nationalitäten, obwohl deutsche angeblich einen Sozialisationsvorteil haben, da es – so schreiben zumindest Harald Kimpel und Johanna Werckmeister in ihrem Buch über Strandburgen – nur in Deutschland Sandkästen gibt, in denen sich üben lässt (Kimpel und Werckmeister 1995, 48). Allerdings sind kindlicher Strandburgenbau und Strandburgenwettbewerbe für Kinder zumindest auch für Großbritannien in der ersten Hälfte des zwanzigsten Jahrhunderts belegt (Walton 2000, 95). Das Entscheidende ist jedoch, dass die britischen Wettbewerbe nur für Kinder veranstaltet wurden, während deutsche Badeorte sie auch für Erwachsene auslobten. Darin liegt die deutsche Besonderheit. So konnte man etwa in der *Westerländer Kurzeitung* vom 26. Juli 1921 folgende amtliche Bekanntmachung lesen, die sich so oder ähnlich in vielen anderen deutschen Nord- oder Ostseebäderzeitungen jener Zeit wiederfindet:

> Der zweite Burgenwettbewerb findet am Donnerstag, den 28. Juli statt. Zur Teilnahme berechtigt sind sämtliche Burgenbauer, sofern ihre Burg den nachstehenden Bedingungen entspricht: 1. Zum Bau der Burg dürfen kein Holz, Treppen usw., kein Dünenhalm, keine größeren Steine verwendet werden. Gestattet zum Bau sind nur Strandkorb, Strandstühle, Flaggen und Wimpel. 2. Die Burg muß frei liegen, d. h. sie darf nicht an andere Burgen angelehnt werden. 3. Die Burg muß durch kleine Steinchen oder dergleichen mit einem Kennwort versehen sein. Es werden ausgezeichnet: a) Die schönste Burg. b) Die beste Blumenburg. c) Die beste Einlegearbeit. d) Die besten Kinderburgen. Die Burgen müssen am Donnerstag, den 28. Juli, nachmittags 3 Uhr, zur Besichtigung bereit sein. Wir hoffen, dass recht viele unserer Gäste an diesem Wettbewerb sich beteiligen werden. (Amtliche

Bekanntmachung im 2. Blatt der *Westerländer Kurzeitung* Nr. 20, 26. Juli 1921, zitiert nach Kimpel und Werckmeister 1995, 27)

Das Zitat enthält wichtige Stichworte zum Thema Strandburgenbau und gibt detaillierten Aufschluss über dessen Praxis. So musste zum Beispiel nicht eigens gesagt werden, dass der Wettbewerb sich an Erwachsene richtete oder wie eine normale Strandburg aussah. Dabei handelte es sich mitnichten um ein burgähnliches Gebilde, sondern vielmehr um einen veritablen Ringwall mit mehreren Metern Durchmesser (Abb. 1). Das war selbstverständliches Strandurlauberwissen.

Abb. 1: Strandburgen im Ostseebad Kellenhusen in Holstein. Postkarte, 1934.

Die vier unterschiedlichen Wettbewerbssparten zeigen die Artenvielfalt, die der Strandburgenbau Anfang der 1920er Jahre aufwies – das deutet darauf hin, dass er eine etablierte und häufig ausgeübte Urlaubsbeschäftigung war. Die Bauten hatten einen ästhetischen, ja: künstlerischen Anspruch. Sie wurden mit Sandskulpturen, Blumen, mit Einlegearbeiten aus Muscheln oder kleinen Steinen, mit Flaggen oder Wimpeln verziert und durften das Strandmobiliar einbeziehen – nicht jedoch andere Materialien: Das Verbot zeigt, dass die Urlauber*innen offenbar allzu gern Treibholz und sonstiges Strandgut als Konstruktionshilfen für ihre Burgen verwendeten. Um verbreitete Zuwiderhandlungen gab es Anfang des zwanzigsten Jahrhunderts immer wieder Konflikte zwischen Burgenbauer*innen und den Kurverwaltungen (Kimpel und Werckmeister 1995, 11).

Bei der Verzierung der Strandburgen waren der Phantasie keine Grenzen gesetzt. Häufig wurden sie mit Inschriften aus Muscheln versehen, aber auch komplexe Muschelintarsien, die etwa bekannte Komponisten darstellten (Abb. bei Diers 1986, 143), oder Filmstars der 1920er Jahre, in Sand auf den Ringwall modelliert (Abb. bei Kimpel und Werckmeister 1995, 22), waren keine Ausnahmen. Ähnlich kunstvolle Motive und Techniken waren auch bei späteren Strandburgenwettbewerben, die es bis in die 1970er Jahre in Ost- und Westdeutschland gab, zu sehen (Abb. 2).

Abb. 2: Strandburg mit Meeresgeschöpf und Bremer Stadtmusikanten. Strandburgenwettbewerb im Ostseebad Laboe bei Kiel, 1963.

Daneben gab es bei den Burgenbauwettbewerben die Variante, dass der Ringwall nur noch der Abgrenzung des Territoriums diente und das eigentliche Kunstwerk aus anderen Sandskulpturen bestand (Abb. 3).

Sand*skulpturen*wettbewerbe wiederum sind kein auf deutsche Strände und deutsche Urlauber*innen beschränktes Phänomen. Seit Anfang der 1990er Jahre werden internationale Sandskulpturenfestivals etwa in den USA, Kanada, Australien und den Niederlanden, seit den 2000er Jahren auch in deutschen Seebädern in kommerzialisierter Form mit professionellen Sandskulpturenkünstler*innen und hohen Eintrittsgeldern veranstaltet. Hier werden ganze Städte und Landschaften in Sand als Miniaturausgabe nachgebaut (Kimpel und Werckmeister 1995, 77–82). Zu dieser Zeit waren die von Urlauber*innen errichteten Ringwallburgen längst von den deutschen Kurverwaltungen an Nord- und

Ostsee verboten worden. Seit den 1970er Jahren erließen immer mehr Bäder generelle Burgenbauverbote, aus Gründen des Natur-, Küsten- und Unfallschutzes und um die Belegungsdichte an den Stränden zu erhöhen (ebd., 11–12, 54).

Abb. 3: Sandskulpturen neben dem Ringwall. Strandburgenwettbewerb im Ostseebad Laboe bei Kiel, 1963.

Heute sieht man Strandburgen an deutschen Stränden daher nur noch selten. Gebaut werden sie allerdings noch an den Sandstränden anderer Länder, sofern dies dort erlaubt ist. Dass sie ein deutsches Spezifikum waren (und sind), lässt sich unter anderem damit erklären, dass die Burgen häufig der Umrundung und ‚Einzäunung' von Strandkörben dienten – einer ebenfalls deutschen Erfindung, die dem Korbmacher Wilhelm Bartelmann in Rostock 1882 zugesprochen wird, wenngleich es vereinzelte Vorläufer gab (Holfelder 1996, 27–34, 39–41). Strandkörbe traten rasch einen Siegeszug in allen deutschen Seebädern an, fanden ihren Weg jedoch nie über die Landesgrenzen hinaus – mit Ausnahme der Niederlande, wo sie im späten neunzehnten Jahrhundert nachweisbar sind (Holfelder 1996, 32–33). Dort wurden sie allerdings niemals mit Strandburgen kombiniert. Doch erklärt die Existenz von Strandkörben allein nicht die landesspezifische Verbreitung von Strandburgen, denn die Burgen wurden in Deutschland auch ohne Strandkörbe gebaut, mehr noch: die Strandburgen konnten den Strandkorb geradezu als Schutzwall gegen die Witterung und gegen neugierige Blicke ersetzen. Es muss also noch andere Erklärungen für die Beliebtheit des Strandburgenbaus gerade bei deutschen Urlauber*innen geben.

2 Bisherige Deutungsangebote des Strandburgenbaus

Den (wenigen) bisherigen kulturwissenschaftlichen Interpretationen zufolge sind Strandburgen eine Manifestation deutschen Nationalcharakters mit insbesondere drei Aspekten. Erstens: Deutsche sind Workaholics und arbeiten selbst im Urlaub (Bausinger 2002, 18; Kimpel und Werckmeister 1995, 37–43). Zweitens: Die Burgen dienen der Abgrenzung gegenüber den übrigen Badegästen (Bausinger 2002, 18; Kimpel und Werckmeister 1995, 17–19; Linke 1999, 87). Drittens: Die Strandburgen werden als Metapher für Schützengräben, Angriffskrieg und Inbesitznahme von Land gedeutet (Bausinger 2002, 18; Kimpel und Werckmeister 1995, 62–68; Linke 1999, 89). Die Interpretationen sind dabei unterschiedlich akzentuiert. Der Kulturwissenschaftler Hermann Bausinger reflektiert darüber, wie der Strandburgenbau deutscher Urlauber*innen im Ausland wahrgenommen wird. Besonders in der Nachkriegszeit sei der Burgenbau „geradezu als Reflex des militärischen Stellungskriegs gedeutet" worden. (Bausinger 2002, 18) Heutzutage würden die deutschen Strandburgen hingegen stärker als „Besitznahme und Zeichen der Abschließung gegen alle anderen verstanden" und als „ein Indiz dafür, dass die Deutschen Workaholics sind, die immer strebend sich bemühen müssen – selbst in ihren Ferien." (Ebd.) Bausinger resümiert: „Wenn gesagt wird, das Bauen von Sandburgen sei typisch deutsch, dann heißt das nicht: Alle Deutschen machen das. Eher ist gemeint: Diese Tätigkeit verweist auf Eigenheiten, die als für alle Deutschen charakteristisch gelten – sei es nun die militärische Orientierung, die Besetzer- und Besitzermentalität oder die hektische Arbeitswut." (Ebd., 18–19)

Die Kunstwissenschaftler*innen Harald Kimpel und Johanna Werckmeister haben eine ganze Publikation der Strandburg gewidmet, in der sie deren Charakteristika und Bedeutungen nachgehen. Dabei reihen sie allerdings empirische Beispiele aus dem gesamten zwanzigsten Jahrhundert aneinander und ziehen daraus Schlüsse mit allgemeinem Geltungsanspruch. Sie konstatieren:

> Wer an ausländischen Küsten eine Strandburg antrifft, kann sicher sein, einen Deutschen darin zu finden [...] Der Drang zum Burgenbauen muss nämlich als Ausdruck einer typisch deutschen Mentalität angesehen werden; keine zweite Nation hat ein vergleichbar

zwanghaftes Verhaltensmuster herausgebildet, um sich die Urlaubsorte überall auf dem Globus untertan zu machen. (Kimpel und Werckmeister 1995, 48)

Ohne nach den jeweils spezifischen Funktionen von Strandburgen in unterschiedlichen historischen Kontexten zu fragen, halten Kimpel und Werckmeister offenbar die Kontinuität dieses erstaunlichen Phänomens für nicht erklärungsbedürftig, sondern nehmen an, es sei Ausdruck einer „typisch deutschen Mentalität", die als gleichbleibend im gesamten zwanzigsten Jahrhundert angenommen wird.

Die Anthropologin Uli Linke bezieht sich in ihrem Buch *German Bodies* auf Kimpel und Werckmeister und betont ebenfalls, Strandburgen würden ausschließlich von Deutschen gebaut (Linke 1999, 87). Ausgehend von einem Zitat Hans Falladas, das sich auf kindliche Kämpfe um Strandburgen im Kaiserreich bezieht[1], folgert sie: „castle building is deeply embedded in the historical semantics of war". Und: „These associations still hold true in postwar Germany." (Ebd., 89) Noch lange nach dem Zweiten Weltkrieg hätten sich Urlauber*innen anderer Nationen, an deren Stränden Deutsche ihre Burgen bauten, unangenehm an das deutsche Expansionsstreben und, besonders in Dänemark und den Niederlanden, an die Besatzungszeit erinnert gefühlt und die germanischen Bauten nach Kräften zerstört (Linke 1999, 89; siehe auch Kimpel und Werckmeister 1995, 48–49; Bausinger 2002, 18). Linke fährt fort: „As an armored extension of the German self, the building of sandcastles seeks to restructure a public terrain. In a symbolic sense, the castle is a material demarcation of identity: a way of space-claiming, of gaining ‚living space' (*Lebensraum*)." (Linke 1999, 89) Illustriert wird der Text mit ganzseitigen Fotografien, die die Mutter und Tante der Autorin 1936 als Kinder auf Juist beim Strandburgenbau zeigen (ebd., 88, 91). Auch Linke verwendet somit historische Beispiele aus ganz unterschiedlichen Zeiten und Zusammenhängen, um daraus generelle Schlüsse zu ziehen, die den Strandburgenbau mit einem „deutschen Selbst" und einer „Lebensraum" beanspruchenden (sprich: deutschen) „Identität" in Verbindung bringen, die sie bis heute zu finden meint.

Da Strandburgen so offensichtlich ein ausschließlich deutsches Phänomen sind, kommt man kaum umhin, sie als ‚typisch deutsch' zu deuten – in dem Sinne, dass sie eine Eigenheit sind, die als für alle Deutschen charakteristisch gilt, indem sie sich von Eigenheiten anderer Nationalitäten unterscheidet (Bausinger 2002, 18–19). Doch gehen mir die vorhandenen Interpretationen zu weit, die wahllos empirische Beispiele aus einem Zeitraum von hundert Jahren

---

1 Auf dieses Fallada-Zitat gehe ich weiter unten ein.

aneinanderreihen, um daraus generelle Schlüsse zu ziehen, die den Strandburgenbau mit einer historisch unveränderlichen ‚deutschen Identität' verknüpfen.

Im Folgenden werde ich eine andere Interpretation entwickeln, die Strandburgen als Metaphern für typische Charakteristika und Funktionsweisen des Tourismus auffasst. Im Rahmen dieser Interpretation werde ich den Strandburgenbau historisieren, indem ich die empirischen Beispiele zur Veranschaulichung und Untermauerung meiner Deutung aus dem Kaiserreich, der Weimarer Republik und dem ‚Dritten Reich' wähle und zeige, welche Bedeutungen und Funktionen Strandburgen im jeweiligen historischen Kontext besaßen.

3 Strandburgen als Metaphern für Charakteristika von Urlaubsreisen

Dass Menschen massenhaft reisen und in den Urlaub fahren, ist keineswegs ein anthropologisches Grundbedürfnis, sondern ein spezifisches Phänomen der Moderne, der Epoche seit dem späten achtzehnten Jahrhundert (Enzensberger 1958, 708; Zuelow 2016, 9–12). In der kulturwissenschaftlichen Tourismusforschung gibt es verschiedene Überlegungen und Theorieangebote, die sich mit grundsätzlichen Fragen nach Funktionen und Charakteristika von Urlaubsreisen befassen (vgl. Hennig 1997). Einige davon möchte ich im Folgenden aufgreifen, andere selbst entwickeln und argumentieren, dass man Strandburgen als eine Metapher für zentrale Funktionsweisen des Tourismus auffassen kann.

Eine Urlaubsreise wird in unserem Alltagsverständnis und in vielen Theorien des Tourismus als das ganz Andere, als Gegenwelt zum Alltag (ebd., 42–44), als Flucht aus dem Alltag und dessen sozialen Normen und Zwängen (Enzensberger 1958, 708) und als ein das Alltagsbewusstsein überschreitender und den eigenen Horizont erweiternder Erfahrungsraum (Hennig 1999, 53–55; Löfgren 1999, 7, 281) aufgefasst. Vieles spricht für diese Konzeption von Alltagswelt einerseits und Gegenwelt Urlaub andererseits, an die sich weitere polare Begriffspaare anschließen:

Vertrautheit – Fremdheit
Nähe – Distanz
Arbeit – Freizeit
Zentrum – Marginalität

Der französische Tourismusgeograph Olivier Lazzarotti hat dagegen die These formuliert, dass ein entscheidendes Charakteristikum touristischer Orte gerade ihre Ambivalenz sei: Sie seien vom Alltagsleben „zugleich stark distanziert und völlig zugänglich", „entfernt", aber nicht „weit weg" (Lazzarotti 2001, 74). Ich möchte diese Überlegung aufgreifen und die These aufstellen, dass diese Ambivalenz auf alle genannten Begriffspaare zutrifft. Urlaubsreisen funktionieren somit nicht, weil sie das ganz Andere sind, sondern gerade wegen ihres ambivalenten Charakters, in dem ihr eigentlicher Reiz liegt. Anhand der genannten Gegensatzpaare werde ich diese Ambivalenzen herausarbeiten und an historischen Beispielen zeigen, wie sie auf den Strandburgenbau im Kaiserreich, der Weimarer Republik und dem ‚Dritten Reich' zutrafen. Dabei beleuchte ich sowohl die sozialen Praktiken als auch die kulturellen Repräsentationen von Strandburgen in Form von Postkarten und Selbstzeugnissen.

3.1 Vertrautheit und Fremdheit

Der Alltag ist das Vertraute, der Urlaubsort das Fremde. Bertolt Brecht formuliert dazu in der Oper *Aufstieg und Fall der Stadt Mahagonny:*

> PAUL: Wenn man an einen fremden Strand kommt
> Ist man immer zuerst etwas verlegen.
> JAKOB: Man weiß nicht recht, wohin man gehen soll
> HEINRICH: Wen man anbrüllen darf
> JOSEPH: Und vor wem man den Hut zieht.
> PAUL: Das ist der Nachteil
> Wenn man an einen fremden Strand kommt.
> (Brecht 1988 [1929], 341)

An einem fremden Strand ist man demnach unsicher, ob die aus dem Alltag vertrauten sozialen Regeln auch dort gelten. Auch der Ort und die Landschaft sind beim ersten Besuch unbekannt. Der Reiz einer Urlaubsreise liegt gerade in der Erfahrung der Fremdheit; und doch versuchen Tourist*innen auf unterschiedliche Art und Weise, sich dieser Fremdheit vor Ort zu entledigen, sich das Fremde anzueignen, es in Vertrautes zu verwandeln oder Inseln von Vertrautem zu suchen oder selbst zu schaffen. Das kann nur funktionieren, wenn der Urlaubsort seinerseits entsprechende Angebote macht, wenn er nicht nur Elemente besitzt, die ausreichend fremd und ‚exotisch' sind, um ihn interessant zu machen, sondern auch solche, die für Tourist*innen einen Wiedererkennungswert besitzen (vgl. Lazzarotti 2001, 75–76).

Der Strandburgenbau veranschaulicht dieses Charakteristikum von Urlaubsreisen gut: Der Urlaubsort Strand ist dem Gast zunächst fremd, als Landschaft wie als Ort, an dem Einheimische und bereits länger anwesende Gäste sich nach sozialen Regeln bewegen, die er noch nicht kennt. Indem neu angekommene Urlauber*innen Strandburgen bauen, verwandeln sie symbolisch die Fremde in ein Stück vertraute Heimat. Innerhalb des Ringwalls können sie sich sicher fühlen und sich von hier aus in der Fremde um sie herum orientieren. Innerhalb ihrer Fluchtburg gelten ihre eigenen, von zu Hause mitgebrachten sozialen Regeln; hier ist ihr Territorium. Die Burg markiert zugleich den Endpunkt ihrer Reise, das Angekommensein am Urlaubsort.[2]

Diese Deutung wird gestützt durch die Aufschriften, Motive, Flaggen und Wimpel, mit denen Strandburgen im späten neunzehnten und frühen zwanzigsten Jahrhundert geschmückt waren. Sehr oft wurden sie mit lokalen, regionalen oder nationalen Flaggen oder Wimpeln versehen (vgl. Abb. 1 und 4 sowie Abbildungen bei Kimpel und Werckmeister 1995, 63). Diese Art von Identitätsbekenntnissen fand sich nach dem Zweiten Weltkrieg nicht mehr, wohl aber die ebenfalls häufig vorkommenden Aufschriften, die die Herkunft der Burgbesitzer*innen anzeigten, indem sie schlicht „Düsseldorf" oder „Hamburg" verkündeten.[3] Aufwändiger waren Sandskulpturen an den Burgen, die heimatliche Motive darstellten, wie etwa die Westfalenhalle oder den Nürburgring, gesehen beim Strandburgenwettbewerb 1928 in Timmendorfer Strand (Kimpel und Werckmeister 1995, 71). Diese Bekenntnisse zum Heimatort und die Demonstrationen von Lokalpatriotismus leiten über zum nächsten Begriffspaar.

3.2 Nähe und Distanz

Nähe und Distanz beziehe ich hier ausschließlich auf soziale Kontakte, nicht auf die geographische Entfernung des Urlaubsortes. Strandburgen besitzen einen ambivalenten Charakter von Abgrenzung und Kommunikation, von Distanzierung und Annäherung. Beides dient der Positionierung der Bewohner*innen im sozialen Mikrokosmos der Urlaubswelt. Strandburgen dienen damit der Orientierung und der Anpassung der/des Einzelnen an die spezifischen sozialen Verhältnisse des Urlaubsortes. (Vgl. auch Kimpel und Werckmeister 1995, 17) Denn Urlauber*innen sind im Mikrokosmos der Urlaubswelt zugleich stärker auf sich selbst gestellt, losgelöst von gewohnten sozialen Bindungen im Alltag, und in eine vergleichsweise überschaubare soziale Welt geworfen, in der die soziale Kontrolle in mancher Hinsicht geringer, in manch anderer jedoch größer ist als zu Hause. So trifft man als Badegast etwa jeden Tag dieselben anderen Gäste am selben Strand wieder.

---

[2] Ähnlich auch Kimpel und Werckmeister (1995, 44–47).
[3] Beispiele bei Kimpel und Werckmeister (1995, 71); Diers (1986, 143).

Die Strandburg als Fluchtpunkt im doppelten Wortsinn erlaubt den Rückzug an einen sicheren, vertrauten, nach eigenen Regeln gestalteten Ort. Von dieser Basis aus jedoch ermöglicht sie Kommunikation: das Sich-Hinauswagen in die soziale Urlaubswelt. So besitzen die massive Zurschaustellung des Herkunftsortes und auch die sonstigen Verzierungen der Strandburg einen Doppelcharakter: Einerseits dienen sie der Abgrenzung und der Demonstration der spezifischen Identität der Burgbewohner*innen. Andererseits kommunizieren sie mit den umliegenden Strandgästen, ermöglichen Gesprächsanknüpfungspunkte und Verbrüderungen, denn die individuelle Gestaltung der Strandburgen lässt Aufschlüsse auf die Mentalität oder Interessen der Besitzer*innen zu.[4]

Im Kaiserreich und in der Weimarer Republik gab es eine Fülle von Aufschriften, die explizit der Charakterisierung ihrer Erbauer*innen dienten oder mit anderen Gästen kommunizierten. So beschreibt der *Sylt-Führer* von 1906 einige der „grüssenden Inschriften" folgendermaßen:

> Lesen wir ‚Servas Schurl' oder ‚Gengans baden', so sind wir sicher, kreuzfidele Urwiener vor uns zu haben, und heißt es ‚Berliner Rangen', so erkennen wir sofort Herkunft, Geschlecht und Gefährlichkeit dieser Burgbewohner; lockt die eine Tafel: ‚Wir sind noch zu haben', so warnt die nächste: ‚Diese Höhlenbewohner dürfen nicht gereizt werden', und so wohnen neben der ‚lustigen Schwiegermutter' friedlich die ‚Harmlosen, G. m. b. H.', und neben der „Feuergefährlichen Strohwitwe" erhebt sich das hagestolze ‚Junggesellenheim', und so gibt es ‚Nichten und Genossen', ‚Süsse Mädel', ‚Unterbrettl', ‚Übermenschen' in lustiger Auswahl die Menge. (*Sylt-Führer* 1906, zitiert nach Diers 1986, 140)

Andere Strandburgen zeigten an, dass hier der „Club der Arbeitsscheuen" residierte (1913, Abb. bei Kimpel und Werckmeister 1995, 40) oder dass es den Bewohner*innen um „Deutsch sein" ging (1929, Abb. bei Kimpel und Werckmeister 1995, 59). Derlei kommunizierende Aufschriften fanden sich bis in die 1970er Jahre an deutschen Stränden.

3.3 Arbeit und Freizeit

Wieso schufteten sich Deutsche im Urlaub ab, indem sie tagelang Sandwälle mit Spaten und Gießkanne auftürmten, dann mühevoll Muscheln und Anderes zusammentrugen, um sich in weiterer tagelanger Kleinarbeit an die Verzierung ihrer Burg zu machen und schließlich den Rest des Urlaubs damit zu verbringen, das Kunstwerk gegen feindliche Witterungseinflüsse und Burgenräuber zu verteidigen? Strandburgenbau kann folglich als Fortsetzung der Arbeits- und

---
[4] Ähnlich auch Kimpel und Werckmeister (1995, 17, 24–25).

Leistungsgesellschaft im Urlaub interpretiert werden, als Bekämpfung der Langeweile, die sich sonst allzu schnell einstellen würde, zumal sich am Strand ansonsten kaum etwas Sinnvolles tun ließ. In einer Epoche, in der die kommerzielle Animation am Strand noch nicht so verbreitet war wie heutzutage, bot sich kreatives Bauen auf Sand geradezu als Ausweg aus dem verordneten Nichtstun an. Das bürgerlich-männliche Arbeitsethos machte bei dieser Betrachtungsweise auch vor dem Urlaub nicht Halt.[5]

Zumindest passte es sich in Debatten des späten neunzehnten und frühen zwanzigsten Jahrhunderts ein, in denen besorgte Experten (Mediziner, Sozialreformer, Arbeitgeber und andere) einerseits über die Notwendigkeit von Erholungsurlaub für Erwerbstätige, andererseits über dessen richtige Nutzung stritten (Schumacher 2002, 37–59, 78–81, 90–103; Reulecke 1976, 221–228). Denn die freie Zeit sollte nicht mit sinnlosem Tun vergeudet, sondern sinnvoll genutzt werden, so dass sie der notwendigen Rekreation der Arbeitskraft zuträglich war. Körperliche Bewegung an frischer Luft galt dabei als beste Erholung. (Schumacher 2002, 35–36) Deshalb hielten es viele Entscheidungsträger im Kaiserreich nicht für notwendig, dass Arbeiter*innen Urlaub erhielten, da sie bereits körperlich arbeiteten und folglich nichts hatten, wovon sie sich erholen mussten. Als erholungsbedürftig galt nur, wer geistig arbeitete. (Reulecke 1976, 226) Das Verhältnis von Arbeit und Urlaub ist also keineswegs ein einfaches und entgegengesetztes, wie so häufig angenommen.

In geschlechtergeschichtlicher Perspektive ist die Trennung zwischen Arbeit und Freizeit/Urlaub mittlerweile ohnehin als hinfällig entlarvt worden. Männer aus dem Bildungsbürgertum und aus den freien Berufen etwa nahmen sich im frühen zwanzigsten Jahrhundert häufig Arbeit mit in den Urlaub (Kolbe 2005, 194). Für sie war Urlaub lediglich die Fortsetzung der Arbeit in angenehmerer Umgebung und selbstbestimmterer Weise. Für eine große Gruppe bürgerlicher Frauen wiederum war die Urlaubsreise „nur der aufs Land versetzte städtische Haushalt, etwas erschwert durch die primitiven ländlichen Einkaufsgelegenheiten und das Kochen auf demselben Herd mit den Bauern", wie Hans Fallada in seinen Kindheitserinnerungen schreibt (2001 [1941], 120–121). Vielleicht erklärt das auch die Geschlechterspezifik des Strandburgenbaus. Denn offensichtlich wurden die Burgen hauptsächlich von Männern und Kindern gebaut, während die Frauen höchstens beim Sammeln von Strandgut und Verzierungsmaterial, eventuell noch beim Verzieren halfen (vgl. die Abbildungen bei Kimpel und Werckmeister 1995, 38–39). Die Geschlechterspezifik scheint sich auch im Laufe des Jahrhunderts nicht verändert zu haben.

---

5 Zum zentralen Stellenwert von (Erwerbs-)Arbeit bei der Identitätskonstruktion bürgerlicher Männer seit der zweiten Hälfte des neunzehnten Jahrhunderts siehe Kessel (2003, 14–16).

3.4 Zentrum und Marginalität

Das Begriffspaar Zentrum und Marginalität hebt auf die Vorstellung ab, dass sich Alltagsleben im Zentrum der Gesellschaft abspielt, während Urlaubsreisen und -orte an der Peripherie anzusiedeln seien. Das heißt nicht, dass sie weniger bedeutsam sind, sondern bezieht sich vielmehr auf ihre vermeintliche Andersartigkeit, auf den Charakter einer lokalen, zeitlichen und sozialen Ausnahmesituation, etwa darauf, dass die gewohnten sozialen Regeln und Zwänge im Urlaub weniger streng und Urlaubsorte „*places on the margin*" seien, wie der Soziologe und Kulturtheoretiker Rob Shields es ausdrückt (Shields 1991). Die Qualität eines *place on the margin* trifft ganz besonders auf den Strand zu, nicht nur im übertragenen Sinne, denn er ist auch geographisch die Übergangszone zwischen Land und Meer und lädt als solche zu alltagsüberschreitenden Träumen und Tätigkeiten geradezu ein (ebd., 75, 84).

Die Tätigkeit des Strandburgenbaus an sich bestätigt den Charakter der sozialen Ausnahmesituation: Nur im Urlaub bauten erwachsene Männer Burgen aus Sand und verzierten sie mit Muscheln, Steinen und Wimpeln. Der Sand mit seinen Gestaltungsmöglichkeiten ließ somit das Kind im Manne erwachen und Erwachsene im Urlaub regredieren. Das zählt der Tourismusautor Christoph Hennig zu den Charakteristika des Strandurlaubs (1999, 28). Die Strand-Kommunikation durch teilweise provozierende Strandburgen-Aufschriften, bei denen auch erotische Untertöne mitklingen konnten, wiederum deutet auf ein freizügigeres Miteinander hin, als es im Alltag möglich war – noch dazu über soziale Grenzen hinweg (die am Strand nicht sofort erkennbar waren).

Fand Strandburgenbau somit einerseits in einem Raum am Rande der Gesellschaft statt, war andererseits die Kommunikation via Strandburgen im frühen zwanzigsten Jahrhundert hoch politisch und stand mitten im Zentrum der Gesellschaft. Zeitgenössische Fotos dokumentieren, dass auch politische Themen zu den Motiven des Strandburgenbaus gehörten, etwa Gefallenendenkmäler nach dem Ersten Weltkrieg oder nationalsozialistische Bekenntnisburgen im ‚Dritten Reich', die Adolf Hitler oder Hermann Göring zeigten.[6] Daneben lassen uns unzählige Berichte, amtliche Erlasse und Klagen der Kurverwaltungen wissen, dass der Flaggenstreit der Weimarer Republik auch vor den Stränden nicht Halt machte.[7] Immer wieder wurde von Beschwerden der Badegäste über die

---

[6] Beispiele bei Kimpel und Werckmeister (1995, 70, 74–76).
[7] Der Flaggenstreit der 1920er Jahre wurde zwischen Republikaner*innen einerseits und Republikgegner*innen andererseits ausgetragen. Die einen waren der Ansicht, dass die allein legitime Flagge die republikanische schwarz-rot-goldene sei, während die anderen die traditionelle schwarz-weiß-rote Flagge des Kaiserreichs wiederbeleben wollten.

‚falschen' Flaggen anderer Gäste oder auch von gegenseitigen Strandburgzerstörungen, Handgreiflichkeiten und dem nächtlichen Entwenden nachbarlicher Flaggen berichtet (z. B. Mühlhausen 2006, 392). Ab Ende der 1920er Jahre gab es dann vermehrt Berichte über Urlaubsgäste, die sich von nationalsozialistischen Flaggen auf Strandburgen gestört fühlten.

Aber nicht nur die Kommunikation via Strandburgen, auch die Bauten selbst können als Politikum gelesen werden. Kein Zufall sei es, so Kimpel und Werckmeister, dass Strandburgen im Kaiserreich ein so überaus beliebtes Postkartenmotiv wurden. Die Burgen hätten den „aggressiven Charakter des geeinten Nationalstaats" symbolisiert (Kimpel und Werckmeister 1995, 62). Die „Erprobung des Ernstfalls unter Urlaubsbedingungen" sei „Ausdruck von Ahnungen des Kommenden", die „Trichterlandschaften von Westerland und Wangerooge" seien „denen von Verdun und Douaumont zum Verwechseln ähnlich" (ebd., 68). Diese Interpretation drängt sich in der Tat auf, wenn man Bilder von Stränden des Kaiserreichs sieht, die wie Kraterlandschaften aussehen.[8]

Auch die zeitgenössische soziale Praxis sowie ihre Repräsentation in Wort und Bild unterstreichen diese ausnahmsweise historisch spezifische Deutung Kimpels und Werckmeisters von Strandburgen als Ausdruck einer hoch militarisierten Gesellschaft: So beschreibt Hans Fallada seine Kindheitsferien in Graal an der Ostsee um 1900 folgendermaßen:

> So war die ganze Baderei eigentlich mehr Pflicht als Vergnügen, und wir waren immer froh, wenn wir wieder in unsern Kleidern steckten und der heimischen Burg zustrebten, stets voller Spannung, ob nicht ein Unbefugter unterdes Besitz von ihr ergriffen hätte. So wenig besucht damals Graal auch noch war, der Kampf um die schönste Burg stand doch schon in voller Blüte, und wir wollten nicht umsonst in tagelangem Bemühen einen Wall und Graben angelegt haben, die auch der stärksten Sturmflut zu trotzen schienen!
> Die Freude, wenn man zur heimischen Burg kam und alles war noch in bester Ordnung, die Empörung, wenn uns der Brettersteg über den Graben gestohlen war (den wir erst gestohlen hatten) oder gar der Balken, der Mutters Sitzplatz bildete! Aufklärungsfahrten wurden organisiert, Spione ausgesandt, und war der Verbleib des Diebesguts ermittelt, so wurde je nach Art und Kraft des neuen Besitzers entweder Bitten oder offene Gewalt oder List beschlossen. (Fallada 2001 [1941], 188)

Zeitgenössische Zitate beschreiben auch, wie Kinder und Jugendliche in Kompanien an den Strand ziehen, um Burgen zu bauen und dann damit Krieg zu spielen, bei dem entweder die Burgen gegenseitig gestürmt bzw. erfolgreich verteidigt oder möglichst lange gegen die einlaufende Flut gehalten werden mussten. Mit solchen Spielen warb etwa ein Jugendpensionat und Ferienheim in einer Anzeige im Sylt-Führer von 1906 (Diers 1986, 140) und Theodor Fontane

---

[8] Vgl. dazu die Beispiele bei Kimpel und Werckmeister (1995, 52–53, 68–69).

beschreibt in einem Brief von Norderney vom 4. August 1883 an seine Frau eine „Spielgesellschaft" aus „lauter Berliner Jungens":

> Hauptaufgabe waren Burgen baun. Sie brachten es darin zu einer wahren Meisterschaft und errichteten am Strand, während der Ebbe, Riesenbauten mit Forts, Wällen, Zugbrücken. Kam dann die Fluth, so bestand der Witz darin, diese Burg durch große Wall- und Deich-Arbeiten vor der Fluth zu schützen, bis dann endlich eine große Welle der ganzen Herrlichkeit ein Ende machte. Das war Vormittags. Nachmittags wurde dann Krieg gespielt [...]. (Fontane und Fontane 1998, 358)

Die Verteidigung von Strandburgen gegen die steigende Flut war offenbar auch ein beliebtes Vergnügen erwachsener Nordseeurlauber*innen, zumindest lassen zahlreiche einschlägige Postkartenmotive, die ganze Familien und Strandgesellschaften mit Spaten bewaffnet gegen die ansteigenden Wassermassen anschaufelnd zeigen, darauf schließen. Sie tragen Titel wie „Die Vertheidigung einer Burg bei Sturmfluth" (Postkarte aus Sylt von 1904) oder „Die letzten 5 Minuten unserer Burg" (Postkarte aus Sylt von 1906).[9] Bei solchen Postkarten drängt sich die Deutung des wehrhaften und kriegsbereiten Volkes geradezu auf: Vom Kind bis zur alten Frau waren alle gerüstet. Solche Motive finden sich nach dem Ersten Weltkrieg nicht mehr. Diese Art der Politisierung und Militarisierung von Strandburgen war demnach spezifisch für das von Imperialismus und Militarismus geprägte Kaiserreich. Nach dem verlorenen Krieg war den Deutschen das Kriegspielen am Strand offenbar vergangen.

Abb. 4: „Am Morgen nach dem Sturm". Ostseebad Brunshaupten in Mecklenburg (seit 1938 Kühlungsborn). Postkarte um 1900.

---

9 Diese und weitere Beispiele bei Kimpel und Werckmeister (1995, 65–67).

4 Historische Spezifika des Strandburgenbaus

Es ist wohl kein Zufall, dass Strandburgen sich gerade im Kaiserreich als Postkartenmotiv solch großer Beliebtheit erfreuten. Neben den Panoramaansichten vom Strand, auf denen zahlreiche Strandburgen unvermeidlich zu sehen waren, stechen besonders die Motive hervor, bei denen es um Grenzüberschreitungen oder Grenzsicherungen geht: Burgen mit besonders frechen Sprüchen oder Burgen, deren Bewohner*innen zur Verteidigung gerüstet sind. Angesichts der historisch spezifischen Bedeutungen und Funktionen von Strandburgen im Kaiserreich als Ausdruck einer militarisierten Gesellschaft ist es erstaunlich, dass sie sich nach dem verlorenen Krieg an deutschen Stränden hielten. Wenngleich Bauweise und Ästhetik dabei unverändert blieben, waren sie dann jedoch entmilitarisiert, nicht aber unpolitisch. Politische Aufschriften und Motive sowie die gehissten politischen Flaggen kommunizierten nach wie vor mit den Strandgästen. Erst nach dem Zweiten Weltkrieg verschwanden die politischen Bekenntnisse an ost- und westdeutschen Stränden. Die Aufschriften wurden unpolitisch und es gab keine Flaggen mehr auf den Strandburgen. Der Nationalsozialismus und der verheerende erneut verlorene Krieg hatten den Deutschen die Lust am Politisieren am Strand genommen. Doch deuteten Angehörige von Nachbarländern die Burgen, die Deutsche an ihren Stränden bauten, in den ersten Nachkriegsjahrzehnten als Ausdruck einer andauernden deutschen Angriffs- und Besitzanspruchsmentalität. Auch diese Deutung war eine historisch spezifische, gespeist aus den Erfahrungen, die sie im Krieg gemacht hatten. Das Hinterfragen der zeitlichen Kontinuität von Strandburgen und die Frage nach ihren jeweils spezifischen Bedeutungen und Funktionen wird der historischen Wirklichkeit eher gerecht als die Annahme, dass die Deutschen, von historischen Kontexten unabhängig, eine seit rund hundert Jahren gleichbleibende ‚Identität' besitzen, die sie nach wie vor Strandburgen bauen lässt.

Literaturverzeichnis

Bausinger, Hermann. *Typisch deutsch. Wie typisch sind die Deutschen?* München: Beck, 2002.
Brecht, Bertolt. *Aufstieg und Fall der Stadt Mahagonny. Oper. Stücke 2. Werke. Große kommentierte Berliner und Frankfurter Ausgabe.* Bd. 2. Hg. Werner Hecht, Jan Knopf, Werner Mittenzwei und Klaus-Detlef Müller. Berlin, Weimar und Frankfurt/Main: Suhrkamp und Aufbau, 1988. 334–392.
Diers, Michael. „Strandburgenbau". *Saison am Strand. Badeleben an Nord- und Ostsee 200 Jahre.* Katalog zur Ausstellung im Norddeutschen Landesmuseum. Hg. Altonaer Museum in Hamburg. Herford: Koehler, 1986. 139–144.

Enzensberger, Hans Magnus. "Vergebliche Brandung der Ferne. Eine Theorie des Tourismus". *Merkur* 12.8 (1958): 701–720.
Fallada, Hans. *Damals bei uns daheim. Erlebtes, Erfahrenes und Erfundenes* [1941]. Berlin: Aufbau, 2001.
Fontane, Theodor, und Emilie Fontane. "„Zuneigung ist etwas Rätselvolles'. Der Ehebriefwechsel. 1873–1898". *Große Brandenburger Ausgabe, Bd. XI/3*. Hg. Gotthard Erler. Berlin: Aufbau, 1998.
Hennig, Christoph. "Jenseits des Alltags. Theorien des Tourismus". *Voyage. Jahrbuch für Reise- und Tourismusforschung* 1 (1997): 35–53.
Hennig, Christoph. *Reiselust. Touristen, Tourismus und Urlaubskultur*. Frankfurt/Main: Suhrkamp, 1999.
Holfelder, Moritz. *Das Buch vom Strandkorb*. Husum: Husum Druck- und Verlagsgesellschaft, 1996.
Kessel, Martina. "„The Whole Man': The Longing for a Masculine World in Nineteenth-Century Germany". *Gender & History* 15.1 (2003): 1–31.
Kimpel, Harald, und Johanna Werckmeister. *Die Strandburg. Ein versandetes Freizeitvergnügen*. Marburg: Jonas, 1995.
Kolbe, Wiebke. "Strandurlaub als liminoider (Erfahrungs-)Raum der Moderne? Deutsche Seebäder im späten 19. und frühen 20. Jahrhundert". *Freizeit und Vergnügen vom 14. bis zum 20. Jahrhundert / Temps libre et loisirs du 14e au 20e siècles*. Hg. Hans-Jörg Gilomen, Beatrice Schumacher und Laurent Tissot. Zürich: Chronos, 2005. 187–200.
Kolbe, Wiebke. "Körpergeschichte(n) am Strand. Bürgerliches Seebaden im langen 19. Jahrhundert". *Tourismusgeschichte(n)*. Hg. Wiebke Kolbe, Christian Noack und Hasso Spode. München und Wien: Profil, 2009. 23–34.
Lazzarotti, Olivier. "Tourismus: Von Orten und Menschen". *Voyage. Jahrbuch für Reise- und Tourismusforschung* 4 (2001): 72–78.
Linke, Uli. *German Bodies: Race and Representation after Hitler*. New York und London: Routledge, 1999.
Löfgren, Orvar. *On Holiday. A History of Vacationing*. Berkeley, Los Angeles und London: University of California Press, 1999.
Mühlhausen, Walter. *Friedrich Ebert 1871–1925. Reichspräsident der Weimarer Republik*. Bonn: Dietz, 2006.
Reulecke, Jürgen. "Vom Blauen Montag zum Arbeiterurlaub. Vorgeschichte und Entstehung des Erholungsurlaubs für Arbeiter vor dem Ersten Weltkrieg". *Archiv für Sozialgeschichte* 16 (1976): 205–248.
Schumacher, Beatrice. *Ferien. Interpretationen und Popularisierung eines Bedürfnisses. Schweiz 1890–1950*. Wien, Köln und Weimar: Böhlau, 2002.
Shields, Rob. *Places on the Margin. Alternative Geographies of Modernity*. London und New York: Routledge, 1991.
Walter, Karin. "Die Ansichtskarte als visuelles Massenmedium". *Schund und Schönheit. Populäre Kultur um 1900*. Hg. Kaspar Maase und Wolfgang Kaschuba. Köln und Wien: Böhlau, 2001. 46–61.
Walton, John K. *The British Seaside. Holidays and Resorts in the Twentieth Century*. Manchester: Manchester UP, 2000.
Zuelow, Eric G. E. *A History of Modern Tourism*. Basingstoke: Palgrave Macmillan, 2016.

Abbildungsverzeichnis

Abb. 1: Strandburgen im Ostseebad Kellenhusen in Holstein. Postkarte. Oldenburg in Holstein: Kunstverlag Julius Simonsen. Poststempel: Kellenhusen, 14. August 1934.

Abb. 2: Strandburg mit Meeresgeschöpf und Bremer Stadtmusikanten. Strandburgenwettbewerb im Ostseebad Laboe bei Kiel, 1963. Foto: Friedrich Magnussen. © Gesellschaft für Kieler Stadtgeschichte. https://commons.wikimedia.org/wiki/File:Sandburgenwettbewerb_in_Laboe_(Kiel_31.099).jpg?uselang=de. Creative Commons Lizenz. Genehmigung: CC BY-SA 3.0 DE, Identity 31.099.

Abb. 3: Sandskulpturen neben dem Ringwall. Strandburgenwettbewerb im Ostseebad Laboe bei Kiel, 1963. Foto: Friedrich Magnussen. © Gesellschaft für Kieler Stadtgeschichte. https://commons.wikimedia.org/wiki/File:Sandburgenwettbewerb_in_Laboe_(Kiel_31.163).jpg?uselang=de. Creative Commons Lizenz. Genehmigung: CC BY-SA 3.0 DE, Identity 31.163.

Abb. 4: „Am Morgen nach dem Sturm". Ostseebad Brunshaupten in Mecklenburg (seit 1938 Kühlungsborn). Postkarte. Brunshaupten: Friedrich Reincke, um 1900.

Robert Bauernfeind
Der Strand als Schauplatz weltweiter Fauna. Exotische *naturalia* auf Stranddarstellungen Jan van Kessels d.Ä.

The contribution interprets representations of the beach by the Flemish painter Jan van Kessel the Elder as iconographic constructs. The discussed paintings show the beach as habitat for numerous exotic animals. After explaining their derivation of the composition from prints of around 1600, these depictions of the beach are contextualized within early modern trade as well as the European culture of collecting. For both, animals as depicted on beaches by van Kessel were of high relevance. Subsequently, the paper identifies relevant motifs van Kessel took from publications of natural history. By representing the variety of exotic maritime fauna, van Kessel's paintings reflect the contemporary European perception of the foreign; in the seemingly precise depiction of an encyclopedic multitude of creatures, they show painting as a medium of scientific insight and, thus, contribute to a better social standing of artists in seventeenth-century Flanders.

Der Beitrag deutet Stranddarstellungen des flämischen Malers Jan van Kessel d.Ä. als ikonographische Konstrukte. Die dafür herangezogenen Gemälde zeigen den Strand als Lebensraum zahlreicher exotischer Tiere. Nach einer Herleitung der Komposition von Strandbildern aus der Druckgraphik um 1600 werden die Bilder zunächst in den Kontext des frühneuzeitlichen Handels sowie des europäischen Sammlungswesens gesetzt. Tieren wie denen, die van Kessels Bilder auf Stränden zeigen, kam darin eine hohe Bedeutung zu. Anschließend werden Motive identifiziert, die van Kessel aus Publikationen der Naturgeschichte übernommen hat. In der Darstellung der exotischen Meeresfauna reflektieren van Kessels Gemälde die zeitgenössische europäische Wahrnehmung des Fremden; in der scheinbar präzisen Wiedergabe einer enzyklopädischen Vielfalt von Lebewesen lassen sie überdies die Malerei als Medium wissenschaftlicher Erkenntnis erscheinen und tragen somit zu einer Steigerung des Ansehens der Künstler im Flandern des siebzehnten Jahrhunderts bei.

1 Einleitung

Obwohl die Küste von jeher zu den zentralen Schauplätzen des Lebens der am Meer gelegenen Länder Europas gezählt hat,[1] wurde der Strand als eigenständiges Motiv der Kunst erst im siebzehnten Jahrhundert etabliert. Zuvor dienten Strände allenfalls als Hintergrund für biblische und mythologische Historien,

---

[1] Siehe hierzu jüngst Baltrusch (2018). Einen knappen Überblick über Meer und Strand gibt im selben Katalog Breymayer (2018). Grundlegend zum Thema sind überdies Baader und Wolf (2010) sowie Richter (2014).

https://doi.org/10.1515/9783110672244-012

die am oder auf dem Meer spielen. Der Strand konnte etwa der Schauplatz der Geburt der Venus oder der Rettung Jonas aus dem großen Fisch sein, blieb diesem Geschehen aber entsprechend der zeitgenössischen Kunsttheorie untergeordnet, die die Umsetzung derartiger Stoffe als erstrangige Aufgabe der Malerei bestimmte. Die Aufwertung des Strandes zu einem selbstständigen Thema hing von der Emanzipation der Landschaft von der Historienmalerei ab. Diese vollzog sich mit einem um die Mitte des sechzehnten Jahrhunderts aufkommenden Interesse an der Gestalt der Erde, das nicht zuletzt von der humanistischen Lektüre antiker Geographen motiviert war. Zur Prüfung und Erweiterung von deren schriftlich tradierten Kenntnissen erwies sich das Bild als eine entscheidende Instanz, da sich mit Bildern eng gefasste Ausschnitte der Erdoberfläche in topographischen Aufsichten und breitere Ausschnitte in der Abstraktion von Karten fixieren ließen. Auf Reisen sammelten Künstler einzelne Ansichten, deren Verarbeitung zu autonomen Landschaftsgemälden aus dieser kartographischen Praxis erklärbar wird, aber auch von einem Wandel in der Wahrnehmung der Natur zeugt, die in zunehmendem Maße ästhetisch erfahren wurde (Büttner 2000).[2] Strand und Meer blieben dabei zunächst untergeordnete Motive. Sie wurden etwa insofern zu eigenständigen Bildthemen, als Künstler – nicht zuletzt als Begleiter auf Seefahrten – aus der Skizzierung von Ufern kartographisches Material gewannen.[3] Einen von der Historienmalerei abhängigen Impuls für ihre Darstellung bildeten zudem repräsentative Bilder von Seeschlachten, aber auch von marinen Herrschaftszeremonien, in Malerei und Graphik. Die ersten selbständigen Strand- und Meereslandschaften wurden von niederländischen Künstlern wie Hendrick Vroom (1566–1640) und seinen Schülern Jan Porcellis (1582–1632) und Simon de Vlieger (1601–1653) um 1600 angefertigt (Giltaij 1996; Sitt 2010). Holländische Strandszenen des siebzehnten Jahrhunderts sind allerdings meist der Darstellung des Meeres untergeordnet. Sie führen den Blick vom Land auf die See und beleben den Übergang mit anonymen Figuren bei gottgefälliger Arbeit wie dem Kalfatern von Schiffen; Strand und Meer bleiben dabei letztlich Objekte des holländischen, von den Zeitgenossen bewunderten Projekts der Meeresbeherrschung.[4] In der flämischen Malerei

---

2 Grundlegend zur Ästhetisierung der Natur als Landschaft Ritter (1974).

3 Berühmte Beispiele hierfür sind etwa die mit monumentalen Karten ausgemalte Guardaroba des Palazzo Vecchio in Florenz sowie der Atlas Blaeu-van der Hem in der Österreichischen Nationalbibliothek in Wien, der zahlreiche Küstenskizzen enthält, die auf Schiffen der niederländischen Ost-Indischen Handelskompanie angefertigt wurden. Siehe hierzu auch Koller (2014).

4 Beispiele hierfür sind etwa Simon de Vliegers Meereslandschaft in der National Gallery of Art in Washington (Inv. Nr. 1997.101.1) und Reinier Nooms' Darstellung des Ij zu Amsterdam im Rijksmuseum (Inv. Nr. SK-A-759). Siehe hierzu auch Corbin (1990, 52–64).

entstand hingegen eine zwischen Landschaft und Stillleben changierende Bildgattung, die den eng gefassten, mit zahlreichen Naturalien angefüllten Ausschnitt eines Strandes zeigt. Ihr prägender Vertreter war der aus der Brueghel-Dynastie stammende Jan van Kessel (1626–1679), der im Stil seines Großvaters Jan Brueghel (1568–1625) malte und auf die Darstellung von Insekten und Exotica spezialisiert war. In besonders eindrucksvoller Weise hat van Kessel Strandbilder mit Naturalien in einen 1664 bis 1666 entstandenen Gemäldezyklus mit dem Thema der vier Erdteile integriert, der als einzig vollständig erhaltene von mehreren Fassungen heute in der Alten Pinakothek in München aufbewahrt wird.[5]

Dieser Zyklus ist ein formal einzigartiges Bildensemble des flämischen Barock. Auf vier Gemälden sind die Personifikationen der damals bekannten Kontinente Europa, Asien, Afrika und Amerika im Ambiente zeitgenössischer Kunstkammern dargestellt; diese vier zentralen Bilder werden von jeweils sechzehn kleinformatigen Landschaften umgeben, in deren Hintergrund die Veduten bedeutender Städte liegen, während der Vordergrund von Tierstaffagen belebt wird. Der Zyklus erweckt so den Eindruck der Repräsentation eines universellen Wissens, versammelt er doch vermeintlich typische Vertreter*innen von Bewohner*innen der gesamten Welt mit ihren jeweiligen kulturellen Erzeugnissen ebenso wie eine Übersicht über die Fauna der Welt. In Orientierung an frühneuzeitlichen Modellen von Repräsentationen des Wissens hat Andreas Gormans in einem diagrammatischen Ansatz aufzuzeigen versucht, dass van Kessels Erdteilbilder in der strengen Organisation ihres Rahmenformulars eine autoritäre Wissensordnung stifteten und diese in der Markierung ihres kombinatorischen Malverfahrens zugleich dekonstruierten (Gormans 2004). Nadja Baadj hat den Zyklus unter materialkundlichen Aspekten in der Antwerpener Sammlungsgeschichte verortet (Baadj 2012, 2016). Die Dissertation des Autors sollte aufzeigen, dass die Disposition von Wissen im Zyklus anhand von Subgenres der niederländischen Malerei erfolgt, die in van Kessels Umfeld geprägt wurden; der Zyklus erscheint aus ikonographischer Sicht als ein Manifest der Repräsentationskraft von van Kessels Kunst (Bauernfeind 2016). Insbesondere die Darstellung von Tieren auf dem Strand – im Zyklus auf vierzehn Randgemälden zu sehen – ist, wie Sabine Giepmans (2001) aufgezeigt hat, ein Spezifikum van Kessels.[6]

---

[5] Zu den einzelnen fragmentarisch erhaltenen Fassungen siehe Ertz (2012, 153–161, dort auch Abbildungen des vollständigen Zyklus).
[6] Giepmans' (2001) These von van Kessel als Inventor des Sujets muss allerdings auf den Bereich der flämischen Malerei beschränkt werden; bereits 1627 hatte etwa Gillis Claesz d'Hondecoeter eine Darstellung von Perseus und Andromeda gemalt, bei der der mythologische Stoff im Hintergrund bleibt, während im Vordergrund ein van Kessels Kompositionen ähnliches, stilllebenhaftes Arrangement von Muscheln und Meeresvögeln das Bild dominiert.

Der folgende Beitrag soll den Strand als Schauort der Wunder in van Kessels Erdteile-Zyklus in Hinsicht auf die Wissenschaftsgeschichte, auf Alteritätsmodelle sowie auf die Sozialgeschichte der flämischen Malerei deuten. Dazu sollen zunächst die Vorläufer der Bildgattung und der Gehalt der Stranddarstellung in der Entdeckerzeit bestimmt werden. Aufzuzeigen gilt es des Weiteren, welche Kenntnisse die Naturgeschichte über exemplarische Objekte bot und welche Deutungen sich um diese rankten. Zum anderen soll nach der Darstellung des Fremden im Zyklus gefragt werden. Die ästhetische Aneignung des Anderen lässt nicht nur auf europäische Besitzansprüche schließen, sondern ist mit einer symbolischen Wertung verbunden, die das Fremde ebenso zu verklären wie herabzuwürdigen vermag. Ein vierter Punkt soll schließlich Momente selbstreferentieller Malerei in van Kessels Zyklus beleuchten, die diesen als Beleg für den wissenschaftlichen Anspruch der Malerei und den damit verbundenen Wunsch nach deren gesellschaftlicher Aufwertung erscheinen lassen.

2 Kompositorische und motivische Vorläufer

Auf der zur Afrika-Allegorie gehörenden Ansicht von Algier hat van Kessel 26 Tiermotive auf einem bühnenartigen Vordergrund zusammengestellt, hinter dem sich jenseits einer Bucht die Stadt erstreckt.

Abb. 1: Jan van Kessels *Algier* (1664–1666).

Auf dem in sich noch einmal abgestuften Vordergrund geben sich unter anderem eine Seenadel, eine Meeres- und eine Landschildkröte, ein Krebs, ein Seestern und sogar ein Seehund ein Stelldichein. Gefahrvoller erscheint die Fauna auf dem unteren Rang des Litorals: Dort geraten eine mehrfach gewundene Schlange, ein Nilpferd und zwei Haie aneinander, um sich – wohl in Hinblick auf einen zu erbeutenden Fisch – anzufeinden. Die Zusammenstellung erscheint schon daher paradox, dass einige Arten wie das Nilpferd nicht in Algerien verbreitet sind. Mehr noch erfährt sie allerdings durch die Darstellung der Fische einen fabelähnlichen Charakter, da diese mit den anderen Tieren zu interagieren scheinen, an Land aber kläglich zugrunde gehen müssten.

Als motivische Vorläufer von van Kessels Strandbildern nennt Giepmans (2001) Fischbuden von Frans Snyders (1579–1657). Bei diesen Bildern handelt es sich um genrehafte Szenen im Monumentalformat, bei denen Snyders das Thema des Marktstands zur Darstellung einer Vielzahl von Meeresbewohnern nutzte, ohne Wirklichkeitsnähe anzustreben; eher wird der Gegenstand der maritimen Vielfalt durch Andeutungen biblischer Themen wie des Zinsgroschens legitimiert (Giepmans 2001, 84–86). Etwa zeitgleich mit van Kessel haben auch holländische Maler wie Abraham van Beijeren Fische an Stränden gemalt; diese Bilder weisen auf die Bedeutung der heimischen Fischerei für den niederländischen Wohlstand hin, wohingegen van Kessels Gemälde in der Darstellung exotischer Motive einen enzyklopädischen Überblick über die maritime Fauna anstreben.[7]

Als kompositorische Vorbilder erscheinen Bilderfolgen aus der niederländischen Graphik. Grundlegend für die Anordnung unterschiedlicher Meerestiere auf einem Uferstreifen sind die *Piscium Vivae Icones*, die Adriaen Collaert (1560–1680) um 1600 angefertigt hat.

Sie beinhalten neben einem Titelblatt 25 Kupferstiche, auf denen insgesamt 104 Fische, Krebse und andere Meerestiere dargestellt sind. Wie bei van Kessel ist dabei jeweils eine Auswahl im bühnenhaft erhöhten Vordergrund nahsichtig dargestellt, während sich im Hintergrund eine Meereslandschaft mit fernen Städten und Schiffen auf dem Wasser erstreckt. Die Kompositionen sind durch horizontale Linien dreifach in die Tiefe gestaffelt, wobei der erhöhte Vordergrund deutlich von Mittel- und Hintergrund abgesetzt ist; der Mittelgrund wird in der Regel von einer Bucht ausgefüllt, der Hintergrund beinhaltet die Stadtvedute. Im Gegensatz zu van Kessels Bildern zeigen Collaerts Landschaften keine identifizierbaren Orte; in der Kombination von offener See, Flüssen, Städten

---

7 Auffällig ist dabei, dass die Fische auf den niederländischen Gemälden als Ausbeute der Fischer erkennbar, mithin tot sind, wohingegen die Tiere auf van Kessels Bildern ohne menschliches Einwirken am Strand zusammengefunden zu haben scheinen (Giepmans 2001, 88–94).

und Bergen erscheinen sie als Weltlandschaften, wodurch die Tierstudien im Vordergrund womöglich durch eine universelle Bedeutung überhöht werden sollten. Auffällig ist im Vergleich allerdings, dass van Kessel das starre Nebeneinander von Collaerts Tierdarstellungen mit der lebhaften Interaktion der dargestellten Tiere ersetzte.

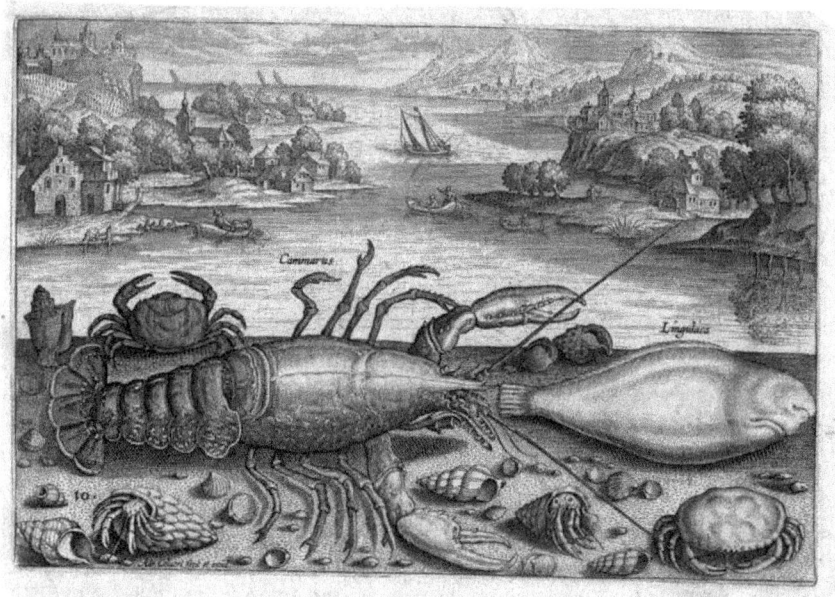

Abb. 2: Adriaen Collaerts *Piscium Vivae Icones* (nach 1598).

Collaerts Serie bot einen Überblick über eine Vielzahl maritimer Lebewesen, doch konnte sich van Kessel auch an Bildern mit einzelnen Tieren orientieren, die Rückschlüsse auf den ikonographischen Gehalt des Litorals im sechzehnten und siebzehnten Jahrhundert zulassen. So zeigt die Darstellung Spitzbergens auf der Asien-Tafel einen Strand, der vom Eismeer der Polarregion umgeben ist.

Zwei Chamäleons, ein Biber, eine Bisamratte und ein Stachelschwein sollen im Vordergrund die regionale Fauna repräsentieren; das markantere Motiv bilden jedoch zwei Wale, die im Mittelgrund gestrandet sind, während im Eismeer ein Segelschiff festgefahren ist. Dies dürfte als Hinweis auf die Grönlandfahrt zu verstehen sein, die frühe Form des europäischen Walfangs, in dessen Rahmen Schiffe nach Spitzbergen vorstießen. Van Kessel hat den Wal nach einem in zahlreichen Varianten publizierten Flugblatt des siebzehnten Jahrhunderts gemalt, das auf die Zeichnung eines gestrandeten Pottwals von Hendrick

Goltzius (1558–1616) zurückgeht. Goltzius hatte den Wal 1598 bei Scheveningen skizziert und sein Schüler Jacob Matham (1571–1631) die Zeichnung in einem Kupferstich reproduziert. Dieser Kupferstich wurde als verbindliche Darstellung eines Wals in naturgeschichtlichen Publikationen und in weiteren Flugblättern kopiert und variiert.[8] Mathams Bild gibt aber auch einen Eindruck vom Strand als Raum des frühneuzeitlichen Monstren- und Prodigienglaubens, da seine Inschrift den Wal nicht nur als naturkundliches Phänomen beschreibt, sondern ihn auch als göttliches Zeichen für den Krieg der Niederlande gegen Spanien deutet. Dieses ambivalente Interesse an der Strandung lässt auf eine Wahrnehmung des Litorals als ungewisse Übergangszone und Imaginationsraum monströser Exzesse und zeichenhafter Erscheinungen schließen (Faust 2002, 42–43).[9] Van Kessels Stranddarstellungen haben mit ihrer Häufung skurriler Wesen Tendenzen dieser Wahrnehmung aufgegriffen.

Abb. 3: Jan van Kessels *Spitzbergen* (1664–1666).

---

8 Grundlegend zur Darstellung von Walen in der Frühen Neuzeit siehe Barthelmeß (1991).
9 Exemplarisch hierfür ist auch ein Flugblatt aus den 1580er-Jahren, das von den Umtrieben eines mordenden Untiers an der Provence-Küste berichtet; der ästhetisch grobe Holzschnitt stellt es als ovales Wesen mit zwölf klauenbewehrten Extremitäten dar, das am Strand zwischen den verstümmelten Leibern seiner Opfer haust. Derartige Darstellungen vermochten nicht zuletzt Erfahrungen von Gräueltaten zu sublimieren, wie sie Frankreich während der Hugenottenkriege erschütterten. Siehe auch Faust (2003, 226).

3 Handel und Sammlungswesen

Über den ikonographischen Gehalt des Strands als Folie für einen allgemeinen Überblick über die maritime Fauna bzw. als Schauplatz von Wunderzeichen hinaus nehmen van Kessels Darstellungen des exotischen Litorals Impulse aus der Bildgeschichte des überseeischen Kulturkontakts auf.

Eine 1648 entstandene Meereslandschaft des flämischen Marinemalers Bonaventura Peeters (1614–1652) lässt die transatlantische Begegnung als lukratives Idyll erscheinen.[10] Vor dem Festland, das von links ins Meer ragt, ist ein Zweimaster unter der Flagge der niederländischen Generalstaaten vor Anker gegangen. Zwei Beiboote steuern auf das Land zu, während ein Kanu mit vier Indigenen in Richtung des Schiffs fährt. Weitere Segelschiffe sind im Hintergrund auszumachen. Im Vordergrund erstreckt sich ein bühnenartiger Uferstreifen, auf dem eine Gruppe von Indigenen die Ankunft der Europäer erwartet. Kronenartiger Federschmuck macht sie auf stereotype Weise als brasilianische Ureinwohner erkennbar. Drei von ihnen recken den Ankömmlingen Schätze ihres Landes entgegen, doch es sind weder Gold noch der in der Kolonisierung Brasiliens bedeutende Zucker, sondern bunt gefiederte Papageien bzw. deren Bälge, die als Zeichen des Warenverkehrs erscheinen.

Peeters' Gemälde reflektiert damit offenbar Erwartungen, die auf die seit 1637 bestehende niederländische Kolonie in Brasilien gerichtet waren.[11] Dieser Verdacht erhärtet sich noch durch den Vergleich mit einem Gemälde Hendrick Vrooms, das mit einer ähnlichen kompositorischen Anlage europäische Schiffe an einer fernasiatischen Küste zeigt.[12] Auch hier steuern Beiboote auf das Ufer zu, an dem ein reger Austausch zwischen Europäern und Indigenen stattfindet; diese werden mit pseudo-orientalischen Gewändern und dem diensteifrigen Einsatz von Sonnenschirmen als Indigene markiert. Es wird vermutet, dass Vrooms Bild während des zwölfjährigen Waffenstillstands zwischen den nördlichen und südlichen Niederlanden entstanden ist und – im friedlichen Nebeneinander von spanischen, englischen und niederländischen Schiffen – die Vorzüge eines innereuropäischen Friedens für den Handel im fernen Osten verherrlichen sollte (Giltaij 1996, 80).

---

10 Heute im Wadsworth Atheneum, Hartford (Inv. Nr. 1940.403).
11 Erik Larsen (1970) vermutete, dass das Bild nach Skizzen entstanden sein dürfte, die Bonaventuras Bruder Gillis Peeters vor Ort in Brasilien gezeichnet hatte. Von Gillis sind topographisch präzise Darstellungen Recifes um 1637 erhalten. Bonaventura Peeters hat mindestens eine frühere, auf 1640 datierte brasilianische Küstenlandschaft gemalt, als deren Wiederholung bei Spiegelung der ursprünglichen Komposition das vorliegende Gemälde erscheint (Larsen 1970, 130).
12 Heute im National Maritime Museum, Greenwich, London (Inv. Nr. BHC0727).

Als visuelle Abbreviatur eines geglückten Welthandels erscheint auf beiden Bildern das Angebot exotischer Waren auf dem Uferstreifen. Naturalien wie Peeters' Papageien und ethnographische Objekte wie Vrooms Sonnenschirme dienten zumeist als Geschenke, die den eigentlichen Handel erst zu initiieren halfen;[13] in diesem Sinne erscheint das Motiv des Warentauschs am Strand bereits auf Holzschnitten, die 1493 zur Illustration von Kolumbus' erstem Brief aus der Neuen Welt angefertigt worden waren (Frübis 1995, 63–65). Derartige Objekte entsprachen als exotische Raritäten aber auch jener Qualität der *curiositas*, die eine zentrale Kategorie der frühneuzeitlichen Sammlungskultur Europas bildete und sich in der erhöhten Aufmerksamkeit gegenüber außergewöhnlichen Phänomenen äußerte. So zählten exotische Naturalien, wie sie van Kessel malte, zum typischen Bestand zeitgenössischer Kunstkammern und Naturalienkabinette, deren Zusammenführung besonders signifikanter Objekte aus Natur und Kunst auf eine Abbildung der gesamten Schöpfung abzielte.[14] Die Gemälde der flämischen Bildgattung der gemalten Kunstkammer reflektieren den hohen ästhetischen Reiz derartiger Sammlungen, deren Ordnung sie im Sinne allegorischer Aussagen abwandeln; eine Kunstkammerwand Frans Franckens d.J. (1581–1642) zeigt etwa eine Vielzahl exotischer Schnecken- und Muschelgehäuse im Nebeneinander mit Gemälden, Kleinskulpturen und Münzen. Als Hommage an den hohen Rang der Wissenschaften und Künste in Antwerpen, auf den unter anderem die Bildnisse von Abraham Ortelius (1527–1598) und Benedictus Arias Montanus (1527–1598) hinweisen, zeigt das Bild auch die Wertschätzung, die den exotischen Conchylien zukam (Schütz 2002).[15]

In der nahsichtigen Darstellung solcher und weiterer exotischer Naturalien auf dem Strand dürften van Kessels Gemälde nicht nur als Bilder zeitgenössischer Sammlungsinteressen verstanden worden sein; formelhaft verweist zugleich der Strand auf den Welthandel als deren grundlegende Bedingung.

4 Naturgeschichte

Vermochte van Kessel Meerestiere, die an den niederländischen Küsten gefischt und auf den heimischen Märkten verkauft wurden, nach dem Leben zu malen, so kopierte der Maler exotische Motive überwiegend nach Illustrationen

---

13 Zur Bedeutung von exotischen Objekten als Geschenke im Fernhandel siehe O'Neil Rife (2013, 132–171).
14 Grundlegend hierzu Bredekamp (2000); Felfe und Lozar (2006); Grote (1994); Minges (1998).
15 Heute in der Gemäldegalerie des Kunsthistorischen Museums in Wien (Inv. Nr. 1048).

naturgeschichtlicher Publikationen (Giepmans 2001, 80). Die Haie am Strand von Algier sind dafür exemplarisch. Van Kessel hat die Motive aus Ulisse Aldrovandis (1522–1605) posthum 1613 erschienenen *De piscibus libri V* übernommen, in denen das bei van Kessel vordere Tier mit dem auffälligen Unterbiss einen Glatthai und das hintere, u-förmig gekrümmte einen Weißen Hai darstellen soll.

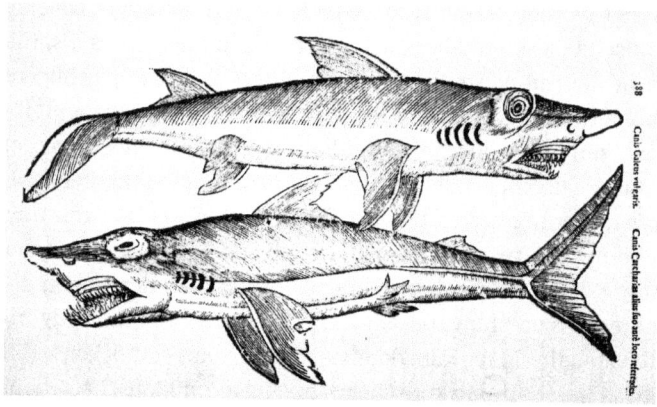

Abb. 4: Anonym. *Glatthai* (1613).

Aldrovandis Holzschnitt zum Weißen Hai ist wiederum eine Kopie nach der entsprechenden Illustration in Konrad Gessners (1516–1565) *Piscium & aquatilium animantium natura* von 1558. Gessner hatte das Bild mit der Beischrift versehen, dass es auf seine Veranlassung hin von einem Präparat gemacht worden sei. Dies erklärt die Verformung des Hais, der offenbar nur notdürftig ausgestopft war und infolge seiner Hängung durchgebogen gewesen sein dürfte; Darstellungen zeitgenössischer Kunstkammern und Kabinette zeigen, dass die Anbringung großer Tierpräparate an der Decke zur Präsentationspraxis gehörte. Van Kessel, der zumindest in der Nordsee verbreitete Haie aus eigener Anschauung gekannt haben dürfte, nutzte jedoch gerade die bizarre Deformation des Hais zu dessen Einsatz in einer Art Tier-Genrebild und ignorierte dabei offenkundig das in den Büchern festgehaltene Wissen über Weiße Haie, weisen doch sowohl Gessner als auch Aldrovandi auf die enorme Größe der Tiere hin, die imstande sein sollten, ganze Menschen zu verschlingen. Auch die von beiden beschriebene Färbung in dunklen Grautönen setzte der Maler nicht um, sondern gab dem Hai silbern und rot schillernde Farben.

Neben naturgeschichtlichen Publikationen zog van Kessel auch Emblembücher heran, in denen naturkundliches Wissen in moralisierendem Sinne überhöht werden sollte. Beispielhaft dafür ist das Bild des Strands bei der brasilianischen Hafenstadt Olinda. Im Vordergrund der in der diesigen Witterung verschwindenden Stadtansicht liegen drei Krokodile am Strand, von denen zwei diagonal von links ins Bild ragen und ein drittes auf einer nahsichtigen Anhöhe ein Nest mit Jungen bewacht. Insbesondere das Verhalten der beiden Krokodile links ist sonderbar: Rinnen dem äußeren Tier Tränen aus den Augen, so hat sich das mittlere auf den Rücken gelegt, während ihm ein Vogel zwischen den Zähnen pickt und eine Manguste auf sein geöffnetes Maul zurennt.

Abb. 5: Jan van Kessels *Olinda* (1664–1666).

Van Kessel hat beide Motive aus den *Symbola et Emblemata* des Joachim Camerarius (1534–1598) übernommen, einer Reihe von Emblembüchern, die ausschließlich Pflanzen und Tiere beschreiben und diese in Abstimmung mit antiker und zeitgenössischer Literatur gleichnishaft deuten (Peil 2004; Vignau-Wilberg 1987).

Van Kessels weinendes Krokodil erscheint bei Camerarius unter dem Lemma „DEVORAT, ET PLORAT" [Es verschlingt und plärrt] als Sinnbild falscher Freundschaft (Schöne 1993 [1964], 73–75). Das Ikon zeigt ein Krokodil an einem felsigen Strand, das über der leblosen Gestalt eines nackten Menschen Tränen vergießt, während ein weiterer Mann nach links Reißaus nimmt. Lemma und

Epigramm beziehen sich auf das bereits in der antiken Naturgeschichte diskutierte Phänomen von Krokodilstränen, die seit dem Mittelalter, etwa im *Buch der Natur* des Konrad von Megenberg (1309–1374), als Zeichen falscher oder verspäteter Reue interpretiert wurden.

Van Kessels mittleres Krokodil verbindet hingegen zwei Embleme aus Camerarius' Büchern. Unter dem Lemma „GRATIS SERVIRE IUCUNDUM" [Freies Dienen ist erfreulich] ist dort zum einen ein Krokodil dargestellt, das auf dem Rücken liegt und einen Vogel zwischen seinen Zähnen stochern lässt. Diese Symbiose zwischen dem sogenannten Krokodilwächter und dem Nilkrokodil findet sich bereits bei Herodot; für Camerarius wird sie zum Sinnbild einer dankenswerten Dienstleistung, denn das Krokodil lässt den Vogel gewähren, der eine sichere Nahrungsquelle im Maul des Raubtiers hat. Anders steht es hingegen um das Tier, das auf das Maul des Krokodils zurennt. Bei ihm handelt es sich um ein Ichneumon, eine Manguste, die schlafenden Krokodilen ins Maul schlüpfen und die Raubtiere von innen heraus zerfressen soll. Unter dem Lemma „NUSQUAM TUTA TYRANNIS" [Die Tyrannei ist nirgends sicher] gerät dies bei Camerarius zum Sinnbild des Widerstands gegen Tyrannen. Bereits bei Plutarch und Plinius d.Ä. überliefert, blieb die Vorstellung im Mittelalter in der Physiologus-Tradition präsent, in der sie als Gleichnis für die Überwindung der Hölle durch den auferstandenen Christus interpretiert wurde; Konrad Gessner hat hingegen die Angriffe des Ichneumons auf das Krokodil als natürliches Verhalten beschrieben (Fischel 2009, 44). Ob allerdings van Kessel Camerarius' Motive nur zur Erweiterung seines Motivrepertoires aufnahm oder sich in der Darstellung ein an die Embleme angelehnter Hintersinn versteckt, bleibt unklar; womöglich sind in der Darstellung noch zu entschlüsselnde Hinweise, etwa auf die niederländisch-portugiesische Rivalität in der Kolonisierung Brasiliens, versteckt.

5 Symbolische Bedeutung

Neben der zeitgenössischen Naturkunde übernahm van Kessel zahlreiche Motive aus der Tradition der flämischen Malerei. Von besonderer Grausamkeit ist dabei das Treiben am Strand von Havanna.

Abb. 6: Jan van Kessels *Havanna* (1664–1666).

Ein Nilpferd hat sich über ein getötetes Krokodil gebeugt, um die Beute gegen ein weiteres Krokodil zu verteidigen, das in gewundener Haltung zum Angriff anzusetzen scheint. Beide Tiere haben die Mäuler aufgerissen, sodass die Zähne deutlich sichtbar sind. Ein drittes Krokodil reckt von rechts den Kopf ins Bild. Unter den Pranken der Streitenden lassen Knochen auf frühere Fressen schließen, darunter ein Eselskinn, das das attackierende Krokodil zu packen scheint, und ein Menschenschädel. Van Kessel hat Krokodil und Nilpferd nach der graphischen Reproduktion von Peter Paul Rubens' (1577–1640) *Jagd auf Nilpferd und Krokodil* kopiert, die der Rubens-Stecher Pieter Claesz. Soutman (1580–1657) angefertigt hat. Dort trampeln die Tiere im Getümmel einer Parforcejagd aufeinander; van Kessel hat sie von Kampfgenossen zu Fressfeinden umgedeutet.

Abb. 7: Pieter Claesz. Soutman nach Peter Paul Rubens. *Jagd auf Nilpferd und Krokodil* (nach 1624).

Das aggressive Verhalten der Tiere scheint jedoch auf mehr als ihren Fressneid hinzudeuten. Der Menschenschädel im Vordergrund weist sie als Anthropophagen aus, als Tiere also, die nicht nur einander, sondern auch Menschen zu fressen imstande sind. Sie entsprechen damit einer Zuordnung wilder Tiere als Attribute, die bereits in den ersten Ausformungen der Erdteil-Ikonographie verbreitet war und ihre vorbildliche Formulierung in der zweiten, illustrierten Ausgabe von Cesare Ripas *Iconologia* gefunden hat. Dort beschreibt Ripa die jugendlich-wilde Gestalt der Amerika-Personifikation als Kannibalin und nimmt damit ein Stereotyp auf, das bereits in den frühesten Beschreibungen Amerikas, den Entdeckerbriefen von Kolumbus und Amerigo Vespucci, etabliert worden war. Ripa forciert den Kannibalismus der Amerika-Personifikation noch, indem er ihr ein Tier als Attribut zuordnet: In Gestalt einer Echse ist einerseits auf die bedrohliche Fauna Südamerikas hingewiesen, andererseits ein Sinnbild für die Anthropophagie der amerikanischen Indigenen gefunden, seien Ripa zufolge doch auch die gewaltigen Echsen Amerikas in der Lage, Menschen zu verschlingen.

Flugblätter und Illustrationen zu Reiseberichten ließen die Anthropophagie amerikanischer Ureinwohner*innen auch im Bild als ein zentrales Problem des frühneuzeitlichen Amerika-Diskurses erscheinen. Dass van Kessel mit dem Kannibal*innen-Stereotyp vertraut war, zeigen Details der Amerika-Allegorie, auf der ein Bild-im-Bild die Vorbereitung einer menschlichen Leiche für den gemeinschaftlichen Verzehr zeigt; van Kessel orientierte sich für diese Darstellung an einer Illustration zum Bericht des hessischen Söldners Hans Staden (1525–1576), der dessen Gefangenschaft bei brasilianischen Ureinwohner*innen beschreibt; das Bild war bei Theodor de Bry (1528–1598) für die Publikation der *Grands Voyages*, einer mehrbändigen Sammlung von Reiseberichten, kopiert und dem Stil der Offizin angeglichen worden.[16] Zudem fügte van Kessel die Figuren zweier Kannibal*innen in das Skulpturenprogramm des Bildes ein, bei denen er sich an der Darstellung eines Tapuya-Paars aus Willem Pisos *Historia Naturalis Brasiliae* (1648) orientierte. Aus dem Tragekorb der Frauenfigur ragt ein Fuß, in der Linken hält sie eine abgeschlagene Hand; beide Attribute lassen den Kannibalismus als gewöhnliche Ernährungsweise der Indigenen erscheinen. Die Tiere, die sich am Strand von Havanna über einem Menschenschädel raufen, scheinen diese Vorstellung symbolisch zu forcieren. Van Kessel relativierte diese Herabwürdigung der amerikanischen Indigenen allerdings dadurch, dass er die eigentliche Personifikation des Erdteils in friedvoller Pose, umgeben von Schätzen ihrer Lande, und die Kannibal*innenszenen ihr gegenüber nur als Bilder-im-Bild malte.

6 Selbstreferentielle Malerei

Im Kontext des Münchner Erdteile-Zyklus erscheint van Kessels Panorama der Fauna der Welt als Beleg für das erkenntnisstiftende Potential der Malerei, da van Kessel die Betrachtung von Tierdarstellungen zum programmatischen Thema der Europa-Allegorie machte. Ihr kompositorisches Vorbild ist die zur Gattung der gemalten Kunstkammer zählende *Allegorie des Sehens* von Peter Paul Rubens und Jan Brueghel, als deren Kernaussage die Vergegenwärtigung der Heilsgeschichte durch die Malerei erscheint: Die heidnische Göttin Juno in ihrer speziellen Funktion als Patronin des Sehsinns wird durch die Betrachtung eines Gemäldes aus ihrer melancholischen Erstarrung gelöst (Müller Hofstede 1984, 254).

---

16 Zum Alteritätsdiskurs bei de Bry siehe Greve (2004).

Analog dazu tritt bei van Kessel eine Männerfigur an die als imperiale Herrscherin charakterisierte Personifikation Europas heran, um ihr mit markantem Zeigegestus ein Gemälde mit Insektendarstellungen in van Kessels eigenem Stil vorzuführen. Als Hommage an Tizians (um 1488–1576) Porträt des Jacopo Strada (1507–1588), das van Kessel aus der Sammlung der Statthalter in Brüssel gekannt haben mag, dürfte diese Figur auf die Tradition der Habsburger als Sammler*innen hinweisen. Indem sie die Europa-Personifikation auf die mimetisch anspruchsvolle Darstellung der Insekten aufmerksam macht, aktiviert sie einen Topos der Naturgeschichte, der bereits bei Plinius d.Ä. (24–79 n.Chr.) formuliert und von neuzeitlichen Autoren wie Aldrovandi und Thomas Muffet (1553–1604) in ihren Büchern aufgegriffen worden war: Gerade in der Betrachtung der kleinsten und unscheinbarsten Geschöpfe offenbare sich das Wesen der Schöpfung und damit die Weisheit Gottes (Vignau-Wilberg 1994, 37–45). Dass dieser Topos in der flämischen Künstlertradition bekannt war, zeigt eine Zeichnung Joris Hoefnagels (1542–1600), deren druckgraphische Reproduktion van Kessel als Vorlage für die Spinne auf dem Insektenbild der Europa-Allegorie gedient zu haben scheint, denn bei Hoefnagel ist das Tier mit einem Psalm überschrieben: „Magnus Dominus noster, et magna virtus eius, et sapientia eius non est numerus." [Groß ist unser Herr und groß ist seine Macht und seine Weisheit ist unermesslich.]

Wollte van Kessel also augenscheinlich das Erkenntnispotential der Malerei für eine theologisch legitimierte Naturgeschichte geltend machen, so konnte er sich auf eine lange Tradition flämischer Maler berufen, die eine Emanzipation ihrer Kunst in den Status der Freien Künste gefordert hatten, indem sie die geistige Konzeption ihrer Arbeiten betonten. In der selbstreferentiellen Darstellung einer Bildbetrachtung gibt die Europa-Allegorie eine Anweisung für die Betrachtung des Zyklus, der Gottes Schöpfung in ihrer Vielfalt vor Augen zu führen scheint.

Van Kessel bediente sich dazu der Breite zeitgenössischer Subgenres, indem er etwa Vögel im Modus des Vogelkonzerts, Amphibien und kleine Reptilien in dem des Sottobosco sowie Versammlungen diverser Tiere nach dem Vorbild von Paradieslandschaften malte; diese Subgenres waren im Verlauf des siebzehnten Jahrhunderts in der flämischen und niederländischen Malerei geprägt worden.[17] Den Strand-Darstellungen kommt dabei schon insofern eine besondere Bedeutung zu, als van Kessel selbst sie als autonome Bildgattung in der flämischen Malerei etabliert hat. Darüber hinaus bieten sie eine in ihrer Plausibilität allerdings brüchige Möglichkeit, Meerestiere darzustellen, die in

---

[17] Zur Geschichte des Vogelkonzerts als Untergattung der Malerei siehe Wepler (2014). Zum Sottobosco vgl. u. a. Leonhard (2013) sowie Seelig (2017).

ihrer natürlichen Umgebung, also unter Wasser, nicht beobachtet werden konnten.

Abb. 8: Jan van Kessels *Europa* (1664).

7 Fazit

Der Strand erscheint in van Kessels Erdteile-Zyklus als ikonographisch aufgeladenes Gebilde, dessen Motivgeschichte die Universalität früherer Weltlandschaften und die Erfahrung monströser Zeichen ebenso beinhaltet wie die Bedeutung des exotischen Litorals als Zeichen und Schauplatz des überseeischen Kulturkontakts und Handels. Kompositorisch nutzte van Kessel den Strand als bühnenhafte Grundlage zur Darstellung exotischer Fauna, für die er sich an Vorlagen aus der Naturgeschichte, der Emblematik und der flämischen Malertradition bediente. Van Kessels Motive entsprechen dabei dem zeitgenössischen Sammlungsinteresse von Kunstkammern und Naturalienkabinetten. Sie werden allerdings immer wieder in narrativen Mustern miteinander verbunden, die mitunter das Wissen unterwandern, das die naturgeschichtlichen Publikationen zu den einzelnen Arten boten. In anderen Fällen sind die Tiermotive als attributive, uneigentliche Darstellung im Sinne der Ikonographie der Erdteile zu verstehen, indem sie etwa als Menschenfresser*innen auf das Kannibal*innen-Stereotyp des Amerika-Diskurses hinweisen. Im Kontext von van Kessels Münchner Erdteile-Zyklus tragen die Strand-Darstellungen zur programmatischen Kernaussage bei, die den Zyklus als Beleg für das erkenntnisstiftende Potential der Malerei erscheinen lässt.

Ausblickend sei darauf hingewiesen, dass van Kessel exotische Kuriosa auf Stränden auch in autonomen Kompositionen darstellte. Beispielhaft dafür ist ein 1661 signiertes und datiertes Gemälde, das sich heute im Städel Museum in Frankfurt (Inv. Nr. 2167.) befindet. Es zeigt eine Anhäufung von Meerestieren im Vordergrund einer Bucht, hinter deren Öffnung zur See Schiffe zu sehen sind; im rechten Hintergrund ragt eine Kirche empor. Das Bild bringt einheimische Tiere mit Exoten und Fabelwesen zusammen; so sind im linken Mittelgrund ein Krokodil und mehrere Pinguine zu erkennen, während im rechten ein monströses Ungetüm an einen Wal erinnert. Insgesamt ergibt sich so auch hier ein symbolisch überhöhter Abriss der weltweiten Meeresfauna, der im Zeichen der europäischen Seefahrt und des christlichen Glaubens als Legitimation europäischer Vorherrschaft in der Welt steht. Als seine Bühne erscheint ein weiteres Mal der Strand.

Literaturverzeichnis

Baader, Hannah, und Gerhard Wolf (Hg.). *Das Meer, der Tausch und die Repräsentation*. Zürich und Berlin: diaphanes, 2010.

Baadj, Nadia. „A World of Materials in a Cabinet Without Drawers. Reframing Jan van Kessel's The Four Parts of the World". *Nederlands kunsthistorisch jaarboek* 62 (2012): 202–237.

Baadj, Nadia. *Jan van Kessel I (1626–79). Crafting a Natural History of Art in Early-Modern Antwerp*. London und Turnhout: Harvey Miller, 2016.

Baltrusch, Ernst. „Antike Horizonte. Die Aneignung des Meeres". *Europa und das Meer*. Katalog zur Ausstellung des Deutschen Historischen Museums. Hg. Dorlis Blume, Christian Brennecke, Ursula Breymayer und Thomas Eisentraut. München: Hirmer, 2018. 14–22.

Barthelmeß, Klaus. *Monstrum Horrendum. Wale und Waldarstellungen in der Druckgraphik des 16. Jahrhunderts und ihr motivkundlicher Einfluß*. 3 Bde. Hamburg: Kabel, 1991.

Bauernfeind, Robert. *Die Ordnung der Dinge durch die Malerei. Jan van Kessels Münchener Erdteile-Zyklus*. Augsburg: Opus Universität Augsburg, 2016.

Bredekamp, Horst. *Antikensehnsucht und Maschinenglauben. Die Geschichte der Kunstkammer und die Zukunft der Kunstgeschichte*. Berlin: Wagenbach, 2000.

Breymayer, Ursula. „Mentalitätswandel. Meer und Strand als Themen der Malerei". *Europa und das Meer*. Katalog zur Ausstellung des Deutschen Historischen Museums. Hg. Dorlis

Blume, Christian Brennecke, Ursula Breymayer und Thomas Eisentraut. München: Hirmer, 2018. 420–431.

Büttner, Nils. *Die Erfindung der Landschaft. Kosmographie und Landschaftskunst im Zeitalter Bruegels*. Göttingen: Vandenhoeck & Ruprecht, 2000.

Corbin, Alain. *Meereslust. Das Abendland und die Entdeckung der Küste*. Berlin: Wagenbach, 1990.

Ertz, Klaus. *Jan van Kessel der Ältere, 1626–1679, Jan van Kessel der Jüngere, 1654–1708, Jan van Kessel der Andere, ca. 1620–ca. 1661. Kritische Kataloge der Gemälde*. Lingen: Luca, 2012.

Faust, Ingrid. *Wale. Sirenen. Elefanten. Zoologische Einblattdrucke und Flugschriften vor 1800*. Bd. 4. Stuttgart: Hiersemann, 2002.

Faust, Ingrid. *Nashörner, Tapire, Pferdeartige, Sammelblätter, Monster. Zoologische Einblattdrucke und Flugschriften vor 1800*. Bd. 5. Stuttgart: Hiersemann, 2003.

Felfe, Robert, und Angelika Lozar (Hg.). *Frühneuzeitliche Sammlungspraxis und Literatur*. Berlin: Lukas, 2006.

Fischel, Angela. *Natur im Bild. Zeichnung und Naturerkenntnis bei Conrad Gessner und Ulisse Aldrovandi*. Berlin: Mann, 2009.

Frübis, Hildegard. *Die Wirklichkeit des Fremden. Die Darstellung der Neuen Welt im 16. Jahrhundert*. Berlin: Reimer, 1995.

Giepmans, Sabine E. „Vissen op het droge. Visstillevens an de waterkant door Jan van Kessel I (1626–1679)". *Standplaats: RDK*. Hg. Ingrid Brons. Zwolle: Waanders, 2001. 77–104.

Gormans, Andreas. „Ein eurozentrischer Blick auf die Welt, die Lust an der Malerei und die Macht der Erinnerung. Die Erdteilbilder Jan van Kessels in der Alten Pinakothek, München". *Das Bild als Autorität. Die normierende Kraft des Bildes*. Hg. Frank Büttner und Gabriele Wimböck. Münster: LIT Verlag, 2004. 363–400.

Greve, Anna. *Die Konstruktion Amerikas. Bilderpolitik in den* Grand Voyages *aus der Werkstatt de Bry*. Köln: Böhlau, 2004.

Giltaij, Jeroen (Hg.). *Herren der Meere – Meister der Kunst. Das holländische Seebild im 17. Jahrhundert*. Katalog zur Ausstellung des Museums Boijmans van Beuningen und der Gemäldegalerie Berlin. Rotterdam: Museum Boijmans van Beuningen, 1996.

Grote, Andreas (Hg.). *Macrocosmos in Microcosmo. Die Welt in der Stube. Zur Geschichte des Sammelns 1450 bis 1800*. Opladen: Leske + Budrich, 1994.

Koller, Ariane. *Weltbilder und die Ästhetik der Geographie. Die Offizin Blaeu und die niederländische Kartographie der Frühen Neuzeit*. Affalterbach: Didymos-Verlag, 2014.

Larsen, Erik. „Some Seventeenth-Century Paintings of Brazil". *The Connoisseur* 175 (1970): 123–131.

Leonhard, Karin. *Bildfelder. Stilleben und Naturstücke des 17. Jahrhunderts*. Berlin: Akademie-Verlag, 2013.

Minges, Klaus. *Das Sammlungswesen der Frühen Neuzeit. Kriterien der Ordnung und Spezialisierung*. Münster: LIT Verlag, 1998.

Müller Hofstede, Justus. „‚Non Saturatur Oculus Visu'. Zur *Allegorie des Gesichts* von Peter Paul Rubens und Jan Brueghel d.Ä". *Wort und Bild in der niederländischen Kunst und Literatur des 16. und 17. Jahrhunderts*. Hg. Herman W. J. Vekeman und Justus Müller Hofstede. Erfstadt: Lukassen, 1984. 243–289.

O'Neil Rife, Ellen. *The Exotic Gift and the Art of the Seventeenth-Century Dutch Republic*. Kansas: KU ScholarWorks, 2013.

Peil, Dietmar. „Das Neue ist das Alte. Antike Traditionen in den Emblembüchern des Joachim Camerarius". *Die Wahrnehmung des Neuen in Antike und Renaissance.* Hg. Achatz von Müller und Jürgen von Ungern-Sternberg. München: Saur, 2004. 134–166.

Richter, Dieter. *Das Meer. Geschichte der ältesten Landschaft.* Berlin: Wagenbach, 2014.

Ritter, Joachim. „Landschaft. Zur Funktion des Ästhetischen in der modernen Gesellschaft". *Subjektivität.* Frankfurt/Main: Suhrkamp, 1974. 141–166.

Schöne, Albrecht. *Emblematik und Drama im Zeitalter des Barock* [1964]. 3. Aufl. München: C. H. Beck, 1993.

Schütz, Karl. Frans Francken d. J. „Kunst- und Raritätenkammer, um 1620–25". *Das flämische Stillleben. 1550–1680.* Katalog zur Ausstellung des Kunsthistorischen Museums Wien und der Kulturstiftung Ruhr Essen. Hg. Wilfried Seipel. Lingen: Luca, 2002. 88.

Seelig, Gero (Hg.). *Die Menagerie der Medusa. Otto Marseus van Schrieck und die Gelehrten.* Katalog zur Ausstellung des Staatlichen Museums Schwerin. München: Hirmer, 2017.

Sitt, Martina (Hg.). *Segeln, was das Zeugt hält. Niederländische Gemälde des Goldenen Zeitalters.* Katalog zur Ausstellung der Hamburger Kunsthalle 2010. München: Hirmer, 2010.

Vignau-Wilberg, Thea. „Naturemblematik am Ende des 16. Jahrhunderts". *Jahrbuch der Kunsthistorischen Sammlungen in Wien* 82/83 (1986/87): 145–156.

Vignau-Wilberg, Thea. *Archetypa studiaque patris Georgii Hoefnagelii. 1592. Natur, Dichtung und Wissenschaft in der Kunst um 1600.* München: Staatliche Graphische Sammlung, 1994.

Wepler, Lisanne. *Bilderzählungen in der Vogelmalerei des niederländischen Barock.* Petersberg: Imhof, 2014.

Abbildungsnachweis

Abb. 1: Jan van Kessel. *Algier.* 1664–1666. Öl auf Kupfer, 14,5 x 21 cm. München, Alte Pinakothek. Abbildung in: Dante Martins Teixeira. *Brasil Holandês. A „Allegoria dos Continentes" de Jan van Kessel „o Velho" (1626–1679). Uma Visão Seiscentista da Fauna dos Quatro Cantos do Mundo.* Rio de Janeiro: Editora Index, 2002. 61.

Abb. 2: Adriaen Collaert. *Piscium Vivae Icones.* Nach 1598. Kupferstich, 12,6 x 18,8 cm. Abbildung in: Ann Diels und Marjolein Leesberg (Hg.). *The New Hollstein Dutch and Flemish Etchings, Engravings and Woodcuts. The Collaert Dynasty Vol. 6.* Ouderkerk aan den Ijssel: Sound and Vision, 2005. 160.

Abb. 3: Jan van Kessel. *Spitzbergen.* 1664 – 1666. Öl auf Kupfer, 14,5 x 21 cm. München, Alte Pinakothek. Abbildung in: Dante Martins Teixeira. *Brasil Holandês. A „Allegoria dos Continentes" de Jan van Kessel „o Velho" (1626–1679). Uma Visão Seiscentista da Fauna dos Quatro Cantos do Mundo.* Rio de Janeiro: Editora Index, 2002. 44.

Abb. 4: Anonym. *Glatthai.* 1613. Holzschnitt, 36,5 x 23,5 cm. Abbildung in: Ulisse Aldrovandi. *De piscibus libri V.* Bologna: Nicolas Thebaldinus, 1613. 388.

Abb. 5: Jan van Kessel. *Olinda.* 1664 – 1666. Öl auf Kupfer, 14,5 x 21 cm. München, Alte Pinakothek. Abbildung in: Dante Martins Teixeira. *Brasil Holandês. A „Allegoria dos Continentes" de Jan van Kessel „o Velho" (1626–1679). Uma Visão Seiscentista da Fauna dos Quatro Cantos do Mundo.* Rio de Janeiro: Editora Index, 2002. 73.

Abb. 6: Jan van Kessel. *Havanna*. 1664–1666. Öl auf Kupfer, 14,5 x 21 cm. München, Alte Pinakothek. Abbildung in: Dante Martins Teixeira. *Brasil Holandês. A „Allegoria dos Continentes" de Jan van Kessel „o Velho" (1626–1679). Uma Visão Seiscentista da Fauna dos Quatro Cantos do Mundo*. Rio de Janeiro: Editora Index, 2002. 92.

Abb. 7: Pieter Claesz. Soutman nach Peter Paul Rubens. *Jagd auf Nilpferd und Krokodil*. Nach 1624. Radierung und Kupferstich, 113,9 x 85,5 cm. Abbildung in: Nils Büttner und Ulrich Heinen (Hg.). *Peter Paul Rubens. Barocke Leidenschaften*. Katalog zur Ausstellung des Herzog-Anton-Ulrich-Museums, Braunschweig. München: Hirmer, 2004. 148.

Abb. 8: Jan van Kessel. *Europa*. 1664. Öl auf Kupfer, 77,6 x 109,8 cm. München, Alte Pinakothek. Abbildung in: Dante Martins Teixeira. *Brasil Holandês. A „Allegoria dos Continentes" de Jan van Kessel „o Velho" (1626–1679). Uma Visão Seiscentista da Fauna dos Quatro Cantos do Mundo*. Rio de Janeiro: Editora Index, 2002. 8.

Nadja Grasselli
SHORELINES & SPACES

This dramaturgy has been performed by Nadja Grasselli and Federico Robol 2018 at the conference *Narrating and Constructing the Beach* in the format of a reading with sounds. Besides being centred on the topic of the beach as liminal space, it focuses on the communication of academic and scientific matters through dramaturgical practice. An experiment of a dramaturgical *mapping* around the image of the beach, in the form of a compact overview: the beach is a border always in motion, between the known and the unknown, between dreams and abysses.

Dieser Text wurde 2018 auf der Konferenz *Narrating and Constructing the Beach* von Nadja Grasselli und Federico Robol in Form einer Lesung mit Sounds aufgeführt. Darin geht es um das Thema Strand als liminaler Raum, wie auch um die Übermittlung akademischer und wissenschaftlicher Inhalte mittels der dramaturgischen Arbeit. Ein Experiment eines dramaturgischen *mapping* rund um den Begriff Strand und seine Welten in Form eines kompakten Überblicks:
der Strand ist eine sich ständig bewegende Schwelle – zwischen Bekanntem und Unbekanntem, zwischen Träumen und Abgründen.

The shoreline between elements making up the world
is the shore space of clashes and folly
here   the precarious state of balance is challenged,
constantly.

Step by step
on the wooden ramp
through the plants
entering
the beach
the sand   burning your feet if you're not running fast enough
the sound   of those animals impossible to see, but always present,
a board with its own alphabet of colours, explaining the flattering flag:
red for sharks or waves or storms
yellow for sharks (but far away), waves (but not so high) or storms (but arriving in an hour)
blue for jelly fish or (yes) war ships
green – and you could risk to...
begin
floating.

Just after the plants,
protecting the continent from sand storms,
protecting the eye from that smashing sight,
protecting the spirit from the fear of the abyss –
the sea opens up.

The impulse to run into the water.
The exhaustion falling on the beach.
Digging with your hands in the dry sand
building   a mountain.
When does the moment come, when we call it a mountain?

Sand running through fingers –
time

millions of grains,
fragments of shells, finely shredded rock particles,
diameter from 0.0625 to 2 millimetres,
as small as I could imagine an atom,
imagine it transformed in glass, then glass in sand again,
imagine it transformed in transistors, in bricks, in concrete,
a house of sand,
by crashing: a cloud of gold dust in the midst of a city,
in front of it: a puddle with sharks.

The ocean is staring at me
like I am staring at the water,
like the person longing for inspiration,
scribbling in a book the lines of the waves,
a portrait of the never still-standing,
in colours,
in all of the different light moods, in all of the different latitudes, snow and tropics, in
all of the different seasons,
staring – for how long? –
erosion over thousands of years, water and wind,
hypnotized by this line far off,
from which traveling water is sent to the beach
in repetition,
same water and yet different,
the tide.
Since when?

Alone, in the middle of the flat beach,
there was a great horse on four wheels,
a wooden horse
with a shimmering golden harness,

a woman screaming
and the souls of dead warriors crowding the beach

a man screaming
and a desperate smell –
wo habe ich den Mann aus Melos ausgesetzt?

A new tide and the Hispaniola has anchored; but sure enough, there was the jolly roger flying from her peak
and a man, who walks in a limp.

I am alone on the beach again.
Not really alone,
the eyes of the crabs are staring at me
as I am still staring at the water.

A woman flying on a giant shell
– *even such a shell the universe itself* –
and in the sand the shellfish, trying to dig deeper,
trying to escape the small fingers
hold them so close to the eye,
hold them so close to the shell of the ear...
where is the sound we are longing for?
Des gärenden Schlammes geheimnisvoller Ton.
Over me screaming seagulls
and the pelican
feeding its progeny with its blood.

Gestrandet.
Stranded on the beach:
big whales, small fish, giant turtles, snakes, monsters,
damned creatures of the darkness tearing each other in pieces or pairing off, leviathans...
big whales, small fish, giant turtles, snakes, monsters,
screaming seagulls and the pelican
feeding its progeny with its blood.
Strandgut.
Dangerous vapours of soda,
plastic,
trash of all kinds.
And vessels of all kinds:
ships, canoes, little colourful boats, rubber boats,
and people on them
arriving from long trips, with bags and bags or with nothing,
and pirates, gentlemen, fishermen,
and people without boats
swimming

and people not swimming anymore,
women children men bodies corpses
and kids playing
a sand burial.

From the observation station beach
a certain amount of political worms is observing
observing   the ship
sinking
feeling   the stable ground under their feet
taking   a picture.

From workers of sand and algae
from the fear of unhealthy, risky, smelling dangerous vapours of soda,
to people in swimsuits,
putting all over around me their towels, chairs, elegant women and men,
– all women on one side, all the men on the other side –
beach machines, beach huts,
more people,
ein Strandkorb! Ist es nicht ein Strandwetter! Heute habe ich so richtig Strandlaune!
Otium and purification, invalids curing from diseases,
where has grandma gone?
Regeneration through water and sea side air –
but getting sick from stress of social formalization or just
bored.
More people!
Bringing now also air mattresses, big umbrellas,
people on surfboards, jet-skies, pedalò, beach outfits,
pronta per la prova costume? Who is that and why does she look like that?
Sometimes I'm afraid our beautiful beach town will lose its peculiarity because of this
coming and going!
Oh! today it is not permitted to bath in Rimini, the water is simply too dirty!
Doesn't matter, beach is not about water.
Beachboys and girls, beachqueens!, beachrats, beachbars, beachvolley, beachclub, sex
on the beach, beach party paradise planet, fireworks!, salsa, house, techno, goa, it's all
inclusive and bay watched;
in one corner, a couple is getting married "secretly",
the soundtrack is getting diamond-romantic,
more couples, but still an insider tip,
giving birth in Thailand
in the womb of the sea, while
the sun   goes down.

Mein Fräulein! sein Sie munter,
Das ist ein altes Stück;
Hier vorne geht sie unter
Und kehrt von hinten zurück.

Two suns come up.
Not taking dreams as reality, nor reality as folly.
Fallen asleep, the water surprised me, if I had not waken up, the tide would have caught me.

At night the beach is the kingdom of crabs.

The first time I came on shore, and began to look about me; how I gave myself over for lost; what dreadful apprehension I had, and how I lodged in the tree all night for fear of being devoured by wild beasts.

At night the beach is the kingdom of crabs,
animals between earth and water,
they come to cut me into pieces and eat me under the moonlight.
Imagination: the mother of all terrors.
They are hundreds, they've reached the beach so desperately crossing the big street,
half of them crashed dead spread on the street,
king crab legs,
the smell of fried shrimps,
after the coconut shrimps a shark steak,
Palm Beach, West Palm Beach, Miami Beach, Vero Beach, Daytona Beach
and the cars are almost parking on my head.

Places that are running against their disappearance,
resorts resorts resorts,
who cares if we demolish the soil, we can import sand from Australia!
The merchant of Venice is pricing a pound of sand.
The cape is sending its spacecrafts in the air,
connecting the elements of the world so absurdly.

There is no part of the world I feel like I am on a planet
more than when lying on the beach,
lying with arms and legs stretched as long as I can,
striving on one side to the sea
on the other to earth.
I put my ear on the sand
...
a deaf sound, millions of lives in fermentation,
the heart boiling sounds like an ocean far away,
together with the sounds of the wind it turns into a kind of apnoea, suffocation,
then   a subtle whistle
– seems stable but vibrates,
endless never ending,
deep sea animals sending messages I cannot get
talking about secrets   I will never discover, but I know they exist
and this is   why I want to know them.

The tide is calling.
The sand ground beneath me so compact,
I do stick to the ground with every cell of my body,
my eyes look up to the sky and on the border I can see the plants
protecting the beach line,
with their roots so deep in the earth, holding it against the strength of the wind, they
grow into my bulbs.
Stranded on this flat line is the only moment in life
I know the world is round,
lying with arms and legs stretched as long as I can,
striving on one side to the sea
on the other to earth,
a planet in the form of the eye of a fish,
the globe a giant living monster, causing with its breath – the one of a whale alike –
the tide.

The waves are touching my toes now.
I sit up in the water, the hands in the wet sand,
I am on the edge
of doubt and decision
leaving the safe harbour or not.
Die Anziehung der Untergänge,
die brennende Neugierde.
Unberechenbarkeit, Gesetzlosigkeit, Orientierungslosigkeit,
state of exception,
the closest to something you can just guess –
the closest to risk,
floods and tsunamis,
I am at the one end of the apparently never ending water,
end and beginning,
we already know we know nothing, but our own complexities.
I am the closest to all that is out of me
the closest to immensity, to the infinite.
The womb calling you back to chaos,
presence of absence, the closest to void,
to birth, to
death.

Where water comes to die on earth
we are caught in between worlds,
scared,
desiring
all of them – and all at the same time
we got sick not risking for even one
but we are still alive until we decide – at least –
to walk in the sand, to dance with Zorba,
to put   our toes carefully   in the water,

to put the ears on the sand – the heart still boiling:
Hier ist der Schlüssel zu allem.

On the threshold of the dream is the production of desires and imagination,
am Strandrand.
State of possibilities where everything bounds with imagination so far to fill the whole spirit and breathe, to fill every cell of your body like the sand you will carry home and find it after ages…
Here all gets to present, now
and already gone.
This liminal space makes us think of death,
survival to and in existence,
the only eternity we can acknowledge is the present,
if it needed a goal, then infinite repetition of the same
but always a bit different,
alterare, alterare, alterare,
like theater
or like
the tide.

Leipzig, early 2018

Quotes

"even such a shell the universe itself": Wordsworth, William: "The Sea Shell." *The Excursion. A Poem*. London: Edward Moxon, 1836. 155.

"[…] des gärenden Schlammes / geheimnisvollen Ton": Storm, Theodor. "Meeresstrand." *Gedichte, Novellen 1848–1867. Sämtliche Werke in vier Bänden, Bd. 1*. Eds. Karl Ernst Laage und Dieter Lohmeier. Frankfurt/Main: Deutscher Klassiker Verlag, 1987. 14–15.

"Mein Fräulein, sein Sie munter / das ist ein altes Stück / hier vorne geht sie unter / und kehrt von hinten zurück.": Heine, Heinrich: "Das Fräulein stand am Meere." *Neue Gedichte. Historisch-kritische Gesamtausgabe der Werke, Bd. 2*. Ed. Manfred Windfuhr. Hamburg: Hoffmann und Campe, 1983. 36–37.

"The first time I came on shore, and began to look about me; how I gave myself over for lost; […] what dreadful apprehension I had, and how I lodged in the tree all night for fear of being devoured by wild beasts.": Defoe, Daniel: *Robinson Crusoe*. London: J. Mawman, 1815. 204.

References to: A. Bioy Casares, H. Blumenberg, Borges and Guerrero, J. Conrad, A. Corbin, Deleuze and Guattari, J. W. Goethe, Homer, H. Ibsen, N. Kazantakis, M. Mari, H. Müller, E. A. Poe, M. Proust, W. Shakespeare, R. L. Stevenson, W. C. Williams.

Bodies in Time: Littoral Rhythms of Death and Desire

Roxanne Phillips
Time and Tide Again. Traces, Permeable Spaces and Sensory Perceptions of the Beach in Theodor Storm's *Aquis submersus* and HBO's *Big Little Lies*

This article traces the acoustic and the visual dimensions of beachscapes in Theodor Storm's *Aquis submersus* and HBO's *Big Little Lies* in order to reveal how the beach is narrated as a space that imprints itself on memory through recurring sensory perceptions. Both the novella and the miniseries construct their narratives around the beach as an acoustic, spatial and temporal aesthetic. To that end, they employ the tides as a figuration of time that collapses the boundary between past and present by merging sound and movement: While *Aquis submersus* translates the back-and-forth dynamic of the tides and thus of time into boundless rhythmic language, in *Big Little Lies* the repetitive and inherently traumatic structure of the waves unfolds in recurring visual and acoustic 'traces' of the past, in crosscutting and in a spectacular final montage sequence. [This article discusses representations of violence and rape.]

Dieser Aufsatz arbeitet die akustischen und visuellen Dimensionen von Strandlandschaften in Theodor Storms *Aquis submersus* und in der HBO-Serie *Big Little Lies* heraus, um offenzulegen, wie Strände darin als Räume erzählt werden, die sich mit wiederkehrenden Wahrnehmungsereignissen in das Gedächtnis einschreiben. Novelle und Miniserie bauen ihr Narrativ jeweils auf dem Strand als einer akustischen, räumlichen und zeitlichen Ästhetik auf und setzen dafür die Gezeiten als Figuration von Zeit ein. Wellengang, Ebbe und Flut lassen die Grenzen zwischen Vergangenheit und Gegenwart kollabieren, indem sie Geräusche und Bewegungen miteinander verschmelzen: Während *Aquis submersus* das Hin-und-Her der (Ge-)Zeiten in unbändige rhythmische Sprache übersetzt, entfaltet *Big Little Lies* die repetitive und inhärent traumatische Struktur wogender Wellen in wiederkehrenden visuellen und akustischen ‚Spuren' der Vergangenheit, in Kreuzschnitten sowie in einer spektakulären abschließenden Parallelmontagesequenz. [Dieser Artikel bespricht Darstellungen von Gewalt und Vergewaltigung.]

1 Sensing the Beach

Sensory perceptions accompany any trip to the shore. Gazing toward the horizon, where the sky and the sea melt into each other, we smell the breeze and taste the salt. When a soft murmuring wave breaks on the beach and retreats, sand oozes out from under our feet. The ground can be sludgy or springy; it may feel hard, at times even crunchy if our toes break through a salt-lined crust of clustered sand. Colors mingle, ever-changing: Does the water appear as light turquoise or as bright teal; is it the shade of midnight blue where its depth

https://doi.org/10.1515/9783110672244-014

increases or is it a stormy yellowish gray? Tiny grains, sharply blown across the beach, hit us like minuscule razor blades. Yet later, once the wind abates, the fine and silky sand softly caresses our skin as the sun warms us to the core.

Each moment spent by the beach and every act performed there augment our physical awareness and ensnare our senses. As Jennifer Webb notes:

> The inevitable engagement with the elements [at the beach] forces us to concentrate on the body as lived rather than as observed, because all the while the burning of sun and water and wind textures the skin itself, the ingestion of salt water affects the interior, and in every way the self turns out to become and to be experienced more as body, less as soul, and certainly less as machine. (Webb 2003, 85)

Our sensory perception is heightened at the beach and every time we visit the seashore, we revisit previous experiences of this physical entanglement with the elements. Even when recalling the beach from memory – when 'visiting' the shore in our imagination –, we might still hear the repetitive cries of seagulls pierce the sound of the roaring ocean. The beach is a space that imprints itself on our (corporeal) memory through an array of overlapping sensory perceptions. The familiar, yet extraordinary sounds, the feeling of wind and sand and water, the movement of the tides with their gentle back and forth: They all are revenants in time and remind us that we have felt, smelled, tasted, heard and seen all of this before, albeit with small differences.

This article explores the sensory perception of invasive acoustics and of visual movement as recurring constituents of beachscapes in literature and television. In what follows, two seemingly remote works of art meet: Theodor Storm's nineteenth-century novella *Aquis submersus* (1876) and HBO's miniseries *Big Little Lies* which first aired in 2017.[1] Separated by a rather tumultuous twentieth century and by virtue of using different media to tell their respective stories, Storm's description of the rugged North Frisian coast and the picture-perfect Californian shore in *Big Little Lies* both narrate and construct beaches that are severely haunted by time. Sensory perceptions – especially the sound, image and movement of waves – recall a complicated past in the novella and in the miniseries. In a way, the tides and the waves appear as a figuration of time

---

[1] HBO has since aired the second season of their Golden Globe- and Emmy-winning TV series *Big Little Lies* (under director Andrea Arnold who replaced Jean-Marc Vallée). While this technically means that it should no longer be considered a miniseries, *Big Little Lies* was initially promoted as one. In what has effectively become the first season of a limited series, the seven episodes unfold several interwoven plots into a continuous narrative arc and provide narrative closure. At the time of writing this article, the second season had not yet aired. Unclear in which direction the show might go, I opted to regard season 1 as a miniseries (Mittell 2010, 225–230).

itself. They collapse the boundaries between past and present by merging different sensory perceptions of the beach. *Aquis submersus* and *Big Little Lies* utilize this figuration of time and tide to explore the potential of the beach as a memoryscape and do so by self-reflexively employing narrative techniques unique to literature and television.

2 Traces in the Sand: The Beach as Memoryscape in *Big Little Lies*

Directed by Jean-Marc Vallée, *Big Little Lies* is set by the beach in Monterey, California, a seaside town seemingly populated by predominantly wealthy professionals and their families. Jane Chapman, a single mother played by Shailene Woodley, moves there with her six-year-old son Ziggy in search of a "better" life ("Serious Mothering" 2017). Ziggy, as it turns out, is the product of a rape, and it appears that Jane might have come to Monterey to find traces of the man who assaulted her. She befriends Madeline (Reese Witherspoon) and Celeste (Nicole Kidman) whose children respectively attend school with Ziggy. Both Madeline and Celeste live in exquisite, mansion-sized beachfront properties, but are financially dependent on their well-earning spouses and feel trapped in their "full-time mommy status" ("Somebody's Dead" 2017).

Celeste Wright seems to live a perfect marriage with Perry, an impression which is fostered by the couple's last name. The Wrights, for all intents and purposes, appear to be Mr. and Mrs. 'Right.' And yet, the *silent* 'w' in the surname subtly indicates not only that there is something *w*rong with their relationship, but also that Celeste keeps *quiet* about it: Under carefully applied makeup, she hides the bruises she sustains as a victim of spousal abuse. Over the course of the episodes, she suffers both physical and psychological harm as well as marital rape by her husband Perry (Alexander Skarsgård). Echoing this violence, there is an issue with bullying at the children's school. A girl is bitten by a classmate and sustains marks on her neck from being choked. Jane's son Ziggy – the new element in Monterey and thus considered with suspicion – is blamed. The marks on Amabella's neck correspond to the bruises on Celeste's body. As the story develops, these marks both converge with the traces that Jane is looking for: The violent behavior at school originates from Max, Celeste and Perry's son, and thus can be traced back to the abusive husband; and finally, it turns out that Perry was the man who raped Jane years before.

With such narrative significance placed on traces, it comes as no surprise that HBO's *Big Little Lies* can be classified as a whodunit. The intertwining stories of the main characters in the narrative present are framed by flash-forwards to a police inquiry into a homicide at the school fundraiser. Calling on the audience to find clues and to pursue traces from the very beginning, the show withholds the identity of both the murderer and the murder victim until episode 7, yet aptly names the first episode "Somebody's Dead" to create suspense and encourage audience participation. The detectives on the case also follow traces, for example, by conducting interviews with witnesses throughout the episodes. The mostly negative assessments made during these witness snapshots contrast starkly with the complexity of the main characters' lives as told over the course of the miniseries. While they contribute nothing to solving the murder, they give shape to a community in which everybody is obsessed with other people's business, constantly judging and monitoring acquaintances, neighbors, other parents and so-called friends.

HBO's miniseries is based on Liane Moriarty's 2014 novel *Big Little Lies*. Several changes were made for the adaptation. Notably, the HBO narrative is more determined to label Jane's one-night stand as rape with forced erotic asphyxiation. Also, representations of thought processes differ in the miniseries to effect a stronger involvement of the audience with respect to the multiple whodunits. Interiorization in the prose version frequently takes the form of free indirect speech: "Then [the two mothers] introduced themselves to Jane, and Jane had a story to tell about Madeline's ankle, and next thing the kindergarten teacher, Miss Barnes, wanted to hear, and Jane found herself the centre of attention, *which was quite pleasant to be honest.*" (Moriarty 2014, 23 [emphasis mine]) In HBO's adaptation, information about the characters' intimate thoughts must be pieced together by the viewers. For example, close-ups or (rearview) mirror shots frame and study the characters' facial expressions but ultimately fail to penetrate their facades and decode the visible signs of emotion. The audience is called upon to participate. Though the viewers cannot know the characters' thought processes with certainty, or rather because such filming techniques make the viewers acutely aware of their lack of knowledge, they are provoked to follow facial traits as if they were traces in order to make deductions that solve the whodunit(s).

However, the most relevant difference for this article concerns the fact that the beach plays a much more pivotal role in the miniseries than it does in Moriarty's novel. Initially, the depiction of pristine beaches and dazzling coastal landscapes in HBO's *Big Little Lies* relies on a well-marketed seaside fantasy (Taussig 2000, 252–257): Following the eighteenth-century 'invention of the beach,' as Alain Corbin (1994, 250–281) puts it, the shore underwent a remarkable career.

Technological developments from rail travel to cruise ships, from cars to affordable airfares democratized tourism ever further, first turning the beach into and then ensuring its continuing appeal as *the* prime holiday destination. Offering aesthetically pleasing landscapes of relaxation as well as sportive enjoyment, how blessed one might be to call the beach one's home! The miniseries draws on this association when it presents the formidable beachfront properties Celeste or Madeline inhabit with their families. Nonetheless, the beaches in *Big Little Lies* often become the stage for family disputes or set the scene for the characters' inner torment. For instance, when Jane spends time by the shore with her son in "Push Comes to Shove" (2017), the scene calls upon the positive image of beachscapes first. Their happy, sun-kissed and fun-filled time is ruptured suddenly (and painfully) when Ziggy is hit in the face by a baseball. Adding insult to injury, Jane tells him soon after that he will be seeing a child psychologist – upon recommendation by his teacher, who suspects Ziggy to be the class bully.

Marking another instance of both inner and physical torment set at the beach, Jane's rape occurs in a hotel room overlooking the ocean. Before the rape is revealed in the third episode, "Living the Dream" (2017), the two previous installments already present short, disjointed flashbacks of that night as well as sequences of Jane running and following shoe prints in the sand. They repeat throughout the episodes. In Jane's recurring visualizations of pursuing the attacker (and his traces) along the beach she is, at times, carrying a revolver. In the episode "Push Comes to Shove," spray splashes noisily as the camera follows a wave arriving on the still surface of the sand. A cut brings the viewer to a close-up of Jane's pensive face, eyes unblinking, as she lies in bed in the narrative present. A series of fast cuts then reveals what she is visualizing: Jane's imagined gaze and by extension the viewer's actual gaze, guided by the subjective camera, follow imprints made by shoes in the sand. As the handheld camera pursues the traces, the translucent image of a man in a suit appears in the center, only to fade away once Jane runs into the shot, barefoot and disheveled. Directed at 'running' Jane, the camera's gaze still corresponds to that of 'imagining' Jane (in bed), thus the doubling of her character implies a dissociative split. In fact, the running sequences represent Jane's coping narrative, a way to distance herself from the rape.

Fig. 1: Jane, with revolver, chasing traces of a fading ghost ("Push Comes to Shove" 2017).

By pulling the viewers in via an initial subjective shot, the camera work allies them with Jane, asks them to participate in her search for the assailant and to follow his (vanishing) traces. As the traces leave clues and alert the audience, they function as one of the main structural elements of the whodunit. But they also serve a purpose for the depiction of memory. Like the marks left on Amabella and Celeste that conspicuously reveal abuse but fade over time, the assailant has faded from Jane's memory. As she is unable to remember his face ("Push Comes to Shove" 2017), his image appears as translucent in her imagination, too, and ultimately escapes her: His shape vanishes. The traces lead nowhere, or rather to a memory blockage.

The materiality of the traces left in the sand varies over the course of *Big Little Lies*. Some imprints have crisp and clear contours, others are washed out by the ocean. Connected as they are with the depiction of remembering the rape, their altering form gives shape to how Jane's memory work is both enabled and blocked specifically *by the beach* as "a remembered place or a place that provokes characters to remember." (Rohdie 2002, 99) Yet, as Sam Rohdie, speaking about Federico Fellini's beachscapes, observes further, the beach "is also where memory may be blocked [...]" (ibid.). In *Big Little Lies*, the beach similarly appears as a location for memory, or more precisely for traumatic memory work. On the one hand, Jane is struggling to remember what her assailant looked like. So when she follows his trace, chasing him across the shore, and the ghost-like apparition vanishes, this representation mirrors her search for and her inability to recall the attacker's face. Her memory is partially blocked. Such gaps in recollection, as is known, can occur when traumatic events have taken place. An event of that sort cannot be "assimilated or experienced fully at the time," as Cathy Caruth (1995, 4) notes. Because it cannot be understood completely, the event (or a part of it) is "marked by its lack of registration" (ibid., 6). Accordingly, the rape is 'present' in the episodes of *Big Little Lies* only as a trace, as a marked absence or a gap at first – untold by Jane and therefore unknown to her friends and the viewers.

On the other hand, the beach also provokes Jane to *remember* the events of the past twofold because the beach is experienced in an inherently physical way. It refers back to the body, to the senses and to perception. As Susan J. Brison (1999, 42) points out, traumatic memories are equally "dependent on sensory representations" because the traumatic experience itself is "tied to the body." So the beach triggers Jane's memory of the rape firstly because she is physically at the beach and experiencing the sound and sight of the waves again, as she did on the night of the rape. And secondly, the fact that the sensory perceptions experienced at the beach repeat constantly – with depictions of waves rolling in and crashing noisily, again and again and again throughout the episodes – prompts the trauma to resurface as it mirrors the structure of traumatic repetition itself. The return of the event then forces the coping narrative to repeat over and over again, too.

The acoustic and visual repetitions connected to the beach and depicted in *Big Little Lies* also form a distinctive sound and viewing experience for the audience. Not only do they appeal to the viewers' sensory perceptions, but they indeed inscribe themselves on the audience over the course of the episodes: Aired in weekly installments, beach sounds and motions leave their own mark. Whenever this specific set of audiovisual traces reappears, imprinted as it becomes on viewers' memories from one week to the next, the audience knows that the miniseries is moving closer and closer to the climactic solving of the whodunit itself and thus closer to filling *their* gap in knowledge.

In the meantime, Jane appears trapped in an endless aural and visual loop as trauma and coping narrative both revolve around the repetitive sensory perceptions connected to the beach. The episode "Push Comes to Shove" (2017) cuts from the coping narrative to Jane actually jogging on the beach, presumably earlier that day, and forward again to the narrative present with her in bed at night; the cross cut repeats. All the while, the only sound that can be heard is that of murmuring waves at a distance mingled with Jane's breathing in the narrative present. The visual movement of the camera – shifting back and forth, mirroring the movement of the waves themselves – is translated or rather *echoed* in a double soundscape: Jane's inhalation and exhalation overlap with the sound of waves rolling up and down the beach.[2] Originally occurring at several points in time and in different locations, the acoustic and visual perceptions merge into one experience of immediacy during which everything happens simultaneously.

Referring to Sigmund Freud, Caruth (1995, 9) states that "the impact of the traumatic event lies [...] in its refusal to be simply located, in its insistent appearance outside the boundaries of any single place or time." It would seem that the beach, in itself an intangible border, lends itself to the representation of trauma for precisely this reason. The visual and the acoustic in *Big Little Lies* converge on one double, repetitive movement that could be considered as symptomatic for both the repetitive structure of traumatic memory and for the beach itself: in and out (breathing), back and forth (camera and time), up and down (waves), on an endless loop. Even the structure of the show as a whodunit relates to this motion. The events in the miniseries are presented in a non-linear fashion with back-and-forth cross cuts between flash-forwards (the police investigation of the homicide), flashbacks (Jane's rape), and the narrative present, i. e., the events leading up to the murder, and thus the upcoming revelation of the murder victim, of the murderer and of Jane's attacker.

3 Revenants in Time: Submerging and Resurfacing in *Aquis submersus*

Halfway around the globe and many years prior, Theodor Storm, the German realist known for his engagement with the porous and ever-changing North Sea scenery, published *Aquis submersus* (1876). As Thomas Mann once noted, when Storm's fiction looks back at the landscapes of his native North Frisia, it does so with pronounced nostalgia. Therein, the past appears as irretrievably lost, often taking the shape of "[das] Versunkene" (Mann 1974, 253)[3] – of something explicitly

---

[2] The French historian Jules Michelet's influential study *La mer* dating from 1861 already calls the tides the 'respiration' of the sea (1875, 31): "The advantage we gain from the cliffs is this, that at the foot of their lofty walls we can appreciate much more sensibly than elsewhere the tidal motion, the respiration, or, let us say, the pulse of the Sea. Imperceptible in the Mediterranean, it is strongly marked in the Ocean. Ocean breathes as we do – in harmony with our internal movement, with that from on high. It compels us to count incessantly with it, to compute the days and hours, to look up to heaven."
[3] Others have drawn similar connections (Detering 2001, 106; Strowick 2013, 55–56). Mann writes: "Um seine [i. e. Storm's] Heimatlichkeit ist es etwas dichterisch Sonderbares, der Philister könnte sie hysterisch finden, sie ist wesentlich Sehnsucht, Nostalgie, ein Heimweh, das

submerged in water, metaphorically speaking. But as seascapes do not appear center stage in *Aquis submersus*, little attention has been drawn to them or to the tides and the waves as figurations of a permeable border between past and present or between life and death so far. The beach, however, emerges at a prominent moment at the very end of the novella and reveals that it was present all along as a barely perceptible sensory trace – as an undercurrent that shapes the poetics of *Aquis submersus*, as I would like to propose.

In the frame story of the novella, an unnamed narrator remembers his childhood in North Frisia. He encounters a *memento mori* portrait of a dead boy adorned by an enigmatic inscription, "C. P. A. S." (Storm 1998, 382), which he cannot decode. After many years, the now adult narrator comes across a manuscript which promises to decipher the inscription. Those papers, dating back to the seventeenth century, contain the memories of the painter of said portrait, an artist named Johannes. Told as story within the story, the two-part manuscript recounts Johannes's life. Having spent time abroad learning the trade, he returns to his foster father Gerhardus, who has passed away unexpectedly. Johannes falls in love with Gerhardus's daughter Katharina; they spend a night together, after which he asks for her hand in marriage. But Johannes is not of aristocratic descent. Once the illicit rendezvous comes to light, Katharina's brother Wulf attacks him and chases him away. When Johannes returns to search for Katharina, she has vanished without a trace. All the while, he is unaware of the fact (as is the reader) that their tryst resulted in a pregnancy.

Years later, Johannes is commissioned to paint a pastor in a coastal village. This priest turns out to be Katharina's husband and raising a young boy who, eerily enough, is named Johannes, too. The painter soon comes to realize that this is *his* son. Johannes finally finds Katharina and professes his love to her. While the biological parents take their eyes off the playing boy, he drowns in a nearby pond. Grief-stricken, Johannes creates a painting of his child's corpse and adds the inscription 'C. P. A. S.,' "Culpa Patris Aquis Submersus," meaning 'drowned' or 'submerged in water through the fault of the father' (ibid., 453).

---

durch keine Realität zu stillen ist, denn sie richtet sich durchaus aufs Vergangene, Versunkene, Verlorene. [...] Es ist gemüthaft oder, wenn man will, sentimental in einem etwas krankhaften Sinn, wenn man die Gleichsetzung von Vergangenheit und Heimat ein wenig krankhaft nennen darf [...]" (Mann 1974, 253). Mann calls Storm's attachment to his native home – "seine Heimatlichkeit" – essentially a longing or a homesickness directed toward that which has passed, that which has sunk and that which is lost. Furthermore, he notes that past and native place are interchangeable for Storm, which is why they can both be viewed as 'sunken.' To my knowledge however, the *Aquis submersus*-scholarship has not focused on "[das] Versunkene" quite in the way I intend here.

The demise of the child is but one death by drowning in the novella. Drowning appears as a curse that haunts Katharina's bloodline and foreshadows the boy's death: One of Katharina's ancestors drowns herself in a pond behind the house after falling in love with a man of the wrong social standing, too, and being cursed for it by her unforgiving mother (ibid., 407–408). The novella has a similar fate in store for Katharina's illicit child. While examining common facial traits in Katharina's ancestral portrait gallery, Johannes realizes the similarly unkind and uncanny physiognomy of Katharina's hostile brother and the cruel ancestor; both possess small, narrow eyes and piercing stares. Not realizing the quasi prophetic nature of his words, Johannes exclaims: "Wie räthselhafte Wege gehet die Natur! Ein saeculum und drüber rinnt es [i. e. das kleine Auge] heimlich wie unter einer Decke im Blute der Geschlechter fort; dann, längst vergessen, taucht es plötzlich wieder auf, den Lebenden zum Unheil."[4] (Ibid., 402) The facial trait of small, cruel eyes, which doubles as a sign for the drowning curse, disappears, only to resurface a century later in another family member (Strowick 2013, 55). Fittingly, the novella describes the submerged, yet resurfacing drowning curse with a water metaphor. The curse 'flows' "drüber," 'over' or maybe 'across' the centuries and simultaneously trickles "heimlich wie unter einer Decke," 'under' or 'below' the surface, like a secret or uncanny undercurrent.[5] Once the eyes emerge again in Wulf, doom follows and Katharina's child drowns. In this contrastive dynamic, the curse figuratively resurfacing from the depths of time causes a literal death by drowning, i. e., by sinking into watery depths. Time and water in *Aquis submersus* are closely linked to each other via this movement of disappearance and emergence. Submerging and resurfacing comprise a curiously inverted and inverting motion throughout the novella.

A second foreboding tale of the past in *Aquis submersus* refers to the disastrous Burchardi flood of 1634 during which an estimated eight thousand people and more than fifty thousand livestock drowned on the North Frisian coast (Wade 1995, 57–58). The flood tore apart the island Strand – literally meaning 'beach' – and thus formed two separate islands, Pellworm and Nordstrand. Taking into account the etymology of the word for beach, this appears as a near

---

[4] Johannes is speaking about a familial trait of small eyes: "What mysterious routes Nature takes! Sometimes, for a century and more, running as though hidden under cover though the blood of generations, then, long forgotten, suddenly emerging again to trouble the living." (Storm 2015, 53)

[5] Storm, as Christian Begemann observes, was acutely aware of and repeatedly staged the nuanced play of the words *heimlich / heimelig* ('secret,' but also 'homey') and *unheimlich* ('uncanny') that Freud was to develop into his conception of the uncanny many years later (Begemann 2013, 35).

performative act. *Strand* is thought to have been appropriated from Scandinavian languages in the late thirteenth century. In Norse, *strind* means 'edge, side, border' (Pfeifer et al. "Strand"); its root being *strā-*, signifying 'spreading, disseminating' (Pfeifer et al. "Streuen").[6] So *Strand* occupies both the edge of the sea and of the land; the beach penetrates into the ocean, simultaneously forming an area that is moved and scattered by the water. In an eerie way, the island Strand called forth its own dispersal.

Furthermore, the etymology suggests that the beach, steadily invaded by the sea, constitutes a permeable and thus constantly changing landscape. Periodically being submerged by water and reemerging again with the rise and fall of sea levels, the beach forms an unsteady border that moves with the tides and is displaced over time to potentially catastrophic results for coastal inhabitants. Storm's fiction is acutely aware of the changing and often destructive nature of beachscapes, thus it comes as no surprise that *Aquis submersus* invokes these strange and unstable boundaries. The description of the 1634 Burchardi flood, for example, connects time and tides to the fragile border between life and death:

> Es mußte eben Fluth sein; denn die Watten waren überströmet und das Meer stund wie ein lichtes Silber. Da ich anmerkete, wie oberhalb desselben die Spitze des Festlandes und von der andern Seite diejenige der Insel sich gegen einander strecketen, wies der Küster auf die Wasserfläche, so dazwischen liegt. "Dort," sagte er, "hat einst meiner Eltern Haus gestanden; aber anno 34 bei der großen Fluth trieb es gleich hundert anderen in den grimmen Wassern; auf der einen Hälfte des Daches ward ich an diesen Strand geworfen, auf der anderen fuhren Vater und Bruder in die Ewigkeit hinaus."[7] (Storm 1998, 436–437)

The sexton's father and brother drown in the raging waters; he himself is miraculously saved. While Helga Bleckwenn (2003, 82) emphasizes the link between the flood, transience, forgetting, and sinking away into the past, it should be noted that the past also *resurfaces* here. The deaths are quite literally a moment of submersion, but the sexton's remembrance allows the dead to reemerge, to

---

[6] Jacob and Wilhelm Grimm's dictionary *Deutsches Wörterbuch* takes the etymology even a step further, noting that the word *Strand* has in and of itself 'spread' or disseminated through the German language (Grimm and Grimm 1957).

[7] "It must have been about high tide; for the mudflats were covered and the sea upon them stood a bright silver. When I remarked how from the other side of the church the tip of the mainland and that of the island stretched towards each other on the surface of the water, the sexton pointed to the extent of water lying between them. 'My parents' cottage once stood there,' he said, 'but in the great flood of '34 it was carried away by the raging waters along with hundreds of others. I was thrown up onto these shores on one half of the roof, but on the other my father and brother were washed into eternity.'" (Storm 2015, 83)

become present once more in words, in narration. The deceased and, more broadly, the past – which had sunk into the depths of both the sea and time – reappear as the tides come into play: Once Johannes observes that it is high tide and the sexton elaborates on the ever-changing shape of the coast, the past resurfaces. As the waves do in *Big Little Lies*, the tides in *Aquis submersus* periodically uncover the past. In the novella, the movement of the water marks the border between past and present as a highly unstable, even porous one. Things from the past can suddenly emerge in the present and haunt it (Detering 2001, 133) – people, curses, facial traits, paintings or even enigmatic inscriptions become revenants in time.

4 Tidal Poetics: Visual vs. Aural Perception in *Aquis submersus*

Time comprises a double movement in *Aquis submersus*. It is a dynamic of repetition staged as a recurring shift back *and* forth, as something rising from the depths *and* falling back into them. However, this operation is not restricted to time alone. Elisabeth Strowick (2013, 55–57) aptly points out that the structural double movement of back and forth is figured in the revenant character of "aquis submersus," i. e., in the formulaic repetition of these words surfacing and disappearing repeatedly throughout the novella. Taking this as a point of departure, I argue that the recurring phrase 'aquis submersus' embodies the poetics of the novella and that it originates in the sensory perception of the waves and the tides.

One painting makes the dynamic movement especially apparent and strikingly reveals a connection to the sea. Working on Katharina's portrait, Johannes describes the process as a flow of rising and falling, as a back and forth:

> [...] dabei blühete *aus dem dunkeln Grund* des Bildes immer süßer das holde Antlitz *auf*; mir schien's, als sei es kaum mein eigenes Werk. – Mitunter war's, als schaue mich etwas heiß aus ihren Augen an; doch wollte ich es dann fassen, *so floh es scheu zurück*; und dennoch *floß es durch den Pinsel heimlich auf die Leinewand*, so daß mir selber kaum bewußt ein sinnberückend Bild entstand, wie nie zuvor und nie nachher ein solches aus meiner Hand gegangen ist.[8] (Storm 1998, 406 [emphasis mine])

---

[8] "[...] and *out of the painting's dark background* the beloved face blossomed ever more sweetly; it seemed to be hardly my own work. Occasionally it was as though there was something warm looking at me in her eyes; yet when I tried to capture it, *it shyly flew away*; although *it flowed secretly through the brush on to the canvas*, so that without my knowing it a deeply

Katharina's face emerges from the dark depths of the painting, rising upward. Johannes is under the impression that something is looking directly at him from 'within' her eyes, yet it retreats as soon as he attempts to capture it. Nonetheless, it secretly 'flows' through his brush and onto the canvas, referencing a stream of water. Such a dynamic of emergence and retreat also constitutes the beach: as the movement of ebb and flow, as the rise and fall, the back and forth of the waves on a sandy surface. It engenders a sensory perception encountered very specifically at the beach where bodies are rocked by waves; where water is both seen and heard submerging the beach and retreating back into the depths of the ocean with the tides.

So how does sensory perception work in the novella? It is paramount to take into account that the narrator of the story within the story, Johannes, is a *painter* – somebody who operates within the visual media. The story is conveyed through his eyes, a painter's eyes, which is why spaces are often described as landscapes that one might paint:[9]

> Als ich auf den Kirchhof kam, trug von der Stadtseite der Wind ein wimmernd Glockenläuten an mein Ohr; ich aber wandte mich und blickte hinab nach Westen, wo wiederum das Meer wie lichtes Silber am Himmelssaume hinfloß, und war doch ein tobend Unheil dort gewesen, worin in einer Nacht des Höchsten Hand viel tausend Menschenleben hingeworfen hatte.[10] (Ibid., 445)

When the novella, which largely consists of the painter's manuscript, talks of the ocean or the beach, it does so by describing and thus creating space; by verbally visualizing a scenery. Johannes focuses on the images the landscapes present and on the stories these images invoke, like the Burchardi flood. For the most part, he is not very attentive to acoustic sensations – in this case, he physically turns away from the sound of the church bells. He is first and foremost a creature of the visual, not of the acoustic.

---

affecting portrait came into being like nothing that ever came from my hand before or since" (Storm 2015, 56 [emphasis mine]). Unfortunately, the translation does not quite capture the movement contained in the original.
9 I would like to thank the 2018 participants of Annette Keck's Oberseminar at LMU Munich for the discussions and observations about the medium of painting in *Aquis submersus*. Their valuable input helped shape this paper in its early stages.
10 "When I came to the churchyard, the wind, from the direction of the town, carried the faint sound of bells to my ear; but I turned and looked down toward the west where the sea like bright silver flowed on continuously into the edge of the sky; and yet had there not been a raging disaster there one night, in which many thousands of human lives had been lost at the hand of the Almighty?" (Storm 2015, 90)

As *Aquis submersus* constantly describes paintings, portraits and images from Johannes's time that appear again in the frame story, initially, the narrative appears to be carried and dominated by the visual media. While visuality certainly encodes the dynamic of a sunken past reemerging, this movement is also expressed in aural perceptions, especially in the sound of water – there is an aural undercurrent that 'leaks' through the entire novella.[11] This sound takes its cue from waves repeatedly submerging the beach and then retreating, from the sea continuously infiltrating the landscape and receding.[12] For instance, in the moment preceding Johannes's realization that the pastor's young boy has Katharina's eyes and she must be close by, he describes his thoughts as restlessly drifting toward her as if on a dark stream, "wie auf einem dunklen Strome" (Storm 1998, 440). Katharina is where his thoughts always find "Rast und Unrast" (ibid., 440), rest and unrest. Firstly, the phrase "Rast und Unrast" illustrates the dynamic of waves themselves, restlessly crashing, as they do, onto the beach, but also resting or halting their movement for a split second before being pulled back in the opposite direction. Secondly, this choice of words mirrors the double movement of a back and forth dynamic by describing two contradictory, yet related terms – a semantic inversion. And thirdly, the syllables themselves are arranged as a to-and-fro *sound* with a turning point: Rast-un-(d)-Un-rast. The aesthetic dynamic of *Aquis submersus* announced here as a flow of moving back and forth, of rising and falling has an often overheard, but distinct acoustic dimension.

Not long after, while painting his child's portrait in a room overlooking the beach, Johannes has an uncanny auditory hallucination. Hoping against reason that an audible trace of life still persists in his son, he hears "leise Odemzüge"

---

[11] The sensory perception of water – the sight, movement *and sound* of water – often converges on Katharina and Johannes (Cunningham 1978, 42): When young Johannes meets Katharina in the forest, her hair looks like cascading water and she leaves a trace of tears. Departing hastily, her movement causes branches to swoosh, "die Zweige rauschen" (Storm 1998, 392) – 'rauschen' is an onomatopoetic word connected to the sound of water in German. When they unwittingly conceive the child, Johannes hears "das Rauschen des Wässerleins, das hinten um die Hecken fließt" (ibid., 419); he hears water outside, presumably close to the pond in which Katharina's ancestor drowned. And later still, after the boy's death, Johannes hears something 'rauschen' behind a door – it is Katharina falling to the ground (ibid., 454).

[12] Helga Bleckwenn (2003, 79) makes note of the fact that in *Aquis submersus* different bodies of water like the ocean and the pond are merged on a metaphorical level. This is less surprising when one considers that the North Frisian landscape is thoroughly marked by the sea: Its brackish waters constantly penetrate the earth, creating ponds, rivulets, swamps and the like (see the article by Christian Begemann in this volume). That being said, I propose that *Aquis submersus* does not stop here, but also incorporates other fluids like tears, paint and even blood into its watery dynamic.

(ibid., 452) coming from the corpse as if the boy was breathing in and out. It is a sound modeled on waves or on the 'respiration' of the sea; a sound that the viewer encounters in *Big Little Lies* as well. Soon after, Johannes adds the enigmatic inscription 'C. P. A. S.' to the portrait:

> Dann *tauchete* ich meinen Pinsel in ein dunkles Roth und schrieb unten in den Schatten des Bildes die Buchstaben: C. P. A. S. Das sollte heißen: Culpa Patris Aquis Submersus, "Durch Vaters Schuld in der Fluth versunken." – Und *mit dem Schalle dieser Worte in meinem Ohre*, die wie ein schneidend Schwert durch meine Seele fuhren, malete ich das Bild zu Ende.[13] (Ibid., 453 [emphasis mine])

The brush is immersed or submerged in the red paint, and once it resurfaces, the letters 'C. P. A. S.' reappear in the novella, too. Johannes traces the letters in red, symbolizing the blood on his hands, on the bottom edge of the portrait. His actions ultimately have effected the child's death by drowning. The inscription 'C. P. A. S.' now no longer represents a string of coded letters, four signifiers without reference – this is the moment in which Johannes deciphers the letters and bestows them with meaning. They become language for the frame narrator reading Johannes's manuscript and subsequently for Storm's readers as well. And thus the phrase is also endowed with a new sound as Johannes hears the words, not the letters painfully reverberating in his mind while he finishes his painting. The manuscript ends with his sensory perceptions shifting away from the visual and toward sound once more as he leaves the village:

> Noch einmal wandte ich mich um und schaute nach dem Dorf zurück, das nur noch wie Schatten aus dem Abenddunkel ragte. Dort lag mein todtes Kind – Katharina – Alles, Alles! – Meine alte Wunde brannte mir in meiner Brust; *und seltsam, was ich niemals hier vernommen, ich wurde plötzlich mir bewußt, daß ich vom fernen Strand die Brandung tosen hörete.* Kein Mensch begegnete mir, keines Vogels Ruf vernahm ich; aber *aus dem dumpfen Brausen des Meeres tönete es mir immerfort, gleich einem finstern Wiegenliede: Aquis submersus – aquis submersus!*[14] (Ibid., 454–455 [emphasis mine])

---

[13] "Then I *dipped* my brush in a dark red and wrote below in the shadow of the picture the letters: C. P. A. S., which was to mean: Culpa Patris Aquis Submersus. 'Drowned through the fault of the father.' *And with these words ringing in my ears* and cutting into my soul like a sharp sword, I finished the painting." (Storm 2015, 98 [emphasis mine])

[14] "I turned once more and looked back towards the village, which looked like a mass of shadows out of the dusk. There lay my dead child – Katharina – everything, everything! My old wound burned in my breast; *and strangely, something I had never been aware of before, I was suddenly conscious that I could hear the breaking of the waves on the distant shore.* I met no one, heard not a bird call; *but the dull roar of the sea constantly sounded in my ears like a grim lullaby: Aquis submersus – Aquis submersus!*" (Storm 2015, 99 [emphasis mine])

Reflecting on the painful memory of having found and yet lost both Katharina and his child, Johannes realizes for the first time that the thunderous roll of the sea must have accompanied him all along. He does not see the beach, but once more the surge evokes the movement of back and forth. It is incorporated in the repetitive sound of the waves and is subsequently translated into the rhythmic intonation of repeated words: "Aquis submersus – aquis submersus!" (ibid., 455), the meter of which might be considered an iambic one. Short long short long short, or fall rise fall rise fall.[15] To pick up on the expression describing the familial curse earlier in the novella, the "aquis submersus"-phrase is hidden within the 'C. P. A. S.'-enigma as a secret, an uncanny undercurrent. Thus, it is unveiled as an aural and rhythmic trace which now accompanies the painter much in the same way as the sound and rhythm of the sea do, too. Phrase and sea both reiterate the twofold movement of Katharina (and the child) resurfacing into Johannes's life again, only to drop out once more. The words echo this narrative dynamic as well as the rhythmic rise and fall of the sea level, the sound and the movement of waves.

Finally hearing and perceiving the sounds of the beach – where time figuratively becomes the tides –, the memory of those who were both literally and metaphorically submerged is repeatedly uncovered. By conjuring up his son's death, which the novella eerily foreshadowed by retelling the story of the Burchardi flood victims (who died in the exact waters that Johannes hears now), the surge in *Aquis submersus* reveals itself as a dynamic of time and tide again.

---

15 The assessment of the meter is tricky business considering the third metric foot is incomplete – so reading it as iambic is just a proposal that takes into account the *muta cum liquida* breve (sub-mer) and that Latin meter is derived from syllable length, not stress. The exact analysis of the meter would raise a series of questions that is nearly impossible to answer: Which style of Latin was Storm familiar with and how might the words '*aquis submersus*' have been pronounced in the nineteenth century? Bearing in mind that the novella differentiates Johannes's seventeenth-century manuscript from the nineteenth-century frame story by use of an antiquated style of German, the narrator Johannes's Latin might even be pronounced as it would have been in the seventeenth century. But as vulgar Latin or as church Latin? The matter is complicated even further if the contentious debate concerning the proper pronunciation of Latin during Storm's lifetime is accounted for – consider the influential volumes by Wilhelm Paul Corssen *Über Aussprache, Vokalismus und Betonung der Lateinischen Sprache* dating from 1857, which won the highly acclaimed prize of the Royal Academy in Berlin. I shall therefore leave the matter to versed scholars of Latin philology.

5 Collapsing Boundaries: Gazes, Voyeurism and Immersion in *Big Little Lies*

'Time and tide again' is a fitting description for narrative structure and haunting loss or memories not only in *Aquis submersus* but also in HBO's *Big Little Lies*. Here, the sensory perception of the waves rolling onto the beach over and over causes traumatic events from Jane's past to resurface. Like the recurring audio-visual images that depict her coping narrative, the fantasy itself repeatedly assembles traces of movement and sound to encode the past. And fantasies, as Freud remarks in a letter to Wilhelm Fließ, are psychic constructions, montages of prior experiences and perceived sounds that act as a protective barrier against memories in order to repress them (Freud 1986, 253–255). But what happens when that protective boundary is constructed around an unstable, porous border? What if the barrier fantasy, a coping narrative such as Jane's imaginary chases after the assailant, occurred on a beach, i.e., a permeable space to begin with – and a space which the traumatic event was also connected to? The repression would surely have to break down at some point. That point, in *Big Little Lies*, could be localized in the moment that Jane returned to Monterey and its beach. One might say that the miniseries not only reveals the beach as a privileged space for memory work, but demonstrates that this is the case because the beach collapses the barriers of sensory perception, allowing flashes of the past to trickle through as visual or aural traces.

While these traces pertain to the characters' (and especially Jane's) subjective sensory perception, they also serve an important narrative function by involving the audience in the whodunit(s), by breaking down the border between viewing and experiencing. In part, this effect arises from the camera work. The gazes it generates seem to oscillate between voyeurism and immersion. Throughout the miniseries, sequences are shot with a handheld, documentary-style shaky camera, which calls into question how reliable the presented perspectives are. The vantage points constituted by the camera work thus appear as highly subjective, divulging and mirroring the community's judgmental gaze. Characters in *Big Little Lies* are always being watched by other characters. Yet this rarely happens during scenes set at the beach[16] which is paradoxical

---

[16] The notable exception being the final scene of the first season, during which characters on the beach are being observed. At first, the viewer cannot determine by whom exactly – society? The audience itself? The vignette-style frame which focuses the attention on the individuals on the beach, scanning and scrutinizing their behavior, indicates they are being observed through binoculars. Finally, the clicking of a lighter implies that the observer is the homicide detective, whom had become associated with that sound earlier on ("You Get What You Need" 2017). By

considering the beach is a space established inherently *by* gazes (Löw 2005, 251–254). Constructed through "the act of looking and being looked at" within "an arena of mass consumption" as Fiona Handyside points out, the beach shares this important aspect with film as a medium: Both beach and film are sites of "spectacle and display" (2014, 13–14). Similarly, the TV series *Big Little Lies* establishes a space constructed and structured by gazes. As noted before, when Madeline, Celeste or Jane are presented at the beach, they mostly appear in scenes of dispute and suffering; and although these scenes are not watched by the community of Monterey, they are on display for the audience itself. The distress experienced by the characters at the beach is the spectacle the viewers have paid to watch. *Their* voyeurism is reflected within the camera work as an array of gazes, for instance, when the shaky camera is combined with shot/reverse shots which pull viewers into the scene as silently observing third parties.

Another example can be found in the repeated depiction of opening and closing blinds that unveil ocean views from Celeste's bedroom window or from the hotel room in which Jane's rape occurs. Like a theater raising its curtains for a show – spectacle and display –, the blinds lift. In "Living the Dream" (2017), Jane now opens up to tell Madeline (and the audience) her story. However, the blinds shut again as Jane begins to speak about the rape, indicating that they also act as a barrier that encloses the most violent aspects of that night and her most traumatic memories. These closed blinds irritate the viewing experience by implying that although the audience is watching a show, a rape is anything but a show. So while the audience's gaze doubles the depicted community's voyeuristic gaze, it is also repeatedly thwarted by encaging viewers in unsettling scenes and finally by pulling them squarely 'into' the characters, immersing them fully into distressing points of view.

When Jane tells Madeline about the rape, at first, the audience observes her lying face down on a bed, clearly distraught. Moving into Jane's point of view, the camera focuses on a pair of men's shoes on the carpeted floor. Feet slip into them in a hurry. The viewers are now watching the same scene as Jane after the rape; they are slipping into her shoes as the rapist is slipping into his. After another switch back and forth, a cross cut brings viewers to the now familiar, distinctive shoe prints on the beach and immerses them back into Jane's vantage point as the camera follows the traces. Coming back to Jane, the image of the rapist appears in her iris against the backdrop of the beach for a split second.

---

this point, the audience has solved the homicide, knows 'who did it' in the whodunit – but the police does not.

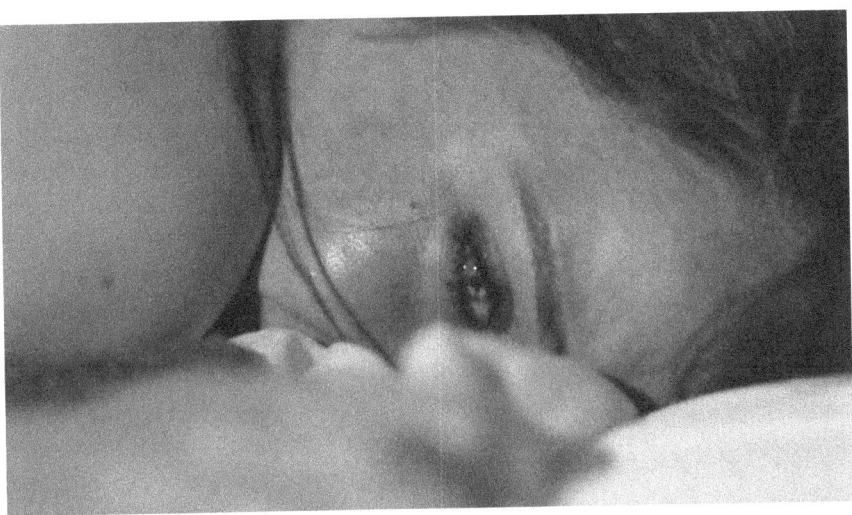

Fig. 2: Immersing the audience into Jane's 'point of view' ("Living the Dream" 2017).

Pictured within the iris and barely perceptible to the audience, Jane's first visualization and distancing act is literally born 'in a blink of an eye.' In the midst of the traumatic incident that cannot be experienced or perceived fully – Jane is still in the hotel room here –, a fleeting visual emerges that represents an act of distancing oneself from the event and simultaneously bears the mark of the traumatic experience. As the attacker's facial traits are lost to Jane's memory, the flash-like image in her eye doubles as a sign for the *lack* of visual inscription; accordingly, we see him from behind only. While the flash in Jane's eye might be barely discernible, its effects unfold over time, looping Jane into an endlessly repeating coping narrative of chasing the assailant across the beach, but never even catching a glimpse of his face. It cannot come as a surprise that the next cut pulls the viewers 'into' Jane's imagination through her iris to chase the vanishing figure across the beach – and that the attacker fades away. A wave washes over his last imprint in the sand, as if visually erasing his trace / his traits from Jane's memory. The focus on the traces here also serves a purpose for the narrative structure. It signals to the audience that the homicide-whodunit set up in the first episode is accompanied by a rape-whodunit – which makes the vantage point of participative voyeurism particularly untenable from here on.

While 'present' Jane narrates the events and visualizes the rape for the viewers to see in "Living the Dream," silent 'past' Jane in those images experiences a split: Sitting in the bathroom, she herself replays the incident in her mind. The camera work projects her rape onto a mirror reflecting the (now empty) bed. The audience watches the disturbing scenes of Jane with Jane, or rather: as Jane. Jane relives not her dream but her nightmare. Implicitly, the viewers also 'live' it as a cut immerses them into Jane's vantage point from the bed *while she is being raped*. As the subjective camera, Jane and the audience stare at the attacker's shoes from there, the image repeatedly moves up and down during the rape, rising and falling with every violent and slightly audible thrust. Camera and thrusts echo the agitation of the waves on the beach outside.[17] The brutal motions are imprinted on Jane's memory like a shoe print in the sand, but unlike her assailant's image, they will not wash away.

During the visual representation of the rape, the camera switches back and forth between past and present. Jane's narration as well as background sounds tie the present moment to sounds and images of the past. Cross cuts juxtapose the images; tied together via soundscapes, the difference between past and present becomes blurry as does the one between coping narrative and traumatic reality. The shaky camera technique underlines how unstable the border between both is, how penetrable: The traumatic past seeps into the present and washes out the boundaries. The further the miniseries progresses, the more pronounced cross-cutting becomes as a representational technique, immersing the audience even further into Jane's unstable point of view of simultaneous, overlapping sensory perceptions and timelines.

6 Boundless Potentiality: Rhythmic Narration and Spectacular Montage

Sensory perception, as was shown earlier, plays an equally important role in *Aquis submersus*. Especially the rhythmic sound of the beach acts as a trigger for the past to resurface in the present; it impacts the experience of reality. As Strowick observes, Storm's fiction constructs reality as a subjective reality and thus always as perceived reality (Strowick 2013, 55). Sensory perception in the present, according to Strowick, is brought forth by the past, or more specifically by what has been irretrievably lost to the past. This means that sensory perception both refers to the past, but also that it has lost what it is referring to. Suspending that reference in turn produces moments of sensory perception as

---

[17] Other noises in Jane's narration of the rape include water repeatedly dripping from an (unseen) tap; waves as an acoustic background trace; the soft plopping noise of champagne in Jane's glass as she stumbles, slightly inebriated.

uncanny doubles, "Wahrnehmungsereignisse [werden] selbst zu Wiedergängern, ihre 'Gegenwart' [...] ist eine gespenstische, und einzig sie ist Ausweis des Wirklichen" (ibid., 56): Sensory perception is 'present' as a ghostly revenant as Strowick notes, and since subjective perception alone indicates reality (as perceived reality), the latter itself becomes uncanny.

The phrase 'aquis submersus' is such a revenant in the form of acoustic perception. It signifies an irretrievably lost past – something which has sunk into the depths of time – that haunts Johannes in the present. 'Aquis submersus' is the sound that sets up the novella in the title and resurfaces within the text (Storm 1998, 383, 453), finally emerging to voice the resounding last words first of the manuscript and then again of the frame story. The ceaseless movement of the tides pours through the novella repeatedly as a ghostly melodic rhythm, as musicality even: Note that the sound of the waves reminds Johannes of a dark lullaby, "ein[] finstere[s] Wiegenlied[]," sounding the sinister, rhythmically repeated words "Aquis submersus – aquis submersus!" (Ibid., 455)

'Aquis submersus,' the phrase echoing throughout the novella, becomes the signifier for rhythmic narration itself and for its boundless potential. It transcends the boundaries of time for Johannes, whose present is haunted by the irretrievable past expressed by the phrase, and even crosses over from the seventeenth-century manuscript into the nineteenth-century frame story. While the rhythmic quality of the text is brought to the forefront by the sound of waves on the beach at the end of the novella, it is contained within from the beginning – from the title *Aquis submersus* onward – and it resurfaces several times like an uncanny revenant, like a ghostly undercurrent rising from the depths. After all, the painter Johannes himself notes that something secretly *flowed* into his painting of Katharina – "dennoch floß es durch den Pinsel heimlich" (ibid., 406). This unnamed and uncanny something could be read as the poetics of rise and fall, as the movement of the tides seeping into the manuscript and into the novella as rhythmic language.

One might even speculate whether the meter of "Aquis submersus – aquis submersus!" (ibid., 455) at the end, i.e., the double 'fall rise fall rise fall' with a caesura in between, echoes the narrative structure of the novella itself. After all, the frame story interrupts the manuscript halfway through the text, hence the caesura, and the 'rises' could be likened to traces of the 'C. P. A. S.'-enigma emerging during the course of the narrative. These appearances result in the frame narrator searching for the meaning of 'C. P. A. S.' in the first place. Therefore, they motivate the whole novella, pushing it forward, while simultaneously foreshadowing the gloomy ending.

Similarly, *Big Little Lies* encourages the audience to hunt for the traces of several enigmas. Like the police searching for the murderer, like Jane following shoe prints on the beach and like the parents trying to figure out which child is responsible for bullying, the audience is also looking for clues to all those questions and to one additional one: Who is that somebody who died at the school fundraiser?

In the last episode, Celeste discovers that her son Max has been hurting girls at school. The spousal abuse she suffers has left an imprint on the children: Max is replicating his father's behavior, becoming his double. Celeste leaves her husband to protect herself and her children, but is confronted by Perry at a school fundraiser in the presence of Madeline, Jane, Renata and Bonnie (the mothers of the girls who are bullied by Max at school). Jane, upon meeting Perry for the first time in that moment, realizes that he is the man who raped her years ago. While this part of the whodunit is solved, the murder at the fundraiser is not yet. Perry makes a sudden move toward the women, but the scene is interrupted and the narrative flashes forward to the police questioning Celeste and the four other women. A funeral service follows, which is being watched by a detective; Perry is dead. The last episode then cuts to a sequence of the aforementioned women at the beach, playing with their children. The mothers are portrayed as sharing a new, unspoken bond as they run with the waves. The camera follows footprints, but this time they are of Jane's (and Perry's) son Ziggy running along the beach. They echo the shoe prints in Jane's imagination and emphasize that the violence experienced by both Celeste and Jane is far from contained. Rather it has permeated to the next generation, possibly to haunt them in turn like the drowning curse in *Aquis submersus*.

The utopian beach scene at the end of the final episode "You Get What You Need" (2017) juxtaposes the climactic sequence that follows, in which Perry and the women physically fight at the fundraiser. This ends with Bonnie pushing Perry down a flight of stairs to protect the others, ultimately causing his death. Prior to his demise, the sound of waves carries the viewer from the utopian beach scene back to Perry confronting the women at the fundraiser in the narrative present. A montage sequence ensues that plays off the now well-formed linkage between the beach and its waves, traumatic memory, and violence, continuously switching between the confrontation and shots of the roaring waves. Perry lunges forward towards Celeste, beating her to the ground. The other women ward him off, pulling, grabbing and yelling at him; he lashes out against them, too. The frames of Perry fighting with the women and of the surge are meticulously pieced together and alternate in rapid succession. With every cross cut between fight and ocean, back and forth movements of hitting, pushing, pulling and falling are picked up by the waves forcefully crashing against the rocks (and vice versa). Well-timed match cuts visually enhance the violence. Simultaneously, the parallel editing interlaces traumatic event and coping narrative, abuse and waves, creating a spectacular and deeply affecting montage sequence.

The accelerating visual movement of punches, thrusts, waves and spray also interacts with the sounds. While the women's screams have been edited out, the mixage superimposes the soundscape of the waves with the flow of the piano piece *September Song* by Agnes Obel (Obel 2014). This composition can be characterized as a (simple) polyrhythm, i.e., a montage of overlapping rhythms in itself, which flow seamlessly into each other. Soundscape, music and frames reverberate off one another. The softer, murmuring parts of the music are reserved for the utopian beach sequence. They fade out into a pause that marks both the switch to the fundraiser and the jump in narrative time while connecting setting and time via the image and sound of waves against rocks. The sudden general rest – both in the music and in the story – creates suspense for the more dramatic part of the piano piece which then guides the rhythmic editing in the climactic montage of violence. The high notes in the melody coincide with the expressive back-and-forth movement of waves and gestures.

In the montage sequence, sensory perceptions are no longer distinguishable from one another: Music and waves flow into visual gesture; movement melts back into sound. The boundaries between them collapse entirely. The intricate montage of sensory perceptions unites television as an art in both space (the visual) and time (narrative, sound) with the beach as a spatial, temporal and acoustic aesthetic: Both are ceaselessly changing 'land-' and soundscapes. *Big Little Lies* self-reflexively puts this on show by celebrating and unveiling their shared potential for spectacle and display.

Beach landscapes, lacking clear demarcations themselves, allow for sensory perceptions to merge and overlap in works of art, thus opening up a unique, permeable aesthetic time-space grounded in the different techniques of representation in literature and television. *Big Little Lies* assembles sound and image, music and movement, creating a spectacular montage sequence that collapses the boundaries of individually distinguishable sensory perceptions and immerses the audience into the intense physicality of a traumatic experience. *Aquis submersus* underlays the movement of rising and falling tides, of a resurfacing yet irretrievable past with an aural, rhythmic dynamic that permeates from the manuscript into the frame story.

Like the violence in *Big Little Lies*, the peculiar dynamic of *Aquis submersus* cannot be contained. The past pierces the present and opens it up into the future when the frame narrator himself repeats "Aquis submersus" in lieu of the more conventional *finis* at the end (Storm 1998, 455). As uncanny repetition and boundless rhythm both, the formulaic reiteration cannot end or enclose the story within the boundaries of the text – instead it evokes the past, the deaths by submersion, which will haunt even the next generation and the next forevermore. The ending of the novella emphasizes that Johannes's paintings have been lost, thus asserting, as Elisabeth Bronfen (1990, 317) suggests, that only words can stand the test of time: Aquis submersus. The evidence presented in this article expands Bronfen's notion further. Not words *per se* stand the test of time, but "finstere[] Wiegenlied[er]," dark lullabies (Storm 1998, 455) – i.e., rhythmic, (re)sounding words. Like the beach, rhythmic narration disseminates endlessly. Of this, the frame story itself is an example, repeating as it does the manuscript word for word as a story within the story; and even the quotations given in this article reiterate the fictional painter's manuscript. In *Aquis submersus*, the movement and the aural perception of the tides, translated into rhythmic narration, collapse the boundaries of time.

Both *Aquis submersus* and *Big Little Lies* present us with questions to solve and an array of traces to follow. These traces lead us up and down the beach as a location severely marked by the past and imbued with memory. Figuratively represented via an aesthetic of ebb and flow, traces of memory – and thus traces of time – are repeatedly uncovered and submerged, albeit the two works of art harness the potential of this back-and-forth motion in different ways. While the novella employs visual media for the dynamic, but conceals it in its rhythmic language as a secret undercurrent, too, the miniseries encodes the movement in its camera work, editing and mixage, ultimately merging them in a spectacular montage sequence. The tides and the waves as sensory and temporal phenomena shape both *Aquis submersus* and *Big Little Lies*: Literature and television, respectively showcasing their own media, explore the dynamic of a past resurfacing in the present through the movement of to-and-fro. In doing so, and each in their own manner, they reveal the beach as a permeable space that erodes the boundaries of perception – time and tide again.

Bibliography

Begemann, Christian. "Figuren der Wiederkehr. Erinnerung, Tradition, Vererbung und andere Gespenster der Vergangenheit bei Theodor Storm." *Wirklichkeit und Wahrnehmung. Neue Perspektiven auf Theodor Storm*. Eds. Elisabeth Strowick and Ulrike Vedder. Bern et al.: Peter Lang, 2013. 13–37.

Big Little Lies. Season 1. Directed by Jean-Marc Vallée. HBO, 2017.
    Episode 1: "Somebody's Dead."
    Episode 2: "Serious Mothering."
    Episode 3: "Living the Dream."

Episode 4: "Push Comes to Shove."
Episode 7: "You Get What You Need."

Bleckwenn, Helga. "*Aquis submersus*. Das Motiv des ertrinkenden Kindes in Storms Novelle und in Goethes Roman *Die Wahlverwandtschaften*." *Schriften der Theodor-Storm-Gesellschaft* 52 (2003): 75–83.

Brison, Susan J. "Trauma Narratives and the Remaking of the Self." *Acts of Memory. Cultural Recall in the Present*. Eds. Mieke Bal, Jonathan Crewe and Leo Spitzer. Hanover/NH and London: University Press of New England, 1999. 39–54.

Bronfen, Elisabeth. "Leichenhafte Bilder – Bildhafte Leichen. Zu dem Verhältnis von Bild und Referenz in Theodor Storms Novelle *Aquis Submersus*." *Die Trauben des Zeuxis. Formen künstlerischer Wirklichkeitsaneignung*. Eds. Hans Körner, Constance Peres, Reinhard Steiner and Ludwig Travernier. Hildesheim, Zurich and New York: Georg Olms, 1990. 305–334.

Caruth, Cathy. "Trauma and Experience. Introduction." *Trauma. Explorations in Memory*. Ed. Cathy Caruth. Baltimore and London: Johns Hopkins University Press, 1995. 3–12.

Corbin, Alain. *The Lure of the Sea. The Discovery of the Seaside in the Western World. 1750–1840*. Translated by Jocelyn Phelps. Berkeley and Los Angeles: University of California Press, 1994.

Cunningham, William L. "Zur Wassersymbolik in *Aquis submersus*." *Schriften der Theodor-Storm-Gesellschaft* 27 (1978). 40–49.

Detering, Heinrich. "Storm oder Die Wiederkehr der Toten. Zur Rahmenerzählung von *Aquis submersus*." *Herkunftsorte. Literarische Verwandlungen im Werk Storms, Hebbels, Groths, Thomas und Heinrich Manns*. Heide: Westholsteinische Verlangsanstalt Boyens, 2001. 106–147.

Freud, Sigmund. "Brief 126, 2. Mai 1897" and "Manuskript L (Beilage zu Brief an Wilhelm Fließ, 2. Mai 1897." *Briefe an Wilhelm Fließ 1887–1904*. Eds. Jeffrey Moussaieff Masson and Michael Schröter. Frankfurt/Main: Fischer, 1986. 253–257.

Grimm, Jacob, and Wilhelm Grimm. "Strand." *Deutsches Wörterbuch, Vol. 19*. http://www.woerterbuchnetz.de/DWB?lemma=strand. Leipzig: S. Hirzel, 1957 (5 February 2019).

Handyside, Fiona. *Cinema at the Shore. The Beach in French Film*. Bern et al.: Peter Lang 2014.

Löw, Martina. "Die Rache des Körpers über den Raum? Über Henri Lefèbvres Utopie und Geschlechterverhältnisse am Strand." *Soziologie des Körpers*. Ed. Markus Schroer. Frankfurt/Main: Suhrkamp, 2005. 241–270.

Mann, Thomas. "Theodor Storm." *Gesammelte Werke in dreizehn Bänden, Vol. 9*. 2nd ed. Frankfurt/Main: Fischer, 1974. 246–267.

Michelet, Jules. *The Sea*. Translated by W. H. D. Adams. London, Edinburgh and New York: T. Nelson and Sons, 1875.

Mittell, Jason. *Television and American Culture*. New York and Oxford: Oxford University Press, 2010.

Moriarty, Liane. *Big Little Lies*. London: Penguin, 2014.

Obel, Agnes. "September Song." *Aventine (Deluxe Version)*. Compact disc. PIAS, 2014.

Pfeifer, Wolfgang et al. (eds.). "Strand." *Etymologisches Wörterbuch des Deutschen (1993)*. Digitized edition, revised by Wolfgang Pfeifer. https://www.dwds.de/wb/Strand. (5 February 2019). [Pfeifer et al. "Streuen"]

Pfeifer, Wolfgang et al. (eds.). "Streuen." *Etymologisches Wörterbuch des Deutschen (1993)*. Digitized edition, revised by Wolfgang Pfeifer. https://www.dwds.de/wb/streuen (5 February 2019). [Pfeifer et al. "Streuen"]

Rohdie, Sam. *Fellini Lexicon*. London: BFI, 2002.

Storm, Theodor. "Aquis submersus." *Novellen. 1867–1880. Sämtliche Werke in vier Bänden, Vol. 2*. Eds. Karl Ernst Laage and Dieter Lohmeier. Frankfurt/Main: DKV, 1998. 378–455.

Storm, Theodor. "Aquis submersus." *A Doppelgänger with Aquis submersus*. Edited and translated by Denis Jackson. London: Angel Books, 2015: 29–99.

Taussig, Michael. "The Beach (A Fantasy)." *Critical Inquiry* 26.2 (2000): 249–278.

Strowick, Elisabeth. "'Eine andere Zeit'. Storms Rahmentechnik des Zeitsprungs." *Wirklichkeit und Wahrnehmung. Neue Perspektiven auf Theodor Storm*. Eds. Elisabeth Strowick and Ulrike Vedder. Bern et al.: Peter Lang, 2013. 55–72.

Wade, Mara R. "The Fifth Horseman. Discourses of Disaster and the 'Burchardi Flut' 1634". *Daphnis. Zeitschrift für Mittlere Deutsche Literatur* 24 (1995): 301–327.

Webb, Jennifer. "Beaches, Bodies and Being in the World." *Some Like it Hot. The Beach as a Cultural Dimension*. Eds. James Skinner, Keith Gilbert and Allan Edwards. Oxford: Meyer & Meyer Sport, 2003. 77–90.

List of Figures

Fig. 1: Still from *Big Little Lies. Season 1, episode 4*: "Push Comes to Shove." Directed by Jean-Marc Vallée. HBO, 2017.

Fig. 2: Still from *Big Little Lies. Season 1, episode 3*: "Living the Dream." Directed by Jean-Marc Vallée. HBO, 2017.

Alberto Napoli
"Stile balneare." Singing the Italian Summer by the Seaside (1960s–1980s)

This article focuses on popular summer songs that dominated Italian charts during the 1960s and the 1980s. Analyzing the music and lyrics of these songs in the 1960s, I show how they create common tropes of temporal continuity and periodicity through their references to *villeggiatura*, or the Italian custom of vacationing in the same second home year after year. In similarly themed songs of the 1980s, conversely, tropes of temporal fragmentation emerged due to changing vacation habits. I also scrutinize the obsession with women's bodies and their transformation on the beach, highlighting its racial implications. Finally, considering these songs as a united corpus, I trace the shift of Italian escapist desires from a domestic environment to more exotic sceneries.

Dieser Artikel beschäftigt sich mit populären Summer Songs, die in den 1960er und 1980er Jahren die italienischen Charts dominierten. In exemplarischen Musik- und Textanalysen möchte ich zeigen, wie die Songs aus den 1960er Jahren durch gezielte Bezugnahmen auf *villeggiatura*, also den italienischen Brauch eines alljährlichen Urlaubs am selben Ferienort, Tropen zeitlicher Kontinuität und Wiederholung entwickeln. Mit sich ändernden Urlaubsgewohnheiten finden sich in den Songs der 1980er auch zunehmend Tropen der zeitlichen Fragmentierung. Dabei lässt sich die in den behandelten Songs auffällige Obsession mit weiblichen Körpern und ihren Verwandlungen am Strand unter Berücksichtigung von rassistischen Implikationen beleuchten. Betrachtet man schließlich diese Songs als einen einheitlichen Korpus, so lässt sich in der italienischen Gesellschaft eine Verschiebung der eskapistischen Wünsche weg von einheimischer Umgebung hin zu eher exotischen Landschaften ausmachen.

> L'estate sta finendo,
> e un anno se ne va,
> sto diventando grande,
> lo sai che non mi va...
> Righeira, *L'estate sta finendo*, 1985[1]

1 Introduction

In July 1985, the popular Italian duo Righeira (Stefano Righi and Stefano Rota) seemed to foreshadow the economic and political crisis that would eventually put an end to the 'Roaring Eighties' in the country, as well as the Italian

---
[1] "The summer is ending / And a year is gone, / I'm growing up, / You know it doesn't suit me." Reference to this and all the songs quoted in this article can be found in the list of recordings at the end of the text.

https://doi.org/10.1515/9783110672244-015

people's lackluster reaction to it in the following decade. In this unconventional summer hit, Righeira sang also of the decline of Italian summer dreams on the beach, and the vacuity of the songs that typically animated those dreams. These songs, characterized by a catchy tune and evocative lyrics celebrating life by the sea and under the sun, would make it to the top-ten charts every summer and provided a major, pervasive contribution to the vacation imaginary on Italian shores. In this article, I will analyze Italian summer hits from the 1960s, 1970s, and 1980s, highlighting their recurrent themes, and outlining their historical trajectory: from a lively artistic expression significantly contributing to Italy's soundscape during the economic boom, to an alienated, but also self-reflective, cluster of musical and literary tropes that still persist today.

Songs about summer vacations on the beach have been predominant in Italy since the end of the 1950s, with the introduction and widespread installation of jukeboxes in bars and dance halls in coastal tourist destinations. The sheer loudness bursting outward from these machines represented the ultimate sonic manifestation of the transformations experienced by the Italian seascape and its beaches after World War II. During the 1950s, the building of new resort facilities made vacation trips available to an empowered middle class, who by the 1960s finally appropriated the beach as a space in which to exercise its values and aspirations. New housing quartiers were planned and built along the coast of the Romagna region. Here, the comfortable and easily accessible Adriatic Sea favored the development of a second-house vacationing culture, very popular among the growing number of Italian families who could afford it (Crainz 2003, 16). This was part of a deliberate plan of a "democratizzazione della vacanza" [democratization of vacation] (Manning 2011, 262) especially in the coastal town of Rimini, establishing a model promoting mass tourism instead of traditional elite resorts (Battilani 2009). The model spread rapidly to the rest of the Italian peninsula, from Liguria to Apulia, and its influence on tourists' imagination extended far beyond national borders. In fact, the Italian summer dream captivated also the German, Austrian, and Swiss middle class, resulting in a significant transalpine seasonal migration every summer (Pagenstecher 2003; Manning 2011).

The study of Italian beach-inspired summer hits is therefore inseparable from the study of tourism culture. Since the publication of John Urry's pivotal study *The Tourist Gaze* (1990), tourist studies have quickly grown in the past decades to become a well-established field of research, with contributions from the most diverse disciplinary perspectives (Lew et al. 2004) and with dedicated journals. Much of this literature reveals that tourist places, that is, places exploited by the tourism industry, are defined less by inherent qualities such as their landscape or their historical heritage, and more by the way travel agents, hotel managers, and tourists themselves produce and consume them (Urry 1990; Franklin and Crang 2001; Urbain, 2003; Bærenholdt et al. 2004). The beach is very often a privileged study case, by virtue of its popularity as a vacation destination and its impact on all human senses, especially sight and touch (Löfgren 1999; Obrador Pons 2003, 2012). As I will show, the visual and tactile appeals of the beach were celebrated in the songs analyzed in the present article. These songs reflected contemporary tourist practices, and their recurring themes changed following concurrent societal shifts.

Provided that "tourism has always been a transnational mode of production," (Löfgren 1999, 8) and given the popularity of some of these songs abroad, I would suggest that my conclusions apply to a certain extent to intersections between popular music and the beach in general. In fact, early-1960s America witnessed the flourishing of so-called 'beach movies,' especially the *Beach Party* series produced by American International Pictures (AIP). These films featured numerous musical numbers and were light-hearted and escapist in tone, combining "clean teens, music, and a lot of exposed young bodies." (Shary 2005, 31) Scholars have especially noticed that "the films' construction of the beach as a 'raceless' utopian landscape worked to naturalize whiteness and to regulate racial, sexual and geographic mobilities." (Stenger 2007, 29; cf. Morris 1998) In contrast with the United States, post-colonial Italy was already imagined as a raceless (i.e. white) country, thanks to cultural and legal strategies enacted to remove non-white individuals after World War II (Patriarca 2015, Deplano 2018). Therefore, as we will see, Italian summer hits not only regulated, but actually reintroduced race in relationship with the landscape of the beach and sexuality.

Finally, envisioning vacationing as "a cultural laboratory where people have been able to experiment with new aspects of their identities, their social relations, or their interaction with nature and also to use the important cultural skills of daydreaming and mindtravelling," (Löfgren 1999, 7) I aim to show that summer hits are a direct product of such a laboratory, bearing witness to its workings in their lines and rhymes, in their melodies and harmonies, and in their structures and arrangements. Moreover, I will argue that the "cultural skills of daydreaming and mindtravelling" were practiced extensively through these songs. Summer hits participated in the re-production of Italian beaches as tourist places, influencing the Italian vacation imaginary and the escapist desires connected to it.

2 Defining Summer Hits

I will consider summer hits as a corpus of songs sharing certain commercial common traits and content similarities. Summer hits were – and are even today – popular songs characterized by a seasonal commercial trajectory. Generally, they came out in late spring, reached the top of the charts over the summer, and then disappeared in fall, leaving space for new hits. In Italy, one of the first examples of this trajectory is Fred Buscaglione's 1959 hit *Guarda che luna!*. Starting from the 1960s, this trend was promoted and guaranteed also by record labels through the establishment of specific festivals. These events capitalized on the fortune of the Sanremo festival (Festival della canzone italiana), a song competition founded in 1951 and still running today, Italy's largest yearly media event (Facci and Soddu 2011). Likewise, the festival Un disco per l'estate, starting each year in spring, lasted for several decades (1964–2003), always in the quest for new hits for the upcoming summer. Another of these events, the early-summer festival Cantagiro (begun in 1964 and still running, with some interruptions), based its success on the unusual format of an itinerant song competition, mimicking the Giro d'Italia, Italy's most popular annual bicycle race. In both Un disco per l'estate and Cantagiro – which still lack scholarly investigation by music historians – major record labels, and especially the Italian branch of the Radio Corporation of America, put forth their best or newest singers and songs.

After the 1960s and up to this day, summer hits never disappeared completely from Italian charts. Yet, I will limit my analysis to songs up to the 1980s, comparing them with songs from the 1960s. After a decrease during the 1970s, in fact, many new summer hits took over Italian charts in the 1980s. The recurring themes of songs from the 1980s paralleled those of hits in the 1960s, but in reverse. As we will see, tropes of temporal continuity were substituted by temporal fragmentation, and exotic sceneries took the place of familiar ones.

From the point of view of content, I will not consider all the popular songs that showed this seasonal economic trajectory, but I will rather focus on those which reflected and reinforced the middle-class vacation imaginary connected to Italian beaches. In his *La grande evasione. Storia del Festival di San Remo*, Gianni Borgna (1980) has shown the strong correlation between Italian postwar mainstream music and the escapism sought after by contemporaneous society and politics, wavering between normativity and liberation. Escapism from the working routine and boredom of winter months was also at the core of the imaginary evoked by summer hits, and was articulated through two equally important elements: love/romance and beach/seascape. By analyzing Italian beach-inspired summer hits produced between the 1960s and the 1980s, it is therefore possible to illustrate the close interplay between representations of the beach and romance narratives.

In my analysis, a concentration of similar themes and tropes related to vacationing will identify a corpus made of songs coming from different musical subgenres. Such songs could be sung by a more conservative 'crooner' like Nico Fidenco, but also by the new generation of so-called *urlatori* [shouters] like Mina and Adriano Celentano. Their arrangements could be conventional in the panorama of popular music of their time, or exude amusing experimentalism thanks to the artistry of composers such as Ennio Morricone, who often participated in the production of these songs. As we will see, summer hits were released even by *cantautori*, singer-songwriters whose songs were generally perceived as more sophisticated than popular trends in mass entertainment (Santoro 2002). That so many different influences could merge into a single, dominant musical practice is inscribed in the very metaphor of the 'mainstream.' (Huber 2013) Yet, the diversity of such influences and the chronological and poetic distance between summer hits from the 1960s and the 1980s prevent me from referring to this corpus of songs as a genre. Instead, I would stress how all these songs based their success on exploiting beach tourism and the cultural, romantic, and sexual tropes attached to it. In other words, they capitalized on what songwriter Franco Battiato, in one of his greatest summer hits, brilliantly called: "stile balneare" [beach style] (Battiato 1981).

3 Evoking the Seascape

Summer hits were always about life on the beach, a characteristic that enhanced their appeal to the public and fulfilled its escapist desires. The beach and its attributes were often signaled in the lyrics, and even in song titles. Natural elements from the seascape were mentioned in many songs, among them: *Sapore di sale* [The taste of salt] (1963), *Con te sulla spiaggia* [With you on the beach] (1964), *Stessa spiaggia, stesso mare* [The same beach, the same sea] (1963), *Legata a un granello di sabbia* [Tied to a grain of salt] (1961), *Guarda che luna!* [Oh, what a moon!] (1959), and many more. Songs also mentioned architecture and artifacts signaling the transformation of Italian beaches into tourist resorts after WWII, as in *Una rotonda sul mare* [A *rotonda* on the sea[2]] (1964),

---

[2] "A *rotonda* on the sea" probably refers to the rotunda on stilts built in the 1930s on the shore of Senigallia, on the Adriatic sea.

Pinne fucile ed occhiali [Flippers, speargun, and goggles] (1962), *Se mi compri un gelato* [If you buy me an ice-cream] (1964).

The beach could occasionally be represented also sonically, by recreating its stereotypical soundscape. For example, Nico Fidenco's *Con te sulla spiaggia* (1964) is introduced by, and ends with the sound of sea waves crashing on the shore and the noise of people playing in the sand. In Giuni Russo's greatest success *Un'estate al mare* [A summer at the beach] (1982), the song fade-out is accompanied by the singer's signature high overtones imitating the cry of a seagull. The contemplation of the sea described in the lyrics of Umberto Bindi's *Riviera* and its B-side *Vento di mare* [Sea wind] (1961) is also evoked with strictly orchestral means. The unusually rich instrumentation characterizing both songs repeats some symphonic clichés dating back to Claude Debussy, known for the frequent musical representations of water and the sea in his compositions. *Vento di mare*'s introduction is reminiscent of the composer's style through the use of typical instruments such as the piccolo, the oboe and the harp, while the choir sings an ascending tetratonic scale. Similarly, the succession of alternating parallel chords in *Riviera*'s intro, together with the lush instrumentation combining the choir with the strings, brass instruments, and timpani of a full symphonic orchestra, suggests the motion of sea waves and recalls some pages of Debussy's symphonic sketches *La mer*.

These elements from the seascape did not only recreate impressions of the coast, suggesting a vacation setting, but they also represented nature's counterpart to the speaker's emotions. For example, in Umberto Bindi's *Riviera*, the sea participates in the two lovers' romantic idyll: "fiori di spuma / l'onda inventa per noi / e si consuma / l'orizzonte negli occhi tuoi" [the waves invent / flowers of foam for us / and the horizon is consumed / in your eyes]. Sadness and jealousy are the dominant feelings in Gianni Morandi's 1966 single *Notte di Ferragosto* [Night of Ferragosto]. Here, the warm summer night contrasts with the man's heart, which is freezing because the beloved one is in someone else's arms. Finally, in *Guarda che luna!*, the moon serves as a beautiful yet somehow unresponsive counterpart for the loneliness of a man regretting having loved a woman who has left. This song also features a simple introduction quoting Beethoven's so-called 'Moonlight' piano sonata, making the moon even more the protagonist of the song.

4 *Villeggiatura* and Summer Hits: Temporal Tropes

In summer hits, feelings connected to romantic experiences were manifold and varied. It is important to note that in the 1960s these feelings were represented as love stories, each with a beginning, an extended duration, and sometimes an ending. Implicitly, they were based on a trope of temporal continuity, a lengthy and uninterrupted stay in the same tourist destination. Within a continuous, extended time frame, the couple could meet, celebrate their love, experience jealousy, and sometimes break up. Each of these moments was captured in different songs. Such time continuity was a direct reflection of the most prominent mode of vacationing of that time: the so-called '*villeggiatura*,' that is, second-house vacationing. Traditionally, *villeggiare* referred to the practice of the wealthy to spend the warmest months of the year in their countryside 'villa.' During the economic boom, the beach had already taken the place of the countryside as a salubrious holiday destination, and it became popular thanks to the vacation democratization plans illustrated above. The term *villeggiatura* was therefore adapted to describe the middle-class migration to their second houses or to rented apartments on the coast. For stay-at-home mothers and their children on summer break, an Italian *villeggiatura* could last up to three months.

Time periodicity, or the recurrence of yearly vacations, was another relevant characteristic of *villeggiatura*. In fact, it could often coincide with the return to the same beach from one year to the other, a characteristic that impacted the romances narrated in summer hits. If continuity was implicit in song lyrics, periodicity was made explicit, and constituted an occasion for the expression of desires, anxieties, expectations. One of the most telling examples in this respect is *Stessa spiaggia, stesso mare*, a song interpreted both by Piero Focaccia and by Mina in 1963.

Per quest'anno, non cambiare:	This year, don't change:
stessa spiaggia, stesso mare,	come to the same beach, the same sea,
per poterti rivedere,	so that I can see you again,
per tornare, per restare insieme a te.	return, spend time with you.
È come l'anno scorso [...].	It's just like last year [...].

The protagonist is asking the beloved one to come back to the same beach resort, in order to spend time together just as they did the previous year. A similar case is represented by Riccardo Del Turco's *Luglio*, featured in the 1968 top-ten summer charts. Here, the protagonist is waiting for a romantic obligation to be honored: the beloved one promised she would be back to the sea by the month of July.

Anche tu, in riva al mare,	Beside the sea,
tempo fa, amore amore,	a while ago, love,
mi dicevi:	you told me:
"Luglio ci porterà fortuna"	"July will bring us luck"
poi non ti ho vista più;	and then I never saw you again;
vieni, da me c'è tanto sole,	come, there's so much sun here,
ma ho tanto freddo al cuore	but my heart is cold
se tu non sei con me.	if you are not with me.

Happily, we learn at the end of the song that the lovers finally meet in July, just a few days in; the long wait has been rewarded.

A case worth a deeper analysis is Petula Clark's single *Ciao Ciao*, which became famous in Italy in the summer of 1965. This was the Italian version of Clark's worldwide success from the previous year, *Downtown*. The original English text by Tony Hatch celebrates the liveliness of a city and the pleasures of consumerism, leaving space for a possible relationship – a friend or a partner – only in the last verse. Significantly, the new Italian lyrics by Vito Pallavicini recount a situation similar to *Luglio*. At the center is the anticipation of the beloved's return, as well as the joy of meeting with him again at the same beach after a long separation:

First section	Verse	Ritorno al mar dove ho sognato con te, e sembra dirmi "Ciao" "Ciao, ciao!" Rivedo ancor i vecchi amici che ho, e mi salutano: "Ciao, ciao!" E sulla spiaggia limpida non è cambiato niente, sotto il sole caldo io ti cerco tra la gente; so che ci sei...	I return to the sea where I dreamed with you, And it seems to tell me "Ciao" "Ciao, ciao!" I see my old friends again, And they greet me: "Ciao, ciao!" And on the clear beach, nothing has changed, Under the hot sun, I search for you in the crowd; I know that you're there…
	Pre-chorus	Ecco, mi hai vista, e tu mi vieni incontro correndo, e stai sorridendomi: "Ciao, ciao!"	Now you've seen me, and you Come running to greet me, And you're smiling at me: "Ciao, ciao!"
	Chorus	grido chiamandoti, "Ciao, ciao!" amore abbracciami, "Ciao, ciao!" sono tornata da te.	I call to you: "Ciao, ciao!" Embrace me, love, "Ciao, ciao!" I've returned to you.
Second section	Verse	Tu non lo sai con quanta ansia aspettai di rivedere te. "Ciao, ciao!" Ora di te non voglio perdere mai neanche un attimo. "Ciao, ciao!" Diventeranno facili i baci dell'estate, passeremo insieme cento ore innamorate; ma poi verrà	You don't know how much I longed To see you again. "Ciao, ciao!" Now I never want to lose you again, Not even for a moment. "Ciao, ciao!" The summer kisses will come freely, We'll spend a hundred hours together, in love; But then the day will come
	Pre-chorus	il giorno che partirò, alla stazione verrai, la mano tu agiti: "Ciao, ciao!"	When I leave, I'll arrive at the station, You'll wave your hand, "Ciao, ciao!"
	Chorus	Io sto per piangere, "Ciao, ciao!" il treno va, io grido "Ciao, ciao!" Non ti scordare di me.	I'm about to cry, "Ciao, ciao!" The train pulls off, I call, "Ciao, ciao!" Don't forget me.

Fig. 1: Vito Pallavicini, Tony Hatch. *Ciao ciao* (lyrics).

The new lyrics outline a typical romance in the context of *villeggiatura*, including many of the common traits that can be found in Italian summer hits of the time. The protagonist, along with all of her friends, has come back to the very same beach where she met her lover the previous year (periodicity); she looks forward to spending the whole summer with him ("cento ore innamorate," continuity); but finally, she must leave again at the end of the season.

Fig. 2: Vito Pallavicini, Tony Hatch. *Ciao ciao*.

The new lyrics match effectively the song structure, consisting of two different sections of lyrics sharing the same music (fig. 2). Everything in the music contributes to the sense of anticipation for the encounter (first section) and for the departure (second section). In the first section, the first part of the verse ("Ritorno al mar..." and "Rivedo ancor...") is in E major, while the melody revolves around the dominant and ends with a half cadence on the words "Ciao, ciao!," thus implying some instability according to the conventions of tonal harmony. The second part of the verse ("E sulla spiaggia limpida...") introduces temporarily the relative minor key (C sharp minor), with the melody revolving mainly around its 5th grade (G sharp, the mediant tone in the original E major key). Here, the protagonist appears happy that everything on the beach stayed as it used to be, but is still looking for her lover. The tension increases suddenly at the pre-chorus ("So che ci sei..."), where a fermata on the dominant introduces a rapid melodic ascent corresponding to the lover running towards the protagonist in the lyrics. The climax is reached at the chorus ("Ciao, ciao! ..."). Significantly, the distinctive "Ciao, ciao!" hits the high dominant – the melodic peak of the song – and the mediant, and the chorus lands on a stable, affirmative tonic only on the final word of the chorus ("sono tornata da te"). The same structure works also for the lyrics in the second section of the song. In the verse, the protagonist enjoys the company of her lover, but the intrinsic instability of the music reminds the listener that this satisfaction is only temporary. The sudden suspense created by the pre-chorus corresponds to a contrasting clause ("Ma poi verrà...") introducing the theme of separation. The subsequent ascending melody leads to the chorus, where "Ciao, ciao!" as a farewell takes the place of the initial greetings for the encounter.

The Italian version of the song takes advantage of the inherent dramaturgy of Hatch's music in a much more articulate way than the original. *Ciao ciao* is therefore an excellent example of a typical Italian summer hit in the *stile balneare*, despite being based on an international song. This version is even more significant precisely because it addresses a completely different topic from the original; the new lyrics were crafted to fit in all the temporal tropes connected to *villeggiatura*. If we want to understand the connection between summer hits belonging to *stile balneare* and the beach, we should therefore look past the occasional sonic mimesis of elements of the seascape. Instead, it is necessary to direct our attention to the ways in which music organizes time – in the case of Clark's *Ciao ciao*, through the repetition of the anticipation-climax pattern. This organization reflects and reinforces on a micro-level the time tropes characteristic of *villeggiatura*, the dominant source of imagination and practice of exploitation of Italian beaches in the 1960s.

5 *Se telefonando*: An Exception to the Tropes of *villeggiatura*

While temporal tropes are typical of most of summer hits in the 1960s, it is possible to find some exceptions to the rule of time continuity and periodicity. This is the case in Mina's *Se telefonando* [If calling], a song where the beach is not mentioned, but there is a reference to the sea at night in the verse. Furthermore, *Se telefonando* was the theme song for the summer TV show *Aria condizionata* in 1966, and its instant popularity makes it worthy of attention under the lens of summer hits. The writers of the TV show, Ghigo De Chiara and Maurizio Costanzo, wrote the text, which was then set to music by Ennio Morricone. The suggestive lyrics and music, and the interpretive talent of Mina, Italy's most renowned popular music diva, have made this song one of the most popular and beloved Italian songs of all time.

In *Se telefonando*, the story narrated is that of a one-night encounter. The setting is significantly by the sea at night, and the perspective adopted is that of a woman who does not see any future for the romance, but is also unable to leave her lover:

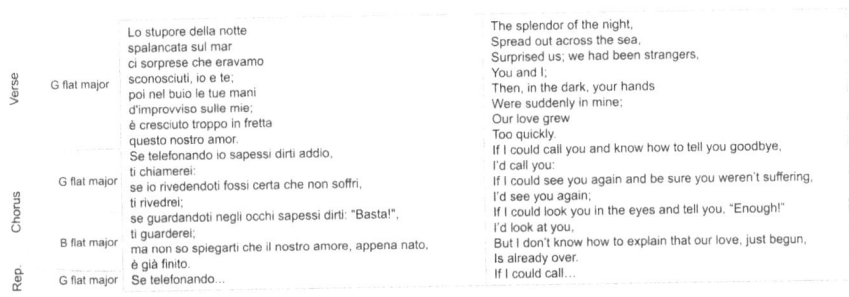

Fig. 3: Ghigo De Chiara, Maurizio Costanzo and Ennio Morricone. *Se telefonando* (lyrics).

The difference between *Se telefonando* and more conventional summer hits is not limited to the lyrics, but also involves the music. Repetition of the verse and the chorus, in fact, is the most common trait of summer hits in the 1960s – as well as of popular music in general. Making the songs more appealing and durable in the memory of the public, the repetition of these musical structures also paralleled the yearly periodicity of vacations. Yet, in *Se telefonando*, repetition is not truly integral to the musical structure. Sure, we can separate the verse ("Lo stupore della notte...") from the emphatic chorus ("Se telefonando..."), and the chorus is indeed repeated. Nonetheless, since the chorus is internally modulating (from G flat major to B flat major, one major third higher, as shown in the table), its repetition must return abruptly to the original key, thus cancelling any increasing tension accumulated in the modulation. In other words, from a harmonic perspective, this repetition does not make sense within the dramaturgy of the song. In fact, it is possible that the chorus was repeated for the sake of duration. Without repetition, the song wouldn't last much longer than two minutes, whereas in its final form it spans over three full minutes – a more suitable duration for a record single.

If the harmonic modulation does not really allow for any repetition, it means that the song structure of *Se telefonando* transgresses the structure of a typical *stile balneare* song just as the lyrics transgress the typical *villeggiatura* setting. Just as the lovers' encounter could not last more than one night, so the music, without the chorus repetition, "just begun, / is already over." On the other hand, the stubborn chorus repetition could musically represent the speaker's inability to leave her casual lover behind. *Se telefonando* proves once more, although differently from other *stile balneare* songs, that the micro-level of the song structure directly relates to the macro-level of the escapist fantasy it fulfills.

6 Female Bodies on the Beach and Escapism

The one-night encounter in *Se telefonando* represents an exception in the panorama of summer hits from the 1960s. Possibly only Mina – whose popularity three years earlier had already fully overcome the scandal of having a child with a married man – could bear its success without suffering from the potential threat to public morality it represented. Nonetheless, the escapist potential of even more conventional summer hits resided precisely in their ability to mix middle-class conservatism with sexual desire. In the 1950s, middle-class values were certainly stricter; in *Guarda che luna!* (1959), the lonely protagonist regrets the passion for his lover as if it were a sin: "Resta soltanto / tutto il rimpianto / perché ho peccato nel desiderarti tanto" [All that remains / is regret / because I have sinned in wanting you so much].

In the 1960s, yet, social norms became looser, and explicit sexual desire was at the center of most songs. Since many of them implied a white (as we will see), heterosexual male perspective, the female body was often the object of desire expressed in the lyrics, and it is precisely in this objectification of the female body that the seascape plays a key role. What is objectified, in fact, is not simply the body of a woman, but rather the body of a woman interacting with the beach. As we will see in the following paragraphs, the beach could be intended as a socialized environment in the era of mass tourism, or as the sum of the natural elements that come together to constitute an escapist fantasy.

In 1961, Nico Fidenco presented a close connection between elements of the seascape and the woman's body in *Legata ad un granello di sabbia*. Here, the protagonist resorts to all the natural elements of the beach to tame the recalcitrant lover. Fidenco's character wants to "cullare / posandoti sull'onda del mare" [cradle you, / resting on the ocean waves], "legandoti a un granello di sabbia" [[tie] you to a grain of sand], and "tenere / legata con un raggio di sole" [hold you / tied to a ray of sun], in order to prevent the lover from disappearing in a veil of fog. Fidenco incarnated a paternalistic male figure, expressing his intention to not-so-metaphorically possess a woman while singing her a lullaby. It is interesting to notice that the connections between the woman's body and the seascape are a matter of bodily contact. The physical desires of Fidenco's character, though mediated through a soft, paternalistic tone, are reflected in the very tangible textures of the beach elements he would use to hold his lover. For him, the beach – with its sea waves, sunrays, and grains of sand – is the site on which to possess the woman, in contrast with the winter fog.

Three years later, Fidenco sang *Con te sulla spiaggia* (1964), in which the beach became less of a friendly prop to sexual desire, and more of a threat. Here, the beach is seen as a stage animated by a multitude of vacationers. At its center, we find the protagonist's partner, whose beauty raises everybody's interest: "[S]e passeggi sotto il sole / [...] poi tutta la spiaggia guarda te" [if you walk under the sun / all those at the beach watch you], "se ti vedono nuotare / da tutta la spiaggia / si buttano nel mare" [if they see you swimming / all those at the beach / throw themselves into the sea]. Consequently, Fidenco's character expresses his jealousy that arises only in summer months, when the couple goes to the seaside:

Tu lo sai, tu lo sai,	You know, you know,
non sono mai geloso, mai;	that I'm never jealous;
tu lo sai, tu lo sai,	you know, you know,
per tutti gli altri mesi mai,	in all the other months of the year,
ma quando sono con te	but when I'm with you,
al mare, al mare	at the sea, at the sea,
son geloso di te...	I'm jealous of you...

The ostensible austerity of Fidenco's character, though, is contradicted by the tone of the music. While Fidenco states at the beginning of the song that "no, quest'anno al mare non andrò / con te sulla spiaggia" [no, this year I won't go to the sea / with you on the beach], the playful violins, and especially the women's choir highlighting only the words "con te sulla spiaggia" and "al mare, al mare," deliberately ignore the singer's protests. The song's irony is built precisely on the tension between the conservative lyrics and the cheerful, allusive arrangement. Therefore, the unveiling of the female body on the beach, far from being repressed, was a necessary, expected ingredient in the vacation imaginary of summer hits.

In *Portala in cantina*, the B-side of *Stessa spiaggia, stesso mare*, Piero Focaccia urged his lover to leave childhood behind by metaphorically putting away her doll ("in cantina") and to finally enter sexual maturity by showing her body in a bikini:

Lascia quella bambola,	Leave that doll behind,
portala in cantina,	put it in the cellar,
non sei più bambina,	you're not a girl anymore,
ora puoi giocare con l'amor.	now you can play with love.
Vieni sulla spiaggia,	Come out on the beach,
mettiti in bikini,	put on your bikini,
lascia che ti vedano,	let them see you
sulla sabbia con me.	on the sand with me.

The threat of, and lust for, female nudity, together with female bodies' contact with elements of the seascape, were the crucial factors in summer hits where a clear male perspective was adopted. In order to mediate between these two apparently divergent forces, many songs in the 1960s fetishized, and obsessed over, the female body and its physical transformations on the beach, under the sun. More often than celebrated, the habit of getting tanned was ridiculed. In *Il peperone* (1965), Edoardo Vianello teased his lover for getting "rossa, spellata / sei come un peperone" [red, peeled / you're like a pepper]. In *Sei diventata nera* (1964) by Los Marcellos Ferial – an Italian group which maliciously alluded to Los Hermanos Rigual of *Cuando calienta el sol* [When the sun is hot] – the protagonist makes fun of his partner because her skin is so tanned that he cannot find her anymore in the night ("Sei diventata nera / come il carbon") [You've become as black / as coal].

The racist implications of such songs could go unnoticed only thanks to the Italian republic's alleged racial innocence (Petrovich Njegosh 2013). However, the fact that a racist attitude and colonial memory were at play is proven by the fetishization and eroticization of the woman's tanned body in one of the most popular summer hits of its time, with a catchy arrangement by Ennio Morricone: *Abbronzatissima* (literally: "very tanned girl"), sung by Vianello in 1963.

A-abbronzatissima,	A-abbronzatissima,
sotto i raggi del sole,	under the sun's rays,
come è bello sognare	how lovely it is to dream
abbracciato con te.	in your arms.
A-abbronzatissima,	A-abbronzatissima,
a due passi dal mare,	just next to the sea,
come è dolce sentirti	how sweet it is to hear you
respirare con me.	breathe with me.
Sulle labbra tue dolcissime,	On your sweet lips,
un profumo di salsedine	I'll smell the scent of dried salt
sentirò per tutto il tempo	for this entire
di questa estate d'amor.	summer of love.
Quando il viso tuo nerissimo	When your dark face
tornerà di nuovo pallido,	turns pale again,
questi giorni in riva al mar	I won't be able to forget
non potrò dimenticar.	these days by the sea.

The woman of *Abbronzatissima*, whose body is celebrated in the lyrics, is a tourist herself. She is someone with whom the male protagonist is more than familiar – his girlfriend or his wife – that he will see back in fall and winter, when her skin will be pale again. Indeed, this was the case for all the women described in songs by Fidenco, Los Marcellos Ferial, and Edoardo Vianello. These customary presences in the life of the songs' protagonists, nonetheless, undergo a radical transformation during the vacation season. The changing color of their skin symbolizes the shift in their function from habitual partner to renewed, almost exotic lovers. In fact, as argued by Richard Dyer, tanning displays "white people's right [...] to incorporate into themselves features of other people" (Dyer 1997, 49). The features appropriated through tanning have not only to do with skin tone, of course, but also the hyper-sexualization associated with it (Giuliani 2013, 2018). In the case of AIP's beach movies, the scripts provided "many diegetic opportunities to literalize the conflation of sexuality and darkness. The most prominent of these is the ritual of tanning." (Stenger 2007, 38) In *stile balneare* songs, the threat of white female (the wife's) nudity dreaded by Fidenco in *Con te sulla spiaggia* was exorcized through tanning, a phenomenon sometimes ridiculed, but then fetishized. In *Abbronzatissima*, this new, transformed, temporarily non-white lover and the seascape can be experienced simultaneously through the senses; the warm sun and the tanned skin through the touch of a hug (first stanza), the sea waves and the woman's breath through hearing (second stanza), the salty water and the sweet lips through smell (third stanza), and finally the full memory of the escapist vacation through sight (fourth stanza).

The same year, a similar dynamic was enacted in Gino Paoli's *Sapore di sale*, an actual ode to the "embodied pleasures" of the beach (Obrador Pons 2012, 48). As the title indicates, here taste is the prevailing sense through which the protagonist lives the escapist fantasy. The relationship between the woman and the seascape is even reverted. In fact, the partner's body is instrumental for the narrating voice to experience the salt, the sea, the sand and the sun:

Sapore di sale,	The taste of salt,
sapore di mare,	the taste of sea,
che hai sulla pelle,	that you have on your skin,
che hai sulle labbra,	that you have on your lips,
[…]	[…]
qui il tempo è dei giorni	here, the time is made up of days
che passano pigri,	that pass lazily,
e lasciano in bocca	and leave the taste of salt
il gusto del sale.	in your mouth.
[…]	[…]
e mentre ti bacio,	and while I kiss you,
sapore di sale,	the taste of salt,
sapore di mare,	the taste of sea,
sapore di te.	the taste of you.

By the end of the song, in the last line, the woman's body is conflated with the surrounding environment, so that the taste of salt and the sea coincides with her very taste. Vincenza Perilli has identified, at the intersection of popular-culture representations of blackness and sexuality, "the black African woman, whose 'availability to be conquered/penetrated' […] becomes a clear metaphor for the availability of the colony to be colonized."[3] (Perilli 2012, 95) In the same way, the woman of *Sapore di sale* is a metaphor of a colonial nostalgia. Significantly, if the colony is typically evoked visually through black skin, the beach and its prominent tactile pleasures are evoked, in *Sapore di sale*, through touch and taste.

In a later interview commenting on *Sapore di sale*, Gino Paoli, a *cantautore*, reclaimed his intellectual engagement as an author while at the same time confirming the escapist purpose of the song:

I've never sought the approval of the general public […]. "Sapore di sale" was seen as a carefree, cheerful song, but it wasn't cheerful at all; […] it was a flash of light, a break

---

[3] "La donna nera africana, la cui 'disponibilità ad essere conquistata-penetrata' […] diviene lampante metafora della disponibilità della colonia ad essere colonizzata." Translated from the Italian by Joanna Helms.

from reality, like a vacation should be, that is, a temporary distancing from established habits.[4] (Paoli 2005)

Sapore di sale fits in perfectly with summer hits from the 1960s, thus confirming that this commercial practice cut across the different statuses and genres ascribed to singers – whether pop singers or singer-songwriters. Summer hits also shared a number of characteristics. The temporal tropes of *villeggiatura* allowed for the reproduction, in vacation destinations, of a micro-society that adhered to middle-class values and shaped the escapist fantasies described in the songs. Once at the beach, the body of the female partner underwent a transformation and became something 'other,' exotic, thanks to the new natural environment. Finally, a tourist (male) gaze – or better, a tourist (male) touch, and taste – was enacted, so that both the environment and the non-white female body became mediators through which to experience escapism in an otherwise familiar setting.

7 The 1970s: Social and Aesthetic Shifts

The escapism permeating summer hits from the 1960s wouldn't last long. Already in 1968 a critical voice was raised by one of the most popular male singers of those years, Adriano Celentano. A so-called '*urlatore*,' soon-to-become guru for his generation, Celentano frequently expressed nostalgia for a pre-industrialized world in his songs, and preached against urbanization. Nostalgia for an imaginary lost past also characterized his summer hit *Azzurro*, with music by another *cantautore*, Paolo Conte, and lyrics by Vito Pallavicini. In *Azzurro*, the beloved woman has left to go to the beach, leaving the narrator alone in the city. In the chorus, Celentano entertains the idea of joining her to escape the alienation and solitude of the urban concrete, but in the end, he admits that such escapism is just an illusion, since the only destination he would like to reach is his past childhood: "E allora io quasi quasi prendo il treno / e vengo, vengo da te / ma il treno dei desideri / nei miei pensieri all'incontrario va" [And then I take the train / And come, come to you / But the train of desire, / In my thoughts, goes backwards].

---

4 "Io non ho mai rincorso il successo del grande pubblico [...]. 'Sapore di sale' poi era vista come una canzone spensierata mentre spensierata non lo era per niente; [...] era un flash, un lampo di luce, uno stacco dalla realtà come dovrebbe essere una vacanza, che significa un allontanamento temporaneo dalle abitudini consolidate." Translated from the Italian by Joanna Helms.

Celentano's hit, together with Mina's *Se telefonando*, sang the decline of the common narrative expressed in songs from the 1960s, a decline confirmed in the 1970s. Summer hits in the *stile balneare* disappeared from the charts, and vacationing was not a frequent topic anymore. During this decade, the nation and its public opinion were shaken by hard changes in the industrial and political fabric of the country, as well as by the emergence of terrorism (Crainz 2012). Such a climate, together with the economic crisis, impacted the expression of escapist desires. In the case of summer hits, it favored the nostalgic tone of songs by Lucio Battisti and Claudio Baglioni, who dominated the Italian charts. In their most popular summer songs – *La canzone del sole* [The song of the sun] (1971) and *Questo piccolo grande amore* [This little big love] (1972) respectively – a youthful summer by the sea is remembered, evoking idealizations of a sexual initiation. Once again, the cliché of a summer romance by the sea is at the center of the songs, but it is set in the past, in a time and age that is lost forever.

8 The 1980s: Exotic Sceneries and the End of Summer Dreams

In the early 1980s, we find an entirely different scenario. First of all, American and British music almost completely take over the Italian popular music scene, leaving less room for Italian artists on the charts. Second, among the Italian titles which make it to the charts, the "Roaring Eighties" witness a new explosion of hits in which vacation themes play a primary role. The new songs are radically different from those of the 1960s. New working conditions allow only for fragmented vacations, whose length no longer spans the entire summer. This is accurately portrayed in contemporary summer songs: in a 1985 hit, the singer Toto Cotugno, who two years earlier had become famous worldwide by claiming to be "Un italiano vero" [a true Italian], impersonated a depressed employee singing *Mi piacerebbe... andare al mare... di lunedì* [I'd like...to go to the sea...on Monday].

Meanwhile, the new affordability of foreign destinations, and the escapist desire they created, generated song titles like *Maracaibo* by Lou Colombo (1981) and *Tropicana* by Gruppo Italiano (1983). In *Maracaibo*, a fictional tropical world populated by criminals and prostitutes, the woman's body was no longer the beloved, familiar body undergoing a perceivable change, but rather a multitude of readymade, anonymous, overtly racialized bodies ("ventitré mulatte" [twenty-three mulattos]) accessible for consumption. More exoticism is featured in *Tropicana*, where the entire scene described is actually a TV commercial for a fictional tropical fruit cocktail: "Mentre la TV diceva, / mentre la TV cantava: / 'Bevila perché è Tropicana, yeah!'" [Meanwhile, the TV was saying, / Meanwhile, the TV was singing: / 'Drink it because it's Tropicana, yeah!']. The distance between this detached, alienated view of the beach and the predominantly tactile experience celebrated in summer hits from the 1960s is striking.

In 1983, the Italian duo Righeira presented *Vamos a la playa*, a hit that made alienation its distinctive trait. In the chorus, the title line was repeated obsessively in an incessant unison that earned this song, for the first time in the press, the epithet of *tormentone*: a derogatory word for 'ear-worm.'[5] In the few lines of the text, sung in Spanish, Righeira manifested their excitement for the explosion of an atomic bomb. They invited the listener to go to the beach, where the radiations would color their skin, brush their hair, and turn the sea into a fluorescent water desert. The song was accompanied by an equally unsettling video, filled with bright, unnatural colors, and featuring an unsynchronized choreography. With this song, Righeira highlighted the vacuity of Italian escapist desires, when confronted with contemporary political and environmental concerns.

Italian summer hits had already expressed the crisis of the *villeggiatura* mode of vacationing in 1979, with Loredana Bertè's *E la luna bussò*. In this song, the moon, the traditional protagonist of a romantic seascape, is personified as a female character and is portrayed as an outcast. Firstly, she is exiled from all the elements of her natural environment (e. g. "E la luna bussò alle porte del buio: / 'Fammi entrare' lui rispose di no" [And the moon knocked at the dark's door: / "Let me come in"; he answered, "no"]). Next, she has to face the indifference of the human beings populating the seaside: "dopo avere pianto un po' / per un altro 'no' / di un cameriere" [after having cried awhile / Over another "no" / From a waiter]. The song criticized the vanity of new ways of living on the *riviera*, and by extension the whole society emerging in those years. In other musical representations of Italian coasts in the 1980s, romance was not at the center anymore. In *Un'estate al mare* by Franco Battiato (1982), the song from which the phrase *stile balneare* is taken, singer Giuni Russo replicated scenarios of prostitution and hallucinations typical of the exoticizing songs ("per le strade mercenarie del sesso / che procurano fantastiche illusioni" [in the streets, sex mercenaries / that provoke fantastic illusions]).

Another critical reflection on summer vacations came in the fall of 1983, when Loredana Berté released her album *Jazz*, giving her voice to Enrico Ruggeri's *Il mare d'inverno*. In this song, the protagonist confesses her inability to

---

[5] The term is used today to define precisely summer hits, '*tormentoni estivi*.'

conceive an alternative mode of interaction with the seascape outside of the season of vacation and its escapist fantasies: "Il mare d'inverno / è un concetto che il pensiero non considera / è poco moderno / è qualcosa che nessuno mai desidera" [The winter sea / Is a concept beyond the possibilities of thought; / It's not very modern / It's something that no one ever wants]. When the season is over, what is left is just "alberghi chiusi / manifesti già sbiaditi di pubblicità" [closed hotels / advertising posters, already faded]. Outside of an escapist frame, the protagonist is disoriented and paralyzed: "ed io, che non riesco nemmeno / a parlare con me" [and I, who can't even / speak to myself]. This new consciousness reveals the end of a myth that the protagonist, and Italian society with her, seems to be unable to cope with.

As a last example, I will turn to the summer hit opening this article. In 1985, Righeira came up with a new *tormentone*: *L'estate sta finendo*. It was released in June, despite its title.

L'estate sta finendo,	The summer is ending
e un anno se ne va;	and a year is gone.
sto diventando grande:	I'm growing up:
lo sai che non mi va.	You know I don't want to.
In spiaggia, di ombrelloni	On the beach, there are barely
non ce ne sono più;	any more umbrellas;
è il solito rituale,	it's the usual ritual,
ma ora manchi tu.	but now you're gone.
La-languidi bri-brividi	Li-listless sh-shivers
come il ghiaccio bruciano	burn like ice
quando sto con te,	when I'm with you,
Ba-ba-ba-ba-baciami, siamo	K-k-k-kiss me, we're
due satelliti in orbita sul mar.	two satellites, orbiting the sea.

The chorus, starting with "La-languidi bri-brividi," is unusually set in a minor key (a melancholic G minor), apparently disconnected from the verses in B-flat major. The chorus clearly references songs from the 1960s, featuring the stuttering on the first syllable of "la-languidi," "bri-brividi;" the same effect is replicated with a sampler on the syllable "ba-ba-ba-ba-baciami," imitating the signature stuttering of *Ba... ba... baciami piccina* – a very popular song from the 1940s which got countless covers between the 1950s and the 1960s – and *Abbronzatissima*. Finally, an emphatic rolling of the "r" ("brividi," "bruciano"), is reminiscent of the style of singers from the 1960s, and especially of Edoardo Vianello. The second verse of the song states: "una fotografia / è tutto quel che ho / ma stanne pur sicura / io non ti scorderò" [a photograph / is all I have / but you can be sure / I won't forget you]. In this song, Righeira was not singing only about the end of summer. Thanks to the minor key and the references to songs from the 1960s, the chorus of *L'estate sta finendo* has the same function as the photograph: a souvenir of many unforgettable *stile balneare* summer hits that cannot be repeated.

9 Conclusions

In this article, I have defined a corpus of songs originating around the early 1960s and scattered among many different artists and genres. Despite their diversity, these songs show certain similarities that have allowed me to group them under the label of *stile balneare*. Part of their similarities resides in their escapist function and in the commercial pattern they tend to follow: these are songs deliberately released in late spring or early summer, reaching a peak in popularity over one season, and then disappearing from the charts in fall. While this trajectory is shared by many summer hits every year, the group of songs that I spotlighted also share certain similarities in their content. With frequent references to the sea, the sun, and generally life at the beach, these songs intertwine elements of the seascape with stories of romantic and sexual relationships taking place during summer holidays.

Considering the shifting holiday habits of Italians from the 1960s to the 1980s, it is possible to identify some parallels between modes of vacationing and the stories in the songs. In the 1960s, long stays in the same beach destination and second-house tourism (*villeggiatura*) resulted in temporal tropes of continuity and periodicity at the base of the romances unfolding in the songs' lyrics and musical structures, with some notable exceptions. These tropes were turned upside down in songs from the 1980s, where sporadic and short-term encounters reflected the contemporary atomization of vacation time for most of Italian society. Not only the type of time, but also the type of places described in these songs changed over the decades. During the 1960s, songs celebrated Italian coasts crowded with familiar faces, where the escapist experience of a summer at the beach was embodied through the transformation of women's skin, unveiled, bronzed, and perfumed with dried salt. The tension between female, racialized nudity and middle-class conservative values was at the core of such escapism. In the 1970s, summer hits almost disappeared and consisted predominantly of memories of idealized sexual initiations, until they flourished again in the 1980s, when the traditional Mediterranean coasts were replaced in the collective imaginary by fictional foreign destinations populated by stereotypically exotic figures. During this decade, the singing of Italian beaches was haunted by a strong sense of alienation and inability to reconnect to the seascape, while at the same time it became embedded in the legacy of summer hits from the 1960s through deliberate literary and sonic references.

The great season of summer hits from the 1960s, animated by the careless optimism of the economic boom, cannot be repeated. In more recent years, one of the most beloved and remembered Italian songs about tourism in Italy is *Vieni a ballare in Puglia* [Come and dance in Puglia] by songwriter and rapper Caparezza (2008), a bitter take on popular summer folk music festivals in Apulia. In this song, which completely excludes any romantic or sexual narrative, the irresistible rhythm of a typical *tarantella* dance is contrasted with lyrics about the poor working and environmental conditions for the inhabitants of the region. Paradoxically, the verb 'to dance' becomes a synonym for 'to die,' and the escapism the music instinctively induces in the listener is turned into a sarcastic, tragic gesture. Today, Italian beaches infamously hit the news worldwide in relation with the immigrant crisis, but mainstream summer hits hardly acknowledge this issue. Instead, the last three years have witnessed a flourishing of new summer hits. These songs have capitalized on the reproduction of many tropes of *stile balneare*, whether in a carefree fashion – like Thegiornailisti, *Riccione* (2017) – or implying a mild critique of contemporary society and politics – like the popular collaboration between rappers and producers J-Ax and Fedez with songs like *Vorrei ma non posto* [I'd like to but I can't (post)] (2016), *Senza pagare* [Without paying] (2017), and *Italiana* (2018). These summer hits are once again an indicator of contemporary Italy, bearing witness to the country's nostalgic relationship with its beaches, and by extension, its inability to conceive new dreams and aspirations.[6]

List of recordings

Year	Title	Singers	Label	Catalog Number
1940	Ba ba baciami piccina / Il primo pensiero	Alberto Rabagliati	Cetra	IT 806
1959	Guarda che luna! / Piangi / Pity Pity / Tu... Non devi farlo più	Fred Buscaglione	Fonit Cetra	EPE 3061

---

[6] All the lyrics quoted in the text have been translated from the Italian by Joanna Helms. I would like to thank the organizers of the conference *Narrating and Constructing the Beach*, and my colleagues and friends Benedetta Zucconi, María Cáceres Piñuel, Valeria Lucentini and Stefano Guerini Rocco for their invaluable input, support, and remarks. I would also like to thank Joanna Helms for her careful revision of the English text.

"Stile balneare." Singing the Italian Summer by the Seaside (1960s–1980s) —— 333

Year	Title	Singers	Label	Catalog Number
1961	*Legata a un granello di sabbia / Ridi ridi*	Nico Fidenco	RCA Italiana	45N-1166
1961	*Riviera / Vento di mare*	Umberto Bindi	Dischi Ricordi	SRL 10-198
1962	*Cuando calienta el sol / La del vestido rojo*	Los Hermanos Rigual	RCA Victor	N 1300
1962	*Pinne, fucile ed occhiali / Guarda come dondolo*	Edoardo Vianello	RCA Italiana	PM45-3100
1963	*Abbronzatissima / Il cicerone*	Edoardo Vianello	RCA Italiana	PM45-3200
1963	*Sapore di sale / La nostra casa*	Gino Paoli	RCA Italiana	PM45-3204
1963	*Stessa spiaggia, stesso mare / Portala in cantina*	Piero Focaccia	CGD	N 9460
1963	*Stessa spiaggia, stesso mare / Ollallà Gigi*	Mina	Italdisc	MH 134
1964	*Con te sulla spiaggia / Mi devi credere*	Nico Fidenco	RCA Italiana	PM45-3255
1964	*Downtown / You'd Better Love Me*	Petula Clark	Pye	7N 15722
1964	*Sei diventata nera / Ora che te ne vai / Piccola timida fragile / Angelita di Anzio*	Los Marcellos Ferial	Vogue Durium	DVEP 95137
1964	*Una rotonda sul mare / Chi ci sarà dopo di te*	Fred Bongusto	Primary	CRA 91934
1964	*Un buco nella sabbia / Se mi compri un gelato*	Mina	Ri-Fi	RFN NP 16061
1965	*Ciao ciao / Se te ne vai*	Petula Clark	Disques Vogue	J 35066
1965	*Il peperone / Nei paesi latini*	Edoardo Vianello e i Flippers	RCA Italiana	PM45-3320
1966	*Notte di Ferragosto / Povera piccola*	Gianni Morandi	RCA Italiana	PM45-3363
1966	*Se telefonando / No*	Mina	Ri-Fi	RFN NP 16146
1968	*Azzurro / Una carezza in un pugno*	Adriano Celentano	Clan Celentano	ACC 40011
1968	*Luglio / Il temporale*	Riccardo del Turco	CGD	N 9682
1971	*La canzone del sole / Anche per te*	Lucio Battisti	Numero Uno	ZN 50132

Year	Title	Singers	Label	Catalog Number
1972	Questo piccolo grande amore	Claudio Baglioni	RCA Italiana	PSL 10551
1979	E la luna bussò / Folle città	Loredana Bertè	CGD	10181
1981	Maracaibo / Neon	Lu Colombo	Carosello Records	CI 20502
1982	Un'estate al Mare / Bing Bang Being	Giuni Russo	CGD	10401
1983	Jazz	Loredana Bertè	CBS	25724
1983	Tropicana / Noi cannibali	Gruppo Italiano	Dischi Ricordi	SRL 10-982
1983	Vamos a la playa / Vamos a la playa (Spanish version)	Righeira	CGD	INT 10457
1985	L'estate sta finendo / Prima dell'estate	Righeira	CGD	10615
1985	Mi piacerebbe... andare al mare... di lunedì... / Come mai?	Toto Cutugno	EMI Italiana	06 1187187
2008	Vieni a ballare in Puglia	Caparezza	EMI Italiana	
2016	Vorrei ma non posto	J-Ax, Fedez	Sony Music, Newtopia	
2017	Riccione	TheGiornalisti	Carosello Records	
2017	Senza pagare	J-Ax, Fedez	Sony Music, Newtopia	
2018	Italiana	J-Ax, Fedez	Newtopia	

Bibliography

Battilani, Patrizia. "Rimini. An Original Mix of Italian Style and Foreign Models?" *Europe at the Seaside. The Economic History of Mass Tourism in the Mediterranean*. Eds. Luciano Segreto, Carles Manera and Manfred Pohl. New York and Oxford: Berghahn Books, 2009. 104–124.

Bærenholdt, Jørgen Ole, Michael Haldrup, Jonas Larsen and John Urry. *Performing Tourist Places*. Aldershot: Ashgate, 2004.

Borgna, Gianni. *La grande evasione. Storia del Festival di Sanremo: 30 anni di costume italiano*. Milano: Savelli, 1980.
Crainz, Guido. *Il paese mancato. Dal miracolo economico agli anni Ottanta*. Roma: Donzelli, 2003.
Crainz, Guido. *Il paese reale. Dall'assassinio di Moro all'Italia di oggi*. Roma: Donzelli, 2012.
Franklin, Adrian, and Mike Crang. "The Trouble with Tourism and Travel Theory?" *Tourist Studies* 1.1 (2001): 5–22.
Deplano, Valeria. "Within and Outside the Nation: Former Colonial Subjects in Post-War Italy." *Modern Italy* 23.4 (2018): 395–410.
Dyer, Richard. *White. Essays on Race and Culture*. London and New York: Routlege, 1997.
Facci, Serena, and Paolo Soddu. *Il Festival di Sanremo. Parole e suoni raccontano la nazione*. Roma: Carocci, 2011.
Giuliani, Gaia. "La sottile linea bianca. Intersezioni di razza, genere e classe nell'Italia postcoloniale." *Studi culturali* 2 (2013): 253–267.
Giuliani, Gaia. "Razza cagna: *Mondo Movies*, the White Heterosexual Male Gaze, and the 1960s–1970s Imaginary of the Nation." *Modern Italy* 23.4 (2018): 429–444.
Huber, Alison. "Mainstream as Metaphor. Imagining Dominant Culture." *Redefining Mainstream Popular Music*. Eds. Sarah Baker, Andy Bennet and Jodie Taylor. London and New York: Routledge, 2013. 3–13.
Lew, Alan A., C. Michael Hall and Allan M. Williams. *A Companion to Tourism*. Malden/MA: Blackwell, 2004.
Löfgren, Orvar. *On Holiday. A History of Vacationing*. Berkeley: University of California Press, 1999.
Manning, Till. *Die Italiengeneration. Stilbildung durch Massentourismus in den 1950er und 1960er Jahren*. Göttingen: Wallstein, 2011.
Morris, Gary. "Surf's up! Beyond the Beach: AIP's Beach Party movies." *Bright Light Films Journal* 21 (1998). https://brightlightsfilm.com/surfs-beyond-beach-aips-beach-party-movies/#.XNBvIhMzaAw (7 May 2019).
Obrador Pons, Pau. "Being-on-holiday. Tourist Dwelling, Bodies and Place." *Tourist Studies* 3.1 (2003): 47–66.
Obrador Pons, Pau. "Touching the Beach." *Touching Space. Placing Touch*. Eds. Mark Paterson and Martin Dodge. Farnham: Ashgate, 2012. 47–70.
Pagenstecher, Cord. "L'immagine dell'Italia nella pubblicità tedesca del dopoguerra. Il Lago di Garda e la Riviera Adriatica nelle brochure del tour operator Scharnow." *Storia del turismo. Annale 2003*. Ed. Istituto per la Storia del Risorgimento Italiano. Roma and Milano: FrancoAngeli, 2004. 105–136.
Paoli, Gino. "Gino Paoli: 'Mi credevo al centro dell'universo'." Interview with Marinella Venegoni. *La Stampa* (9 August 2005): 27. http://archivio.lastampa.it/m/articolo?id=06eb372b02bef6de9a12a4a8695a1c59fbe44309 (28 January 2019).
Patriarca, Silvana. "'Gli italiani non sono razzisti': costruzioni dell'italianità tra gli anni Cinquanta e il 1968." *Il colore della nazione*. Ed. Gaia Giuliani. Firenze: Le Monnier, 2015. 32–45.
Perilli, Vincenza. "'Sesso' e 'razza' al muro. Razzismo e sessismo in pubblicità." *Specchio delle sue brame. Analisi socio-politica delel pubblicità: genere, classe, razza, età e eterosessimo*. Ed. Laura Corradi. Roma: Ediesse, 2012. 91–126.
Petrovich Njegosh, Tatiana. "La linea del colore nella cultura di massa." *Studi culturali* 2 (2013). 47–54.

Santoro, Marco: "What is a 'cantautore?' Distinction and Authorship in Italian (popular) music." *Poetics* 30 (2002). 111–132.
Shary, Timothy. *Teen Movies. American Youth on Screen.* London: Wallflower, 2005.
Stenger, Josh. "Mapping the Beach. Beach Movies, Exploitation Film and Geographies of Whiteness." *The Persistence of Whiteness. Race and Contemporary Hollywood Cinema.* Ed. Daniel Bernardi. London and New York: Routledge, 2007. 28–50.
Urbain, Jean-Didier. *At the Beach.* Minneapolis and London: University of Minnesota Press, 2003.
Urry, John. *The Tourist Gaze. Leisure and Travel in Contemporary Societies.* London: SAGE Publications, 1990.

List of Figures

Fig. 1: Vito Pallavicini, Tony Hatch. *Ciao ciao* (lyrics).
Fig. 2: Vito Pallavicini, Tony Hatch. *Ciao ciao* (my melodic transcription).
Fig. 3: Ghigo De Chiara, Maurizio Costanzo and Ennio Morricone. *Se telefonando* (lyrics).

Jack Parlett
The Boys on the Beach: Andrew Holleran's Fire Island

This article discusses the relationship between the beach culture of Fire Island, a famous gay vacation spot, in the 1970s, and a mode of tragic fatalism that is traditionally associated with gay literature. It brings these concerns together by examining Andrew Holleran's 1978 Fire Island novel *Dancer from the Dance*, where "death and desire" are placed in a constitutive bind. By suggesting that the beach offers a fertile analogy for considering the historical re-emergence of particular corporeal tropes in accounts of gay life, the article proposes that Holleran's novel is haunted not only by what has preceded it, such as W. H. Auden's 1948 poem "Pleasure Island" but, more uncannily, by the devastation of the HIV/AIDS epidemic that followed in the 1980s.

Der vorliegende Aufsatz verhandelt das Verhältnis zwischen der Strandkultur von Fire Island in den 1970er Jahren – einem damals bei Schwulen besonders beliebten Urlaubsort – und einem Modus des tragischen Fatalismus, der traditionell mit schwuler Literatur assoziiert wird. Diese beiden Themen werden anhand einer Lektüre von Andrew Hollerans Fire Island-Roman *Dancer from the Dance* (1978) verknüpft, in welchem „Tod und Begehren" in eine konstitutive Verbindung zueinander gesetzt werden. Am Ende des Aufsatzes steht die Schlussfolgerung, dass der Strand eine fruchtbare Analogie für die Betrachtung der Rückkehr besonderer körperlicher Tropen in Darstellungen des schwulen Lebens bietet, und dass Hollerans Roman nicht nur von dem heimgesucht wird, was ihm zeitlich vorausging, wie etwa W. H. Audens Gedicht „Pleasure Island" von 1948, sondern – umso unheimlicher – auch von der verheerenden HIV/AIDS Epidemie, die in den 1980er Jahren folgen sollte.

1 Introduction

Recalling summers spent in the 1970s and 1980s on the beach at Fire Island Pines, a gay vacation spot around fifty miles away from New York City, the American photographer Tom Bianchi writes:

> Over the years, I chronicled a cultural phenomenon – an awakening – as more and more gay men found gyms and transformed themselves into our collective sexual fantasies. Early each season I'd see men on the beach, emerging newly buff after a winter in a New York gym. Most of us had suffered boyhoods as secret or not so secret sissies. The demonstration of physical beauty and strength was a natural part of the gay pride movement, then in full throttle. Many who had the desire to do it, discovered they could create themselves. When the transformation was coupled with an intelligent generous spirit, the result was fine indeed. What some saw as narcissism, I saw as healthy self-regard – no need to apologize for our personal and cultural transformation. (Bianchi 2013, 16)

Bianchi's celebratory account of beach body culture and its "natural" relation to "gay pride" is disarmingly simple, its only caveat being the nature of the "intelligent generous spirit" which ensured the order of the day was "healthy self-regard" instead of "narcissism." What such generosity might mean in this context is left unsaid, and Bianchi's Polaroid images of men on Fire Island attest to a milieu that seems by design exceptional rather than inclusive, its primary commitment being to "physical beauty," populated by chiselled Adonis types. Bianchi's account is appealing, at least, for so eagerly providing a positive spin upon the standards of this culture. It rehearses a defence of beauty that he has made throughout his photographic career, suggesting that these macho transformations are acts of defiance, mutually affirming responses to the shame and suffering of repressed "boyhoods." A highly aesthetic photographer of the male body, Bianchi seems unfazed in this recollection by the theoretical warfare which surrounds the gay-macho style he is known for capturing. When invoking the gendered nature of this performance, which substitutes a "buff," athletic masculinity in place of the feminised abjection of the sissy boy, Bianchi stops short of considering this as a subversive practice that toys with gender norms. But neither does he trouble over the opposing critique, of which Leo Bersani's essay "Is the Rectum a Grave?" is perhaps the classic example. Bersani argues that the gay-macho style, centred around "looks" and "muscles," failed to transcend its own reverence for machismo and thus have any tangible "effects" on "the heterosexual world that provides the models" upon which it is based (Bersani 1987, 207). Instead, it risks "complicities with a brutal and misogynous ideal of masculinity" (ibid., 206), the same oppressive ideal that propagates derogatory terms like "sissy" in the first place.

In the years following gay liberation, then, the culture of the beach body involved distinctly *unhealthy* forms of self-regard, too, contrary to the sunny naivety of Bianchi's account. The associations of the beach body were indeed further confounded by the ravages wrought upon the body by the HIV/AIDS crisis during the 1980s, when the emaciation of illness became a ubiquitous body type in the gay community. In this regard Bianchi's photographs seem resolutely *pre*-AIDS, for there is a simplicity in their devotion to pleasure, and they possess the idyllic valence of the calm before a storm, ripe for nostalgic appropriation as tantalising glimpses of the utopic. As a form of visual documentary, they register as a retro iteration of what the sociologist Henning Bech describes as a "stock theme" in the "homosexual experience," the sense that happiness is located somewhere on the horizon, in "another country," a place both real and imagined, with a landscape "appropriate to pleasure and play" (Bech 1997, 37). This gay pastoralism infuses Bianchi's images, for it is not only bodily ideals that they convey but the ideal of the natural paradise, the clear skies and sandy beaches of Fire Island, offering plentiful spaces for acts of cruising and dancing. The utopic resonance of Bianchi's visual record is thus not only palpable retrospectively, as the product of a post-AIDS vantage, but also relates to Fire Island's long-standing associations as a refuge from the everyday, a place which each summer would play host, away from the potential hostility of the dominant culture, to the community's "awakening." Such a place then sustains an illusion of exemption not only from the political restrictions or inequities of the mainland, but other forms of drudgery or labour that underpin that place's functioning. The beach foregrounds the spectacle of having the right kind of body whilst simultaneously obscuring, as a space of leisure, the exertion involved in obtaining it, just as the "winter in a New York gym" is excluded from Bianchi's showcase of the results. The labour-intensive *how* and the potentially problematic *why* of such bodily transformations are only ever implicit in these images, which are absorbed instead in the sheer beauty of the *what*, the sculpted male body as a corporeal *a priori* that seems part and parcel of the naturally beautiful setting. As such, they only tell a part of the story.

Compare, for example, Bianchi's account of gym-going to the following moment from Andrew Holleran's 1978 novel *Dancer from the Dance*, where the narrator recalls

> [the] summer gym shorts had become fashionable as bathing suits, the summer Frank Post (who each spring contemplated suicide because he could not rise to the occasion – of being the most voluptuous, beautiful man on the Island, the homosexual myth everyone adored – but managed to go to the gym, take his pills, and master yet another season) shaved his body and wore jockstraps to Tea Dance, and his lover died of an overdose of Angel Dust and Quaaludes. (Holleran 1990 [1978], 31)

Appropriating the syntax of fashion, this passage measures memories by "season" and describes annual shifts in what is "fashionable," diffusing the charge of its more serious moments, which lose their significance when rendered as so many entries in a list of transient tastes. The effect of such a list is that the differences between its formulaically brief units are elided, suggesting an unquestioned simultaneity where trends in "bathing suits" and the shadow of "suicide" co-exist. Frank Post's serial contemplation of killing himself while working on his beach body forms the larger part of his description but is written as a long parenthetical aside, as if offering a glimpse behind the scenes of what is taken as given "every spring," an impulse that arises like clockwork amid changing vogues. It might read merely as comically overwrought, a campy exaggeration of priorities that is meant no more seriously than the vogue of "gym shorts," were it not for the revelation that Post's lover "died of an overdose." This is the kind of fatality that is perhaps ambiguously suicidal, and it inflects

Post's earlier contemplation with a retrospective gravity. Post himself seems precariously suspended as the sentence's subject, awaiting the completion of the verb from which he is kept distant by the parenthesised activities that constitute his exterior self. Punctuated by death, this passage offers an altogether different account of "personal and cultural transformation" (Bianchi 2013, 16) to Bianchi's, illuminating how this impulse toward transformation might in turn be destructive, or lead to destruction. Whilst it is in one sense oriented toward a future ("yet another season"), Post's desire to "rise to the occasion" seems simultaneously to risk annihilation, thus foregoing futurity altogether.

The Fire Island beach, as this article will explore, is a consummate landscape for futurity under threat. The narrator of *Dancer from the Dance* earlier describes the island as "nothing but a sandbar, as slim as a parenthesis, enclosing the Atlantic, the very last fringe of soil on which a man might put up his house, and leave behind him all – absolutely all – of that huge continent to the west" (Holleran 1990 [1978], 24). This description is alive to the precariousness of the place, its diminutive topography and geographical marginality meeting with an implicit inclination toward negation and finality: "nothing," "the very last," leaving "behind." In this regard, such a place might seem analogously suited to the contemplated finality of Frank Post's suicidal urges, even if this fatalism is spurred by the desire, ironically, to be more, to be in one's body desirably "voluptuous" as opposed to "slim as a parenthesis." *Dancer from the Dance* asks us to take seriously the notion that the culture of the beach body is a matter of life and death for gay men on Fire Island in the 1970s. As the site where the body is showcased and exposed, Fire Island and by extension the space of the beach more generally make this peculiar sense of morbidity legible. The narrator's recollections of Frank Post and his dead lover occur in a reverie that is spurred on by a "sudden wish to feast on the past" and takes place from the vantage of "the steps leading to the beach" (ibid., 30). In this section of the novel (examined in more detail below), the beach is cast as a landscape that emphasises the close relationship between "death and desire" (ibid., 31).

Holleran's fixation upon such morbidity raises other questions about the moral presumptions of this novel, which in some respects appears to suggest that both gay male sexuality, and the attendant work involved in obtaining a sexually desirable body, are synonymous with a sense of doom. Although this is rooted in characters' anxieties about physical beauty and aging, it also feels eerily proleptic of the age of HIV/AIDS, when the relation between "death and desire" came to be framed as a constitutive part of the disease, a moralistic projection of death as a consequence of reckless sexual activity. In this sense Holleran's novel has something in common with Larry Kramer's *Faggots*, which was published the same year and loudly derided by many gay readers for its perceived moralism with regards to sex and promiscuity. Accounting for the similar and different ways Holleran and Kramer treat these issues would be the remit of another article, but suffice it to say here that both novels express a set of pessimistic reservations about the sexual culture of the post-Stonewall 1970s, and both feature a dramatic denouement on Fire Island where such pessimisms play out. I will conclude by suggesting that this crux of concerns is not unique to Holleran's work, or even this period of writing about Fire Island. W. H. Auden's 1948 poem "Pleasure Island," for example, paints a similar picture. Such echoes before and after the historical moment of *Dancer from the Dance* point to the beach's particular resonance for reflecting upon the vexed corporeal tropes of gay life and resonate with a connection between death and Fire Island first drawn by David Bergman in his account of the island's literary history, where he writes of it as a 'place of and for extremes'; a potentially fatal 'precipice' (Bergman 2004, 164–165).

2 A Visual People

Dancer from the Dance is structured around a novel-within-a-novel called *Wild Swans*, which is narrated by an unnamed denizen of the New York gay scene who introduces the novel through a series of framing letters to Paul, a friend who has vacated the city for a quieter life in the Deep South. The opening of *Wild Swans* begins after the events of its denouement, and sees the narrator returning to Fire Island in the "last week of October" (Holleran 1990 [1978], 23) to collect the possessions of Malone, the novel's protagonist, who was last seen wading "into the bay" at a Fire Island party that summer (ibid., 232). This episode's water-side vantage, late October setting and maudlin fixation upon the passing of time are evidently borrowed from the poem that provides *Wild Swans* with its title, W. B. Yeats's 1919 "The Wild Swans at Coole," and the Fire Island beach is here figured as a haunted space, ushering in a funereal pageant of summers past.[1] As for Malone, numerous fates are suggested; whether his disappearance was a suicidal act, whether he survived, or whether he made it back to the city but then died in a fire at the Everard Baths, all remain unknown. A closeted corporate lawyer from Ohio, Malone first moves to New York in the early 1970s in search of love. After a tempestuous love affair with Frankie, a married man from New Jersey, he is swept up by the campy older queen

---

[1] The title of the novel proper is taken from a line in another Yeats poem, "Among School Children" (1926), which reads: "O body swayed to music, O brightening glance / How can we know the dancer from the dance?" (Yeats 1997, 222)

Sutherland, who helps him become a darling of the scene, a prodigiously handsome realization of the community's desires. By the end of the novel, he is a disillusioned escort who feels he has wasted his life searching for love in an environment devoted above all to youth and pleasure. Although his final words before swimming away suggest that he plans to go "out west" to "some little town in Idaho," the narrator worries as to Malone's urges, having heard "his reflections on the young man who had killed himself in Manhattan that afternoon" (Holleran 1990 [1978], 232). Graphic talk of a young man's suicide had dominated beach conversations earlier in the chapter; talk of a "boy from Idaho – who had slashed his wrists, and then his throat, and then hurled himself nine floors from the top of his apartment building to the steaming pavement below on this hottest of all hot afternoons" (ibid., 220).

Among several more or less ambiguous suicides referred to throughout the novel, which include numerous drug overdoses and the case of "a nameless ribbon clerk" who died from sniffing "a popper at the bottom of a pool" (ibid., 32), the stark case of the "boy from Idaho" casts the longest shadow, and has Malone reflecting that "When we're all so terribly alone" the "least we can do in this life is love one another" (ibid., 221). His own disappearance is shot through with the fatalism of this earlier suicide, and in this light his choice of "Idaho" as the generic town "out west" to which he claims to be fleeing feels deliberate, offering the suggestion that he might follow in the footsteps of the young man who hailed from there. Just as Malone's disappearance is positioned in relation to an event preceding it, the morbid return to Fire Island at the opening of *Wild Swans* is re-contextualised by this ending, which chronologically precedes it. For this reason, and for the sake of clarity, this article will examine examples from the novel in the chronological order of their unfolding. Although this goes against the novel's structure, it is my contention that its ending casts light upon the spectral textures of its opening, and provides a narrative context for the co-presence of "death and desire" that so infuses the narrator's recollection on the beach. Approaching examples in this order is also consonant with the principle of syntactical retroactivity that runs throughout, where clauses in the narrator's lists inflect and re-contextualise what has come before, often turning the trivial into the tragic. Frank Post's contemplation of suicide, for example, loses its comic resonance when listed alongside his lover's overdose. These non-linearities in structure and syntax speak to the novel's sense of its own haunting, and the beach emerges, I will conclude, as a landscape of spectral return.

The eighth and final chapter of *Wild Swans* takes place on Fire Island, a place "for madness, for hot nights, kisses, and herds of stunning men: a national game preserve annually replenished" (ibid., 206–207). This description of the island's corporeality pre-empts Malone's melancholic diatribe, addressed to

John Schaeffer, a young man vying for his affections, later that evening at the party:

> You must remember one thing, if I can leave you with anything, if my years out here can benefit you at all, then let it be with this. Never forget that all these people are primarily a visual people. They are designers, window dressers, models, photographers, graphic artists. They design the windows at Saks. Do you understand? They are a visual people, they value the eye, and their sins, as Saint Augustine said, are the sins of the eye. And being people who live on the surface of the eye, they cannot be expected to have minds or hearts. It sounds absurd but it's that simple. Everything is beautiful here, and that is all it is: beautiful. Do not expect anything else, do not expect nourishment for anything but your eye. (Ibid., 228)

A great deal of work is done here by the phrase "all it is," holding within it the suggestion that a given virtue is sacrificed when it becomes "all" an object is. Something that is only beautiful, it suggests, is in fact not beautiful at all. Malone is hardly the first thinker to get here; his statement rehearses an age-old "political critique" which, Elaine Scarry writes, "urges that beauty, by preoccupying our attention, distracts attention from wrong social arrangements" and "makes us inattentive, and therefore eventually indifferent, to the project of bringing about arrangements that are just" (Scarry 1999, 58). Contrary to Scarry's well-known debunking of such an argument through the idea that "perceiving beauty confers" on both the perceiver and on the object the "gift of life" (ibid., 90), Malone, who has often been both object and perceiver, sees only beauty's lack of affective substance, its visuality over vitality, its spurning of justice, of "minds and hearts." Fire Island nourishes the eye, not the I; as Malone pondered earlier that afternoon, upon seeing a beautiful boy in the park, beauty had become "an impersonal fact, as impersonal as the beauty of a tree, or a sky, or a seacoast" (Holleran 1990 [1978], 214), catalysing his decision to leave behind the life he has been living.

It is in these climactic moments that *Dancer from the Dance* recalls F. Scott Fitzgerald's *The Great Gatsby*, a classic intertextual shorthand for the diagnosis of a lifestyle that favours style over substance (Schopp 2016). Edmund White once stated that Holleran's novel "accomplished for the 1970s" what Fitzgerald's did "for the 1920s ... the glamorization of a decade and a culture" (Holleran 1990 [1978], book jacket). If such a claim seems at odds with Malone's disillusioned lament, it is worth noting that this lament is rooted in his own exclusion from a way of life that had before both protected and beguiled him. Your invite may get lost in the post, but the party will continue to be beautiful. This is why, when stood facing the island's "impersonal [...] sea-coast," he and "people he had known for years [...] were looking at the new faces" at the party "with an odd sensation of death, for they had all been new faces once" (ibid., 226). What Malone's demise turns upon is ultimately an anticipated failure in looking, not only the failure to maintain the good looks and physical form required to be a "star" of the island, nor the failure to look good enough "to get any of these stars into bed" (ibid.), but a failure to look upon the island's beauties and feel anything, to obtain what Scarry identifies as "the gift of life." This exclusion from the spoils of a transient culture, the novel's conclusion suggests, is tantamount to death, which is why Malone disappears before he can be made invisible.

3 Death and Desire

Some months later at the novel's "beginning," upon his return to Fire Island to sort Malone's possessions, the narrator reflects upon those "boys in New York whose lovers die of drugs, and who give the dead lover's clothes to their new lover without a second thought" (Holleran 1990 [1978], 29). Walking through the house, he thinks of the "succession of houseboys" who "had passed through the place" and been "replaced as casually as fuses," including "a dancer from Iowa" who "had been discovered renting rooms to strangers for fifty dollars a day during the week" and "later had his head blown off on St. Marks Place by a Mafia hit man when he started a new career as a drug dealer; his funeral had been more glittering than any party of the winter" (ibid.). This past as conjured up by the silent house is mediated, like the world of "visual people," by a callous economy of replacement, where the clothes of the dead quickly find new wearers and the houseboys are as interchangeable as "fuses." The story of the dead house-boy gestures to a milieu outside of the novel's gaze, a realm of precarious work and criminality which the relatively moneyed protagonists seem largely distant from. He is invoked, like many of the sentence-long cameo roles in *Dancer*, in relation to his hometown. The "dancer from Iowa" who met a grisly end; it is in these compact, even throwaway instances that Holleran's prose seems to engage the mode of the obituary, glimpsing momentarily at the back-story of a lost life. And like most of the deaths in the novel, the demise of the houseboy is also brought flippantly into the service of the scene's larger glamour, his send-off a "glittering" substitute for a winter party.

Moving through the house to the beach, the narrator describes that the reason "I loved the beach in autumn [...] was that now the false social organism had vanished and left it what Malone had always wished it to be: a fishing village, in which, presumably, no one lied to one another" (ibid., 30). The turn of the season replaces Fire Island's very ecosystem, from party-town to pastoral, from a "false social organism" to a wholesome, honest desertedness that is all the better for reflection:

> A sudden wish to feast on the past made me sit down on the steps leading to the beach for a moment, the steps where in the hot August sunlight we had rested our feet from the burning sand and shaded our eyes to look out at the figures in the dazzling light. There had been a dwarf that summer, a squat hydrocephalic woman who wandered up and down the beach among those handsome young men like a figure in an allegory. And there had been the Viet Nam veteran who had lost a leg, and walked along the water's edge in a leather jacket in the hottest weather, hobbling with a cane. He had drowned that Sunday so many swimmers had drowned. Not twenty feet from the steps on which I sat now, a corpse had lain all afternoon beneath a sheet because the police were too busy to remove it, and five feet away from the corpse, people lay taking the sun and admiring a man who had just given the kiss of life to a young boy. Death and desire, death and desire. (Ibid., 30–31)

This is one of the strangest moments in *Dancer from the Dance*. By introducing incongruous figures whose presences are avowedly allegorical, the narrator employs the spectacle of the freak show to create a more general sense of dread. Concisely, these figures invoke the political realities of deformation, disability and war, forms of difficulty and conflict which seem outside of the novel's universe. The "squat hydrocephalic" woman and the "Viet Nam veteran" both seem as if they are borrowed from another time and place, or another discourse altogether, like a pulp novel or a sensational news story. They are in this sense deviant bodies, which is to say you would not find them in a photograph by Tom Bianchi, and in this moment, they serve to disrupt the beach's worship of youth and virility (in which able-bodied-ness is taken as given) by offering palpable signs of the body's vulnerability. Yet these intrusions are also unable to penetrate the surface and the beach community's love thereof. Beyond it, the police are "too busy" with some other emergency, too busy to remove the corpse of an amputee, a dead body whose presence is little more than an inconvenience in the face of more appealing spectacles, like the "man who had just given the kiss of life to a young boy."

Whilst the elegiac mood of this reflection is rooted in the context of Malone's disappearance, it also seems to identify, more synoptically, a larger, more sordid sense of doom at the Fire Island beach. The community's apparent predilection for death and destruction is here given sinister, symbolic form right under its nose, but people are too busy sun-bathing to notice. It also speaks to the narrator's admission, in one of the framing letters which closes *Dancer*, of the novel's own circumspection:

> That day we marched to Central Park and found ourselves in a sea of humanity, how stunned I was to recognise no more than four or five faces? (Of course our friends were all at the beach, darling; they couldn't be bothered to come in and make a political statement.) (Ibid., 249)

The beach here becomes idiomatic for a certain leisurely apathy, a glamorous reprieve from the banal work of political engagement. This moment somewhat disturbs the novel's own mythologization of gay life by exposing the specificity of its plot, which mostly renders a whole way of life in broad and tragic terms but in fact, as admitted here, represents just one beach from amidst a "sea of humanity." There were so many other "men in that city who weren't on the circuit, who didn't dance, didn't cruise, didn't fall in love with Malone [...] We never saw them" (ibid.). The tragedy of *Wild Swans* thus becomes one of a community, or one part of a community, intoxicated by its own pathos: as Paul, the narrator's epistolary interlocutor writes in an introductory letter, the "world demands that gay life, like the life of the Very Rich, be ultimately sad, for everyone in this country believes, down deep in their heart, that to be happy you must have a two-story house in the suburbs and a FAMILY" (ibid., 15). The men seeking to approximate such domesticity are among those the narrator "never saw," forced out of view like the rest of the world, and this binary between the domestic and the destructive implies, in a sex-negative manner, that the sadness felt by the novel's characters is somehow inherent to an outgoing and promiscuous way of living. This is the central ambivalence of *Dancer from the Dance*, a novel which seems to be eulogising a way of life, rendered as tragic and therefore beautiful, whilst also remaining suspicious of that way of life and its perceived irresponsibility. Andrew Schopp argues that Paul's delineation of "the addictive consequences that result when one allows the frame within which one lives to determine one's existence" should be used to defend Holleran's novel from "critiques" which "disregard the message inherent in Malone's rejection of that life and in Paul's final missive," thus "ignor[ing] the novel's irony" (Schopp 2016, 169–170). The novel's late-hour acknowledgment of the world outside it, and of the previously unknown capaciousness of the world inside it, serves to undercut some of its cautionary melancholy. But can the novel's hard-and-fast play with lived experiences of death and desire, a relation given allegorical shape by figures of abject deformity and militarised death, be recuperated by "irony" alone?

4 The Boys on the Beach

Holleran is not the first writer to light upon a connection between the body cult of Fire Island and broader social ills. During the late 1940s, W. H. Auden summered for several years in Cherry Grove, a neighbouring gay community to the west of Fire Island Pines (the two are separated by the Meat Rack, an infamous wooded cruising spot). Auden's 1948 poem on the subject, "Pleasure Island," tells a familiar story of "an outpost where nothing is wicked / But to be sorry or sick" (Auden 1976, 266). The poem centres upon a temptation scene, and charts the fate of a well-intentioned visitor who is seen

> [...] improving his mind
> On the beach with a book, but the dozing
> Afternoon is opposed
> To rhyme and reason and chamber music,
> The plain sun has no use
> For the printing press, the wheel, the electric
> Light, and the waves reject
> Sympathy: soon he gives in, stops stopping
> To think, lets his book drop
> And lies, like us, on his stomach watching
> As bosom, backside, crotch
> Or other sacred trophy is borne in triumph
> Past his adoring by
> Souls he does not try to like; then, getting
> Up, gives all to the wet
> Clasps of the sea or surrenders his scruples
> To some great gross braying group
> That will be drunk till Fall. The tide rises
> And falls [...]
> (ibid.)

There's a self-reflexive quality to the voice narrating this scene; we don't know much about the "us," the community of voyeuristic bathers into which this unwitting writer is initiated, but the poem makes conceivable that perhaps they were once writers too, subject to this same fate of surrendering to revelry "till Fall." By taking up the American English word for autumn, Auden also introduces, somewhat histrionically, a Biblical valence to this transgression of scruples, consonant with what Richard Bozorth identifies as the poem's "unironized Christian mythos, in which life devoted [...] to sexual bliss is not paradise but hell" (Bozorth 2001, 242). One of the beach lifestyle's greatest sins, after all, is its lack of substance, privileging "bosom" over "book." In this sense Auden's poem resembles Sutherland's account of what distinguishes the beaches of Fire

Island from those of the Hamptons, where the "homosexuals tended to be fatter, older, and attired in pastel-colored slacks," but "they could at least discuss [...] Samuel Beckett, or the latest novel of Iris Murdoch" (Holleran 1990 [1978], 207). Fire Island is a place where the intellect goes to die, where even the educated succumb to its deleterious effects, and Holleran later recalls being both observer and participant in a culture where the "thing that had not seemed important at Harvard – the body – was now crucial." Where he once would have "wondered what Henry James had meant in *The Ambassadors*," Holleran was now "wondering how to combine brewers' yeast with my morning milkshake because I needed extra protein for the body-building I was doing at the gym" (Holleran 2018 [1994], 144–145).

This substitution of bodies for books has become a standard joke in representations of Fire Island, made up of works that inhabit the ironic position of rendering textually, from the perspective of a participant, a place that is supposedly anti-literary, a place which distracts you from "improving" your "mind." The speaker of "Pleasure Island" is hardly agnostic about this trade-off, and Richard Bozorth suggests that the poem also gravely registers Auden's "sense of his own aging body," at age forty-one, in the face of "the worship of youth that permeates gay male subculture" (Bozorth 2001, 240). The "unruly sea" and "great gross braying group" of body worshippers are indeed comparable threats to one's autonomy (Auden 1976, 266). The island is a "Place of the skull, a place where the rose of/Self-punishment will grow." This pastoral image of Golgotha draws upon an unspoken sense of the dreadful and the hellish, gesturing implicitly to historical precedents where the beach body is coded as the site of possible annihilation, and "Pleasure Island" finds an analogue in Auden's 1933 masque play *The Dance of Death*, a cautionary satire that is also set on the beach. In the opening scene, the play's Chorus worship the mysterious figure of the Dancer, a sinister cult leader and advocate of bodily health who they claim can "give you a grecian figure," instructing new recruits to "Lie down on the sand" and feel "the sun on your flesh" (Auden 1933, 9). The ominously benign imperatives of physical improvement in *The Dance of Death* contain shadows of the *Freikörperkultur*, the free-body naturist movement that had flourished in Germany since the nineteenth century but became increasingly intertwined with National Socialism in the years leading up to the Second World War. Auden's play thus suggests how easily a culture of the body which advocates freedom from societal and sartorial constraints can be co-opted into a body cult whose aims lead troublingly, by extension, to the sought-after *purity* of the body politic.

This texture of Auden's writing, the overlay of his respective experiences in Germany and America at different but proximate historical moments, touches at last upon that ubiquitous and troubling metaphor of body fascism. Mickey Weems writes that *"body fascists,"* the "men who judge others solely on physical beauty," are one of the consummate "stereotypes" (Weems 2008, 1) of the Circuit, the hedonistic gay party culture that began to bloom in the late 1970s, around the time Holleran's novel was published. In its drastic associations, the notion of body fascism seems a world away from the "healthy self-regard" that Bianchi identifies in the same culture. In a 2000 review of David Morgan's *The Beach*, a collection of male nudes shot on the beach at Fire Island, Holleran writes "whatever you think of this – whether you call it body fascism or absently leaf through a book like this while waiting for a friend to get off the phone – such collections [...] are basically eye candy" (Holleran 2000). Bodies, he continues, are "paraded at the beach to exercise power" and "advertise the details of one's need in a partner," a beach which "presents a constant tension between reality and image, invitation and exclusion," for the "paradox of the Pines" is like the "double message of these bodies: on the one hand, hot, on the other, oh so cold" (ibid.). In *Dancer from the Dance*, however, the stakes of hotness and *froideur* seemed considerably higher. The puritanical melancholia of *Dancer* and "Pleasure Island" make good upon the metaphorical weight of body fascism, less as a fanciful analogy than as a present menace of annihilation that seems immanent in the very atmosphere of the beach. As Auden has it, it is as if "our / Lenient amusing shore / Knows in fact about all the dyings" (Auden 1976, 266), playing upon dying's orgasmic and organic meanings and rendering the numerous *petits morts* of a Fire Island weekend in relation to spectres of historical "fact."

The problem with this rendering of fatalism as immanent is the inference that it is somehow pre-determined, the inevitable price of gay pleasure on the "lenient" shore. However much these literary works invest in or ironize such a conflation, a tragic trope of gay life, the example of something like "The Boys on the Beach," the infamous 1980 essay by Midge Decter from which this article, with some irony, borrows a title, demonstrates how readily available such a trope is to moralistic and homophobic rewriting. Decter bemoans the changes she has witnessed to "the homosexual community I used to know" from her summers spent at the Pines in the 1960s, the pre-Stonewall years during which the Pines was still a mix of gay and straight (Decter 1980). These gays "were characterized by nothing so much as a sweet, vain, pouting, girlish attention to the youth and the beauty of their bodies," a "worship of youth" that was particularly "inescapable to the eye" on the beach, a catwalk for the "tanning flesh" which was never "permitted to betray any of the ordinary signs of encroaching mortality" (ibid.). Although Decter believes such preening was primarily intended as a mockery of the straight men at the beach, for "homosexuality paints" such men "with the colour of sheer entrapment," it was at least an improvement upon the community "nowadays" (ibid. 1980), in 1980. These gays are newly politicised and increasingly "engaged in efforts at self-obliteration," animated by the "increasing longing to do away with themselves – if not in an actual physical sense then at least spiritually – a longing whose chief emblem, among others, is the leather bar" (ibid.). Another such "emblem" might be Decter's once-beloved beach at the Pines, which is also shorthand for promiscuity, an arena that makes visible the community's penchant for physical perfection and self-destruction.

"The Boys on the Beach" seems wilfully naïve about the reasons gay men might display self-destructive tendencies, seldom going further than the suggestion that it is because of some latent *hamartia*, as opposed to the insidious effects of hate speech like its author's. In "Some Jews & The Gays," an inspired and incisive response to Decter, Gore Vidal suggests that her thesis can be defined thus: "since homosexualists choose to be the way they are out of idle hatefulness, it has been a mistake to allow them to come out of the closet to the extent that they have," leaving them "no choice but to face up to their essential hatefulness and abnormality and so be driven to kill themselves with promiscuity, drugs, S-M and suicide" (Vidal 1981). "Not even the authors of *The Protocols of the Elders of Zion*," he continues, referring to the 1903 text that provided the blueprint for fascistic anti-Semitism, "ever suggested that the Jews who were so hateful to them, were also hateful to themselves" (ibid.). Decter is hardly, in her bigotry and circumspection, the most reliable narrator of this history, but it is fair to say that *Dancer from the Dance* seems situated between the older fixation upon youth and beauty, on the one hand, and the muscular, high-octane pursuits of the post-Stonewall 70s on the other. Holleran's novel may flirt with the notion of there being something potentially fascistic and in turn annihiliatory about the gay beach culture of this period, but Decter turns any such notion of the fascistic upon its head by her own example, a "virtuoso of hate" (Vidal 1981) who singles out that culture as perverse and other-worldly. And "thus," Vidal writes, do "pogroms begin" (ibid.).

Although it is not mentioned by name, one can imagine that *Dancer from the Dance* might belong on Decter's list of "Gay Lib 'literature' [that] is now characterized by an earnestness and callowness and crudity that are the very last qualities one who knew them would have associated with homosexuals" (Decter 1980). The cultural fate of Holleran's novel is indeed curiously marked by its capacity to rub both gay and homophobic readers up the wrong way. Its status as a classic of gay American literature is relatively secure, with a Vintage Books re-print appearing in 2019, featuring a Bianchi cover and a new foreword by Alan Hollinghurst, to commemorate the fiftieth anniversary of Stonewall.

But numerous critics over the years have identified problems with the novel's melancholic portrait of gay life (Raphael 1995), not to mention its political flippancies, recently summarised by Les Fabian Braithwaite thus: "Holleran's depiction of gay life is very specific – it's very white, it's very middle class, it's very melodramatic, and it's very depressing" (Braithwaite 2018). It remains to be seen how *Dancer* will fare in the eyes of a "2018 view" (and beyond) that is "steeped in a political and social correctness that ebbs and flows with the tides and presidents" (ibid.). Yet to view this novel as merely *of its time* is to historicize prematurely and exonerate the present, while ignoring the stubborn longevity of the novel's implications. Holleran writes in his review of Morgan's *The Beach* that what is "odd is that AIDS did not call into question the gym culture's values [...] Gym culture has only expanded" (Holleran 2000), and works as recent as Matthew Lopez's 2018 play *The Inheritance* continue to frame Fire Island as a place where, one character states, "the last thing anyone comes [...] to do is read"; they come to "dance," "drink" and "get fucked up" (Lopez 2018, 211). The same character, during a drug-fuelled orgy of "hot" (ibid., 215) bodies in the next scene, expresses a familiar desire for ecstatic surrender: "This moment, this feeling. I want to live in this moment for the rest of my life" (ibid.). Today, the persistence of body image issues, along with 'dangerous' sexual practices like chem-sex, all too easily feed the narrative of the gay community's death-drive. Yet this tragic mythos of hedonism, which has re-emerged haphazardly at different historical moments, is not solely the product of conservative propaganda. It can be found alive and well in the literary tradition of writing about Fire Island, a place where 'love and death', and the 'ecstatic and the fatal', are 'inseparable' (Bergman 2004, 164).

The beach itself then provides a fertile final analogy for this phenomenon. That the beach is a site of haunting is something of a littoral truism; a sense of the residual, symbolically taken up as the spectral, is endemic to its definition. As the threshold between land and sea, or here and elsewhere, the sediment or matter of the past arrives there – is beached – in hiding or in full view, depending on your vantage. Trafficking in bodies in states of leisure, disrepute or death, the beach is an ambivalent meeting point for the pleasures of recreation and the harsh geopolitical realities of travel and exile. "Spectrality," Carla Freccero writes, "is, in part, a mode of historicity," describing "the way the past or the future presses upon us with a kind of insistence or demand, a demand to which we must somehow respond" (Freccero 2006, 70). The beach is not exactly the site where "thinking and responding ethically within history" takes place (ibid.); as Holleran's novel, and the literature of Fire Island more broadly, demonstrate, the beach is associated numerously with accusations of narcissism, hedonism and anti-intellectualism. Nonetheless, as a space of liminality, it might in the first instance make the call of history sensible. Manifesting as a temporal "insistence or demand," this call goes beyond linearity, a trajectory whereby the past penetrates the present, and catalyses the impression made by the future too. The "lenient amusing shore" of Auden's poem "knows" about the already dead, the casualties of the global conflicts preceding it, but also foreshadows "dyings" yet to come (Auden 1976, 266). This uncanny intersection of historical motifs within the precarious space of the Fire Island beach troubles its dominant iconography as a gay paradise. These concerns can thus at last be traced back to the simple tableau of Frank Post before a mirror, where he yearns to be "the most voluptuous, beautiful man on the Island, the homosexual myth everyone adored," leaving us to wonder if that "homosexual myth" (Holleran 1990 [1978], 31) in fact refers to the man who will, in one way or another, die trying.

Bibliography

Auden, W. H. *The Dance of Death*. London: Faber & Faber, 1933.
Auden, W. H. *Collected Poems*. New York: Random House, 1976.
Bech, Henning. *When Men Meet: Homosexuality and Modernity*. Translated by Teresa Mesquit and Tim Davies. Chicago: University of Chicago Press, 1997.
Bergman, David. *The Violet Hour. The Violet Quill and the Making of Gay Culture*. New York: Columbia University Press, 2004.
Bersani, Leo. "Is the Rectum a Grave?" *October* 43 (1987): 197–222.
Bianchi, Tom. *Fire Island Pines: Polaroids 1975–1983*. Bologna: Damiani, 2013.
Bozorth, Richard. *Auden's Games of Knowledge: Poetry and the Meanings of Homosexuality*. New York: Columbia University Press, 2001.
Braithwaite, Les Fabian. "What It Means to Be a Gay Who is Free: Reflecting on *Dancer from the Dance*." *Out* (August 2018). https://www.out.com/art-books/2018/8/07/being-gay-man-who-free-reflecting-dancer-dance (21 January 2019).
Decter, Midge. "The Boys on the Beach." *Commentary* (September 1980). https://www.commentarymagazine.com/articles/the-boys-on-the-beach/ (21 January 2019).
Freccero, Carla. *Queer/Early/Modern*. Durham/NC: Duke University Press, 2016.
Holleran, Andrew. *Dancer from the Dance* [1978]. London: Penguin, 1990.
Holleran, Andrew. "Men in Black (Speedos)." *The Gay and Lesbian Review* 7.4 (2000). https://www.thefreelibrary.com/Men+in+Black+(Speedos).-a077712288 (21 January 2019).
Holleran, Andrew. "As the '70s World Turned." *In Search of Stonewall: The Riots at 50, 'The Gay & Lesbian Review' at 25, Best Essays, 1994–2018*. Ed. Richard Schneider Jr. Boston: The Gay & Lesbian Review Worldwide, 2019. 142–146.
Lopez, Matthew. *The Inheritance*. London: Faber & Faber, 2018.
Raphael, Lev. "Why are They Bashing *Dancer from the Dance*?" *Lambda Book Report* 4.8 (1995): 10–13.
Scarry, Elaine. *On Beauty and Being Just*. Princeton/NJ: Princeton University Press, 1999.

Schopp, Andrew. "The Gay *Great Gatsby*: Andrew Holleran's *Dancer from the Dance* and the Dismantling of Normative Frames." *Lit: Lit Interpretation Theory* 27.2 (2016): 153–171.

Vidal, Gore. "Some Jews & The Gays." *The Nation* (November 1981). https://www.thenation.com/article/some-jews-gays/ (21 January 2019).

Weems, Mickey. *The Fierce Tribe: Masculine Identity and Performance in the Circuit*. Logan, UT: Utah State University Press, 2008.

Yeats, William Butler. *The Poems. The Collected Works of W. B. Yeats*. Vol. 1. Ed. Richard J. Finneran. New York: Simon and Schuster, 1997.

Christian Begemann
Stimmen über der Tiefe, gärender Schlamm, Wasserleichen – Theodor Storms Strände

In Theodor Storm's (1817–1888) oeuvre, beaches are sites of a cultural imaginary and serve as spaces for negotiating fundamental contemporary problems. This article examines the topography and the diverse semantization of beaches in Storm's texts. They are spaces of a 'transcendental homelessness' (Lukács) and illustrate what 'life' means in a post-metaphysical world. On the beach, and especially in the mud, life and death overlap in an eternal cycle. Storm, thus, seems to take up contemporary theories about primeval mud aiming to explain the autogenesis of life. However, metaphysical aspects have not completely disappeared but survive as relics that also transform the beach into a space of the uncanny. Similar structures apply, after all, where sea and beach reflect the dynamics of forgetting and remembering, which is a central theme for Storm.

Strände fungieren im Werk Theodor Storms (1817–1888) als Verhandlungsorte grundsätzlicher zeitgenössischer Problemlagen und sind Schauplätze eines kulturellen Imaginären. Der Beitrag untersucht die Topographie und die vielfältigen semantischen Besetzungen, die Strände bei Storm annehmen können. Sie sind Räume einer „transzendentalen Obdachlosigkeit" (Lukács) und illustrieren, was ‚Leben' in einer nachmetaphysischen Welt bedeutet. Am Strand, und insbesondere im Schlamm, überlagern sich Leben und Tod im Sinne eines ewigen Kreislaufs. Storm scheint dabei an Theorien des Urschleims in seiner Epoche anzuknüpfen, die die Autogenese des Lebens klären wollten. Metaphysische Aspekte sind jedoch nicht gänzlich verschwunden, sondern leben als Relikte fort, die den Strand auch zum Raum eines Unheimlichen machen. Strukturell Ähnliches gilt schließlich, wo Meer und Strand die Mechanismen von Vergessen und Erinnern spiegeln, ein zentrales Thema Storms.

Strände haben die menschliche Einbildungskraft aufgrund ihrer Beschaffenheit und ihres semantischen Potentials seit jeher besonders angeregt. Für unsere Wahrnehmung sind sie nicht nur von ‚objektiven' Faktoren wie Geographie und Klima geprägt, sondern auch von einer langen Imaginationsgeschichte, von kulturellen Denkmustern, Sehweisen und Bildwelten. Sie sind daher über ihre physische Gegebenheit hinaus immer auch „kulturelle Tatsachen" (Konersmann 2006, 190). Unter den deutschsprachigen Autoren und Autorinnen des neunzehnten Jahrhunderts ist Theodor Storm derjenige, der sich mit dem Thema Strand – unter Einschluss von Ufer, Küste und Deich – am ausführlichsten und am entschiedensten auseinandergesetzt hat. Dabei ist der Strand keineswegs nur Schauplatz. Vielmehr nutzt Storm seine spezifische Topographie für die Verhandlung sehr grundsätzlicher zeitgenössischer Problemlagen. Es geht hier weder um Fragen der ökonomischen Nutzung noch um koloniale Kulturkonflikte oder ‚Landnahmen' und ebenso wenig um die Usurpation des Strandes durch sonnenhungrige und badelustige Touristen. Was ich akzentuieren möchte, hängt eher mit Storms Diagnose eines ‚modernen' Bewusstseins und eines kulturellen Imaginären zusammen, wie sie sich im Spannungsfeld von Szientismus, Säkularismus und Religionskritik ausbilden (vgl. Begemann 2019). Storms Texte zeigen ein sehr dezidiertes ‚constructing the beach', das auf dieses Problemfeld zugeschnitten ist.

1 Storms Imagination des Strandes („Meeresstrand")

Einen prägnanten Eindruck von Topographie, Beschaffenheit und Atmosphäre der Strände bei Storm bietet das bekannte Gedicht „Meeresstrand" von 1856:

> An's Haf nun fliegt die Möwe,
> Und Dämm'rung bricht herein;
> Über die feuchten Watten
> Spiegelt der Abendschein
>
> Graues Geflügel huschet
> Neben dem Wasser her;
> Wie Träume liegen die Inseln
> Im Nebel auf dem Meer.
>
> Ich höre des gärenden Schlammes
> Geheimnisvollen Ton,
> Einsames Vogelrufen –
> So war es immer schon.
>
> Noch einmal schauert leise
> Und schweiget dann der Wind;
> Vernehmlich werden die Stimmen,
> Die über der Tiefe sind.[1]

Dieses scheinbar schlichte Gedicht wirft bei näherem Zusehen viele Fragen auf. Wovon spricht es überhaupt? Schildert es einen bloßen Natureindruck? Ist es eine realistisch präzise Darstellung einer ruhigen, sehr norddeutschen Abendlandschaft oder schildert es eine düstere, ja abgründige Szenerie? Zeigt es

---
1 Storm (1987/88, Bd. 1, 14–15). Diese Ausgabe wird im Folgenden mit der Sigle LL, Band- und Seitenzahl im Text zitiert.

Naturverbundenheit oder vielmehr Entfremdung von der Natur? Dass sich das so schwer sagen lässt, wie sich an der Forschung zeigt, die hier die verschiedensten Positionen bezogen hat (s. u.), hängt ganz offenbar auch mit dem Sujet des Gedichts zusammen, das zwischen Gegensätzen changiert und Übergänge thematisiert, also gerade Eindeutigkeit vermeidet. Schon die Tageszeit und die Lichtverhältnisse weisen darauf hin: Es ist weder Tag noch Nacht, sondern vielmehr die Zwischenzeit der „Dämm'rung". Der heraufziehende abendliche Nebel trübt die Wahrnehmung und verunklart die Beschaffenheit der Dinge. Ähnlich verhält es sich mit der Topographie. Der Meeresstrand wird nicht als klare Demarkation von Land und Meer gezeigt, sondern als eine hybride Übergangszone. Das Watt bildet keine scharfe Grenze, sondern ist ein breites Gebiet, das bei Ebbe freiliegt, aber bei Flut überschwemmt, also mal Land, mal Meer ist (vgl. Forster 1976, 39). Diese Übergänglichkeit der Topographie wird enggeführt im Boden, den das „Ich" unter den Füßen hat: „Schlamm" ist geradezu das Inbild des Unklaren, Unreinen und Vermischten, das der ‚poetische Realismus' sonst eher auszuschließen neigt. Im weiteren Umfeld des eigentlichen Strandbereichs setzt sich dieser Befund fort. Im Meer liegen Inseln als Exklaven, versprengte Außenposten des Festlands, und für dieses gilt Analoges. ‚Haff' ist im üblichen Sprachgebrauch ein vom Meer abgetrennter, im Land liegender Brackwasserbereich, also quasi eine Enklave. Auch wenn man hier feststellen muss, dass Storm einem abweichenden niederdeutschen Sprachgebrauch folgt, demzufolge „Haf" das Wattenmeer selbst meint (LL 1, 766; vgl. LL 3, 756), bleibt der Befund in den meisten seiner Texte derselbe. Immer wieder ist dort die Rede von den „Wehlen", Teichen und Tümpeln, die durch Wassereinbrüche ins Festland entstanden sind, die quasi den Inseln im Meer umgekehrt entsprechen und sich sogar auf diesen selbst wiederfinden – als Einschluss im Einschluss (LL 2, 53, 55). Auf diese Weise also wird die hybride Strandzone in beide Richtungen ausgeweitet: Land und Meer sind auf beiden Seiten ihrer unklaren Ränder durch abgerissene Fetzen, Einsprengsel des jeweils gegenteiligen Elements, und das heißt durch *reentries*, perforiert.

Angesichts der ostentativen Akzentuierung eines solchen ‚dritten Raums' vom Gedicht Eindeutigkeit zu erwarten, und sei es nur hinsichtlich seiner ‚Stimmung', wäre ein Missverständnis. Will der Text seinen Gegenstand nicht dementieren, so muss er sich ihm anpassen: Strand, so ließe sich sagen, wird hier auch zu einem Textmodell. Darauf deuten auch jene Elemente, die ein Unheimliches nicht nur als Teil der diegetischen Welt benennen, sondern vielmehr textuell evozieren. Vom ‚Geheimnis' wird nicht nur geredet, der Text selbst stellt eines dar. Es sind nur vage Andeutungen, die in die ruhige Strandszene buchstäblich einen doppelten Boden einziehen und die Position des Ichs destabilisieren. Da ist zunächst die fliegende Möwe, die eine Strophe später vom huschenden „grauen Geflügel" ersetzt wird, das an das schauerromantische „Geflügel der Nacht" aus dem Tieck'schen *Runenberg* (1804) erinnert (Tieck 1985, 186); in der 3. Strophe verbinden sich dann die Vogelrufe mit dem „geheimnisvollen Ton" des gärenden Schlammes. Davon unterschieden sind jene „Stimmen", von denen in der 4. Strophe die Rede ist. Diese werden erst jetzt „vernehmlich", nachdem der Wind erst leise „schauert" und dann schweigt, als sei er ein lebendiges Wesen. Was also sind das für „Stimmen, die über der Tiefe sind"? Und was für eine „Tiefe" wird angesprochen – im Flachland *par excellence*? Topographisch wird hier die Horizontale um eine vertikale Achse ergänzt, die eine Ebene über und unter der Position des Sprechers einzieht. Der Sprecher scheint sich in einem Raum zu befinden, unter dem ein anderer liegt. Das erinnert an ein anderes Gedicht von Storm, das „Über die Heide" (1875) heißt und mit den eindrucksvollen Versen beginnt: „Über die Heide hallet mein Schritt; / Dumpf aus der Erde wandert es mit" (LL 1, 93). Das erklärt sich, bei allem Realismus Storms, wohl kaum hinlänglich aus der trockenen Beschaffenheit des resonierenden und nachhallenden Heidebodens (LL 1, 871), der dann in einer Art Echoeffekt dazu führt, dass das, „was aus der Erde mitwandert, [...] die bloße Verdopplung der Bewegung" (Schönert 2000, 182) ist.[2] Hier wie dort eröffnet sich, so scheint es vielmehr, ein Tiefenraum, der allerdings unbestimmt bleibt wie die Stimmen über ihm.[3] Woher kommen sie? Wem gehören sie? Wollen sie etwas mitteilen? Wenn ja, so bleibt die Botschaft unverstanden, denn „vernehmlich" heißt nicht ‚verständlich' (vgl. Kaiser 1994, 289).

Mit den „Stimmen, / Die über der Tiefe sind", hat sich die Forschung intensiv und aufgrund der extremen Unterdeterminiertheit des Bildes höchst kontrovers befasst. Das sei hier kurz kommentiert, weil sich das, was man als ‚Textmodell Strand' bezeichnen könnte, im Ensemble der extrem divergenten Forschungspositionen spiegelt. Man hat zur Erklärung der „Stimmen" in bemerkenswerter

---

[2] Treffender bei Müller und Mecklenburg (1970, 36): „Die zweite Zeile [...] schildert zwar sachlich-präzise den Widerhall der Schritte auf dem dumpfen Heideboden, doch gleichzeitig trägt die Natur unheimliche Züge: Da Bewegung und Geräusch die Subjekte tauschen – der Schritt wandert nicht, sondern er ‚hallt'; es hallt nicht aus dem Boden, sondern es ‚wandert' –, wird das grammatische Subjekt ‚es' substanziell aufgeladen, steigert sich zu einem in der Außenwelt nicht mehr aufweisbaren ‚mitwandernden' Wesen."

[3] Eine sehr ähnliche Konstellation begegnet in *Auf dem Staatshof*. Auch hier ist von einer „wüsten geheimnisvollen Tiefe" die Rede, dieses Mal der des Meeres, die enigmatisch und trostlos ist: „In diese heimlichen Laute der Nacht drang plötzlich von der Gegend des Deiches her der gellende Ruf eines Seevogels, der hoch durch die Luft dahin fuhr. Da mein Ohr einmal geweckt war, so vernahm ich nun auch aus der Ferne das Branden der Wellen, die in der hellen Nacht sich draußen über der wüsten geheimnisvollen Tiefe wälzten und von der kommenden Flut dem Strande zugeworfen wurden. Ein Gefühl der Öde und Verlorenheit überfiel mich". (LL 1, 423)

Vereindeutigung auf „Schicksalsmächte", auf „Kräfte chthonischer Gewalten" und die „gegen Mitternacht aufstehende Geisterwelt" zurückgegriffen und die Frage gestellt, ob es sich bei den „Stimmen" um die „von Naturgeistern, von Seelen Verstorbener, von himmlischen Wesen" handle (Merker 1942, 280–281) – jedenfalls seien sie „nicht irdischer Herkunft" (Schneider 1954, 111; ähnlich Bernd 2005, 146) und deuteten auf eine „mystische Dimension" (Gräff 2000, 131) und ein „Hinübergleiten aus der konkreten Welt in die Welt des Unheimlichen": „[B]efinden wir uns bereits im Jenseits?", fragt Tamara Silman (1976, 50–51) mit Bezug auf die letzte Strophe. Joachim Rickes hat solche Interpretationen akkurat aufgelistet, um sie als Belege zu entlarven, die Germanistik habe „das Interpretieren verlernt" (Rickes 2005, 5). Seine entgegengesetzte Deutung ist allerdings nach so viel Aufwand von erstaunlicher Schlichtheit: Die „Stimmen" seien die Geräusche des Meeres, die erst nach dem Verstummen des Windes hörbar würden (ebd., 9–11). Warum es sich dabei um „Stimmen" handelt, warum hier also eine Anthropomorphisierung vorgenommen wird, bleibt nach wie vor ungeklärt, ebenso, was es mit der geheimnisvollen „Tiefe" auf sich hat. In Auseinandersetzung mit diesem *down to earth*-Ansatz erlebte der „theologische und mythologische Konnotationsraum" des Gedichts schon kurz darauf ein theoretisch ambitioniertes Revival in der Untersuchung von Michael Baum, der zur semantischen Füllung der „Stimmen" auf den „Zusammenhang von Hören und Offenbarung" hinweist (2005, 251). Obwohl die Referenz der „Stimmen" „leer", „unlesbar" und „unausgesprochen" bleibe, konstatiert er aufgrund der „Spurung im Raum von Hören und Transzendenz": „Storms Raum öffnet sich gen Himmel." (Ebd., 255, 256, 259, 257, 260) Umstritten ist aber nicht nur der sozusagen ontologische Status der „Stimmen", sondern auch das Verhältnis von Subjekt und Natur. Rickes (2005, 10–11) sieht im Gedicht den Ausdruck von „Verbundenheit" mit der Natur, ja ein „beglückendes Naturerlebnis", und Jörg Schönert (2000, 183) leitet aus der „Korrespondenz im Kosmos" zwischen den „Tönen aus dem Bereich der Erde" und den „Vogelrufe[n] aus der Luft" ein „Ordnungsmuster der Natur" ab. Demgegenüber folgern ansatzweise Franz Forster (1976, 30–31), sehr viel dezidierter dann Gerhard Kaiser (1994, 288–289) und Heinrich Detering aus der Unverständlichkeit der Naturlaute, Heimat werde hier „fremd und unheimlich", das Ich erweise sich als „ausgeschlossen aus der Landschaft, ihren unverständlichen Zeichen und ihren Bewegungen, die einem rätselhaften Eigenleben folgen" (Detering 2013, 226–228). Im Raum einer „metaphysische[n] Enttäuschung" opponiere das Gedicht damit gerade der „Gewissheit einer Übereinstimmung zwischen äußerer und innerer Welt" (ebd., 228–229).

Weiter kann die interpretatorische Diskrepanz kaum getrieben werden. Angesichts ihrer bleibt zunächst nur festzuhalten: Das Gedicht und seine

Atmosphäre leben von überaus vagen Andeutungen, die man nicht festzuzurren versuchen sollte, weil sie ihre Unverständlichkeit ja gerade ostendieren. Wenn der Text die Stellung des Ichs „über der Tiefe" situiert und auf ein ‚Geheimnis' hinweist, dann darf man das vielleicht auch als doppeldeutige Anspielung auf eine subtextuelle Dimension verstehen.

Halten wir also versuchsweise einmal fest, was sich hier in nebelhaften Umrissen abzeichnet. Ein einziges Mal taucht hier ein „Ich" auf, ziemlich exakt in der Mitte des Gedichts. Aber von einer Mittenstellung im erzählten Raum kann keine Rede sein. Das Ich befindet sich vielmehr ‚mitten' in einer Welt, in der Polaritäten nicht greifen, es keine eindeutigen Koordinaten gibt und alle klaren Parameter sich aufgelöst haben: Es befindet sich, auf gärendem Schlamm stehend, während einer Übergangszeit in einem Grenzland und über einem diffusen Raum der „Tiefe" und ist konfrontiert mit einer geheimnisvollen Natur, die andeutungsweise animistische Züge trägt, einer Natur, die „immer schon" so war, also auch vor unserem, dem menschlichen Erscheinen. „So war es immer schon" – das allein auf die Lebensdauer und -erfahrung des Sprechers zu beziehen, schiene mir verkürzt. Vielmehr gibt der Satz der Strandzone eine urweltliche, eine archaische Dimension.[4] Sie ist durchsetzt mit geheimnisvollen Tönen und unverständlichen Stimmen, die ein hohes Maß an Fremdheit, Ungeborgenheit und Ausgesetztheit vermitteln. Anders als in der Romantik ist das lyrische Ich hier keine Instanz mehr, die die Hieroglyphen der Natur verstehen könnte. Wenn die Inseln „wie Träume" auf dem Meer liegen, dann verstärkt das den ohnehin phantasmatischen Charakter des Textes: Statt von einem realistischen Bild einer norddeutschen Seelandschaft zu sprechen, könnte man ebenso gut sagen, dass das Ich hier seine Position in der Welt überhaupt anhand der Gegebenheiten des „Meeresstrandes" imaginiert. So problematisch solche Vokabeln wegen ihrer Abgegriffenheit und ihrer prekären Implikationen sind – aber hier ist man doch versucht, von einer ‚existenziellen' Dimension und einem Welt-Bild zu sprechen.

Dazu passt, dass der Blick gegen alle Erfahrung mit Seelandschaften strikt auf den Boden gerichtet bleibt – anders als z. B. in Caspar David Friedrichs berühmtem Gemälde *Der Mönch am Meer* (1808–10). Signifikant ist gerade auch, was das Gedicht *nicht* zeigt. Üblicherweise fallen Meer und Himmel gemeinsam ins Auge – hier nicht. Zwar wird von den Vögeln gesprochen, die oben sind, zunehmend aber nur noch in ihrer akustischen Präsenz – der Himmel fällt dabei aus. Selbst der Abendschein kommt nur in seiner Spiegelung im Watt in den Blick.[5]

---

[4] In diesem Sinne die Bemerkungen bei Merker (1942, 280).
[5] Gegen Baum (2005, 260) ist also zu sagen: „Storms Raum öffnet sich" eben gerade nicht „gen Himmel."

2 Tod und Leben

Es soll nun versucht werden, Storms Imagination des Strandes über einen weiteren Text zu ergänzen. Es handelt sich um einen kleinen, aber signifikanten Ausschnitt aus der Erzählung *Carsten Curator* von 1878. Der Plot ist hier nicht relevant, es genügt zu wissen, dass der sprichwörtlich redliche und rechtliche Protagonist Carsten Carstens einen Konflikt mit seinem Sohn Heinrich hat, der geschäftlich unsolide und liederlich ist und sich zudem auch noch als ein Trinker herausgestellt hat. Das bringt den Vater um den Schlaf. Unruhig im Bett, gehen ihm alte Erinnerungen durch den Kopf:

> Seine Gedanken flogen zurück in Heinrich's Kinderzeit; er suchte sich das glückliche Gesicht des Knaben zurückzurufen, wenn es hieß: „Am Deich spazieren gehen"; er suchte seinen Jubel zu hören, wenn ein Lerchennest gefunden oder eine große Seespinne von der Flut ans Ufer getrieben wurde. Aber auch hier kam etwas, um seinen kargen Schlaf mit ihm zu teilen. Nicht nur, wenn es von den Nordsee-Watten her an seine Fenster wehte, sondern auch in todstiller Nacht, immer war jetzt das eintönige Tosen des Meeres in seinen Ohren; wie zur Ebbezeit von weit draußen, hinter der Schmaltiefe [d. i. Priel, Wasserlauf im Meer] schien es herzukommen; statt des glücklichen Gesichtes seines Knaben sah er die bloßgelegten Strecken des gärenden Wattenschlammes im Mondschein blänkern, und daraus flach und schwarz erhob sich eine öde Hallig. Es war dieselbe, bei der er einst mit Heinrich angefahren, um Möwen- oder Kiebitzeier dort zu suchen. Aber sie hatten keine gefunden; nur den aufgeschwemmten Leichnam eines Ertrunkenen. Er lag zwischen dem urweltlichen Kraut des Queller [d. i. ein Gänsefußgewächs], von großen Vögeln umflogen, die Arme ausgestreckt, das furchtbare Totenantlitz gegen den Himmel gekehrt. Schreiend, mit entsetzten Augen hatte bei diesem Anblick der Knabe sich an den Vater angeklammert.
>
> Immer wieder, ja selbst im Traum, wohin diese Vorstellungen ihn verfolgten, suchte der Greis seine Gedanken nach friedlicheren Orten hinzulenken; aber jedes Wehen der Luft führte ihn zurück auf jenes furchtbare Eiland. (LL 2, 511–512)

Auch hier trägt die Erinnerung an die Strandlandschaft phantasmatische Züge, ist traumartig zwischen Wachen und Schlaf angesiedelt und gehorcht einer unbewussten Logik. Sie beginnt mit einem heiteren Deichidyll in Heinrichs Kindheit.[6] Der Deich ist ein schöner und sicherer Ort, an dem man vergnügt spazieren gehen und die Vögel beim Brüten beobachten kann. Diese Konnotation des Deichs hängt mit seiner Funktion zusammen. Der Deich ist die markanteste Konfiguration der Natur-Kultur-Grenze. Er ist ein Bollwerk, er markiert und schützt den menschlichen Lebensraum gegenüber dem Bereich eines amorph Elementaren. Er ist daher mit dem Leben und seiner Reproduktion verbunden,

---

6 Mit dem Deich beginnt auch die Textgeschichte von *Meeresstrand*, das ursprünglich *Am Deich* heißen sollte (LL 1, 766).

den Vogelnestern und -eiern. Zugleich bietet der Deich den erhabenen oder auch nur unheimlichen Ausblick aus dem Geborgenen auf's Ungeborgene; er ist die paradigmatische Aussichtsplattform auf das Toben der Elemente oder den ‚Schiffbruch mit Zuschauer'. Diese Gewalt ist nämlich noch in der heitersten Deichidylle impliziert. Der Deich schützt mit technischen Mitteln das Leben vor der Vernichtung,[7] er hat aber nicht nur eine defensive Funktion, sondern auch ein konfrontatives, agonales und quasi darwinistisches Moment, denn er expandiert den kulturellen auf Kosten des elementaren Raums.[8] Die wechselhafte und unübersichtliche Geschichte der Schleswig-Holsteinischen Küste, auf die viele Texte Storms zurückblicken, illustriert eindrucksvoll das ständige Vor und Zurück des Landes im ‚Kampf' mit dem Meer und bestätigt die ‚Fluidität' von Küstenverläufen, wie sie sich an der Mikrostruktur des Strands gezeigt hat, auch in ihrer Makrostruktur.

Noch dort also, wo der Deich als Ort des Lebens imaginiert wird, impliziert er notwendig den Gedanken an Untergang, Vernichtung und Tod. Daher können Carstens Gedanken so schnell umkippen, sich metonymisch-assoziativ verschieben zum Gegenteil des heiteren Lebensbilds. Topographisch durchlaufen sie – „in todstiller Nacht" bezeichnenderweise und begleitet vom „eintönigen Tosen des Meeres" – „die bloßgelegten Strecken des gärenden Wattenschlamms", um dann auf einer Hallig zu landen, wo der Konflikt noch einmal enggeführt wird. Gesucht werden am Strand die Garanten eines fortdauernden Lebens, die „Möwen- und Kiebitzeier", gefunden aber wird eine Wasserleiche. Am Strand berühren und überlagern sich Leben und Tod, und insofern muss festgehalten werden, dass der Strand generell bei Storm gegensätzlicher Akzentuierungen fähig ist – je nachdem, welche seiner Seiten hervorgehoben wird. Die Todesursache des „Ertrunkenen" ist das Wasser, der Untergang im Elementaren. Es durchbricht und flutet die Körpergrenze, wie es im *Schimmelreiter* den Deich durchbricht und den dahinter liegenden menschlichen Lebensraum verwüstet. Meer und Wasser, so ließe sich ein erster Befund formulieren, sind bei

---

7 Für Volker Hoffmann (1990, 361) markiert der Deich „die Grenzlinie zwischen Leben und Tod".
8 Hauke Haiens Deichbauprojekt im *Schimmelreiter* wird in seiner darwinistischen Dimension in jener Szene angekündigt, in der Hauke – bezeichnenderweise auf dem Deich – selbst wie ein „Raubtier" mit dem Kater um seine „Beute" kämpft (LL 3, 647). Das setzt sich dann darin fort, dass am Ende das Tosen des Meeres dem „Schrei alles furchtbaren Raubgetieres der Wildnis" ähnelt (LL 3, 748). – *Eine Halligfahrt* schildert an der untergegangenen Stadt Rungholt das Moment einer provokativen Vermessenheit beim Deichbau: „zur Zeit der Äquinoktialstürme stiegen die Männer, wenn sie von ihren Gelagen kamen, vorerst noch einmal auf ihre hohen Deiche, hielten die Hände in den Taschen und riefen hohnlachend auf die anbrüllende See hinaus: ‚Trotz nu, blanke Hans!'" (LL 2, 43) Mit dieser Hybris besiegeln sie ihren – buchstäblichen – Untergang.

Storm mit dem Tod assoziiert, allerdings in ambivalenter Weise. Durchaus begegnet man in seinem Werk gelegentlich der Vorstellung vom Tod als „Heimgang des Menschen in eine elementare, ‚ewige' Natur", die man, je nach Sichtweise, als naturmystisch oder regressiv begreifen kann (Blödorn 2016, 266, 270, 272). Das Meer kann dabei „als Verkörperung der Mutterinstanz" (Neumann 2002, 117) figurieren, wie die Forschung unter psychoanalytischer Perspektive verschiedentlich behauptet hat, und auch der Deich gewinnt in diesem Horizont eine psychodynamische Dimension (vgl. ebd., 117, 132–133 u. ö.). Nur selten allerdings gleicht das „Brausen des heimatlichen Meeres" dem „Wiegenliede, womit einst die Mutter das Tosen der Welt von ihrem Kinde fern gehalten hatte".[9] Kann das Meer in solchen tendenziell idyllischen Zusammenhängen als natürlicher „Gegenpol zum bürgerlichen Leben" erscheinen (Blödorn 2016, 266), so erschreckt es jedoch zumeist durch eine „latente Todesdrohung" (ebd., 271), die auch sehr manifest ausfallen kann. Die Mutterbeziehungen in Storms Texten sind überwiegend problematisch und gestört, sodass vom „mütterlichen Bereich Meer" die „Vernichtungsbedrohung durch eine aggressive Mutterimago" ausgeht (Fasold 1997, 155; vgl. Neumann 2002, 116–120, 129–140; Roebling 2012c, 333, 343, 347). Das Meer als „verschlingende Mutter" (Neumann 2002, 139) ist in bedrohlicher Weise mit dem Tod verknüpft.[10]

Es ist von daher nicht überraschend, dass die häufigste Todesursache in Storms Texten das Ertrinken ist. Menschen ertrinken im Meer, sie ertrinken aber ebenso häufig in Kanälen, Wehlen, Teichen und Gewässern, die zum Teil als Abkömmlinge des Meeres den belebten, bebauten und bewohnten Raum des Festlands durchsetzen, oder sie stürzen in Brunnen. In *Aquis submersus*[11] ertrinken nicht nur zwei Menschen, in insistierender Präsenz ist auch stets das Meer am Horizont zu sehen. Wenn der Protagonist und Erzähler der im siebzehnten Jahrhundert spielenden Novelle, der Maler Johannes, täglich zu jenem Ort wandert, an dem durch sein Verschulden sein Sohn in einem Teich den Tod finden wird, dann begleitet ihn permanent das Bild des Meeres und mit diesem die Erinnerung an die gewaltige Flut von 1634 (vgl. LL 2, 437):

> Als ich auf den Kirchhof kam, trug von der Stadtseite der Wind ein wimmernd Glockenläuten an mein Ohr; ich aber wandte mich und blickte hinab nach Westen, wo wiederum das Meer wie lichtes Silber am Himmelssaume hinfloß, und war doch ein tobend Unheil

---

9 Theodor Storm, *Zerstreute Kapitel: Der Amtschirurgus – Heimkehr* (LL 4, 159–174, hier 169).
10 Aus diesem Rahmen fällt das Märchen *Die Regentrude* von 1864, in dem das Wasser primär als lebensstiftende Kraft erscheint – bezeichnenderweise aber fern vom Meer. Vgl. dazu Roebling (2012a, 39–42) sowie Roebling (2012b, 218–228).
11 Vgl. dazu den Beitrag von Roxanne Phillips in diesem Band.

dort gewesen, worin in einer Nacht des Höchsten Hand viel tausend Menschenleben hingeworfen hatte. (LL 2, 445)[12]

Die vielleicht schockierendste Todesszene findet sich in der Novelle *Auf dem Staatshof*, wo eine junge Frau einfach durch den Boden eines über eine „Graft", einen Wassergraben, gebauten Gartenpavillons bricht und verschlungen wird:

> Noch auf einen Augenblick sah ich die zarten Umrisse ihres lieben Antlitzes vor einem Strahl des milden Lichtes beleuchtet; dann aber geschah etwas und ging so schnell vorüber, daß mein Gedächtnis es nicht zu bewahren vermocht hat. Ein Brett des Fußbodens schlug in die Höhe; ich sah den Schein des weißen Gewandes, dann hörte ich es unter mir im Wasser rauschen. Ich riß die Augen auf; der Mond schien durch den leeren Raum. (LL 1, 425)

Hier gibt es keinen Deichbruch und keine chthonische Tiefe unter den Füßen, aber das todbringende Wasser ist mitten im und unter dem menschlichen Lebensraum, dem Ort des Kaffeetrinkens und gemütlichen Plauderns – ein Bild äußerster Gefährdung, ständiger Unsicherheit und Ungeborgenheit.

3 Schlamm und Schleim

An Carsten Curator und seinen Nachtgedanken hat sich gezeigt, dass sich am Deich und am Strand Leben und Tod nicht nur berühren, sondern dass sie sich überlagern. Noch deutlicher, schon rein topographisch, ist das im Watt, der erweiterten Strandzone. Wie bereits im Gedicht *Meeresstrand* wird dem „Wattenschlamm" das Epitheton „gärend" zugeordnet. Das scheint Storm wichtig gewesen zu sein. Aber warum? Die Übergangszone von Land und Meer, der Schlamm, ist für Storm mehr als nasser Sand. Ob Storm den Begriff „gärend" in einem präzis wissenschaftlichen oder eher in einem metaphorischen Sinne verwendet hat, ist schwer zu entscheiden. Vielleicht kann man vorläufig und stark vereinfachend festhalten, dass ‚Gärung' in Storms Epoche als ein biotischer Prozess verstanden wird, der mit Lebensprozessen von „Mikro-Organismen" zu tun hat, aber auch mit „Zersetzung", „Fäulnis und Verwesung" (Brockhaus 1894–1896, 562–563). Insofern kann man mit Blick auf Storm zunächst an die Verwesungsvorgänge von Fischen, Kleintieren und Plankton im Schlick denken (vgl. Schneider 1954, 108). Aber das reicht nicht aus.

Der mögliche Bedeutungshorizont des gärenden Schlamms konturiert sich, so scheint mir, mit Blick auf die zeitgenössische Debatte um den Ursprung des

---
[12] Vgl. *Auf dem Staatshof* (LL 1, 423).

Lebens, auf die daher etwas ausführlicher eingegangen werden soll. Diese Frage stellt sich im Zeichen eines säkularen Szientismus, der eine göttliche Schöpfung weithin leugnet, mit besonderer Brisanz, denn nun geht es darum, den problematischen Übergang vom Anorganischen ins Organische zu erklären. Eine Bilanz der verschiedenen Positionen in dieser Diskussion bietet unter dem zeittypischen Titel „Urzeugung" beispielsweise Ludwig Büchners *Kraft und Stoff*, in erster Auflage 1855 erschienen und dann mehrfach erweitert, ein Hauptwerk des Materialismus der Epoche (Büchner 1898 [1855], 159–177). Das neunzehnte Jahrhundert findet, kurz gesagt, keine Antwort auf diese Frage, aber es gibt in den verschiedenen Lösungsversuchen doch eine bemerkenswerte Schnittmenge. Zu dieser gehört die maßgebliche Rolle des Wassers, und insbesondere des Meerwassers, für die Entstehung von Leben. Diese Auffassung reicht bis in die Antike zurück. Bei Thales von Milet, so berichtet Aristoteles, hat das Leben seinen Ursprung im Wasser (vgl. Aristoteles 1995, A 3, 983b), und noch Goethe lässt Thales im *Faust II* ausrufen: „Alles ist aus dem Wasser entsprungen!! / Alles wird durch das Wasser erhalten! / Ocean gönn' uns Dein ewiges Walten" (Goethe 1997, 230, V. 8435–8437). In diesem Punkt stimmen Philosophie und Mythos überein. Für Homer steht Okeanos im Anfang, und bei Hesiod erfolgen Zeugung und Geburt der Aphrodite aus Blut und Samen des Uranos im Element des Meeres. Sandro Botticellis berühmtes Gemälde dieses Vorgangs (1484–1486) siedelt bezeichnenderweise *La nascita di Venere* am Strand an, lässt das Prinzip des Begehrens und der Prokreation also selbst in der liminalen Uferzone geboren werden und aus dem Wasser ans Land steigen, um dort das Leben fortzupflanzen. Dass das Leben aus dem mütterlich-väterlichen Element des Wassers und insbesondere des Meeres stammt, bleibt die dauerhafte Überzeugung einer populären Naturphilosophie, wie man sie – um nur eines von vielen möglichen Beispielen zu nennen – etwa in Carl Gustav Carus' *Zwölf Briefe[n] über das Erdleben* von 1841 ausgedrückt findet (vgl. Carus 1841, 37, 134–137). Es ist ein bemerkenswertes Phänomen, dass die säkularen Naturwissenschaften, und insbesondere die Evolutionstheorien, seit dem achtzehnten Jahrhundert diese uralte Vorstellung letztlich nur umkodieren und mit einem neuen Begründungsrahmen versehen, wenn sie auf der Suche nach einer ‚Urzeugung' die Autogenese des Lebens in einem Urmeer ansiedeln.

Zu den besonderen Bedingungen der Entstehung des Lebens gehören dabei Schleim und Schlamm. Ein semiwissenschaftlicher Text, der dies besonders eindrucksvoll schildert, ist das große Werk *La Mer* des Historikers Jules Michelet von 1861, das im selben Jahr auch ins Deutsche übersetzt wurde. Michelet geht von der emphatisch beschriebenen Anschauung des Meeres und seiner substanziellen Zusammensetzung aus, die er als weißlich, klebrig, gallertartig und unendlich fruchtbar beschreibt. Dieser „Schleim des Meeres" stellt „sowohl ein Endstadium, als auch zugleich einen Ausgangspunkt" dar. Er besteht, unter dem Mikroskop betrachtet, unter anderem aus Ausscheidungen, „unzähligen Rückständen des Todes" (Michelet 2006 [1861], 93), aus Mikroalgen und insbesondere aus „der unermeßlichen Welt lebendiger Atome – mikroskopisch kleiner Tiere –, jenem wahren Grund des Lebens, der" – und auch hier begegnen wir Storms Assoziation – „im Schoß des Meeres gärt" (ebd., 88). Dieser Schleim ist „das universelle Lebenselement schlechthin", ja „das Leben selbst" (ebd., 92). Mit den allerprimitivsten Wesen, einem „belebte[n] Gallert" im Meer, habe die Schöpfung auf dem Planeten begonnen, er ist der „erste, vage Entwurf des Lebens" (ebd., 96). Anders als viele naturwissenschaftlich versiertere Zeitgenossen, die die ,Urzeugung' auf einen an die besonderen Bedingungen der Frühzeit gebundenen zeitlich befristeten Akt beschränken – Ludwig Büchner etwa, Ernst Haeckel oder Wilhelm Wundt –, behauptet Michelet eine im Element des Meeresschleims sich perpetuierende „Urschöpfung" (ebd., 94), die sich in der Folge gerade „aus den aufgelösten Elementen des vorausgehenden Lebens" speist: „Der Tod gebiert das Leben" (ebd., 103).

Michelet bietet damit zugleich eine Erklärung für die Gründung und den enormen Zulauf der Seebäder, die seit der Mitte des achtzehnten Jahrhunderts zunächst in England, dann auch auf dem Kontinent entstehen. Den Anregungen des Hippokrates (*De liquidorum usu*) folgend, wird die Heilkraft von Meerwasser und Meeresschlamm, Seeluft und Strandleben ,entdeckt'. Der breite medizinische Diskurs darüber wird sogleich in die Praxis umgesetzt und mündet in eine therapeutische Meer- und Strand-Emphase (Corbin 1990, 83–120, 319–357; Richter 2014, 145–161). Vor der touristischen Erschließung der Strände im neunzehnten Jahrhundert, deren Voraussetzung die verkehrstechnische Anbindung der Küsten durch die Eisenbahn ebenso ist wie die allmähliche Etablierung von Freizeit, herrscht hier zunächst ein kurförmiger Gebrauch von Meer und Strand, der von einer neuen Naturerfahrung flankiert und unterstützt wird, die die Natur nicht nur in den Kategorien des Schönen und Erhabenen feiert, sondern in ihr das Heilende schlechthin sieht. Michelet legt den geheimen Kern dieser Faszination von Meer und Strand offen: Noch vor allen empirischen Evidenzen liegt den Meerwasser- und Thalasso-Kuren die Vorstellung zugrunde, dass das, woraus das Leben entstanden ist, auch der Aufrechterhaltung und Heilung des Lebens dienen müsse. Im Kapitel „Der Ursprung der Seebäder" unterstreicht Michelet nicht allein die „reinigenden Tugenden", die das „heilende Element" besitzt, sondern führt diese Heilkraft darauf zurück, dass das Meer die „universelle Grundlage des Lebens" „so reichhaltig" besitze, „daß es wie das Leben selbst ist". „Sein nährender Reichtum wird Euch in Strömen erquicken." (Michelet 2006 [1861], 253–256)

Michelet formuliert hier letztlich einen zeitgenössischen Konsens. Theorien des Urschleims bzw. Urschlamms haben Konjunktur. Bereits in seiner Auseinandersetzung mit Georg Forster zitiert Kant dessen These von der „kreißende[n] Erde [...], welche Tiere und Pflanzen ohne Zeugung von ihresgleichen, aus ihrem weichen, vom Meeresschlamme befeuchteten Mutterschoße, entspringen ließ"[13] (Kant 1975,164, A 128), wobei der Akzent weniger auf der Fruchtbarkeit des Meeres allein als auf einer Koproduktion von Meer und Erde liegt. Die weitere Theorie des Urschleims geht dann auf Lorenz Oken zurück, der bezeichnenderweise bereits ein Frühwerk von 1805 *Die Zeugung* betitelt hatte. Schon in der ersten Auflage seines *Lehrbuchs der Naturphilosophie* von 1810 formuliert Oken lapidar: „Der Urschleim, aus dem alles Organische erschaffen worden, ist der Meerschleim"[14], und in der zweiten Auflage, erschienen 1831, lässt er den „Urschleim" „an der Gränze zwischen Wasser und Erde" entstehen.[15] Diese Lokalisierung bezieht ihre Attraktivität zweifellos auch aus ihrem Symbolwert: Der zeitliche Ursprung wird durch die Überblendung mit einer räumlichen Grenze quasi ins Bild gesetzt. Ihre größte Prominenz erlangt die Theorie des Urschleims unter einem neuen Namen im Zeichen des Darwinismus. Ihren kurzen Siegeszug tritt sie 1857 an, nachdem bei der Verlegung von transatlantischen Telegrafenkabeln auf dem Meeresboden eine zähe gallertartige, mutmaßlich aus Protoplasma bestehende Masse aufgefunden wurde, die die Eigenschaften einer extrem einfachen Lebensform zu zeigen schien. Ihre Erforschung verdankt sie einerseits Thomas Henry Huxley, der sie ‚Bathybius' bzw. zu Ehren von Ernst Haeckel ‚Bathybius Haeckelii' nannte (Huxley 1868, 210), andererseits Haeckel selbst, der diese Hypothese ausbaut und den ganzen Meeresboden mit Urschleim überzogen vermutet, bestehend aus ‚Moneren', den allereinfachsten Eiweißkörpern (Abb. 1).[16] Die Bedeutung dieser Theorie fasst Haeckel zusammen:

---

13 In Georg Forsters Aufsatz „Noch etwas über die Menschenraßen" heißt es wörtlich: „Wer hat die kreißende Erde betrachtet in jenem entfernten und ganz in Unbegreiflichkeit verschleyerten Zeitpunkt, da Thiere und Pflanzen ihrem Schoße in vieler Myriaden Mannigfaltigkeit entsprossen, ohne Zeugung von ihres Gleichen, ohne Samengehäuse, ohne Gebärmutter? Wer hat die Zahl ihrer ursprünglichen Gattungen, ihrer Autochthonen, gezählt? Wer kann uns berichten, wie viele Einzelne von jeder Gestalt, in ganz verschiedenen Weltgegenden sich aus der gebärenden Mutter weichem, vom Meere befruchteten Schlamm organisirten? Wer ist so weise, der uns lehren könne, ob nur einmal, an einem Orte nur, oder zu ganz verschiedenen Zeiten, in ganz getrennten Welttheilen, so wie sie allmälig aus des Oceans Umarmung hervorgiengen, organische Kräfte sich regten?" (Forster 1969, 87)
14 Oken (1810 [Kapitel „Urschleim"], 15, § 841).
15 Oken (1831 [Kapitel „Gestaltung des Urorganismus"], 153, § 949).
16 Haeckel (1870, 499–519 [Bathybius und das freie Protoplasma der Meerestiefen]). Zu diesem Konzept vgl. Rehbock (1975); Rupke (1976); Gould (1980).

Mit diesem formlosen Ur-Organismus einfachster Art, der zu Milliarden vereinigt den Meeresboden mit einer lebendigen Schleimdecke überzieht, schien ein neues Licht auf eine der schwierigsten und dunkelsten Fragen der Schöpfungsgeschichte zu fallen, auf die Frage von der Urzeugung, von der ersten Entstehung des Lebens auf unserer Erde. Mit dem Bathybius schien der berüchtigte ‚Urschleim' gefunden zu sein, von dem Oken vor einem halben Jahrhundert prophetisch behauptet hatte, dass alles Organische aus ihm hervorgegangen, und dass er im Verfolge der Planeten-Entwickelung aus anorganischer Materie im Meeresgrunde entstanden sei. (Haeckel 1878, 73)

Noch zu Storms Lebzeiten, nämlich in seiner Ausgabe von 1885–92, resümiert auch *Meyers Konversationslexikon*: „Die Entdeckung des B.[athybius] erregte bei allen Naturforschern das größte Aufsehen, weil man in ihm den Anfang alles Lebens gefunden zu haben glaubte." (Meyer 1885–1892, 448) Das Lexikon verweist aber auch schon auf den empirischen Anfang vom Ende dieser Theorieblase, die mit der zwischen 1872 und 1876 durchgeführten ozeanographischen Expedition der *Challenger* zerplatzte, die die Welt umrundete, ohne erneut Bathybius-Schlamm zu finden. Huxley widerrief seine Theorie, während Haeckel, darüber einigermaßen indigniert, sie lediglich einschränken und modifizieren wollte und zu dem Resultat kam, „dass die ‚Nicht-Existenz des Bathybius nicht erwiesen' ist" (Haeckel 1878, 73–82).[17]

---

[17] Das Konzept des Bathybius ist keineswegs die einzige Theorie von Schlamm und Schleim im neunzehnten Jahrhundert. Die Verbreitung, Geltung und Abhängigkeit dieser Theorien ist, soweit ich sehe, noch nicht geklärt. An dieser Stelle soll nur ein weiterer Hinweis erfolgen, um diese Denkform zu belegen. Vom ganzen Ansatz, dem Ziel wie der Methode nahezu unvergleichbar mit Oken, Huxley und Haeckel ist Johann Jakob Bachofens 1861 erschienenes Hauptwerk *Das Mutterrecht. Eine Untersuchung über die Gynaikokratie der alten Welt nach ihrer religiösen und rechtlichen Natur*. Umso bemerkenswerter ist, dass auch hier eine Denkfigur begegnet, die den Ursprung des Lebens im Schlamm auffindet, ‚Leben' allerdings primär verstanden im Sinne der menschlichen Gesellschaft. Bachofens (1975 [1861], 194) teils historische, teils geschichtsphilosophische und teils selbst mythisierende Überlegungen konstruieren eine der Ära des gynaikokratischen Ackerbaus vorausgehende „älteste Stufe des Mutterrechts, auf welcher die Mutter nicht nur über den Mann hervorragt, sondern nach Maßgabe des Sumpflebens gar keinen bestimmten Begatter sich gegenüber sieht, sondern der männlichen Kraft in ihrer Allgemeinheit angehört". Hier herrscht ein hetärischer „Sumpfkult" und eine „wilde Erdzeugung", die letztlich der aphroditischen Natur des ‚Weibes' entsprechen (ebd., 193–194). Mythologisch verweist der Sumpfkult auf „die Schlamm- und Sumpfgründe, in welchen sich die Mischung von Erde und Wasser gewissermaßen verkörpert, und die eben darum als das Urchaos, aus welchem alles Leben hervorgeht, angesehen werden." Dies erfolgt durch den „einigenden Liebestrieb der Materie", eine „Selbstumarmung der Materie." (Ebd., 187–188)

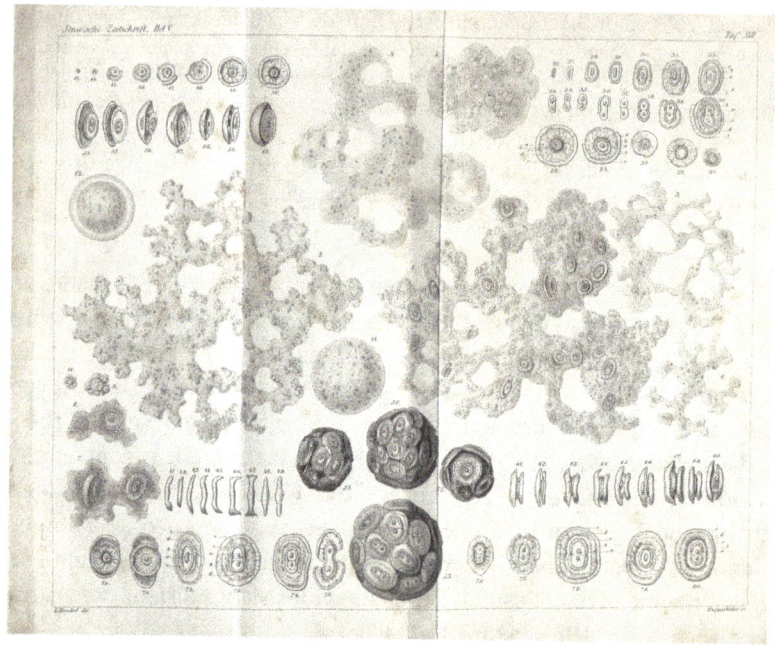

Abb. 1: Bathybius Haeckelii in Haeckels „Beiträge zur Plastidentheorie".

Storm, so die These, bewegt sich im Imaginationsraum der zeitgenössischen Theoriebildung zum Thema Urschlamm, er ist aber offensichtlich kein Anhänger der uralten und seit dem achtzehnten Jahrhundert erneut aktivierten Wasseremphase. Während bei ihm das durch Deiche zu schützende Kulturland die Bedingung des Lebens zu sein scheint, ist das Meer tendenziell eher mit Tod konnotiert. Doch bemerkenswerterweise ist gerade der Grenzbereich zwischen beiden ein bevorzugter Ort des Lebens und seiner Selbstgeneration. Man kann daraus folgern, dass der Tod eben nicht nur Tod ist, sondern zugleich eine notwendige Bedingung, ein Agens des Lebens selbst. Folgt man der hier dargelegten Assoziationskette, so ist gerade Storms Wattenschlamm – wie der Oken'sche Urschleim angesiedelt im notorischen Überlagerungsbereich „zwischen Wasser und Erde" – das Medium, in dem zwar die Endprodukte der destruktiven Gewalt der Elemente, die Leben vernichtet und zersetzt, sich sammeln und verwesen, wo aber gerade darum zugleich aus toter Materie neues Leben entsteht. Im Bild des gärenden Schlammes wird so der ewige Naturkreislauf enggeführt und als ‚Geheimnis' markiert. Und dass mit dem „urweltlichen Kraut des Queller" auch in *Carsten Curator* eine Dimension des Archaischen, Uranfänglichen ins Spiel kommt, passt ins Bild: „so war es immer schon" – das Leben nämlich, seitdem es besteht.

Storm entfaltet diese Doppeldeutigkeit des Strandes als Interferenz von Leben und Tod immer aufs Neue: nicht nur im zitierten Gegeneinander von Wasserleiche und Vogelnest, sondern auch mit speziellerem Bezug auf den „gärenden Schlamm" selbst. Auf die dem Tod zugewandte Seite dieser Konstellation gehört, dass Menschen bei Storm nicht nur ertrinken, sondern auch vom Schlamm verschlungen werden, wie der Sohn der Trien' Jans im *Schimmelreiter*, der „im Schlick versank" (LL 3, 649). Die lebensnah-heilsame Seite des Schlamms reklamiert dagegen – mehr auf der Landseite – der problematische Herr Etatsrat, als Deichkonstrukteur bezeichnenderweise dem Schutz des Landes verpflichtet, mit seinem „Erdbad" am Strand. Mit dem allerdings fraglichen Rekurs auf die „Heilkraft unserer guten Mutter Erde", in deren „Schoß" er sich bis zum Kopf eingraben lässt, will er „gegen irgendwelchen Ungehorsam seines Leibes" angehen. (LL 3, 27–28) Seine Freistiltherapie ist schwer dingfest zu machen, doch erkennbar steht sie in der Tradition der diversen Meer- und Strandkuren seit dem achtzehnten Jahrhundert,[18] der Thalasso-Therapie, deren Begriff Joseph La Bonnardière 1865, sechzehn Jahre vor Storms Erzählung, kreiert hatte (La Bonnardière 1865), oder der Experimente mit Schlamm- und Moorbädern, die eine bis in die Antike zurückreichende Tradition haben, im neunzehnten Jahrhundert allerdings überwiegend erst etwas später an breiterer Bedeutung gewinnen, z. B. durch Adolf Just (1859–1936) oder den homöopathischen ‚Lehmpastor' Emanuel Felke (1856–1926) (vgl. Jütte 1996).[19]

Storm hat den Kreislauf der Natur in einem anderen bekannten Gedicht ausgesprochen:

---

[18] Es soll hier lediglich diese Traditionslinie markiert werden. Textuell sind die Sachverhalte erwartungsgemäß komplizierter. Einerseits wird die Kompetenz des Deichbauers explizit (LL 3, 11, 57) und dann auch implizit in Zweifel gezogen, insofern er ein Alkoholiker ist und ‚Trinken' und ‚Ertrinken' in mehreren Texten Storms korreliert sind (*Carsten Curator, John Riew*). Andererseits trägt seine Rückkehr in den Schoß der Mutter inzestuöse Züge und bestärkt darin die naheliegende Vermutung, der Etatsrat habe auch seine eigene Tochter missbraucht. Das bestätigt Storms Selbstdeutung des Themas der Novelle als „die Zerstörung der Familie", dessen also, was das soziale Leben perpetuiert, „oder vielmehr ‚die Familie in der Zerstörung' [...] durch den Vater" (LL 3, 776).
[19] Nur am Rande sei darauf hingewiesen, dass Schlammbäder auch in der Literatur gelegentlich Erwähnung finden, etwa in Jean Pauls *Quintus Fixlein*, Börnes *Briefe[n] aus Paris* oder Stifters *Nachkommenschaften*.

> Wie wenn das Leben wär nichts Andres,
> Als das Verbrennen eines Lichts!
> Verloren geht kein einzig Teilchen,
> Jedoch wir selber gehn ins Nichts!
>
> Denn was wir Leib und Seele nennen,
> So fest in Eins gestaltet kaum,
> Es löst sich auf in Tausendteilchen
> Und wimmelt durch den öden Raum.
>
> Es waltet stets dasselbe Leben,
> Natur geht ihren ewgen Lauf;
> In tausend neuerschaffnen Wesen
> Stehn diese tausend Teilchen auf.
> [...] (LL 1, 253)

Formuliert wird hier eine tendenziell materialistisch-monistische Weltsicht, in der es keine substanzielle Differenz von „Leib und Seele" gibt und das menschliche Individuum nach dem Tod unwiderruflich „ins Nichts" geht. Die materiellen „Teilchen" aber, aus denen es gebildet war, verschwinden nicht, sie bleiben in der Welt und gehen ein in neue Lebewesen. Storm folgt darin – in auf die Biologie übertragener Form – dem Satz der Erhaltung der Masse in geschlossenen Systemen. Diesen hatte der Chemiker Antoine Laurent de Lavoisier 1789 in seinem *Traité élémentaire de chimie* ausgesprochen, und zwar ausgerechnet in einem Kapitel über „Gährung" („fermentation vineuse"):

> [...] denn nichts wird weder in den Operationen der Kunst, noch in jenen der Natur erschaffen, und man kann als Grundsatz annehmen, daß in jeder Operation eine gleiche Menge Stoff vor und nach der Operation vorhanden sey; daß die Eigenschaft und die Menge der Bestandtheile ebendieselbe bleibe, und daß nur Abänderungen und Modifikationen entstehen. (Lavoisier 1803, I, 180)

Neben der Gärung spielt die Verbrennung organischer Stoffe in diesem Zusammenhang eine zentrale Rolle (ebd., I, 139–157 u. ö.). Darauf mag sich implizit Storms Metapher der verbrennenden Kerze beziehen. Ludwig Büchner stellte den Massenerhaltungssatz dann ohne konkreten Verweis auf Lavoisier unter der bezeichnenden Überschrift „Unsterblichkeit des Stoffs" popularisiert dar – ergänzt um ein auf den ersten thermodynamischen Hauptsatz bezogenes Kapitel zur „Unsterblichkeit der Kraft" (Büchner 1898 [1855], 17–24). Hier heißt es u. a.: „Der Stoff als solcher ist unsterblich, unvernichtbar; kein Stäubchen im Weltall kann verloren gehen, keines hinzukommen"; die „Verwandlung und Umgestaltung der Dinge" bestehe „in nichts Anderem [...], als in einem beständigen und unausgesetzten Kreislauf derselben Grundstoffe, deren Menge und Beschaffenheit an sich stets dieselbe und für alle Zeiten unveränderliche bleibt" (ebd., 17–18). Und mit Blick auf die Verwesung:

> Der äußere Anschein erweckt den Glauben, als ob von den ehemaligen Bestandtheilen des einst der Erde übergebenen Körpers außer jenen Ueberresten [d. i. Knochen] nichts mehr vorhanden sei; aber die Wissenschaft sagt, daß in Wirklichkeit auch nicht das kleinste Stäubchen davon verloren gegangen ist, sondern daß die ganze Veränderung nur darin besteht, daß die Grundstoffe jener Bestandtheile ihre ehemaligen Verbindungen verlassen haben und wieder in den allgemeinen Kreislauf der Stoffe zurückgekehrt sind, um heute in dieser morgen in jener Gestalt ihre ewigen Bahnen weiter zu verfolgen. (Ebd., 19)

In Storms damit bis ins Detail übereinstimmender Lesart formiert der Kreislauf der Materie stets neue Lebewesen und perpetuiert so das „Leben" überhaupt. Im Bild des gärenden Schlamms verdichtet er sich quasi in *einer* hybriden Substanz.

4 Nach der Metaphysik

Es ist dies die einzige Form der Unsterblichkeit, die nach dem Ende der Metaphysik bleibt. Man hat in der Forschung mit gutem Recht beschrieben, dass und wie Storm sich sehr dezidiert gegen das Christentum gewendet hat (vgl. Jackson 1989; Demandt 2010; Laage 2010), und mit halbem Recht behauptet, er sei ein Antimetaphysiker und Agnostiker. Mit nur *halbem* Recht – denn die Dinge liegen bei Storm und generell im neunzehnten Jahrhundert komplizierter. Übersehen werden gerne die Spuren, Reste und Überlebsel der alten Metaphysik, die sich dem kulturellen Imaginären eingeschrieben haben. Der Himmel wird bei Storm im Rahmen eines immanenten Weltbilds zu einem topographischen, physikalischen und meteorologischen Phänomen, aber es bleibt ihm zugleich die Absenz der symbolisch-transzendenten Dimension eingeschrieben, die man früher einmal in ihm gesehen hatte. In dem bereits zitierten Gedicht „Über die Heide" heißt es: „Schwarz ist das Kraut und der Himmel so leer" (LL 1, 93). Der Ertrunkene, den Carsten und sein Sohn am Strand der Hallig finden, hat „das furchtbare Totenantlitz gegen den Himmel gekehrt". Die Formulierung – „*gegen* den Himmel" – scheint mehr zu sein als eine Richtungsangabe; sie klingt nach einer Anklage, als lägen dem Toten die letzten Worte Jesu am

Kreuz auf den Lippen: „Mein Gott, mein Gott, warum hast Du mich verlassen?"[20] (Mk 15,34; Mt 27,46) Im anklagenden Blick der Leiche schwingt nicht nur die Verlorenheit angesichts eines sinnlosen Todes mit, sondern – noch vor Freuds Analyse der drei großen menschheitsgeschichtlichen Kränkungen durch Kopernikus, Darwin und die Psychoanalyse selbst (Freud 1969 [1916–1917], 283–284) – vielleicht auch etwas wie eine weitere narzisstische Kränkung, nämlich eine religiöse: die Ent-Setzung aus dem Zentrum einer göttlichen Schöpfung. Hier scheint es weder Euphorie einer befreiten Diesseitigkeit (wie bei Ludwig Feuerbach) noch areligiösen Gleichmut (wie bei Gottfried Keller) noch das Pathos des Lebenskreislaufs als ewige Wiederkunft (wie bei Friedrich Nietzsche) zu geben, eher wird eine Art Phantomschmerz der verlorenen Metaphysik artikuliert. Die Wasserleiche am Strand – das ist der Tod des Menschen in einer entgötterten Welt, ein buchstäblich elementarer Vorgang, und der „gärende Wattenschlamm" ist das Bild des Lebens im Zeichen der „transzendentalen Obdachlosigkeit" (Lukács 1988 [1916], 32): Materie, die sich selbst reproduziert ohne Schöpfung von außen.

Ein besonders prominentes Bild des Strandes wird darin überschrieben: Wie kein anderes könnte der Strand ein Inbild der alttestamentlichen Genesis sein, der Ort, an dem Gott am dritten Schöpfungstag Wasser und Erde scheidet (1. Mose 1,9–10); hier jedoch ist er der urweltlich anmutende Schauplatz einer rein immanenten Lebensschöpfung. So scheint es. Doch diese Überschreibung ist keine vollständige; das Überschriebene wird nicht einfach getilgt, sondern bleibt in und unter der Überschreibung palimpsestartig erhalten, so wie im Blick des Toten gegen den Himmel dessen Leere mit artikuliert wird. An biblische Vorstellungskomplexe als alte Bildwelten erinnert Storm häufig und mitunter ganz ausdrücklich, wenn etwa im *Schimmelreiter* Überschwemmung und Deichbruch als „Sündflut" und „Weltenuntergang" (LL 3, 752–753) erscheinen – freilich perspektivisch gebrochen und in metaphorischem Gebrauch. Es sind gerade die Perspektiven der Figuren, nicht zuletzt in den historischen Erzählungen, die die alten Weltdeutungsparadigmen sozusagen semantisch im Spiel halten. Auch dort, wo ‚das *Elementare*' an die Stelle der alten Schöpfung tritt, leben so metaphysische Restbestände fort. Der Lebensprozess der Natur überhaupt refiguriert ‚Unsterblichkeit', so wie der Ausblick ins Unendliche und das Meeresrauschen als stete Wiederkehr des Gleichen an jene andere, verlorene ‚Ewigkeit' erinnern; und der Streif des Meeres am Horizont lässt die christliche Eschatologie anklingen, indem er mal silbrig-verheißungsvoll erglänzen und „im ersten Sonnenstrahl entbrennen" (LL 2, 442), mal als „schreckende Unendlichkeit"

---

20 Vergleichbar die letzten Worte des sterbenden jungen Mannes in „Geh nicht hinein": „Hilf! / Ach, Vater, lieber Vater!" (LL 1, 94)

(LL 2, 437) düster-apokalyptisch drohen kann. Die metaphysische Transzendenz wird also nicht schlechterdings verabschiedet, sondern überlebt bzw. kehrt wieder in semantischen Restbeständen und Besetzungen der Dinge. *Etwas* von dem, was nach dem Ende der Metaphysik verschwunden sein müsste, die Spur eines Etwas, von dem sich nicht sagen lässt, ob es numinos, dämonisch oder nur unheimlich ist, bleibt noch unter dem ‚leeren Himmel' präsent.

In diesem Zusammenhang ist noch einmal auf die unauflösbaren Geheimnisse, Töne und „Stimmen" über der „Tiefe" zurückzukommen, die am Meeresstrand zwar „vernehmlich" werden, aber fremd und unverständlich bleiben wie die dumpf mitwandernden Schritte aus der Tiefe des Heidebodens. Es scheint mir völlig plausibel, ihre Unverständlichkeit als Indikator für ein entfremdetes Naturverhältnis in einer entzauberten, nicht mehr durch metaphysische oder naturphilosophische Sinnzusammenhänge getragenen Welt zu interpretieren, wie Heinrich Detering (2013, 227–229) das getan hat. Aber woher rührt dann das Moment einer anthropomorphen bzw. animistischen Belebtheit und Intentionalität, die von den Stimmen wie von anderen Details der Szene ausgehen? In ihnen lässt sich, so kann man vielleicht sagen, die heimliche Persistenz eines Anderen des bloß Säkularen und Immanenten vernehmen. Strand und Meer bilden gewissermaßen eine metaphysische Landschaft, aber, anders als etwa bei Caspar David Friedrich, eine metaphysische Landschaft ohne Metaphysik. Damit kommt man nicht einfach auf die zitierten älteren Deutungen einer ‚schicksalhaften' oder ‚mystischen' Dimension des Gedichts zurück, die defizitär bleiben, soweit sie nicht sehen, dass diese Züge erst auf der Kehrseite einer gegenmetaphysischen ‚Weltanschauung' entstehen. Sie verweisen vage und andeutungshaft auf eine „innerirdische, immanente Form der Transzendenz" (Blödorn 2016, 270). Es wäre verführerisch zu sagen, dass sich alte Dualismen in Form eines *reentry* als immanente Transzendenz in die säkulare Welt hinübergerettet und dabei transformiert hätten und dass die religiös-vertikale Polarität von Erde und Himmel, Diesseits und Jenseits sozusagen in eine immanent-horizontale von Land und Meer umkippe. Doch wäre sogleich zu korrigieren, dass mit dem Ende der traditionellen Metaphysik auch die Denkfigur des Dualismus verabschiedet wird, allerdings ohne von einem eindeutigen Monismus ersetzt zu werden, wie er die materialistischen Wissenschaften der Epoche prägt. Land und Meer sind zwar nicht dasselbe, aber sie greifen ineinander über, überlagern und durchdringen sich, bis sie im Schlamm ununterscheidbar werden. Der Strand, die Übergangszone zwischen Land und Meer wie zwischen Leben und Tod, verbildlicht wie kaum etwas anderes Storms Stellung zwischen Abweisung und Wiederkehr der Metaphysik, Monismus und Dualismus.

Dass der Strand derart ein Ort des Übergangs, Fortlebens, der Wiederkehr und des Unheimlichen ist, zeigt sich auch an der anklagenden Wasserleiche in

Carsten Curator. In einer schwer greifbaren Weise scheint ihr ein allerletzter Rest von Intentionalität innezuwohnen, eine Art paradoxes Restleben. Wie das Watt ein Zwischenraum ist und wie im gärenden Schlamm Leben und Tod interferieren, so scheint auch der Tote in einer Uferzone des Übergangs zu verbleiben, nicht mehr lebendig, aber auch nicht völlig tot, in einem Raum des Gespenstischen und Unheimlichen. Dieses gespenstische Moment ergreift auch vom Text selbst Besitz, denn die Wasserleiche hat eine proleptische Funktion: Sie deutet auf das spätere Ertrinken von Heinrich, der hier den Toten gefunden hat, voraus, sodass die zitierte Strandszene nicht nur in einem allgemeinen Sinne von Leben und Tod handelt, sondern auch das gesamte Leben Heinrichs von der Kindheit bis zu seinem Untergang in einer Sturmflut zusammenzieht. Ohne es zu wissen, halluziniert Carsten, wenn er sich nachts im Bett an die Vergangenheit erinnert, die Zukunft und wird so zum ‚Spökenkieker' (vgl. Theisohn 2014), der auch noch in einem anderen Sinne Grenzen durchlässig macht, die nämlich von Vergangenheit, Gegenwart und Zukunft, und die Zeitschichten überblendet.

Diese Überlegungen würden vielleicht etwas forciert und überfrachtet wirken, wenn es nicht noch andere Indizien in diese Richtung gäbe. Tatsächlich sind die Schwellenräume Strand und Deich beim realistischen Autor und vermeintlichen Agnostiker Storm Orte gespenstischer Erscheinungen – auch wenn diese zumeist perspektivisch gebrochen werden oder im Sinne einer phantastischen Literatur offen bleiben. Im *Schimmelreiter* glaubt der junge Hauke Haien vom Deich aus, im Watt „die Geister der Ertrunkenen" (LL 3, 645) zu sehen, und die abergläubischen Knechte rätseln über das Pferdegespenst auf Jevershallig. Wenn Hauke später auf dem Deich, den er selbst gebaut hat, als gespenstischer Reiter umgehen muss, dann bietet der Text dafür eine frappante Erklärung an, in der man eine geisterhafte Parodie des materialistischen Lebenskreislaufs, aber auch der alten Metaphysik sehen kann: Da Hauke und seine Familie bei einer Sturmflut ertrinken und nicht mehr gefunden werden, vermutet der Erzähler: „die toten Körper werden von dem abströmenden Wasser durch den Bruch ins Meer hinausgetrieben und auf dessen Grunde allmählich in ihre Urbestandteile aufgelöst sein" (LL 3, 754). An dieser Stelle könnte das zitierte Gedicht *Wie wenn das Leben wär nichts Andres* den Lebenskreislauf fortschreiben. Doch eine – leider gestrichene – Variante des Schlusses gibt dem Ganzen eine überraschende Wendung. Polemisch reformuliert der Erzähler die Volksmeinung über den Deichgrafen Hauke: „bei Hochfluthen müssen seine verstäubten Atome sich zu einem Scheinbild wiederum zusammenfinden" (LL 3, 1061). Auch Gespenster gehorchen bei ihrer Auferstehung im Diesseits offenbar dem Erhaltungssatz der Materie, und das belegt, wie nahe die materialistische Vorstellung eines Lebensrecyclings am Phantasma einer gespenstischen Wiederkehr liegt.

Was also ist der Strand? Er ist, wie schon erwähnt, bei Storm immer auch ein Welt-Bild, ein Ort der Verhandlung darüber, was es mit Leben und Tod, Immanenz und Transzendenz auf sich hat. Die säkulare Weltsicht wird durch sinnliche Konkretion ebenso unterstrichen wie durch die Anspielungen auf wissenschaftliche Paradigmen. Doch zeigt sich, dass sie Spuren und Restbestände des Metaphysischen nicht loswird und vielleicht auch gar nicht loswerden will. Sie bleiben in den drei Modi der Negation, der Fortdauer und der Wiederkehr erhalten: als anklagende Betonung der Absenz, als assoziative Besetzungen, als Geheimnis, Stimme oder Gespenst. „Wo keine Götter sind, walten Gespenster", bemerkt Novalis (1983, 520) – vielleicht ein bisschen zu lapidar. Anders als Götter bieten Gespenster keine metaphysischen Garantien oder Sinnversprechen mehr, aber sie markieren die Leerstelle dieser Garantie und halten so die Erinnerung daran wach. Etwas bleibt oder kehrt wieder, etwas, das vom säkularen Denken nicht erfasst wird und eine Lücke in diesem markiert – sei es Ahnung eines Geheimnisses, das sich aber nicht mehr metaphysisch oder ‚romantisch'-naturphilosophisch fixieren lässt, sei es Ungenügen an der entzauberten Welt oder auch eine heimliche Hoffnung auf eine andere Dimension des Wirklichen. Aufgrund seiner topographischen Struktur als ein Raum der Übergänge und des Dazwischen ist der Strand die ideale Chiffre für solche Konstellationen. Der Strand wird so zugleich auch Schauplatz und Bild eines in sich gespaltenen säkularen Bewusstseins der Moderne, das von dem heimgesucht wird, was es aus sich auszuschließen sucht und darum mit Spuren, Resten, Relikten und Wiedergängern durchsetzt ist.

5 Vergessen und Erinnern (*Eine Halligfahrt*)

Dieser Aspekt ist abschließend durch eine weitere Dimension des Strandes zu ergänzen, die an Storms Erzählung *Eine Halligfahrt* von 1871 erläutert werden soll. Es handelt sich um die fiktive Erinnerung eines Ich-Erzählers, der aus weiter zeitlicher Distanz von einem Ausflug auf eine Hallig, dem Besuch bei einem unverheirateten alten Vetter und einer sich anbahnenden, dann aber nicht eingetretenen Liebesbeziehung mit dem Mädchen Susanne berichtet. Trotz ruhiger See und heiteren Wetters werden auch hier die destruktiven und todbringenden Kräfte des Meeres betont, das die Stadt Rungholt verschlungen und in der „großen Flut" „vor einem halben Jahrtausend" die Hallig des Vetters nebst anderen „Inselbrocken" vom nordfriesischen Festland abgerissen hat (LL 2, 45). Zugleich aber ist auch hier wiederum der Strand der Ort des sich selbst erneuernden Lebens: Die Insel ist von „einem ungeheuren schwebenden Gürtel" von

Silbermöwen umgeben (LL 2, 45), die am Strand nisten. Hierhin führt ein Spaziergang das potenzielle Liebespaar, um die Brutplätze zu besichtigen, und hier hält die einer Beziehung offenbar stärker zugeneigte Susanne ein Ei ans Ohr, „als wolle sie das keimende Leben belauschen" (LL 2, 57). Auch das Winseln eines jungen Seehunds, „der seine Mutter such[t]" (LL 2, 60), fügt sich in das um Prokreation, Ehe und Familie zentrierte Szenario, aus dem hier allerdings „keine Frucht" erwächst (LL 2, 61). Dass der Ausflug mit einem nächtlichen Blick auf „den von der eintretenden Ebbe bloßgelegten Schlamm" endet (LL 2, 61), unterstreicht die Bildlogik in Storms Erzählen.

Diese bereits ausführlich erläuterte Dimension von Strand und Meer wird nun überlagert von einer weiteren, in der die Vorstellungen von Untergang, Tod und Leben eine metaphorische Qualität zugewiesen bekommen, indem sie mit Konzepten von Vergessen und Erinnerung verknüpft werden, bekanntlich einem zentralen – und hier auch formgebenden – Thema bei Storm (vgl. Laage 1985; Pastor 1988; Schilling 1995; Lee 2005; Onken 2009). Charakteristischerweise beginnt die Erzählung mit einem die eigentliche Erinnerung einleitenden Sonntagsspaziergang am Deich bzw. am Strand, dessen Saum „gegen die nagende Flut" mit einer „neue[n] Strohbestickung" geschützt ist (LL 2, 41). Hier erfolgt eine doppelte Wiederkehr. Zum einen wird berichtet, wie man gelegentlich „aus schwarzen Moorgründen oder aus dem Schlamm der Watten noch eine versteinte Wurzel" (LL 2, 41) jener Urwälder gräbt, die einst die Küste bedeckt haben, Relikt einer Urzeit und ihrer Stürme. Damit öffnet sich – auch hier wieder – eine Tiefendimension in die Vorzeit, in der auch die jetzt lebenden Menschen ihre Wurzeln haben. Zum anderen taucht in der Uferzone plötzlich der eigentliche Erzählgegenstand auf: „Und siehe! – während das Wasser weich, fast lautlos zu meinen Füßen anspülte, plötzlich mit leichten Schritten ging die Erinnerung neben mir" (LL 2, 41), und zwar in Gestalt von Susanne, als sei sie wie Aphrodite Anadyomene soeben dem Schaum des Meeres entstiegen. Da das Erinnerte vergangen und tot ist, zugleich aber fortlebt, liegt seine Identifizierung als Gespenst nahe (vgl. Begemann 2013), wenngleich als „Gespenst[]" des Glückes" (LL 2, 41), eines Glückes, das der Erzähler zwar ausgeschlagen hat, das aber als unabgegoltenes Versprechen bis in die Gegenwart hineinreicht. Wenn der Strand andernorts der Landeplatz der Wasserleichen und ihrer mutmaßlichen Geister ist, und wenn der untote Deichgraf Hauke Haien auf seinem Lebenswerk umgeht, so ist auch hier wieder der Strand, die Schwellenzone zwischen Tod und Leben, ein Ort der Gespenster. Anhand der räumlichen Konstellation um Meer, Land und den Übergangsraum zwischen beiden werden damit Fragen des individuellen wie kulturellen Gedächtnisses verhandelt. Das Meer gewinnt Züge eines amorphen Reservoirs von ehemaligen Bewusstseinsinhalten, die „unsichtbar und verschollen" (LL 2, 44) auf seinem Boden lagern wie das versunkene Rungholt, aber nach Willkür freigegeben werden und am Ufer in den Raum des Bewusstseins übertreten können, wo sie vom Tod zu einem Scheinleben erwachen und gleichsam auferstehen.[21] Es ist nur konsequent, dass gerade mit Bezug auf die untergegangene Stadt auch auf eine andere Form des Fortlebens verwiesen wird, nämlich auf die Präsenz nichtintegrierter ‚ungleichzeitiger' Inhalte eines kulturellen Imaginären. Mit Blick auf die Tiefe des Meeres bemerkt der Erzähler, dass das mythisch denkende „rotwangige Heidentum [...] hier noch in uns Allen spukt" (LL 2, 43), d. h. auch und gerade im säkularen Bewusstsein. Dieses erweist sich als gespalten und widersprüchlich, weil durchzogen von Relikten älterer Bewusstseinsformen, abgesunkenen kulturellen Reminiszenzen, die obsolet scheinen, aber in bestimmten Situationen dann eben doch gewissermaßen an Land gehen können.

Der Strand figuriert damit auch als Schwelle des Bewusstseins. Doch wie sich an dem Petrefakt im Uferschlamm zeigt, geht es nicht allein um immaterielle, individuelle oder kollektive Erinnerungen, sondern auch um deren materielle Träger, um Dinge, die das Gedächtnis der Vergangenheit evozieren.[22] Während der Blick durch das Fenster auf ein kürzlich auf der Hallig gestrandetes Schiff fällt (LL 2, 47–48), das damit dem Strandrecht unterliegt, wird dem Leser mitgeteilt, dass nahezu der gesamte, mit zahllosen kulturellen Artefakten ausgestattete Hausrat des Vetters vom Haushund bis zum Tischwein aus „Strandgut" besteht (LL 2, 48) – wobei offen bleibt, ob es sich um wirkliches oder nur metaphorisches Strandgut handelt. Dieses tritt jetzt ins eigene Leben ein, stammt aber aus anderen Leben und anderen Zeiten und setzt sich darum immer auch aus „Gedächtnisstücken" zusammen (LL 2, 62) – „Gedächtnisstücken" in dem Doppelsinn, dass sie einerseits Memorialdinge sind, die die Erinnerung an Vergangenes speichern und eine Geschichte zu erzählen haben, und die andererseits selbst nur Bruchstücke eines umfassenden Gedächtnisses sind, wie die Hallig ihrerseits ein „Inselbrocken" ist und daher diese Konstellation des Versprengtseins von einem verlorenen Ursprung spiegelt. So werden die in die Zukunft weisenden Mächte Leben und Prokreation ergänzt von den die Vergangenheit konservierenden Faktoren der Erinnerung und des Erbes.

Darin steckt eine kleine Kulturtheorie. „Was überhaupt war hier nicht Strandgut?" (LL 2, 48): Das gesamte materielle, mentale und emotionale Leben bewegt sich im Horizont der Erbschaft, in den Relikten, den Überbleibseln und

---

[21] Das Meer symbolisiere „das absolute Vergessen wegen seiner unbegrenzten Speicherkraft", bemerkt Jean Lefebvre (2004, 75).
[22] Vgl. dazu grundsätzlich Vedder (2013). Eine solche Zeitkapsel ist hier am prononciertesten der Geigenkasten des Vetters, den dieser nicht öffnen will aus Furcht vor dem Überflutetwerden durch die Erinnerung: „Siehst du denn nicht, daß das ein Särglein ist? Man soll die Toten ruhen lassen" (LL 2, 49).

Überlebseln der Vergangenheit, die man zwar zu „Sammlungen" ordnen kann (LL 2, 47), die aber darum ihren kontingenten Charakter nicht verlieren und später erneut zu Treibgut an anderen Stränden werden können. So wie das Meer ganz beliebig manches preisgibt und manches nicht, so teilen einige „Gedächtnisstücke" ihre Geschichte mit, während andere sie für sich behalten. Das gesamte Leben wird so quasi zu einer Strandzone, und darin verbinden sich die kulturelle und die anthropologisch-existenzielle Dimension. Über den Vetter heißt es, er habe sich später auf seiner Hallig beerdigen lassen auf die Gefahr hin, selbst zu Treibgut zu werden und sich im ozeanischen Kreislauf der Materie aufzulösen – so wie das bei Hauke Haien und seiner Familie der Fall sein wird: „Er hat es gewagt, sich hier zur Ruhe zu begeben, wohl wissend, daß der Sturm die Flut zu seinem Grabe treiben, daß die Flut es aufwühlen und ihn in seinem schmalen Ruhebette auf das weite Meer hinaustragen könne." (LL 2, 62) So zirkulieren die kulturellen Dinge in der Welt wie die Atome; der kulturelle Kreislauf wird in Analogie zum Lebenskreislauf gedacht.

Auch die Bibliothek des Vetters ist

> Strandgut; fast Alles Antiquaria! Die einstigen Besitzer sind gescheitert oder zu Grunde gegangen; ihre Bücher sind in alle Welt getrieben, von geschäftigen Leuten aufgefischt und verkauft; und nun stehen sie hier eine Weile, bis auch ihren jetzigen Besitzer das gleiche Los ereilt. (LL 2, 48)

Wenn diese Bibliothek nebst den Aufzeichnungen des Vetters dem Erzähler vererbt wird (LL 2, 62), dann zeigt sich auch die poetologische Komponente dieses kulturellen Konzepts. Denn wie der Hausrat des Vetters, so ist auch der gesamte Text durchsetzt mit Relikten und Reminiszenzen, versprengten Zitaten und Allusionen.[23] Nicht nur werden am Ende der Erzählung die Aufzeichnungen des Vetters angehängt; es werden auch Sagen und Mythen aufgerufen, Daniel Defoe, Jean Paul, Novalis, Eichendorff, Hoffmann, Heine und manche andere zitiert und zu einem intertextuellen Patchwork neu zusammengefügt, dessen selbstreflexives Bild der Hausrat und speziell die Bibliothek des Vetters darstellt: Strandgut als Textprinzip.

Über die in den vorherigen Kapiteln skizzierten Aspekte hinaus und sie ergänzend, zeigt die *Halligfahrt*, wie vielfältiger semantischer Besetzungen die Strandzone fähig ist. Ging es zunächst um die existenzielle Stellung des Subjekts in der Welt, sodann um das Verhältnis von Leben, Tod und Metaphysik, so wird hier dem Tableau das Thema Gedächtnis hinzugefügt. Dabei gewinnt die gesamte Topographie eine quasi anthropomorphe Dimension. Über Meer und Land werden Versinken und Auftauchen, Vergessen und Erinnern verhandelt,

---

[23] Das intertextuelle Verfahren der Erzählung rekonstruiert Onken (2009, 209–258).

und der Strand ist die Schwelle des Übertritts von einem zum anderen. Er ist in dieser Hinsicht der Ort nicht nur von Leben und Fortpflanzung überhaupt, sondern auch der Verlebendigung eines vermeintlich Toten, weil Vergessenen, das quasi aus dem Meer des Unbewussten wiederkehrt.[24] Diese anthropomorphe Struktur bestätigt sich auch am Verhältnis der Insel zu ihrem Bewohner, dem alten Vetter. Wie sich die Hallig in heftigen Stürmen als „Inselbrocken" vom Festland abgetrennt hatte, so hat sich auch der Vetter von der defizitären gesellschaftlichen Welt losgerissen. Die topographische Insellage ist auch ein Bild des abgeschlossenen, weltabgewandten, gleichsam a-sozialen Subjekts (vgl. Borgards 2018, 10–12, 35). Dass es sich dabei erneut um ein literarisches Zitat handelt, insofern hier eine zentrale Konstellation aus Adalbert Stifters Erzählung *Der Hagestolz* (1844/50) aufgenommen wird, zeigt die Engführung der diegetisch-topographischen, metaphorischen und poetologischen Ebenen der Erzählung. Wenn der ehe- und kinderlose und damit dem ‚Leben' abgewandte Zölibatär, der vor langer Zeit mit der Liebe abgeschlossen hat und ihre seltsamen Wirrungen am Strand nur noch durch das Fernglas beobachtet (LL 2, 59), selbst ein abgerissener „Inselbrocken" und mit seinem Wohnort identisch ist, dann verbindet sich das strukturell mit dem Motiv des Treibguts, denn auch seine Insel und er selbst sind gleichsam Treibgut im Meer. Und zugleich spiegelt sich darin das literarische Verfahren des Textes. Denn auch mit der intertextuellen Wiederkehr des Insel-Motivs auf der Ebene des *discours* wird ein Stück Treibgut aus der literarischen Überlieferung aufgefischt und rekontextualisiert, was auf der Ebene der *histoire* wiederum dem Lebenskonzept des Vetters korrespondiert und zugleich ein kulturelles Konzept exemplifiziert. In einem ganz umfassenden Sinn wird der Strand zu einer Lebens- und Textlandschaft.

Literaturverzeichnis

Aristoteles. „Metaphysik". *Philosophische Schriften*. Nach der Übersetzung von Hermann Bonitz, bearb. von Horst Seidl. Hamburg: Edition Kramer, 1995.

Bachofen, Johann Jakob. *Das Mutterrecht. Eine Untersuchung über die Gynaikokratie der alten Welt nach ihrer religiösen und rechtlichen Natur. Eine Auswahl* [1861]. Hg. Hans-Jürgen Heinrichs. Frankfurt/Main: Suhrkamp, 1975.

„Bathybius". *Meyers Konversationslexikon, Bd. 2*. http://www.retrobibliothek.de/retrobib/seite.html?id=101692. Leipzig und Wien: Verlag des Bibliographischen Instituts, 1885–1892 (01.04.2019).

---

[24] Das Verhältnis von Meer und Unbewusstem untersucht unter psychoanalytischer Perspektive Neumann (2002, 129–140).

Baum, Michael. „Storms *Meeresstrand* und die Grenzen der Interpretation". *1955–2005: Emil Staiger und ‚Die Kunst der Interpretation' heute*. Hg. Joachim Rickes, Volker Ladenthin und Michael Baum. Bern et al.: Peter Lang, 2007. 243–260.

Begemann, Christian. „Figuren der Wiederkehr. Gespenster, Erinnerung, Tradition und Vererbung bei Theodor Storm". *Wirklichkeit und Wahrnehmung: Neue Perspektiven auf Theodor Storm*. Hg. Elisabeth Strowick und Ulrike Vedder. Bern et al.: Peter Lang, 2013. 13–37.

Begemann, Christian. „Nachtgespenster – Überlebsel. Zum Verhältnis von Moderne und kulturellem Imaginärem bei Theodor Storm". *Konventionen und Tabubrüche. Theodor Storm als widerspenstiger Erfolgsautor des deutschen Realismus*. Hg. Louis Gerrekens, Valérie Leyh und Eckart Pastor. Berlin: Erich Schmidt, 2019. 201–231.

Bernd, Clifford A. *Theodor Storm. The Dano-German Poet and Writer*. Bern, Oxford und New York: Peter Lang, 2005.

Blödorn, Andreas. „Meeresrauschen. Immanente Transzendenz und anti-bürgerliche Fluchtimpulse bei Theodor Storm und Thomas Mann". *Verirrte Bürger: Thomas Mann und Theodor Storm*. Hg. Heinrich Detering, Maren Ermisch und Hans Wisskirchen. Frankfurt/Main: Vittorio Klostermann, 2016. 265–281.

Borgards, Roland. „‚…und endlich stieg ein grünes Eiland vor uns auf'. Theodor Storms *Eine Halligfahrt* (1871) und die Geschichte der Inselbiogeographie". *Schriften der Theodor-Storm-Gesellschaft* 67 (2018): 9–36.

Büchner, Ludwig. *Kraft und Stoff oder Grundzüge der natürlichen Weltordnung* [1855]. Leipzig: Theodor Thomas, 1898.

Carus, Carl Gustav. *Zwölf Briefe über das Erdleben*. Stuttgart: P. Balz'sche Buchhandlung, 1841.

Corbin, Alain. *Meereslust. Das Abendland und die Entdeckung der Küste*. Berlin: Wagenbach, 1990.

Demandt, Christian. *Religion und Religionskritik bei Theodor Storm*. Berlin: Erich Schmidt, 2010.

Detering, Heinrich. „Die Stimmen und die Stimmung. Storms Naturgedichte". *Stimmung und Methode*. Hg. Friederike Reents und Burkhard Meyer-Sickendiek. Tübingen: Mohr Siebeck, 2013. 219–234.

Fasold, Regina. *Theodor Storm*. Stuttgart und Weimar: Metzler, 1997.

Forster, Franz. „Theodor Storms *Meeresstrand* und *Die Stadt*. Probleme der Lyrikdefinition. Zur Gattungspoetik und einigen Fragen ihrer Systematik". *Jahrbuch der Grillparzer-Gesellschaft* 12.3 (1976): 27–37.

Forster, Georg. „Noch etwas über die Menschenraßen". *Werke in vier Bänden, Bd. 2*. Hg. Gerhard Steiner. Frankfurt/Main: Insel, 1969. 71–101.

Freud, Sigmund. „Vorlesungen zur Einführung in die Psychoanalyse" [1916–1917]. *Studienausgabe, Bd. 1*. Hg. Alexander Mitscherlich, Angela Richards und James Strachey. Frankfurt/Main: Fischer, 1969.

„Gärung". *Brockhaus Konversationslexikon, Bd. 7*. http://www.retrobibliothek.de/retrobib/seite.html?id=126981&imageview=true. Berlin und Wien: F. A. Brockhaus, 1894. 562–561 (01.04.2019).

Goethe, Johann Wolfgang. „Faust. Der Tragödie zweiter Teil". *Sämtliche Werke nach Epochen seines Schaffens. Münchner Ausgabe, Bd. 18.1: Letzte Jahre. 1827–1832*. Hg. von Karl Richter in Zusammenarbeit mit Herbert G. Göpfert, Norbert Miller, Gerhard Sauder und Edith Zehm. München und Wien: Hanser, 1997. 103–351.

Gould, Stephen Jay. „Bathybius and Eozoon". *The Panda's Thumb*. New York und London: W. W. Norton Company, 1980. 236–244.

Gräff, Thomas. *Lyrik von der Romantik bis zur Jahrhundertwende*. München: Oldenbourg, 2000.

Haeckel, Ernst. „Beiträge zur Plastidentheorie". *Jenaische Zeitschrift* 5.3 (1870): 492–550. https://reader.digitale-sammlungen.de/de/fs1/object/display/bsb11018338_00007.html (01.04.2019).

Haeckel, Ernst. *Das Protistenreich. Eine populäre Uebersicht über das Formengebiet der niedersten Lebewesen*. https://www.biodiversitylibrary.org/item/119851#page/1/mode/1up. Leipzig: Ernst Günther's Verlag, 1878 (01.04.2019).

Hoffmann, Volker. „Theodor Storm, Der Schimmelreiter. Eine Teufelspaktgeschichte als realistische Lebensgeschichte". *Erzählungen und Novellen des 19. Jahrhunderts, Bd. 2*. Stuttgart: Reclam,1990. 333–370.

Huxley, Thomas Henry. „On Some Organisms Living at Great Depths in the North Atlantic Ocean". *Quarterly Journal of Microscopical Science* 8 (1868): 203–212. https://www.biodiversitylibrary.org/page/13766309#page/213/mode/1up (01.04.2019).

Jackson, David A. „Storms Stellung zum Christentum und zur christlichen Kirche". *Theodor Storm und das 19. Jahrhundert*. Hg. Brian Coghlan und Karl Ernst Laage. Berlin: Erich Schmidt, 1989. 41–99.

Jütte, Robert. *Geschichte der Alternativen Medizin. Von der Volksmedizin zu den unkonventionellen Therapien von heute*. München: C. H. Beck, 1996.

Kaiser, Gerhard. „Im Geflüster der Stimmen oder vom Selbstgenuss der Verlassenheit". *1000 deutsche Gedichte und ihre Interpretation, Bd. 4: Von Heinrich Heine bis Friedrich Nietzsche*. Hg. Marcel Reich-Ranicki. Frankfurt/Main: Insel, 1994. 288–290.

Kant, Immanuel. „Über den Gebrauch teleologischer Prinzipien in der Philosophie". *Werke in zehn Bänden, Bd. 8*. Hg. Wilhelm Weischedel. Darmstadt: Wissenschaftliche Buchgesellschaft, 1975. 139–170.

Konersmann, Ralf. „Die Philosophen und das Meer". *Kulturelle Tatsachen*. Frankfurt/Main: Suhrkamp, 2006. 190–205.

Laage, Karl Ernst. „Das Erinnerungsmotiv in Theodor Storms Novellistik". *Theodor Storm. Studien zu seinem Leben und Werk*. Berlin: Erich Schmidt, 1985. 1–19.

Laage, Karl Ernst. *„Wenn ich doch glauben könnte!" Theodor Storm und die Religion*. Heide: Boyens Medien, 2010.

La Bonnardière, Joseph. *Introduction à la thalassothérapie. Thèse pour obtenir le grade de docteur en médecine*. Montpellier: Boehm & Fils, 1865.

Lavoisier, Anton Lorenz [Antoine Laurent de]. *System der antiphlogistischen Chemie [Traité élémentaire de chimie, 1789]*. 2 Bde. 2. Aufl. Berlin und Stettin: Friedrich Nicolai, 1803.

Lee, No-Eun. *Erinnerung und Erzählprozess in Theodor Storm frühen Novellen (1848–1859)*. Berlin: Erich Schmidt, 2005.

Lefebvre, Jean. „Schuld und Scheitern in Theodor Storms Novelle *Eine Halligfahrt*". *Schriften der Theodor-Storm-Gesellschaft* 53 (2004): 63–80.

Lukács, Georg. *Die Theorie des Romans. Ein geschichtsphilosophischer Versuch über die Formen der großen Epik* [1916]. Neuwied: Luchterhand, 1988.

Merker, Paul. „Theodor Storm: *Meeresstrand*". *Gedicht und Gedanke*. Hg. Heinz Otto Burger. Halle/Saale: Max Niemeyer, 1942. 274–287.

Michelet, Jules. *Das Meer [La Mer, 1861]*. Übersetzt und hg. von Rolf Wintermeyer. Frankfurt/Main und New York: Campus, 2006.

Müller, Harro, und Norbert Mecklenburg. „Theodor Storms Gedicht *Über die Heide*. Versuch einer kritischen Interpretation". *Schriften der Theodor-Storm-Gesellschaft* 19 (1970): 35–42.

Neumann, Christian. *Zwischen Paradies und ödem Ort. Unbewusste Bedeutungsstrukturen in Theodor Storms novellistischem Spätwerk*. Würzburg: Königshausen & Neumann, 2002.

Novalis. „Die Christenheit oder Europa". *Schriften, Bd. 3: Das philosophische Werk II*. Hg. von Richard Samuel in Zusammenarbeit mit Hans-Joachim Mähl und Gerhard Schulz. 3. Aufl. Darmstadt: Kohlhammer, 1983. 507–524.

Oken, Lorenz. *Lehrbuch der Naturphilosophie*. Jena: Friedrich Frommann, 1810.

Oken, Lorenz. *Lehrbuch der Naturphilosophie*. 2. Aufl. Jena: Friedrich Frommann, 1831.

Onken, Aiko. *Erinnerung, Erzählung, Identität. Theodor Storms mittlere Schaffensperiode (1867–1872)*. Heidelberg: Winter, 2009.

Pastor, Eckart. *Die Sprache der Erinnerung. Zu den Novellen von Theodor Storm*. Frankfurt/Main: Athenäum, 1988.

Rehbock, Philip F. „Huxley, Haeckel, and the Oceanographers: The Case of *Bathybius haeckelii*". *Isis* 66 (1975): 504–533.

Richter, Dieter. *Das Meer. Geschichte der ältesten Landschaft*. Berlin: Wagenbach, 2014.

Rickes, Joachim. „Hat die Germanistik das Interpretieren verlernt? Vom Schiffbruch an Storms *Meeresstrand*. Eine Streitschrift". *Wirkendes Wort* 55 (2005): 5–13.

Roebling, Irmgard. „‚Es rauscht kein Wald, es schlägt im Mai / Kein Vogel ohn Unterlaß'. Storms Naturdichtung im Lichte der Einfühlungsästhetik". *Theodor Storms ästhetische Heimat. Studien zur Lyrik und zum Erzählwerk Storms*. Würzburg: Königshausen & Neumann, 2012a. 15–65.

Roebling, Irmgard. „Prinzip Heimat – eine regressive Utopie? Eine psychoanalytische Interpretation von Theodor Storms *Regentrude*". *Theodor Storms ästhetische Heimat. Studien zur Lyrik und zum Erzählwerk Storms*. Würzburg: Königshausen & Neumann, 2012b. 209–228.

Roebling, Irmgard. „‚Von Menschentragik und wildem Naturgeheimnis'. Die Thematisierung von Natur, Aberglauben und Weiblichkeit in Storms *Schimmelreiter*". *Theodor Storms ästhetische Heimat. Studien zur Lyrik und zum Erzählwerk Storms*. Würzburg: Königshausen & Neumann, 2012c. 311–356.

Rupke, Nicolaas A. „Bathybius Haeckelii and the Psychology of Scientific Discovery". *Studies in the History and Philosophy of Science* 7 (1976): 53–62.

Schilling, Michael. „Erzählen als Arbeit am kollektiven Gedächtnis. Zu Theodor Storms Novellen nach 1865". *Euphorion* 89 (1995): 37–53.

Schneider, Wilhelm. „Theodor Storm, *Meeresstrand*". *Liebe zum deutschen Gedicht*. Hg. Wilhelm Schneider. 2. Aufl. Freiburg: Herder, 1954. 105–113.

Schönert, Jörg. „‚Am Himmel fährt ein kalt Gewölk daher!'. Zu Anspruch und Krise des Erfahrungs- und Deutungsmodells ‚Natur' in der deutschsprachigen Lyrik 1850–1890". *Das schwierige neunzehnte Jahrhundert*. Hg. Jürgen Barkhoff, Gilbert Carr und Roger Paulin. Tübingen: Niemeyer, 2000. 171–185.

Silman, Tamara. „Theodor Storms Gedicht *Meeresstrand*". *Schriften der Theodor Storm-Gesellschaft* 25 (1976): 48–52.

Storm, Theodor. *Sämtliche Werke in vier Bänden*. Hg. Karl Ernst Laage und Dieter Lohmeier. Frankfurt/Main: Deutscher Klassiker Verlag, 1987/1988.

Theisohn, Philipp. „Spökenkieken. Storm und das Wissen der Geister". *Schriften der Theodor Storm-Gesellschaft* 63 (2014): 23–39.

Tieck, Ludwig. „Der Runenberg". *Schriften in zwölf Bänden. Bd. 6: Phantasus*. Hg. Manfred Frank. Frankfurt/Main: Deutscher Klassiker Verlag, 1985. 184–209.

Vedder, Ulrike. „Dinge als Zeitkapseln. Realismus und Unverfügbarkeit der Dinge in Theodor Storms Novellen". *Wirklichkeit und Wahrnehmung: Neue Perspektiven auf Theodor Storm.* Hg. Elisabeth Strowick und Ulrike Vedder. Bern et al.: Peter Lang, 2013. 73–90.

Abbildungsverzeichnis

Abb. 1: Bathybius Haeckelii. Illustration in: Haeckel 1870, Tafel XVII.

Social and Material Transformations

Florian Auerochs
Sisyphos am Strand: Beachcleaning und die litoralen Figurationen fossiler Energiekultur in der zeitgenössischen Umweltfotografie

The petro-ecological discussion of the global littoral in Alejandro Durán's photo series *Washed Up*, with its playful account of global plastic pollution, and Allan Sekula's *Black Tide: Fragments for an Opera*, close-up images of an oil spill in Galicia, reads both waste and oil spill photography as pictorial petro-texts. Hereby, the littoral can be understood as the materially inflected in-between of petrolic and plastic contamination in order to grasp those spill events as mutual petrochemical embodiments countering the obscured becoming-plastics of oil and the eclipsed petrochemical descent of synthetic waste. From the perspective of an extended *spill*-concept, plastic and pellet spills are examined as an iteration of the oil spill to emphasize the 'crescive troubles' (Thomas Beamish) of global beaches. In my petrocritical reading, the beach as 'human-ocean-interface' will be legible as a toxic landscape of bodily backflows and epistemic feedback whose documentarily framed material-semiotic entanglement provides valuable perspectives on the beach in terms of Anthropocenic environmental development and cultural transformation.

Die hier vorgeschlagene petro- und ökokritisch informierte Lektüre von Strandrepräsentationen in Alejandro Duráns Fotoserie *Washed Up* und Allan Sekulas fotodokumentarischem Projekt *Black Tide: Fragments for an Opera* begreift die kleinen umweltfotografischen Genres der Müll- und Energiefotografie als visuelle Auseinandersetzung mit den dissipierenden Resten fossiler Energiekultur. Der Strand wird als Raum der Überlagerung und wechselseitigen Durchdringung verschiedener *spill*-Ereignisse begriffen, der die diskursive Leerstelle einer petrochemischen Ableitung von Kunststoffen aufhebt. Dieser extensive *spill*-Begriff betrachtet Plastikmüllverschmutzungen als strukturelle Wiederholung von Ölverschmutzungsszenarien, um die langwierige Gewalt gegen litorale Ökosysteme nachdrücklicher zu bestimmen. Über die fotografisch umgesetzten materiell-semiotischen Verflechtungen des Strandes als ‚human-ocean-interface' wird dieser als toxische Landschaft lesbar, der die ökologischen und kulturellen Transformationen des Anthropozäns eingezeichnet sind.

1 *Oil Spill Photography* zwischen Sein und Simulakrum

Als böse Variante des populären Kartenspiels offeriert das *Öltanker & Bohrinseln-Quartett* dem spielerisch-kompetitiven Datenvergleich unter anderem die Kategorien ‚Tote Seevögel' und ‚Verschmutzte Küste'. Was als morbide Geschmacklosigkeit erscheint, pointiert in der enumerativen Eintönigkeit der Motivkarten wesentliche medienkulturelle Merkmale mariner Ölkatastrophen und

„spill reports" (Juhasz 2017, 318): Gerade über die enervierende Wiederholbarkeit der narrativen und optischen Struktur der ‚Auslaufmodelle' lässt sich die Begegnung mit der verletzten Umwelt, mit dem *spill*, gar nicht mehr nur zur Sensation, sondern vielmehr zum *Spiel* verkehren. Der Kartenwert des gewaltigsten Desasters sticht (*Prestige*, Galizien: „Verschmutzte Küste 3 000 km"), ohne sich vom ‚geringsten' zu unterscheiden (*Atlantic Empress*, Tobago: „Verschmutzte Küste 10 km" [Kittel und Wagner 2011]). Der Verlust biodiverser Natur-, Kultur- und Lebensräume wird zum Sieg in einem *jeu de familles*[1] degradiert, das auf ungenierte Weise den Kampf um Aufmerksamkeit jener vergifteten Küstengemeinden imitiert, „that struggle to distinguish their spill as worthy of notice, by virtue of being the largest, involving the highest number of fatalities of people and/or other living things" (Juhasz 2017, 320).

Erfahrungsgemäß ist der Strand einem positiv konnotierten Bilderrepertoire und Gefühlsregime zwischen Erholung, Abenteuer und Erotik verpflichtet. Doch marine Lebensräume wie das globale Litoral, Strände und Küstenabschnitte, in denen sich die Effekte fossiler Energieproduktion manifestieren, sind meist, so Stephanie LeMenager (2014, 123), „unhappy ones", glücklose Räume, die ebenso drastisch wie rhythmisch petrochemisch, also von der Erdöl- und Kunststoffindustrie, affiziert werden.[2] Als „human-ocean-interface[]" (Yaeger 2010, 539) und *naturkulturelle* Membran tragen Strände die (un-)sichtbaren, schlagartig ins Bildfeld rückenden oder graduell anwachsenden Spuren fossiler Energiekultur, wofür die bedrückende Ikonizität von Ölverschmutzungsszenarien, *oil spills*, und ihre nekrotischen Valenzen einstehen. Es ist jedoch genau diese, meist fotojournalistisch aufbereitete Ikonizität, der trotz der hartnäckig wiederkehrenden spektakulären Bildlichkeit und exzessiven Visibilität von Tankerunglücken, eingerissenen Pipelines und explodierenden Bohrinseln eine zeitweise trügerische Optik attestiert wird, die das Scheitern fotografischer Realismen an der Großmaßstäblichkeit fossiler Energieregime vermuten lässt. Und schließlich spult auch der Fächer aus Motivkarten des Spielequartetts dokumentarisches Bildmaterial von frei zugänglichen Bilddatenbanken im Internet ab: eine Bildreihe, die immer wieder den gleichen Moment des Brechens, Brennens und Sinkens wuchern lässt.[3]

Schon vor gut zwei Jahrzehnten zog der deutsch-niederländische Ethiker Jean-Pierre Wils die kollektive Rezeptionsfähigkeit – oder eher -unfähigkeit –

---

1 So die französische Bezeichnung für das populäre Kinder- und Gesellschaftsspiel.
2 Einen naturwissenschaftlichen Überblick zu litoraler Plastikmüllverschmutzung geben Galgani, Hanke und Maes (2015, 32–35).
3 Das Bildmaterial stammt ohne Verweis auf den/die Fotograf*in und Kontexte medialer (Erst-)Verwertung von den Bildagenturen *dpa Picture-Alliance* oder *Getty Images*.

einer Ölkatastrophe als Beispiel heran, um die krisenhafte Perzeption in „neuen Medienwelten" (Wils 2000, 11) aufzuzeigen; ein umfassendes Erodieren des phänomenal Realen durch medial überbrachte Ontologien und eine „Übermacht ikonischer Weltbegegnung" (ebd., 11). So lesen wir etwa von der Unentscheidbarkeit, ob

> eine Ölpest reale oder nur ‚phänomenale' Verursacher hat, bzw. ob es die wahrgenommene Ölpest überhaupt noch gibt, sobald eine Mehrheit der Zuschauer das ‚Phänomen', also ihr Erscheinen, als Ausfluß lediglich miteinander geteilter Wahrnehmungsgewohnheiten bezeichnet, die nun dringend – angesichts möglicher Folgekosten – gelöscht werden sollten. Man könnte dann irgendwann zur Schlußfolgerung kommen, eine Ölpest müsse eher als ein gigantisches Öko-Gemälde betrachtet werden [...]. (Ebd., 20)

Die Gefahr, ökologische Risikoszenarien in ihrer medialen Verfasstheit als lediglich konstruierte Wahrnehmungsweisen auf dem technologischen oder kortikalen Bildschirm verstanden zu wissen, liegt schließlich in einem sozialkonstruktivistischen Missverstehen des Umweltskandals als Diskursivkonstrukt oder Beinahe-Halluzination:

> In this, its [social constructionism's, F. A.] most far reaching form, ‚objective reality' is denied a place at the table. Even if objective reality exists ‚out there', this phenomenological outlook contends that we cannot experience it directly. Thus, ‚reality' is fruitfully dealt with as an ontological phenomenon rooted squarely and solely in the mind. (Beamish 2002, 41)

Dabei müssen sich auch bildwissenschaftliche Vertreter*innen der Petrokritik (*Petrocriticism*)[4] mit den perzeptiven Dissonanzen einer fossilen Energiedependenz als Bild- und Wahrnehmungsstörung auseinandersetzen; mit der – sicherlich zu diskutierenden – Impasse, dass jede situierte fotografische Bemühung um eine anthropogen geschädigte Umwelt in ihrem Nexus aus ökologischen

---

4 Als Subdisziplin der themen- und produktionszentrierten kulturwissenschaftlichen Energieforschung (*Energy Humanities*) interessiert sich das noch sehr junge inter- und transdisziplinäre Forschungsfeld des *Petrocriticism* in seiner literatur- und medienkulturwissenschaftlichen Ausprägung dafür, was fiktionale bis dokumentarische (Medien-)Texte und deren (Re-)Lektüre zum kulturellen Ort des Treib- und Rohstoffs im materiellen Universum des westlichen Industriekapitalismus und seines Energie-Imaginären, will heißen: kollektiven Bilderrepertoires, äußern oder aussparen: „Petrocriticism [...] is that branch of literary criticism specializing in petromodernity for which the concept of the ‚energy regime' is the most significant mode of historical and literary-historical periodizing. [...] A petrocritic may be someone looking to say something about texts about oil; she may also be looking for oil in cultural places where it is otherwise unspoken or unspeakable [...]; and she may be looking, in fictions, for the profoundly uneven distribution of oil's benefits and consequences to peoples and territories around the globe." (Rubenstein 2017, 50)

und symbolischen Faktoren unweigerlich in eine Landschaftsdarstellung überführt wird, in ein „cultural image, a pictorial way of representing, structuring or symbolising surroundings" (Cosgrove und Daniels 2007, 1), das sich seiner physischen Referenz in der materiellen Realität entledigt hat. Ironischerweise: Der vielbeschworene materielle Schwund des Öls – *Peak Oil* –, mit dem sich ein Signifikant tatsächlich seines (roh-)stofflichen Referenten entledigt, sieht sich in der geopolitischen und -kulturellen Zentralität des Öls einer penetranten Sichtbarkeit und semiotischen Profusion gegenübergestellt, in der sich Öl in Medienbildern von Pipeline-Explosionen, Ölteppichen, Bergeteichen und monumental aufgeschrammten Landschaften diskursiv ereignet, „excessively visible, publicly present, and politically charged" (Boetzkes 2017, 223).

Die kanadische Kunstwissenschaftlerin Amanda Boetzkes erkennt in der zwei ideologischen Lagern entstammenden schizoiden Bilderflut mit entsprechend faktualen Bildrhetoriken und -archiven eine dokumentarisch verfasste ‚Schlacht der Objektivitäten' (ebd., 226): Auf der einen Seite die „upward counterfactual narratives" (Gordon 2016, LI) der Propagierung wirtschaftlicher und sozialer Rentabilität sowie ökologischer und marktethischer Kompetenz durch die fossile Energiebranche; auf der anderen Seite die aktivistisch intendierte dokumentarische Enthüllung der biosozialen Folgen genau der gleichen industriellen Strukturen und Kreisläufe durch die Porträtierung vulnerabler (Industrie-) Landschaften, die einem (Bild-)Speicher der „downward counterfactuals" (ebd., LIII) angehören, der dokumentarischen Kritik an der extraktiven Inbesitznahme von Naturressourcen durch den menschlichen Konsumdrang.

Bildstürmerisch verkündet Boetzkes das Scheitern der kritisch-dokumentarischen Bildgebungsverfahren des Petrorealismus[5] und damit der ökologisch motivierten Dokumentation anthropogener Landschaft durch die gegenwärtige Umweltfotografie, deren emblematische Strategie der An- oder Aufsicht nicht in der Lage sei, petrokulturelle Inkorporationsleistungen im ökologischen Imaginären einzuschreiben – eben weil der erdölbasierte Kunststoff als Ober- und Überallfläche bereits die gesamte materielle Realität abdichtet:

---

5 „*Petro-* is meant to posit that all texts produced within petroculture are functionally marked by the ontology of oil, even as they anticipate a world after oil. *Realism* emphasizes the forms of mediation of the various scales simultaneously implicated in specific instances within a larger whole." (Bellamy 2017, 260) Dabei bezieht sich Bellamy mit Verweis auf Allan Sekula, Max Brook und Steven Soderbergh ausdrücklich auf dokumentarische (Bewegt-)Bildwerke in ihrem Vermögen, „[m]aps of energy presents" zu entwerfen, ohne ein Wissen vom unhintergehbaren Eingebundensein in das molekulare und planetarische Technikzeitalter zu unterschlagen: „Petrorealism attempts to come to terms with petromodernity from within. There is no external vantage from which to write about its flows and limits." (Ebd., 261)

But the real cartography of petrocultures cannot be subsumed into an external view of either the structure or the system so that the viewing subject is positioned outside or above, as is always the case with a landscape. Petroculture is lived from within, and thus the line between it and the potential for an altered sensorial field is as fine as that between my eye and the plastic contact lens through which I read. (Boetzkes 2017, 226)

Während Wils im „Sinnbild des typischen Umweltskandals" (Soentgen 2014, 279) die unhintergehbare Oberflächigkeit eines ikonischen Überschusses imaginiert, an dessen simulierten Zeichen der menschliche Geist abgleitet, und Boetzkes die raum- und körpergreifende Tiefe von Öl- und Kunststoffprodukten beschwört, unternimmt dieser Beitrag einen rehabilitierenden Ausblick auf die Umweltfotografie und hält sich für diese Form ökologisch motivierter Bildproduktion an die nüchterne Einschätzung des Wissenschaftshistorikers Thomas Beamish: „These are questions of quality (what is said), not quantity (how many times it is said) [or shown, F. A.]." (Beamish 2002, 31) Dies vor allem hinsichtlich der Überzeugung, dass die fotografische Repräsentation anthropogener Landschaften jene Schattenorte (*shadow places*) vergegenwärtigen kann, die die ökofeministische Theoretikerin Val Plumwood definiert hat als „all those places that produce or are affected by the commodities you consume, places consumers don't know about, don't want to know about, and in a commodity regime don't ever need to know about or take responsibility for." (Plumwood 2008, 146–147)[6] Die fotografische Begegnung mit diesen kontaminierten Räumen, die im Übrigen einen Resonanzraum aktiver Kontemplation des Selbst in Bezug auf das landschafliche Objekt ermöglicht, darf so Jennifer Peeples, keinesfalls ausbleiben, denn „[i]n dealing with environmental problems, a lack of

---

[6] Die Apologet*innen der dokumentarischen Energie- und Umweltfotografie lagern sich um das Vermögen des fotografischen Bildes, visuell unzugängliche Verschmutzungsereignisse zu vergegenwärtigen („creating a presence" [Peeples 2011, 387]), von Extraktivismus abstrahierte Landschaften zu versinnlichen („address[ing] us as sentient, material subjects" [Banita 2017b, 431]) und durch das multiskalare Durchschreiten globaler Erdölnetze einer anthropozänen Bildkomparatistik zu dienen: „from resource site to incidental body, from polluted ‚foreign' locale to domestic suburb, from atmosphere to biosphere and back again" (McDonald 2017, 65–66). Anders als in Boetzkes Kritik an der ökologisch engagierten, aber analgetischen Industriefotografie, wird hier die dokumentarästhetische Bannung der Landschaft nicht als täuschende Suggestion eines abstandnehmenden Blicks *von außen* auf die Kohlenwasserstoffgesellschaft (*hydrocarbon society*) begriffen. Gerade die komplexe Entstehung der fotografischen Apparatur in fossilen Ressourcen gibt Aufschluss darüber, wie ökotoxikologisch persistente Materien der sichtbaren Realität semiotische Persistenz im fotografischen Bild verleihen: „Yet the origin of photography in the inscription and its continuing reliance on energy-intensive technologies invite a material approach to the photographic image that highlights how energy gives shape to visible reality and rescues it from the passage of time." (Banita 2017a, 263)

visual representation can mean a lack of social or political power as there is nothing to show, no compelling visual evidence of the extent or severity of the problem" (Peeples 2011, 374). Dabei hat gerade das ‚kleine' umweltfotografische Genre der „oil spill photography" (LeMenager 2014, 35) – und sicherlich auch die Müllfotografie – den Vorteil, sichtbare Stofflichkeiten visuell herstellen zu wollen, während andere umweltfotografische Projekte von chemisch-residualen Agenten herausgefordert werden, die unterhalb der Schwelle visueller Wahrnehmung codieren.

Unter diesen Voraussetzungen untersucht der Beitrag sowohl die Strand- und Küsteninszenierung von Alejandro Duráns Bildzyklus *Washed Up*, dessen inszenierte Fotografien von Plastikmüll-Installationen die kollektive Bildlichkeit des pittoresken Strandparadieses zwar visuell zitieren, aber produktionszentriert unterlaufen, als auch jene von Allan Sekulas Fotoserie *Black Tide: Fragments for an Opera*, die mit dem visuellen Vokabular der Erschöpfung die Ölkatastrophe vor der Nordwestküste Spaniens 2002 dokumentiert. Dabei frage ich nach den Möglichkeiten und Grenzen des fotografischen Bildes, die petrochemischen Onto- und Epistemologien nachzuzeichnen, die sich am Strand als materiell-semiotischem Index einer schmutzigen Streuung manifestieren. Dadurch weitet sich der Blick vom unschuldigen Strandparadies auf die symbolische Signifikanz der Strände als materieller Manifestationsfläche petrochemischer Kultur.

2 Pest und Dissipation: *spill*-Ereignisse zwischen Öl- und Plastikfluss

Die Auseinandersetzung mit der Imaginationskraft oder einem punktuellen Imaginationsverlust einer Gesellschaft, die durch vielerlei rhetorische und diskursive Inszenierungsprinzipien ein phantasmatisch durchschossenes Rearrangement des Materiellen und als ‚natürlich' gedachter Systeme herrichtet, kann sich der intrikaten Selbstorganisation des Stofflichen nicht entziehen, das als (an-)organischer Subtext bereits vor seinem Spürbarwerden im industriellen Defekt immanenter Bestandteil multipel selbsttätiger Körper und Medien in ihrer technologischen Herstellung war. Dies verlangt eine Einsicht darin, „how the physical environment structures, feeds back into, and refashions discourse and hence choice sets and decisions" (Beamish 2002, 41). Ein *spill*-Ereignis verlangt schließlich, in seinen materiell heterogenen und phänomenal übereinstimmenden Ausformungen als eine materiell-semiotische ‚Figuration' (*figure*) erkannt zu werden, in der „diverse bodies and meanings coshape one another" (Haraway 2008, 4). In Anlehnung an Haraway versteht auch die feministische Posthumanitätstheoretikerin Astrida Neimanis ‚Figurationen', die das konzeptuelle Gewicht der Verschmelzung von gelebter Realität und zeichenhafter Bedeutungsentstehung (er-)tragen, als „embodied concepts", „importantly grounded in our material reality" (Neimanis 2017, 5). Roh- und Mineralölgüsse, die das globale Litoral inflammieren, Kunststoffrelikte, die es interpungieren, bilden in ihrem schmerzlichen Durchwandern von Körpern und Symbolsystemen solch materiell-semiotische Verknotungen, die es konsequenter aufeinander zu beziehen gilt. Denn obgleich sich die emotionalen und geo-spatialen Arrangements der dokumentierten bis imaginierten litoralen Naturzonen in der auf Strandverschmutzung abhebenden Umwelt- und Landschaftsfotografie formal und affektiv ähneln, thematisiert das dokumentarische Genre bislang nicht oder nur peripher im Binnenraum einer ästhetischen Artikulation die petrochemische Herkunft und Rohstoffgeschichte von erdölbasiertem Plastik am Beispiel litoraler *spill*-Vorkommen.[7]

Plastik(-müll) ist erdölbasiert und hat einen fossil-chemischen Ursprung, den es in seinem Farb- und Formenüberfluss wirkungsvoll verschleiert, so wie Erdöl seit den 1950er Jahren der wichtigste Rohstoff der Kunststoffindustrie ist, die der Urmasse durch Polymerchemie eine Reihe von Kunststoffen entzieht. Bereits 1957 bringt Roland Barthes in den *Mythen des Alltags* das durch eine visuelle Leerstelle und für die sinnliche Wahrnehmung unzugängliche, nicht-intelligible Verhältnis der beiden Materien auf die Formel: „Auf der einen Seite der tellurische Rohstoff, auf der anderen der perfekte Gegenstand. Zwischen diesen beiden Extremen nichts, nichts als ein zurückgelegter Weg."

---

7 Soentgen weist auf einen wesentlichen Unterschied zwischen der in ihrem empirischen Kontext partikularen Ölkatastrophe und der richtungslosen Simultanität synthetischer Stoffflüsse, die einen Hinweis für das Auseinandertreten der Risikomaterien innerhalb ästhetisch-dokumentarischer Gebilde liefern könnte: „Sie [d. i. die Ölkatastrophe] lässt sich skandalisieren, weil es einen sichtbaren (industriellen) Verursacher gibt, auf den man zeigen kann, weil es ein Ereignis gibt und weil die Dissipation plötzlich vor sich geht. Die weitaus wichtigeren Mobilisierungsprozesse aber geschehen alltäglich, sie sind nicht industriell, sondern zum Beispiel landwirtschaftlich, nicht punktuell, sondern diffus, sie haben zahlreiche Verursacher und lassen sich daher nicht oder kaum skandalisieren." (Soentgen 2014, 279) Die Mehrfachadressierung petrochemischer Auswürfe scheitert an der wichtigen skalaren Unterscheidung zwischen *dem einen* identifizierbaren Verursacher aus der Ölwirtschaft bei einem Petroleumunglück und *der einen* verursachenden Spezies des müllproduzierenden Menschen, des *homo detritus*, für die Plastikmüllproblematik (obwohl es Vorfälle gibt, wie das Beispiel *Sinopec* zeigen wird, die diese Unterscheidung selbst verunreinigen).

(Barthes 1964 [1957], 79)[8] Innerhalb eines weit gefassten *spill*-Begriffs ‚verrät' sich diese toxische Liaison gerade durch den ‚gemeinsam zurückgelegten Weg' über marine und litorale Räume in einen ähnlich dissipativen Phänotyp, der über die Beschreibung kultureller Gegenstände eingeholt werden kann, denn „petro-paths produce petro-texts" (Sullivan 2017, 414).[9]

Als Beispiel lässt sich die *Sinopec*-Katastrophe von 2012, das sogenannte ‚Hong Kong Plastic Disaster' (Gottlieb 2012), anführen, bei der sieben Schiffscontainer, die 168 Tonnen Mikroplastik, genauer: Polypropylen-Kügelchen, transportierten, während eines Sturms beschädigt wurden und ihren Inhalt in die südlich gelegenen Gewässer Hongkongs verschütteten, der nach und nach an die umliegenden Strände gespült wurde. Verantwortlich für die desaströse Fracht zeigt sich das chinesische Erdgas- und Mineralölunternehmen *Sinopec*, was ahnen lässt, dass die stoffliche Matrix des Kunststoffs Polypropylen Propen bildet, ein Pyrolyseprodukt von Erdöl. Und es ist morbiderweise die Funktion dieses *spills* – denn als *plastic spill* wurde das Ereignis in der internationalen Berichterstattung adressiert –, als Wiederholung des materiell-diskursiven Schemas eines *oil spills* den organischen Subtext und das petrochemische Unbewusste[10] der Kunststoffkultur zu obduzieren: Schließlich liest sich auf den angeschwemmten und aufgerissenen Pellet-Säcken selbst ‚SINOPEC Shanghai Petrochemical Co., Ltd', was in einer lapidaren optischen Mitteilung die sonst so leicht zu übersehende chemisch (tiefen-)strukturelle und industriell so potente Kontiguität von Grund-, Kraft- und Kunststoffen registrieren lässt.

Als menschlich hervorgerufenes Verschmutzungsereignis meist durch Roh- oder Mineralölprodukte und insbesondere mariner Umwelten kennzeichnet das

---

[8] Der von Greenpeace angefertigte *Öl-Report 2016* spricht für das Jahr 2015 von einer dreizehnprozentigen Beteiligung der Petrochemie am globalen Erdölverbrauch und erläutert: „In der Petrochemie werden Grundchemikalien wie Ethylen oder Propylen aus den leichten Bestandteilen von Erdöl hergestellt. Sie dienen der Herstellung von Kunststoffen aller Art." (Bukold und Feddern 2016, 7) Für die tatsächliche Kunststoffherstellung führt Kaiser einen Bedarf von vier bis sechs Prozent am globalen Erdöl- und Erdgasverbrauch an, der großteils als Brenn- oder Treibstoff zum Einsatz kommt (Kaiser 2015, 4). Die Wissenschaftsphilosophin Bernadette Bensaude-Vincent legt die rohstoffliche Herkunft von Plastik tiefenzeitlich aus und erinnert dabei an den Konnex von Geologie und Gedächtnis, an dessen Auflösung die Petroindustrie arbeitet: „Plastics irreversibly consume the vestiges of plants accumulated over thousands of years. [...] It is the tip of a heap of memory, the upper layer of many layers of the past that have resulted in crude oil stored in the depths of the soil and the sea." (Bensaude-Vincent 2013, 24)
[9] Zum Begriff *Petrotext*: „These tales make visible the mostly hidden facts of how our current cultures are shaped by petroleum and fossil fuels generally." (Sullivan 2017, 420)
[10] In Anlehnung an Patricia Yaegers Demonstration sozialer und kultureller Energievergessenheit, die sie vorsichtig als ein *energy unconscious* bezeichnet hat, „culture's silence about the energy that powers it, and the unsignifying opacity of the modern concept" (Soni 2017, 133).

englische Substantiv *spill* „a downpour of liquid [...], no particular agency, a blurring of cause and effect, the possibility of both human error and atypical natural occurence" (LeMenager 2017, 322), womit dem Begriffsinhalt eine Konturlosigkeit eignet, die kaum die großtechnisch-systematischen Extraktionskulturen hinter dem Ereignis assoziieren lässt (Juhasz 2017). Die deutschen Bezeichnungen ‚Ölpest' und ‚Ölverseuchung' weisen durch das Konnotat des Kontagiösen eine wesentlich problematischere Metaphorik auf, während ‚Ölunfall' menschlich-industrielles (Mit-)Verschulden unterbietet, ‚Ölkatastrophe' den fatalistischen Vergleich mit anderen Naturkatastrophen herausfordert und ‚Ölteppich' zwar ein interessantes Bildfeld des Verwebens und Vernetzens eröffnet, aber kaum eignet, semantisch den toxischen Überschuss von Petroleum zu absorbieren.

Für den „geteilten inneren Drang, [...] sich über die Welt zu zerstreuen, sich nach eigenem Plan im Raum zu verteilen, zu dissipieren" (Soentgen 2014, 276–277), reserviert Jens Soentgen den Begriff ‚Dissipation' und spricht von ‚direkter Mobilisierung', „[w]enn Stoffen durch menschliches Handeln Gelegenheit gegeben wird, sich in der Umwelt zu verteilen" (ebd., 279). Der chemisch-physikalische Fachterminus entstammt der Wissenschaftssprache und ist daher medienkulturell weitestgehend unberührt, daneben lässt er sich auf die Verstreuungs-, Entströmungs- und „Zerrüttungstendenz" (ebd., 275) aller (petroindustrieller) Risikomaterien anwenden. Obgleich sich ‚Dissipation' dezidiert als Begrifflichkeit durch keine (medien-)kulturelle Signifikanz ausweist, kommt sie der englischsprachigen *spill*-Terminologie in der Weite ihres stofflichen Spektrums am nächsten und wird stückweise für diese Untersuchung übernommen.

Die partielle Verwendung der englischen *spill*-Terminologie erscheint mir deshalb attraktiv, da in der anglophonen Umweltberichterstattung mittlerweile nicht nur die episodisch einsickernden schwarzen Fluten des Petroleums, sondern auch die kunterbunten und nicht weniger fatalen Plastik- und Pelletfluten als *spill* bezeichnet werden (*plastic spill, pellet spill*), die darüber in ein Ähnlichkeitsverhältnis mit ihrem schwerflüssigen Counterpart treten, das sich der dualistischen Logik von Identität und Differenz entzieht. An LeMenagers Minimaldefinition anknüpfend, bietet es sich schließlich an, am Strand den semiotisch gewendeten Echoraum zwischen den toxischen Ereignissen der Erdöl- und Plastikkontamination abzulesen und jene sich wechselseitig verkörpern zu lassen: „Spills are often multiply sited, difficult to grasp as precise causes and effects. The spill categorically defies endings, persisting in space and time through its effect on ecosystems and bodies." (LeMenager 2017, 324) Litorale Plastikakkumulationen figurieren als Quasi-Iterationen von Ölteppichen und halten die Transtemporalität und -lokalität petrochemischer Hinterlassenschaften deutlicher im Bewusstsein. *Spill* wird so zu einer Figuration, die erlaubt,

Ähnlichkeiten zwischen Verschmutzungsereignissen in ihrer kulturpoetischen Verstetigung durch visuelle Petro-Texte herauszustellen. Aggressive Öl- und Plastikfrachten letztlich neben- und ineinander zu vergegenwärtigen, erinnert schließlich daran, dass eine symbolische Investition in das extraktive Begehren erdölbasierter Ökonomien immer auch ein materielles Zugeständnis an petrochemische Kunststoffe ist.

In Anbetracht der kontextresistenten Einreihung uniformer Ölkatastrophen, die einander verlängern und wiederholen, nur um ihre resolute Konformität im ökologischen Imaginären abzuspulen, fasst LeMenager das mediale *spill*-Verhalten ins Gedankenbild einer aussichtslosen Iteration, in der Memorisierung in Vergessen übergeht: „Every oil spill remembers every other, from the mid-twentieth century onward. These iterative events spill across history to happen again as if they are happening for the first time." (Ebd., 64–65) Die literarische Annäherung an diese kollektive Auffassung fossiler Dissipation durch den kulturtheoretisch ambitionierten Roman *Satin Island* des britischen Autors Tom McCarthy legt eine eigene Theorie der „oil spill media" (ebd., 17) vor und kommt jener monomorphen *spill*-Emblematik sehr nahe: „There's always an oil spill happening", so der solipsistische Protagonist, „[t]he Oil Spill – an ongoing event whose discrete parts and moments, whatever their particular shapes and vicissitudes [...], have run together, merged into a continuum in which all plurals drown." (McCarthy 2015, 128)

Die kulturelle Einschmelzung einer Katastrophenkette in das zeitlos schimmernde Schaubild einer ölverklebten Küste macht einen auf Analogien basierenden *spill*-Begriff für eine Analyse der visuellen Kultur der Erdölgesellschaft, der von einer materiellen Verschränkung vergangener und gegenwärtiger petrochemischer Dissipationsprozesse ausgeht, wünschenswert. Dies bedarf eines „Verständnis[ses] von ästhetischen Werken [...], in dem erfinderisch Korrespondenzen gesucht werden, um disparate Texte miteinander zu verbinden, um Bezüge herzustellen zwischen kulturellen Gegenständen, die oberflächlich betrachtet nicht übereinstimmen und nicht vergleichbar sind" – so Elisabeth Bronfen (2004, 14) für die Rehabilitierung analogisierender Lektüreverfahren, die den „imaginativen Sprung durch Raum und Zeit" (ebd., 12–13) wagen, der hier um ein Changieren zwischen materiellen Prozessen erweitert wird. Daher die Attraktivität, zwei Fotoprojekte vergleichend zu betrachten, die jenseits ihres umweltthematischen Bezugs generisch auseinanderliegen und jeweils ‚verschiedene' Verschmutzungsszenarien fotografisch umschreiben, handelt es sich doch bei der Fotografie um eine Art der „Übertragung von kontingenter Materialität in eine ästhetische Formalisierung" (ebd., 14) par excellence. Es gilt, innerhalb der kollektiven Bildlichkeit einer dissipativen

„similarity-in-difference" (Stafford 1999, 9) die Vergleichsmöglichkeiten zwischen umweltfotografischen Arbeiten zu befragen.

3 Fels, „vom Öl akribisch umgestaltet"[11]: *Black Tide: Fragments for an Opera* (2003)

Mit groß angelegten essayistischen Foto- und Videoarbeiten zum „techno-ocean" (Yaeger 2010, 526), dem anthropogen durchgearbeiteten Ozean und seinen spätmodernen Schwellenräumen, kreiert der 2013 verstorbene und einer ebenso sozial- wie auch umweltkritischen Praxis des fotografischen Realismus verpflichtete Künstler und Foto-Theoretiker Allan Sekula ohne ökologisches Pathos ein, so Celina Jeffery, visuelles Archiv des ‚Ozeanozids', eines Ab- oder Aussterbens – oder besser, eines Aus-sich-Herausgetrieben-Werdens – mariner Landschaften in materieller und imaginärer Hinsicht (Jeffery 2017, 238). Gerade aufgrund seines Beitrags zu einer visuellen Kultur der Ölförderung und ihrer giftigen Stoffbewegungen kann Sekula als Vertreter eines fotodokumentarischen Realismus verstanden werden, der die Möglichkeit bietet, über das fotografische Bild materiellen Kontexten nachzuspüren, die auf verdeckte (bio-)soziale Verhältnisse schließen lassen; dies insbesondere durch die als äußerst zuträglich rezipierte Koaleszenz von Sekulas produktionszentrierter Herangehensweise eines ‚kritischen Realismus' – des Versuchs einer ästhetisch-politischen Praxis, die jene petrifizierenden „narratives about globalization as immaterial and unrepresentable" (Szeman und White 2012, 46) herausfordert – und eines themenzentrierten Petrorealismus, der Kartografierung einer anhaltenden Abhängigkeit von Erdöl, seinen Nach- und Nebenprodukten.

Der Fotoessay *Black Tide: Fragments for an Opera* besteht aus rund fünfzehn Fotografien und einem dramatischen Begleittext, der als Aufführungsskript zu einer Theaterperformance absurde Bühnenkonventionen zitiert. Es handelt sich um eine Auftragsarbeit des spanischen Künstlers und Kurators Carles Rojas und der katalanischen Tageszeitung *La Vanguardia*, in deren Wochenbeilage *Culturas* die Arbeit im Februar 2003 erstmals auf Spanisch publiziert wurde. Thema ist die durch den Öltanker Prestige verursachte Ölkatastrophe vor der Küste Galiziens im November 2002 (man mag die entsprechende Spielkarte zücken: „Verschmutzte Küste 3 000 km", „Tote Seevögel 250 000" [Kittel und Wagner 2011]), der bisher größten Havarie eines Öltankers vor spanischen und

---

11 Das Zitat ist der deutschen Übersetzung von Tom McCarthys *Satin Island* entnommen (vgl. McCarthy 2016, 138).

französischen Küsten. Anhand einer Satellitenfotografie kommentiert Sekula die schwindelerregende Großmaßstäblichkeit des *spills*, der, skopisch entrückt, eine regelrechte Öl-Vertigo hervorzurufen in der Lage ist: „It was almost impossible from looking at the photo to tell the scale. I didn't really know if I was looking at something that covered a distance of 50 km or one meter." (Sekula zit. nach Rojas 2017, 141) Anstatt diese delirierende Wahrnehmung mit defigurierenden Bildmitteln einzulösen, schreitet Sekula einen am Einzelfall orientierten Maßstab ab, der sich entschlossen an der „Körperlichkeit von sozialem Agieren" (Kastner 2003, 80) und jenem Individuum ausrichtet, das sich in greifbarer Auseinandersetzung mit einer litoralen Landschaft verkörpert – in diesem Fall freiwillige Katastrophenhelfer*innen beim strapaziösen Säubern von Strand- und Küstenabschnitten. Sekulas kritisch-petrorealistischem Bildprogramm entsprechend, das mit narrativer Sequenzialisierung, bildrhetorischer Varianz unter Zurschaustellung einer partikularen Realitätskonstruktion und am (an-)organischen Detail ausgerichteten Verfremdungseffekten operiert (Szeman und White 2003, 50), erfasst *Black Tide* die Küstentopographie durch den holprigen Wechsel von eng bis weit gehaltenen Bildausschnitten: nahe bis halbnahe Porträts der Säuberungsarbeiter*innen, Großaufnahmen anscheinend belangloser Bruchstücke des Geschehens (die sich mitunter als Vogelleichenteile entpuppen) und Landschaftsfotografien, in diesem Fall der diesigen galizischen Felsenküste, auf der unter dem viskosen Schwarz des Rohöls jegliche soziale (Kastner 2003, 80), aber auch materielle Differenz zwischen menschlichen, tierlichen und landschaftlichen Körpern zu kollabieren scheint.

Ich möchte die Fotostrecke durch eine erste Figur, die des ‚Containers', betrachten, um zu einer fotografisch verwirklichten materiell-semiotischen Signifikanz der besudelten Strand- und Küstenlandschaft vorzudringen. LeMenager richtet sich im Bild eines genuin porösen Containments an die eitlen Deponierungs- und Einhegungsversuche, die die wilde Mobilität in Dissipationsprozessen rahmen und deren chronisches Scheitern sich als Effekt der beständigen Herausforderung darstellt, den antriebsstarken Giftcocktail aus immer absurderen geologischen Tiefen und geographischen Weiten heranzutransportieren: „The inadequate or negligent containerization of oil figures strongly in spill events, speaking to the broad connotations of *spill* as an inability to contain. An oil tanker holds potentially decades of contamination – a bomb exploding slowly over time." (LeMenager 2017, 323)[12] Auch der vor Galizien gekenterte Öltanker Prestige war ein solch scheiternder Container, der 64 000 Tonnen Schweröl an spanische und französische Strände und Küsten schwemmte, damit diese, um

---

[12] Auch Soentgen (2014, 281–282) beschreibt missglückende Containment-Versuche als wesentlichen Bestandteil von Dissipationsprozessen.

im Bild zu bleiben, Container fänden; nicht nur die Lastwägen zum Abpumpen und Abtransportieren des Öls sowie die Bergeteiche im Landesinneren, sondern auch das Litoral selbst, das nun jene „decades of contamination" (aus-)halten und in sich bergen muss.

Bei Sekula begegnen nun verschiedene Räume des Containments, in materieller und semiotischer Hinsicht: Strand und Küste als, es wurde bereits gesagt, vulnerable Räume, denen durch petrochemische Prekarisierung die Identität als multispeziär belebtes Ökosystem, Kultur- und Freizeitstätte ausgetrieben wird (Abb. 1). Denn wie bei jedem Container ist auch das Fassungsvermögen des litoralen Strandes begrenzt, dessen Artenreichtum durch die fossilen Reste organischen Lebens ersetzt wurde. Der US-amerikanische Umweltautor John Keeble etwa deutet die Trauer, die sich nach einem *spill*-Desaster bei den Küstengemeinden einstellt, als Reaktion auf die abrupte Abwesenheit tierischen Lebens, das von Strömen flüssiger Energie fortgespült wurde: „The grief", schreibt er, „was a response to the removal of a presence from a thousand miles of beach and thousands of miles of near-shore waters." (Keeble 1999, 126) Die zudringliche Sichtbarkeit des Öls wird mit der auch visuell zu verstehenden Abwesenheit des nicht-menschlichen Anderen bezahlt[13] und schreibt dem Strand einen Mangel ein[14], womit sich das Litoral kaum mehr von dem ebenso für bildwürdig erachteten kraterähnlichen Bergeteich auf einem Industriegelände 57 Kilometer von der Küste entfernt unterscheiden lässt: die Kippfigur des verölten Strandes, der von der Funktion und den visuellen Zeichen der Grubendeponie als Totzone bereinigt werden muss (Abb. 2).

---

13 Sekula widersteht der vertrauten Ikonografie sich gegen den Schlick aufbäumender Seevögel und lässt die tierischen Küstenbewohner*innen zuallererst als Bilderrätsel auftreten: Was wie die Nahaufnahme eines Teerballens aussieht, ‚entpuppt' sich als veröltes Vogelei, aus dem die rosa Gliedmaßen eines nicht zu Ende geschlüpften Kükens ragen, rein visuell mehr pinkes Plastik als Fleisch, das in das mit Flechten überzogene Küstengestein mineralisiert.

14 Der Mangel, den das Fehlen des Tieres in die Küstenlandschaft schlägt, lässt sich für eine Betrachtung von Landschaftsrepräsentationen auch semiotisch bestimmen, wird einer entsprechenden Auffassung von Landschaften als System materieller Zeichen auch in der phänomenalen Realität gefolgt: „Landscapes are seen as sign systems, that is, diverse landscape phenomena are thought to form a coherent systemic whole in which each of the elements is related to each other and where individual signs can be combined into sequences according to certain codes." (Kull, Lindström und Palang 2014, 113–114) Ein *spill* entfernt ‚Elemente' des Überartlichen aus der landschaftlichen ‚Sequenz' und nähert den Strand über das Moment des Artensterbens einem auch symbolischen ‚Tod'.

Abb. 1: Allan Sekula. *Shellfishers Working and Army preparing*, 2003.

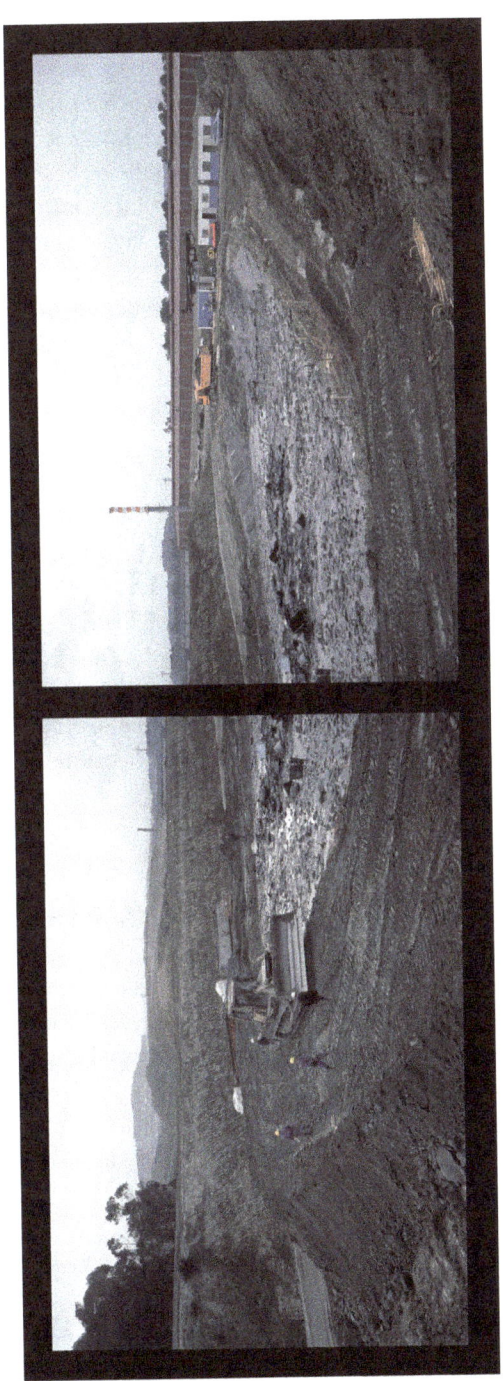

Abb. 2: Allan Sekula. *Disposal Pit*, 2003.

Die beiden Landschaftspanoramen wurden zu einem Triptychon und einem, in seinen Teilstücken inkongruenten, Diptychon zergliedert, deren Segmente als untereinander auswechselbar erscheinen und die plötzliche Verwechslungsgefahr von Abraum und Küstenraum in ein visuelles Raster übersetzen: „Where a larger natural area loses its character through a natural catastrophe or human destruction it lacks the unity necessary for being a landscape. It turns into an expressionless heterogeneity, into a non-place or landscape garbage." (Krebs 2017, 106)

Neben einem Transport- und Einlagerungsproblem in der materiellen Realität führt LeMenager die ästhetische Herausforderung an, *spill*-Ereignisse erzählerisch-bildkünstlerisch zu ‚containern' und zu bewahren: „The material problem of how to move oil, in what sort of container, complements the communications problem of containing oil spills within transmissible stories when the spill's effects persist over lengthy time frames, as they always do." (LeMenager 2017, 323) In Sekulas nicht-indexikalischer Fototheorie codiert das Medium des fotografischen Bildes selbst als Container und Transporter – dazu Jens Kastner (2003, 76): „Allan Sekula versteht die Fotografie als Transporter, der zwar nicht neutral im Sinne von beliebig zu beladen ist, aber dennoch kein eigenes Wesen besitzt." Aus dieser Perspektive könnte die Fotografie *Dripping Black Trapezoid*, auf dem eine von schwerem, silbrigem Ölschlick überzogene Lastertür, die formal die Rahmung der Fotografie selbst wiederholt, abgebildet ist, metaphorisch für den Versuch der Fotoserie stehen, das Öl zu bergen, endlich festzuhalten und einzuhegen.

4 Künstliche Paradiese: *Washed Up* (2010–2014)

Bei Alejandro Duráns Fotoprojekt *Washed Up: Transforming a Trashed Landscape* handelt es sich nicht um dokumentarische, sondern um inszenierte Fotografien mit einer Bildwirklichkeit, deren Herstellung „allein und ausschließlich im Hinblick auf das Fotografiertwerden erfolgt[e]" (Weiß 2010, 50) – in diesem Fall vom ins Bild setzenden Fotografen selbst angefertigte Land-Art-Installationen, die Durán aus aufgelesenem Plastikmüll kreiert, der an Mexikos karibische Küste Sian Ka'an gespült wurde, größtes staatlich geschütztes Naturschutzgebiet und UNESCO-Weltkulturerbe.

In den fotografisch festgehaltenen Kunststoffinstallationen akkumuliert sich das Plastik wie selbsttätig zu einem quasi-natürlichen Arrangement, das sich in die litorale Umgebung schmiegt. Nicht nur die naturähnliche morphologische Anordnung der Müllberge, auch die Titel der einzelnen Installationen bzw. Fotografien vollführen eine vivikatorische Mimikry, die für eine Semiotik des Plastikmülls bezeichnend ist; neigt doch das frei bewegliche Plastik dazu, Bewegungsmuster des Lebendigen anzunehmen oder gar wie eine organische Substanz auszusehen, und sich darüber mit insbesondere tierlichen Körpern zu verbinden – im Fall des ‚Hong Kong Plastic Spills' etwa milchig-weiße Pellets, die von Raubfischen für Fischeier und somit eine Nahrungsquelle gehalten wurden.

Aus dieser Perspektive spiegeln die Fotografien keine surreale oder fantastische Landschaft wider, sondern ökologischen Realismus. Die Geologin Patricia Corcoran und ihr interdisziplinäres Team haben die Bezeichnung ‚Plastiglomerat' für jene hybrid zusammengesetzte Neomaterie geprägt, die bei der Agglutination geschmolzener Kunststoffabfälle mit Sand, Korallen, Basaltgestein und anderen organisch-mineralischen Bruchteilen entstehen (Corcoran, Jazvac und Moore 2014, 5–6). Erforscht hat sie das Phänomen auf Kamilo Beach, Hawaii, dem „dirtiest beach on earth" (Corcoran und Jazvac 2017, 276). Bei diesen verwilderten, nicht verwitternden Plastikexistenzen wird zwischen einem (groß-)flächig stratisch gebundenen *in-situ*-Typ unterschieden, bei dem sich das Plastik mit Gesteinsaufschlüssen verbindet, und einem losen, klastischen Vertreter, bei dem natürliche Rückbleibsel in einer Plastikmatrix zusammenfinden und verklumpen. „Einmal hart wird Kunststoff dauerhaft und buchstäblich Teil der Geologie. Kunststoff wird tatsächlich zu Gestein" (Davis 2016, 100) – oder eher: zu Strandsediment, und damit Echofigur jener konglomerierenden Teerbälle, die nach natürlichen oder industriellen Ölaustritten stranden und, in ihrer Befallsqualität dem Plastik verwandt, als „fusion of Earth/pollution" (Corcoran und Jazvac 2017, 277) hybrider Teil sandiger Uferstreifen werden (Golik 1982, 1).

Duráns naturmetaphorisch anmutende Bildtitel wie *Algas (Algae), Cocos (Coconuts)* und *Raíces (Roots)* greifen dieses geo- und biomimetische – oder symbiotische – Potential des Plastikmülls auf, phänomenal im landschaftlichen Raum aufzugehen, ohne tatsächlich jemals in ihn einzugehen oder aus diesem zu verschwinden. Im Gegensatz zur melancholisch-monochromen, bereits farblich erschöpften *oil spill*-Fotografie von Allan Sekula erfreut sich Duráns *plastic spill*-Fotografie am visuellen Kontrast zwischen den giftigen Farben der Petroleumprodukte und dem litoralen Raum, von dem sie sich trotz der formbezogenen Adaptionsleistung visuell abheben. Anders als der In-situ-Typ von synthetischem Beachrock, der die immobilisierenden Valenzen von Plastik als sklerotischem ‚Feststoff' unterstreicht, der sich trotz des gewaltigen Fluktuationspotentials von Plastik dauerhaft in Körpern und Ökosystemen ‚festsetzt', bleiben Duráns artifizielle Gefüge vor allem in der isolierenden fotografischen Rahmung sonderbar freigestellt – und damit vom Strand abgesondert. Über seine Betitelung als

‚Verbundstoff' hinaus behält er das Vermögen, über eine beinahe-parasitäre Verbindung mit elementaren Kräften, der Meeresströmung oder der permeablen Strandgeologie, transgeographisch wie -temporal beweglich zu bleiben.

Die Fotografien *Mar (Sea)*, *Gota (Drop)*, *Espuma (Foam)* oder *Vena (Vein)* setzen metaphorische Bild- und Körpergebungsverfahren um, die eine liquide Beweglichkeit und Agentialität konnotativ in den skulpturalen Plastikmengen halten. Die Bildtitel markieren nicht nur den bioakkumulativen Synthetisierungstrieb der bewegten Stoffe, sondern zapfen eine letale Ölsemiotik an, die auf den latenten petrochemischen Flüssigkeitshaushalt ölbasierter Kunststoffe verweist. Die korallenrote Kunststoffader *Vena* signifiziert nicht nur, dass sich über den diskret energiesaugenden Leichtstoff[15] das anatomische Geflecht globaler Infrastrukturen materialisiert, sondern auch, dass durch die synthetischen Polymere Petroleum ‚fließt'. *Gota (Drop)* macht das noch deutlicher, will man in dem gummiartigen Tropfen aus schwärzlichen Plastikerzeugnissen jene dickflüssige „*unter*-substance" (MacDonald 2017, 38) erkennen, die seine Bestandteile erst ermöglicht. (Abb. 3)

Abb. 3: Alejandro Durán. *Gota (Drop)*, 2011.

---

15 „These light, colourful and cheap materials, apparently liberated from the constraints of gravity, from rigid shapes and duration, are inextricably linked to the accumulation of huge quantities of matter and energy." (Bensaude-Vincent 2013, 24)

In der Installation *Derrame (Spill)*, der Name verrät es bereits, kulminiert die petrochemische Signifikanz von *Washed Up* und bedient einen extensiven *spill*-Begriff, der über die literale Bedeutung von ‚to spill' ein liquides Bild-, Bedeutungs- und Bewegungsspektrum des Fließens, Strömens und Sickerns aktiviert, das für die Besprechung permeabler Materien und mariner Natur- und Kulturräume interessante Zeichenkontaminationen in Gang setzt. In die felsige Bucht strömt diesmal nicht, wie bei Sekula, die ‚schwarze Flut', sondern eine kunterbunte Plastikschwemme, die das regenbogenfarbige Schillern verschütteten Benzins zitiert. (Abb. 4)

Abb. 4: Alejandro Durán. *Derrame (Spill)*, 2010.

Durán bewahrt dabei das materiell-semiotische Substrat des *spills* in einem ambivalenten Bewegungsmuster zwischen kontingenten Gesten des Fließens und Ausströmens chemischer Sturzbäche zum oder auf dem Strand einerseits und optisch verklumpten, ebenso monolithischen wie monochromen Anordnungen andererseits, deren Bewegungslosigkeit in der statischen Eigenzeitlichkeit des fotografischen Bildes gefriert. Letztere bergen ebenso die Hoffnung auf ein Aufsammeln und Einhegen des Mülls sowie sie auch die maliziöse Dauer von Plastik als potentiellem Beachrock und die unfreiwillige geochemische Speichertätigkeit des Strandes in die visuelle Dauer der ästhetischen Formalisierung übersetzen.

5 Sisyphos am Strand: Landschaftsarbeiten

Um von Durán zurück zu Sekula zu gelangen, möchte ich die den Bildformeln des Containments so implizite Figur der körperlichen Arbeit als Effekt einer Dissipation einführen, denn wenn „dieses Sich-Umverteilen durch Einsammeln [...] wieder in begrenztem Umfang rückgängig gemacht werden" (Soentgen 2014, 277) kann, ist diese Sammeltätigkeit vor allem als bodennahe, und interessanterweise dem Fördereifer so ähnliche, Interferenz von Natur und Arbeit zu verstehen.

Wie die *dramatis personae* aus Allan Sekulas *Black Tide*, die strandsäubernden Katastrophenhelfer*innen, ist auch Alejandro Durán ein Beachcleaner, bei dem jedoch der körperliche Arbeitsprozess, der den Kunst- und Bildwerken als Ergebnissen dieser Arbeit vorausgeht, in den Hintergrund tritt. Es ist der Künstler selbst, der den Strand von Sian Ka'an nach synthetischem Strandgut abschreitet, dabei säubert, um seine Monumente, die selbst vom Stigma des Abfalls gesäubert sind, zu errichten: „When it is cleaned", sagt er, „more trash is guaranteed to arrive the next day. Cleaning the beach is quite literally a Sisyphean task." (Durán zit. nach Harlan 2016, 4) Den mythologischen, hier aber sehr materiellen und in den litoralen Raum verlegten Topos der Sisyphosarbeit, in dem sich endliche Energie und unendlicher Energieaufwand begegnen,[16] bemüht auch Sekula: Im die Fotoserie *Black Tide* begleitenden Theatertext sind die im Chor zusammengefassten Strandarbeiter*innen einer „Sisyphean labor" vorgespannt, „a collective Sisyphus, the chorus trailing across the dark beach in a ragged line, passing unwelcome cargo from hand to hand up the slope of the raking stage" (Sekula 2017 [2003], 133–134). Die Abbildung jener Sisyphosarbeit, die bei Durán konstitutiv, aber bildlich abwesend ist, wird bei Sekula zur eigentlichen dokumentarischen Aufgabe, da er sich mehr auf die Säuberungsarbeiter*innen konzentriert als auf die ökologischen Auswirkungen von 64 000 Tonnen Rohöl selbst. Diese Form der Arbeit jedoch, das Küsten- und Beachcleaning, produziert in scheinbar sinnloser Wiederholung kein sichtbares Produkt außer den Zustand körperlicher Erschöpfung: „These ‚boring' images aim to become emblems of the individual struggle against global economic

---

[16] Als dritte Energieform ließe sich mit Stiegler jene eines ‚unendlichen' Begehrens anführen, das dieser Beitrag thematisch ausklammert: „Was Bestand hat, was *konsistiert*, ist das mehr oder weniger sublimierte Objekt des Begehrens. Es existiert nicht, da es unendlich ist, und weil nur existiert, was endlich und insofern berechenbar ist. Aber nur das Begehren kann die Individuationen in all ihren Formen in Bewegung setzen, nur das Begehren kann also die *energeia* als noetische Individuation, *d.h. auch als Sorge*, entzünden." (Stiegler 2013, 103) Aus dieser Perspektive lässt sich der Akt der Strandsäuberung auch als Ausdruck der Sorge und einer *love of place* (Yi Fu Tuan) verstehen.

forces, carried out on a beach or a rock", so die Kuratorin Gabriele Mackert (2017, 154). Denn es ist der Fels, das Küstengestein, von dem die galizischen Katastrophenhelfer*innen bis zur Kraftlosigkeit das Rohöl schrubben und der wie jener von Duráns Beachcleaning an seiner Entstehung gehinderte Beachrock eine Brücke zur Mühsal des mythologischen Sisyphos schlägt, den Finburgh und Lavery in einer ökokritischen Lesart von Camus' *Der Mythos von Sisyphos* gar als mehr-als-menschliche „creature of the rock" (Finburgh und Lavery 2015, 27) bezeichnen, ein geo-soziales Mythologem einer lithischen Intimität.[17]

Es ist diese transformative und differenzüberschreitende Form körperlicher Arbeit, die Stephanie LeMenager durch die elektrische Arbeit des fossilen Rohstoffes verdrängt sieht und die potentiell aus dem im Meer verschleuderten Energierohstoff Erdöl sublimiert worden wäre. Nicht nur der schmutzige *spill*, auch der semantisch saubere, gänzlich transzendierte Begriff der ‚Energie' ist Bestandteil eines kritisch zu befragenden Vokabulars:

> ‚[E]nergy' becomes a way to talk about how humans and nonhumans do work. I would add that ‚energy' also functions as a metaphor that obscures our laboring bodies, offloading work as a grounding concept of our species onto other entities, such as water, wood, coal, and oil. (LeMenager 2014, 191)

Sowie:

> Energy becomes a way to talk about how both humans and nonhumans do work – and avoid it. (LeMenager 2014, 4)

Energetisch konnotierte Substanzen sind auf mehrfache Weise entstofflicht. Die fossilen ‚Energieträger' werden in Motoren verbrannt, so wie sie in Text und Bild ‚entnannt' sind.[18] Indem muskuläre in ‚mineralischer' Arbeit verschwindet, wird nicht nur Körperarbeit entsinnlicht, da absentiert, sondern auch die potentiell sinnliche Stofflichkeit jener Roh- und Brennstoffe – tatsächlich ein Naturerbe –, die dieses abstrakte Tätigwerden in erster Linie ermöglichen und aus denen sich die Infrastruktur des „fossil-chemischen Industriekomplexes"

---

17 „Sisyphus looks to establish a new relationship with ‚nature', a kind of impossible intimacy, in which the foreignness of the world, its ‚strange strangeness' is affirmed. [...] A major component of Sisyphus's happiness, Camus proposes, arises from his sudden awareness of immanence, his acceptance that he is part of, and tied to, a complex world of matter from which he can neither escape nor transcend." (Finburgh und Lavery 2015, 25)

18 „Indeed, energy has been the great not-said (or, in terms of reception, not-seen, unsaid) in cultural production during the unprecedented and unrepeatable moment of abundant energy in the past century or more. This is the great paradox of fossil fuel imaginaries: in literature as in life, oil in particular is at once everywhere and nowhere, indispensable yet largely unapprehended, not so much invisible as unseen." (Wenzel 2017, 11)

(Steininger 2013, 296) zusammensetzt. Aus dieser Perspektive lässt sich der Küstenbereich, auf dem die ‚Sisyphosarbeit' des Beachcleaning performiert ist, als Ort der Rückkehr jener manuellen Körperleistung bestimmen, die von fossilelektrischer Arbeitsleistung ersetzt wird – und somit beschreibt der ölig oder plastikbunt fluoreszierende Strand auch ein sensationelles Auftauchen jener Materialitäten, die sich sonst in einer Vielzahl von Trieb- und Kraftwerken (oder, wie Boetzkes [2017, 226] pointiert anmerkt, in der Kontaktlinse) ‚verflüchtigen'.

Die Arbeit des/der Beachcleaner*in, ob nun am verölten oder am vermüllten Strand, ist keine Form der Arbeit, die den Strand performativ als Ort der Rekreation – im Sinne menschlich-erbaulicher Erholungs- und Freizeitkultur – anruft. Als Ort einer Re-Kreation wird der Strand als Ort seiner eigenen Wiederherstellung zum Kulturraum paradoxerweise gerade durch das, was ihn als landschaftlich attraktive „vacationscape" (Kluwick und Richter 2015, 7) ausstreicht: nämlich Arbeit. In Albert Camus' *conditio humana* des Absurden heißt es: „Man gebe die Hoffnung auf, aus ihnen [den Bruchstücken einer vormals ganzheitlichen (Um-)Welt, F. A.] jemals die vertraute, ruhige Oberfläche, die uns den Frieden des Herzens geben würde, wiederherzustellen." (Camus 2015 [1942], 30) An dieser Stelle lässt sich im Beachcleaning jener Schnitt orten zwischen der Natur, die ersehnt wird, und dem, was eine toxische Landschaft überhaupt noch an ideellen und materiellen Ressourcen bereitzustellen in der Lage ist. Beachcleaning als Versuch der Wiederherstellung eines, zumindest auf den ersten Blick, nicht-anthropogenen Litorals codiert diesen Schnitt in der gleichen Bewegung, in der es diesen vernäht. Raymond Williams konstatiert, dass Arbeit und ihre Objektbezüge in oder an der Natur ‚Landschaft' als genuin ideologischen Wahrnehmungsmodus eines umweltlichen Arrangements verunmöglicht, wenn er verkündet: „A working country is hardly ever a landscape." (Williams 1973, 120) Unter diesem Aspekt lässt sich fragen, ob sich der *spill*-Effekt des Beachcleaning zwischen materieller Restaurierung und Ausfall der Landschaftsfunktion wider Willen als symbolische Fortsetzung jener vorgängigen Zerstörung durch petrochemische Gewalt lesen lässt, durch die der Strand nun doppelt ‚kontaminiert' ist: landschaftssemiotisch gerade durch den Versuch, ihn materiell zu bergen.

Die hier vorgestellten Figuren, der Container und die Arbeit, stehen nicht unverbunden nebeneinander, sondern durchschnüren die kulturpoetisch gewendete Dissipationskette eines weiten *spill*-Begriffs, der über eine materiell-semiotische Analogie die gekippten „petrochemical landscapes" (Misrach und Orff 2014, 129) globaler Uferzonen als symptomatische Schwellenräume evoziert, in denen sich nicht nur Mensch, Meer und Müll begegnen, sondern in

Form materieller Rückflüsse und epistemischer Rückführungen auch Kunststoffe und fossile Energierohstoffe selbst.

Um die diffuse phänomenologische Beschaffenheit umweltlicher Körper im Phasenraum des Anthropozän zu beschreiben, greift Timothy Morton auf den philosophischen Topos der ‚Paradoxie des Haufens' zurück, mit dem sich die Konturlosigkeit phänomenaler Objekte – ihre *weirdness* – im Hinblick auf ein immanentes Potential zur Aufhebung von Selbstpräsenz ausdrücken lässt; am Beispiel einer Wiese fragt Morton:

> [A]n existing thing is something that is present in such a way that it can be subdivided – it is constantly there, so there can be parts of a thing, whose removal will at some point drastically alter that thing's existence. Say, for example, I am an ecologist studying a meadow. If I think that the meadow is constantly present, I can remove pieces of it – a blade of grass here, a blade of grass there. At some point I imagine that the meadow will not exist anymore. The trouble is, when exactly is that? (Morton 2016, 67)

Wieviel Prozent an Sandkörnern müssen durch Mikroplastikpartikel ersetzt werden, damit einem Strand unter dem (Ver-)Formungsdruck giftiger Gegenwartsgeologie eine abweichende (*deviant*) Existenzform attestiert werden muss? Schon heute, so der Umweltphänomenologe Jens Soentgen, bestehen die Sandstrände bestimmter Meeresbuchten zu bis zu drei Prozent aus Kunststoffkügelchen (Soentgen 2019, 7). „Preventing a thing from deviating is called destroying it", schreibt Morton (2016, 78), und ironisiert damit das Bedürfnis, in ein fürsorgliches Verhältnis zu diesen sonnenbeschienenen ‚Schattenorten' (Val Plumwood) zu treten. Der topophile Rettungsimpuls aber, „[t]he desire to touch damaged objects", ist Teil unserer ökologischen Identität, so die US-amerikanische Literaturwissenschaftlerin Ruth Salvaggio (2014, 392), die am Beispiel des verölten Pelikans die Idee eines körper- und artenübergreifenden Spürens (*shared sensorium*) stark machen will. Im schleichenden Unähnlichwerden von Landschaften aber, das sich auch in den hier besprochenen fotografischen Arbeiten ankündigt, gehen Denaturierung und Renaturierung bis zur Unkenntlichkeit ineinander über; dies fordert eine sinnlich-ästhetische Arten- und Ortsverbundenheit sowie das visuelle Vokabular der Landschaftsfotografie gleichermaßen heraus.

Literaturverzeichnis

Banita, Georgiana. „Photography". *Fueling Culture: 101 Words for Energy and Environment*. Hg. Imre Szeman, Jennifer Wenzel und Patricia Yaeger. New York: Fordham University Press, 2017a. 263–266.

Banita, Georgiana. „Sensing Oil: Sublime Art and Politics in Canada". *Petrocultures: Oil, Politics, Culture*. Hg. Adam Carlson, Imre Szeman und Sheena Wilson. Montreal: McGill-Queen's University Press, 2017b. 431–457.

Barthes, Roland. *Mythen des Alltags* [1957]. Frankfurt/Main: Suhrkamp, 1964.

Beamish, Thomas. *Silent Spill: The Organization of an Industrial Crisis*. Cambridge/MA: The MIT Press, 2002.

Bellamy, Brent Ryan. „Petrorealism". *Fueling Culture: 101 Words for Energy and Environment*. Hg. Imre Szeman, Jennifer Wenzel und Patricia Yaeger. New York: Fordham University Press, 2017. 259–262.

Bensaude-Vincent, Bernadette. „Plastics, Materials and Dreams of Dematerialization". *Accumulation: The Material Politics of Plastic*. Hg. Jennifer Gabrys, Gay Hawkins und Mike Michael. London: Routledge, 2013. 17–29.

Boetzkes, Amanda. „Plastic Vision and the Sight of Petroculture". *Petrocultures: Oil, Politics, Culture*. Hg. Adam Carlson, Imre Szeman und Sheena Wilson. Montreal: McGill-Queen's University Press, 2017. 222–241.

Bronfen, Elisabeth. *Liebestod und Femme fatale. Der Austausch sozialer Energien zwischen Oper, Literatur und Film*. Frankfurt/Main: Suhrkamp, 2004.

Bronfen, Elisabeth. „Visuelles Lesen als kritische Intervention im kulturellen Imaginären". *Crossmappings. Essays zur visuellen Kultur*. Zürich: Scheidegger & Spiess, 2009. 7–41.

Brown, Mark. A. „Sources and Pathways of Microplastics to Habitats". *Marine Anthropogenic Litter*. Hg. Melanie Bergmann, Lars Gutow und Michael Klages. Cham et al.: Springer Open, 2015. 229–244.

Bukold, Steffen, und Jörg Feddern. *Öl-Report 2016*. Hg. Greenpeace e. V., 2016. https://www.greenpeace.de/sites/www.greenpeace.de/files/publications/oel-report-2016-greenpeace-20160108_0.pdf/ (3. September 2018).

Camus, Albert. *Der Mythos des Sisyphos* [1942]. Reinbek/Hamburg: Rowohlt, 2015.

Corcoran, Patricia L., Charles J. Moore und Kelly Jazvac. „An Anthropogenic Marker Horizon in the Future Rock Record". *GSA Today* 24.6 (2014): 4–8.

Corcoran, Patricia L., und Kelly Jazvac. „Plastiglomerate". *Fueling Culture: 101 Words for Energy and Environment*. Hg. Imre Szeman, Jennifer Wenzel und Patricia Yaeger. New York: Fordham University Press, 2017. 275–277.

Cosgrove, Denis, und Stephen Daniels. „Introduction: Iconography and Landscape". *The Iconography of Landscape: Essays on the Symbolic Representation, Design and Use of Past Environments*. Hg. Denis Cosgrove und Stephen Daniels. Cambridge: Cambridge University Press, 2007. 1–10.

Davis, Heather. „Plastikgeologie". *Mensch macht Natur. Landschaft im Anthropozän*. Hg. Gabiele Mackert und Paul Petritsch. Berlin und Boston: de Gruyter, 2016. 94–123.

Durán, Alejandro. „Washed Up: Transforming a Trashed Landscape". http://www.alejandroduran.com/washedupseries/ (18. Januar 2019).

Finburgh, Clare, und Carl Lavery. „Introduction: Greening the Absurd". *Rethinking the Theatre of the Absurd: Ecology, the Environment and the Greening of the Modern Stage*. Hg. Clare Finburgh und Carl Lavery. London: Bloomsbury, 2015. 1–58.

Golik, Abraham. „The Distribution and Behaviour of Tar Balls Along the Israeli Coast". *Esturiane, Coastal and Shelf Science* 15 (1982): 267–276.

Gordon, Jon. *Unsustainable Oil: Facts, Counterfacts and Fictions*. Edmonton: The University of Alberta Press, 2016.

Gottlieb, Benjamin. „Hong Kong's Plastic Pellet Problem". *The Washington Post* (6. August 2012): https://www.washingtonpost.com/blogs/blogpost/post/hong-kongs-plastic-pellet-problem/2012/08/06/6bbc018a-dfe3-11e1-a19c-fcfa365396c8_blog.html (3. September 2019).
Hanke, Georg, François Galgani und Thomas Maes. „Global Distribution, Composition and Abundance of Marine Litter". *Marine Anthropogenic Litter*. Hg. Melanie Bergmann, Lars Gutow und Michael Klages. Cham et al.: Springer, 2015. 29–56.
Haraway, Donna. *When Species Meet*. Minneapolis und London: University of Minnesota Press, 2008.
Harlan, Becky. „This is not a Mirage: Colorful Art Installations That Delight, Then Horrify". *National Geographic* 10. Juni 2016: https://www.nationalgeographic.com/photography/proof/2016/06/an-oceans-trash-is-an-artists-treasure/ (18. Januar 2019).
Jeffery, Celina. „Dismal Science: Narratives of Violence and Extinction in the Age of the Anthropocene". *Allan Sekula: Okeanos*. Hg. Cory Scozzari und Daniela Zyman. Berlin: Sternberg Press, 2017. 234–239.
Juhasz, Antonia. „Spill". *Fueling Culture: 101 Words for Energy and Environment*. Hg. Imre Szeman, Jennifer Wenzel und Patricia Yaeger. New York: Fordham University Press, 2017. 318–320.
Kaiser, Wolfgang. *Kunststoffchemie für Ingenieure: Von der Synthese bis zur Anwendung*. München: Hanser, 2015.
Kastner, Jens. „‚Gegen die Abstraktion des globalen Kapitals'. Das Foto als Transporter: Allan Sekula und postmoderne Fotografie ohne Postmoderne". *kritische berichte – Zeitschrift für Kunst- und Kulturwissenschaften* 31.3 (2003): 76–82.
Keeble, John. *Out of the Channel: The Exxon Valdez Oil Spill in Prince William Sound*. New York: HarperCollins, 1999.
Kittel, Jürgen, und Jörg Wagner. *Öltanker-Quartett: Die katastrophalsten Auslaufmodelle der Weltmeere auf 32 Spielkarten*. Kartenspiel. Hamburg: Weltquartett, 2011.
Kluwick, Ursula, und Virginia Richter. „‚Twixt Land and Sea': Approaches to Littoral Studies". *The Beach in Anglophone Literatures and Cultures: Reading Littoral Space*. Hg. Ursula Kluwick und Virginia Richter. London: Routledge, 2015. 1–20.
Krebs, Angelika. „The Ethics and Aesthetics of Landscape". *Ecological Thought in German Literature and Culture*. Hg. Gabriele Dürbeck, Urte Stobbe, Hubert Zapf und Evi Zemanek. London: Lexington Books, 2017. 101–118.
Kull, Kalevi, Kati Lindström und Hannes Palang. „Landscape Semiotics: Contribution to Culture Theory". *Estonian Approaches to Culture Theory* 4 (2014): 110–132.
LeMenager, Stephanie. *Living Oil: Petroleum Culture in the American Century*. New York: Oxford University Press, 2014.
LeMenager, Stephanie. „Spills". *Fueling Culture: 101 Words for Energy and Environment*. Hg. Imre Szeman, Jennifer Wenzel und Patricia Yaeger. New York: Fordham University Press, 2017. 321–324.
Mackert, Gabriele. „Sisyphus's Prestige: On Allan Sekula's *Marea Negra: fragmentos para una ópera*". *Allan Sekula: Okeanos*. Hg. Cory Scozzari und Daniela Zyman. Berlin: Sternberg Press, 2017. 152–159.
Misrach, Richard, und Kate Orff. *Petrochemical America*. New York: Aperture, 2010.
McCarthy, Tom. *Satin Island*. New York: Penguin, 2015.
McCarthy, Tom. *Satin Island*. Übersetzt von Thomas Melle. München: Deutsche Verlags-Anstalt, 2016.

McDonald, Graeme. „Containing Oil: The Pipeline in Petroculture". *Petrocultures: Oil, Politics, Culture*. Hg. Adam Carlson, Imre Szeman und Sheena Wilson. Montreal: McGill-Queen's University Press, 2017. 36–77.

Morton, Timothy. „All Objects Are Deviant: Feminism and Ecological Intimacy". *Object-Oriented Feminism*. Hg. Katherine Behar. Minneapolis und London: University of Minnesota Press, 2016. 65–81.

Neimanis, Astrida. *Bodies of Water. Posthuman Feminist Phenomenology*. London und New York: Bloomsbury, 2017.

Peeples, Jennifer. „Toxic Sublime: Imaging Contaminated Landscapes". *Environmental Communication: A Journal of Nature and Culture* 5.4 (2011): 373–392.

Plumwood, Val. „Shadow Places and the Politics of Dwelling". *Australian Humanities Review* 44 (2008): 139–150.

Rojas, Carles Guerra. „Arrested Flow: Allan Sekula in Galicia". *Allan Sekula: Okeanos*. Hg. Cory Scozzari und Daniela Zyman. Berlin: Sternberg Press, 2017. 138–143.

Rubenstein, Michael. „Petrocriticism". *Futures of Comparative Literature: ACLA State of the Discipline Report*. Hg. Ursula K. Heise. New York: Routledge, 2017. 49–50.

Salvaggio, Ruth. „Imagining Angels on the Gulf". *Oil Culture*. Hg. Ross Barrett und Daniel Worden. Minneapolis und London: University of Minnesota Press, 2014. 384–403.

Sekula, Allan. „Black Tide: Fragments for an Opera". *Allan Sekula: Okeanos*. Hg. Cory Scozzari und Daniela Zyman. Berlin: Sternberg Press, 2017. 132–137.

Soentgen, Jens. „Dissipation". *Stoffe in Bewegung: Beiträge zu einer Wissensgeschichte der materiellen Welt*. Hg. Kijan Espahangizi und Barbara Orland. Zürich: diaphanes, 2014. 279–287.

Soentgen, Jens. *Konfliktstoffe. Über Kohlendioxid, Heroin und andere strittige Substanzen*. München: Oekom Verlag, 2019.

Soni, Vivasvan. „Energy". *Fueling Culture: 101 Words for Energy and Environment*. Hg. Imre Szeman, Jennifer Wenzel und Patricia Yaeger. New York: Fordham University Press, 2017. 132–135.

Stafford, Maria. *Visual Analogy: Consciousness as the Art of Connecting*. Cambridge/MA: The MIT Press, 1999.

Steininger, Benjamin. „Zum Energiewert der Zeit". *Prometheische Kultur. Wo kommen unsere Energien her?* Hg. Claus Leggewie, Ursula Renner und Peter Risthaus. München: Fink, 2013. 293–308.

Stiegler, Bernd. „Sorgfältige Arbeit". *Prometheische Kultur. Wo kommen unsere Energien her?* Hg. Claus Leggewie, Ursula Renner und Peter Risthaus. München: Fink, 2013. 95–109.

Sullivan, Heather I. „Material Ecocriticism and the Petro-Text". *The Routledge Companion to the Environmental Humanities*. Hg. Jon Christensen, Ursula K. Heise und Michelle Niemann. London: Routledge, 2017. 414–423.

Szeman, Imre, und Maria Whiteman. „Oil Imag(e)inaries: Critical Realism and the Oil Sands". *Imaginations: Journal of Cross-Cultural Image Studies* 3.2 (2012): 46–67.

Weiß, Matthias. „Was ist ‚inszenierte Fotografie'? Eine Begriffsbestimmung". *Die fotografische Wirklichkeit: Inszenierung – Fiktion – Narration*. Hg. Lars Blunck. Bielefeld: transcript, 2010. 35–52.

Wenzel, Jennifer. „Introduction". *Fueling Culture: 101 Words for Energy and Environment*. Hg. Imre Szeman, Jennifer Wenzel und Patricia Yaeger. New York: Fordham University Press, 2017. 1–16.

Williams, Raymond. *The Country and the City*. New York: Oxford University Press, 1973.

Wils, Jean-Pierre. „Medien-Welten. Vernichtung oder Verdichtung der Sinne?". *Vom Sinn multipler Welten. Medien und Kunst.* Hg. Volker Demuth und Robin Wagner. Würzburg: Königshausen & Neumann, 2000. 9–38.

Yaeger, Patricia. „Sea Trash, Dark Pools, and the Tragedy of the Commons". *PMLA* 125.3 (2010): 523–545.

Abbildungsverzeichnis

Abb. 1: Allan Sekula. *Shellfishers Working and Army preparing*, 2003. Abdruckgenehmigung erteilt durch Allan Sekula Studio.

Abb. 2: Allan Sekula. *Disposal Pit*, 2003. Abdruckgenehmigung erteilt durch Allan Sekula Studio.

Abb. 3: Alejandro Durán. *Gota (Drop)*, 2011. Abdruckgenehmigung erteilt durch den Fotografen.

Abb. 4: Alejandro Durán. *Derrame (Spill)*, 2010. Abdruckgenehmigung erteilt durch den Fotografen.

Konstantin Butz
The Ephemeral Beachscape: Skateboarding and the Appropriation of Suburban Concrete

This essay examines how American teenagers, from the late 1950s onwards, have been using the four-wheeled device of the skateboard to disentangle the stable and rigid elements of suburban organization and replace them with ephemeral moments of fluid mobility that are genealogically linked to the beachside activity of surfing. Informed by Gilles Deleuze and Félix Guattari's concept of *smooth* and *striated space* and its specification as a *Maritime Model*, this evaluation of skateboarding opens an analytic perspective on the mediating qualities of the beach. By transferring maneuvers from a water-bound activity to the onshore environment of suburbia, it argues, young skateboarders performatively mirror specific notions of the beach and generate emancipatory effects momentarily disrupting the conservative environment of their concrete surroundings.

In dem vorliegenden Aufsatz wird untersucht, wie Skateboardfahren seit den späten 1950er Jahren Jugendlichen in amerikanischen Vorstädten dazu dienen konnte, die unflexiblen und konservativen Strukturen suburbanen Lebens aufzuweichen und durch ephemere Momente fluider Mobilität zu ersetzen, die sich genealogisch an die Aktivität des Surfens knüpfen lassen. Die Untersuchung des Skateboarding eröffnet dabei eine Perspektive, die sich auf die vermittelnden Eigenschaften des Strandes konzentriert und diese Anhand von Gilles Deleuze und Félix Guattaris Konzept von *glattem* und *gekerbten Raum* – bzw. dessen Spezifizierung als *Modell des Meeres* – erörtert. Es wird gezeigt, wie Bewegungen, die ursprünglich auf dem Wasser stattfinden, von jungen Skateboarder*innen auf das Festland übertragen und im suburbanen Raum angewendet werden. Dort spiegeln sie konkrete Eigenschaften des Strandes und generieren emanzipatorische Effekte, die das konservative Umfeld der Vororte in Frage stellen und stören.

> Don't be afraid to try the newest sport around
> It's catching on in every city and town
> You can do the tricks the surfers do
> Just try a "Quasimodo" or "The Coffin" too
> Grab your board and go sidewalk surfin' with me
> Jan & Dean (1964)

1 Introduction

Jan & Dean's 1964 song "Sidewalk Surfin" provides a very perceptive observation of the interconnection of the two activities of surfing and skateboarding. It musically accounts for the fact that, at some point in the evolution of both movements, Californian surfers had started to reapply and transfer their tricks and skills from the oceanic action of surfing to the dry land movement of skateboarding.[1] They had embarked on an itinerary that was rooted in the site-specific locale of the beach and from there would spread out into the American continent.

Although it is hardly possible to pinpoint the exact moment the skateboard itself was invented,[2] there is solid evidence that skateboarding was in fact massively influenced by surf culture and concrete adaptations from surfing actions. Already during the late 1950s, the first commercially produced skateboards were known and marketed as *sidewalk surfboards* while, particularly with the "more physical and dynamic style of surfing" (Zarka 2011, 22) emerging during the 1970s, skateboarders started to imitate the movements and maneuvers of their surfing idols. The so-called "Bertlemann-style" constitutes a frequently referenced example of a very influential way of skateboarding that explicitly mimicked Hawaiian surfer Larry Bertlemann's aggressive surfing approach characterized by touching the water with his hands while turning on a breaking wave (see e. g. Wayland 2002, 47; Zarka 2011, 22). By performing sudden turns and wheel slides on the ground, such surfing movements could be applied to the land and it really became possible to "do the tricks the surfers do," as the lyrics of Jan & Dean's song suggested.

Many of the water-bound tricks that were performed on a surfboard *washed up* on the shore of California where a huge surfing scene intermixed with the burgeoning teen culture of the postwar years and skateboarding took on to become a popular activity among young people. Skateboarding was "largely imagined as a suburban, middle class pursuit" (Yochim 2010, 20), Emily Chivers Yochim points out, and, as architectural historian Iain Borden adds, particularly in the post-sixties, "the suburban modernism of Los Angeles and other Californian Oceanside cities allowed frustrated surfers to re-enact the sense of being on the sea" (Borden 2005, 29). In what follows, I analyze the attributes of skateboarding that make it much more than a sportive activity of teenagers and enhance the movement on the four-wheeled device with a potential to disrupt, resist, and re-imagine the site-specific locale of suburban California. I do so by concentrating on the interconnections between skateboarding and surfing as they help to underscore the emancipatory moments that pervade skateboarding and its transfers of a beachside activity to the dry-land environments of suburbia and beyond. What exactly does it mean to skateboard in an environment

---

[1] The "Quasimodo" and the "Coffin" mentioned in the lyrics of Jan and Dean's "Sidewalk Surfing" are names for tricks that can be performed both on a surfboard or a skateboard.
[2] The first industrially manufactured skateboards entered the market during the mid to late 1950s (Brooke 2005, 16; Zarka 2011, 12).

that, at least in its initial figuration, constitutes a habitat that particularly provides a mythologically charged retreat for citizens of the middle class? How does skateboarding intervene in the often monotonous, boring, and dreary landscape of conservative suburban life? To what extent can it generate resistant potential and in how far does it still reflect the aquatic features of oceanic surfing and the latter's reliance on the beach?

2 Antipedestrian Suburbia

Suburbia is often characterized by its conformist architecture, an emphasis on property and prosperity, privatized and isolated domesticity, security and surveillance, and an anti-pedestrian traffic pattern that particularly binds teenagers to this orthodox environment of fixity. This fixity, by definition, has tremendous consequences for the mobility of people, and particularly of young people, as it hinders free and unrestricted movement and binds teenagers to their parents' suburban retreat while preventing the creation of "a powerful, nuanced, diverse, and authentic local culture" (Hansen and Ryan 1991, 184); a lack that Debra Gold Hansen and Mary P. Ryan exemplarily propose as a reason for the "relative paucity of public life" in Southern California's Orange County (ibid., 184). Dennis P. Sobin's remarks concerning life in American suburbs, although already published in 1971, still provide a revealing anticipation of these problems while paralleling Hansen and Ryan's description of Californian suburbia and combining it with a special focus on teenage life:

> Suburbia was originally considered to be a utopia for the young, at least for young couples with children to raise. [...] It was viewed as an ideal place to raise children. For very young children this was somewhat true. The suburban problems did not emerge until these youngsters became adolescents. The teenagers were the first to sense the inadequacies of suburbia. Life in the suburbs was limited and dull to young people who were anxious to experiment and explore the world. (Sobin 1971, 80)

The exploration of the world that Sobin attributes to teenage aspirations directly reflects the importance that mobility and movement have for young people. Suburbia, at least in the conservative areas of Southern California – and despite being connected to artificial networks and flows of (automobile) traffic – constitutes an immobile and restricted if not isolated environment suffering from antipedestrian fragmentation (see Kling et al. 1991, X). Consequently, resistance to such a rigid organization must concentrate on mobilizing actions that fight the inertia of this spatial setup. The activity of skateboarding, I argue, provides a comprehensive, material, and *concrete* strategy that counters and indeed liquefies the stable, immobile, and fixed characteristics of suburban living – particularly in view of its genealogical reliance on the aquatic fluidity of surfing motions.

3 Skateboarding within the *Maritime Model*

In order to emphasize the liberating potential that skateboarding offers to its activists, it is revealing to specify the suburban landscape by approaching it through a focused reading of what Gilles Deleuze and Félix Guattari introduce or, more precisely, juxtapose as *smooth* and *striated* space.[3] In their conception they define the former as "nomad" and the latter as "sedentary space" (Deleuze and Guattari 2005, 524), thereby incorporating notions of movement and suggesting the existence of two spatial poles: one that implies the mobility of nomadic movement (smoothness) and one that implies the immobility of rigid fixity (striation). According to such a rendering of space, for skateboarding to generate liberating, i.e. mobilizing, potential within the restricted and fixed locale of suburbia, it needs to engage in the production of a smooth space that counters the immobility affecting suburban dwellers and particularly young people in their everyday lives. For the purpose of locating such moments of a production of smooth space, i.e. moments of smoothing, within the activity of skateboarding, it is helpful to reference Deleuze and Guattari's initial conception of what they call a *"Maritime Model"* (ibid., 528) and consider what they regard as "a smooth space par excellence" (ibid., 529) – the sea. "Of course, there are points, lines, and surfaces in striated space as well as in smooth space" (ibid., 528), they set out to explain, but then specify that "[i]n striated space, lines or trajectories tend to be subordinated to points: one goes from one point to another. In the smooth, it is the opposite: the points are subordinated to the trajectory" (ibid.). Paralleling the ever shifting and moving seascape, a space where "the ground constantly changes direction" (ibid., 545), this model foregrounds an *in-between* that indicates trajectories of movement countering the striated immobility of fixed and stable points. As opposed to the sea, Deleuze and Guattari define the city as "the striated space par excellence" (ibid., 531), and with the extreme order of conservative habitation and carefully planned housing and traffic patterns in mind, it seems as if suburbia received a particular role in this

---
3 I first introduced an analysis of skateboarding in connection to Deleuze and Guattari's elaborations on smooth and striated space in my book *Grinding California: Culture and Corporeality in American Skate Punk* (particularly see Butz 2012, 233 ff.).

attribution: Within a *Maritime Model* it constitutes the epitome of striation, discipline, and fixity, and thus the opposite of smoothness.

Deleuze and Guattari suggest to what extent such a sedentary environment can in fact be challenged:

> Even the most striated city gives rise to smooth spaces: to live in the city as a nomad, or as a cave dweller. Movements, speed and slowness, are sometimes enough to reconstruct a smooth space. Of course, smooth spaces are not in themselves liberatory. But the struggle is changed or displaced in them, and life reconstitutes its stakes, confronts new obstacles, invents new paces, switches adversaries. (Ibid., 551)

Although cautioning that one should "[n]ever believe that a smooth space will suffice to save us" (ibid., 551), their statement – particularly their reference to the life of the nomad and thus nomadism – introduces movements, speed and slowness, i. e. variations of mobility, as programmatic options that, if not saving us, should at least foster moments of resistance against fixity. Mobility, it seems, constitutes an important prerequisite for the production of smooth space and, while the mentioned confrontation of "new obstacles" and the invention of "new paces" already seems to parallel important aspects of skateboarders' approaches to their surroundings, it is Deleuze himself who, at least within the scope of this essay, prepares an almost direct connection to skateboarding by mentioning the activity of surfing in his work on "Mediators" (Deleuze 1992): "Many of the new sports – surfing, windsurfing, hang gliding – take the form of entry into an existing wave" (ibid., 281), Deleuze states, and continues:

> There's no longer an origin as starting point, but a sort of putting into orbit. The basic thing is how to get taken up in movement of a big wave, column of rising air, to 'come between' rather than be the origin of an effort. (Ibid., 281)

What Deleuze describes here is the injection of the human body into smooth space. The *coming between* an already existing wave in surfing constitutes an entry into a trajectory that is not defined by two points but rather shoots across the smooth space of the sea as a line of flight without a fixed origin or terminal point. Since the activity of surfing has had a tremendous influence on skateboarding both culturally and in view of its physical maneuvers and movements – as pointed out, the early sobriquet of *sidewalk surfing* summarizes this influence – it becomes possible to also transfer Deleuze's anticipation of surfing as a new sport characterized by its occupation of the *between* to the activity of skateboarding within the context of suburban California and beyond. Deleuze's take on surfing and the application of the Deleuzo-Guattarian diction developed in the *Maritime Model* open a perspective that reads skateboarding as a kind of mediator enabling a transmission and transgression between smooth and striated spaces.

4 Passages between Sea and Land

Iain Borden's implications concerning the mobility that skateboarders induce in seemingly static, i. e. striated, architecture illustrate the transmissive and transgressive qualities that skateboarding holds:

> By focusing only on certain elements (ledges, walls, banks, rails) of the building, skateboarders deny architecture's existence as a discrete three-dimensional indivisible thing, knowable only as totality, and treat it instead as a set of *floating*, detached, physical elements isolated from each other. (Borden 2005, 145 [emphasis mine])

Describing skateboarders' treatment of their surroundings as *"floating"* elements, Borden suggests the way they perceive their environment as, or indeed make it: mobile. The bodily engagement of the Californian landscape seems to momentarily turn the striated space into a floating seascape and, thus, into the ultimate paradigm of smoothness. As Deleuze and Guattari define, smooth space is "a space constructed by local operations involving changes in direction" (Deleuze and Guattari 2005, 528), and the movement on the four-wheeled board constitutes precisely that, a local activity that constantly produces a changing of directions: up, down, left, right, and through a variety of tricks and jumps also into the air and onto the concrete. But to what extent do these movements generate resistant interventions? And how do they relate to the qualities of surfing?

Jeff Lewis, in his essay "In Search of the Postmodern Surfer: Territory, Terror and Masculinity," sets out to examine the "relationship between the phenomenal world of surfing and its representation in language and text" (Lewis 2003, 59). He also refers to Deleuze's comment on surfing and explains in what way the activity "can be seen as part of a 'de-territorializing' process in which institutional power is effectively deconstructed by the nomadic experiences of new subjectivities" (ibid., 61). Lewis points towards surfing's potential for resistance by describing it "as a rebel flow [that] contrasts with the ossifying of institutionalized language which would fix identity and ideas into specific ideologies and structure" (ibid., 62). "[T]he act of surfboard riding," he explicates, "becomes transgressive inasmuch as it unleashes an aesthetic of immediate pleasure and 'immersion' in the experience of the phenomenal (everyday) world" (ibid., 65). Lewis's allusion to pleasure establishes a link to John Fiske's analysis of the beach and surfing and its reliance on a semiotic approach in the vein of Roland Barthes. Fiske, in the chapter "Reading the Beach" of his monograph *Reading the Popular*, departs from a clear and exclusive differentiation between the sea and nature on the one hand and the city and culture on the other hand. In the establishment of binary diagrams, he ascribes body, physical sensation, and the signifier to the former, while classing mind, conceptual construction, and the signified with the latter. He thus introduces a setting within which surfing becomes a subversive journey from culture to nature, from mind to body, from city to sea.

The site-specific setting of the beach, in this conception, constitutes a particular in-between stage as it is not only located right at the border of landlocked "civilization" and the "untamed, uncivilized, raw" nature of the sea but also "mediates this terrifying boundary" (Fiske 1990, 45). Fiske goes on and elaborates:

> The beach, then, is an anomalous category, overflowing with meaning because it is neither land nor sea, neither nature nor culture, but partakes of both. It is therefore the appropriate place for anomalous behavior, behavior that is highly significant because it pushes the cultural as far as it can go toward Nature. It explores the boundary of what it is to be social, to be cultured, that is the nonphysical part of the human condition. (Ibid., 56)

This understanding of the beach as an "anomalous" category, i.e. a place for "anomalous behavior," emphasizes its role in the generation of deviant and thus potentially resistant activities and movements, particularly for young people. "The beach," Fiske specifies, "plays an important part in youth culture, because youth, too, is an anomalous category, the one between child and adult" (ibid., 58). He undergirds the interconnections of youth and deviance that characterize beachside activities such as surfing and therefore implicitly hints at their reverberations in skateboarding. Explicitly analyzing it for critical potential, Fiske explains that the "subversion of surfing lies in its apparent escape from the control of the signified, from social power" (ibid., 73). He presents an approach paralleling the experience of surfing with Barthes's descriptions of blissful moments in the reading of text:

> The wave is that text of bliss to the surfie [i. e. the surfer], escape from the signified, potential reentry into nature, constantly shifting, needing rereading for each loss of subjectivity. It contradicts, defines momentarily, the ideological subjectivity through which discourses exert their control. (Ibid., 76)

By focusing on the ocean as an escape from sites of control, Fiske strictly allocates the subversive momentum of surfing within the wave, i.e. on the water and away from the land. Lewis summarizes the situation by reading it in view of the binary opposition between nature and culture that Fiske prescribed: In surfing, "the body and the sensory (nature) are wedded in opposition against the reasoned hegemonies of domination (civilization)," and "in this sense, [surfing] becomes a strategic immersion which enables surfers to escape, however briefly, the controlling powers of work, state, capitalism and institutional regulations" (Lewis 2003, 66). This reading implicitly suggests that a transfer of surfing to the land and to the city would carry and import possibilities of subversion, opposing discourses of surveillance and ultimately generating "a tactical attempt to evade the social control of meaning" (Fiske 1990, 76), including the restrictive setup of suburban organization. For an analysis of skateboarding as a concrete opportunity to transfer surfing's liberating potential to the four-wheeled device and thus to the dry-land locale of suburbia, however, it is important to question the dichotomy that follows from Fiske's inquiries and becomes apparent in his analysis of surfing media, particularly surf journals.

Fiske juxtaposes and describes the actual activity of surfing as enmeshed in "physical sensation" on the one hand, and in the discourses that draw the surfer "back into dominant culture by the very journals, competitions, and manufacturers that apparently serve his interests" (Fiske 1990, 61, 67–68) on the other. In this regard, the medial stylization undermines the potentially rebellious and liberating subculture of surfing by drawing it back from its physical engagement into a media discourse:

> What the culture is trying to do to the surf is to defuse its potential radicalism. By incorporating it into TV sports and news, into the advertising of banks, or soft drinks, or electronic hardware, it is pulling the surfie back from the brink of becoming nature into the comfortable security of the natural. (Ibid., 74)

The radical potential of surfing is entirely located within nature, or at least the brink of becoming nature, and thus far away from any dry-land application. Lewis summarizes the binary opposition that Fiske establishes by labeling surfing's immersion in the ocean as "pre-discursive" and thus diametrically opposed to the "institutionally constrained language" of media such as the "surfie journal" (Lewis 2003, 66). This dichotomous distinction, despite its very relevant and appropriate critique of the commercialization of surfing, leads away from the evaluation of surfing's subversive potential *beyond* a strict localization within and on the waves of the ocean. The installation of a definite border between sea and city that follows from the differentiation between "pre-discursive" surfing and its linguistic-discursive representation on land fixates and immobilizes the potentiality of the activity and the moments of lived intensity that it possibly generates. It isolates the mobilizing potential of surfing within an essentialized space of strictly defined otherness: the sea as essential nature.

Particularly with regard to Deleuze and Guattari, the strong dichotomization that Fiske introduces and which reverberates in Lewis's introduction of the "pre-discursive" appears extremely confining. It is important to note that Deleuze and Guattari do not establish the antagonistic concepts of *smooth* and *striated* space by a strict polarity but emphasize that, "we must remind ourselves that the two spaces in fact exist only in mixture: smooth space is constantly being translated, transversed into a striated space; striated space is constantly being reversed, returned to a smooth space" (Deleuze and Guattari 2005, 524). This statement puts the "primordial duality between the smooth and the striated" (ibid., 547) in perspective and in fact provides the prerequisite for an approach to surfing that unhinges its mobilizing, nomad, and smoothing generations from the oceanic wave and makes it applicable to other, more striated environments in the first place. It proves that an essentializing binary between sea and land ignores the potentiality that lies in their interconnection, an interconnection that is most vividly incorporated in the mediating qualities of the beach.

While Fiske's description of surfing seems very invested in a binary conception of sea and land that places the riding of waves in essential opposition to everything ashore, Deleuze and Guattari point towards the fact that despite its paradigmatic role as smooth space, the sea was "the first to encounter the demands of increasingly strict striation" (ibid., 529), which was imposed by navigation, bearings, and the cartographic plottings of the map. They reveal to what extent smooth and striated spaces always interact and mix, while implying that the dualistic differentiation between sea and city falls short of the transmissions, transgressions, translations, transversals, reversals, and returns that constantly interconnect them or at least prolong the trajectories of lines of flight that emerge in either locale.

Within such a multidirectional conception, the beach acts as a spatial mediator, which constantly reminds us of the fact that a definite distinction between the qualities of land and ocean is neither fruitful nor possible. Through reciprocal interconnections of sea and city, the beach generates opportunities of mobility that surpass any appointed function of a definite border. The beach does not fix or separate but, just as Fiske himself declares, "[t]he beach *mediates*" (Fiske 1990, 45 [emphasis mine]). This flexible understanding of smoothness and striation in dynamic oscillation opens a perspective on skateboarding as a continuity of the trajectory that the movement of surfing launches – a trajectory "sometimes causing a passage from the smooth to the striated, sometimes from the striated to the smooth, according to entirely different movements" (Deleuze and

Guattari 2005, 524). Skateboarding relies on surfing's floating in the smooth space of the ocean and imports it to the striated space of suburbia by deploying a new approach to movement.[4] It constitutes a passage from the ocean to the city and indicates a potential line of flight that cuts across both spaces. Thereby, the skateboard turns into a tool that picks up on the mediating qualities of the beach and itself becomes a mediator putting striated structures into a dynamic exchange with smooth mobilities.

5 A Portable Beach

A decisive difference between maritime surfing and dry-land skateboarding becomes manifest in the role of the body, which is crucial for both activities: While the body in surfing literally enters a flow of energy in form of the aquatic wave, in skateboarding the energy is brought to a static place by the body itself. The skateboarder, via the skateboard, introduces movement to an otherwise *striated space*, e. g. the concrete driveway of a suburban mansion, and thus operates precisely along the notion of a *production* of *smooth space*, i. e. the bodily initiated development of smoothness. While actual water-bound surfing is dependent on the topology of the beach, as the beach constitutes the highly site-specific environment where water meets land and oceanic waves break,[5] the sidewalk surfer – i. e. the skateboarder – basically turns the locale of the beach into a mobile and even portable feature that can be resurrected almost everywhere: at every driveway, every street, every sidewalk, and every pavement. Borden very aptly summarizes this phenomenon by providing a highly significant and suggestive title for his influential essay on skateboarding as a performative critique of architecture: "Another Pavement, Another Beach" (Borden 2018, 246 ff.). This caption does not only directly associate the built environment of streets and sidewalks with the potentialities of the beach but, of course, also references the 1968 revolts in Paris and the urban tactics of the Situationist International as they popularized a very similar, oftentimes spray-painted

---

[4] Of course, nowadays, skateboarding is much more 'emancipated' from its wave-bound influences and includes a whole variety of tricks and maneuvers that surpass the early surfing-style by far. However, the basic parallel, i. e. the (floating) movement of a body on a board, remains. The evolution of skateboarding beyond surfing actually supports a reading of the phenomenon as a continuation of a line of flight that brings forth "entirely different movements," "confronts new obstacles," and "invents new paces" (Deleuze and Guattari 2005, 524, 551).

[5] Waves that can be surfed may also break further away from the beach when they hit reefs in open water, however, beach breaks constitute the most common, usually easier accessible, and thus more frequented spots for surfing.

slogan: "Beneath the pavement, the beach" (see Wark 2011, 149–150; Borden 2018, 263).

In her comprehensive study of the Situationist International titled *The Beach Beneath the Street*, McKenzie Wark follows the beach references of the Situationists and concludes that the projects of the involved artists, activists, and authors did not end in May 1968 but still reverberate in the present: "Wherever the boredom with given forms of art, politics, thought, everyday life jackhammers through the carapace of mindless form," she proclaims, "the beach emerges" (Wark 2011, 159). The interconnections between paved surface and sandy underground, i. e. the pavement and the beach, that the Situationists established through their famous aphorism do hardly find a more nuanced and practically applied fulfillment than in skateboarding. While Wark, shaping her argument in the vein of Situationism, still requires a metaphorical jackhammer to dig through to the beach underlying the boring forms of everyday life, skateboarders directly carve it out of the built environment and eagerly start to ride the concrete waves they produce on its surfaces. They practically implement the potential that the 1968 protesters sensed in the beach beneath the street by simply turning around the most essential prerequisite of the water-bound beachside activity of surfing: While surfers are dependent on breaking waves and therefore still have to go to the actual beach to perform their practice, skateboarders literally carry the beach with them: to the suburbs and to the cities. Their skateboard constitutes a device that can be brought anywhere into the urban and suburban landscape where it confronts the concrete striations of streets, sidewalks, parking lots, paved surfaces, and buildings with physical mobility and therefore "gives rise to smooth spaces" (Deleuze and Guattari 2005, 551). As opposed to the beach *beneath* the street it gives rise to the beach *on* the street.

6 Conclusion

My initial question concerning skateboarding's intervention in a specific suburban environment can be answered by a concentration on the floating and liquefying potentialities it transfers to the striations of this spatial setting (and beyond). Although the suburban locale ostensibly appears to embody the direct opposite of a free, unrestricted, and mobile space, skateboarding offers an alternative that does not circumvent the fixating striations by the mere implementation of an *escape* but by an active production of a momentary *seascape*. While Fiske reads surfing in the ocean as a brief yet effective escape from restrictive environments and discourses, in skateboarding no exodus is necessary: Instead of abandoning the bleak concrete environments they are faced with in their everyday lives, instead of setting sails to look for a better place beyond the horizon, skateboarders stay put and produce liberating and mobilizing alternatives *on the spot*. Prolonging a line of flight that the riding of oceanic waves set into motion with the activity of surfing, skateboarders, through the movement of their bodies and their boards, seize the opportunity to unhinge the rigid points of their surroundings and subordinate them to free floating trajectories of movement.

Author and skateboarder Anthony Pappalardo, in the book *Live...Suburbia*, a publication on suburban youth culture, exemplifies to what extent this potential can function in the most remote regions. From his first experiences of skateboarding he remembers that when "my [...] wheels hit the rough pavement of Salem, New Hampshire, I was telepathically transported to Venice Beach" (Pappalardo 2011, 79). With the movement of his skateboard, so it seems, Pappalardo departs on a maritime voyage. Right at his feet, under the rolling, moving, and floating skateboard, he senses – and I would add: he (re-)produces – the Californian coast and the roaring surf of its beaches. In the scope of this essay, I would re-read Pappalardo's experience and claim that as much as he felt *telepathically* transported to Venice Beach, one could also argue the other way around and conclude that he *physically* transported Venice Beach, i. e. the California beachside, to the streets of New Hampshire and thus: to his feet. For a brief moment, while surfing the sidewalk of his suburban neighborhood, he encounters the whole potentiality of unrestricted mobility that the *smooth space* of the Pacific Ocean promises. With his skateboard, he generates a mobile moment in the limited and dull environment of suburbia by creating what I would like to label a momentary beach or, more precisely, an *ephemeral beachscape*.

Bibliography

Borden, Iain. *Skateboarding, Space and the City: Architecture and the Body*. Oxford: Berg, 2005.

Borden, Iain. "Another Pavement, Another Beach: Skateboarding and the Performative Critique of Architecture." *Skateboard Studies*. Eds. Konstantin Butz and Christian Peters, 2018. 246–266.

Brooke, Michael. *The Concrete Wave: The History of Skateboarding*. Toronto: Warwick Publishing Inc., 2005.

Butz, Konstantin. *Grinding California: Culture and Corporeality in American Skate Punk*. Bielefeld: transcript, 2012.

Deleuze, Gilles. "Mediators." *Incorporations*. Eds. Jonathan Crary and Sanford Kwinter. New York: Zone Books, 1992. 281–294.

Deleuze, Gilles and Félix Guattari. *A Thousand Plateaus*. London: Continuum, 2004.

Fiske, John. *Reading the Popular*. London: Routledge, 1990. Digitalization by Taylor & Francis e-Library, 2005.

Hansen, Debra Gold, and Mary P. Ryan. "Public Ceremony in a Private Culture: Orange County Celebrates the Fourth of July." *Postsuburban California*. Eds. Rob Kling, Spencer Olin and Mark Poster. Berkeley: University of California Press, 1991. 165–189.

Jan & Dean. *Sidewalk Surfin'*. 7" Single. 1964.

Kling, Rob, Spencer Olin and Mark Poster. "Beyond the Edge: The Dynamism of Postsuburban Regions." *Postsuburban California*. Eds. Rob Kling, Spencer Olin and Mark Poster. Berkeley: University of California Press, 1991. vii–xx.

Lewis, Jeff. "In Search of the Postmodern Surfer: Territory, Terror and Masculinity." *Some Like It Hot: The Beach as a Cultural Dimension*. Eds. James Skinner, Keith Gilbert and Allan Edwards. Oxford: Meyer & Meyer Sport, 2003. 58–76.

Pappalardo, Anthony. "The Ramp Locals." *Live... Suburbia!* Eds. Anthony Pappalardo and Max G. Morton. Brooklyn/NY: powerHouse Books, 2011. 79.

Sobin, Dennis P. *The Future of the American Suburbs*. Port Washington/NY: Kennikat Press, 1971.

Wark, McKenzie. *The Beach Beneath the Street: The Everyday Life and Glorious Times of the Situationist International*. London and Brooklyn/NY: Verso, 2011.

Weyland, Jocko. *The Answer is Never: A Skateboarder's History of the World*. London: Century, 2002.

Yochim, Emily Chivers, *Skate Life: Re-Imagining White Masculinity*. Ann Arbor/MI: University of Michigan Press, 2010.

Zarka, Raphaël. *On a Day with No Waves: A Chronicle of Skateboarding 1779–2009*. Paris: Édition B42, 2011.

Sebastian Haselbeck
Beached. The Awkward Beginnings of Weimar Democracy

This essay traces the political dimension of the beach and the curious afterlife of a notorious beach photograph in the political imaginary of the Weimar Republic, focusing on elements of emergence, collage, and circulation that connect sea, sand, and mass leisure to political and aesthetic dimensions of representational practice in the period. The picture of President Friedrich Ebert and Gustav Noske, Minister of Defense, in bathing trunks wading in the Baltic Sea dominated the newspaper headlines just around the time of the new government's inaugural ceremony in Weimar. This image seems to have encapsulated a certain aesthetic discomfort with the new form of democratic governance, and registered a deep-rooted fear of the disintegration of social and political order. The site of the beach may thus be understood not just as a background for the emerging democratic Republic, but rather as cypher of tensions in Weimar Germany between new and old political orders.

Ein einzelnes Foto sucht die politische Einbildungskraft der Weimarer Republik heim: Das Bild zeigt Reichspräsident Ebert und Kriegsminister Noske ungelenk in Badehosen an einem Ostseestrand. Das ästhetische Unbehagen gegenüber der neuen Staatsform, die Angst vor der Nivellierung alter Ordnungen in einer demokratischen Gesellschaft verdichten sich scheinbar in diesem Strandbild aus dem Jahr 1919. Der Strand bildet dabei nicht nur den demokratisierenden Hintergrund, er wird vielmehr in den folgenden Reaktionen auf die Fotografie zum Schauplatz einer Auseinandersetzung über das Wesen demokratischer Repräsentation und zu einem Ort, der wie kaum ein anderer in den Jahren der Weimarer Republik den scharfen Kontrast zwischen der alten und der neuen politischen Ordnung zur Anschauung bringt. Dieser Aufsatz verfolgt die politische Dimension und Funktionalisierung des Strandes und das schicksalhafte Nachleben des Strandfotos im politisch Imaginären der Weimarer Republik.

1 A Photograph

The inauguration of the first democratically elected German government was haunted by a beach photograph. A picture of President Friedrich Ebert and Gustav Noske, Minister of Defense, in bathing trunks wading in the shallow waters of the Baltic Sea dominated the newspaper headlines just a few days after the new government's inaugural ceremony in Weimar: "Ebert und Noske in der Sommerfrische" [Ebert and Noske during the summer holidays] read the mocking subtitle to the photograph that graced the front page of the *Berliner Illustrirte* [sic] *Zeitung* (*BIZ*) on 24 August 1919, Germany's illustrated newspaper

https://doi.org/10.1515/9783110672244-020

with the greatest circulation at the time.[1] Although the picture was published after the inauguration ceremony at the Weimar Nationaltheater, the issue of the weekly paper had already been circulated on the day of the inauguration, presumably in order to deal a perfect blow to the legitimacy of the new democratic government by undermining what might be called its aesthetic authority. As if watching from the beach, the beholder could recognize the newly elected politicians semi-naked, wading through the knee-high water, somehow awkward in their nakedness, but in no way intimidated or surprised by the presence of a camera. Between the two politicians, the head of an anonymous person[2] emerges from the water, his hair covered in seaweed holding up a fork imitating Poseidon's trident. This half-hearted mythological allusion adds a certain self-awareness or sense of self-deprecation to the picture, which might otherwise not have been taken for granted. The "Sommerfrische" of the title plays on the summer vacation, from which the reading public and the unassuming politicians would have returned, in August, as well as on the political hiatus after the subdued revolutionary uprisings and the elections in February of that same year.

The original photograph taken at the Seebad Haffkrug in the bay of Lübeck by the local photographer Wilhelm Steffen showed more than just the two heads of state: a group of well-known Social Democrats visiting the resort in mid-May can be seen along with two *Badewagen* or *Strandkarren* [bathing machines] in the background.[3] The beach where the picture was taken is also visible, at least in part as a sandy patch in the upper left-hand corner. The picture in its 'original' version – only slightly cropped around the edges – had actually already been published before the scandal erupted by the anti-democratic *Deutsche Zeitung* on 9 August 1919, without causing much excitement. Its subtitle on the front page of the *Deutsche Zeitung* betrayed similar intentions to those of the *BIZ*, it read "Die Repräsentanten des *Neuen* Deutschland" [The Representatives of the *New* Germany] (*Deutsche Zeitung*, 9 August 1919, 1). The political agenda seems even more obvious in the short text that follows, which ridicules the politicians with unconcealed glee (ibid.). Nevertheless, only the cropped version of the *Berliner Illustrirte Zeitung* would create the outrage that would

---

[1] A very detailed account of this famous press scandal and its aftermath can be found in Albrecht (2002). On the importance of political imagery in the Weimar Republic as a modern "Bildgesellschaft," see Mergel (2007). Mergel (2007, 531) claims that the *Badebild* was a solitary incident that quickly lost its importance, but the long list of images that reference the *Badebild* – well into the early 1930s – would suggest otherwise.

[2] He is usually identified as Josef Rieger, a Social Democrat from Hamburg.

[3] For a short history on where the photograph was actually taken and how it found its way to the editors of the Berlin newspaper, see Koszyk (1988, 88–95).

reverberate throughout the early years of the new republic.⁴ Which begs the question, what exactly lay at the root of this indignation?

Fig. 1: The title page of the *BIZ* with the clipped image.

---

4 A small exhibition of the Friedrich-Ebert-Gedenkstätte traced the afterlife of the photograph in Weimar Germany caricatures, as documented in the catalogue Sonnabend and Mühlhausen (2010). Ebert would go on to accuse many of the newspapers, magazines, and caricaturists of defamation and even sue a number of them, including the photographer Wilhelm Steffen and the *Deutsche Zeitung*, for libel. For a detailed account, see Albrecht (2002).

What the cropping of the image did was to transform the panoramic beach photograph into an enlarged almost vignette-like image of Ebert and Noske enclosed by water. Without any sign of the beach or other bathers around them, only the Poseidon-parody cowering between them, they are given the unfavorable appearance of two small beached whales who, having wandered into the shallows, found themselves stranded. Moreover, by turning the horizontal panorama of the original into a vertical plane, the clipped image zooms in on the politicians' bellies which seem to become the *pars pro toto* of a new body politic[5], slightly ridiculous and seemingly helpless: an image that would come to mark what Hannah Höch and other Dadaists would call the 'Weimarer Bierbauchkulturepoche' [Weimar Beer Belly Cultural Epoch].

Fig. 2: The original photograph.

The suggestive helplessness of the photograph's protagonists is exacerbated by the fact that we do not see Ebert's and Noske's hands. The very posture of carefully wading through the water while clasping their hands behind their backs, leaves them bereft of agency; with no means of extracting themselves out of the watery shallows either by their hands or submerged feet, they appear stuck, apparently unable to move either forward or backward.[6] Postcards were circulated in the weeks after the image's publication that juxtaposed the half-naked

---

5 For further exploration of this synecdochical figuration, see Doherty (1998).
6 See the entry on "Hand" in the *Handbuch der politischen Ikonographie* (Springer 2011).

democrats with their aristocratic counterparts of the *ancient regime*, which had so quickly disintegrated with the end of the Great War, the Kaiser and his Field Marshall von Hindenburg, dressed in uniform. The satirical magazine *Satyr* would go on accordingly to rhyme: "Ordenlos, nur nacktes Fell, ohne Hofzeremoniell."[7] The juxtaposition helped to materialize the aesthetic discontent or discomfort with the new form of polity, at the sight of the protruding belly of their newly elected president and his leptosomatic minister of Defense. The dignified head of the abdicated emperor appears in sharp contrast to the stomach of the new president.

In this essay, I argue that the notorious beach image can be read as a cypher of tensions in Weimar Germany between new and old political orders. The beach allowed for new forms of political figuration and representation, whose awkwardness may be understood in tandem with unease over the political form of democracy itself. The image becomes an unassuming Weimar pendant to Hans Christian Andersen's fairy tale about *The Emperor's New Clothes* (Frank, Koschorke, Lüdemann, and Matala de Mazza 2002): It reveals more about Germany's political imaginary than many of its heated political debates. Here, the beach not only functions as the background to this scenography of democratic representation, it gives form to a new idea of representation that allows for an inversion of traditional models of political order and authority. The political promise of democratic equality, which is encapsulated in the rather ordinary snapshot, is then realized, I shall suggest, in Hannah Höch's collage *Staatshäupter* [Heads of State] from 1920, which makes use of the newspaper clipping by reintegrating Ebert and Noske into a very different beach setting.

2 "Peinliche Pause." Ungraceful Beginnings

On Thursday evening, 21 August 1919, Harry Graf Kessler, one of the most attentive diarists of the period, would write down the following observations in his diary, after attending the new government's inaugural ceremony in Weimar during the day:

> Nachmittags um 5 Vereidigung Eberts in der Nationalversammlung. Die Bühne war festlich geschmückt mit den neuen Reichsfarben, Blattpflanzen und Blumen, Gladiolen und Chrysanthemen, unter denen ein Theaterteppich, offenbar der Moosboden aus dem

---

[7] The poem, from which the line is taken, was written by the editor of the magazine Alexis Schleimer (1919, 1). The line translates roughly as "No medals, just naked skin, without ceremonial form."

Sommernachtstraum, ausgebreitet war. Die Orgel spielte und Alles drängte sich im schwarzen Rock zwischen den Blattpflanzen wie bei einer besseren Hochzeit. Das Haus war dicht besetzt bis auf die Deutsch-Nationalen und Unabhängigen Bänke, die ostentativ leer blieben. Einige Sekretäre und Stenographen verteilten sich als Statisten auf die Plätze der Deutschnationalen. Ebert im schwarzen Bratenrock, klein und breitschulterig mit einer goldenen Brille kam nach einem Orgelvorspiel auf die Bühne vor, gefolgt vom hinkenden Reichskanzler Bauer und den Reichsministerien, die alle ebenfalls sehr feierlich schwarz waren. Ullsteins Berliner Illustrierte hatte es passend gefunden, gerade heute das Bild von Ebert u Noske in Badehosen zu bringen; Ebert wie der Wassermann aus der "Versunkenen Glocke." Das Bild schwebt bei der feierlichen Handlung über den Bratenröcken in der Luft. Als Ebert den Eid leisten soll, fehlt das Manuscript. Es muss erst gesucht werden. Peinliche Pause, da die Orgel aufgehört hat zu spielen. Fehrenbach wird nervös. Schließlich kommt jemand mit dem Blatt durch die Bratenröcke nach vorne gedrängt. Ebert spricht den Eid mit einer ganz sympathischen, hellen Stimme. Fehrenbach begrüßt ihn. Ebert redet. Alles sehr anständig, aber schwunglos, wie bei einer Konfirmation in einem gutbürgerlichen Hause. Die Republik sollte Zeremonien aus dem Wege gehen; diese Staatsform eignet sich nicht dazu. Es ist wie wenn eine Gouvernante Ballett tanzt. Trotzdem hatte das ganze etwas Rührendes und vor allem Tragisches. Dieses kleinbürgerliche Theater als Abschluss des gewaltigsten Krieges und der Revolution![8] (Kessler 2007, 265)

In Kessler's eye-witness account the image from the beach follows the political protagonists wherever they go. It cannot be separated from them and from the

---

[8] Translations from German provided in footnotes and square brackets are mine. "5 p. m. Ebert's inauguration at the Weimar National Assembly. The stage was festively decorated with the new colors of the German Reich and with plants and flowers, gladioli and chrysanthemums under which a theater carpet, which had obviously served as the mossy turf of *Midsummer Night's Dream* had been laid out. The organ played and all the people dressed in frock coats made their way through the potted plants like guests at a better-class wedding. The house was tightly packed save for the seats that were reserved for the Nationalists and the Independent Socialists, which remained ostentatiously empty. A number of secretaries and stenotypists took the seats of the Nationalists as extras. Ebert, small and broad-shouldered, with gold-rimmed spectacles, appeared on the stage after an organ prelude, followed by the hobbling Chancellor Bauer and the remaining cabinet, all dressed likewise in solemn black. Ullstein's *Berliner Illustrirte [BIZ]* saw fit to publish today, out of all days, the photograph of Ebert a[nd] Noske in bathing trunks: Ebert like the Water Spirit in the *The Sunken Bell*. The picture hovered in the air above the frock coats during the solemn ceremony. When Ebert was supposed to take the oath, the text was nowhere to be found. A search ensued, which created an awkward pause, as the organ stopped playing. Fehrenbach [German politician, first President of the National Assembly] starts to get nervous. Finally, someone pushes his way through the frock coats with the page in hand. Ebert speaks the oath with a clear and agreeable voice. Fehrenbach welcomes him. Ebert talks. Everything appears very respectable, but it lacks drive, like a Protestant confirmation in a bourgeois household. The Republic should avoid any ceremonial forms; this form of polity is not suited for it. It is as if a governess would give a ballet performance. Still it is somehow moving, yet even more tragic. Such a petits bourgeois drama at the end of such a horrendous war and as the conclusion to the revolution."

new form of polity, which it has come to represent; it hovers over every public appearance, no matter how remote the occasion might seem. Kessler's account veers between mild contempt and affectionate derision. His paratactic style and his use of the historical present enhances the clash of two, in his eyes, irreconcilable things: democracy and ceremonial form. Democracy appears, according to Kessler, as downright unaesthetic. It lacks appropriateness, propriety, grace, and the necessary grandeur and gravitas. The petty-bourgeois mediocrity of the maritime scene prevents any notion of historical greatness from taking hold of Kessler's aristocratic imagination. He, therefore, focuses on the theatricality of the ceremony itself and its unintended interruptions and gaffes: Ebert and the new government's appearance on the political stage is ruined because it lacks timing and tactfulness. In Kessler's view, it even acquires a tragic quality, which seems to stem from its anti-triumphalist appearance and sheer ordinariness in stark contrast to the unimaginable violence of the war and desperation of the revolution.[9] Two literary intertexts, *A Midsummer Night's Dream* and Gerhart Hauptmann's, at the time popular drama, *Die versunkene Glocke* [*The Sunken Bell*], help to reinforce the image of Germany's new political protagonists as hapless actors on a public stage. The "Theaterteppich" [theater carpet], as a second-hand prop, on which the politicians are sworn in is incidentally the same ground on which Shakespeare's half-assed-fool Bottom and his group of amateur actors are trying to practice their parts, a place where opposites coalesce, social order is inverted, and where reason gets twisted if only for one long night. Ebert squeezed in his frock coat reminds Kessler of the figure of the Wassermann in Hauptmann's "Deutschem Märchendrama" [German fairy drama], whom the play from 1896 introduced as "ein Wassergreis, Schilf im Haar, triefend von Nässe, lang ausschnaufend wie ein Seehund. Er zwinkert mit den Augen, bis er sich an das Tageslicht gewöhnt hat"[10] (Hauptmann 1897, 4). The two theatrical scenes and the image are connected not only by tropes of awakening and transitions from dark to light, their protagonists' lack of material weight seems to comically inhibit a political *Standhaftigkeit* [steadfastness] reiterated through ceremonial ritual.

The social-democratic daily *Vorwärts* was similarly reserved when describing the inauguration ceremony to its readers the next day:

---

9 Juliane Vogel has demonstrated how this anti-triumphalist entrance or appearance on stage ("anti-triumphaler Auftritt") can often be understood as a generative moment of modern tragedies (Vogel 2018, 26–27).
10 "a water-spirit emerges, weeds clinging to his head, streaming with water, he snorts like a seal. He blinks with his eyes, adjusting to the daylight."

> Der Reichspräsident hat gestern den vorgeschriebenen Eid auf die Verfassung geleistet. Es war eine einfache, aber doch feierliche Veranstaltung. Die Republik sucht noch tastend nach ihren äußeren Formen, die keinen Pomp und Prunk vertragen. Sie appelliert nicht an die Sinne und den Instinkt, sondern an den Verstand und die tieferen sittlichen Kräfte, kann aber eine stärkere Heraushebung und Unterstreichung der wichtigeren Augenblicke ihres jungen Daseins nicht entbehren. Wer mit dem Herzen an den großen Spielen hängt, die das Kaiserreich dem schaulustigen Volk zu geben liebte, wird die Feier von Weimar arm finden. Wer jeder überkommenen äußeren Form abhold ist, wird meinen, die Anleihe aus den Mitteln des alten Systems sei immer noch zu groß gewesen. Gleichwohl war es richtig, etwas Klang und Farbe in diesen Tag zu bringen, um zu zeigen, dass er kein Alltag war.[11] (*Vorwärts*, 22 August 1919, 1)

With palpable restraint, the article's author manages to address the aesthetic incongruity of the scene, which Kessler's diary makes explicit, without being too critical of its protagonists. For the editors of *Vorwärts* everything that appeals to the senses must have a destabilizing, if not harmful, effect on a form of polity that calls on reason and morality. By implication, monarchies are, thus, characterized as appealing to instincts and the sensual. Still, the author sees an apparent need for an aesthetic experience that would present the political event as something *extra*ordinary. The scandal of the beach photograph would only find an echo in *Vorwärts* a week later on 29 August under the headline "Grobe Geschmacklosigkeit" [Gross Tastelessness]. To calm the nerves of its readers, the short note on page three claims that the picture was not intended for the public, that it was taken out of its intimate and private context by the corrupt "bürgerliche Presse" [bourgeois press] (*Vorwärts*, 29 August 1919, 3), with the intention of harming the reputation of the depicted politicians and that of the Social Democratic Party at large.

All the images that Kessler's text conjures out of the mis-timed inauguration ceremony, from the allusions to Shakespeare and Hauptmann, to an upper-crust wedding or a confirmation, to a petty bourgeois drama, lead back to the beach photograph and to two half-naked politicians wading at the seashore. They all share the same sense of incongruity and inappropriateness. The beach

---

[11] "Yesterday, the President swore an oath on the constitution as provided by law. It was a simple yet solemn event. The Republic is still looking tentatively for the appropriate form of appearance, which does not allow for pomp or the display of splendor. The form of democracy does not address the senses, it addresses reason and the deeper moral forces. But it somehow seems necessary for this still very young form of polity to emphasize the important moments and events. The person who clings to the past splendor of the *Kaiserreich*, will find the Weimar inauguration ceremony lacking. While the person who abhors rituals and ceremonies of any kind, will still find that there are too many elements adopted from the old regime. Be that as it may, it was certainly the right decision, to add some color to this day, to make clear that this was not an ordinary day."

photograph confronted the reading public not with a voyeuristic glimpse behind the scenes and into the machinations of political power, but with a strangely private view of the new representatives of state sovereignty.

At the time, there would have been no better place than a public beach to visualize this conflict between the political and the private body of a democratically elected representative. Beaches were more intimate places than a bus or tram car, people encountered each other in a state of increasing undress, which made maintaining 'cool conduct' difficult. Around 1900 the public beach was evolving as a place of heightened 'intimate anonymity' (Geisthövel 2005, 127; also see Edgerton 1979); increasingly, it was seen both as a space of erotic projection and as a source of vitality, where children and ailing adults alike would be sent to regain or retain their health (Edgerton 1979, 1–10). Public beaches had become "pleasure grounds" and reservoirs of health for a mass public (see Cross and Walton 2005, 11–58), strangely ambivalent in the way in which they confronted a mass public with the private lives (and unclothed bodies) of the individuals constituting the mass: private citizens appeared in public for everyone to see in a decidedly intimate setting. At least in Hannah Arendt's seminal understanding (Arendt 1998 [1958]), beaches could not be considered public spaces in a political sense; they ought rather to be seen as belonging to the social realm of mass society that does not allow for actual political discourse to take place. But the very awkwardness of the beach photograph and the reactions in the press seem to point to the beach's uniquely public and surprisingly political significance in Weimar Germany. They seem to point at a deep-felt discomfort with democracy as a form of appearance. This discomfort with democracy's aesthetic form becomes, in the image, associated with the beach – or at least to how this aesthetic is perceived to be staged at the beach. It might be difficult to tell though whether democracy's aesthetic form *appears* awkward in the photograph at the beach, or whether the photograph records an inherent awkwardness. Arendt's distinction between the public and the private realm centers on the necessity for some human activities to remain hidden and others "to be displayed publicly if they are to exist at all" (ibid., 73). For Arendt, there is a certain natural progression in this, as "each human activity points to its proper location in the world" (ibid.). Shame and honor are associated with the private and the public realm respectively. The *skandalon* of the beach photograph seems to consist in something that is considered shameful, showing yourself in a state of undress in public, crossing over into the political sphere by entering the public realm. A new form of 'democratic nakedness' is staged on the beach.

3 Assembling the Social. The Political Dimension of the Beach

> Part of the problem of discovery of a public capable of organization into a state is that of drawing lines between the too close and intimate and the too remote and disconnected. (Dewey 1927, 39)

The war had left many of the German *Strandbäder* financially depleted although they appeared outwardly untouched by the war, compared to the parts of Germany that had suffered from severe food shortages or revolutionary conflicts in the aftermath of the military defeat. The number of visitors that came to resorts had dwindled and it would take a few years until the numbers returned to pre-war levels.[12] The *Badekarren* [bathing machine] (Prignitz 1977, 97), an invention of the nineteenth century, two of which can be seen in the background of the image, had already acquired the status of a beach relic. As a "Strandrequisit des kühlen Nordens" [beach prop of the cold North] they were not longer in demand (ibid.), but they could still be found in some beach resorts. These clunky vehicles shielded the bathers from cold winds as well as the gaze of others since one could roll in the *Badekarren* to the water's edge and disembark without having to walk across the beach. They, therefore, worked towards preserving privacy in the public realm in the name of decorum and dignity.

The group of politicians in the photograph seems to have made use of the two *Badekarren*, but they are not dressed according to the beach etiquette of the time; at least they would not have been allowed in one of the so-called *Familienbäder* introduced around the turn of century, which welcomed all classes, sexes, and children, given they were dressed in appropriate bathing suits.[13] Those bathing suits, *Badeanzüge*, covered most parts of the body ("bis zum Halse schließen") and were made from fabrics that were neither "hell, durchsichtig oder durchbrochen" [bright, see-through, or openwork].[14] Soon these old-fashioned suits were replaced by the *Trikots*, which came quite close to today's bathing attire. These newly established inclusive, but regulated, public bathing beaches were imagined as chaste places that would repel any kind of

---

[12] On the history of the *Badekarren*, see the chapter about them in Prignitz (1977).
[13] These family bathing resorts were first introduced in 1901 (Timm 2000, 55–65).
[14] Cited in Timm (2000, 56). Timm concludes his chapter about the *Familienbäder* with Ringelnatz' poem, which is also cited here.

"sinnliche Reizung" [sensuous stimulus].[15] "Und im Familienbade," as Joachim Ringelnatz's "Enttäuschter Badegast" [Disappointed Bather] states in a poem of the same name, "Geht die Erotik fort. Wohin / Weiß Gott. Wie Schade."[16] In the reactions to the photograph of Ebert and Noske, however, the question of whether democratically elected representatives should be erotically appealing or not seems to have infected the political imagination of their contemporaries. The politicians in the photograph are clearly wearing undergarments, still typical attire for all-male beaches at the time, but not considered appropriate in the mixed *Familienbäder*. Like the parliament prior to 1919, when women entered as elected representatives,[17] the beach had generally appeared as an exclusively male space during and oftentimes before the war. If one leafs through the pages of the *BIZ* of the previous (war) years, one finds only beach photographs featuring German soldiers frolicking in the waves of European beaches. The image of Ebert and Noske calls to mind, though it is never mentioned explicitly in any of the reactions, both the loss of this male beach community at the front and the loss of Germany's colonial beaches.[18] Images of beaches may well, therefore, have reminded the reading public in 1919 of both this loss and the necessity to find new ways of "organizing" a public into a state. For the "Republik ohne Gebrauchsanweisung" [Republic without instructions or directions] (Döblin 1972 [1921], 100) the need to find suitable forms of representation became increasingly urgent. The beach seems to have been one of the places – to represent the new form of polity – that suggested itself to a new, emerging democratic public. The transitory space between land and sea has been ascribed with a variety of attributes, as this volume gives ample evidence of, and proclaimed to be either a *tabula rasa* or a protean place of metamorphosis. Alain Corbin and others have described the ascent of the public beach in terms of a democratization process (Corbin 1994, 277–278). Cultural historians have pointed out that beaches played a decisive role in the democratizing of recreational spaces and vacations in general. Some have gone so far as to speak of nineteenth century beaches as

---

15 Until the mid-twenties the strict pre-war dress codes of the *Familienbäder* remained in place. Most beach resorts did not allow its visitors to undress outside of a *Strandkorb*, *Badekarren* or *Strandkabine* (Timm 2000, 73). Gradually, it became more important to be seen at the beach and to present oneself to others. This tendency is best captured by looking at the changing *Bademoden* of the time.
16 The poem was first published in Ringelnatz (1929, 130). The line translates roughly as "In the family bathing resort, eroticism disappears, whereto, God knows where. What a pity."
17 The first elected female parliamentarians joined the German parliament in February 1919. The Social democrat Marie Juchacz would be the first woman to address the Reichstag on February 19, 1919.
18 For a closer look at the strong hold that the imperial imaginary had on German society, see Eley 2014.

"classless spaces."[19] Even with a dose of skepticism towards this narrative, the simple fact that more and more people were actually able to visit the beaches marks a historical shift in the history of the beach as a public place.

This historical shift transformed the beaches of Weimar Germany into spaces where the plurality of the population could be seen and observed, and into spaces where, in Hannah Arendt's words, given favorable weather conditions, "everything that appears in public can be seen and heard by everybody and has the widest possible publicity" (Arendt 1998 [1958], 50). New or improved railway connections to the beach resorts and longer holidays meant that more and more people were able to visit the beaches of the German Reich (Prignitz 1977, 127–134).[20] Beaches were democratic 'contact zones,'[21] the only places where the body or bodies of the purported new 'sovereign' (i. e. the people, both singular and plural), the subject of the *pouvoir constituant* could be seen exposed and at least to certain extent equal in their state of leisurely undress. The promise or the possibility of equality could, one might argue, thus be best embodied *and* envisioned on the beaches of Weimar Germany. This form of assembling the social on the beaches went beyond the simple freedom of assembly, guaranteed by the Weimar constitution (*Die Verfassung des Deutschen Reiches* 1919, Artikel 123, 1406). It was not exercised under the right protected by state power[22], it was a form of assembly exercised mostly unrestricted by state power and executive authority. In response to the demilitarization of German society, the beach appeared as a site of peace and simple pleasures. Haffkrug, the beach resort, where the picture of Ebert and Noske was taken, was described by contemporary guide-books as a small and uneventful place, conveniently located, "gegen die Nordwinde geschützt" [protected against the north winds]:

---

[19] James Freeman questions this frequently found assumption in his ethnographic field study on the beaches of Rio de Janeiro (Freeman 2002).

[20] Until 1910, the percentage of workers who were entitled to take paid recreational leave was just about ten percent, compared to 85 percent in 1920: "Bis 1910 hatten etwa zehn Prozent der Arbeiter einen Anspruch auf Erholungsurlaub erkämpft, doch zählten zu den Besuchern vor dem ersten Weltkrieg ausschließlich wohlhabende Gäste" (Prignitz 1977, 131). This situation changes drastically during the years of the Weimar Republic: "Es gelang der großen Masse der arbeitenden Bevölkerung, ihre Forderung nach Urlaub durchzusetzen. Im Jahr 1920 hatten 85 Prozent der Arbeiter und 1929 97,8 Prozent einen tariflich festgelegten Erholungsurlaub" (ibid., 134). 97,8 percent were entitled by collective agreement to take paid holidays in 1929.

[21] The term, referring to intercultural zones of contact and spaces of hybridity, was introduced into academic discourse by Mary Louise Pratt (1992).

[22] Judith Butler draws attention to the slightly paradoxical notion of the right to assembly, that is granted by modern constitutions, since it is meant to be protected from "governmental interference" by the government (Butler 2015, 158).

> Der Badestrand ist schmal, zum Teil mit Kieseln bedeckt (starke Seetang-Anschwemmungen nicht selten), der Badegrund feinsandig und sanft abfallend, der Wellenschlag nur mäßig. Das Badeleben ist ruhig, doch fehlt es nicht an Geselligkeit. Besondere Unterhaltungen gibt es nicht, man macht Boot- und Wagenpartien oder jagt und fischt auf den Binnenseen.[23] (as cited in *Ostseebäder und Städte der Ostseeküste* 1910, 263)

War-weariness and a strong rejection of the militaristic and authoritarian regime of the *Kaiserreich* enhanced the image of the beach as a modern-day *locus amoenus*. Foreign visitors would famously speak of the sun as "a social force" in Weimar Germany (Spender 1951, 109) and muse about the new German *Körperkultur* or *Körperkult* displayed on the shores.[24]

> Thousands of people went to the open-air swimming baths or lay down on the shores [...]. The sun healed their bodies of the years of war, and made them conscious of the quivering and fluttering life of blood and muscles covering their exhausted spirits like a pelt of an animal [...]. (Ibid.)

In the aftermath of the first 'industrial war' that shattered not just the expectations of traditional warfare but killed and impaired millions of soldiers, beaches attained a redeeming yet somehow ambiguous quality: On the one hand they provided a space to aestheticize the unscathed, sun-tanned, and lively bodies of young beach-goers, while on the other they exposed the maimed and debilitated bodies of the soldiers returning from the battlefields. Beaches assembled the social in its plurality and created a form of visibility characterized by uncompromising directness and openness, while simultaneously revealing the internalized, normative expectations and restrictions against which this democratic society presented itself.[25]

---

[23] "The bathing beach is narrow, covered in parts with pebbles (at times there is a lot of washed-up kelp). The beach has fine grained sand with a gentle slope and the waves are not too strong. Life at the beach resort is quiet, but there are opportunities to enjoy the company of others, though no special entertainment is offered, except for trips by boat or carriage and hunting or fishing excursions in the nearby lakes."

[24] This well-known passage from Stephen Spender's autobiography has been cited frequently. Even though Spender refers to a later period of the Weimar Republic, the late 1920s and early 1930s, the general observation seems to hold true also for the earlier period directly after the war.

[25] The interactions and social expectations are of course far more complicated than these insinuations suggest. Erving Goffman's famous study about *Behaviour in Public Places* makes multiple references to the beach as a public place and its specific mix of informal behavior and self-involved actions (Goffman 1966, 67, 201). A sequence from Robert Sidomak's and Edgar G. Ulmer's documentary or essay film *Menschen am Sonntag* (1930) at the *Strandbad* Wannsee, which juxtaposes mass scenes with anonymous portraits of bathers taken by a beach photographer, exemplifies this dynamic.

Beaches in Germany were not private property in most cases. Since the property laws of the new republic showed a strong interest in protecting the rights of the community, the access to lakes, rivers, and the sea was usually granted to everyone.[26] Individual property owners were reminded of their social obligation and were expected to use the land accordingly, enabling access to the shore. But the democratic promise of the beach photograph of Ebert and Noske would inevitably also be linked to the promises not kept and to the violence perpetrated under the new government's name: the murder of Karl Liebknecht and Rosa Luxemburg by *Freikorps* soldiers and the violent end of the revolution had a lasting effect on the image of the new government, a government, which according to some historians, missed its chance to create a powerful founding myth (Peukert 1987, 15). The *Badebild* could not have helped to repair an already tarnished public image. Instead, caricatures like George Grosz' "Nach Hamburg und Sachsen" helped to remove any remaining shred of dignity from the image. Published in the magazine *Die Pleite* (Grosz 1923, 6), Ebert and Noske can be seen in Grosz' image wading through a sea of corpses, broken bones, and crushed skulls. But at the same time, and in spite of the massive critique of the image's shortcomings, one could also observe how the *Badebild* helped a notion of public assembly and public sovereignty to resurface, which the violent outcome of the revolution had almost pushed into oblivion; this notion was the idea that in a democracy popular sovereignty is never identical with state sovereignty.

4 Naked Democrats. Modern Beaches and Aesthetic Form

The political sovereign dominating the elements and defying nature constitutes a traditional trope in political iconography; the image of the swimming sovereign is a case in point.[27] The infamous *Badebild* of Ebert and Noske takes up this iconography to use as precedent both against and for the new form of polity, which it came to represent. Charles Baudelaire had declared that the ubiquitous frock coats of nineteenth-century-politicians bore witness "to an expression of universal equality" (Baudelaire 1981, 118), the image of two

---

[26] The new constitution promised to guarantee property but it did not consider property a basic right, unlike today's German *Grundgesetz*.
[27] On the iconography of this *topos* from Charlemagne to Mao Tse-tung, see Bredekamp (2014).

semi-naked heads of state takes this idea a step further. The nakedness of the politicians has a specific quality to it: It renders them average citizens, without exposing them in a pornographic or demeaning way. Albrecht Koschorke has observed that this kind of awkward or 'embarrassing nakedness' (Koschorke 2007, 242),[28] compared to other forms of political nakedness – he distinguishes between 'imperial,' 'Christological,' 'pornographic,' and 'embarrassing nakedness' – concerns foremost the public or official persona of a politician. Unlike 'pornographic nakedness,' which aims at the private persona in order to damage the *aura* of the person who is holding an office, 'embarrassing nakedness' is aimed at the office the person, who is depicted, is holding (ibid.). Ebert's and Noske's nakedness is one that induced a feeling of shame into the political sphere of the German Reich. This peculiar shame resulted from the simple recognition that democratic representatives were not in any way extraordinary and that the office of a democratically elected representative was not imbued with the same *aura* as that of a monarch. The *BIZ* had used a similar image a few years earlier, although it was a photomontage with painted elements, not an actual photograph, of Reichskanzler Bethmann-Hollweg bathing in the Tiber on their front page in 1910.[29] The image of Ebert and Noske, insofar as it was clearly recognizable as an actual photograph, hit a more serious note. Between the form of the land and the formlessness of the sea, the nakedness of the democratic protagonists seems to expose an issue which is foremost an aesthetic problem, the question of the appropriate form of democratic representation and democratic appearance. The strong reactions towards the image of Ebert and Noske in bathing trunks reveal an underlying discourse about a new understanding of the body politic and simultaneously a quest to find the appropriate aesthetic form for this new form of polity.

The *BIZ* pursued a strangely consistent *Bildprogramm* in 1919 almost akin to a visual education in democracy, starting with the series "Charakterköpfe der

---

[28] This seems particularly helpful in this context, since the *Badebild* cannot be understood in the tradition of satirizing portraits of rulers by showing them naked or in pornographic poses. Ebert's and Noske's semi-nakedness clearly falls under the fourth category 'embarrassing nakedness': "Die peinliche Nacktheit hebt sich von der pornographischen insofern ab, als sie das offizielle, nicht das private Erscheinungsbild des Herrschers betrifft. Ihr Problem ist nicht der Voyeurismus der Beherrschten, sondern dessen *Versagen*. Herrscherpornographie zehrt von der Wirkung eines auratischen Körpers, selbst wenn sie ihn seiner Aura beraubt (was diese Macht-Aura nicht dauerhaft, sondern nur in kritischen historischen Konstellationen gefährdet). Peinliche Bloßstellung dagegen führt einen depotenzierten einsamen Körper vor" (Koschorke 2007, 242).
[29] The image was a photomontage and framed as an "Aprilscherz" [April fool's trick] by the editors, which seems to have reduced its satirical impact at the time (*Berliner Illustrirte Zeitung*, Nr. 14, 1 April 1910. 1).

Gegenwart" [Political Types of the Present], which began with an imposing image of Ebert on the front page, followed by an image of Noske, and one of Hugo Preuß.[30] This programmatic series was based on a surprisingly antiquated form of physiognomic thought, best encapsulated in an article entitled "Der neue politische Kopf" ['The New Political Head' or 'The new Political Physiognomy'] and published that same year:

> Die Regime, die Systeme sind in den gesellschaftspolitischen Köpfen ihrer Repräsentanten so scharf charakterisiert, daß es einem geübten Auge genügt, die Photographien der leitenden Männer eines Landes zu sehen, um danach allein zu bestimmen, welches Regime in diesem Lande besteht.[31] (*Berliner Illustrirte Zeitung*, 23 Februar 1919, 58)

The reason for this introductory course in political physiognomy seems to have been a growing uncertainty about how to judge or read the heads or faces of democratically elected representatives. In this series the beach photograph of Ebert and Noske marks a disruptive point in an emerging discourse. They became "synecdochical figurations of the body politic as a pseudorevolutionary republican belly," as different Dadaist publications proclaimed (Doherty 1998, 64–68). The belly of the President as *pars pro toto* was showcased for the first time on the beach at Haffkrug and inscribed into the collective memory of the Weimar Republic by the BIZ's publication of the *Badebild*. After that, no other German politician would volunteer or pose to have his or her picture taken clothed in nothing but swimwear, except for Franz Josef Strauß in 1971 for a *home story* by the magazine *Stern* (Höpfinger, Henning and Scheutle 2015, 58).

5 The Beach as the *Klebegrund* of Democracy. Hannah Höch's Collage *Staatshäupter*

The figures of the two bathing *Staatshäupter* [Heads of State] become part of the world of a very different beach in Hannah Höch's collage, which measures 16.2 x 23.3 centimeters. Ebert and Noske, cut-outs from the same *BIZ* issue, are fitted

---

30 See the front page of the *BIZ* on February 23 (Ebert), March 2 (Noske), and March 23 (Preuß). The front page on March 9 showed a photograph of the two sisters Marie Juchacz and Elisabeth Röhl, who had both been elected to parliament.
31 The underlying assumption of the article is that one could recognize a specific form of polity by looking at the heads and faces of its representatives.

into a beach setting with blurred boundaries where the figure of a mermaid-like woman with a parasol surrounded by butterflies and flowers floats behind them, cut-out waves lapping against the knees of the two politicians. Originally an iron-on embroidery pattern, of the kind that Höch had been designing for the Ullstein magazine *Die praktische Berlinerin*[32], the materiality of the sand-colored paper, the *Klebegrund* [adhesive paper ground] for her collage, is not concealed by the glued-on newspaper-clippings. Rather, it is foregrounded. The pattern and the color of the paper dominate the scene. As cut-outs, the two politicians have neither depth nor statesman-like gravitas. They haplessly float on the sticky *Klebegrund* of the collage where the beholder is not offered the comfort of watching from a discrete distance. The position of the beholder is not contemplative and objective, but instead is drawn in close to a ground that is at once sandy (colored) and sticky, a surface upon which various images have affixed themselves, cut and reassembled out of items of mass circulation. This particular perspective and its materiality hints at once to qualities of the beach ('Strandgut' [flotsam and jetsam] washed ashore a yellow-brown ground) as well as a participatory quality: Höch's beach is not structured hierarchically and its underlying structure is that of repetition in the sense that the pattern refers the beholder back to the repetitive and gendered work of creating mass-produced iron-on patterns that could be bought and duplicated countless times while the photographic images are themselves mimetic reproductions. The patterns that were printed in the weekly issues of *Die praktische Berlinerin* were attributed to their creators, mostly female artists like Höch, although the artists did not own the copy right to the embroidery patterns which remained with the Ullstein Verlag (incidentally the same publishing house as that of the *BIZ*) meaning that once they were published, they circulated freely for appropriation in the public domain.

---

[32] Every issue of *Die praktische Berlinerin* contained images of embroidery patterns. The actual iron-on patterns could be bought at the *Verkaufsstellen* of the Ullstein-Verlag in Berlin.

Fig. 3: Hannah Höch *Staatshäupter* (1919–1920).

Compared to Höch's better known collages, like *Schnitt mit dem Küchenmesser Dada durch die letzte Weimarer Bierbauchkulturepoche* [Cut with the Kitchen Knife Dada through the Last Weimar Beer Belly Cultural Epoch of Germany], which uses the same cut-outs of Ebert and Noske, *Staatshäupter* is characterized by a strange serenity and the near absence of allegorical suggestiveness. Whereas Höch's other collages tend to create an abundance of allegorical suggestions, with different clipped objects, mechanical devices, bodies or body parts strewn over the *Klebegrund*, *Staatshäupter* belongs to a group of collages that appear more reserved or reduced in the way they integrate the photographic elements within the collage. Höch's collage not only foregrounds the *Klebegrund* itself, it reminds its beholder of its constitutive function: Höch's *Klebergund* represents the beach as a place of public assembly and as an unregulated place, where the forces of public sovereignty are displayed and circulated. Höch's collage draws our attention to an aspect of sovereignty in a modern democratic state that Judith Butler has described as an aspect of popular sovereignty "that remains untranslatable, nontransferable, and even unsubstitutable" (Butler 2015, 162):

As much as popular sovereignty legitimates parliamentary forms of power, it also retains the power to withdraw its support from those same forms when they prove to be illegitimate. If parliamentary forms of power require popular sovereignty for their legitimacy, they also surely fear it, for there is something about popular sovereignty that runs counter to, and exceeds or outruns, every parliamentary form that it institutes and grounds. [...] This is an extraparliamentary power without which no parliament can function legitimately, and that threatens every parliament with dysfunction or even dissolution. We may again want to call it an "anarchist" interval or a permanent principle of revolution that resides within democratic orders, one that shows up more or less both at moments of founding and moments of dissolution, but is also operative in the freedom of assembly itself [...]. (Ibid., 162–163)

The collage as an artistic medium connects two very different practices with each other, cutting and pasting (Heesen 2006, 193–198). In the self-descriptions of the Avant-garde the two practices have been imbued with allegorical meaning by their practitioners (Vogel 2011, 166), in *Staatshäupter* they seem to acquire a blatantly political meaning. Democratically elected representatives can be replaced and rearranged in the electoral practice of democracy, the new body politic is a social collage of sorts, it is not a closed-off hierarchical entity. It is a product of a new mass-culture like the newspaper clippings and iron-on patterns that Höch uses for her work.

In the summer of 1919, the "permanent principle of revolution that resides within democratic orders," as Judith Butler (2015, 163) puts it, manifests itself on the Weimar beach. Hannah Höch's collage reminds its viewers of the uncontrollable forces of popular sovereignty, the beach it creates is a space of future possibilities past. In Höch's collage, the photograph of two Weimar politicians on the beach becomes both a founding moment and a moment of dissolution.

Bibliography

Albrecht, Niels H. M. *Die Macht einer Verleumdungskampagne. Antidemokratische Agitationen der Presse und Justiz gegen die Weimarer Republik und ihren ersten Reichspräsidenten Friedrich Ebert vom "Badebild" bis zum Magdeburger Prozess* [Masch. Dissertation]. Bremen, 2002.
Arendt, Hannah. *The Human Condition* [1958]. With an Introduction by Margaret Canovan. Chicago: University of Chicago Press, 1998.
Baudelaire, Charles. *Art in Paris 1845–1862: Salons and Other Exhibitions*. Edited and translated by Jonathan Mayne. Oxford: Phaidon, 1981.
Berliner Illustrirte Zeitung 14 (1 April 1910).
Berliner Illustrirte Zeitung 8 (23 February 1919).

Berliner Illustrirte Zeitung 34 (23 August 1919).
Bredekamp, Horst. *Der schwimmende Souverän. Karl der Große und die Bildpolitik des Körpers*. Berlin: Wagenbach, 2014.
Bredekamp, Horst. "Elemente einer politischen Ikonologie des Schwimmens." *Politische Repräsentation und das Symbolische. Staat – Souveränität – Nation*. Eds. Paula Diehl and Felix Steilen. Wiesbaden: Springer, 2016. 195–224.
Butler, Judith. *Notes Toward a Performative Theory of Assembly*. Cambridge, MA and London: Harvard University Press, 2015.
Corbin, Alain. *The Lure of the Sea. The Discovery of the Seaside in the Western World*. Translated by Jocelyn Phelps. Berkeley and Los Angeles: University of California Press, 1994.
Cross, Gary S., and John K. Walton. *The Playful Crowd. Pleasure Places in the Twentieth Century*. New York: Columbia University Press, 2005.
Dewey, John. *The Public and Its Problems*. Chicago: Swallow Press, 1927.
Die praktische Berlinerin. Wochenschrift für Haushalt und Mode. Berlin: Ullstein, 1905–1927.
Deutsche Zeitung (9 August 1919).
Döblin, Alfred. "Der Deutsche Maskenball." [1921] *Der Deutsche Maskenball von Linke-Poot: Wissen und Verändern! Ausgewählte Werke in Einzelbänden*. Eds. Walter Muschg and Heinz Graber. Olten and Freiburg/Br.: Walter Verlag, 1972. 94–105.
Doherty, Brigid. "Figures of the Pseudorevolution." *October* 84 (1998): 64–89.
Edgerton, Robert B. *Alone Together. Social Order on A Public Beach*. Berkeley and Los Angeles: University of California Press, 1979.
Eley, Geoff. "One Empire by Land or Sea? Germany's Imperial Imaginary." *German Colonialism in A Global Age*. Eds. Bradley Naranch and Geoff Eley. Durham and London: Duke University Press, 2014. 19–45.
Frank, Thomas, Albrecht Koschorke, Susanne Lüdemann and Ethel Mathala de Mazza (eds.): *Des Kaisers neue Kleider. Über das Imaginäre politscher Herrschaft. Texte, Bilder, Lektüren*. Frankfurt/Main: Fischer, 2002.
Freeman, James. "Democracy and Danger on the Beach. Class Relations in the Public Space of Rio de Janeiro." *Space and Culture* 5,1 (2002): 9–28.
Geisthövel, Alexa. "Der Strand." *Orte der Moderne. Erfahrungswelten des 19. und 20. Jahrhunderts*. Eds. Alexa Geisthövel and Habbo Knoch. Frankfurt/Main and New York: Campus, 2005. 121–130.
Goffman, Erving. *Behaviour in Public Places. Notes on the Social Organization of Gatherings*. New York: The Free Press, 1966.
Grosz, George. "Nach Hamburg und Sachsen." *Die Pleite*. 2,8 (1923): 6.
Hauptmann, Gerhart. *Die versunkene Glocke. Ein deutsches Märchendrama*. Berlin: Fischer, 1897.
Heesen, Anke te. *Der Zeitungsausschnitt. Ein Papierobjekt der Moderne*. Frankfurt/Main: Fischer, 2006.
Höpfinger, Renate, Henning Rader and Rudolf Scheutle (eds.): *Stadtmuseum: Franz Josef Strauß. Die Macht der Bilder*. München: Allitera Verlag, 2015.
Kessler, Harry Graf. *Das Tagebuch. Siebter Band 1919–1923. Das Tagebuch 1880–1937, Vol. 7*. Ed. Angela Reinthal. Stuttgart: Cotta, 2007.
Koschorke, Albrecht. "Der nackte Herrscher." *Des Kaisers neue Kleider. Über das Imaginäre politscher Herrschaft. Texte, Bilder, Lektüren*. Eds. Thomas Frank, Albrecht Koschorke, Susanne Lüdemann and Ethel Mathala de Mazza in collaboration with Andreas Kraß. Frankfurt/Main: Fischer, 2002. 233–243.

Koszyk, Kurt. "Wie Ebert und Noske baden gingen – oder was passiert, wenn ein Chefredakteur Urlaub macht." *Beruf und Berufung. Zweite Festschrift für Johannes Binkowski.* Ed. Rolf Terheyden. Mainz: v. Hase & Koehler, 1988. 88–85.

Lavin, Maud. *Cut with a Kitchen Knife. The Weimar Photomontages of Hannah Höch.* New Haven and London: Yale University Press, 1993.

Mergel, Thomas. "Propaganda in der Kultur des Schauens. Visuelle Politik in der Weimarer Republik." *Ordnungen in der Krise. Zur politischen Kulturgeschichte Deutschlands.* Ed. Wolfgang Hardtwig. München: Oldenbourg, 2007. 531–560.

Peukert, Detlev: *Die Weimarer Republik. Krisenjahre der Klassischen Moderne.* Frankfurt/Main: Suhrkamp, 1987.

Pratt, Mary Louise. *Imperial Eyes: Travel Writing and Transculturation.* London: Routledge, 1992.

Ostseebäder und Städte der Ostseeküste. Mit 22 Karten, 27 Plänen und zwei Tafeln. 4. Aufl. Leipzig and Wien: Bibliographisches Institut, 1910.

Prignitz, Horst. *Vom Badekarren zum Strandkorb. Zur Geschichte des Badewesens an der Ostseeküste.* Leipzig: Koehler & Amelang, 1977.

Ringelnatz, Joachim. *Flugzeuggedanken.* Berlin: Rowohlt, 1929.

Schleimer, Alexis. "Die Kommunisierung des Geschmacks." *Satyr* 25 (1919): 1.

Sonnabend, Gaby, and Walter Mühlhausen (eds.). *Darüber lacht die Republik. Friedrich Ebert und seine Reichskanzler in der Karikatur.* Begleitband zur Ausstellung in der Reichspräsident-Friedrich-Ebert-Gedenkstätte, 26. Januar–6. Juni 2006. Heidelberg: Stiftung Reichspräsident-Friedrich-Ebert-Gedenkstätte, 2010.

Spender, Stephen. *World Within World. The Autobiography of Stephen Spender.* London: Hamish Hamilton, 1951.

Springer, Peter. "Hand." *Abdankung bis Huldigung. Handbuch der politischen Ikonographie.* Vol. 1. Eds. Uwe Fleckner, Martin Warnke and Hendrik Ziegler. München: C. H. Beck, 2011. 443–450.

Timm, Werner. *Vom Badehemd zum Bikini. Bademoden und Badeleben im Wandel der Zeit.* Husum: Husum Druck und Verlagsgesellschaft, 2000.

Die Verfassung des Deutschen Reiches. Reichs-Gesetzblatt 152 (1919): 1383–1418.

Vogel, Juliane. "Anti-Greffologie. Schneiden und Kleben in der Avantgarde." *Impfen, propfen, transplantieren.* Eds. Uwe Wirth and Emmanuel Alloa. Berlin: Kadmos, 2011. 159–172.

Vogel, Juliane. *Aus dem Grund. Auftrittsprotokolle zwischen Racine und Nietzsche.* Paderborn: Fink, 2018.

Vorwärts. Berliner Volksblatt. Zentralorgan der Sozialdemokratischen Partei Deutschlands 427 (22 August 1919).

Vorwärts. Berliner Volksblatt. Zentralorgan der Sozialdemokratischen Partei Deutschlands 441 (29 August 1919).

List of Figures

Fig. 1: Titelblatt der *Berliner Illustrirten Zeitung*, 23 August 1919: 1.

Fig. 2: Foto von Wilhelm Steffen. 1919. Bundesarchiv Koblenz, Bild 146-1987-076-13.

Fig. 3: Hannah Höch, *Staatshäupter*. 1919–1920. Collection of IFA, Stuttgart. Fotostudio Liedtke & Michel. © VG Bild-Kunst, Bonn 2019.

Barbara Vinken
Der Strand: What to wear on the beach / Was am Strand anziehen?

The image of a Muslim woman, forced by the police to take off her long-sleeve top in the summer of 2016, the burkini and subsequent discussions show that beachwear has become political again. What one wears at the beach and how one presents one's body expresses the relationship between body and shame. The discourse around the beach, characterized by the polarity between clothes unto life and clothes unto death, between deadly waters and the nudity of passion, on the one hand, and sweet waters of life, on the other, comes to the fore in Bernardin de Saint-Pierre's *Paul et Virginie* and in Theodor Fontane's *Effi Briest*. The 'beach body' in its nudity functions as a cipher for the establishment of the new man, the recovery of paradisiac innocence, and not as a shameful body fallen into desire, sexual difference and death.

Das Bild einer muslimischen Frau, die im Sommer 2016 von der Polizei gezwungen wird, ihr langärmliges Oberteil auszuziehen, der Burkini und daran anknüpfende Diskussionen zeigen, dass die Bademode wieder politisch geworden ist, denn was man am Strand trägt und wie man seinen Körper in Szene setzt, ist Ausdruck eines Verhältnisses von Körper und Scham. Das von den Polaritäten zwischen Kleidern zum Leben wie zum Tod, tödlichem Wasser und Nacktheit der Leidenschaft einerseits und süßem Wasser des Lebens andererseits gekennzeichnete Diskursfeld des Strandes zeigt sich besonders klar in Bernardin de Saint-Pierres *Paul et Virginie* und Theodor Fontanes *Effi Briest*. Der ‚beach body' fungiert in seiner Nacktheit als Chiffre für das Anlegen des neuen Menschen oder die Wiedererlangung paradiesischer Unschuld und nicht als schambehafteter, in sein Begehren, sexuelle Differenz und Tod gefallener Körper.

„Irgendwo wartet immer ein Strand auf Sie." „Life is better at the beach." „Sea, sex and sun / le soleil au zénith" (Serge Gainsbourg). ‚The beach': der Ort, wo alle immer sein wollen. Weil alle möglichst immer einen Platz an Sonne und Meer wollen, wurde der Strand in die Städte getragen: Paris Plages verwandelt das Seine-Ufer für die Sommermonate in einen Meeresstrand. Allüberall Strände auch in München; Sand, Sonnenschirme, Strandkörbe, Drinks. Manchmal ein paar Palmen. Fuhr die Stadt bisher an den Strand, so kommt seit ein paar Jahren der Strand im Trend der Renaturierung der Städte – als Garten, Wald, wilde Wiesen – in die Stadt.

1

Im Sommer 2016 wurde das Strandidyll – der Strand als Schutzzone eines zivilisierten, eingehegten Vergnügens, paradiesischen Einswerdens mit der Natur – ausgerechnet am Strand der Strände, der Baie des Anges an der Côte d'Azur in Nizza, gestört: Polizisten am Strand, die Sittenpolizei unterwegs. Schlechte Nachrichten. Die Bürgermeister*innen hatten eine Kleiderordnung für den Strand ausgegeben: Verhüllt geht gar nicht. Der Bürgermeister von Cannes verfügte, dass man – und vor allen Dingen frau – beim Baden und Sonnenbaden am Meer nicht etwa verhüllt erscheinen dürfe. Und obwohl das französische Verfassungsgericht die kommunalen Verbotsdekrete aufhob, kam es in der Zwischenzeit zu hässlichen Szenen. Der Schnappschuss, auf dem zu sehen war, wie volluniformierte Polizisten am Strand von Nizza eine Frau nötigten, ihr langärmliges Oberteil *coram publico* auszuziehen, ging um die Welt.

Prompt wurden aus den Archiven Photos der 1950er-Jahre ausgegraben, auf denen ein ebenfalls vollbekleideter Polizist einer nur mit einem Bikini angetanen Schönheit ein Strafmandat ausstellt. Beides sittenwidrig? Einmal zu viel, einmal zu wenig. Die Staatsgewalt beschämt und bestraft Frauen; Polizisten kontrollieren, wieviel Haut frau zu zeigen und wieviel sie zu bedecken hat. Im *Corriere della Sera* vom 19. August 2016 sah man kurz darauf Nonnen mit Schleier und Habit in den Wellen planschen.

In der *beachwear* hat sich etwas getan: Ein neuer Typ von Badeanzug ist auf den Markt gekommen, der Burkini. Bei Marks & Spencer konnte man den aus der *sportswear* stammenden Burkini (Wort-Kombination aus ‚Burka' und ‚Bikini') kaufen. Er verhüllt Körper und Haare auch beim Schwimmen. Wenn frau aus dem Wasser steigt, schmiegt er sich nicht so an den Körper, als wäre sie nackt. Nichts mit schaumgeborener Venus. Nichts mehr mit Meerjungfrau. Die alle am Strand ohne Unterlass umtreibende Frage nach einer streifenlosen Bräune und umgekehrt die nach Sonnenschutz für Haut und Haare stellt sich nicht mehr. Der gebräunte, schlanke, leicht trainierte ‚beach body', den ja mittlerweile, in Frankreich jedenfalls, auch Präsidentschaftskandidatinnen wie Ségolène Royal zeigen, scheint keine Frage mehr zu sein.

In der anglophonen Welt wird diese neue *beachwear* weitgehend nicht nur als ein gutes Geschäft, sondern auch als eine inklusive, liberale Maßnahme verstanden. Eine Muslima kann die konventionellen Verschleierungsregeln beachten und Rettungsschwimmerin werden, am gemischten Schwimmunterricht teilnehmen und joggen, kurz: an den Strand gehen wie alle anderen. Hautärzt*innen haben längst weltweit, vor allem in den heliophoben USA, darauf hingewiesen, dass sie grundsätzlich zum Tragen solcher Kleidungsstücke raten würden – nicht der Scham, sondern des effektiven Sonnenschutzes wegen.

Was man am Strand trägt, ist plötzlich, nach einer längeren Ruhephase, wieder politisch geworden. Was am Strand zu tragen sei, getragen werden darf und was nicht, bewegt die Gemüter. Nacktheit und Wasser sind in aller Munde, ein *clash* der Kulturen wird nicht nur heraufbeschworen, sondern führt am Strand zu Schlägereien. Wem gehört der Strand und was hat am Strand zu passieren? Am Strand – auch im Bad – droht die saubere Parzellierung der Klassen aufzubrechen: Die Vorstädte dringen ein und mit der Vermischung der Klassen und Rassen, mit der Verschiedenheit der Religionen drängen sich Fragen nach dem Verhältnis von Kultur und Natur auf. Mehr aber als um die Frage der *banlieues*, also der Klassen, scheint es mir um die Rückkehr der Dame am Strand zu gehen. Die kehrt zurück nicht als Frau aus den *banlieues*, arm, muslimisch und unterprivilegiert, sondern als ostentativ verhüllte Muslima. Die Verhüllung ist hier auch Frage der Klassendistinktion. Die von Kopf bis Fuß elegant verhüllte Dame – gerade im Ungererbad, *awfully stilish*, in einem schwarzen Ganzkörperanzug mit wunderbarem, auch schwarzem Turban – ist klar keine Frage der *banlieues*, sondern einer Distinktion des Weiblichen, die von einem anderen Verhältnis von Körper und Scham, von Verhüllen und Entblößen erzählt.

Sonne, Wasser und Haut sind plötzlich nicht mehr nur Versprechen eines glücklicheren, schöneren, natürlicheren und sexuell erfüllteren Lebens. Was erwartet uns, wenn überall und immer ein Strand auf uns wartet? Was ist das inzwischen über zweihundert Jahre alte Versprechen des Strandes?

Von Anfang an begleitet die Frage, ob und wie man sich in die Fluten stürzen sollte, den Aufstieg von Seebad und Strand. Die Frage der Klassen stellte sich noch nicht so drängend, weil das Strandvergnügen zuerst aristokratisch bis großbürgerlich war. Die Geschlechtertrennung mehr als die Klassentrennung war zentral. Damen und Herren waren beim Baden getrennt: „jetzt wo ‚Damenbad' und ‚Herrenbad' keine scheidenden Schreckensworte mehr waren" (Fontane 1998 [1894], 149), heißt es in Fontanes *Effi Briest* 1894, als Effi in der Nachsaison – die Geschlechtersegregation in Sachen Baden ist aufgehoben – mit Ehemann und späterem Geliebten den Strand entlangjagt. Auf die ‚beach novel' *Effi Briest* ist noch zurückzukommen.

Das Baden hatte zuerst hygienische Gründe und wurde von Ärzten überwacht: von Kneipp bis Thalasso alles Badekuren. Besonders das Kaltbaden stand hoch im Kurs. Man badete nackt, aber so, dass einen niemand sah. Ein Badewagen, der als Umkleidekabine fungierte, wurde ins Wasser gezogen und fern aller Blicke ging man schwimmen, unterstützt von einer Baderin. Nackt oder in Unterkleidern, ein Usus, den die britische Unterschicht bis in die 1990er-Jahre beibehielt.

Abb. 1: Badekarren 1893.

Ich weiß nicht, ob das heute noch so ist; ich bin der Klassensegregation gefolgt und gehe nicht mehr an solche Strände. Am Strand nahm man, wenn man nicht ins Wasser ging, kein Sonnenbad im Badeanzug, sondern war durchaus bekleidet. Die Aristokratie, die Bourgeoisie, wie am Strand bei Manet, Renoir, Boudin zu sehen, wirkt eigenartig *overdressed*. Im Badekleid jedenfalls ist dort niemand anzutreffen. (Abb. 2)

Erst Coco Chanel machte, mit weiten Matrosenhosen und *marinière*, die Haare im Wind, Kleider aus Jersey, dem Material der Herrenunterwäsche, den Strand zu einem ebenso lässigen wie eleganten Ort, wo man alle Konvention hinter sich lässt. Als Chanel Paris verließ, um während des Ersten Weltkriegs eine Boutique in Deauville und später in Biarritz zu eröffnen, war der Strand endgültig zu einem supermodischen Ort geworden – vor allem deshalb, weil man hier alles Einschnürende, Einengende abwerfen und endlich ein freier Mensch in der Natur sein könne. Mit den Hüllen ließ man auch die Distinktion der Klassen, nicht dagegen alle feinen Unterschiede hinter sich. Das einfache Leben teilte man gerne mit den Matrosen, Fischern, Meerleuten, die man nicht schlicht arm, sondern romantisch fand. Noch heute zehrt die Mode von den

Capri-Fischerhosen und den weiten Hosen der Seeleute. Die *marinière* ist sogar und genauso eindrücklich wie die Jeans zur Kurzformel für die Mode der Moderne insgesamt geworden (von Anfang an Jean Paul Gaultiers Markenzeichen, vor ein paar Jahren hatten alle im Sommer in den Seminaren eine *marinière* an). Die Mode des Strandes, der Strand als Mode gingen Hand in Hand und machten die freie Unkonventionalität, das Ablegen aller Konventionen zur Konvention schlechthin. Eine Konvention, deren Konventionslosigkeit die strengen Regeln eines *self-fashioning* befolgen musste.

Abb. 2: Édouard Manets *Sur la plage de Boulogne* (1873).

Seit der Erfindung der Schwimmmode aus den Bloomers heraus um die 1870er-Jahre schien, bis vor kurzem jedenfalls, weniger mehr zu sein: weniger Stoff, mehr Reize. Die Schwimmbekleidung wurde nicht nur immer knapper, sondern auch immer leichter und anschmiegsamer. Der endgültige Durchbruch kam durch die Erfindung von Lycra in den 1960er-Jahren. Die Schwimmanzüge aus Wolle oder Baumwolle waren, voll Wasser gesogen, schwer. Heute fühlt man den Bikini, den Badeanzug kaum noch. Und er trocknet in Windeseile auf der Haut.

Abb. 3: Badebekleidung um 1900.

Aus Badekleidern wurde der Badeanzug mit Rockschößchen, die den Beinansatz, und Ärmeln, die die Oberarme und Achselhöhlen bedeckten. Aus dem Einteiler wurde der Bikini, für den man immer wieder antike Beispiele, beispielsweise auf den Mosaiken der Villa Romana del Casale auf Sizilien aus dem vierten Jahrhundert, gefunden hat, aus dem taillierten Höschen der String, Rudi Gernreich erfand den Monokini. Der aus vier Dreiecken bestehende Bikini war, priesen sich seine Erfinder, aus so hauchdünnem Stoff, dass man ihn durch einen Ring ziehen konnte. Aber zu Anfang wollte kein Mannequin ihn vorführen – zu gewagt, zu viel nackte Haut; das übernahmen Varieté-Tänzerinnen. Diese Strandkleider, die das Exotisch-Aufregende, wie eine Bombe Einschlagende mit dem Bikini-Atoll verband, das in den bahnbrechenden Atomversuchen als Kurzchiffre für einen Durchbruch in einer alles verändernden Technik stand, waren bis in die 1970er-Jahre nie unumstritten. Als schamlos sorgten sie nicht nur für Aufregung, sondern auch für das Eingreifen der Sittenpolizei. Überhaupt wurde die Badekleidung ein Lieblingsobjekt öffentlicher Regulierungen. Und diese betrafen fast immer ein Verbieten einer zu erregenden Aufladung. Zu viel nackte Haut, zu viel Fleisch. Badeanzüge hatten Ende der 1930er-Jahre einen Beinanschnitt zu haben: Anständige Deutsche, in freiem Einklang mit Wasser, Luft und Licht, sind selbstverständlich nicht prüde, aber noch weniger verführerisch-lasziv.

Die 1970er-, 1980er- und 1990er-Jahre sind dann eine liberale Zeit, in der man ungestört Körperteile und Ausschnitte zeigen darf: Pobacken, Hüften bis zur Taille, Anfang der Scham, Busen. An der Côte d'Azur badete und sonnenbadete man oben ohne, und zwar alle durcheinander, Männer und Frauen, Damen nur mit Höschen und diejenigen, die außer einem String gar nichts trugen. Allerdings hätte man nie und nimmer nackt gebadet; das tat man nur an den hauptsächlich von Deutschen aufgesuchten FKK-Stränden, man denke an Houellebecqs (1998) Beschreibung von Cap d'Agde in den *Particules élémentaires*. Ein Zeichen der Zivilisation, eine Anerkennung der Gefallenheit im Feigenblatt, eine Markierung der Geschlechtlichkeit war und blieb und ist in der Romania unumgänglich. Ganz nackt, das ist nicht so sehr schamlos als barbarisch. In den romanischen Ländern, anders als in Deutschland ging es nicht um ein Zurück zu einer mit Barbarei und Unzivilisiertheit konnotierten Natur, sondern um das Übersteigen der Ersten Natur in eine Zweite, schönere Natur.

,Oben ohne' war und ist selbstverständlich in den USA ganz und gar undenkbar. Undenkbar dort auch FKK und bis heute in Kalifornien nur von ein paar Deutschen fernab klandestin praktiziert. Am planmäßigsten ist die Kleiderordnung in der ehemaligen DDR und daran hat sich bis jetzt auf Rügen nichts geändert: „FKK", „Hunde", „Badebekleidung" heißen die feinsäuberlich getrennten Badestrände. FKK und damit die Vorstellung einer natürlichen, unverstellten, von gesellschaftlichen Zwängen befreiten Geschlechtlichkeit ist eine Spezialität der Deutschen geblieben, eine blauäugige Verleugnung der Bedrohung, die im geschlechtlichen Unterschied liegt. *Ab hier FKK erlaubt*, erinnere ich mich an einen satirischen Titel von Thomas Palzer, der das Paradox von verordneter Freiheit auf den Punkt bringt.

Der Trend ,weniger Stoff ist mehr' scheint sich in den letzten Jahren umzukehren, auch wenn man nicht Burkini trägt. Der Trend in der *beachwear* geht wie auch sonst in der Mode zu mehr Stoff: Typ ,Königin von Saba', Damen in hauchdünne, weite, leuchtende Schleier, vom Wind gebauscht, gehüllt, aber auch, prosaischer, das Raufrutschen des Höschens bis über die Taille gehen in diese Richtung.

2

Nackt oder angezogen, und wieviel Stoff? Wasser und Scham, ein heikles Thema. Im ,finsteren' Mittelalter scheint das überhaupt kein Problem gewesen zu sein. Nackt badeten Männer und Frauen durcheinander. Die immer beliebter werdenden Badehäuser, die sich auf die antike Tradition bezogen, wurden allerdings mit dem Aufkommen der Syphilis in Europa als Orte öffentlicher Promiskuität geschlossen. Und sie scheinen eher Vergnügungsorte gewesen zu sein, deren Tradition bis in die 1970er-Jahre in den *dark rooms* untergründig weiterwirkte, die dann mit dem Aufkommen der Aids-Epidemie schlossen.

Was das Nackte und das Angezogene, den Unterschied der Geschlechter und die Scham angeht, so ist das ein traditionell hochbesetztes Thema. Am Strand, beim Baden und Sonnenbaden, stellt es sich mit besonderer Dringlichkeit. Im Paradies waren Adam und Eva nackt, aber unwissend ohne Scham. Erst aus dem Paradies vertrieben entdeckten sie ihre Blöße und damit, dass sie Mann und Frau waren, und bedeckten sich. Die Kleider sind also nachwirkende Zeichen des Sündenfalls. Gleichzeitig sind Kleider, Gewänder aber auch, nämlich doppelcodiert, Zeichen der verlorenen Reinheit und Verklärung, einer Aufhebung des Fleisches und seiner Triebe in vergeistigten, himmlischen Körpern. In der Hölle sind auf den mittelalterlichen Bildern alle in ihrer verdammten Fleischlichkeit nackt, während die, die in den Himmel kommen, prächtig in die üppigsten Falten gehüllt sind.

Abb. 4: Hans Memlings *Das jüngste Gericht* (ca. 1467–1471).

Diese Verwandlung des Kleides von einem Zeichen von Scham und Sünde zu seiner Aufwertung als Vorschein eines vom sündigen Fleisch erlösten Leibes hängt, denke ich, an der Figur der Konversion, nach der man den alten

Menschen ablegt, den neuen anzieht. Nackt wird man zum ersten Mal aus dem Fleisch zum Tod und zur Sünde geboren; zum zweiten Mal wird man, gereinigt durch das Wasser der Taufe, in makelloses weißes Tuch gehüllt, durch die Kirche, durch die Herzwunde Jesu zum ewigen Leben geboren (Bynum 2007). Das Kleid ist hier Zeichen einer Vergeistigung, der Aufhebung der erbsündlichen Gefallenheit des Fleisches.

Wasser, Nacktheit, Scham. Eine der berühmtesten Szenen der europäischen Literatur in diesen Dingen kommt aus Bernardin de Saint-Pierres Bestseller *Paul et Virginie* von 1789. Nackt oder angezogen, das ist hier eine Frage von Leben und Tod. Virginie, *nomen est omen*, reist zur Zeit der großen Stürme von Frankreich zurück zur Isle de France, dem heutigen Mauritius, wo sie aufgewachsen ist: zurück aus der verderbten Zivilisation, nach Hause, zur Mutter und dem brüderlich-unschuldigen Geliebten. Kurz vor der Küste von Mauritius, im wild aufgewühlten Meer erleidet die Saint-Géran – vom Strand aus gut zu sehen – in einem apokalyptischen Gewitter Schiffbruch mit Zuschauern, an Weihnachten wohlgemerkt, am 25. Dezember. Vor den turmhohen, pechschwarz dräuenden brüllenden, wild schäumenden Wasserbergen hilft nur der rettende Sprung ins Wasser.

NAUFRAGE DE VIRGINIE.
Elle parut un ange qui prend son vol vers les cieux.

Abb. 5: Pierre-Paul Prud'hons *Le naufrage de Virginie* (1806).

Die im Wasser Treibenden können nicht an den Strand schwimmen – schwimmen konnte keiner, am allerwenigsten die Matrosen, die ihr Leben auf dem Wasser verbrachten. Aber vom Strand aus können sie in Fässern gerettet werden. Alle die, die erwähnt werden – Männer der unteren Schichten, Matrosen –, ziehen sich für den rettenden Sprung in die Wellen aus und sind nackt. Allein Virginie weigert sich, ihre Kleider, die im Wasser schwer werden und ihren sicheren Tod bedeuten würden, auszuziehen. Sie trägt übrigens keinen Reifrock, sondern die *mode à la grecque* aus hellem Musselin, wie sie sich am Ende des achtzehnten Jahrhunderts durchgesetzt hatte; ein Kleid, das in einem neuerwachten Klassizismus die ‚edle Einfalt, stille Größe' einer reinen Seele durchschimmern ließ. Von dem nackten Matrosen, der versucht, ihr Leben zu retten und ihr die Kleider auszuziehen, wendet Virginie würdevoll die Augen ab:

> Il n'en restait plus qu'un sur le pont, qui était tout nu et nerveux comme Hercule. Il s'approcha de Virginie avec respect: nous le vîmes se jeter à ses genoux, et s'efforcer même de lui ôter ses habits; mais elle, le repoussant avec dignité, détourna de lui sa vue. [...] et Virginie, voyant la mort inévitable, posa une main sur ses habits, l'autre sur son cœur, et levant en haut des yeux sereins, parut un ange qui prend son vol vers les cieux.[1] (Saint-Pierre 1999 [1789], 241)

Virginie nimmt den Tod sehenden Auges in Kauf. Der Text betont in der Wiederholung von Virginies Weigerung sich auszuziehen, dass sie Scham und Tugend über das Leben stellt. Besser angezogen und tot als nackt und lebendig: „cette digne demoiselle qui n'a jamais voulu se déshabiller comme moi" (Saint-Pierre 1999 [1789], 242) [„jenes edle Fräulein [...], das sich nicht entkleiden wollte wie ich" (Saint-Pierre 1987, 223)], sagt der Matrose, der nicht nackt zum Wurm, sondern nackt zum Herkules wird und keine lächerlich verheerende, obszöne, würdelose, sondern eine heroisch-antike Nacktheit zeigt.

Das Aufkommen von Virginies Sinnlichkeit, das Erwachen des Fleisches zum Zeitpunkt der Pubertät war schon vorher im Roman mit dem feuchten Element assoziiert worden. Ein Quellbad, in das Virginie vermutlich nackt – als *pars pro toto* fungieren die nackten Arme – eintaucht, kann ihre erwachende Sinnlichkeit nicht löschen: Von einem brennenden Feuer verzehrt flieht sie die kühle Quelle. Diese Wasser, „ces eaux plus brûlantes que les soleils de la zone

---

[1] „Nur noch ein einziger war auf dem Deck zurückgeblieben; er war ganz nackt und muskulös wie ein Herkules. Ehrerbietig trat er zu Virginie heran; wir sahen, wie er sich auf die Knie vor ihr niederwarf und sich bemühte, ihr ebenfalls die Kleider auszuziehen; sie aber wies ihn mit Würde zurück und wandte den Blick von ihm weg. [...] und Virginie, die den unvermeidlichen Tod vor Augen sah, legte die eine Hand an ihre Kleider, die andere auf ihr Herz, und mit heiteren Augen nach oben blickend, schien sie ein Engel, der seinen Flug gen Himmel nimmt." (Saint-Pierre 1987, 221–222)

torride" (Saint-Pierre 1999 [1789], 174) [„jene Wasser, heißer als die Sonnenstrahlen der sengenden Zone" (Saint-Pierre 1987, 106)] werden zur Metapher für das Brennen der sinnlichen Leidenschaften. Das Mitternachtsbad besiegelt den Verlust ihrer unschuldigen Liebe und die Vertreibung aus dem exotischen Paradies, als das Bernardin die Isle de France stilisiert. „Et in arcadia ego" ist hier nicht der Tod, sondern der fatale Sex, das Übel, der *mal*, der *trouble*, die weibliche Krankheit im Paradies, schon bevor Virginie in die verderbte Zivilisation aufbricht. Das reine Quellwasser wäscht nicht rein, sondern es befördert das Brennen der Leidenschaften. Das tosende Meer wird vollends Metapher für den Sturm der tödlichen, nackten, überrollenden Leidenschaften, die alles zu verschlingen und in den Abgrund zu reißen drohen.

Weil Virginie nicht mehr unschuldig, weil sie durch Sinnlichkeit affiziert ist, kann sie nicht mehr paradiesisch nackt sein. Auch die antike heroische Nacktheit, die Fleisch in Muskeln und Sehnen, in Kraft verwandelt und im Text einhergeht mit einer ausgesprochenen Einfachheit des Gemütes, ist ihr nicht gegeben. Virginie, nackt, wäre begehrtes und begehrendes Fleisch, gezeichnet von Sünde und Tod: der alte Adam, die alte Eva.

Aber das bittere, tödliche Wasser wird, weil es sie in den Himmel entrückt, zum Wasser des Lebens. Indem sie ihre Kleider anbehält, ist ihr Tod zwar sicher, aber gleichzeitig zieht sie dadurch auch den neuen Menschen an. Durch ihren Tod wird sie zum wirklichen Leben geboren. Ihre keusche, tugendhafte Scham – eine Hand auf ihre Kleider, eine Hand aufs Herz – sublimiert ihr fleischliches Begehren ins Engelhafte. Sie fährt nicht in den abgründigen Tod der fleischlichen Lust – nackt, tobendes Meer –, sondern in die himmlische Erlösung. Das Zeichen der Sünde, die Kleider verwandeln sich hier in den neuen Menschen, den sie mit der Weigerung, ihre Kleider abzulegen, jungfräulich anlegt.

Heiter, vom Tod nicht entstellt, vollkommen bekleidet – „une main sur ses habits" [„eine Hand an ihre Kleider"] – und vollkommen intakt, mit dem Sand wie mit einem Tuch bedeckt, wird ihr Leichnam am Strand gefunden. Die Rosen der Scham mischen sich auf ihren Wangen mit den Veilchen des Todes – wobei die duftenden Veilchen Blumen des ewigen Lebens waren. Wie eine Heilige, begleitet von den Palmen des Martyriums, wird sie, von der ganzen Insel beweint, betrauert und verehrt, begraben (Saint-Pierre 1999 [1789], 247). Die unglückliche Tugend vereint alle Nationen, alle Geschlechter, Rassen und Klassen und ihre verschiedenen Trauergebräuche in ihrer Verehrung. Die Mutter, der Geliebte folgen ihr bald in den Tod.

Kleider zum Tod, Kleider zum Leben, tödliches, bitteres Wasser der verschlingenden Leidenschaften, Wasser und Nacktheit, die die Leidenschaften brennend entzünden, süßes Wasser des Lebens, der alte Mensch, der ausgezogen wird, um den neuen Menschen anzuziehen – in diesem Diskursfeld bewegen wir uns am Strand. Sea, sex and sun – Is life better at the beach?

Die Ehebruchsgeschichte *Effi Briest* spielt in einem Badeort, „alles da herum ist Badeort" (Fontane 1998 [1894], 12), in einem Seebad an der Ostsee. Passend zu der „Seestadt" tritt Effi Innstetten, der eben um ihre Hand angehalten hat, im „Matrosenkostüm" (ebd., 15) unter die Augen, als ein „Schiffsjunge" (ebd., 14), „Midshipman" (ebd., 15), ein Mädchen auf dem Meer. Fontanes durchgehende Metapher für den tödlichen Sog der Leidenschaften, in dem Effi untergeht, ist das Wasser, Meer: wild, wogend, anbrandend, aufschäumend. Crampas, ihr späterer Geliebter, kommt „vom Strand her" am „27. September" (ebd., 144) mit nassen Haaren aus dem Meer. Und das Örtchen Crampas auf Rügen, das Effi wieder in den Erinnerungsfluten des Ehebruchs untergehen lässt, ist selbstverständlich ein Seebad am Strand. Der Major Crampas ist ein Mann, der bei neun Grad in den wogenden Wellen badet, und ihm ist daher alles zuzutrauen. „[O]hne Furcht vor der Götter Eifersucht" (ebd., 145) wagt er, sich ins Meer zu stürzen, das eben erst vor vier Wochen den Bankier Heinersdorf ohne Respekt vor seinen Millionen verschlungen hat (ebd., 144–145). Überhaupt diskutieren Innstetten und Crampas am Meer meistens über die Todesart, die Crampas ereilen wird – und am Strand wird Crampas dann tatsächlich im Duell erschossen (ebd., 285–286). Effi ist „selig, am Strande hinjagen zu können" (ebd., 149). In weiten Ritten durch Dünen und schäumende Brandung kommen Effi und Crampas sich, und damit ihrem Tod, näher. Im Schloon, der unterirdisch ins Land dringenden Ostsee, träumt Innstetten, werden seine Frau und sein Freund in den Sog der Leidenschaften gezogen und untergehen (ebd., 190). Die Nachricht von der Entdeckung ihres Ehebruches erreicht Effi natürlich auch in einer Wasserstadt, in Bad Ems, wo sie kurt, um noch einmal schwanger zu werden. Im Wasser werden die untreuen Haremsdamen ertränkt, im Wasser, dem Herthasee, die ehebrecherischen Frauen, die im Hertha-Kult geopfert werden. Fatale Fluten. (Vgl. Vinken 2016)

Wie ist aus Strand und Meer, der See, dem wogenden Meer der fatalen Leidenschaften, ein neues Paradies, ein Eden, ein Arkadien geworden? Vielleicht ist daran zu erinnern, dass die Seebäder und die Bäder überhaupt als therapeutisch wertvoll galten. Wasser, Luft und Sonne galten als etwas, das Leib und Seele natürlich heilt: von allen Zivilisationskrankheiten, die ja irgendwie auch Liebeskrankheiten waren. Die Säfte des Körpers sollten wieder richtig in Fluss geraten. Kalte Bäder etwa waren durchaus dazu gedacht, von der Krankheit der Leidenschaften, Hysterie und überhaupt, zu heilen.

Die Nacktheit des Körpers, der aus Scham vor dem, was Alain Corbin (1988, 97) „le viol oculaire" [Vergewaltigung durch Blicke] nennt, versteckt wurde, wurde antik sublimiert. Das Ausziehen, die Nacktheit wird schon in *Paul et*

Virginie – ‚Hercule' –, wie später in den See- und Strandbädern, immer mit der edlen, der reinen Antike assoziiert, einer reinen Schönheit vor dem Fall. Die Badenden sind Nymphen oder Meerjungfrauen bis hin zu Matisse. Die Damenbäder in Dieppe hießen Bain de Diane; sie standen unter dem Schutz der keuschen Jagdgöttin, deren Nacktheit nur der Mond sehen darf. Die Mädchen am Strand, etwa in Prousts *À l'ombre des jeunes filles en fleurs*, tauchen – auch das ein typisch antikes Motiv, wie ich von Hanna Sohns (2018) gelernt habe – immer in Scharen, in Schwärmen auf.

Meine These wäre also, dass unsere Körper nicht immer nackter geworden sind, sondern dass diese Nacktheit als Chiffre entweder für das Anlegen des neuen Menschen oder als Chiffre für das Wiederfinden der Unschuld des Paradieses oder das Wiederfinden einer edlen, reinen Antike gesehen wird, die nicht, Nietzsche paraphrasierend, angekränkelt ist von christlicher Scham oder Verklemmtheit. Kurz, ich neige, was den *beach body* angeht, eher zu Max Weber und Theorien der Säkularisierung – der *beach body* ist säkularisiertes Heilsversprechen – als zu Norbert Elias und dessen These der zunehmenden Triebbeherrschung und -kontrolle, die den nackten Körper möglich machen würde, ohne dass sich alle auf ihn stürzen.

Denn der *beach body* soll ganz dezidiert nicht der schambehaftete, aus der Unschuld des Paradieses in sein Begehren, in sexuelle Differenz und Tod gefallene Körper sein. Er ist im Gegenteil ein Körper, der die Nacktheit wie eine zweite Haut trägt und hofft, sich mit der Nacktheit ein Säkularisat des neuen Menschen überzustreifen oder in die Unschuld des Paradieses zurückzukehren. Moderner gesagt, einen *beach body* hat man nicht, man konstruiert ihn als einen natürlich un-konstruierten. Am Strand zeigen wir nicht unser nacktes Fleisch. Die Haut muss durch den richtigen Sonnenschutz und alle möglichen anderen Vorbereitungen goldbraun sein, Muskeln und Rundungen richtig ausgebildet werden, der Winterspeck abgeschmolzen, die Haare je nach Mode, *Brazilian, bikini* etc., entfernt, die Nägel lackiert, evtl. Piercing und Tattoo hinzugefügt, Augen und Haare geschützt, und schließlich der ‚ihre Linie sublimierende' Bikini oder Badeanzug – wie es in der Reklame des Bon Marché so schön heißt – angelegt werden. Wenn Roland Barthes (1967) gesagt hat, die Mode sei immer keusch, so ist der nackte und der fast nackte Körper in Sand, Wind und Wellen eben dies: ein Körper so keusch wie der der Virginie auf der Saint-Géran. Ein Körper, der erst, wenn er seine Kleider ablegt, in den Stand der Befreiung von Zwang, Einengung und Entstellung kommt, barfuß, mit Sand zwischen den perfekt pediküren und mit kratzfreiem Schellack glänzend lackierten Zehen. Ein Körper, für den man sich nicht zu schämen braucht und der sich vor aller Augen zeigen darf. Der Strand – ‚life is better at the beach' – verspricht das Gesunden an Leib und Seele, den Einklang von Mensch und Natur durch die Erlösung des Körpers vom Obszönen, dem Dunklen seiner den Trieben ausgelieferten, schambeladenen Nacktheit. Es ist ein von obtuser Fleischlichkeit befreiter, sublimierter Körper. Unter freiem Himmel, im Licht der Sonne, im Spiel der Wellen kann er sich zeigen, weil er seine paradiesische Unschuld im Bad, in den ihn durch- und umspülenden Wassern wiedergefunden hat. Oder weil seine Nacktheit, die der neue Mensch anzieht, ihn so kleidet wie die Kleider Virginie.

Das Auftauchen des Burkinis am Strand zeigt dann folgendes: Die, die ihn tragen, haben die sublimierende Leistung, die in den *beach body* eingeht, nicht verstanden. Sie glauben nicht daran, sie verstehen das Säkularisat nicht. Sie glauben nicht an das Versprechen von Sand und See; sie verstehen nicht, dass der *beach body* kein nacktes Fleisch ist. Weil das Fleisch für sie ein Zeichen von Scham und Schuld, von fataler Versuchung geblieben ist, müssen sie es bedecken. Unsere Nacktheit finden sie schlicht vulgär – und vielleicht würde uns ein zweiter Blick auf das Phänomen ganz guttun. Und sie sehen nicht, dass unser Strandkörper beansprucht, den gefallenen Körper hinter sich gelassen zu haben, dass wir mit unserer Nacktheit den neuen Menschen angelegt haben, der sich sehen lassen kann, darf, soll. Nichts ist unverzeihlicher als diese Häresie.

Literaturverzeichnis

Barthes, Roland. *Système de la mode*. Paris: Seuil, 1967.
Bernardin de Saint-Pierre, Jacques-Henri. *Paul et Virginie* [1789]. Paris: Librairie Générale Française, 1999.
Bernardin de Saint-Pierre, Jacques-Henri. *Paul und Virginie*. Übersetzt von Karl Eitner. München: Winkler, 1987.
Bynum, Caroline Walker. *Jesus as Mother. Studies in the Spirituality of the High Middle Ages*. Berkeley, Los Angeles und London: University of California Press, 2007.
Corbin, Alain. *Le territoire du vide. L'Occident et le désir du rivage (1750–1840)*. Paris: Aubier, 1988.
Fontane, Theodor. „Effi Briest" [1894]. *Das erzählerische Werk. Große Brandenburger Ausgabe*, Bd. I/15. Hg. Christine Hehle. Berlin: Aufbau 1998.
Houellebecq, Michel. *Les particules élémentaires*. Paris: Flammarion, 1998.
Sohns, Hanna. *Weibliche Scharen* [Unveröffentlichtes Manuskript des Habilitationsprojekts], 2018.
Vinken Barbara. „,Schlusen'. Effi Briest und die ‚rechte Liebe'". *Allegorie. DFG-Symposion 2014*. Hg. Ulla Haselstein. Berlin und Boston: de Gruyter, 2016. 499–527.

Abbildungsverzeichnis

Abb. 1: *Frau verlässt eine Badekarre*. 1893. Foto: Wilhelm Dreesen. https://commons.wikimedia.org/wiki/File:Woman_in_bathing_suit_(1893).jpg.

Abb. 2: Édouard Manet. *Sur la plage de Boulogne*. 1868. Öl auf Leinwand. Richmond, Virginia Museum of Fine Arts. https://commons.wikimedia.org/wiki/File:%C3%89douard_Manet_-_Sur_la_plage_de_Boulogne.jpg.

Abb. 3: *Badebekleidung für Frauen um 1900*. Foto in: *Nordisk Mønster-tidende* 11/1898: 84. https://commons.wikimedia.org/wiki/File:Badedragter_for_damer.jpg.

Abb. 4: Hans Memling. *Das jüngste Gericht*. Ca. 1470. Öl auf Holz. Danzig, Nationalmuseum. https://commons.wikimedia.org/wiki/File:Das_J%C3%BCngste_Gericht_(Memling).jpg.

Abb. 5: Pierre-Paul Prud'hon. *Le naufrage de Virginie*. 1806. Radierung der Edition Didot. https://commons.wikimedia.org/wiki/File:Paul_virginie_1806_6_naufrage_prudhon.jpg.

Mark Olival-Bartley
Revisited

Because no scene is set in black and white
(in the truest sense), I trace the beaches
along Kailua's storied bay: Each is,
in its way, a hued process – a honed fight
of turquoise and dun; a fondant sea meets
the saline granules of sharp coral cards,
which are a kind of not-quite-white, mere shards
that once were and are now naught.

                              Memory eats
this up like a sponge. (The simile veils
the hunger of the trope.) Color does bleed
into a mud of whorls, misted motes borne
falling fell-fast into the whole shopworn
gamut of burnt blues that have lost green mead
foam, like the eyes of a cabbie one hails.

Notes on Contributors

FLORIAN AUEROCHS is PhD candidate and lecturer in the Faculty of German and Cultural Studies at the University of Vechta. He holds a Master's degree in Comparative Literary and Media Studies from Otto-Friedrich-University Bamberg. His fields of study include contemporary fiction from Germany and the US, Ecocriticism and Environmental Humanities, and Petrocriticism.

ROBERT BAUERNFEIND is research assistant at the University of Augsburg. He has studied History of Art at Augsburg, Eichstätt, Munich and Vienna and completed his PhD in 2015. His fields of study are Netherlandish painting as well as illustrations of early modern natural history.

CHRISTIAN BEGEMANN is Full Professor of Modern German Literature at LMU Munich. His major publications include monographs on the relationship of enlightenment, anxiety and fear (*Furcht und Angst im Prozeß der Aufklärung*, 1987) and on Adalbert Stifter (*Die Welt der Zeichen*, 1995). He is the editor of a volume on the metaphorics of procreation and the birth of art (*Kunst – Zeugung – Geburt*, co-edited with David E. Wellbery, 2002), on German Realism (2007) and on Vampyrism (*Dracula Unbound*, co-edited with Britta Herrmann and Harald Neumeyer, 2008), as well as of the Adalbert-Stifter-Handbook (co-edited with Davide Giuriato, 2017). Furthermore, he published numerous articles on German literature from the eighteenth to the twentieth century (Goethe, Kleist, Tieck, Arnim, Mörike, Richard Wagner, Keller, Storm, Fontane or Robert Müller). He is co-editor of the journal *Internationales Archiv für Sozialgeschichte der deutschen Literatur*. Currently, he is working on a book about 'Ghosts and Spirits of Realism.'

CARINA BREIDENBACH, M.A., studied Comparative Literature, Modern German Literature, English and American Literature, and Philosophy in Munich, London, and Berkeley. She received her M.A. in Modern German Literature from LMU Munich with a final thesis about the narratibility of death. Since 2017, she has been PhD candidate at the Graduate School Language & Literature at LMU Munich and Research Associate (Wissenschaftliche Mitarbeiterin) and lecturer at the Institute of Comparative Literature at LMU Munich. She is currently completing her PhD thesis in Comparative Literature about the 'poetics of anxiety' in twentieth and twenty-first century German and Anglophone narrative fiction with a focus on texts by Kafka, Beckett, Pynchon and DeLillo. Her research interests include emotions and their representation in and evocation by literature, narratology, theories of fictionality, and the intersections of literary studies with psychoanalysis, psychology, and philosophy.

CAROL BUNCH DAVIS is Associate Professor of English at Texas A & M University at Galveston. She earned a PhD in English at the University of Southern California. Her research examines representations of African American identity in contemporary U. S. cultural production. Her publications include *Prefiguring Postblackness: Cultural Memory, Drama and the African American Freedom Struggle of the 1960s*. Jackson/MS: University Press of Mississippi, 2015; and "'Be Loyal to Yourselves': Jim Crow Segregation, Black Cultural Nationalism, and U. S. Cultural Memory in Ossie Davis' *Purlie Victorious*." *Critical Insights: Civil Rights Literature, Past & Present*. Ed. Christopher Allen Varlack. Amenia/NY: Gray House Press, 2017. 36–52.

KONSTANTIN BUTZ is researcher and lecturer at the Academy of Media Arts Cologne. He has studied American Studies and Cultural Studies at the University of Bremen and at Dickinson College in Carlisle, Pennsylvania. He holds a doctorate degree in American Studies from the University of Cologne. His research interests include subcultures, youth cultures, and (un-)popular literature and music. His publications include *Grinding California: Culture and Corporeality in American Skate Punk*. Bielefeld: transcript, 2012; "The Authenticity of a T-shirt: Ryan Gosling, Roddy Dangerblood, and the Rebellious Genealogy of Thrasher Magazine." *American Rock Journalism*. Eds. Marcel Hartwig and Ulf Schulenberg. London: Routledge, 2017. 47–56; *Skateboard Studies*. Eds. Konstantin Butz and Christian Peters. London: Koenig Books, 2018.

ELSA DEVIENNE is lecturer in U. S. History at Northumbria University (Newcastle upon Tyne). She received her PhD in History from the École des Hautes Études en Sciences Sociales, Paris. Devienne was Postdoctoral Fellow at Princeton University from 2016–2017 and lecturer in American Studies at Paris Nanterre University from 2015–2019. Her research interests are the history of the U. S., California and Los Angeles; environmental and coastal history; urban history; history of gender, sexuality and the body. Her publications include: "The Life, Death, and Rebirth of Muscle Beach: Reassessing the Muscular Physique in Postwar American (1940s–1980s)." *Southern California Quarterly* 100.3 (2018): 324–367; "Urban Renewal by the Sea: Reinventing the Beach for the Suburban Age in Postwar Los Angeles." *The Journal of Urban History* 45.1 (2019): 99–125; *La ruée vers le sable: Une histoire environnementale du littoral de Los Angeles*. Paris: Sorbonne Editions, 2020.

THÉRÈSE DE RAEDT is Associate Professor of French in the department of World Languages and Cultures at the University of Utah in Salt Lake City. After studying Art History at the University of Louvain-la-Neuve, she got a PhD in French Literature with a Designated Emphasis in Critical Theory from the University of California at Davis. Her research has focused on three major areas clustered around the broad theme of 'otherness': the representation of Africans in French literature and in the plastic arts in the eighteenth and nineteenth centuries; holiday resorts conceived of as post-colonial utopian spaces; and the intercultural links established voluntarily and by force in the Francophone world. Reflecting her research interests, her primary teaching fields at the University of Utah have been the eighteenth and nineteenth centuries, the representation of the foreigner, the link between visual and textual cultures, and Francophone literatures and cultures.

JEANNOT MOUKOURI EKOBE is PhD candidate at the LMU Munich. He studied German Literature at the University of Yaoundé 1 (Cameroon). He covers topics like Philosophy, Cultural Studies and especially post-colonial literature (in French, German and English). The topic of his dissertation project is: 'The (Re-)Imagination of the National and Aesthetic in the Context of Transformation.' He is currently working on establishing a Center for Transnational Imagination which will be dedicated to new modes of imagining and conceptualizing social life in relation to transnational and post-national formations.

DIETRICH ERBEN teaches as a professor for Theory and History of Architecture, Art and Design at the Technical University of Munich. His fields of research are political iconography since the early modern era and architectural theory. His recent book publications include *Politikstile und die Sichtbarkeit des Politischen in der Frühen Neuzeit*. Eds. Dietrich Erben and Christine Tauber. Passau: Klinger 2016; *Architekturtheorie. Eine Geschichte von der Antike bis zur Gegenwart*. München: C. H. Beck, 2017; *Das eigene Leben als ästhetische Fiktion. Berufsautobiographien und Professionsgeschichte*. Eds. Dietrich Erben and Tobias Zervosen. Bielefeld: transcript, 2018; *Das Buch als Entwurf. Textgattungen in der Geschichte der Architekturtheorie. Ein Handbuch*. Ed. Dietrich Erben. Paderborn: Fink, 2019.

TAMARA FRÖHLER, M.A. M.A., studied Comparative Literature, Modern German Literature and Middle Eastern Studies in Tübingen, Istanbul, Munich and

Berkeley. Since 2017, she has been a Research Associate (Wissenschaftliche Mitarbeiterin) at the German Department of LMU and PhD candidate at the Graduate School Language & Literature at LMU Munich. Currently, she is writing her PhD thesis in Modern German Literature on 'Captivating Extras and the Materialization of tragic Entanglement in end of Nineteenth Century Dramatic Figures.' Recent publications on sexuality in Ovid's *Metamorphoses*, the poetic function of hair in nineteenth century drama and the recurrence of tragic forms in contemporary theater.

Nadja Grasselli grew up in Trento (Italy), studied in Bologna and Berlin, and is based in Leipzig since 2014. Her work is born at the interaction between arts and society and takes different hybrid forms: theatre, writing, radio, video, performance and new forms of communication. Currently, she is mainly working in Germany and Italy, cooperating with universities, NGOs and theater groups. In 2012, she founded *LMN Liminale Räume*, an international project developing social, cultural and artistic actions: *LMN* aims to create liminal/border spaces (whether on an online-platform, in a book, on the stage, on the streets, in a school), where common rules are questioned and where new situations or new meanings can be born.

Sebastian Haselbeck is Wissenschaftlicher Mitarbeiter and teaches at the Ruhr-Universität Bochum. He studied Comparative Literature and Classics at the University of Vienna and Trinity College Dublin and received his PhD in German Literature from the University of California, Berkeley. He was junior fellow at the *Internationales Forschungszentrum Kulturwissenschaften* (IFK) in Vienna and has formerly taught at LMU Munich. His dissertation *Gespenstische Souveränität. Zur politischen Einbildungskraft zwischen 1910 und 1920* is forthcoming with Konstanz University Press (2020). Recent publications include: "Gespenstische Souveräniät in Kafkas China." *Kafkas China. Forschungen der Deutschen Kafka-Gesellschaft*. Eds. Harald Neumeyer and Agnes Bidmon. Würzburg: Königshausen Neumann, 2017. 51–65; with Sasha Rossmann: "Das Reale der Gummihandschuhe. Zur Taktilität in Robert Wienes *Orlac's Hände*." *AugenBlick. Passionen des Realen. Bilder des Menschen zwischen den Kriegen. Konstanzer Hefte zur Medienwissenschaften* 69/70 (2017): 31–48.

Wiebke Kolbe is professor for History at Lund University (Sweden), since 2012. She studied History, German Language and Literature, Scandinavian and Finno-Ugric Languages at the Universities of Kiel, Uppsala and Bielefeld (1984–1991), and received her M.A. in 1991 and her PhD in History from Bielefeld University in 1999, with a PhD thesis about West German and Swedish parental politics from 1945–2000. She was assistant professor in Gender History from 1999–2004 and 2006–2007 at Bielefeld University, Lise Meitner research fellow from 2004–2006, researcher at the Institute of Contemporary History in Hamburg (FZH) from 2008–2010, and guest researcher at Stockholm University from 2011–2012. Her fields of study are tourism history, especially the history of spas and seaside resorts and battlefield history, gender history and comparative welfare state history. Recent publications include *Turismhistoria i Norden*. Uppsala: Kungl. Gustav Adolfs Akademien för svensk folkkultur, 2018 (editor); and "Trauer und Tourismus. Reisen des Volksbundes Deutsche Kriegsgräberfürsorge 1950–2010." *Zeithistorische Forschungen/Studies in Contemporary History* 1 (2017): 68–92.

Désirée Mangard has been employed as a pre-doc at Leopold-Franzens-Universität Innsbruck, Austria, since February 2016. She studied German Language and Literature and History as well as History of Arts at Leopold-Franzens-Universität Innsbruck. She primarily teaches Middle High German and Medieval German Literature and is working on her dissertation about objects in transitional contexts in medieval German literature. Her other research interests include linguistic history and relations of literature and the arts. She has frequently contributed to regional historical projects including publications and exhibitions. Together with Miriam Strieder she has recently published the article "Paradise Perverted? The Garden as the Nucleus of Ungodliness in Gottfried's of Strassburg *Tristan*." *Enchanted, Stereotyped, Civilized: Garden Narratives in Literature, Art and Film*. Eds. Feryal Cubukcu and Sabine Planka. Würzburg: Königshausen & Neumann, 2018. 63–78.

Alberto Napoli has recently completed a PhD in Musicology at the University of Bern. He studied Musicology at Pavia University (Cremona) and at the University of North Carolina at Chapel Hill. He collaborated with the Centre d'Études Supérieures de la Renaissance in Tours, and was awarded a scholarship from the Paul Sacher Stiftung in Basel. Spanning different eras, his research investigates the imaginaries associated with, and generated by, music in Italy. More specifically, his dissertation assesses the role of musical events in great expositions of industry and arts in liberal Italy as well as the impact of great expositions on the musical culture of that time. He is also one of the editors of the upcoming volume: *Branding 'Western Music,'* discussing how the notion of a musical tradition of "the Western world" came into being and is still used to promote people, products, and nation branding.

MARK OLIVAL-BARTLEY studied Applied Linguistics at Hawaii Pacific University, attaining B.A. and M.A. degrees in TESOL. He is currently writing a dissertation on the poetics of E. A. Robinson's meta-sonnet at LMU Munich's Department of English and American Studies, where he tutors composition. With Amy Mohr, he co-edited *New Interpretations of Harper Lee's 'To Kill a Mockingbird' and 'Go Set a Watchman'* (Cambridge Scholars, 2019). He is also the resident poet at EcoHealth, where his science-themed verse is regularly featured.

JACK PARLETT is a Junior Research Fellow in English at University College, Oxford. He completed his PhD on gay cruising and New York poetry at Cambridge University and is in the process of adapting this into a monograph. His other project, a trade non-fiction book about the queer history of Fire Island, is forthcoming in 2022 from Granta Books in the UK and Hanover Square Press in the US.

DOMINIK PENSEL, M.A., studied Modern German Literature, Musicology, Ethnomusicology and Cultural Studies in Munich and Dublin. Since 2016, he has been Research Associate (Wissenschaftlicher Mitarbeiter) at the German Department of LMU Munich and is writing his PhD thesis at the Graduate School Language & Literature on 'The Unconscious in German Realism Literature.' Recent publications, among others, on artistic self-reflections of aesthetic production in literature and music, concepts of the 'open form' in the New York School, on spaces of the unconscious in German Romanticism and Realism, or on trauma in Fontane, Storm, and Ludwig. A monograph on E. T. A. Hoffmann and Jacques Offenbach's opera *Les Contes d'Hoffmann* is currently in preparation.

ROXANNE PHILLIPS, Research Associate (Wissenschaftliche Mitarbeiterin) at the German Department of LMU Munich, studied Modern German Literature, Philosophy and Modern & Contemporary History in Munich and Amsterdam. After a term at New York University as a Visiting Scholar, she is currently completing her PhD project *Die Regierung der Menschen erzählen. Figurationen der Gouvernementalität* at the Graduate School Language & Literature. Her research deals with eighteenth to twenty-first century German literature and focuses on poetics of knowledge, governmentality, gender studies, and representations of authorship, among others. Recent publications include an article on medical poetics in *Komparative Ästhetik(en)*. Eds. Ernest W. B. Hess-Lüttich et. al. Berlin: Peter Lang, 2018; on techniques of the self in *Privates Erzählen*. Eds. Steffen Burk et. al. Berlin: Peter Lang, 2018; and collaborating on the anthology

Kulturwissenschaftliche Perspektiven der Gender Studies. Eds. Manuela Günter and Annette Keck. Berlin: Kadmos, 2018.

Virginia Richter is Full Professor of Modern English Literature at the University of Bern. She holds a doctoral degree in Comparative Literature from LMU Munich, where she also completed her habilitation on literary representations of Darwinism. She was a Visiting Fellow at the University of Kent at Canterbury and at the University of Leeds, and a Visiting Professor at the University of Göttingen. In spring 2018, she was a Visiting Research Fellow at the IASH, University of Edinburgh, where she worked on a monograph about the beach in modernist literature. Her most recent publications include: *The Beach in Anglophone Literatures and Cultures: Reading Littoral Space*. Ed. Ursula Kluwick and Virginia Richter. Farnham and Burlington/VT: Ashgate, 2015; *Modern Creatures*. Special issue of the *European Journal of English Studies* (*EJES*). Ed. Virginia Richter and Pieter Vermeulen (2015).

Katharina Simon, M.A., studied Art History, Comparative Literature and Theater Studies in Munich and Paris (2015, Magister Artium in Art History with a thesis in Film Studies). In 2016, Katharina Simon joined the Graduate School Language & Literature Munich with a PhD project in Comparative Literature on the spatialization of affective relations to the past and passing of time in Baudelaire, Duras (texts and films) and Angela Carter. From 2016 to 2019, she was a Research Associate (Wissenschaftliche Mitarbeiterin) with the Graduate School, since 2019, she has been working as a Research Associate at the Romance Department of the LMU. Publications on Keun and Baudelaire in the context of Freudian theories on fetishism, on spatial formations in Verne, and scenes of reading in Perec (both 2020), as well as an edited volume on visuality in textual and visual media (with Katharina Rajabi, also forthcoming).

Miriam Strieder is pre-doc at the German Department of the LFU Innsbruck, Austria. She studied English and German at the JGU Mainz, Germany, and York University Toronto, Canada. Her fields of research are the European heroic from the early medieval period to the thirteenth century, theories of cultural memory, and myth and reception of myths. Her recent publications include: "Der staunende Blick auf das weit entfernte Fremde: Das Spanien der Mauren in Konrad Flecks *Flore und Blanscheflur* (um 1220?)." *Spanische Städte und Landschaften in der deutschen (Reise)Literatur / Ciudades y paisajes españoles en la literatura (de viajes) alemana*. Eds. Berta Raposo Fernández and Walther L. Bernecker. Frankfurt/Main: Peter Lang, 2017. 183–195; Strieder, Miriam and Mangard, Désirée. "Paradise Perverted? The Garden as the Nucleus of Ungodliness in Gottfried's of Strassburg *Tristan.*" *Enchanted, Stereotyped, Civilized: Garden Narratives in Literature, Art and Film.* Eds. Feryal Cubukcu and Sabine Planka. Würzburg: Königshausen & Neumann, 2018. 63–78.

Yoko Tawada is a writer. Born in Tokyo, she moved to Germany at the age of 22. She first majored in Russian Literature at Waseda University in Tokyo, studied German Literature in Hamburg and received her PhD under Sigrid Weigel in Zurich. Ever since she published her first collection of prose and poetry in 1987, she has been writing both in Japanese and German. She has also been active in giving readings and performances in collaboration with musicians, travelling extensively throughout the world. Tawada is the recipient of numerous fellowships and awards, including the Kleist Prize, and two of Japan's most-sought literary awards, the Akutagawa Prize and Tanizaki Prize. The English version of *Kentoshi* or *The Emissary* (2018) has won the U.S. National Book Award for Translated Literature.

Florian Telsnig, Mag., is PhD candidate at the LMU Munich. He studied Comparative Literature, Philosophy and Theatre, Film and Media Studies in Vienna, Paris and Lisbon, taught as a Research Associate (Wissenschaftlicher Mitarbeiter) at the LMU Munich and currently teaches at the University of Vienna. Publications, among others, on the notion of destruction in literature and politics, philosophy of time and, especially, philosophy of language.

Carmen Ulrich teaches German Literature at the LMU Munich and also works as a freelance business coach. She studied Modern German Literature, Ethnology and Philosophy at the LMU Munich and completed her PhD in Modern German Literature in 2003 and her Habilitation in 2012. She worked on a DFG-Project about Literature of the GDR, was DAAD-Lecturer at Universities in Latvia (2003–2005) and India (2010–2015), and project manager for the internationalization of the PhD-Program at the University of Wuppertal (2016–2019). Her publications include: *'Bericht vom Anfang.' Der Buchmarkt der SBZ und frühen DDR im Medium der Anthologie.* Bielefeld: Aisthesis, 2013; *Sinn und Sinnlichkeit des Reisens. Indien(be)schreibungen von Hubert Fichte, Günter Grass und Josef Winkler.* München: iudicium, 2004; articles on Wolfgang Koeppen, Elias Canetti, Bertolt Brecht, Adalbert Stifter, Paul Pörtner et al. She is the editor of several journals, e.g. *German Studies in India.*

Barbara Vinken is Chair of French and Comparative Literature at LMU Munich. She received her doctoral degree of Dr. phil. from the University of Konstanz in 1989 and a PhD from Yale University in 1991. In 1996, she took her Habilitation at the University of Jena and was appointed full professor (Ordinaria) at the Universities of Hamburg (1999) and Zurich (2003). Barbara Vinken taught as a Visiting Professor at New York University, Humboldt University, Berlin, the ENS Paris, the FU Berlin, the University of Chicago, Dartmouth College, Johns Hopkins University, Baltimore, and the EHESS Paris. Her main fields of research are French and Italian Renaissance, the French Novel from the eighteenth to the twentieth century, as well as Deconstructive Feminism and Fashion Theory. Most recent publications include: *Flaubert Postsecular. Modernity Crossed Out*. Stanford: Stanford University Press, 2015; *Die Blumen der Mode. Klassische und neue Texte zur Philosophie der Mode*. Stuttgart: Klett-Cotta, 2016; Gustave Flaubert: *Trois contes. Nouvelle édition critique de Barbara Vinken, avec trois essais*. Berlin: De Gruyter, 2020.

Martin Wittmann, M.A., studied Comparative Literature and Philosophy in Munich. In 2015 he received his Master title in Comparative Literature with a thesis on concepts of the face in Deleuze/Guattari and Paul de Man. Since 2016 he has been a graduate student at the Graduate School Language & Literature's Class of Literature and is currently also a Research Associate (Wissenschaftlicher Mitarbeiter) at the Graduate School. His dissertation thesis is concerned with the 'Theory and Poetics of *Alien Discourse* in Valentin Vološinov and Mikhail Bakhtin.'

www.ingramcontent.com/pod-product-compliance
Lightning Source LLC
Chambersburg PA
CBHW070746230426
43665CB00017B/2268